Bioethics

The International Library of Essays in Public and Professional Ethics
Series Editors: Seumas Miller and Tom Campbell

Bioethics

Edited by

Justin Oakley

Monash University, Australia

ASHGATE

Published by
Ashgate Publishing Limited
Wey Court East
Union Road
Farnham
Surrey
GU9 7PT

Ashgate Publishing Company
Suite 420
101 Cherry Street
Burlington, VT 05401-4405
USA

Ashgate website: http://www.ashgate.com

British Library Cataloguing in Publication Data
Bioethics. – (The international library of essays in public
    and professional ethics)
    1. Bioethics
    I Oakley, Justin, 1960–
    174.9 '57

Library of Congress Control Number:2008926063

ISBN: 978-0-7546-2597-1

Mixed Sources
Product group from well-managed
forests and other controlled sources
www.fsc.org Cert no. SGS-COC-2482
© 1996 Forest Stewardship Council
FSC

Printed and bound in Great Britain by
TJ International Ltd, Padstow, Cornwall

Contents

PART III REPRODUCTIVE ETHICS

PART IV END-OF-LIFE ISSUES

PART V PROFESSIONAL INTEGRITY AND THE GOALS OF MEDICINE

PART VI RESEARCH ETHICS

PART VII ETHICS AND THE PHARMACEUTICAL INDUSTRY

PART VIII BIOETHICS AND PUBLIC POLICY

Acknowledgements

The editor and publishers wish to thank the following for permission to use copyright material.

BMJ Publishing Group Ltd for the essays: Onora O'Neill (1984), 'Paternalism and Partial Autonomy', *Journal of Medical Ethics*, **10**, pp. 173–78. Copyright © 1984 BMJ Publishing Group Ltd; John Harris (1997), '"Goodbye Dolly?" The Ethics of Human Cloning', *Journal of Medical Ethics*, **23**, pp. 353–60. Copyright © 1997 BMJ Publishing Group Ltd; A. Schafer (2004), 'Biomedical Conflicts of Interest: A Defence of the Sequestration Thesis – Learning from the Cases of Nancy Olivieri and David Healy', *Journal of Medical Ethics*, **30**, pp. 8–24. Copyright © 2004 BMJ Publishing Group Ltd; Daniel Wikler (1999), 'Can We Learn from Eugenics?', *Journal of Medical Ethics*, **25**, pp. 183–94. Copyright ©1999 BMJ Publishing Group Ltd.

Canadian Journal of Philosophy for the essay: Jim Stone (1987), 'Why Potentiality Matters', *Canadian Journal of Philosophy*, **17**, pp. 815–30. Copyright © 1987 Canadian Journal of Philosophy.

Hastings Center for the essays: Bruce L. Miller (1981), 'Autonomy and the Refusal of Lifesaving Treatment', *Hastings Center Report*, **11**, no. 4, pp. 22–28; Joseph Fletcher (1972), 'Indicators of Humanhood: A Tentative Profile of Man', *Hastings Center Report*, **2**, pp. 1–4; Larry R. Churchill (1989), 'Reviving a Distinctive Medical Ethic', *Hastings Center Report*, **19**, pp. 28–34; Franklin G. Miller and Howard Brody (1995), 'Professional Integrity and Physician-Assisted Death', *Hastings Center Report*, **25**, pp. 8–17; Participants in the 2001 Conference on Ethical Aspects of Research in Developing Countries (2004), 'Moral Standards for Research in Developing Countries: From "Reasonable Availability" to "Fair Benefits"', *Hastings Center Report*, **34**, pp. 17–27; Amy Gutmann and Dennis Thompson (1997), 'Deliberating about Bioethics', *Hastings Center Report*, **27**, pp. 38–41; Robert M. Veatch (1972) 'Models for Ethical Medicine in a Revolutionary Age', *Hastings Center Report*, **2**, pp. 5–7; John Hardwig (1990), 'What about the Family?', *Hastings Center Report*, **20**, pp. 5–10; Rebecca Dresser (1995), 'Dworkin on Dementia: Elegant Theory, Questionable Policy', *Hastings Center Report*, **25**, pp. 32–38; Dena S. Davis (1997), 'Genetic Dilemmas and the Child's Right to an Open Future', *Hastings Center Report*, **27**, pp. 7–15.

Massachusetts Medical Society for the essays: Norman Daniels (1986), 'Why Saying No to Patients in the United States is So Hard: Cost Containment, Justice, and Provider Autonomy', *New England Journal of Medicine*, **314**, pp. 1380–83. Copyright © 1986 Massachusetts Medical Society; George J. Annas (2005), '"Culture of Life" Politics at the Bedside – The Case of Terri Schiavo', *New England Journal of Medicine*, **352**, pp. 1710–15. Copyright © 2005 Massachusetts Medical Society; Benjamin Freedman (1987), 'Equipoise and the Ethics of Clinical Research', *New England Journal of Medicine*, **317**, pp. 141–45. Copyright ©

Series Preface

'Ethics' is now a considerable part of all debates about the conduct of public life, in government, economics, law, business, the professions and indeed every area of social and political affairs. The ethical aspects of public life include questions of moral right and wrong in the performance of public and professional roles, the moral justification and critique of public institutions and the choices that confront citizens and professionals as they come to their own moral views about social, economic and political issues.

While there are no moral experts to whom we can delegate the determination of ethical questions, the traditional skills of moral philosophers have been increasingly applied to practical contexts that call for moral assessment. Moreover this is being done with a degree of specialist knowledge of the areas under scrutiny that previously has been lacking from much of the work undertaken by philosophers.

This series brings together essays that exhibit high quality work in philosophy and the social sciences, that is well informed on the relevant subject matter and provides novel insights into the problems that arise in resolving ethical questions in practical contexts.

The volumes are designed to assist those engaged in scholarly research by providing the core essays that all who are involved in research in that area will want to have to hand. Essays are reproduced in full with the original pagination for ease of reference and citation.

The editors are selected for their eminence in the particular area of public and professional ethics. Each volume represents the editor's selection of the most seminal essays of enduring interest in the field.

SEUMAS MILLER AND TOM CAMPBELL
Centre for Applied Philosophy and Public Ethics (CAPPE)
Australian National University
Charles Sturt University
University of Melbourne

Introduction

Bioethics examines and challenges existing and likely future practices in health care, reproduction, genetics, biotechnology and biomedical research. Of all the areas in applied and professional ethics, bioethics is the oldest and most diverse, and it contains debates that are often more philosophically sophisticated than those in other areas. While many of the particular concerns of contemporary bioethics – such as abortion, prenatal diagnosis, cloning, informed consent and voluntary euthanasia – have been prompted by advances in medical and reproductive technologies in recent decades, they commonly raise deep issues of perennial importance, about when life begins, the value of parenthood, the notion of respect for others and what it means to be human. Consequently, there is a rich and varied literature from which to choose the best and most influential essays.

This volume contains many of the most important and influential essays that have set the agenda for key debates in bioethics or have changed the face of those debates. The essays address ethics in clinical practice, issues at the outset of life, reproductive ethics, end-of-life issues, professional integrity and the goals of medicine, ethics and the pharmaceutical industry, research ethics, and bioethics and public policy. Many of the essays presented here made a contribution by opening up new lines of debate, by revealing shortcomings in received wisdom on these issues or simply by the quality of their arguments and their exceptional clarity. There are, of course, other important essays in bioethics, but I have excluded those which have already been widely anthologized. Also, I have included some short essays by notable figures in the field, which outline approaches or applications that these authors subsequently developed in monographs. The volume demonstrates what is at stake in many current controversies in bioethics, and shows the breadth and richness of work in the field.

Ethics in Clinical Practice

More work has been done to develop a framework of ethical principles for the health care professions than has been done for any other profession. A widely used ethical framework for health care consists of four ethical principles: the principles of autonomy, privacy, beneficence and justice. This basic framework is a variant of a substantially similar framework developed by American bioethicists Tom Beauchamp and James Childress, whose highly influential book *Principles of Biomedical Ethics* (2009) is into its sixth edition after having initially been published in 1979. The principles employed by Beauchamp and Childress themselves drew heavily on those contained in the 'Belmont Report' of the US National Commission for the Protection of Human Subjects of Biomedical and Behavioural Research. This section looks at essays on respecting patient autonomy, acting in patients' best interests and acting justly.

A significant factor in the emergence of bioethics as a discipline was the critique by many philosophers of paternalistic practices in medicine. This critique led to a new emphasis on the importance of patient autonomy in medical decision-making, and philosophers such as Gerald

Dworkin (1976) developed conceptions of autonomy to underpin this value. Chapter 1, Bruce Miller's influential essay on patient autonomy in the context of end-of-life decision-making, demonstrates the importance of developing the positive features of autonomy, which include, for example, a more robust notion of authenticity than those extant at the time. A very large literature has subsequently emerged on the question of what conception of autonomy most plausibly grounds the demand to respect autonomous decisions by patients.

But while discussions of ethical issues in health care went on to make much use of philosophical accounts of autonomy, the notion of patients' best interests was still surprisingly under-theorized in bioethics. A rich debate in prudential value theory had developed in philosophy, with contrasting approaches to analysing what it means to promote a person's welfare or well-being. However, as David Degrazia points out in Chapter 2, bioethical discussions about best interests in patient care had not engaged much with these philosophical debates. Degrazia demonstrates how the three main value theories – mental state accounts, desire-based accounts and objectivist accounts – have quite different implications for justifying treatment withdrawal from severely disabled neonates and persistent vegetative state patients. Thus, Miller and Degrazia draw on philosophical theories of the key concepts of autonomy and beneficence, respectively, to enrich our understanding of ethical decision-making in clinical practice.

Autonomy and beneficence conflict in medical paternalism, which involves interfering with a patient's liberty in order to benefit or protect them. Paternalistic interventions in patient care range from subtle attempts to protect patients by withholding material information from them, to outright coercion, such as threatening to institutionalize a patient of diminished competence who fails to comply with a treatment regimen. Both of these interventions infringe patient autonomy in some sense, but spelling out what would count as respecting patient autonomy is not necessarily a straightforward matter. Kantians offer one approach, emphasizing rationality and acting on consistent principles. However, Kantian accounts of autonomy have been criticized as excessively abstract and idealized, and so as ill-suited to patient care. Onora O'Neill has developed an influential contemporary form of Kantian ethics that attempts to overcome such concerns.[1] In Chapter 3, O'Neill focuses on respecting patient autonomy through obtaining informed consent from patients. She argues that Kantians should understand informed consent not as a matter of disclosing information that some hypothetical abstract reasonable person would find relevant, but as providing the information that this particular patient, with their 'limited and determinate capacities' would regard as relevant to their decision.

In Chapter 4, Steve Clarke and I extend the ethical doctrine of informed consent into new territory. We argue that because one's risks in a surgical procedure depend partly upon which surgeon performs it, obtaining a patient's informed consent therefore requires providing surgeon performance information to patients who regard this as relevant to their decision. Some critics reject this argument because of, for example, concerns about the quality of clinician performance information, but others have used this discussion as a way of bringing ethical debates about transparency and accountability into closer contact with the clinical

---

[1]   Onora O'Neill has subsequently changed her views on autonomy and informed consent considerably. For her more recent position, see O'Neill (2002). See also Manson and O'Neill (2007).

practice literature on these matters (see, for example, the contributions in Clarke and Oakley, 2007).

The rejection of paternalistic practices in medicine and the establishment of informed consent in clinical practice were two early achievements of bioethics. This emphasis on doctors helping patients make more informed decisions led some clinicians to assume that their proper role is to be understood as simply the providers of facts, which patients then use in drawing on their own values to make a decision about treatment options. However, as Robert Veatch's influential essay (Chapter 5) demonstrates, this is only one of several different models of an ethical doctor–patient relationship, and it has serious limitations. Veatch argues that the notion of a contract or covenant provides a more ethically defensible model of good doctor–patient relationships, whereby ethical authority and responsibility for medical decisions is shared between patients and their doctors. On this model, patients have grounds for rationally trusting their doctor to act on a value framework guided by the patient's own values and interests, and, therefore, ethical decision-making in medicine does not demand that patients must participate in the many minute decisions about their care that doctors are called upon to make.[2]

Both of these models place the emphasis squarely on the patient and their interests. While this seems entirely appropriate in hospital-based care, the greater utilization in many countries of home-based care involving family caregivers prompted some bioethicists to question whether this patient-centred approach is always the most ethically defensible. Some have argued that health professionals have a moral duty to rescue family caregivers who are being exploited or over-burdened (see, for example, Post, 1993). In Chapter 6, John Hardwig reminds us that patients can often be quite self-absorbed and are sometimes less vulnerable than their carers, particularly given the dynamics existing in some families. Hardwig argues that the interests of the family and the patient must be regarded as of fundamentally *equal* weight, and so should be treated impartially. According to Hardwig, there should be a presumption in favour of giving the comparable medical interests of the patient and their family members equal weight, and someone advocating special consideration for a family member must meet the burden of proof of demonstrating why this should be the case here.

Advance directives have been thought to present an ethically unproblematic method of respecting patients' autonomous choices about future circumstances they may find themselves in, where they foresee that their autonomy will be diminished by internal or external obstacles and wish to document their views about what sorts of interventions they are prepared to have. However, the ethics of advance directives are less straightforward than they might seem. As Rebecca Dresser argues in Chapter 7, to honour a patient's advance directive might not actually be to respect their autonomous wishes, because patients' genuine values can sometimes change due to their new circumstances, such as facing a more restricted range of options or, conversely, the emergence of new treatments that were not available when the directive was drawn up. Dresser also argues that in some extreme cases of dementia, we might question whether the later individual is still the same *person* as the earlier individual, in which case it would be no more legitimate to apply the directive to this new person than to apply it to a patient in the next ward.

---

[2]   This model has been extended further in a well-known essay by Emanuel and Emanuel (1992). Emanuel and Emanuel argue that doctors should offer patients advice and recommendations, and should help guide patients to deliberate well in making their health care decisions. Providing this sort of assistance, they argue, does not amount to medical paternalism.

Questions about justice in health care go beyond concerns about autonomy, beneficence and ethical doctor–patient relationships, and situate a patient's interests within a broader perspective. For example, issues of justice in health care resource allocation consider whether a beneficial procedure that a patient autonomously requests ought actually to be provided for them, given the competing interests of other patients for the resources used by such a procedure. At the very least, justice in health care requires that decisions to give certain patients priority in access to treatment are not made on grounds that are morally irrelevant. The landmark contributions of Norman Daniels have shaped debates about justice in health care for over two decades (see, for example, his highly influential *Just Health Care*, 1985). Daniels' work extends John Rawls' contractarian theory of justice (1972) to health care, and Chapter 8 presents an early example of some practical implications of Daniels' approach. Daniels argues that when doctors and hospitals are encouraged by cost-containment measures to deny beneficial care to patients in the US free-market health care system, there are no assurances that the resources thereby saved will go to patients who have stronger justice-based claims on those resources. By contrast, health care providers responding to cost-containment measures by denying a patient beneficial care in universal health care systems like that in the UK can justify their decisions on the grounds that to provide such care would unfairly deprive other patients of resources that would more effectively restore the opportunities of those other patients.

Issues at the Outset of Life

Some of the earliest writing in bioethics focused on the ethics of abortion and questions of fetal moral status, and issues about the moral status of human embryos again loom large in debates about the ethics of embryonic stem cell research. But what significance, if any, should be attached to the fact that an individual, whether an embryo, a fetus or an infant, is a *human* being? Peter Singer (1976, 1993) has famously argued that mere membership of the human species does not by itself confer any special moral status. Nevertheless, there might be particular morally significant characteristics that are commonly associated with human beings. In Chapter 9, Joseph Fletcher presents a list of plausible candidates for morally valuable human characteristics, which might be used to develop an account of what it means to live a flourishing human life.

One well-known type of argument in discussions about the morality of abortion claims that a human fetus has a certain moral status because it has the potential to develop morally valuable human characteristics, such as the capacity to experience various emotions, the capacity to form meaningful social relationships with others and the capacity for moral agency. But what does talk of such potential mean? In Chapter 10, Stephen Buckle provides a sensible assessment of what is at stake in debates about potential in the context of abortion. Buckle points out that there are two different notions of potential, the potential to *become* something that actualizes what it is in one's nature to be, and the potential to *produce* something quite different. Buckle argues that most arguments from potentiality in bioethics are about the former. He also makes the important point that it only makes sense to speak of an entity having the potential *to become* something where that entity preserves its numerical identity throughout its development – that is, it remains, in some sense, the same individual.

Arguments about the meaning of potential, however, leave open the question of what the moral significance of a fetus's potential to develop morally significant capacities might be.

Some bioethicists (and particularly those who take a Utilitarian approach) are sceptical of talk about potential, as invoking appeals to some metaphysically obscure notion of entities having inherent powers. However, Jim Stone (Chapter 11) provides a strong defence of the importance of potentiality in the context of abortion. Stone argues that we have a prima facie duty to all creatures not to deprive them of the conscious goods – such as sentience and self-awareness – that it is in their nature to realize under normal developmental conditions. Of course, as a prima facie duty, this can still be overridden by a woman's right to control what happens to her own body. This argument from potentiality might nevertheless place the burden of justification for abortion on the pregnant woman, such that the rightness or wrongness of a particular abortion would depend on an evaluation of her reasons for seeking it.

The early discussions of the ethics of abortion led to something of an impasse between the competing rights of the mother and the fetus, until the publication of Rosalind Hursthouse's illuminating application of a virtue ethics approach to abortion (Chapter 12). Hursthouse argues that people can exercise their rights virtuously or viciously, and that the morality of abortion revolves around the reasons or character traits that a woman acts on in aborting her fetus, rather than the rights of mother and fetus here. For example, Hursthouse suggests that an adolescent girl displays the virtue of humility when she decides to have an abortion because she realizes that she is not psychologically ready for motherhood, whereas a woman who is well-positioned to become a parent but aborts her pregnancy because she is overcome by fear of motherhood displays the vice of cowardice. Whether or not one agrees with these examples of the virtues or vices that can be displayed in abortion decisions, it is clear that Hursthouse's discussion does better at conveying the moral complexity of abortion decisions than familiar rights-based approaches, and it opened up a useful new perspective on the morality of abortion.

One of the most hotly debated topics in contemporary bioethics is the ethics of embryonic stem cell research. In Chapter 13, Søren Holm surveys a range of important ethical concerns about stem cell research. Holm argues that many of these concerns simply reprise arguments about embryonic and fetal moral status that are already familiar from unresolved debates about abortion, and that the challenges lie in formulating justifiable public policy regarding practices about which there is deep ethical disagreement.

The first live birth of a cloned sheep, named 'Dolly', in 1997 prompted a number of bioethicists to consider whether the reproductive cloning of a human being is necessarily immoral, as many people have assumed. An important early discussion of the ethics of human cloning is the essay by John Harris (Chapter 14). Harris surveys a range of ethical objections to human cloning, and argues that the instinctive aversion which many feel towards reproductive cloning lacks any solid ethical foundation. Harris also argues that current prohibitions on human cloning restrict our interest in procreative autonomy without sufficient reason, and so may themselves violate human dignity.

Reproductive Ethics

In 2002, a deaf lesbian couple in Washington DC obtained sperm from a family friend who was deaf, and used this to fertilize an egg that resulted in a baby that was born deaf. (Deafness has a genetic origin in around 50 per cent of cases.) Is it immoral to deliberately conceive a child that will be deaf? Anticipating such a scenario, Dena Davis (Chapter 15) argues that it is immoral to take steps to ensure that the child one wishes to conceive will be deaf, as this violates what she calls the child's right to an open future by substantially narrowing the scope of their career, marriage and cultural choices and prospects. Davis' argument has been widely discussed in the ensuing literature on the ethics of prenatal and pre-implantation genetic diagnosis (PGD).

Chapter 16, Julian Savulescu's provocative and strongly argued essay on the ethics of PGD, has been the focus of lively debate. Savulescu extends the consequentialist demand to maximize good outcomes to the procreative decisions that couples make. He argues that couples making embryo selection decisions in the context of PGD are morally obliged to choose the embryo that is likely to have the best life, in light of the information available at the time. This argument could also be used to support the claim that it is immoral to deliberately select an embryo that will be deaf, but for Savulescu this is because of the maximizing 'principle of procreative beneficence', rather than Davis' concerns about unduly limiting the future autonomy or options of the resulting child. Savulescu's principle imposes very stringent ethical demands on procreative decision-making, and has attracted much subsequent discussion and critique.

In Chapter 17, political philosopher Michael Sandel argues that worries about threats to children's autonomy, collective harms and fairness do not get to the core of what is wrong with genetic enhancements. Sandel accepts the similarity between parents using environmental influences and genetic influences on their children's characteristics, but he questions the impulse often expressed in both – that is, the move towards 'hyperparenting', which he says 'misses the sense of life as a gift'. Sandel then uses this idea of preserving a sense of the 'giftedness' of life as a basis for his critique of genetic enhancement. Sandel objects to routinely practised genetic enhancement for several reasons, including the Communitarian grounds that genetic enhancement undermines social solidarity.

Another topic in reproductive ethics that has been much discussed by bioethicists is surrogate motherhood. A recurrent concern in the literature on commercial surrogacy – where a woman is paid a fee to gestate another couple's biological child – is that such arrangements exploit the surrogate mother. In Chapter 18, Stephen Wilkinson presents a detailed analysis of this concern. Wilkinson argues there is good reason to believe a commercial surrogate mother is exploited by the commissioning couple, in the sense that the couple take unfair advantage of her. According to Wilkinson, commercial surrogate mothers are plausibly thought exploited because they are underpaid, relative to the risks and benefits involved, and because the relatively poor remuneration casts doubt on the validity of their consent to undertake the surrogacy arrangement in the first place. Nevertheless, Wilkinson concludes that these concerns about exploitation are not sufficient reason to prohibit commercial surrogacy.

End-of-Life Issues

Ethical issues about the end of life have been an important part of bioethics since its inception. Because of developments in medical technology and disease control, patients can be kept alive longer and longer, and this has prompted many health professionals, bioethicists and people in the broader community to question whether this is always appropriate.

Peter Singer and Helga Kuhse have written many influential critiques of the notion of the sanctity of human life, the idea that all human life is equally valuable. In Chapter 19, Peter Singer argues that the traditional sanctity of life ethic is in its death throes, because recent legal developments have shown how its directives are morally indefensible. For example, the UK House of Lords decision to allow life support to be withdrawn from Tony Bland, a teenager in persistent vegetative state after the 1989 Hillsborough Football Stadium tragedy, was based on quality of life considerations rather than on the idea of the sanctity of human life. Singer also argues that the move to redefine death in terms of brain-death is an unacceptably expedient response to the increased demand for viable organs for transplantation. In Chapter 20, Helga Kuhse criticizes the claim, on which advocates of the sanctity of life doctrine heavily rely, that there is an asymmetry between killing a patient and letting them die because only the former involves the intentional causation of death. Kuhse rejects this asymmetry, and argues that a doctor who deliberately refrains from preventing the death of a Down syndrome infant with an intestinal blockage causes the death of this infant. According to Kuhse then, whether death is brought about by killing or letting die is not directly relevant to its moral permissibility; rather, its moral permissibility depends on extrinsic factors, such as whether continued life is in an infant's best interests.

Margaret Battin has been another prominent contributor to debates about ethical and public policy issues concerning assisted suicide and voluntary euthanasia. In Chapter 21, Battin compares the official toleration (and subsequent legalization) of voluntary euthanasia in the Netherlands with assisted suicide in Germany and in the United States. Battin carefully considers several objections to each of these practices, and argues in favour of the legalization of physician-assisted suicide, rather than voluntary euthanasia, in the US. This is due, Battin explains, to factors such as the lack of universal health care in the US and doctor–patient relationships that are typically more distant than those in the Netherlands.

End-of-life decisions with incompetent patients raise further ethical issues. The 2005 US case of Terri Schiavo, whose life support was legally withdrawn after she had been in persistent vegetative state for 15 years, received considerable publicity. George Annas (Chapter 22) points out the similarities between the Schiavo case and the earlier cases of Karen Quinlan and Nancy Cruzan. He argues that the legal procedures established in those earlier cases should have been followed with Terri Schiavo, so that Congress did not intrude on a decision that should be made on the basis of the patient's own values (if they can be determined) or their best interests (if their values cannot be established).

These arguments all assume that death can sometimes be in the best interests of the person who dies. Yet as Epicurus famously asked, how can death be either good or bad for us when at death we cease to exist? In Chapter 23, Jeff McMahan develops a plausible answer to this question based on the 'deprivation approach', initially sketched by Thomas Nagel (1979). McMahan argues incisively that the badness of death can be understood in a context-dependent way, whereby we look at the goods that death deprived the person of, considering the trajectory that their life was most likely to take at the time.

Professional Integrity and the Goals of Medicine

Some bioethicists saw the prevalence of unjustifiable medical paternalism as symptomatic of the insularity of professional role-based ethical standards themselves, and so argued that doctors should reject a professionally generated ethic altogether and rely for guidance solely on broad-based ethical theories such as Kantianism or Utilitarianism (see, for example, Veatch, 1981). Others, however, saw this as an overreaction, and argued that an appropriate conception of the internal morality of medicine could be legitimately invoked by doctors without condoning the unethical behaviour of the past. Larry Churchill's essay (Chapter 24) was a key contribution to this reappraisal of medical ethics. Churchill argues that doctors should be guided in their professional behaviour not only by universalist ethical theories such as Utilitarianism and Kantianism but also by a sense of what it is right for them, *qua doctor*, to do in a situation, considering the specific values and goals of medicine. Churchill illustrates this by describing the different rationales that a paediatrician could appeal to in deciding whether he should report a case of child abuse to the proper social service authorities.

The idea that there can be a defensible distinct ethic for various professions has been taken up by many philosophers writing on professional ethics.[3] Indeed, partly because of a reaction to increased commercial and consumerist pressures upon doctors, there has been a renewed emphasis by the medical profession itself on the idea that acting on certain requests would be inconsistent with the proper goals of medicine. When doctors consider whether the proper goals of medicine may or may not allow them to do something, *qua doctor*, they are appealing to the notion of professional integrity. A key focus of debates about the goals of medicine has been the provision of voluntary euthanasia to patients. In Chapter 25, Leon Kass provides an influential presentation of the argument that doctors must not perform voluntary euthanasia because they are healers not killers. Kass criticizes the model of the doctor as 'highly competent hired syringe', which he sees as implicit in a medical ethic which gives primacy to respect for patient autonomy, and he goes on to argue that the absolute obligation upon doctors not to kill patients can be inferred from a conception of medicine as the art of healing the sick. That is, Kass argues that doctors should not kill their patients because this is contrary to the essential ethic of medicine, which is to heal patients or make them whole. Kass then argues that wholeness and healing are never compatible with intentionally killing the patient.

Franklin Miller and Howard Brody (Chapter 26) provide a well-argued and influential response to Kass. Like Kass, Miller and Brody take seriously the notion of professional integrity in medicine, explaining clearly how it differs from conscientious objection, but they offer a broader interpretation of the proper goals of medicine. On this conception, physician-assisted suicide is in certain circumstances compatible with the goals of medicine and thus with professional integrity.

There has been a tendency for some bioethicists to regard physician refusals to provide certain procedures on grounds of personal or professional integrity as examples of unwarranted medical paternalism. However, as Jeffrey Blustein (Chapter 27) clearly explains, doctors who refuse to provide futile interventions on the grounds that they have no mandate to perform procedures that fail to serve patients' best interests are not thereby acting paternalistically. Blustein's emphasis on the role of personal and professional integrity in medicine also helps bring out the limitations of a thoroughly consumerist model of doctor–patient relationships.

---

[3]   Some philosophers have argued that virtue ethics is best positioned to provide an underlying rationale for these distinct ethics of various professions. See, for example, Oakley and Cocking (2001) and Radden (2007).

Research Ethics

Ethical issues in research on humans have been central concerns of bioethics from the very beginning, due to the egregious experiments on concentration camp inmates carried out by the Nazis and to publicity about a number of scandalous experiments that have been carried out in subsequent years. Early discussions of research ethics focused on the importance of informed consent and international statements of the rights of research subjects, such as the Nuremberg Code and the Declaration of Helsinki.

Along with these issues, bioethicists have more recently raised ethical concerns about other aspects of research. One important debate is about the meaning and moral significance of 'equipoise' in a clinical trial. Roughly speaking, a clinical trial has reached a state of equipoise when the results in the experimental groups have become sufficiently promising that there is now genuine uncertainty about whether the standard treatment or the experimental treatment is superior. This raises ethical issues about which treatment should then be offered to research subjects and to patients. One of the most influential essays on this topic is by Benjamin Freedman (Chapter 28). Freedman rejects the subjectivity of the then-prevalent conception of equipoise in terms of the investigator's own uncertainty about the relative merits of the two treatments. Instead, Freedman argues that equipoise should be understood as a lack of consensus among experts in the clinical community about the relative merits of the two drugs or treatments under investigation. Freedman argues that clinical trials can be ethically commenced only if such a state of 'clinical equipoise' exists.

In Chapter 29, Philip Pettit issues a salutary warning against human research ethics committees (HRECs) being inherently conservative. Pettit argues that such committees develop an internal dynamic which is unduly risk-averse and reactive, as getting things right goes unrewarded, while getting things wrong is heavily penalized. He also argues that committee members will have a better understanding of the negative consequences of research that goes awry than they will of the overall benefits of a particular project, and thus of the opportunity costs of rejecting the proposal. Some have used Pettit's argument to call for greater accountability by HRECs for their decisions.

Many writers on the ethics of research hold that it is unethical to pay people a fee to become research subjects. The reason most commonly given for this view is that payments undermine the voluntariness of a person's decision to become a research subject. Against this orthodoxy, Martin Wilkinson and Andrew Moore (Chapter 30) argue that payments to induce people to become research subjects need not be unethical. Wilkinson and Moore argue strongly that such payments need not undermine the voluntariness of a person's decision to become a research subject, and that potential research subjects along with investigators will often be better off overall if subjects are allowed to be paid. Wilkinson and Moore also reject the idea that desperate need removes the possibility of giving autonomous consent.

One of the most controversial debates in contemporary bioethics focuses on research conducted on people in developing countries. Should clinical drug trials that would not be permitted in developed countries be allowed in developing countries, in cases where such trials provide patients in developing countries with their only opportunity to obtain a promising but expensive new drug? A major catalyst of this debate was a series of placebo-controlled trials held in the mid-1990s to test the effectiveness of a variety of interventions in preventing mother-to-child transmission of HIV in developing countries. Trials in the US had already shown AZT to be the most effective way of preventing the transmission of HIV from infected pregnant women to their fetuses, but the placebo-controlled trials in developing countries were testing less expensive interventions, such as vitamin A, immunotherapies and different AZT regimens. Peter Lurie and Sidney M. Wolfe (Chapter 31) criticize these placebo-controlled trials in developing countries as involving an unethical double standard. HIV-infected women who were randomly assigned to the placebo group would receive no intervention whatsoever, whereas all of the women participating in the US trials had access to AZT or other antiretrovirals. Lurie and Wolfe's essay stimulated much lively debate. In defence of this trial, the investigators argued that these women were made no worse off than they otherwise would have been, as AZT would have been too expensive for them anyway. Others, however, agreed with Lurie and Wolfe, and argued that such trials exploit research subjects in developing countries, because the investigators and trial sponsors take unfair advantage of research subjects, even if those subjects gave their informed and voluntary consent to participate (see, for example, Ballantyne, 2005; Wertheimer, 1996).

Some bioethicists argue that overcoming concerns about exploitation of developing country research subjects requires an agreement between developing country governments and clinical trial investigators and sponsors that these subjects' communities will be provided with a reasonable opportunity to gain access to the drug after the trial has been completed, should the drug be shown safe and effective (see Macklin, 2004). However, the Participants in the 2001 Conference on Ethical Aspects of Research in Developing Countries (Chapter 32) argue for a broader criterion of non-exploitative clinical trials, whereby avoiding exploitation does not require providing post-trial access to the drug being tested ('reasonable availability'), but rather requires the provision of 'fair benefits' of various kinds, such as health benefits to research subjects, employment for members of the community, capacity development (for example physical infrastructure, training and so on) and opportunities to share the financial rewards associated with the intervention being evaluated.

Ethics and the Pharmaceutical Industry

Even after clinical trials have shown drugs to be safe and effective, there are further ethical concerns that have been raised about the pharmaceutical industry. There is an emerging debate about the ethics of differential access to medication, as people in developing countries typically have less access to necessary drugs than do people in developed countries. In 2001, 20 per cent of South African adults had AIDS, but AIDS drugs imported from the US were prohibitively expensive. South African pharmaceutical companies sought to manufacture cheaper, generic copies of these AIDS drugs via a process known as compulsory licensing, however, multinational pharmaceutical companies used court action to prevent this. Thomas Pogge (Chapter 33) proposes an innovative incentive scheme for pharmaceutical companies to change their priorities. Pogge does not question the moral legitimacy of drug patents but argues that an alternative system of drug patenting should be developed, whereby pharmaceutical companies are given a financial reward from public funds in developed countries in accordance with the extent of the drug's impact on the global disease burden. Pogge argues that such a scheme would not be impossibly costly (his rough estimate is US$45–90 billion annually) and that governments (or international government organizations) could develop and implement this scheme relatively easily, with citizens in developed countries being persuaded on moral grounds that this is a legitimate use of their taxes (roughly US$70 per person annually).

There has also been considerable discussion about the links many doctors have with the pharmaceutical industry and the resulting problems that physician conflicts of interests can create in patient care.[4] The pharmaceutical industry is also capable of exercising considerable power over the conduct and ethical oversight of clinical trials, as the 1996 case of Nancy Olivieri demonstrates. Apotex proposed to conduct a trial of a new thalassaemia drug, deferiprone, at the Toronto Hospital for Sick Children. Oliveiri was a member of the combined University of Toronto/Hospital for Sick Children research ethics committee, and she asked for the patient information forms in the trial to be altered to better reflect the risks of deferiprone. Olivieri was vilified by the ethics committee, and was eventually dismissed by the University of Toronto, to whom Apotex had promised new buildings worth several million dollars (see Naimark, Knoppers and Lowy, 2000). In Chapter 34, Arthur Schafer analyses the Olivieri case and another case involving responses by the same university and pharmaceutical company Eli Lilly to concerns expressed publicly by prominent psychiatrist David Healy about the drug Prozac, manufactured by Eli Lilly. Schafer argues that these cases demonstrate that maintaining public confidence in biomedical research requires prohibiting universities and hospitals from conducting industry-funded research altogether, and that such research ought instead to be supported entirely from public funds.

In response to these and other ethical concerns, some pharmaceutical companies have attempted to restore their public images by employing bioethicists, subsidizing professorial chairs in bioethics and similar measures. Carl Elliott's lively and widely read discussion (Chapter 35) provides valuable insights into the variety of subtle and not-so-subtle means used by pharmaceutical companies to positively influence public opinion about their products. Elliott brings out vividly how such sponsorship threatens to undermine the independence of bioethicists and can jeopardize public trust in their pronouncements.

Bioethics and Public Policy

The most practical side of bioethics is, perhaps, its engagement with public policy. Many bioethicists have contributed influential discussions about policy recommendations on the basis of ethical arguments, such as those mentioned above, or certain political moralities, along with considerations about democracy and political legitimacy. Dan Wikler's essay (Chapter 36) shows what is and is not ethically troublesome about eugenics programmes. After demonstrating what is objectionable about the directions that were taken by the early twentieth-century eugenics movement, Wikler argues that eugenics need not be taken in such directions, and so its infamous past does not reveal something inherently wrong with eugenics. Wikler then provides a very helpful review and analysis of more fundamental objections to eugenics (including some directed at contemporary practices in clinical genetics), and sorts out which of these are most serious and which are based on faulty reasoning or misunderstandings of the essential claims of eugenics. The essay ends by usefully pointing out how decisions about genetic intervention in individual cases can often result in others being burdened or benefited

---

[4] Two comprehensive empirical studies of these links are Brennan et al. (2006) and Wazana (2000).

in various ways, and that such decisions therefore raise important questions of distributive justice, which deserve much more discussion.

In Chapter 37, Judith Jarvis Thomson builds on her classic argument about the ethics of abortion by considering what the law on abortion should be. Thomson indicates how embryos and fetuses might coherently be thought to have moral rights, but goes on to argue against those who seek to protect any such rights by prohibiting abortion. Thomson argues that such a prohibition is a gross violation of women's liberty, and that in forcing the views of one section of society on others who through their reason have reached different conclusions, it arbitrarily excludes this latter group from public policy decision-making, and precludes their rationally assenting to such a law.

The development of democratic public policy on these issues of life and death, reproduction, genetics and biotechnology highlights the tensions between populist and deliberative conceptions of democracy. Populist approaches hold that the will of the majority serves as the appropriate reference point for law-making, because uneducated people are as capable of using their reason to judge what is right and wrong as are educated people (see Devlin, 1962). However, Mary Warnock (Chapter 38) argues that popular moral belief may be ill-informed, and in that case would not seem to be an appropriate basis for law-making. For example, Warnock suggests that people's views about the morality of experimenting on human embryos are often based on ignorance about what a human embryo is or what such experimentation involves, and she argues that a democratic society should not base its laws on the views of people who are ignorant about such matters. Warnock also argues that on many issues there may be no consensus in the community, but rather a plurality of views on both the morality of a certain practice and the justifiability of any proposed government regulation of such a practice. Warnock suggests that democratic governments engaged in law reform can legitimately look to properly constituted expert committees for advice, especially in making laws to regulate some of the novel practices that advancements in health care and reproduction have created.

In a more recent contribution to this debate, Amy Gutmann and Dennis Thompson (Chapter 39) draw on emerging deliberative conceptions of democracy and demonstrate how they can be fruitfully applied in bioethics. Gutmann and Thompson argue that members of expert committees should not think of themselves merely as delegates of some interest group, but should approach their task with public-spiritedness and should be open-minded to reasoned moral argument.

Future Directions in Bioethics

As the essays in this volume demonstrate, the field of bioethics is developing in a range of different directions. At a broad level, there is a distinction emerging between bioethical issues facing current health professionals and bioethical issues involving future applications of various biotechnologies, some of which remain fairly speculative. We are likely to see much new work on what theories of justice demand in terms of access to stem cell therapies and genetic enhancements, in cases where those interventions are shown to be safe and effective. It is also possible that recent advances in de-differentiating somatic cells might defuse debates about the ethics of stem cell research, by obviating the need to destroy human embryos for their stem cells. However, it remains unclear whether stem cells obtained through de-differentiation hold the same promise as embryonic stem cells. By contrast, ethical and policy debates about embryo selection decisions in pre-implantation genetic diagnosis will probably intensify, as demand for this technique is likely to increase. And recent threats of pandemics from SARS and avian flu are prompting new approaches to the ethics of various public health responses to infectious diseases in an era of increasing globalization. Of course, there will continue to be ethical debates about more familiar issues in clinical practice, such as the limits of informed consent, the meaning of medical futility and end-of-life decision-making, along with new discussions about the pros and cons of moves towards greater transparency, particularly in light of innovative uses of information technology in health care. In any case, a broad division between familiar questions and more speculative issues is no threat to the overall integrity of the discipline and, indeed, is crucial to maintaining its vitality. After all, many (though not all) of the ethical issues that confront health professionals have arisen from the application of new technologies once regarded as speculative, so it is important to understand how these ethical debates inform each other.

Whichever directions eventuate, bioethics has now become an established field of inquiry and clearly has an exciting future ahead. In selecting these essays, I wanted to convey the quality and vitality of debates in this field. I hope this volume demonstrates how, in providing answers to questions of continuing relevance, bioethics enriches our appreciation of issues that matter to us all.

References

Ballantyne, Angela (2005), 'HIV International Clinical Research: Exploitation and Risk', *Bioethics*, **19**, nos 5–6, pp. 476–91.

Beauchamp, Tom and Childress, James (2009), *Principles of Biomedical Ethics* (6th edn), New York: Oxford University Press.

Brennan, T.A. *et al.* (2006), 'Health Industry Practices that Create Conflicts of Interest: A Policy Proposal for Academic Medical Centers', *Journal of the American Medical Association*, **295**, no. 4, pp. 429–33.

Clarke, Steve and Oakley, Justin (eds) (2007), *Informed Consent and Clinician Accountability: The Ethics of Report Cards on Surgeon Performance*, Cambridge: Cambridge University Press.

Daniels, Norman (1985), *Just Health Care*, Cambridge: Cambridge University Press.

Devlin, Patrick (1962), 'Law, Democracy, and Morality', *University of Pennsylvania Law Review*, **110**, no. 5, pp. 635–49.

Dworkin, Gerald (1976), 'Autonomy and Behavior Control', *Hastings Center Report*, **6** (February), pp. 23–28.

Emanuel, Ezekiel J. and Emanuel, Linda L. (1992), 'Four Models of the Physician–Patient Relationship', *Journal of the American Medical Association*, **267**, no. 16, pp. 2221–26.

Macklin, Ruth (2004), *Double Standards in Medical Research in Developing Countries*, Cambridge: Cambridge University Press.

Manson, Neil C. and O'Neill, Onora (2007), *Rethinking Informed Consent in Bioethics*, Cambridge: Cambridge University Press.

Nagel, Thomas (1979), 'Death', in Thomas Nagel, *Mortal Questions*, Cambridge: Cambridge University Press.

Naimark, A., Knoppers, B.M. and Lowy, F.H. (2000), *Clinical Trials of L1 (deferiprone) at The Hospital for Sick Children: A Review of Facts and Circumstances*, Toronto: The Hospital for Sick Children.

O'Neill, Onora (2002), *Autonomy and Trust in Bioethics*, Cambridge: Cambridge University Press.

Oakley, Justin and Cocking, Dean (2001), *Virtue Ethics and Professional Roles*, Cambridge: Cambridge University Press.

Post, Stephen G. (1993), 'Can Familial Caregiving be Required?', in Rosalie A. Kane and Arthur L. Caplan (eds), *Ethical Conflicts in the Management of Home Care*, New York: Springer.

Radden, Jennifer (2007), 'Virtue Ethics as Professional Ethics: The Case of Psychiatry', in R.L. Walker and P.J. Ivanhoe (eds), *Working Virtue: Virtue Ethics and Contemporary Moral Problems*, Oxford: Clarendon Press.

Rawls, John (1972), *A Theory of Justice*, Oxford: Oxford University Press.

Singer, Peter (1976), *Animal Liberation*, London: Jonathan Cape.

Singer, Peter (1993), *Practical Ethics* (2nd edn), Cambridge: Cambridge University Press.

Veatch, Robert M. (1981), *A Theory of Medical Ethics*, New York: Basic Books.

Wazana, A. (2000), 'Physicians and the Pharmaceutical Industry: Is a Gift Ever Just a Gift?', *Journal of the American Medical Association*, **283**, pp. 373–80.

Wertheimer, Alan (1996), *Exploitation*, Princeton: Princeton University Press.

Part I
Ethics in Clinical Practice

[1]

Autonomy & the Refusal of Lifesaving Treatment

by BRUCE L. MILLER

Contemporary, normative ethics—both theoretical and applied—has reacted against utilitarianism because of its tendency to regard the individual as little more than a recipient of good and evil. To avoid the pernicious effect of this notion, many philosophers have insisted that the concept of a person as an autonomous agent must have a central and independent role in ethical theory.[1] From this position there is firm ground to resist coercion and its less forceful, but more pervasive, cousins: manipulation and undue influence. It also provides a warrant for treating a person's own choices, plans, and conception of self as generally dominant over what another believes to be in that person's best interest.

In biomedical ethics, the concept of a person as an autonomous agent places an obligation on physicians and other health professionals to respect the values of patients and not to let their own values influence decisions about treatment. The conflict of patient values and physician values becomes most troublesome when a patient refuses treatment needed to sustain life and a physician believes that the patient should be treated. The conflict can be resolved by taking a firm line on autonomy: any autonomous decision of a patient must be respected. On the other hand, the physician's obligation to preserve life can be placed above the patient's right to autonomy and refusals of treatment can then be overridden when they conflict with "medical judgment."[2] The notion of medical judgment used here is not clear, and it may only be a gloss for "what doctor thinks best." Neither extreme position is tenable; both are insensitive to the complexities of such cases, and the second removes the right to autonomy altogether. But, the conflict between autonomy and medical judgment is not as sharp as it seems.

Four Cases

Consider the following cases.

CASE 1. *A doctor, sixty-eight years of age, had been retired for five years after severe myocardial infarction. He was admitted to a hospital after a barium meal had shown a large and advanced carcinoma of the stomach. Ten days after palliative gastrectomy was performed, the patient collapsed with a massive pulmonary embolism and an emergency embolectomy was done on the ward. When*

BRUCE L. MILLER *is professor of philosophy, Medical Humanities Program, Michigan State University.*

the patient recovered, he asked that if he had a further cardiovascular collapse no steps should be taken to prolong his life, for the pain of his cancer was more than he would needlessly bear. He wrote a note to this effect in his case records and the hospital staff knew of his feelings.[3]

CASE 2. *A forty-three-year-old man was admitted to the hospital with injuries and internal bleeding caused when a tree fell on him. He needed whole blood for a transfusion but refused to give the necessary consent. His wife also refused. Both were Jehovah's Witnesses, holding religious beliefs that forbid the infusion of whole blood. The hospital lawyer brought a petition to the home of a judge. The patient's wife, brother, and grandfather were present to express his strong religious convictions. The grandfather said that the patient "wants to live very much . . . He wants to live in the Bible's promised new world where life will never end. A few hours here would nowhere compare to everlasting life." The judge was concerned with the patient's capacity to make such a decision in light of his serious condition. She recognized the possibility that the use of drugs might have impaired his judgment. The hospital lawyer replied that the patient was receiving fluid intravenously but no drugs that could impair his judgment. He was conscious, knew what the doctor was saying, was aware of the consequences of his decision, and had with full understanding executed a statement refusing the recommended transfusion and releasing the hospital from liability. The judge went to the patient's bedside. She asked him whether he believed that he would be deprived of the opportunity for "everlasting life" if transfusion were ordered by the court. His response was, "Yes. In other words, it is between me and Jehovah; not the courts . . . . I'm willing to take my chances. My faith is that strong . . . . I wish to live, but not with blood transfusions. Now get that straight." The patient had two young children. There was a family business and money to provide for the children, and a large family willing to care for them.*[4]

CASE 3. *A thirty-eight-year-old man with mild upper respiratory infection suddenly developed severe headache, stiff neck, and high fever. He went to an emergency room for help. The diagnosis was pneumococcal meningitis, a bacterial meningitis almost always fatal if not treated. If treatment is delayed, permanent neurological damage is likely. A physician told the patient that urgent treatment was needed to save his life and forestall brain damage. The patient refused to consent to treatment saying that he wanted to be allowed to die.*[5]

CASE 4. *A fifty-two-year-old married man was admitted to a medical intensive care unit (MICU) after a suicide attempt. He had retired two years earlier because of progressive physical disability related to multiple sclerosis (MS) during the fifteen years before admission. He had successfully adapted to his physical limitations, remaining actively involved in family matters with his wife and two teenage sons. However, during the three months before admission, he had become morose and withdrawn. On the evening of admission, while alone, he had ingested an unknown quantity of diazepam. When his family returned six hours later, they found the patient semiconscious. He had left a suicide note. On admission to the MICU, physician examination showed several neurologic deficits, but no more severe than in recent examinations. The patient was alert and fully conversant. He expressed to the house officers his strong belief in a patient's right to die with dignity. He stressed the "meaningless" aspects of his life related to his loss of function, insisting that he did not want vigorous medical intervention should serious complications develop. This position appeared logically coherent to the MICU staff. However, a consultation with members of the psychiatric liaison service was requested. During the initial consultation the patient showed that the onset of his withdrawal and depression coincided with a diagnosis of inoperable cancer in his mother-in-law, who lived in another city. His wife had spent more and more time satisfying her mother's needs. In fact, on the night of his suicide attempt, the patient's wife and two sons had left him alone for the first time to visit his mother-in-law.[6]*

In the first two cases, the most compelling intuition is to respect the refusal of treatment. The patients are competent, exercising their right of autonomy to refuse treatments they believed not in their interest. The patient in Case 1 believed further resuscitation was needless, for it would only briefly prolong a life of great suffering. His concern was for life on earth. The patient in Case 2 believed the transfusions would deprive him of salvation. His concern for life hereafter made whatever life on earth he could get from the transfusions insignificant. In Case 2 the Superior Court and the Court of Appeals recognized the patient's right to refuse transfusion and none was given. Though the patient's chances were thought very slim, he recovered and was discharged from the hospital. In Case 1, two weeks after the embolectomy the patient suffered acute myocardial infarction; his heart was restarted five times in one night. He recovered to linger for three weeks in a coma. On the day his heart stopped, plans were being made to put him on a respirator. The Jehovah's Witness was fortunate, retaining his life on earth without risking the loss of life everlasting. The physician was not so lucky; his right to an autonomous decision concerning the manner of his own death fell victim to the technological imperative—"If you *can* do it, you *should* do it."

Cases 3 and 4, however, incline to the view that patient autonomy may be overriden by medical judgment. In Case 3 there is no apparent reason to justify the death of this otherwise healthy victim of meningitis. His medical condition is not hopeless, as was the condition of the doctor in Case 1, nor does he have a religious objection to treatment like the Jehovah's Witness in Case 2. Our intuition is to treat him against his will. In Case 4 the patient's disability may give us pause; it does prevent a full life, yet he had managed until his mother-in-law became ill and the family began attending to her needs. We might expect that family discussion of the problem could lead to a resolution that would restore the patient's desire to live.

At first glance the position that although there is a right to autonomy from which patients can refuse lifesaving treatment, the right is not absolute and sometimes medical judgment can override it is a tenable one; for there is nothing surprising about a right that is not absolute.[7] However, acknowledging the limits of rights does not mean that rights can be overriden when their exercise conflicts with others' judgments. If medical judgment can override the right to refusal of treatment, then all four patients should have been treated against their will, for in each case a physician believed that the patient should be treated. If this is implausible, given our intuitions on Cases 1 and 2, then we have to say that autonomy is supreme and the refusals of lifesaving treatment should have been respected in all four cases.

One way around this impasse is to develop a list of conditions that must be taken into account to determine whether a refusal of treatment should be respected,[8] for example, age of the patient, life expectancy with and without treatment, the level of incapacity with and without treatment, the degree of pain and suffering, the effect of the time and circumstances of death on family and friends, the views of the family on whether the patient should be treated, the views of the physician and other medical staff, and the costs of treatment. This is a plausible approach; with it the refusal of treatment for meningitis can be justifiably overriden and the refusal of treatment for the doctor suffering from cancer justifiably respected. The meningitis patient is young and will recover without residual defect to lead a full life; the cancer patient will die soon in any case, is suffering greatly, and even though resuscitated is not likely to survive with a capacity for conscious awareness.

The problem with this approach is twofold. First, the list of characteristics is so vague, and hence subject to alternative interpretations, that the right to autonomy, and with it the right to refuse lifesaving treatment, can again be overruled. In practice it might turn out that refusals of treatment would be respected only if there were few negative consequences and everyone agreed with the decision. Second, this view shifts the focus from the patient's refusal to the patient's condition. Appealing to a list of diagnostic and prognostic features and to the consequences for others of treatment versus nontreatment makes the decision one *about* the patient rather than one *by* the patient. The patient's refusal becomes simply one of many factors to weigh in arriving at a decision. But the thrust of placing the patient's right to autonomy in the forefront of medical ethics is to counteract just that tendency to secure those decisions *for* patients that are appropriately theirs. An approach that preserves this priority must be developed.

Four Senses of Autonomy

If the concept of autonomy is clarified, we will have a more rigorous understanding of what the right to autonomy is and what it means to respect that right, thus illuminating the problems regarding refusals of lifesaving treatment. At the first level of analysis it is enough to say that autonomy is self-determination, that the right to autonomy is the right to make one's own choices, and that respect for autonomy is the obligation not to interfere with the choice of another and to treat another as a being capable of choosing. This is helpful, but the concept has more than one meaning. There are at least four senses of the concept as it is used in medical ethics: autonomy as free action, autonomy as authenticity, autonomy as effective deliberation, and autonomy as moral reflection.[9]

Autonomy as free action. Autonomy as free action means an action that is voluntary and intentional. An action is voluntary if it is not the result of coercion, duress, or undue influence. An action is intentional if it is the conscious object of the actor. To submit oneself, or refuse to submit oneself, to medical treatment is an action. If a patient wishes to be treated and submits to treatment, that action is intentional. If a patient wishes not to be treated and refuses treatment, that too is an intentional action. A treatment may be a free action by the physician and yet the patient's action is not free. If the meningitis victim is restrained and medication administered against his wishes, the patient has not voluntarily submitted to treatment. If the patient agrees to pain relief medication, but is given an antibiotic without his knowledge, the patient voluntarily submitted to treatment, but it was not a free action because he did not intend to receive an antibiotic. The doctrine of consent, as it was before the law gave us the doctrine of *informed* consent, required that permission be obtained from a patient and that the patient be told what treatment would be given; this maintains the right to autonomy as free action. Permission to treat makes the treatment voluntary and knowledge of what treatment will be given makes it intentional.

Autonomy as authenticity. Autonomy as authenticity means that an action is consistent with the person's attitudes, values, dispositions, and life plans. Roughly, the person is acting in character. Our inchoate notion of authenticity is revealed in comments like, "He's not himself today" or "She's not the Jane Smith I know." For an action to be labeled "inauthentic" it has to be unusual or unexpected, relatively important in itself or its consequences, and have no apparent or proffered explanation. An action is unusual for a given actor if it is different from what the actor almost always (or always) does in the circumstances, as in, "He always flies to Chicago, but this time he took the train." If an action is not of the sort that a person either usually does or does not do, for example, something more like getting married than drinking coffee, it can still be a surprise to those who know the person. "What! George got married?"

A person's dispositions, values, and plans can be known, and particular actions can then be seen as not in conformity with them. If the action is not of serious import, concern about its authenticity is inappropriate. To ask of a person who customarily drinks beer, "Are you *sure* you want to drink wine?" is to make much of very little. If an explanation for the unusual or unexpected behavior is apparent, or given by the actor, that usually cuts off concern. If no explanation appears on the face of things or if one is given that is unconvincing, then it is appropriate to wonder if the action is really one that the person wants to take. Often we will look for disturbances in the person's life that might account for the inauthenticity.

It will not always be possible to label an action authentic or inauthentic, even where much is known about a person's attitudes, values, and life plans. On the other hand, a given disposition may not be sufficiently specific to judge that it would motivate a particular action. A generous person need not contribute to every cause to merit that attribute. If a person's financial generosity is known to extend to a wide range of liberal political causes, not making a contribution to a given liberal candidate for political office may be inauthentic. On the other hand, most people have dispositions that conflict in some situations; an interest in and commitment to scientific research will conflict with fear of invasive procedures when such an individual considers being a subject in medical research. Many questions about this sense of autonomy cannot be explored here, for example, whether there can be authentic conversions in a person's values and life plans.

Autonomy as effective deliberation. Autonomy as effective deliberation means action taken where a person believed that he or she was in a situation calling for a decision, was aware of the alternatives and the consequences of the alternatives, evaluated both, and chose an action based on that evaluation. Effective deliberation is of course a matter of degree; one can be more or less aware and take more or less care in making decisions. Effective deliberation is distinct from authenticity and free action. A person's action can be voluntary and intentional and not result from effective deliberation, as when one acts impulsively. Further, a person who has a rigid pattern of life acts authentically when he or she does the things we have all come to expect, but without effective deliberation. In medicine, there is no effective deliberation if a patient believes that the physician makes all the decisions. The doctrine of *informed* consent, which requires that the patient be informed of the risks and benefits of the proposed treatment and its alternatives, protects the right to autonomy when autonomy is conceived as effective deliberation.

Gerald Dworkin has shown that an effective deliberation must be more than an apparently coherent thought process.[10] A person who does not wear automobile seat belts may not know that wearing seat belts significantly reduces the chances of death and serious injury. Deliberation without this knowledge can be logically coherent and lead to a decision not to wear seat belts. Alternatively, a person may know the dangers of not wearing seat belts, but maintain that the inconvenience of wearing them outweighs the reduced risk of serious injury or death. Both deliberations are noneffective: the first because it proceeds on ignorance of a crucial piece of information; the second because it assigns a nonrational weighting to alternatives.

It is not always possible to separate the factual and evaluative errors in a noneffective deliberation. A patient may refuse treatment because of its pain and inconvenience, for example, kidney dialysis, and choose to run the risk of serious illness and death. To say that such a patient has the relevant knowledge, if all alternatives and their likely consequences have been explained, but made a nonrational assignment of priorities, is much too simple. A more accurate characterization may be that the patient fails to appreciate certain aspects of the alternatives. The patient may be cognitively aware of the pain and inconvenience of the treatment, but because he or she has not experienced them, may believe that they will be worse than they really are. If the patient has begun dialysis, assessment of the pain and inconvenience may not take into account the possibilities of adapting to them or reducing them by adjustments in the treatment.

In order to avoid conflating effective deliberation with reaching a decision acceptable to the physician, the following must be kept in mind: first, the knowledge a patient needs to decide whether to accept or refuse treatment is not equivalent to a physician's knowledge of alternative treatments and their consequences; second, what makes a weighting nonrational is not that it is different from the physician's weighting, but either that the weighting is inconsistent with other values that the patient holds or that there is good evidence that the patient will not persist in the weighting; third, lack of appreciation of aspects of the alternatives is most likely when the patient has not fully experienced them. In some situations there will be overlap between determinations of authenticity and effective deliberation. This does not undercut the distinctions between the senses of autonomy; rather it shows the complexity of the concept.

Autonomy as moral reflection. Autonomy as moral reflection means acceptance of the moral values one acts on.[11] The values can be those one was dealt in the socialization process, or they can differ in small or large measure. In any case, one has reflected on these values and now accepts them as one's own. This sense of autonomy is deepest and

most demanding when it is conceived as reflection on one's complete set of values, attitudes, and life plans. It requires rigorous self-analysis, awareness of alternative sets of values, commitment to a method for assessing them, and an ability to put them in place. Occasional, or piecemeal moral reflection is less demanding and more common. It can be brought about by a particular moral problem and only requires reflection on the values and plans relevant to the problem. Autonomy as moral reflection is distinguished from effective deliberation, for one can do the latter without questioning the values on which one bases the choice in a deliberation. Reflection on one's values may be occasioned by deliberation on a particular problem, so in some cases it may be difficult to sort out reflection on one's values and plans from deliberation using one's values and plans. Moral reflection can be related to authenticity by regarding the former as determining what sort of person one will be and in comparison to which one's actions can be judged as authentic or inauthentic.

Resolving Apparent Conflicts

The distinction of four senses of autonomy can be used to resolve the apparent conflict between autonomy and medical judgment that the four cases generate. The action of the Jehovah's Witness in Case 2 is autonomous in at least three of the senses. It was a free action because it was voluntary and intentional. The patient was not being coerced and knew what he was doing. It was an authentic action because it was demanded by a strongly held religious belief. A Jehovah's Witness who accepted transfusion under the circumstances would be regarded as one who lacked the strength of commitment to resist earthly temptations; this would not be cause for blame, for it is understandable and, if you are not a Jehovah's Witness, commendable. The action was the result of effective deliberation because the patient knew he had a choice, was aware of the alternatives and their consequences, evaluated them on his values, and made a choice. The situation was so clear and his belief so strong that the deliberation probably did not take much time and thought; effective deliberation is long and painstaking only when the matter for decision is perceived to be difficult. Whether the patient engaged in moral reflection is difficult to determine. The case is not sufficiently detailed to know whether the patient ever carefully reflected on his religious beliefs. One can have strong beliefs without ever having thought carefully about them. Further, since no position has been taken on just what the standards for adequate moral reflection are, it is not possible to make a determination even if all the facts were there. Whether one can, or should, choose a life plan or a religious belief by reasoned inquiry (effective deliberation at the most general level) is a matter of controversy in philosophy and theology.

In Case 1, the physician with cancer, the refusal of treatment was a free action, authentic, and the result of effective deliberation. The decision to treat the patient after he had refused resuscitation in the event of cardiovascular collapse was clearly a violation of his autonomy. He did not voluntarily submit to treatment; he was treated against his will even though no force or threat of force had to be used. He did not intend to submit to treatment, his conscious desire was not to be treated. The authenticity of the refusal of treatment is less a matter of identifying a particular strong belief and showing that the action is in accord with it, than it is a matter of the patient announcing that further resuscitation would incur needless suffering. Because this patient is a physician who has seen such suffering and is now undergoing it, it is more likely that the assertion is coming from the patient's values, and not as something that is not an authentic expression of himself. The refusal also appears to be the result of effective deliberation: the patient knew the alternatives and their consequences, his assessment and weighting of them cannot be regarded as nonrational or a lack of appreciation. Again we do not know whether and how this patient has reflected on the fundamental values that determine his judgment, but to require that he subject them to some sort of reflection before his wishes have to be respected would be to set the standards of autonomy too high.

In Case 4, the man with MS who attempted suicide, the action of the patient is a free action, that is, voluntary and intentional, and it is the result of effective deliberation, but it is not authentic. This was the outcome of the case:

The patient had too much pride to complain to his wife about his feelings of abandonment. He was able to recognize that his suicide attempt and his insistence on death with dignity were attempts to draw the family's attention to his needs. Discussion with all four family members led to improved communication and acknowledgment of the patient's special emotional needs. After these conversations, the patient explicitly retracted both his suicidal threats and his demand that no supportive medical efforts be undertaken.[12]

It is tempting to say that the actions of the patient, the suicide attempt and the refusal of treatment, were not free actions because they were neither voluntary nor intentional. Even though the patient was not coerced directly by another, he was pressured into the actions by his condition and the circumstances of his mother-in-law's terminal illness. Further, it was not an intentional action because he did not *really* want to die; he wanted attention and support. This position is not defensible. First, the claim that the actions were not voluntary rests on the fact that the pressure of circumstances as a motivating factor can be as strong as the direct threat of another person. Indeed, it is easy to imagine cases where it would be stronger. It is important to preserve a clear and distinct concept of voluntariness, and treat similar but distinguishable situations under a different rubric.

Second, the claim that his action was not intentional, that is, not his conscious object, is wrong for two reasons. It fails to distinguish the action of taking the overdose of diazepam from his saying that he wanted no treatment and that he wanted to die with dignity. It was his conscious desire to take the diazepam and to refuse treatment; whether it was his conscious desire to die with dignity is a separate matter. Its answer requires adducing considerations that belong to the notion of autonomy as authenticity. The belief that the patient did not want to die depends on knowing that he had gotten on very well for many years, that his change of view was coincident to the illness of his mother-in-law and the family's attention to her, that a desire to die is not consistent with the values revealed by the past several years of the patient's life, and that there is no apparent or proffered explanation of a change in values but instead an explanation of the alleged desire for death with dignity as a way of asserting his demands on his family. His suicide attempt, the taking of diazepam, and refusal of treatment were free actions, but they were not authentic.

The claim that the patient's taking of diazepam was the result of effective deliberation is more difficult to defend. The hospital staff regarded the explanation as logically coherent, but the appearance of logical coherence is not sufficient for effective deliberation. If the patient lacked relevant knowledge, made a nonrational assignment of weights to alternatives or failed to appreciate one of the alternatives or its consequences, then the decision to take an overdose and request that lifesaving measures not be started would not be the result of effective deliberation. The case description lacks the detail required to reach a definite conclusion on all of these. The most difficult is whether the patient overestimated the difficulty of continuing his life as a victim of MS; it is hard to imagine that he lacked knowledge, and even though we might regard his weighting of death versus continued life in his condition as mistaken, the severity of his condition and the difficulty of coping with it do not readily support a claim that it is not a rational weighting. Further, he is the person with MS and he is the one who has suffered it for fifteen years; for another person to believe that the patient fails to appreciate the severity of his condition seems on its face to discount the most relevant experience. On the other hand, his appreciation at the time of the attempted suicide might be said to have been altered by the perceived threat to his care and comfort. More information is required to decide this; even if his action is ultimately regarded as the result of effective deliberation, it is still not authentic. One might even say that the lack of authenticity influences the effectiveness of the deliberation. More strongly, if an action is not authentic, whether it is the result of effective deliberation becomes somewhat irrelevant; it is rather like asking whether a person effectively decided a matter based on values or plans that were not his own. As in the other cases, we have no clear evidence that the patient ever engaged in moral reflection, or if he did that the values and life plans he reflected about had direct bearing on the issues presented by his attempted suicide. It does seem that a person who has had to manage his life with a seriously debilitating illness must have given some thought to what is important to him and what sort of life plan is suited to him.

In the case of the patient in the emergency room with meningitis, his refusal of treatment is autonomous in the sense of free action. But is it authentic and the result of effective deliberation? This is difficult to determine unless someone in the emergency room knew the patient well or is able to get to know the patient well. Presumably no one knows him and there is not enough time to get to know him; if treatment is delayed there is risk of brain damage and death. Assuming that the patient has the capacity for autonomy in all four senses, treating him would be contrary to his autonomy in the sense of free action; whether it would be a violation of his autonomy in the senses of authenticity, effective deliberation, and moral reflection cannot be determined. Treating him would make possible his further deliberation on whether he wished to live. On balance, it is more respectful of autonomy, given all four senses, to treat him against his will. On the other hand, it might be argued that meningitis has made the patient incompetent. Though the patient has voluntarily and intentionally refused treatment, his disease has removed his capacity to act authentically or to effectively deliberate. If this is so, then the patient's refusal is not an autonomous action, and the obligation to respect the autonomy of patients would not be abridged by treating the patient against his wishes.

A Bridge between Paternalism and Autonomy

This discussion shows that there is no single sense of autonomy and that whether to respect a refusal of treatment requires a determination of what sense of autonomy is satisfied by a patient's refusal. It also shows that there need not be a sharp conflict between autonomy and medical judgment. Jackson and Youngner argue that preoccupation with patient autonomy and the right to die with dignity pose a "threat to sound decision making and the total (medical, social and ethical) basis for the 'optional' decision."[13] Sound decision making need not run counter to patient autonomy; it can involve a judgment that the patient's refusal of treatment is not autonomous in the appropriate sense. What sense of autonomy is required to respect a particular refusal of treatment is a complex question.

If a refusal of lifesaving treatment is not a free action, that is, is coerced or not intentional, then there can be no obligation to respect an autonomous refusal. It is important to note that if the action is not a free action then it makes no sense to assert *or* deny that the action was autonomous in any of the other senses. A coerced action cannot be one that was chosen in accord with the person's character and life plan, nor one that was chosen after effective deliberation, nor one that was chosen in accord with moral standards that the person has reflected upon. The point is the same if the action is not intentional. When a refusal of treatment is not autonomous in the sense of free action, the physician is obliged to see that the coercion is removed or that the person understands what he or she is doing. Is it possible that coercion cannot be removed or that the action cannot be made intentional? This could be the case with an incompetent patient, not externally coerced, but subject to an internal compulsion, or who lacked the capacity to understand his or her situation. For incompetent patients the question of honoring refusals of treatment does not arise; it is replaced by the issue of who should make decisions for incompetent patients, an issue beyond the scope of this article.

If a refusal of treatment is a free action but there is reason to believe that it is not authentic or not the result of effective deliberation, then the physician is obliged to assist the patient to effectively deliberate and reach an authentic decision. This is what happened in Case 4. It is not required that everyone bring about, make possible, or encourage another to act authentically and/or as a result of effective deliberation. Whether such an obligation exists depends on at least two factors: the nature of the relationship between the two persons and how serious or significant the action is for the actor and others. Compare the relationships of strangers, mere acquaintances, and buyer and seller on the one hand, with those of close friends, spouses, parent and child, physician and patient, and lawyer and client. To borrow, and somewhat extend, a legal term, the latter are fiduciary relationships; a close friend, parent, spouse, physician, or lawyer cannot treat the other person in the relationship at arms' length, but has an obligation to protect and advance the interests of the other. For example, we have no obligation to advise a mere acquaintance against making an extravagant and unnecessary purchase, though it is an option we have so long as we do not go so far as to interfere in someone else's business. The situation is different for a good friend, a close relative, or an attorney who is retained to give financial advice.

The other factor, the seriousness of the action, is relevant to medical and nonmedical contexts. If, inspired by the lure of a "macho" image, my brother impulsively decides to buy yet another expensive automobile, how I respond will depend on how it will affect him and his dependents. If a patient refuses a treatment that is elective in the sense that it might benefit him if done but will not have adverse consequences if not done, a physician can accept such a refusal even though it is believed not to be the result of effective deliberation. On the other hand, if the refusal of treatment has serious consequences for the patient, the physician has the obligation to at least attempt to get the patient to make a decision that is authentic and the result of effective deliberation. For the patient with meningitis who refuses treatment (Case 3) the consequences of the refusal are indeed serious, but there is no opportunity to determine whether the decision is authentic and the result of effective deliberation and, if not, to encourage and make possible an authentic and effectively deliberated decision.

A crucial issue is whether a refusal of lifesaving treatment that is autonomous in all four senses can be justifiably overridden by medical judgment. It will help here to compare the Jehovah's Witness case with a somewhat fanciful expansion of the meningitis case. The former's refusal is autonomous in three of the four senses and could be judged autonomous in the sense of moral reflection if we knew more about the patient's acceptance of his faith and had a clear idea of the criteria for moral reflection. Though the belief of Jehovah's Witnesses are not widely shared, and many regard as absurd the belief that accepting a blood transfusion is prohibited by biblical injuncton, their faith has a fair degree of social acceptance. Witnesses are not regarded as lunatics. This is an important factor in the recognition of their right to refuse transfusion. Suppose that the meningitis victim had a personal set of beliefs that forbid the use of drugs, that after years of reflection he came to the view that it was wrong to corrupt the purity of the body with foreign substances. Suppose that he acts on this belief consistently in his diet and medical care, that he has carefully thought about the fact that refusal in this circumstance may well lead to death, but he is willing to run that risk because his belief is strong. This case is parallel to the Jehovah's Witness case; the principal difference is that there is no large, organized group of individuals who share the belief and have promulgated and maintained it over time. One reaction is to regard the patient as mentally incompetent, with the central evidence being the patient's solitary stance on a belief that requires an easily avoided death. An alternative approach is to not regard the patient as incompetent, but to see treatment as justified paternalism. Finally, the position could be that a refusal of lifesaving treatment that is fully autonomous, that is, in all four senses, must be respected even though the belief on which it is founded is eccentric and not socially accepted. Which approach to take would require an analysis of incompetence, a definition of paternalism, and an examination of when it is justified.[14] Defining paternalism as an interference with autonomy in one or more of the four senses might be an illuminating approach.

The conflict between the right of the patient to autonomy and the physician's medical judgment can be bridged if the concept of autonomy is given a more thorough analysis than it is usually accorded in discussions of the problem of refusal of lifesaving treatment. In some cases where medical judgment appears to override autonomy, the four senses of autonomy have not been taken into account.

REFERENCES

[1] Alan Donagan, *The Theory of Morality* (Chicago: The University of Chicago Press, 1977); Ronald Dworkin, *Taking Rights Seriously* (Cambridge: Harvard University Press, 1977); John Rawls, *A Theory of Justice* (Cambridge: Harvard University Press, 1971).
[2] David L. Jackson and Stuart Youngner, "Patient Autonomy and 'Death with Dignity,'" *The New England Journal of Medicine* 301 (1979), 404.
[3] This case is drawn from W. St. C. Symmers, Sr., "Not Allowed to Die," *British Medical Journal* 1 (1968), 442; it is reprinted in Tom L. Beauchamp and James F. Childress, *Principles of Biomedical Ethics* (New York: Oxford University Press, 1979), p. 263.
[4] This case is drawn from *In Re Osborne*, 294 A.2d 372 (1972).
[5] This case is drawn from Eric J. Cassell, "The Function of Medicine," *Hastings Center Report* 6 (1976), 16.
[6] This case is drawn from Jackson and Youngner, p. 406.
[7] *Ibid.*, p. 408.
[8] Mark Siegler, "Critical Illness: The Limits of Autonomy" *Hastings Center Report* 8(1977), 12-15.
[9] Beauchamp and Childress, pp. 56-62; Donagan, p. 35; Gerald Dworkin, "Autonomy and Behavior Control," *Hastings Center Report* 6(1976), 23; and "Moral Autonomy" in H. Tristram Engelhardt and Daniel Callahan, *Morals, Science and Society*, (Hastings Center, 1978), p. 156; Harry G. Frankfurt, "Freedom of the Will and the Concept of a Person," *The Journal of Philosophy* 68(1971), 5; Bernard Gert and Timothy J. Duggan, "Free Will as the Ability to Will" *Nous* 13 (1979), 197; Charles Taylor, "Responsibility for Self" in Amelie Rorty, ed. *The Identities of Persons* (Berkeley: University of California Press, 1976).
[10] Gerald Dworkin, "Paternalism," in Richard A. Wasserstrom, ed. *Morality and the Law* (Belmont: Wadsworth Publishing Co., 1971).
[11] This brief account draws on Dworkin, "Moral Autonomy," and Taylor.
[12] Jackson and Youngner.
[13] *Ibid.*, p. 405.
[14] Dworkin, "Paternalism"; Bernard Gert and Charles M. Culver, "Paternalistic Behavior," *Philosophy and Public Affairs* 6(1976), 45; and "The Justification of Paternalism," in Wade L. Robison and Michael S. Pritchard, eds. *Medical Responsibility: Paternalism, Informed Consent, and Euthanasia* (Clifton, N.J.: Humana Press, 1979), pp. 1-14.

[2]

VALUE THEORY AND THE BEST INTERESTS STANDARD[1]

DAVID DEGRAZIA

ABSTRACT

The idea of a patient's best interests raises issues in prudential value theory — the study of what makes up an individual's ultimate (nonmoral) good or well-being. While this connection may strike a philosopher as obvious, the literature on the best interests standard reveals almost no engagement of recent work in value theory. There seems to be a growing sentiment among bioethicists that their work is independent of philosophical theorizing. Is this sentiment wrong in the present case? Does value theory make a significant difference in interpreting best interests? In pursuing this question, I begin with a quick sketch of broad kinds of value theories, identifying representatives that are plausible enough to count as contenders. I then explore what each account suggests in (1) neonatal treatment decisions, and (2) decisions for patients in persistent vegetative states. I conclude that while these accounts converge somewhat in their interpretations of best interests, they also have importantly different implications.

I INTRODUCTION

Contemporary bioethics generally assumes the following hierarchy of medical decision-making standards: (1) informed consent; (2) substituted judgment; and (3) best interests. In other words, if a patient lacks decision-making capacity, an appropriate surrogate should attempt to determine what the patient would have wanted in her present circumstances;[2] but if that question cannot reasonably

---

[1] I would like to thank an anonymous reviewer and Aaron Mackler for numerous insightful comments about an earlier draft of this paper.

[2] Under this standard I include advance directives, executed while the patient had decision-making capacity, declaring her preferences for particular treatment options in the event of losing capacity or competence. Such directives are a particularly strong form of evidence about what the patient would have wanted.

be answered (say, if the patient's values and preferences are entirely unknown), an attempt must be made to determine what course of action optimally promotes her interests. Now the idea of a patient's best interests raises issues in prudential value theory — the study of what makes up an individual's ultimate (nonmoral) good or well-being. While this connection may strike a philosopher as obvious, the literature on the best interests standard reveals almost no engagement of recent work in value theory. Discussions of patients' best interests are often naive, begging questions by presupposing some account of prudential value without defending it against plausible alternatives (or even showing any awareness of alternatives or of the philosophical issues involved).[3]

There seems to be a growing sentiment among bioethicists that their work is independent of philosophical theorizing.[4] Is this sentiment wrong in the present case? Does value theory make a significant difference in interpreting best interests? In pursuing this question, I begin with a quick sketch of broad kinds of value theories, identifying representatives that are plausible enough to count as contenders. I then explore what each account suggests in (1) neonatal treatment decisions, and (2) decisions for patients in

---

[3] Bioethics anthologies generally reflect the state of the broader bioethics literature at any given time. A search through all of the introductory sections in three leading bioethics anthologies uncovers, at most, a few implicit discussions of value theory in relation to this standard; even in these discussions there is no reference to recent work in value theory. See Thomas A. Mappes and Jane S. Zembaty, eds. *Biomedical Ethics*, 3rd ed., New York: McGraw-Hill, 1991, pp. 47–48; Tom L. Beauchamp and LeRoy Walters, eds. *Contemporary Issues in Bioethics*, Belmont, California: Wadsworth, 1989; and John Arras and Nancy Rhoden, eds. *Ethical Issues in Modern Medicine*, 3rd ed., Mountain View, California: Mayfield, 1989, pp. 135–36. Even journal articles authored by philosophers frequently display the naivete to which I refer. (See, e.g., Daniel Wikler, "The Definition of Death and Persistent Vegetative State", *Hastings Center Report* 18, February–March 1988: 44–47.) For an exception to the rule that the best interests literature ignores value theory, see Dan W. Brock, "Quality of Life Measures in Health Care and Medical Ethics", in Martha Nussbaum and Amartya Sen, eds. *The Quality of Life*, New York: Oxford University Press, 1993: 95–132.

[4] See, e.g., Albert R. Jonsen and Stephen Toulmin, *The Abuse of Casuistry: A History of Moral Reasoning*, Berkeley, California: University of California Press, 1988; and John D. Arras, "Getting Down to Cases: The Revival of Casuistry in Bioethics", *Journal of Medicine and Philosophy* 16, 1991: 29–51. For scepticism about the value of moral theorizing in works that do not focus on bioethics, see, e.g., Alasdaire MacIntyre, *After Virtue*, 2nd ed, Notre Dame, Indiana: University of Notre Dame Press, 1984; Annette Baier, *Postures of the Mind*, Minneapolis, Minnesota: University of Minnesota Press, 1985; and Bernard Williams, *Ethics and the Limits of Philosophy*, Cambridge, Massachusetts: Harvard University Press, 1985.

52 DAVID DEGRAZIA

persistent vegetative states. I conclude that while these accounts converge somewhat in their interpretations of best interests, they also have importantly different implications.

Because discussions of the best interests standard tend to beg questions of prudential value that are deeply and systematically explored in the value theory literature, here is an area within bioethics in which philosophical theorizing is potentially very enriching. Greater awareness of the theoretical issues, of plausible options, and of the implications of each leading option is likely to enhance the integrity of future efforts to unpack the concept of a patient's best interests. Philosophers and other ethicists who address this concept in their lectures, writings, and consultations should take advantage of this well-developed and highly relevant body of philosophical thought. (Because I do not attempt to resolve the difficult question of which leading option is superior, I do not recommend specific policies to guide clinicians and courts.)

II QUICK SKETCH OF THEORETICAL OPTIONS

What, in general, makes up an individual's ultimate (nonmoral) good or well-being?[5] What is prudential value? Today, the customary classification divides value theories into "mental statism", desire accounts, and objective list accounts. Mental statism takes the good to be the having of certain conscious mental states. The classical "hedonists" Bentham and (on one reading) Mill took the good to be pleasure and the absence of pain. For a variety of reasons that I will not review, most theorists have found this account inadequate.[6] Is there a version of mental statism that may be considered a contender today? Has this approach been dismissed too quickly by contemporary theorists?

I think so. A few moves can produce a contender. First, substitute some notion of satisfaction or enjoyment for pleasure, and suffering or distress for pain, for a more plausible overall account of the conditions that make us better off and worse off, respectively.[7] A

---

[5] "Ultimate" is intended to exclude instrumental value. Thus, we are not looking for "all-purpose means" or Rawlsian primary goods (see John Rawls, *A Theory of Justice*, Cambridge, Massachusetts: Harvard University Press, 1971).

[6] For a penetrating discussion of the criticisms, see James Griffin, *Well-Being*, Oxford: Clarendon, 1986, ch. 1. Perhaps the most prominent exception to the rule of abandoning mental statism is R.B. Brandt (*A Theory of the Good and the Right*, Oxford: Clarendon, 1979).

[7] See L.W. Sumner, "Welfare, Happiness, and Pleasure", *Utilitas* 4(2), 1992, esp. pp. 207–14. This article contains a very insightful discussion of mental statism generally.

priest might have pleasures (say, bodily ones) without thinking they
make him better off; he does not find them satisfying and has trouble
enjoying them. But he is likely to consider whatever he enjoys and
finds satisfying to augment his prudential good. Conversely, pain is
a sensation that is arguably not always minded, even *ceteris paribus*,
especially if slight; it might even be enjoyed (say, when one touches
a bruise). Not so for suffering and distress, which are states of the
whole person and seem to be aversive by definition.

But the account may still seem inadequate. Consider Nozick's
imaginary Experience Machine, which you can preprogram to give
you all the mental states you would like: sensations, emotions, even
beliefs that you are doing things of value in the world and not just
sitting in a machine.[8] Though perhaps very satisfying, a life spent
in Nozick's machine would hardly seem to be flourishing.
Moreover, satisfaction is partly a function of expectations. And
expectations are notoriously susceptible to dampening by poverty,
oppression, socialization and so on — so that one might feel fairly
satisfied with a lot that, intuitively, seems pretty poor. Then why not
require a condition of informedness? Perhaps my good is a matter of
satisfaction with my life when I am basically informed about my
circumstances (unlike someone who doesn't know he is in Nozick's
machine, or a slave who is unaware of how profoundly oppression
has affected his expectations).[9]

But how can the theorist deal with another problem — that
mental statism seemingly implies that someone in the full flush of life
is not harmed by being painlessly and unwittingly killed, since such
killing does not cause suffering or distress? One might stipulate that,
in addition to actual satisfaction, opportunities for future satisfaction
matter. That would confirm that death is generally a harm, since
death robs one of such opportunities.

Worries about mental statism have driven most value theorists in
the direction of desire accounts, according to which an individual's

---

[8] See Robert Nozick, *Anarchy, State, and Utopia*, New York: Basic Books, 1974,
pp. 42–45.

[9] Wayne Sumner brought this possibility to my attention in conversation.
Perhaps a condition of informedness reduces the present problem without solving
it. It is conceivable that a slave's becoming fully informed of the way in which
oppression has lowered his expectations might not alter them and, thereby, his state
of satisfaction. One might insist that he is poorly off even if satisfied. (Others might
argue that he is doing well, displaying rare virtues of stoicism.) Especially troubling
are cases in which someone's low expectations are entrenched due to psychological
pathologies (such as irreparably damaged self-esteem). Such cases might motivate
expanding a condition of "informedness" into one requiring basic psychological
health. But I cannot pursue these complexities here.

good consists in the satisfaction of her desires or preferences. The objects of this value theory, then, are states of affairs and not necessarily mental. My desire to be an architect is satisfied only if I really am an architect, so even convincing fantasies in Nozick's machine will not pass muster. But sometimes what we desire is not in our interests. Consider the psychotic who wants to jump through a window to escape an imagined demon, or the child who wants to finish a bottle of pills that taste good. Most desire theorists have adopted conditions for "correcting" actual desires, moving toward informed-desire or rational-desire accounts.[10] Those who have made this move may comprise the largest group of value theorists today.

One issue that divides this camp is whether to adopt the Experience Requirement — which states that only things that affect our consciousness affect our good. Many of the things we desire are not mental states but states of the world. Now is there any reason why desire-satisfaction or frustration must affect our consciousness, in order to count as affecting our good? Maybe not. If I am maliciously slandered, perhaps I am *ipso facto* worse off, even if I don't know about the unkind words. Similarly if I am cheated out of an inheritance without my ever realizing it.[11] On the other hand, without the Experience Requirement, the desire account can ride away like a wild horse. To pick up Parfit's example, if I meet a stranger on the train, form the desire that he succeed in his plans, and then forget about him entirely, am I really better off if — years later — he succeeds?[12] And if my desire for animal liberation is fulfilled two hundred years after my death, am I, the dead person, better off? Surely the desire account needs reigning in. What is controversial is whether the Experience Requirement reins in too much.[13] I simply leave it open whether the most plausible corrected-desire account adopts the Experience Requirement; in effect, we have two contenders here (though they have not been specified in detail).

[10] See Robert Goodin, "Laundering Preferences", in John Elster and Aanund Hylland, *Foundations of Social Choice Theory*, Cambridge: Cambridge University Press, 1986: 75—101. For what may be the most developed corrected-desire approach, see Griffin, *Well-Being*.

[11] Griffin, *Well-Being*, pp. 16—17.

[12] Derek Parfit, *Reasons and Persons*, Oxford: Oxford University Press, 1984, Appendix 1.

[13] Griffin argues for rejecting the Experience Requirement (*Well-Being*, pp. 16—19). Sumner defends the Requirement, but takes it to motivate a move away from desire accounts back in the direction of mental statism ("Welfare, Happiness, and Pleasure", pp. 221—23).

Mental statism and desire accounts may be understood as subjective accounts of prudential value; what figures in an individual's good is a function of that individual's specific desires or the quality of her mental states. In contrast, objective list accounts identify prudential value with certain kinds of states of affairs, regardless of whether one desires them and whether they are satisfying or enjoyable. Since the kinds of states of affairs are considered valuable for anyone, they can, in principle, be listed. Thus, a theory might hold that health is objectively good, even if (strangely) one did not desire health and health did not tend to give one satisfaction.

But probably no item could plausibly be included on a list unless it tended to be the sort of thing individuals enjoy and prefer, when informed. Otherwise it is unclear how the item could be thought to have prudential value — value to the subject. In addition to health, plausible items might be autonomy, deep personal relationships, accomplishment, and enjoyments.[14] Notice that this list makes important concessions to subjective theories. First, the inclusion of autonomy suggests leaving a lot of space to the individual to determine what is in her interests. Second, including enjoyments entails that this particular objective account is pluralistic; it overlaps with mental statism and, assuming we desire enjoyments, with desire accounts.[15] Notice also that a plausible account would contain at least one objective bad, if only implicitly — for suffering or distress seems to lower one's well-being, not just fail to increase it.

Setting aside the issue of how to defend particular items on a list, I simply note that even plausible variants of this approach will have different lists. Should one include conscious life *per se*? How about life itself, whether or not conscious? Either would ground the judgment that death is usually a harm. And if my good can be affected even if I am permanently unconscious, should one include some notion of "dignity" as an objective good? Whatever the answers to these questions, surely any objective list account that is a contender will be pluralistic, making concessions to subjective theories.

---

[14]   Despite classifying himself as an informed-desire theorist, Griffin defends each of these items (except health), suggesting that he could be placed in the objective list camp. That he straddles the divide between these two approaches is most evident in "Well-Being and its Interpersonal Comparability", in Douglas Seanor and N. Fotion, eds. *Hare and Critics: Essays on Moral Thinking*, Oxford: Clarendon, 1990: 73–88.

[15]   Brock defends such a pluralistic account in "Quality of Life Measures in Health Care and Medical Ethics". Brock is influenced here by Amartya Sen ("Plural Utility", *Proceedings of the Aristotelian Society* 81, 198: 193–218).

56 DAVID DEGRAZIA

III IMPLICATIONS FOR NEONATAL TREATMENT DECISIONS

Some infants are born with such severe medical complications that survival may not be in their interest. In such cases, parents and health care providers must decide whether to initiate potentially life-extending treatments (using this term so as to include nutrition and hydration). Since the standards of informed consent and substituted judgment are inapplicable to infants, who have never had decision-making capacity, decision-makers must employ the best interests standard.[16] Do different value theories yield different best interests judgments for newborns with hydrocephaly, spina bifida, or HIV?

In determining the best interests of a seriously impaired infant, a plausible version of mental statism would focus on the infant's experiential welfare — whether her experiences are generally aversive or "attractive" to her — while taking into account opportunities for future experiences. The condition of informedness seems irrelevant, since a newborn could make no use of additional information. Mental statism would attempt to determine whether survival would result in a life of more satisfaction, enjoyments, or the like than suffering and distress.

The desire account has trouble getting off the ground with neonatal treatment decisions. Requiring the desires of infants that count to be informed or rational makes no sense, given their limited cognitive capacities. Moreover, it is debatable whether newborns have desires at all. For the sake of argument, let us assume that they do. Still, it would be implausible to attribute to an infant desires about whether to have particular treatments, or about possible outcomes such as survival with such-and-such conditions or death. It would be more plausible to attribute desires about THIS (this experience — perhaps that it stop or that it continue). But such relatively simple desires would seem ascribable only on the basis of the phenomenological quality of the experiences in question. Thus, while the desire approach may get a footing in determining an infant's best interests, it appears to do so only by collapsing into a

---

[16] The substituted judgment standard is inapplicable to infants because they have not yet developed their own values and treatment preferences — the standard's basis for determining what individuals would have wanted. One might argue that the basis for substituting a judgment for an infant is what we assume any infant would want in a given set of circumstances. The idea of a non-individualized substituted judgment, if not an oxymoron, at least departs from the spirit of the decision-making standard.

version of mental statism.[17] So far, there is no difference between value theories.

Differences appear with certain objective list accounts. Any plausible one will regard experiential well-being as intrinsically valuable; some such concession to subjective approaches seems necessary. But the details of different lists matter crucially. Assume, for example, that our account lists deep personal relationships and conscious life itself. Then it might justify extending the life of a newborn with numerous severe handicaps and a short life expectancy (say, no more than ten years). She might survive into childhood, and love and be loved, even if her life is predicted to include somewhat more suffering than enjoyment.

Not that such a judgment would be easy. Predictions of this sort are a difficult empirical matter; and there is the problem of having to weigh the goods of conscious life and deep personal relationships against the bad of suffering.[18] But such a prediction and value judgment are perfectly intelligible. (Indeed, I participated in an ethics committee meeting in which it appeared most reasonable to

[17] One might argue the converse, that mental statism earns plausibility only by reducing to a version of the desire account — since the former's focus is on mental states that are "attractive" (i.e. desired) and those that are "aversive" (i.e. undesired). The point is a good one and supports the thesis that a plausible mental statism borrows from the spirit of desire approaches. But, unlike the desire approach, mental statism is committed, by definition, to the Experience Requirement. Since the Requirement seems reasonable in neonatal cases, it is most natural to think of the desire account reducing to mental statism in this context.

Note that if the infant grows into a child, her desire-satisfaction might not (when she is older) be collapseable into a mental statist analysis. But we do not know what she will later desire. One might object that evidence gathered from children sharing her disability could enable us to guess what the infant will desire if she grows into childhood — say, to be allowed to die. This logical possibility is not, in my opinion, very important. First, quite arguably (though I cannot review arguments here), the desires that matter, or at least matter most, on a desire account are an individual's present ones. Second, we cannot reasonably guess that the infant will, as a child, have certain desires unless we assume she will grow into a child — begging a practical question at issue. Third, evidence suggesting that children with conditions like the infant's typically have a particular preference may vary in strength. If it is rather weak, showing that these children more often than not have a particular preference (although many do not), our confidence about what the present infant would want as a child will be correspondingly weak. If, however, the evidence is quite powerful — say, that virtually all children in this class have a particular preference — it is very difficult to see how this could be so if the desire account diverged from mental statism. If, say, virtually all children with condition X wanted to die, how could that be so unless they were miserable?

[18] No objective list approach in the literature of which I am aware explicitly tackles the problem of weighing goods and bads. Perhaps such comparisons can be made only intuitively, a fact that would, for some theorists, count against this kind of value theory.

58 DAVID DEGRAZIA

predict such a future for a handicapped infant. The maddening complexity of interpreting his best interests provided one of the motivations for this paper.)

Now consider a theorist who ascribes objective value to autonomy, deep personal relationships and accomplishment — and disvalue to their lack in a human (calling such a lack an "indignity"). She might regard the promise of a relatively contented life for a well-cared-for but extraordinarily mentally impaired individual, insufficient to justify life-saving treatments. In neonatal treatment decisions, objective list accounts can diverge not only from mental statism and desire accounts, but also from each other.

IV IMPLICATIONS FOR DECISIONS REGARDING PVS PATIENTS

What do contending value theories suggest about the best interests of PVS patients (patients in persistent vegetative states)? PVS patients are permanently unconscious. While the determination of permanent loss of consciousness raises difficult medical — and epistemological — issues, let us assume that decision-makers reasonably take the patient in question to be permanently unconscious. Assume also that there is no basis for a substituted judgment. Using the best interests standard, should any and all life-supports (e.g. respirator, feeding tube) be discontinued?

According to mental statism, the patient has no interests at all because she is permanently unconscious. Thus, the best interests standard recommends neither continuing life-supports nor discontinuing them; the decision will have to be made on other grounds, such as the family's wishes or economic considerations.

Many commentators, not all of the mental statists, agree that PVS patients have no interests. Buchanan and Brock confidently assert that "the best interest principle does not apply to beings who have no capacity for consciousness and whose good can never matter to them [including PVS patients]".[19] I have often heard this claim asserted in conversation as if it were obvious. Is it?

Because people sometimes have desires about what will happen to them after they lose consciousness, some desire accounts suggest that PVS patients can have interests. For example, it might be argued that a particular PVS patient has an interest in the removal of life-supports, because that is what she wanted in the event that she became permanently unconscious. Some commentators thought this

[19] Allen Buchanan and Dan W. Brock, "Deciding for Others". *Milbank Quarterly* 64, Supp. 2, 1986, p. 73.

VALUE THEORY AND BEST INTERESTS   59

was true of Nancy Cruzan, the American PVS patient whose parents fought for removing her feeding tube, arguing that some of Cruzan's prior statements evinced a desire not to live in conditions like PVS.[20] Alternatively, a person might have an interest in continued treatment based on her desire for any measures that could extend her life. Desires of both sorts can be fully informed and rational (in light of the patient's values).

But several points must be noted. First, the thesis that PVS patients can have interests is open to desire theorists only if they reject the Experience Requirement. Second, for those who do, any specific evidence that a PVS patient would have wanted such-and-such could be used for a substituted judgment, so that appeal to best interests would be unnecessary.[21]

Objective list theorists could also argue that PVS patients have interests, but even those who think so may disagree in their assessment of patients' best interests. Some will argue that it is in the best interests of patients like Cruzan to have life-supports continued indefinitely — due to the intrinsic value of being alive (and the fact that PVS patients do not suffer).[22] Others will argue that some PVS patients are better off dead than surviving with such "indignities" as emaciation, highly contorted postures, and compromised privacy. They would argue that simply being alive is not intrinsically valuable, or at least not enough to outweigh the disvalue of the

[20] This case is the first right-to-die case to go to the United States Supreme Court, who argued that Cruzan's state, Missouri, did not violate her constitutional rights by applying a "clear and convincing" standard of evidence for determining what she would have wanted in PVS. The Court also upheld Missouri's judgment that the petitioners for removing Cruzan's feeding tube did not meet this standard of evidence. The case is important in part because the Supreme Court recognized the right to refuse unwanted medical treatment (as firmly established in common law but never before affirmed by this high court). See United States Supreme Court, *Cruzan v. Director, Missouri Department of Health*, in *United States [Supreme Court] Reports* 497, 1990: 261–357. For a commentary that rejects the relatively strong "clear and convincing" standard, see John D. Arras, "Beyond *Cruzan*: Individual Rights, Family Autonomy and the Persistent Vegetative State", *Journal of the American Geriatric Society* 39, 1991: 1018–24.

[21] If there is no such evidence about what a particular PVS patient would have wanted, the desire theorist might still argue that the patient would, say, want life-supports discontinued because virtually anyone would in the circumstances. However, I suspect that such an argument would fail. At least I know of no reason to think people's treatment preferences would converge to this degree. Also, the idea of a non-individualized substituted judgment seems to run against the spirit of this decision-making standard (see note 16).

[22] Naturally, the assertion is inconsistent with higher-brain definitions of death, according to which individuals who have permanently lost consciousness have died. Presently, no jurisdiction uses this standard.

above-mentioned "indignities". Then again, the lists of some theorists may imply that PVS patients have no interests — making the best interests standard inapplicable. What is striking here is how differently these objective list approaches might interpret a PVS patient's best interests, without any of them being clearly unreasonable.

V CONCLUDING REFLECTIONS

I close with a few reflections. To begin with an aside about the value theories themselves, the now-classic division into mental statism, desire accounts, and objective list accounts may be inadequate. A plausible desire approach that adopts the Experience Requirement may have more in common with up-dated mental statism than it does with a desire approach that rejects the Requirement; an objective list approach with significant concessions to subjectivism may look more like some desire approaches than certain alternative objective list views.[23]

This further motivates our central question: restricting ourselves to genuine contenders, do different value theories really make a difference in interpreting best interests? Our investigations support a qualified affirmative answer. Regarding neonatal treatment decisions, objective list accounts can lead us to different decisions from those supported by mental statism and desire accounts, which converge. Indeed, plausible objective list accounts can diverge from each other in their implications for newborns. And theories differ considerably over whether PVS patients have interests and, if so, whether continued existence is in their interests in particular cases.

Nor are these medical contexts just occasions for theoretical fun. Our increasing capacity to extend life on both ends of human existence amplifies the urgency of questions about the best interests of impaired newborns and PVS patients — and, of course, other categories of patients. There will be many more such patients (and many formerly competent patients will not have left behind advance directives or other evidence supporting substituted judgments). Because plausible value theories can yield different best interests judgments in such cases, bioethics cannot afford to exempt itself from the philosophical enterprise of value theory. The better informed and more insightful the discussion, the more likely we are

---

[23] Using different arguments, Shelly Kagan also questions the dominant classification scheme ("The Limits of Well-Being", *Social Philosophy and Policy* 9, 2, 1992: 169–89).

VALUE THEORY AND BEST INTERESTS   61

to have a sensible, fruitful debate about how to interpret the best interests of patients who are unable to tell us what to do for them.

Department of Philosophy
The George Washington University

[3]

Paternalism and partial autonomy

Onora O'Neill   *Department of Philosophy, Essex University*

Author's abstract

A contrast is often drawn between standard adult capacities for autonomy, which allow informed consent to be given or withheld, and patients' reduced capacities, which demand paternalistic treatment. But patients may not be radically different from the rest of us, in that all human capacities for autonomous action are limited. An adequate account of paternalism and the role that consent and respect for persons can play in medical and other practice has to be developed within an ethical theory that does not impose an idealised picture of unlimited autonomy but allows for the variable and partial character of actual human autonomy.

Autonomous action, understood literally, is self-legislated action. It is the action of agents who can understand and choose what they do. When cognitive or volitional capacities, or both, are lacking or impaired, autonomous action is reduced or impossible. Autonomy is lacking or incomplete for parts of all lives (infancy, early childhood), for further parts of some lives (unconsciousness, senility, some illness and mental disturbance) and throughout some lives (severe retardation). Since illness often damages autonomy, concern to respect it does not seem a promising fundamental principle for medical ethics. Medical concern would be strangely inadequate if it did not extend to those with incomplete autonomy. Concern for patients' well-being is generally thought a more plausible fundamental principle for medical ethics.

But it is also commonly thought implausible to make beneficence the only fundamental aim of medical practice, since it would then be irrelevant to medical treatment whether patients possessed standard autonomy, impaired autonomy or no capacity for autonomous action. All patients, from infants to the most autonomous, would be treated in ways judged likely to benefit them. Medical practice would be through and through paternalistic, and would treat patients as persons only if beneficence so required.

Recurrent debates about paternalism in medical

Key words

Paternalism; autonomy; consent; informed consent; respect for persons; Kantian ethics.

ethics show that the aim of subordinating concern for autonomy to beneficence remains controversial. The group of notions invoked in these debates – autonomy, paternalism, consent, respect for persons, and treating others as persons – are quite differently articulated in different ethical theories. A consideration of various ways in which they can be articulated casts some light on issues that lie behind discussions of medical paternalism.

1. Paternalism and autonomy in result-oriented ethics

Most consequentialist moral reasoning does not take patients' autonomy as a fundamental constraint on medical practice. Utilitarian moral reasoning takes the production of welfare or well-being (variously construed) as the criterion of right action. Only when respect for patients' autonomy (fortuitously) maximises welfare is it morally required. Paternalism is not morally wrong; but some acts which attempt to maximise welfare by disregarding autonomy will be wrong if in fact non-paternalistic action (such as showing respect for others or seeking their consent to action undertaken) would have maximised welfare. Only some 'ideal' form of consequentialism, which took the maintenance of autonomy as an independent value, could regard the subordination of autonomy to beneficence as wrong. In utilitarian ethical thinking autonomy is of marginal ethical importance, and paternalism only misplaced when it reflects miscalculation of benefits.

This unambiguous picture is easily lost sight of because of an historical accident. A classical and still highly influential utilitarian discussion of autonomy and paternalism is John Stuart Mill's *On Liberty* (1). Mill believed both that each person is the best judge of his or her own happiness and that autonomous pursuit of goals is itself a major source of happiness, so he thought happiness could seldom be maximised by action which thwarted or disregarded others' goals, or took over securing them. Paternalists, on this view, have benevolent motives but don't achieve beneficent results. They miscalculate.

Mill's claims are empirically dubious. Probably many people would be happier under beneficent policies even when these reduce the scope for autonomous action. Some find autonomous pursuit of goals more a source of frustration and anxiety than of satisfaction. In particular, many patients want relief from hard decisions and the burden of autonomy. Even when they don't want decisions made for them they may be unable to make them, or to make them well. The central place Mill assigns autonomy is something of an anomaly in result-oriented ethical thought (2). It is open to challenge and shows Mill's problem in reconciling liberty with utility rather than any success in showing their coincidence.

2. Paternalism and autonomy in action-oriented ethics

Autonomy can have a more central place only in an entirely different framework of thought. Within a moral theory which centres on action rather than on results, the preconditions of agency will be fundamental. Since autonomy, of some degree, is a presupposition of agency, an action-centred ethic, whether its fundamental moral category is that of human rights, or of principles of obligation or of moral worth, must make the autonomy of agents of basic rather than derivative moral concern. This concern may be expressed as concern not to use others, but to respect them or 'treat them as persons', or to secure their consent and avoid all (including paternalistic) coercion.

A central difficulty for all such theories is once again empirical. It is obvious enough that some human beings lack cognitive and volitional capacities that would warrant thinking of them as autonomous. But where autonomous action is ruled out what can be the moral ground for insisting on respect or support for human autonomy (3)? The question is sharply pointed for medical ethics since patients *standardly* have reduced cognitive and volitional capacities.

Yet most patients have some capacities for agency. Their impairments undercut some but not all possibilities for action. Hence agent-centred moral theories may be relevant to medical ethics, but only if based on an accurate view of human autonomy. The central tradition of debate in agent-centred ethics has not been helpful here because it has tended to take an abstract and inaccurate view of human autonomy. The history of these discussions is revealing.

Enlightenment political theory and especially Locke's writings are classical sources of arguments against paternalism and for respect for human autonomy. Here the consent of citizens to their governments is held to legitimate government action. In consenting citizens become, in part, the authors of government action: the notion of the sovereignty of the people can be understood as the claim that they have consented to, and so authorised, the laws by which they are ruled. In obeying such laws they are not mere subjects but retain their autonomy.

This picture invited, and got, a tough focus on the question 'What constitutes consent?' An early and perennial debate was whether consent has to be *express* – explicitly declared in speech or writing – or can be *tacit* – merely a matter of going along with arrangements. In a political context the debate is whether legitimate government must have explicit allegiance, or whether, for example, continued residence can legitimate government action. A parallel debate in medical ethics asks whether legitimate medical intervention requires explicit consent, recorded by the patient's signing of consent forms, or whether placing oneself in the hands of the doctor constitutes consent to whatever the doctor does, provided it accords with the standards of the medical profession (4).

The underlying picture of human choice and action invoked by those who advocate the 'informed consent' account of human autonomy is appropriate to a contractual model of human relations. Just as parties to commercial contracts consent to specific action by others, and have legal redress when this is not forthcoming, and citizens consent to limited government action (and may seek redress when this is exceeded), so patients consent to specified medical procedures (and have cause for grievance if their doctors do otherwise). Those who argue that informed consent criteria are not appropriate in medical practice sometimes explicitly reject the intrusion of commercial and contractual standards in medical care.

The contractual picture of human relations is clearly particularly questionable in medicine. We may think that citizenship and commerce are areas where we are autonomous decision-makers, enjoying what Mill would have called 'the maturity of our faculties'. In these areas, if anywhere, we come close to being fully rational decision-makers. Various well-known idealisations of human rationality – 'rational economic man', 'consenting adults', 'cosmopolitan citizens', 'rational choosers' – may seem tolerable approximations. But the notion that we could be 'ideal rational patients' cannot stand up to a moment's scrutiny. This suggests that we cannot plausibly extend the enlightenment model of legitimating consent to medical contexts. Where autonomy is standardly reduced, paternalism must it seems be permissible; opposition to medical paternalism appears to reflect an abstract and inaccurate view of human consent which is irrelevant in medical contexts.

3. The opacity of consent: a reversal of perspective

However, the same picture might be seen from quite a different perspective. Human autonomy is limited and precarious in many contexts, and the consent given to others' actions and projects is standardly selective and incomplete. *All* consent is consent to some proposed action or project *under certain descriptions*. When we consent to an action or project we often do not consent even to its logical implications or to its likely results (let alone its actual results), nor to its unavoidable corollaries and presuppositions. Put more technically, consenting (like other propositional attitudes) is *opaque*. When we consent we do not necessarily 'see through' to the implications of what we consent to and consent to these also. When a patient consents to an operation he or she will often be unaware of further implications or results of that which is consented to. Risks may not be understood and post-operative expectations may be vague. But the opacity of patients' consent is not radically different from the opacity of all human consenting. Even in the most 'transparent', highly-regulated, contractual arrangements, consent reaches only a certain distance. This is recognised whenever contracts are voided because of cognitive or volitional disability, or because the expectations of the 'reasonable man' about the further implications of some activity do not hold up. Medical cases may then be not so much anomalies, with which consent theory cannot adequately deal, as revealing cases which highlight typical limits of human autonomy and consent (5).

Yet most discussions of consent theory point in the other direction. The limitations of actual human autonomy aren't taken as constraints on working out the determinate implications of respect for autonomy in actual contexts, but often as *aberrations* from ideally autonomous choosing. The rhetoric of the liberal tradition shows this clearly. Although it is accepted that we are discussing the autonomy of '*finite* rational beings', finitude of all sorts is constantly forgotten in favour of loftier and more abstract perspectives.

4. Actual consent and 'ideal' consent

There are advantages to starting with these idealised abstractions rather than the messy incompleteness of human autonomy as it is actually exercised. Debates on consent theory often shift from concern with dubious consent actually given by some agent to a proposed activity or arrangement to concern with consent that would hypothetically be given by an ideally autonomous (rational and free) agent faced with that proposal. This shift to hypothetical consent allows us to treat the peculiar impairments of autonomy which affect us when ill as irrelevant: we can still ask what the (admittedly hypothetical) ideally autonomous patient would consent to. This line of thought curiously allows us to combine ostensible concern for human autonomy with paternalistic medical practice. Having reasoned that some procedure would be consented to by ideally autonomous patients we may then feel its imposition on actual patients of imperfect autonomy is warranted. But by shifting focus from what has (actually) been consented to, to what would (ideally) be consented to, we replace concern for others' autonomy with concern for the autonomy of hypothetical, idealised agents. This is not a convincing account of what it is not to use others, but rather to treat them as persons (6).

If we don't replace concern for actual autonomy with concern for idealised autonomy, we need to say something definite about when actual consent is

genuine and significant and when it is either spurious or misleading, and so unable to legitimise whatever is ostensibly consented to. Instead of facing the sharp outlines of idealised, hypothetical conceptions of human choosing we may have to look at messy actual choosing. However, we don't need to draw a sharp boundary between genuine, morally significant consent and spurious, impaired consent which does not legitimate. For the whole point of concern for autonomy and hence for genuine consent is that it is not up to the *initiator* of action to choose what to impose: it is up to those affected to choose whether to accept or to reject proposals that are made. To respect others' autonomy requires that we make consent *possible* for them (7), taking account of whatever partial autonomy they may have. Medical practice respects patients' autonomy when it allows patients as they actually are to refuse or accept what is proposed to them. Of course, some impairments prevent refusal or acceptance. The comatose and various others have to be treated paternalistically. But many patients can understand and refuse or accept what is proposed over a considerable range. Given some capacities for autonomous action, whatever can be made comprehensible to and refusable by patients, can be treated as subject to their consent – or refusal. This may require doctors and others to avoid haste and pressure and to counteract the intimidation of unfamiliar, technically bewildering and socially alien medical environments. Without such care in imparting information and proposing treatment the 'consent' patients give to their treatment will lack the autonomous character which would show that they have not been treated paternally but rather as persons.

5. 'Informed consent' and legitimating consent

There is a long-standing temptation, both in medical ethics and beyond, to find ways in which consent procedures can be formalised and the avoidance of paternalism guaranteed and routinised. But if the ways in which human autonomy is limited are highly varied, it is not likely that any set procedures can guarantee that consent has been given. Early European colonialists who 'negotiated treaties' by which barely literate native peoples without knowledge of European moral and legal traditions 'consented' to sales of land or cession of sovereignty reveal only that the colonialists had slight respect for others' autonomy. Medical practice which relies on procedures such as routine signing of 'consent forms ' may meet conditions for avoiding litigation, but does not show concern for human autonomy as it actually exists. Such procedures are particularly disreputable given our knowledge of the difficulties even the most autonomous have in assimilating distressing information or making unfamiliar and hard decisions.

Serious respect for autonomy, in its varied, limited forms, demands rather that patients' refusal or consent, at least to fundamental aspects of treatment, be made possible. The onus on practitioners is to see that patients, as they actually are, understand what they can about the basics of their diagnosis and the proposed treatment, and are secure enough to refuse the treatment or to insist on changes. If the proposal is accessible and refusable for an actual patient, then (but only then) can silence or going along with it reasonably be construed as consent. The notions of seeking consent and respecting autonomy are brought into disrepute when the 'consent' obtained does not genuinely reflect the patient's response to proposed treatment.

6. Partial autonomy, coercion and deception

Once we focus on the limited autonomy of actual patients it becomes clear that consent to *all* aspects and descriptions of proposed treatment is neither possible nor required. Only the ideally, unrestrictedly autonomous could offer such consent. In human contexts, whether medical or political, the most that we can ask for is consent to the more *fundamental* proposed policies, practices and actions. Patients can no more be asked to consent to every aspect of treatment than citizens can be asked to consent to every act of government. Respect for autonomy requires that consent be possible to *fundamental* aspects of actions and proposals, but allows that consent to trivial and ancillary aspects of action and proposals may be absent or impossible.

Treatment undertaken without consent when a patient could have reached his or her own decisions if approached with care and respect may fail in many ways. In the most serious cases the action undertaken uses patients as tools or instruments. Here the problem is not just that some partially autonomous patient couldn't (or didn't) consent, but that the treatment precluded consent even for ideally autonomous patients. Where a medical proposal hinges fundamentally on coercion or deception, not even the most rational and independent can dissent, or consent. Deceivers don't reveal their fundamental proposal or action; coercers may make their proposal plain enough but rob *anyone* of choice between consent or dissent. In deception 'consent' is spurious because cognitive conditions for consent are not met: in coercion 'consent' is spurious because volitional conditions for consent are not met.

However, some non-fundamental aspects of treatment to which consent has been given may have to include elements of deception or coercion. Use of placebos or of reassuring but inaccurate accounts of expected pain might sometimes be non-fundamental but indispensable and so permissible deceptions (8). Restraint of a patient during a painful procedure might be a non-fundamental but indispensable and so permissible coercion. But using patients as unwitting experimental subjects or concealing fundamental aspects of their illness or prognosis or treatment from them, or imposing medical treatment and ignoring or preventing its refusal, would always use patients, and

so fail to respect autonomy. At best such imposed treatment might, if benevolent, constitute impermissible paternalism; at worst, if non-benevolent, it might constitute assault or torture.

7. Partial autonomy, manipulation and paternalism

Use of patients is an extreme failure to respect autonomy; it precludes the consent even of the ideally autonomous, let alone of those with cognitive or volitional impairments. Respect for partial autonomy would also require medical practice to avoid treatment which, though refusable by the ideally autonomous, would not be refusable by a particular patient in his or her present condition. Various forms of manipulation and of questionable paternalism fail to meet these requirements. Patients are manipulated if they are 'made offers they cannot refuse', given their actual cognitive and volitional capacities. For example, patients who think they may be denied further care or discharged without recourse if they refuse proposed treatment may be unable to refuse it. To ensure that 'consent' is not manipulated available alternatives may have to be spelled out and refusal of treatment shown to be a genuine option. 'Consent' which is achieved by relying on misleading or alarmist descriptions of prognosis or uninformative accounts of treatment and alternatives does not show genuine respect. Only patients who are quite unable to understand or decide need complete paternalist protection. When there is a relationship of unequal power, knowledge or dependence, as so often between patients and doctors, avoiding manipulation and unacceptable paternalism demands a lot.

Avoiding unacceptable paternalism demands similar care. Manipulators use knowledge of others and their weaknesses to impose their own goals; paternalists may not recognise either others' goals, or that they are *others'* goals. Patients, like anyone with limited understanding and capacity to choose, may be helped by advice and information, and may need help to achieve their aims. But if it is not the patients' but others' aims which determine the limits and goals of medical intervention, the intervention (even if neither deceptive nor coercive) will be unacceptably paternalistic. Handicapped patients whose ways of life are determined by others may not be deceived or coerced – but they may be unable to refuse what others think appropriate for them. This means that patients' own goals, medical and non-medical, and their plans for achieving these, are constraints on any medical practice which respects patients' autonomy. Since return to health is often central to patients' plans, this constraint may require little divergence from the treatment that paternalistic medical practice would select, except that patients would have to be party to fundamental features of their treatment. But where patients' goals differ from doctors' goals – perhaps they value quality of life or avoiding pain or dependence more than the doctor would – respect for the patient requires that these goals not be overridden or replaced by ones the patient does not share, and that the patient's own part in achieving them not be set aside.

Debates on medical paternalism often assume that the goals of medical action can be determined independently of patients' goals. But in action-oriented ethical thinking morally required goals are not given independently of agents' goals. Paternalism in this perspective is simply the imposition of others' goals, (perhaps those of doctors, nursing homes or relatives) on patients. These goals too must be taken into account if we are to respect the autonomy of doctors, nursing homes and relatives. But imposing their goals on patients capable of some autonomy does not respect patients. The contextually-sensitive, action-oriented framework discussed here does not reinstate a contractual or consumer-sovereignty picture of medical practice, in which avoiding deceit and coercion is all that respect requires. On the contrary, it insists that judgements of human autonomy must be contextual, and that what it takes to respect human autonomy will vary with context. When patients' partial autonomy constrains medical practice, respect for patients may demand action which avoids not only deceit and coercion but also manipulation and paternalism; but where autonomy is absent there is no requirement that it be respected.

8. Respecting limited autonomy

Medical paternalism has been considered within three frameworks. Within a result-oriented framework of the standard utilitarian type it is not only permissible but required that concern for human autonomy be subordinated to concern for total welfare. Within an action-oriented framework that relies on an abstract, 'idealising' account of human autonomy, medical practice is too readily construed as ruling out all paternalism and permitting only treatment that would be consented to by 'idealised' autonomous agents. Within an action-oriented framework that takes account of the partial character of human autonomy we can sketch patterns of reasoning which draw boundaries in given contexts between permissible and impermissible forms of paternalism. This account yields no formula, such as the requirement to avoid coercion and deception may be thought to yield for abstract approaches. But the inadequacies of that formula for guiding action when impairment is severe speak in favour of a more accurate and contextual view of human autonomy.

By trying to incorporate concern for actual, partial capacities for autonomous action into an account of respect for patients and medical paternalism we find that we are left without a single boundary-line between acceptable and unacceptable medical practice. What we have are patterns of reasoning which yield different answers for different patients and for different proposals for treatment. One patient can indeed be expected to come to an informed and autonomous (if idiosyncratic) decision; another may be too confused to take in what his options are. A third may be able to understand the issues but too dependent or too distraught to make decisions. Attempts to provide uniform guidelines for treating patients as persons, respecting their autonomy and avoiding unacceptable medical paternalism are bound to be insensitive to the radical differences of capacity of different patients. A theory of respect for patients must rely heavily and crucially on actual medical judgements to assess patient's current capacities to absorb and act on information given in various ways. But it does not follow that 'professional judgement' or 'current medical standards' *alone* can provide appropriate criteria for treating patients as persons. For if these do not take the varying ways in which patients can exercise autonomy as constraints on permissible treatment, they may institutionalise unjustifiable paternalism. Professional judgement determines what constitutes respect for patients only when guided by concern to communicate effectively what patients can understand and to respect the decisions that they can make.

9. Issues and contexts

Sections 1, 2 and 3 above discussed some ways in which treatment of autonomy, paternalism and respect for patients are articulated in result-oriented ethics and in action-oriented approaches which take an abstract view of cognition and volition, and hence of autonomy. The alternative account proposed in sections 4 to 8 is that only consideration of the determinate cognitive and volitional capacities and incapacities of particular patients at particular times provides a framework for working out boundaries of permissible medical paternalism. If such judgements are contextual, there is no way to demarcate unacceptable paternalism in the abstract. The following headings only point to contexts in which these issues arise and have to be resolved. Which resolutions are justifiable will depend not only on following a certain pattern of reasoning but on the capacities for autonomous action paticular patients have at the relevant time.

A. TEMPORARILY IMPAIRED CAPACITY FOR AUTONOMY

If respect for autonomy is morally fundamental, restoring (some) capacities is morally fundamental. Survival is necessary for such restoration; but not sufficient. If patients' autonomy constrains practice, survival can never be foregone in favour of autonomy, but it is an open question whether survival with no or greatly reduced capacities for autonomy can be a permissible goal. Risky surgery may sometimes reasonably be imposed for the sake of restoring capacities, even when mere survival would be surer without surgery.

Temporary loss of autonomy offers grounds for paternalistic intervention to restore autonomy – but not for all paternalistic interventions. It might be better for an unconscious sportsman if advantage were

178   *Onora O'Neill*

taken of his temporary incapacity to perform some non-urgent operation or to make some non-medical intervention in his affairs. But if restoration of autonomy is likely, an action-oriented ethic offers no ground for such paternalism.

B. LONG TERM OR PERMANENT IMPAIRMENT OF AUTONOMY

This is the standard situation of children, and so the original context of paternalism. Those with long and debilitating illnesses, physical as well as mental, may suffer very varied impairments of autonomy. Hence consideration of parental paternalism may illuminate these cases. While the law has to fix an age to end minority, parents have to adapt their action to a constantly altering set of capacities for autonomous action. Choices which cannot be made at one stage can at another; autonomy develops in one area of life and lags in another (9). Unfortunately, medical trajectories may not be towards fuller capacities. Medical and other decisions may then have to be to some extent imposed. But there is no general reason to think that those who are unable to make some decisions are unable to make any decisions, and even when full return of capacities is unlikely, patients, like children, may gain in autonomy when an optimistic view is taken of their capacities.

C. PERMANENT LOSS OF AUTONOMY

Here decisions have (eventually) to be made that go beyond what is needed for restoring (some) autonomy. Sometimes medical staff and relatives may be able to make some use of a notion of hypothetical consent. But what they are likely to be asking is not 'What would the ideally autonomous choose in this situation?', but rather 'What would this patient have chosen in this situation?' If this can be answered, it may be possible to maintain elements of respect for the particular patient as he or she was in former times. But usually this provides only vague indications for medical or other treatment, and respect for absent autonomy can be at best vestigial.

D. LIFELONG INCAPACITY FOR AUTONOMY

For those who never had or will have even slight capacities for autonomous action the notion of respect is vacuous. There is no answer to the hypothetical question 'What would he or she have chosen if able to do so?' and the hypothetical question 'What would the ideally autonomous choose in this situation?' may have no determinate answer. Here, unavoidably, paternalism must govern medical practice indefinitely and the main questions that arise concern the appropriate division of authority to make paternalistic decisions between relatives and medical staff and legally appointed guardians.

References and notes

(1) Mill J S. On liberty. In: Warnock M, ed. *Utilitarianism and on liberty, etc.* London: Fontana, 1972.

(2) This has been a recurrent criticism of Mill from Stephen J F, *Liberty, equality, fraternity,* London: Smith, Elder, 1873, to Dworkin G. Paternalism. *The monist* 1972; 56: 64–84 and reprinted in Sartorius R, ed. *Paternalism.* Minneapolis: University of Minnesota Press, 1983: section IV.

(3) Broader worries mushroom here too: what grounds the moral status of non-autonomous humans in action-oriented ethics? For recent discussion see Haksar V. *Liberty, equality, perfectionism.* Oxford: Clarendon Press, 1979; Clark S. *The moral status of animals.* Oxford: Clarendon Press, 1977; Dennett D Conditions of personhood. In: Rorty A, ed. *The identity of persons.* Berkeley and Los Angeles: University of California Press, 1976, and reprinted in Dennett D. *Brainstorms.* Hassocks, Sussex: The Harvester Press, Ltd 1979.

(4) Here US and British practice differ. US legislation and debates often stress the need to secure informed consent from patients (or their guardians). Cf. discussions and bibliography in Veatch R M. *Case studies in medical ethics.* Cambridge Mass: Harvard University Press, 1977. British law holds that 'what information should be disclosed, and how and when, is very much a matter of professional judgement', and that 'there is no ground in English law for extending the limited doctrine of informed consent outside the field of property rights'. See Sidaway v Board of Governors of the Bethlem Royal Hospital and the Maudsley Hospital and Others, Law Report, *The Times,* 1984 Feb 24. However, medical paternalism may be more practised in the US than it is praised by those who write on medical ethics. See Buchanan A E Medical paternalism. *Philosophy and public affairs* 1978; 7: 371–390, and reprinted in Sartorius, see reference (2).

(5) For further comments on the limitations of 'normal' abilities see Wikler D. Paternalism and the mildly retarded. Reprinted in Sartorius, see reference (2).

(6) A point made long since by Isaiah Berlin in Two concepts of liberty. *Four essays on liberty.* Oxford: OUP, 1969.

(7) For the interpretation of Kantian ethics offered here see also O'Neill O. Kant after virtue. *Inquiry* 1984; 26: 387–405; Consistency in action. In: Potter N, Timmons M, eds. *New essays in ethical universalizability.* Dordrecht, the Netherlands: Reidel publishing company, forthcoming, and Between consenting adults, unpublished.

(8) Bok S. *Lying: moral choice in public and private life.* New York: Harvester Press, Random House, 1978: 234. Bok points out that sometimes the use of placebos may be more than ancillary, (61–68), and also discusses fundamental forms of deception such as hiding from the patient that the illness is terminal. On the latter point see also Kubler-Ross E. *On death and dying.* New York: Macmillan 1969, and the bibliography in Veatch, reference (4).

(9) For discussions of some distinctive features of children's partial autonomy see Leites E. Locke's liberal theory of fatherhood; Slote M A. Obedience and illusions and Katz S N, Schroeder W A, Sidman L. Emancipating our children – coming of legal age in America. In: O'Neill O, Ruddick W, eds. *Having children: philosophical and legal reflections on parenthood.* New York: OUP, 1979.

For a more recent position taken by the same author see: Onora O'Neill *Autonomy and Trust in Bioethics,* Cambridge University Press, 2002.

[4]

Informed Consent and Surgeons' Performance

Steve Clarke[1] and Justin Oakley[2]
[1]Centre for Applied Philosophy and Public Ethics, Charles Sturt University, Canberra, Australia, and [2]Centre for Human Bioethics, Monash University, Melbourne, Australia

ABSTRACT

This paper argues that the provision of effective informed consent by surgical patients requires the disclosure of material information about the comparative clinical performance of available surgeons. We develop a new ethical argument for the conclusion that comparative information about surgeons' performance – surgeons' report cards – should be provided to patients, a conclusion that has already been supported by legal and economic arguments. We consider some recent institutional and legal developments in this area, and we respond to some common objections to the use of report cards on the clinical performance of surgeons.

Keywords: disclosure, informed consent, professional obligations, quality of care, risk, surgeons' report cards

I. RISK AND DISCLOSURE

In order to qualify as an instance of informed consent, a patient's decision to consent to an operation needs to be grounded on an adequate basis of relevant information. Without such a basis of relevant information, a patient's decision to consent to an operation is not an effective informed consent, and is not, therefore, sufficient to authorise that operation. Because many of the categories of information that inform effective decisions by patients to consent to an operation are categories of specialist medical information, patients must rely on the disclosure of such information by medical professionals. A patient must receive an adequate disclosure of a variety of categories of information that are relevant to their decision to undergo an operation, as a precondition to the provision of effective informed consent.

Address correspondence to: Justin Oakley, Ph.D., Centre for Human Bioethics, PO Box 11A, Monash University, Victoria, 3800, Australia. E-mail: Justin.Oakley@arts.monash.edu.au

Exactly which categories of information should be disclosed, for the purposes of providing informed consent, is in dispute.[1] What is not disputed by any commentators who accept a doctrine of informed consent is that a necessary component of disclosure, for the purposes of informed consent, is disclosure of the reasonably foreseeable risks of an operation. In this paper we argue that disclosures made for the purposes of obtaining patients' informed consent to an operation ought to include material information about a subcategory of risk information: that is, information about the ability of available surgeons to perform the operation in question. Disclosures that do not include at least some relevant, material information about the performance ability of available surgeons are an inadequate basis for the provision of effective informed consent. Our argument is for the disclosure of a class of information that has not hitherto been recognised in standard treatments of disclosure in informed consent.[2] However, we do not understand ourselves to be opposed to standard treatments of disclosure in informed consent, such as those provided by Faden and Beauchamp (1986), Appelbaum, Lidz, and Meisel (1987), and Wear (1998). The disclosure requirement that we argue for is a hitherto unrecognised consequence implied by these treatments of disclosure, which can be made explicit when we think carefully about risk, one of the "elements of disclosure".

Our main point is simple and, we think, very hard to deny. The risks that should be disclosed to patients are the risks that we can reasonably expect that patients will face when undergoing an operation. These risks will vary, *inter alia*, according to the level of ability of the surgeons who are available to perform that operation. So, information about the performance ability of surgeons is a necessary component of the disclosure of the reasonably foreseeable risks of a surgical intervention. And, as the disclosure of the reasonably foreseeable risks of a surgical intervention is a necessary requirement for the provision of effective informed consent, the disclosure of information about the performance ability of available surgeons is a necessary requirement for the provision of effective informed consent to a surgical intervention.

Before we go on, we should stress that we fully accept the "received view", that the overriding purpose of the doctrine of informed consent in medical ethics is to ensure that patient autonomy is respected in medical decision making. Faden and Beauchamp state that an "... analysis of the nature of autonomy provides the essential foundation for our analysis of the nature of informed consent" (1986, p. 235). According to Appelbaum, Lidz, and Meisel, informed consent is "an ethical value rooted in our society's cherished value of autonomy" (1987, p. 3). We share these sentiments. It is because we ought to uphold the value of patient autonomy, that material information about a surgeon's ability should be disclosed to patients as a part of the informed consent process.[3] We best uphold a patient's autonomy by enabling that patient to properly understand the risks that they are exposing themselves to when choosing to be operated on by a particular surgeon.

Appelbaum et al. (1987, p. 51) provide a useful analysis of the disclosure of risks, identifying the following four components: (1) the nature of the risk; (2) the magnitude or seriousness, of the risk; (3) the probability that the risk might materialise; and (4) the imminence of the risk. The following example is a simple application of their analysis. Recently Clarke was diagnosed with a cartilage tear in his right knee. He was advised that arthroscopic surgery could be conducted on his knee to alleviate the condition, and that this would involve the risk of severing a nerve in the knee area causing permanent numbness in that region, immediately. The likelihood of this happening was reported, by Clarke's surgeon, as 1 in 1000. The nature of the risk (1) was severing a nerve. The magnitude or seriousness (2), is determined by understanding the consequences of the risk occurring and depends, *inter alia*, on how much Clarke values feeling in his right knee.[4] The probability of the risk materialising (3) was reported to be 1 in 1000, and the consequences of the operation going wrong would be experienced immediately (4).

What does it mean to say that the probability of this risk materialising was 1 in 1000? The surgeon advising Clarke appeared to be asserting that if he (call him Bloggs) were to operate on Clarke, the probability of severing a nerve would be 1 in 1000. But why would Bloggs have thought this? Presumably, because he was in possession of information about the success rates of actual instances of arthroscopic surgery performed by a suitably large class of surgeons, of which he is a member (let us suppose this class is the class of Australian surgeons), on a suitably large class of patients, of which Clarke is a member (let us suppose that this is the class of Australians). Furthermore, Bloggs presumably believed that the probability of severing a nerve, if he were to perform arthroscopic surgery on Clarke, would be no different, *ceteris paribus*, from the probability of severing a nerve when any given Australian surgeon performs this form of surgery on any given Australian.

Measures of the probability that a risk might materialise as a result of an operation are typically presented as if it were unproblematically the case that the probability of a risk materialising in a particular operation simply was the average probability for operations performed by all surgeons within a suitably large reference class, on all patients within the same suitably large reference class. However, this will not always be the case. It might be, for example, that Clarke is member of a subclass of the population, which has a different probability of the risk materialising from the risk for the population as a whole. Suppose that Clarke is a Torres Strait Islander, and that for Torres Strait Islanders it has been demonstrated that there is a significantly higher probability of this risk materialising – say 1 in 100, rather than 1 in 1000. As an Australian, Clarke has a 1 in 1000 chance of ending up with a severed nerve in his knee, but as a Torres Strait Islander, Clarke has a 1 in 100 rate of ending up with a severed nerve in his knee if he goes ahead with the operation. Which rate should Bloggs quote when disclosing the risks of the operation to Clarke? If Bloggs is aware of the substantially higher risk rate for Torres Strait Islanders, then Bloggs should cite this information. Bloggs should provide Clarke with the information available that most closely reflects his actual circumstances. All things being equal, the information that will more closely approximate the actual rate at which a risk to Clarke can be expected to materialise will be information about the most specific reference class to which Clarke belongs and, clearly, information about Torres Strait Islanders is information about a more specific reference class than is information about Australians generally.[5]

Just as specific information about Clarke may be relevant to the rate at which a risk materialises, so too information about Bloggs can be relevant. In particular, information about Bloggs' ability to perform the operation will surely affect the rate at which injuries can be expected to occur. Suppose, for the sake of argument, that Bloggs has performed arthroscopic surgical operations of the type being contemplated 10,000 times, and 100 of these operations have resulted in severed nerves – i.e., 1 in every 100 times. If Clarke is to be operated on by Bloggs then is the expected risk of a severed nerve for Clarke closer to 1 in 1000 or closer to 1 in 100? Surely, all things being equal, 1 in 100 is the more accurate figure, because it represents the probability of the occurrence of an event that is closer in description to the event that is actually being contemplated. It is more fine-grained information, and as we have already argued, all things being equal, we ought to provide more fine-grained information where it is available, because it more closely approximates to the actual probability of the relevant possible event.

The actual probability of a severed nerve, when Bloggs operates on Clarke, will depend on many factors, such as the quality of the lighting in the operating theatre, peculiarities about Clarke's right knee, the occurrence of unforeseen events that interrupt the operation and even whether or not Bloggs slept properly the night before the operation.[6] To provide precise information about the actual probability of a risk materialising, for a particular operation, we would have to anticipate the probability of all such relevant effects and make appropriate adjustments to our assessment of the probability of a risk. As a complete list of factors that can potentially affect the probability that a risk may materialise would be extremely long, if not infinite, this would be impractical, if not impossible. Furthermore, even for those factors that we can anticipate, we will be unable to provide reliable information about some of them. Suppose that Clarke is a member of a distinct population group with, say, less than 100 members. Even if we have reason to suspect that members of this group may be susceptible to the risk in question at a rate which is different to that for the overall population, we may simply be unable to obtain enough reliable information about such a small group to confirm this suspicion.

It is not reasonable for a patient to expect medical professionals to anticipate all factors relevant to a given risk. And nor is it reasonable for patients to expect that medical professionals will be able to provide reliable information about all such factors, even if they are made aware of the materiality of such factors to the decision making of a particular patient. However, it surely is reasonable to expect medical professionals to make the effort to anticipate some of the factors that will be most important for the decision-making of the majority of patients. And it surely is reasonable to expect medical professionals to collect such information about those important factors and to provide it to patients for the purpose of enabling effective informed consent. With many operations, a surgeon's level of performance will be one of the most important factors causing risks to patients; and so it is plausible to believe that many patients will appreciate having such information available (see Marshall, Shekelle, Leatherman, Brook, & Owen, 2000, pp. 60–62). So it is reasonable to require that relevant information about surgeons' performance abilities be made available to patients for the purpose of enabling effective informed consent. Commonly, surgeons already maintain records of their performances in operations, so it would not be an onerous administrative imposition to require that material information derived from such records be made available so that it may be provided to patients for the purposes of enabling informed consent.

II. RECENT INSTITUTIONAL AND LEGAL DEVELOPMENTS

We are unaware of other philosophers who have explicitly advocated the provision of material information about the performance of surgeons for the purpose of disclosure in informed consent in medicine, but we are not the first advocates of the provision of information about the performance of surgeons. In some American hospitals information about the performance of surgeons is already collected and made publicly available on the internet. The best known and longest established such internet site is one maintained by the New York State Department of Health, which issues annual reports, known as "report cards", comparing the mortality rates of individual surgeons who have conducted coronary artery bypass graft operations.[7] This is a commonly recommended form of surgery for people with severe atherosclerotic coronary artery disease. There are also sites available providing data about the performance of heart surgeons in Pennsylvania, and of the results of patient satisfaction surveys of practitioners of general medicine, obstetrics, surgery and intensive care in Cleveland.[8]

There are moves under way to introduce report cards into the public health care systems in both the United Kingdom and in Australia. In 1998, the UK Department of Health released a comprehensive set of performance indicators against which to measure hospital data for the purposes of developing report cards on hospitals, and general practitioners have access to data that enable them to give their patients detailed information about the success rates for a given procedure in a particular hospital, and how that compares with the national average (Department of Health, 1998). The case for public reporting in Britain has gained considerable impetus as a result of the Bristol Royal Infirmary scandal. In response to a recommendation of the subsequent public inquiry into the events at Bristol, *inter alia*, the UK Department of Health has decided that data on the mortality rates for individual cardiac surgeons will be made available to the public in 2004.[9]

In Australia the use of report cards on hospitals has been strongly advocated in the State of Victoria. The Health Services Performance Review, carried out in 1999 under the leadership of Professor Stephen Duckett, produced a discussion paper recommending that a set of comprehensive consumer-oriented performance indicators be developed and that the Victorian Department of Human Services publish annual data on the comparative performance of individual hospitals and day centres for specific procedures.[10] This data on the comparative performance of hospitals has now been made available to the public in Victoria. Although the information contained in report cards on hospitals is not as fine-grained as information contained in report cards on individual surgeons, provision of such information is a step in the right direction. Information about the likelihood of a risk materialising, if an operation is performed at a particular hospital, is more fine-grained information than information about the likelihood of such a risk materialising if the reference class in question is all surgeons performing that operation in an entire nation.

Consider the recent scandal at the Bristol Royal Infirmary. In that case the anaesthetist "whistleblower", Dr. Stephen Bolsin collected figures which showed that two surgeons had mortality rates for two particular operations that were well above the British national average for those operations. The data collected by Dr. Bolsin throw into sharp relief the importance of providing to patients (and hospital administrators) sufficiently fine-grained information about surgeons' performance. For paediatric cardiac operations in 1990–1992, the mortality rate at the Bristol Royal Infirmary was three to four times higher than the national average. For one of the surgeons at the centre of the scandal, Mr. Wisheart, the mortality rate for paediatric cardiac operations in that period was five to six times the national average.[11] Clearly, parents who were informed about the mortality rate of paediatric cardiac surgery, for operations conducted by Mr. Wisheart, would be in a better position to give effective informed consent to a paediatric cardiac operation conducted by Mr. Wisheart than would parents who had been told only about the mortality rate for all surgeons conducting paediatric cardiac operations at the Bristol Royal Infirmary. And parents in the latter group would, in turn, be in a better position to give effective informed consent than those parents who were only told about the national average mortality rate for all surgeons operating in the United Kingdom.

Our view is also broadly in line with the ruling in a recent Australian legal case, *Chappel v Hart* (1998) whose details are as follows. Mrs. Hart consulted an ear, nose and throat specialist, Dr. Chappel, following a sore throat that she had had for a period of nine months. It turned out that Mrs. Hart had a pharyngeal pouch and this had caused a narrowing of her oesophagus. Dr. Chappel recommended surgery, but failed to warn Mrs. Hart that surgery would involve a slight risk of vocal damage, despite the fact that Mrs. Hart had indicated to him that she considered such a risk material to her, informing him that she "didn't want to end up with a voice like Neville Wran" (the ex-premier of New South Wales, who had a famously croaky voice). Surgery was performed by Dr. Chappel, and while he was deemed by the court not to have performed the surgery negligently, Mrs. Hart's oesophagus was inadvertently perforated during the operation, an accident that indirectly caused the permanent impairment of her voice. Mrs. Hart's concern about the state of her voice was particularly well motivated because her position as an Education Officer required that she be able to speak clearly. Following the operation she was assessed as medically unfit to continue her work and had no option but to retire.

Mrs. Hart was awarded a sum of AUS$172,500 in damages by the NSW Supreme court, a decision which was subsequently upheld by the High Court of Australia. Mrs. Hart did not contend that she would not have undergone the operation had she known about the risk to her voice. Instead she contended that she would have gone ahead with the operation, but with a more experienced surgeon – the most experienced surgeon in the field available, whom, Mrs. Hart believed, would be the best performing surgeon.[12]

It seems clear from the context of the court's decision that, had Dr. Chappel advised Mrs. Hart merely of the average risk of such a complication for any Australian patient being operated on by any Australian surgeon, he would not have done enough to escape liability. Because the court's decision turned on accepting Mrs. Hart's claim that, had she known of the risk to her voice, she would have sought the most experienced surgeon in the field available, it seems the court believed that Dr. Chappel had an additional obligation to inform Mrs. Hart that his experience was limited. One of the presiding judges, Justice Gaudron, argued that if the risk to Mrs. Hart is understood as a loss of an opportunity to undergo surgery at the hands of a more experienced surgeon, then Dr. Chappel should be understood to have had a duty to inform Mrs. Hart that there were more experienced surgeons practising in the field.

Both the High Court of Australia's judgment and Mrs. Hart's reasoning appear to be premised on the assumption that greater experience straightforwardly equates to better performance. Here we must demur.[13] While, all things being equal, performance and experience are positively correlated, the relationship between the two is far from straightforward, exceptionless and linear. Some very experienced surgeons may be "past their prime", and in such cases marginal increases in experience will negatively correlate with performance. In some cases performance ability may "plateau" and further experience may make little or no difference to it. In his skeptical study of professional psychology and psychotherapy, Robyn Dawes cites evidence, due to Howard Garb (1989), of such plateauing. In professional psychology, once the rudiments of technique are mastered, experience does not produce any measurable increase in diagnostic performance (Dawes, 1996, pp. 106-107).

The overall relationship between experience and performance is extremely complicated and can be expected to vary across different areas of human endeavour. According to Dawes, one generalisation that is reliable, is that experience enhances performance when practitioners are given regular and explicit feedback about performance and are thus prompted to alter their practices in light of failure (Dawes, 1996, pp. 118–121). Potentially, report cards could have a role in improving overall performance and in making experience correlate more positively with performance. In any case, report cards can be used to indicate performance levels without recourse to indications of experience. Had Dr. Chappel had ready access to reliable statistical information about surgeons' performance, he would have been able to provide Mrs. Hart with very accurate information about his ability to perform the operation that she underwent, as well as accurate information about the relative ability of other surgeons in his field.

It should be noted here, however, that the fact that particular details about an individual surgeon would be material to a given patient's decision about whether or not to consent to that surgeon operating upon them does not by itself suffice to show that those details ought to be provided to the patient. Patients may regard all manner of details about an individual surgeon as material to their decisions about whether or not to consent to that surgeon operating upon them, but the surgeon's privacy is another important factor to be considered in determining what sorts of disclosures are justifiable. Some facts about surgeons are justifiably kept private, even when those facts might be considered material to a particular patient's decision about whether to be operated upon by a given surgeon. For instance, a homosexual surgeon, who preferred that his sexual orientation be kept from his patients, would surely be justified in keeping such information private, even where a patient would regard this information as being material to her decision about whether to be operated upon by this surgeon. The promotion of patient autonomy is justifiably limited by the value of respect for a surgeon's privacy here.

The value of privacy clearly licences the withholding of certain sorts of information about individual surgeons, even where this information would be material to a given patient's decision. However, it is hard to see how this sort of rationale could plausibly be applied to mount an argument for the withholding of information about a surgeon's performance. Even if some surgeons actually do regard details about their surgical performance as equally personal and private as information about, say, their sexual orientation, the moral foundations of professional obligations provide good reason for thinking that, while the public may not have a claim on the latter information, they do have a strong claim on the former. It seems very plausible to hold that, in exchange for the community entrusting professionals with a monopoly of expertise on the provision of certain key goods, professionals owe the community the means to ascertain and monitor whether the requisite expertise is indeed being provided. And surely the provision of information about professional performance is a key way of meeting this demand.[14]

III. TWO OBJECTIONS

Although we see our argument as based on drawing out a logical implication of the doctrine of informed consent, a doctrine that enjoys widespread support, the argument's consequences ensure that it will be controversial. So, it is important that we examine some objections to our position. Two objections seem to us especially worthy of consideration.

A. The Threshold Objection

It might be argued that surgeons can meet their professional obligations by providing performance data regarding their ability, up to a particular threshold, and that it is supererogatory for surgeons to provide further performance data beyond that threshold, even where a surgeon is aware that this further information is material to a particular patient. If this is right, then surgeons need merely to demonstrate that they have met this threshold. If this is to be a low threshold, then a mere demonstration that they are entitled to be called competent might be all that is sufficient, or so our objector may tell us. This objection is plausibly motivated by a general view about professional obligations. According to this view, those of us in need of the services of a professional have a right to know only that the skills of the particular professional in question pass a certain standard of competence and we are not entitled to be given any further details about the individual characteristics of different practitioners.[15] This sort of view is sometimes claimed to be well-suited to contemporary professional practice, given that doctor-patient relationships tend to be more impersonal than they have been previously, and given that what those seeking the help of a professional need to know, above all, is that the professional will adhere to a certain charter of norms and values, no matter what their personal characteristics may be (see Dare, 1998a; Veatch, 1985).

To evaluate this sort of objection properly, we would need to be told more about the point at which it is said to become supererogatory for surgeons to provide data on their performance that was material to a particular patient. If this threshold for surgeons was set quite high, then we might not find this suggestion particularly problematic. Nevertheless, we do find rather implausible the general suggestion that our rights to know details about the performance of individual professionals extend only as far as the information necessary to establish that they meet some threshold of basic competence. Sometimes, the services that we are engaging a professional to provide are of a relatively high level of significance to us. In fact, this is typically the case when we are choosing a surgeon. In such situations, the suggestion that a surgeon who has demonstrated their basic competence has no obligation to provide any further performance information that would be material to our decision seems particularly implausible. Indeed, in some professions it has been thought appropriate to make information available to the public about individual members that goes beyond their meeting a baseline of competence. For example, in Anglophone countries a barrister's advanced level of skill is indicated by their being accepted as a Senior Counsel or a Queen's Counsel. At the very least, we think it is appropriate that surgeons be required to disclose (to patients for whom this is material) core information about their own rates for mortality and major morbidities (including their risk-adjusted mortality and morbidity rates). How far a surgeon should be expected to go beyond this is open to further debate.

B. Justice Issues

A second line of objection raises concerns about justice, regarding the cost of collecting surgeons' performance data, and about the impact of publicly accessible report cards on the availability of medical care. It would be very costly to attempt to cater to every need, because different patients' informational needs regarding the performance of surgeons in a given specialisation may well vary enormously, and can sometimes be quite idiosyncratic. For example, information about different cardiac surgeons' rates for some outcomes of coronary artery bypass grafts, such as the average chest scar width after healing, might be material to the decisions of some patients about which surgeon to choose, but not material to other patients. Indeed, there may appear to be almost no limit to the types of information that could be collected about the clinical

22   STEVE CLARKE & JUSTIN OAKLEY

performance of a given class of surgeons, that different patients may conceivably regard as material to their decision about whom is to operate upon them. The costs of collecting such a diversity of systematic performance data, so as to cater for the wide variety of different patients' informational needs, could plausibly be objected to as an unfair allocation of state resources. After all, it is likely that funds used in the collection of such data would have to be found by reducing levels of funding allocated to certain other areas of health care.

Clearly, given considerations of cost, the sort of data about surgeons' performance that the state can legitimately be expected to collect must be limited in some ways. Specifying in detail where considerations of justice and fairness would limit the collection of systematic performance data is a large task, which we will not undertake here. There is probably considerable diversity in the sort of surgeons' performance data that different patients will regard as material. However, it does not follow that to collect *any* systematic data on the performance of surgeons would be an unjustifiable use of the state's resources. Some sorts of surgical outcomes will surely be regarded by most potential patients as highly material to their decision about which surgeon to operate on them (if they found themselves in a position to make such a choice). Cardiac surgeons' mortality rates for coronary artery bypass surgery is one such example. Given the stakes involved here for such patients, why should the collection of information to help patients make a more informed choice of surgeon be thought any less worthy of state funding than is, say, the collection and dissemination of information about how to prevent coronary artery disease in the first place? It is very hard to see why considerations of costs to the state would rule out expenditure on the provision of surgeon performance information in any reasonably well-funded medical system.[16] The annual collection (and publication) of systematic performance data on the surgical outcomes of different practitioners is certainly not regarded by the New York State Department of Health nor by the UK Government (in their response to the Bristol Inquiry) as an unjustifiable use of state resources. Indeed, quite apart from the value of such information in enhancing the quality of patients' decisions about surgery, the community may well view the expenditure of government funds on the collection and provision of surgeon performance information as justifiable on the grounds that the public availability of such information is an important way of keeping surgeons accountable to the general public.

But what about the impact on the practice of medicine of the transmission of information about surgeons' performance to patients? Green and Wintfeld raise the possibility that the publicising of the cardiac bypass mortality rates for individual surgeons in New York State may have led some surgeons to avoid operating on critically ill patients, so as to protect themselves against any increase in their mortality rates (Green & Wintfeld, 1995, p. 1231). It has also been claimed that the more widespread use of public report cards will result in surgeons becoming much more reluctant to operate on patients who require relatively complex procedures. A response to these concerns is that the development of surgeons' report cards has been driven partly by a desire to improve the practice of medicine. Furthermore, it may be achieving this objective. In their latest listing of cardiac surgeons' mortality rates for bypass surgery, the New York State Department of Health asserts that the publication of this sort of data (on the internet) has improved the quality of care that cardiac patients receive, a judgement supported by Hannan, Sone, Biddle, and DeBuono (1997). This has occurred, it is suggested, partly because the publication of these data has enabled both hospitals and surgeons to identify which practitioners need to improve, and then to take steps to bring about appropriate improvements.[17]

Fully to address concerns about the impact of surgeons' report cards on the practice of medicine would require extensive empirical research. Some such research is now being carried out (Chassin, Hannan, & DeBuono, 1996; Erickson, Torchiana, Schneider, Newburger, & Hannan, 2000; Green & Wintfeld, 1995; Peterson, De Long, & Jollis, 1998). A noteworthy point to emerge from this research is that fears that report cards may have led surgeons to avoid operating on high-risk patients have not been borne out by any of the systematic empirical studies into this matter that we are aware of (Marshall et al., 2000, pp. 68–70). Clearly, though, this is a matter that requires ongoing investigation.

However, even if it turned out that the publication of surgeons' performance data did have certain deleterious effects on the practice of medicine generally, this would not necessarily warrant the conclusion that the publicising of such data was ethically unjustified, all things considered. Different ethical theories might well provide different answers here. If the publication of surgeons' report cards is shown to result in a reduction in medical utility overall, utilitarians would regard this as a strong reason to reject the use of report cards, while some Kantians might (depending, perhaps, on the extent of this reduction) view this as a price worth paying in order to uphold respect for patient autonomy. In any case, our argument has not been directed at giving an overall ethical assessment of surgeons' report cards. Rather, we aim to show that standard requirements of informed consent and respect for patient autonomy entail that the information contained in these report cards ought to be provided to potential patients, for whom it would be material when they make decisions about surgery. To settle conclusively whether surgeons' report cards should be made publicly available for all would require further argument, which is beyond the scope of this paper.

IV. PRACTICAL CONSIDERATIONS

Let us now consider some practical difficulties that have been raised about the implementation of surgeons' report cards, and suggest some ways in which these might be dealt with. A fairly common objection to the implementation of report cards is that it is likely that patients will misinterpret such data, because they will fail to appreciate the difficulties and complexities involved in assessing surgeons' performance.[18] Indeed, it is sometimes suggested that patients should *not* be provided with performance data about individual surgeons, since these data are likely to be so misleading that patients will make *mis*informed decisions about which surgeon to engage. For example, patients might infer, from the fact that a particular surgeon has a relatively high mortality rate for a given procedure, that this surgeon is poorly skilled at this procedure. But such an inference would be mistaken, as different surgeons' mortality rates for a given procedure are affected not only by their levels of surgical skill, but also, *inter alia*, by variations in the health conditions of the patients they operate on, the degree of surgical support available at the institution where they practise, and the sort of post-operative care provided to each patient. A high mortality rate need not indicate a lack of surgical skill. In fact, some very skilful surgeons may actually have quite high mortality rates, since they may be more likely than other surgeons to be called on to perform high-risk operations.

A related problem is that the presentation of performance data can be deliberately manipulated in order to create the impression that a surgeon is considerably more skilled than he or she actually is. Surgeons with objectively poor outcomes may be able to find ways of framing their performance data, in an attempt to mislead patients into believing that they are more successful surgeons than they in fact are. Attempts to counter such distortions by providing additional information threaten to compound the difficulties facing patients. If patients are already confused by the data they are presented with, then they may be further confused by being given more information.

We think these problems can be alleviated, to a large extent, by the use of processed rather than raw data, which is intended to take into account the particular difficulties faced by doctors in particular circumstances. In addition to publishing raw mortality rates, the New York State Department of Health also publishes "risk-adjusted" mortality rates, which indicate what a particular surgeon's mortality rate would have been had he or she had a mix of patients identical to the state average. An analogy that can be made here is to the difference between a raw batting or bowling average in the game of cricket, and the "processed" rating that the Price Waterhouse Coopers' (PWC) rankings provide.[19] The raw batting average fails to take into account various factors such as the difficulty of batting conditions on particular grounds that a particular batsman may be more likely to encounter, and the quality of bowling attack that he may happen to face. PWC ratings account for these factors by statistically adjusting raw data to take into account the ways in which the overall conditions that a batsman faces deviate from the norm.[20]

It is unlikely that risk-adjusted statistics could be so well adjusted as to fully represent the complete range of variables that a surgeon encounters. However, it is surely absurd to insist that anything less than perfectly accurate information about surgeons' performance should be withheld from patients. From a patient's point of view, information that is reasonably accurate and fairly representative can be of significant value, despite its imperfections, and is usually better than having no performance data at all.

From the point of view of surgeons and health policymakers, it may appear justifiable to withhold certain sorts of imperfect performance information from patients, if the provision of such information is likely to have highly deleterious effects on the availability and practice of surgical care generally. But the question of the extent – if at all – to which imperfect performance data can be justifiably withheld from an individual patient to whom it would be material, in order to maintain or promote better overall medical practice, will depend importantly on how one balances such factors as patients' rights to medical information, rights to treatment, surgeons' duties as professionals to make their services broadly available, and the promotion of medical utility overall. And the bearing such factors will have on one's answer here will depend importantly on whether one relies on, for example, a Kantian or a Utilitarian ethical theory. Thus, Kantians may argue here that the public has a right to know about surgeons' performance data, imperfect or not, particularly if such data can enhance the autonomy of patients' decisions about surgery. Utilitarians, on the other hand, might argue that imperfect performance information should not be released to patients, where the provision of such information is likely to lead patients to make decisions that are contrary to their best interests, or is likely to result in a lowering of the quality of surgical care offered to the community overall.

In any case, the worry that patients may misuse or fail to comprehend performance information contained in report cards can be addressed by considering the nature of the informed consent process itself. In standard models of the informed consent process, such as the account given by Wear (1998, chap. 6), the doctor provides relevant information to the patient and then takes reasonable measures to ensure that the patient comprehends that information. Comprehension typically involves placing the significance of the information provided in an appropriate context for the patient to interpret. Consistent with this approach, cardiologists in New York State are encouraged by the Department of Health to discuss and contextualise the different risk-adjusted mortality rates of various cardiac surgeons, as part of the development of an appropriate treatment plan. Report cards made publicly available may well be improperly interpreted by the public at large. However the relevant issue, for the purposes of providing for informed consent, is not whether to make such information available to the public generally, but whether to provide such information to patients who are contemplating the surgical procedure in question.

It might seem unrealistic to expect surgeons with poor report cards and a lack of plausible explanations for those poor results, to own up and say that they are poor surgeons. Some might suggest it is more likely that such surgeons will provide implausible explanations, but dress them up in such a way as to make them appear plausible to patients. This problem prompts thinking about ways in which the informed consent process might be adjusted to minimise the potential for surgeons to mislead patients as to their ability. One idea is to involve third parties in the informed consent process. Although it may be unrealistic to expect a surgeon to divulge that he or she is of poor ability when it comes to performing a particular operation, there is no reason why a third party might not be able to indicate that the surgeon's reports are poor and that his or her explanations for these poor results are inadequate. To an extent, third parties are already involved in the informed consent process in situations where patients seek a "second opinion". Further, in the UK, Patient Care Advisers are now employed by the National Health Service to assist cardiac patients with making various decisions about surgery. The role of these advisers currently includes assisting cardiac patients who have been awaiting surgery for over six months to decide whether to be transferred to another cardiac unit (elsewhere in the UK), which can provide surgery sooner than the unit that the patient is currently listed with. In assisting patients with their decisions, these advisers help patients to consider a range of information, including performance data on individual cardiac units. All indications are that these advisers will also be asked to assist patients with considering performance information on individual cardiac surgeons, once that information becomes publicly available in 2004.[21] Another consideration is that surgeons with merely average performance data might be able to make their services more attractive to patients, offering their services at cheaper rates than those of surgeons with better results, and might be prepared to acknowledge their average results to patients, as a way of explaining their lower fees. In public hospital situations where doctors' fees are not at issue, surgeons with merely average performance results may be able to offer patients reduced waiting times for non-emergency operations.[22]

Another practical issue to consider is the impact of report cards on the training of new surgeons.[23] It takes a long time to become a fully-qualified surgeon. Practitioners will typically spend many years as surgical residents, performing operations under close supervision, before they are permitted to play a leading role in a surgical procedure.[24] It seems to follow from our argument that a surgeon's status as a trainee, or as a newly-qualified practitioner, should be disclosed to those patients who would regard this as material to their decisions about whether or not to be operated upon by a given practitioner.[25] Likewise, where significant data are collected on a trainee's performance in order to monitor the trainee's progress, our argument seems to imply that these data should be made available to those patients who would regard these as material information. However, there may not be sufficient data on an individual practitioner, during their training and immediately after qualifying as a surgeon, to enable a satisfactory report card on their performance to be created. Typically, a satisfactory report card will need to be based on data collected over several years. Attempts to construct a report card on fledgling surgeons, who have conducted only a small number of surgical procedures, can be expected to yield data that are very unreliable.

The problem of adequately informing patients about the performance of trainees and newly-qualified surgeons, in a way that minimises the chance of such information being misinterpreted, is a difficult one to resolve. Much research is currently being done on ways of improving and possibly standardising measures of trainee surgeons' progress along the learning curve, but the problem of how to adequately inform patients about trainee surgeons' performance is widely acknowledged, and the medical profession itself has not so far been able to come up with a solution to this problem.[26] Close supervision of trainees is clearly important, as are the proliferation of skills laboratories where trainees can practice under simulated conditions. However, there will still be occasions where the trainee must perform a procedure themselves for the first time, and outcomes for patients in such cases are commonly worse than if the procedure was carried out by a fully-qualified surgeon (Gawande, 2002, pp. 21–30). Nevertheless, the difficulties of adequately informing patients about trainees may not be entirely intractable. Perhaps there are better ways of helping patients to understand a trainee surgeon's performance than by attempting to develop statistically valid report cards on trainees. After all, records are kept to enable a trainee's progress to be monitored by their superiors, and if suitably contextualised, these records could be provided to patients who see this information as material to their decision about surgery. Because performance information on trainees and newly-qualified surgeons is particularly likely to mislead those unfamiliar with the circumstances and procedures surrounding surgical training,[27] it is especially important to assist patients who are provided with such information to properly contextualise that information.

However, disclosing information to patients about a trainee surgeon's status and their level of performance, raises a further concern. That is, such disclosures may lead patients to avoid the trainee in favour of more experienced practitioners, and this will potentially impede the trainee's development of those surgical skills that can be effectively learnt only by operating on actual patients. Given these implications, we need to address the question of whether there are any reasons that would suffice to justify withholding such information about trainee surgeons from patients who would regard this as material to their decision about surgery.

An argument that some might advance for withholding such information appeals to the notion of justice as reciprocity. According to this argument, because each of us has been or is likely to be the beneficiary of a practitioner's surgical skills at some stage in our lives, there is a reciprocal (*prima facie*) moral obligation upon each of us to accept a trainee surgeon, on some occasion, when we need surgery. Analogous reciprocity-based arguments are sometimes put in the context of medical experimentation, and in regard to blood donation (see for instance, Caplan, 1988). To accept the benefits of medical experimentation or donated blood, without being prepared to make comparable sacrifices, is to act as a "free rider".

Such arguments, while intuitively appealing, are controversial, because they assume that free riding must be wrong in all contexts, and this assumption has been strongly challenged.[28] However, even if we agreed that free riding is always immoral, and so accepted that these reciprocity-based arguments create obligations in the case of medical experimentation or blood donation, this would not justify withholding information about a trainee surgeon's status or their performance from patients who would regard such information as material to their decision about surgery.

The provision to patients of materially relevant information about trainees follows from standard informed consent requirements, and none of the reciprocity-based arguments about medical experimentation or blood donation hold that our obligations here require us to sacrifice our right to be informed about the risks of a particular experiment or of donating blood. In any case, accepting the services of a surgeon might not create any reciprocal obligation on the patient's part, since, as we have argued earlier, surgical services can be seen as something that practitioners are obligated to make broadly available to society, in exchange for society granting surgeons a monopoly of expertise on the provision of these services. Perhaps there are other arguments for creating exceptions to standard informed consent requirements in the case of trainee surgeons. But in the absence of such arguments, we hold that such exceptions would be unjustified.

A consequence of disclosing trainee surgeons' status and performance information to those patients who see this as material information, may be that it begins to take longer to train surgeons. This would be a significant public policy issue, which each community would have to confront for themselves, with reference to the particular health care system in place there. There are many issues raised here. Several measures might be considered, to help mitigate this effect. The community might decide that greater resources ought to be invested in the training of surgeons, to ensure that their progress is not unduly delayed by a possible reduction in the number of patients willing to have surgery performed by a trainee.[29] Thus, closer supervision of trainees by highly proficient surgeons could be made a mandatory part of surgical training regimes, and this could be clearly explained to patients. Also, the distinction between experience and performance could be emphasised, so that patients do not automatically assume (before seeing a trainee's performance data) that an inexperienced trainee surgeon will have poor performance data, and so that patients may be attracted to the services of trainees with good performance data. Another possibility would be to offer certain incentives to patients who are prepared to have surgery by trainees, such as shorter pre-operative waiting periods.[30] Communities with fee-for-service health systems might also consider requiring lower fees to be charged for surgery carried out by trainees, though patients would need to be assured that they would not have to bear any added costs that might eventuate, should extra follow-up procedures prove to be necessary.[31]

V. CONCLUSION

We have argued that a proper understanding of the doctrine of informed consent, in conjunction with a proper understanding of the concept of risk, implies that we should support the use of performance assessment of surgeons as part of the informed consent process. We have considered some commonly voiced objections to this chain of implication and found them to be lacking in substance. We have not shown how our proposal could be turned into sound policy – that would be a major undertaking – but we have addressed some common practical objections to its implementation.[32]

NOTES

1. Those who adopt a maximal approach include Faden and Beauchamp (1986), Appelbaum, Lidz, & Meisel (1987), Wear (1998), and the state of Georgia legislature, which requires a disclosure of the nature of a treatment, the likelihood of its success, practical alternatives to a treatment as well as a prognosis if treatment is declined. In Georgia this information is legally required to be transmitted to a patient even if the doctor providing the disclosure does not have the information available at the time of the proposed treatment. A minimal approach is adopted by most other United States legislatures, such as the state of New York legislature, which only requires information about reasonably foreseeable risks and alternative treatments to be disclosed (Schuck, 1994, p. 917). In an interesting recent move away from the minimal approach, hitherto dominant in the state of New York, the New York State Health Department has recently required a cardiac surgeon with hepatitis C to disclose this to patients before attempting operations (Lambert, 2002). We see this decision as being in accordance with our argument. The fact that a particular surgeon has hepatitis C, and so is likely to have an increased chance of passing on this infection to patients, is information about risks that patients would find material to their decision about whether or not to undergo an operation with that surgeon.
2. One of us has argued against standard treatments of disclosure in informed consent on very different grounds (Clarke, 2001).

3. While it is widely agreed that the overriding purpose of the doctrine of informed consent, in medicine is to ensure that patient autonomy is respected, the nature of autonomy itself is less than transparent. See Clarke (2001) for a discussion of the relationship between different conceptions of autonomy and the doctrine of informed consent. Rival conceptions of autonomy are analysed further by Dworkin (1988).

4. The magnitude to which Clarke values feeling in his right knee may not be completely transparent to him. Nevertheless, we hold, it is reasonable to think that someone can estimate the magnitude of this subjective value, roughly, at least.

5. Schuck (1994, pp. 917-918) provides references to some American legal cases that raise the issue of the relative size of populations to which risks could refer.

6. In a recent simulation of an operation, surgeons who had been awake all night made 20% more errors than surgeons who had had a full night sleep (Taffinder, McManus, Gul, Russell, & Darzi, 1998).

7. New York State Department of Health (2002). The mortality rates for angioplasty procedures performed by different cardiologists has also recently been added to the New York State Department of Health (2003).

8. See Pennsylvania Health Care Cost Containment Council: 'Pennsylvania's Guide to Coronary Artery Bypass Graft (CABG) Surgery 2000'. See also Quality Information Management Corporation, The Greater Cleveland Consumer Report of Hospital Performance (1998).

9. See *The Bristol Royal Infirmary Inquiry*, available: http://www.bristol-inquiry.org.uk/index.htm and, for the UK government response, www.doh.gov.uk/bristolinquiryresponse/statement.htm. In the UK, these report cards will be administered through the newly-established Office for Information on Health Care Performance, within the Commission for Health Improvement, at the National Health Service.

10. See Duckett, Casemix Consulting, & Hunter (1999). We argue that there is a compelling case for the use of such performance indicators as a component of the disclosure requirement in the provision of informed consent. However, this is not to claim that this is the only consideration in favour of report cards, nor to claim that the movement for the use of report cards is being driven by a concern to better enable patients to provide informed consent. The report cards movement appears to be driven by a number of interrelated concerns. One is a concern for public accountability as a means of ensuring public confidence in the health system. A second is an economic argument, which is particularly important in the Victorian case, that links the public provision of information relevant to health care decisions to the more effective operation of the health care system, understood in free market terms. A third is also economic, being the view that the use of performance indicators will motivate hospitals and individual surgeons to improve their overall performance.

11. These figures are extrapolated from Bolsin (1998, p. 370).

12. An American case somewhat similar to *Chappel v Hart* is *Johnson v Kokemoor* (1996), a Wisconsin case in which a patient, Ms. Johnson sued her surgeon, Dr. Kokemoor, as a result of severe side-effects caused by aneurysm surgery. Ms. Johnson contended that Dr. Kokemoor had exaggerated his degree of experience at performing the type of surgery that he proposed, and under-represented the risks associated with that surgery. Expert witnesses for the plaintiff argued that a reasonable physician in Dr. Kokemoor's circumstances would have advised the plaintiff of the availability of more experienced surgeons at a nearby clinic (Heinemann, 1997).

13. A failure to distinguish clearly between performance and experience is also present in the judgement of the Wisconsin High Court in *Johnson v Kokemoor*, and in Heinemann's (1997) discussion of that judgement. The connection between a surgeon's experience and ability is discussed by Freckleton (1999), who also recognises that *Chappel v Hart* provides an impetus towards "report cards".

14. It is also worth noting here that a surgeon who refused to disclose his sexual orientation to a patient for whom this is material may well *restrict* that patient's autonomy in regard to her decision about surgery, but he does not thereby *violate* that patient's autonomy in that regard. A patient's autonomy is violated when it is restricted *unjustifiably*, and if our above argument is sound, a surgeon who refuses to disclose his sexual orientation to a patient for whom this is material does *not* restrict that patient's autonomy unjustifiably. Such a refusal, unlike the case with information about a surgeon's performance, is perfectly compatible with the requirement to respect patient autonomy, for this requirement demands that health professionals do not unjustifiably restrict the autonomy of their patients – it does not demand that health professionals meet whatever informed and voluntary requests (for information, or for services) that patients make. A similar point could be made about a justice-based refusal to meet a patient's autonomous request. For instance, an end-stage renal failure patient who is not provided with the only available dialysis machine certainly has their autonomy restricted here; but if justice requires that this dialysis machine be provided to another patient with end-stage renal failure instead – because, say (as some principles of justice would have it), this patient's prospects with dialysis are much better than the other's – then failing to provide the dialysis machine to the first patient does not count as a violation of their autonomy. (For further discussion of this point, and of other values that properly govern professional roles, see Oakley & Cocking, 2001.)

15. This view has been put to us in conversation by Michael Davis, among others.

16. A conclusive answer to these sorts of resource allocation questions would require details about the costs of collecting performance data, and some principle of health care resource allocation that would enable us to judge whether preventative health measures ought to received funding priority over measures to promote informed decision-making by patients in acute care. Examining these issues would take us too far afield here.

17. See *Coronary Artery Bypass Surgery in New York State 1997–1999*, New York State Department of Health, September 2002, p. 1.

18. This concern was expressed by the Australian Medical Association, and the Royal Australasian College of Surgeons, in their submissions to the Victorian Department of Human Services Health Services Policy Review. See Duckett, Casemix Consulting, & Hunter (1999, 114–117).

19. See "PricewaterhouseCoopers Cricket Ratings" Available: http://cricketratings.pwcglobal.com/cricket/cricket.htm [accessed Sept. 2003].

20. PWC use purely mechanical processing procedures to take account of abnormal conditions, when producing weighted batting and bowling averages. This is not the only way to weight raw data. It may be that additional non-mechanical processing is appropriate in some cases, including the development of risk-adjusted surgeons' report cards.

21. The NHS booklet, *Extending choice for patients – Heart surgery: Your guide to your choices* (2003), explains that the Patient Care Adviser's "...job is to work for you. Although they work closely with the cardiac team in your local hospital they do not answer to them. Your Adviser is managed by the local Patient Advocacy and Liaison Service to ensure that he or she is an independent voice acting on your behalf".

22. Of course, the implementation of such strategies is complicated, considerably, by the involvement of the insurance industry in the financing of medical procedures.
23. Thanks to an anonymous referee for raising this concern.
24. See Gawande (2002) for a lively personal account of the difficulties commonly encountered in learning to perform surgery.
25. Note that, as explained earlier, there is no simple and direct correlation between experience and performance. Some very experienced practitioners may have declining levels of surgical performance, and some inexperienced trainees may have relatively high levels of surgical performance. Also, obtaining statistically valid figures on risks for individual surgeons would seem to require that they have performed a minimum number of operations.
26. It is not only novice surgeons whose performance follows a learning curve. Even well-qualified surgeons face a learning curve when mastering new surgical techniques into surgical practice. So, the question of how to adequately inform patients about where a surgeon's level of performance is in relation to that surgeon's learning curve is more pervasive than might initially be apparent.
27. This point is clearly made by Tony Eyers (2003) in a paper describing a first-hand account of surgical training.
28. This assumption is challenged, *inter alia*, by Cullity (1995), and Dare (1998b).
29. Indeed, given that the increased surgical risks posed by trainees are commonly borne disproportionately by lower socioeconomic groups in society, there is a strong distributive justice argument for greater societal investment in surgical training, to enable these increased risks to be spread more evenly across different socioeconomic groups in the community. (See for instance, Eyers, 2003, on this point.)
30. There is some evidence from the UK that cardiac patients are prepared to make certain sorts of trade-offs – such as travelling significant distances to have surgery at a different cardiac unit – in order to shorten their wait for surgery. See *Extending choice for patients – Heart surgery: Your guide to your choices* (2003).
31. The implications of such incentives for private health insurance would also need to be considered. Further, careful attention would need to be given to each suggested incentive, on a case-by-case basis, to minimise the possibility that such incentives would impair a patient's judgement about the surgery.
32. We would like to thank the anonymous referees for their helpful comments on a previous draft of this paper. For useful feedback on earlier drafts, we also wish to thank Joe Ibrahim, Hugh Martin, David Neil, Tim Van Gelder, the Melbourne-Monash bioethics journal club, and audiences at the Children's Hospital, Westmead NSW, the Australian Association for Professional and Applied Ethics annual conference 2001 and CAPPE Melbourne and Wagga Wagga. Research that led to this paper was supported in part by National Health and Medical Council Project grant no. 236877.

REFERENCES

Appelbaum, P.S., Lidz, C.W., & Meisel, A. (1987). *Informed consent: Legal theory and clinical practice*. New York: Oxford University Press.
Bolsin, S.N. (1998). Professional misconduct: The Bristol case. *Medical Journal of Australia*, *169*, 369–372.

Caplan, A.L. (1988). Is there an obligation to participate in biomedical research? In: S.F. Spicker, I. Alon, A. de Vries, and H.T. Engelhardt, Jr. (Eds.), *The use of human beings in research, with special reference to clinical trials*. Dordrecht: Kluwer.

Chappel v Hart, High Court of Australia HCA 55, 2 September 1998, 195 CLR 232.

Chassin, M.R., Hannan, E.L., & DeBuono, B.A. (1996). Benefits and hazards of reporting medical outcomes publicly. *New England Journal of Medicine, 334*, 394–398.

Clarke, S. (2001). Informed consent in medicine in comparison with consent in other areas of human activity. *The Southern Journal of Philosophy, 39*, 169–187.

Coronary Artery Bypass Surgery in New York State 1997–1999. (2002). New York State Department of Health.

Cullity, G. (1995). Moral free riding. *Philosophy and Public Affairs, 24*, 3–34.

Dare, T. (1998a). The secret courts of men's hearts: Legal ethics and Harper Lee's *To Kill a Mockingbird*. In: K. Economides (Ed.), *Ethical challenges to legal education and conduct*. Oxford: Hart Publishing.

Dare, T. (1998b). Mass immunisation programmes: Some philosophical issues. *Bioethics, 12*, 125–149.

Dawes, R.M. (1996). *House of cards: Psychology and psychotherapy built on myth*. New York: The Free Press.

Department of Health. (1998). *The new NHS performance tables 1997/98* [On-line]. Available: http://www.doh.gov.uk/tables98/index.htm

Duckett, S., Casemix Consulting, & Hunter, L. (1999). *Health Services Policy Review: Final Report*, Victorian Government Department of Human Services [On-line]. Available: http://www.dhs.vic.gov.au/ahs/archive/servrev/

Dworkin, G. (1988). *The theory and practice of autonomy*. Cambridge: Cambridge University Press.

Erickson, L.C., Torchiana, D.F., Schneider, E.C., Newburger, J.W., & Hannan, E.L. (2000). The relationship between managed care insurance and use of lower-mortality hospitals for CABG surgery. *Journal of the American Medical Association, 283*, 1976–1982.

Eyers, T. (2003). Teaching trainee surgeons how to operate. Unpublished manuscript.

Faden, R.R., & Beauchamp, T.L. (1986). *A history and theory of informed consent*. New York: Oxford University Press.

Freckelton, I. (1999). Materiality of risk and proficiency assessment: The onset of report cards? *Journal of Law and Medicine, 6*, 313–318.

Garb, H.N. (1989). Clinical judgement, clinical training and professional experience. *Psychological Bulletin, 105*, 387–392.

Gawande, A. (2002). *Complications: A surgeon's notes on an imperfect science*. London: Profile Books.

Green, J., & Wintfeld, N. (1995). Report cards on cardiac surgeons – Assessing New York State's approach. *New England Journal of Medicine, 332*, 1229–1232.

Hannan, E.L., Sone, C.C., Biddle, T.L., & DeBuono, B.A. (1997). Public release of cardiac surgery outcomes data in New York: 'What do New York State cardiologists think of it?' *American Heart Journal, 136*, 1120–1128.

Heinemann, R.A. (1997). Pushing the limits of informed consent: *Johnson v Kokemoor* and physician-specific disclosure. *Wisconsin Law Review, 1079*, 1083.

Lambert, B. (2002). Infected doctor told to get patients' consent. *The New York Times*, April 19th, 2002.

Marshall, M.N., Shekelle, P., Leatherman, S., Brook, R., & Owen, J.W. (2000). *Dying to know: Public release of information about quality of health care*. Los Angeles: RAND Corporation/Nuffield Trust.

New York State Department of Health. (2002). *Coronary artery bypass surgery in New York State 1997–1999* [On-line]. Available: http://www.health.state.ny.us/nysdoh/heart/1997–99cabg.pdf

New York State Department of Health. (2003). *Percutaneous coronary interventions (PCI) in New York State 1998–2000* [On-line]. Available: http://www.health.state.ny.us/nysdoh/reports/pci_1998–2000.pdf

NHS. (2003). *Extending choice for patients – heart surgery: Your guide to your choices* [On-line]. Available: http://www.doh.gov.uk/heart/choice/index.htm

Oakley, J., & Cocking, D. (2001). *Virtue ethics and professional roles*. Cambridge: Cambridge University Press.

Pennsylvania Health Care Cost Containment Council. (2000). 'Pennsylvania's Guide to Coronary Artery Bypass Graft (CABG) Surgery 2000' [On-line]. Available: http://www.phc4.org/reports/cabg00/default.htm

Peterson, E.D., De Long, E.R., & Jollis, J.G. (1998). The effects of New York's bypass surgery provider profiling on access to care and patient outcomes in the elderly. *Journal of the American College of Cardiology, 32*, 993–999.

Quality Information Management Corporation, *The Greater Cleveland Consumer Report of Hospital Performance*, Cleveland, Ohio (1998) [On-line]. Discussed at http://www.insightsandoutcomes.com/cgi-bin/article.cgi?article_id = 55

Schuck, P.H. (1994). Rethinking informed consent. *The Yale Law Journal, 103*, 899–959.

Taffinder, N.J., McManus, I.C., Gul, Y., Russell, R.C.G., & Darzi, A. (1988). Effect of sleep deprivation on surgeon's dexterity on laparoscopy simulator. *The Lancet, 352*, 1191.

The Bristol Royal Infirmary Inquiry [On-line]. Available: http://www.bristol-inquiry.org.uk/about/issues/brisiss.htm

Veatch, R.M. (1985). The physician as stranger: The ethics of the anonymous patient–physician relationship. In: E. Shelp (Ed.), *The clinical encounter*. Dordrecht: Reidel.

Wear, S. (1998). *Informed consent: Patient autonomy and physician beneficence within health care* (2nd edn.). Dordrecht: Kluwer.

[5]

Models for Ethical Medicine in a Revolutionary Age

What physician-patient roles foster the most ethical relationship?

by **ROBERT M. VEATCH**

Most of the ethical problems in the practice of medicine come up in cases where the medical condition or desired procedure itself presents no moral problem. Most day-to-day patient contacts are just not cases which are ethically exotic. For the woman who spends five hours in the clinic waiting room with two screaming children waiting to be seen for the flu, the flu is not a special moral problem; her wait is. When medical students practice drawing bloods from clinic patients in the cardiac care unit—when teaching material is treated as material—the moral problem is not really related to the patient's heart in the way it might be in a more exotic heart transplant. Many more blood samples are drawn, however, than hearts transplanted. It is only by moving beyond the specific issues to more basic underlying ethical themes that the real ethical problems in medicine can be dealt with.

Most fundamental of the underlying themes of the new medical ethics is that health care must be a human right, no longer a privilege limited to those who can afford it. It has not always been that way, and, of course, is not anything near that in practice today. But the norm, the moral claim, is becoming increasingly recognized. Both of the twin revolutions have made their contribution to this change. Until this century health care could be treated as a luxury, no matter how offensive this might be now. The amount of real healing that went on was minimal anyway. But now, with the biological revolution, health care

Dr. Robert Veatch is Associate for Medical Ethics at the Hastings Center and Research Associate in Medicine at Columbia University College of Physicians and Surgeons.

really is essential to "life, liberty, and the pursuit of happiness." And health care is a right for everyone because of the social revolution which is really a revolution in our conception of justice. If the obscure phrase "all men are created equal" means anything in the medical context where biologically it is clear that they are not equal, it means that they are equal in the legitimacy of their moral claim. They must be treated equally in what is essential to their humanity: dignity, freedom, individuality. The sign in front of the prestigious, modern hospital, "Methadone patients use side door" is morally offensive even if it means nothing more than that the Methadone Unit is located near that door. It is strikingly similar to "Coloreds to the back of the bus." With this affirmation of the right to health care, what are the models of professional-lay relationships which permit this and other basic ethical themes to be conveyed?

1. **The Engineering Model.** One of the impacts of the biological revolution is to make the physician scientific. All too often he behaves like an applied scientist. The rhetoric of the scientific tradition in the modern world is that the scientist must be "pure." He must be factual, divorcing himself from all considerations of value. It has taken atomic bombs and Nazi medical research to let us see the foolishness and danger of such a stance. In the first place the scientist, and certainly the applied scientist, just cannot logically be value-free. Choices must be made daily—in research design, in significance levels of statistical tests, and in perception of the "significant" observations from an infinite perceptual

field, and each of these choices requires a frame of values on which it is based. Even more so in an applied science like medicine choices based upon what is "significant," what is "valuable," must be made constantly. The physician who thinks he can just present all the facts and let the patient make the choices is fooling himself even if it is morally sound and responsible to do this at all the critical points where decisive choices are to be made. Furthermore, even if the physician logically could eliminate all ethical and other value considerations from his decision-making and even if he could in practice conform to the impossible value-free ideal, it would be morally outrageous for him to do so. It would make him an engineer, a plumber making repairs, connecting tubes and flushing out clogged systems, with no questions asked. Even though I strongly favor abortion reform, I am deeply troubled by a physician who really believes abortion is murder *in the full sense* if he agrees to either perform one or refer to another physician. Hopefully no physician would do so when confronted with a request for technical advice about murdering a postnatal human.

2. **The Priestly Model.** In proper moral revulsion to the model which makes the physician into a plumber for whom his own ethical judgments are completely excluded, some move to the opposite extreme, making the physician a new priest. Establishment sociologist of medicine Robert N. Wilson describes the physician-patient relationship as religious. "The doctor's office or the hospital room, for example," he says, "have somewhat the aura of a sanctuary;" "...the patient must view his doctor in a manner far removed from the prosaic and the mundane."

The priestly model leads to what I call the "As-a syndrome." The symptoms are verbal, but the disease is moral. The chief diagnostic sign is the phrase "speaking-as a...." In counseling a pregnant woman who has taken Thalidomide, a physician says, "The odds are against a normal baby and "speaking-as-a-physician that is a risk you shouldn't take." One must ask what it is about medical training that lets this be said "as-a-physician" rather than as a friend or as a moral man or as a priest. The problem is one of generalization of expertise: transferring of expertise in the technical aspects of a subject to expertise in moral advice.

The main ethical principle which summarizes this priestly tradition is "Benefit and do no harm to the patient." Now attacking the principle of doing no harm to the patient is a bit like attacking fatherhood. (Motherhood has not dominated the profession in the Western tradition.) But Fatherhood has long been an alternative symbol for the priestly model; "Father" has traditionally been a personalistic metaphor for God and for the priest. Likewise, the classical medical sociology literature (the same literature using the religious images) always uses the parent-child image as an analogy for the physician-patient relationship. It is this paternalism in the realm of values which is represented in the moral slogan "benefit and do no harm to the patient." It takes the locus of decision-making away from the patient and places it in the hands of the professional. In doing so it destroys or at least minimizes the other moral themes essential to a more balanced ethical system. While a professional group may affirm this principle as adequate for a professional ethic, it is clear that society, more

---

The priestly model

leads to the

"as-a" syndrome

generally, has a much broader set of ethical norms. If the professional group is affirming one norm while society affirms another for the same circumstances, then the physician is placed in the uncomfortable position of having to decide whether his loyalty is to the norms of his professional group or to those of the broader society. What would this larger set of norms include?

a. Producing Good and Not Harm. Outside of the narrowest Kantian tradition, no one excludes the moral duty of producing good and avoiding harm entirely. Let this be said from the start. Some separate producing good and avoiding evil into two different principles placing greater moral weight on the latter, but this is also true within the tradition of professional medical ethics. The real difference is that in a set of ethical norms used more universally in the broader society producing good and avoiding harm is set in a much broader context and becomes just one of a much larger set of moral obligations.

b. Protecting Individual Freedom. Personal freedom is a fundamental value in society. It is essential to being truly human. Individual freedom for both physician and patient must be protected even if it looks like some harm is going to be done in the process. This is why legally competent patients are permitted by society to refuse blood transfusions or other types of medical care even when to the vast majority of us the price seems to be one of great harm. Authority about what constitutes harm and what constitutes good (as opposed to procedures required to obtain a particular predetermined good or harm) cannot be vested in any one particular group of individuals. To do so would be to make the error of generalizing expertise.

c. Preserving Individual Dignity. Equality of moral significance of all persons means that each is given fundamental dignity. Individual freedom of choice and control over one's own life and body contributes to that dignity. We might say that this more universal, societal ethic of freedom and dignity is one which moves beyond B.F. Skinner.

Many of the steps in the hospitalization, care, and maintenance of the patient, particularly seriously ill patients are currently an assault on that dignity. The emaciated, senile man connected to life by IV tubes, tracheotomy, and colostomy has difficulty retaining his sense of dignity. Small wonder that many prefer to return to their own homes to die. It is there on their own turf that they have a sense of power and dignity.

d. Truth-telling and Promise-keeping. As traditional as they sound, the ethical obligations of truth-telling and promise-keeping have retained their place in ethics because they are seen as essential to the quality of human relationships. It is disturbing to see these fundamental elements of human interaction compromised, minimized, and even eliminated supposedly in order to keep from harming the patient. This is a much broader problem than the issue of what to tell the terminal carcinoma patient or the patient for whom there has been an unanticipated discovery of an XYY chromosome pattern when doing an amniocentesis for mongolism. It arises when the young boy getting his measles shot is told "Now this won't hurt a bit" and when a medical student is introduced on the hospital floor as "Doctor." And these all may be defended as ways of keeping from harming the patient. It is clear that in each case, also, especially if one takes into account the long range threat to trust and confidence, that in the long run these violations of truth-telling and promise-keeping may do more harm than good. Both the young boy getting the shot and the medical student are being taught what to expect from the medical profession in the future. But even if that were not the case, each is an assault on patient dignity and freedom and humanity. Such actions may be justifiable sometimes, but the case must be awfully strong.

e. Maintaining and Restoring Justice. Another way in which the ethical norms of the broader society move beyond concern for helping and not harming the patient is by insisting on a fair distribution of health services. What we have been calling the social revolution, as prefigurative as it may be, has heightened our concern for equality in the distribution of basic health services. If health care is a right then it is a right for all. It is not enough to produce individual cases of good health or even the best aggregate health statistics. Even if the United States had the best health statistics in the world (which it does not have), if this were attained at the expense of inferior health care for certain groups within the society it would be ethically unaccepable.

At this point in history with our current record of discriminatory delivery of health services there is a special concern for restoring justice. Justice must also be compensatory. The health of those who have been discriminated against must be maintained and restored as a special priority.

3. The Collegial Model. With the engineering model the physican becomes a plumber without any moral integrity. With the priestly model his moral authority so dominates the patient that the patient's freedom and dignity are extinguished. In the effort to develop a more proper balance which would permit the other fundamental values and obligations to be preserved, some have suggested that the physician and the patient should see themselves as colleagues pursuing the common goal of eliminating the illness and preserving the health of the patient. The physician is the patient's "pal." It is in the collegial model that the themes of trust and confidence play the most crucial role. When two individuals or groups are truly committed to common goals then trust and confidence are justified and the collegial model is appropriate. It is a very pleasant, harmonious way to interact with one's fellow human beings. There is an equality of dignity and respect, an equality of value contributions, lacking in the earlier models.

But social realism makes us ask the embarrassing question. Is there, in fact, any real basis for the assumption of mutual loyalty and goals, of common interest which would permit the unregulated community of colleagues model to apply to the physician-patient relationship?

There is some proleptic sign of a community of real common interests in some elements of the radical health movement and free clinics, but for the most part we have to admit that ethnic, class, economic, and value differences make the assumption of common interest which is necessary for the collegial model to function are a mere pipedream. What is needed is a more provisional model which permits equality in the realm of moral significance between patient and physician without making the utopian assumption of collegiality.

4. The Contractual Model. The model of social relationship which fits these conditions is that of the contract or covenant. The notion of contract should not be loaded with legalistic implications, but taken in its more symbolic form as in the traditional religious or marriage "contract" or "covenant." Here two individuals or groups are interacting in a way where there are obligations and expected benefits for both parties. The obligations and benefits are limited in scope, though, even if they are expressed in somewhat vague terms. The basic norms of freedom, dignity, truthtelling, promise-keeping, and justice are essential to a contractual relationship. The premise is trust and confidence even though it is recognized that there is not a full mutuality of interests. Social sanctions institutionalize and stand behind the relationship, in case there is a violation of the contract, but for the most part the assumption is that there will be a faithful fulfillment of the obligations.

Only in the contractual model can there be a true sharing of ethical authority and responsibility. This avoids the moral abdication on the part of the physician in the engineering model and the moral abdication on the part of the patient in the priestly model. It also avoids the uncontrolled and false sense of equality in the collegial model. With the contractual relationship there is a sharing in which the physician recognizes that the patient must maintain freedom of control over his own life and destiny when significant choices are to be made. Should the physician not be able to live with his conscience under those terms the contract is not made or is broken. This means that there will have to be relatively greater open discussion of the moral premises hid-

The real, day-to-day

ethical crises

are not so exotic

ing in medical decisions before and as they are made.

With the contractual model there is a sharing in which the patient has legitimate grounds for trusting that once the basic value framework for medical decision-making is established on the basis of the patient's own values, the myriads of minute medical decisions which must be made day in and day out in the care of the patient will be made by the physician within that frame of reference.

In the contractual model, then, there is a real sharing of decision-making in a way that there is realistic assurance that both patient and physician will retain their moral integrity. In this contractual context patient control of decision-making in the individual level is assured without the necessity of insisting that the patient participate in every trivial decision. On the social level community control of health care is made possible in the same way. The lay community is given and should be given the status of contractor. The locus of decision-making is thus in the lay community, but the day-to-day medical decisions can, with trust and confidence, rest with the medical community. If trust and confidence are broken the contract is broken.

Medical ethics in the midst of the biological and social revolutions is dealing with a great number of new and difficult ethical cases: in vitro fertilization, psychosurgery, happiness pills, brain death, and the military use of medical technology. But the real day-to-day ethical crises may not be nearly so exotic. Whether the issue is in an exotic context or one which is nothing more complicated medically than a routine physical exam, the ethos of ethical responsibility established by the appropriate selection of a model for the moral relationship between the professional and the lay communities will be decisive. This is the real framework for medical ethics in a revolutionary age.

[6]

We are beginning to recognize that the prevalent ethic of patient autonomy simply will not do. Since demands for health care are virtually unlimited, giving autonomous patients the care they want will bankrupt our health care system. We can no longer simply buy our way out of difficult questions of justice by expanding the health care pie until there is enough to satisfy the wants and needs of everyone. The requirements of justice and the needs of other patients must temper the claims of autonomous patients.

But if the legitimate claims of other patients and other (non-medical) interests of society are beginning to be recognized, another question is still largely ignored: To what extent can the patient's family legitimately be asked or required to sacrifice their interests so that the patient can have the treatment he or she wants?

This question is not only almost universally ignored, it is generally implicitly dismissed, silenced before it can even be raised. This tacit dismissal results from a fundamental assumption of medical ethics: medical treatment ought always to serve the interests of the patient. This, of course, implies that the interests of family members should be irrelevant to medical treatment decisions or at least ought never to take precedence over the interests of the patient. All questions about fairness to the interests of family members are thus precluded, regardless of the merit or importance of the interests that will have to be sacrificed if the patient is to receive optimal treatment.

Yet there is a whole range of cases in which important interests of family members are dramatically affected by decisions about the patient's treatment; medical decisions often should be made with those interests in mind. Indeed, in many cases family members have a greater interest than the patient in which treatment option is exercised. In such cases, the interests of family members often ought to *override* those of the patient.

John Hardwig is associate professor of Medical Ethics at James H. Quillen College of Medicine, East Tennessee State University, Johnson City, TN.

What About the Family?

by John Hardwig

The prevalent ethic of patient autonomy ignores family interests in medical treatment decisions. Acknowledging these interests as legitimate forces basic changes in ethical theory and the moral practice of medicine.

The problem of family interests cannot be resolved by considering other members of the family as "patients," thereby redefining the problem as one of conflicting interests among *patients*. Other members of the family are not always ill, and even if ill, they still may not be patients. Nor will it do to define the whole family as one patient. Granted, the slogan "the patient is the family" was coined partly to draw attention to precisely the issues I wish to raise, but the idea that the whole family is one patient is too monolithic. The conflicts of interests, beliefs, and values among family members are often too real and run too deep to treat all members as "the patient." Thus, if I am correct, it is sometimes the moral thing to do for a physician to sacrifice the interests of her patient to those of nonpatients—specifically, to those of the other members of the patient's family.

But what is the "family"? As I will use it here, it will mean roughly "those who are close to the patient." "Family" so defined will often include close friends and companions. It may also exclude some with blood or marriage ties to the patient. "Closeness" does not, however, always mean care and abiding affection, nor need it be a positive experience—one can hate, resent, fear, or despise a mother or brother with an intensity not often directed toward strangers, acquaintances, or associates. But there are cases where even a hateful or resentful family member's interests ought to be considered.

This use of "family" gives rise to very sensitive ethical—and legal—issues in the case of legal relatives with no emotional ties to the patient that I cannot pursue here. I can only say that I do not mean to suggest that the interests of legal relatives who are not emotionally close to the patient are always to be ignored. They will sometimes have an important financial interest in the treatment even if they are not emotionally close to the patient. But blood and marriage ties can become so thin that they become *merely* legal relationships. (Consider, for example, "couples" who have long since parted but who have never gotten a divorce, or cases in which the next of kin cannot be bothered with making proxy decisions.) Obviously, there are many important questions about just whose interests are to be considered in which treatment decisions and to what extent.

Connected Interests

There is no way to detach the lives of patients from the lives of those who are close to them. Indeed, the intertwining of lives is part of the very meaning of closeness. Consequently, there will be a broad spectrum of cases in which the treatment options will have dramatic and different impacts on the patient's family.

I believe there are many, many such cases. To save the life of a newborn with serious defects is often dramatically to affect the rest of the parents' lives and, if they have other children, may seriously compromise the quality of their lives, as well...The husband of a woman with Alzheimer's disease may well have a life totally dominated for ten years or more by caring for an increasingly foreign and estranged wife...The choice between aggressive and pal-

Hastings Center Report, March/April 1990

liative care or, for that matter, the difference between either kind of care and suicide in the case of a father with terminal cancer or AIDS may have a dramatic emotional and financial impact on his wife and children... Less dramatically, the choice between two medications, one of which has the side effect of impotence, may radically alter the life a couple has together... The drug of choice for controlling high blood pressure may be too expensive (that is, requires too many sacrifices) for many families with incomes just above the ceiling for Medicaid...

Because the lives of those who are close are not separable, to be close is to no longer have a life entirely your own to live entirely as you choose. To be part of a family is to be morally required to make decisions on the basis of thinking about what is best for all concerned, not simply what is best for yourself. In healthy families, characterized by genuine care, one wants to make decisions on this basis, and many people do so quite naturally and automatically. My own grandfather committed suicide after his heart attack as a final gift to his wife—he had plenty of life insurance but not nearly enough health insurance, and he feared that she would be left homeless and destitute if he lingered on in an incapacitated state. Even if one is not so inclined, however, it is irresponsible and wrong to exclude or to fail to consider the interests of those who are close. Only when the lives of family members will not be importantly affected can one rightly make exclusively or even predominantly self-regarding decisions.

Although "what is best for all concerned" sounds utilitarian, my position does not imply that the right course of action results simply from a calculation of what is best for all. No, the seriously ill may have a right to special consideration, and the family of an ill person may have a duty to make sacrifices to respond to a member's illness. It is one thing to claim that the ill deserve special consideration; it is quite another to maintain that they deserve exclusive or even overriding consideration. Surely we must admit that there are limits to the right to special treatment

by virtue of illness. Otherwise, everyone would be morally required to sacrifice all other goods to better care for the ill. We must also recognize that patients too have moral obligations, obligations to try to protect the lives of their families from destruction resulting from their illnesses.

Thus, unless serious illness excuses one from all moral responsibility— and I don't see how it could—it is an oversimplification to say of a patient who is part of a family that "it's his life" or "after all, it's his medical treatment," as if his life and his treatment could be successfully isolated from the lives of the other members of his family. It is more accurate to say "it's their lives" or "after all, they're all going to have to live with his treatment." Then the really serious moral questions are not *whether* the interests of family members are relevant to decisions about a patient's medical treatment or *whether* their interests should be included in his deliberations or in deliberations about him, but how far family and friends can be asked to support and sustain the patient. What sacrifices can they be morally required to make for his health care? How far can they reasonably be asked to compromise the quality of their lives so that he will receive the care that would improve the quality of his life? To what extent can he reasonably expect them to put their lives "on hold" to preoccupy themselves with his illness to the extent necessary to care for him?

The Anomaly of Medical Decisionmaking

The way we analyze medical treatment decisions by or for patients is plainly anomalous to the way we think about other important decisions family members make. I am a husband, a father, and still a son, and no one would argue that I should or even responsibly could decide to take a sabbatical, another job, or even a weekend trip *solely* on the basis of what I want for myself. Why should decisions about my medical treatment be different? Why should we have even *thought* that medical treatment decisions might be different?

Is it because medical decisions,

uniquely, involve life and death matters? Most medical decisions, however, are not matters of life and death, and we as a society risk or shorten the lives of other people— through our toxic waste disposal decisions, for example—quite apart from considerations of whether that is what they want for themselves.

Have we been misled by a preoccupation with the biophysical model of disease? Perhaps it has tempted us to think of illness and hence also of treatment as something that takes place *within* the body of the patient. What happens in my body does not— barring contagion—affect my wife's body, yet it usually does affect her.

Have we tacitly desired to simplify the practice and the ethics of medicine by considering only the *medical* or health-related consequences of treatment decisions? Perhaps, but it is obvious that we need a broader vision of and sensitivity to *all* the consequences of action, at least among those who are not simply technicians following orders from above. Generals need to consider more than military consequences, businessmen more than economic consequences, teachers more than educational consequences, lawyers more than legal consequences.

Does the weakness and vulnerability of serious illness imply that the ill need such protection that we should serve only their interests? Those who are sick may indeed need special protection, but this can only mean that we must take special care to see that the interests of the ill are duly considered. It does not follow that their interests are to be served exclusively or even that their interests must always predominate. Moreover, we must remember that in terms of the dynamics of the family, the patient is not always the weakest member, the member most in need of protection.

Does it make *historical*, if not logical, sense to view the wishes and interests of the patient as always overriding? Historically, illnesses were generally of much shorter duration; patients got better quickly or died quickly. Moreover, the costs of the medical care available were small enough that rarely was one's future mortgaged to the costs of the care of family members. Although this was once

Hastings Center Report, March/April 1990

truer than it is today, there have always been significant exceptions to these generalizations.

None of these considerations adequately explains why the interests of the patient's family have been thought to be appropriately excluded from consideration. At the very least, those who believe that medical treatment decisions are morally anomalous to other important decisions owe us a better account of how and why this is so.

Limits of Public Policy

It might be thought that the problem of family interests *is* a problem only because our society does not shelter families from the negative effects of medical decisions. If, for example, we adopted a comprehensive system of national health insurance and also a system of public insurance to guarantee the incomes of families, then my sons' chances at a college education and the quality of the rest of their lives might not have to be sacrificed were I to receive optimal medical care.

However, it is worth pointing out that we are still moving primarily in the *opposite* direction. Instead of designing policies that would increasingly shelter family members from the adverse impact of serious and prolonged illnesses, we are still attempting to shift the burden of care to family members in our efforts to contain medical costs. A social system that would safeguard families from the impact of serious illness is nowhere in sight in this country. And we must not do medical ethics as if it were.

It is perhaps even more important to recognize that the lives of family members could not be sheltered from all the important ramifications of medical treatment decisions by *any* set of public policies. In any society in which people get close to each other and care deeply for each other, treatment decisions about one will often and *irremediably* affect more than one. If a newborn has been saved by aggressive treatment but is severely handicapped, the parents may simply not be emotionally capable of abandoning the child to institutional care. A man whose wife

is suffering from multiple sclerosis may simply not be willing or able to go on with his own life until he sees her through to the end. A woman whose husband is being maintained in a vegetative state may not feel free to marry or even to see other men again, regardless of what some revised law might say about her marital status.

Nor could we desire a society in which friends and family would quickly lose their concern as soon as continuing to care began to diminish the quality of their own lives. For we would then have alliances for better but not for worse, in health but not in sickness, until death appears on the horizon. And we would all be poorer for that. A man who can leave his wife the day after she learns she has cancer, on the grounds that he has his own life to live, is to be deplored. The emotional inability or principled refusal to separate ourselves and our lives from the lives of ill or dying members of our families is *not* an unfortunate fact about the structure of our emotions. It is a desirable feature, not to be changed even if it could be; not to be changed even if the resulting intertwining of lives debars us from making exclusively self-regarding treatment decisions when we are ill.

Our present individualistic medical ethics is isolating and destructive. For by implicitly suggesting that patients make "their own" treatment decisions on a self-regarding basis and supporting those who do so, such an ethics encourages each of us to see our lives as simply our own. We may yet turn ourselves into beings who are ultimately alone.

Fidelity or Fairness?

Fidelity to the interests of the patient has been a cornerstone of both traditional codes and contemporary theories of medical ethics. The two competing paradigms of medical ethics—the "benevolence" model and the "patient autonomy" model—are simply different ways of construing such fidelity. Both must be rejected or radically modified. The admission that treatment decisions often affect more than just the patient thus forces major changes on both

the theoretical and the practical level. Obviously, I can only begin to explore the needed changes here.

Instead of starting with our usual assumption that physicians are to serve the interests of the patient, we must build our theories on a very different assumption: The medical and nonmedical interests of both the patient and other members of the patient's family are to be considered. It is only in the special case of patients without family that we can simply follow the patient's wishes or pursue the patient's interests. In fact, I would argue that we must build our theory of medical ethics on the presumption of equality: the interests of patients and family members are morally to be weighed equally; medical and nonmedical interests of the same magnitude deserve equal consideration in making treatment decisions. Like any other moral presumption, this one can, perhaps, be defeated in some cases. But the burden of proof will always be on those who would advocate special consideration for any family member's interests, including those of the ill.

Even where the presumption of equality is not defeated, life, health, and freedom from pain and handicapping conditions are extremely important goods for virtually everyone. They are thus very important considerations in all treatment decisions. In the majority of cases, the patient's interest in optimal health and longer life may well be strong enough to outweigh the conflicting interests of other members of the family. But even then, some departure from the treatment plan that would maximize the patient's interests may well be justified to harmonize best the interests of all concerned or to require significantly smaller sacrifices by other family members. That the patient's interests may often outweigh the conflicting interests of others in treatment decisions is no justification for failing to recognize that an attempt to balance or harmonize different, conflicting interests is often morally required. Nor does it justify overlooking the morally crucial cases in which the interests of other members of the family ought to override the interests of the patient. Changing our basic assumption about

Hastings Center Report, March/April 1990

how treatment decisions are to be made means reconceptualizing the ethical roles of both physician and patient, since our understanding of both has been built on the presumption of patient primacy, rather than fairness to all concerned. Recognizing the moral relevance of the interests of family members thus reveals a dilemma for our understanding of what it is to be a physician: Should we retain a fiduciary ethic in which the physician is to serve the interests of her patient? Or should the physician attempt to weigh and balance all the interests of all concerned? I do not yet know just how to resolve this dilemma. All I can do here is try to envision the options.

If we retain the traditional ethic of fidelity to the interests of the patient, the physician should excuse herself from making treatment decisions that will affect the lives of the family on grounds of a moral conflict of interest, for she is a one-sided advocate. A lawyer for one of the parties can not also serve as judge in the case. Thus, it would be unfair if a physician conceived as having a fiduciary relationship to her patient were to make treatment decisions that would adversely affect the lives of the patient's family. Indeed, a physician conceived as a patient advocate should not even *advise* patients or family members about which course of treatment should be chosen. As advocate, she can speak only to what course of treatment would be best for the patient, and must remain silent about what's best for the rest of the family or what should be done in light of everyone's interests.

Physicians might instead renounce their fiduciary relationship with their patients. On this view, physicians would no longer be agents of their patients and would not strive to be advocates for their patients' interests. Instead, the physician would aspire to be an impartial advisor who would stand knowledgeably but sympathetically outside all the many conflicting interests of those affected by the treatment options, and who would strive to discern the treatment that would best harmonize or balance the interests of all concerned.

Although this second option contradicts the Hippocratic Oath and

most other codes of medical ethics, it is not, perhaps, as foreign as it may at first seem. Traditionally, many family physicians—especially small-town physicians who knew patients and their families well—attempted to attend to both medical and nonmedical interests of all concerned. Many contemporary physicians still make decisions in this way. But we do not yet have an ethical theory that explains and justifies what they are doing.

Nevertheless, we may well question the physician's ability to act as an impartial ethical observer. Increasingly, physicians do not know their patients, much less their patients' families. Moreover, we may doubt physicians' abilities to weigh evenhandedly medical and nonmedical interests. Physicians are trained to be especially responsive to medical interests and we may well want them to remain that way. Physicians also tend to be deeply involved with the interests of their patients, and it may be impossible or undesirable to break this tie to enable physicians to be more impartial advisors. Finally, when someone retains the services of a physician, it seems reasonable that she be able to expect that physician to be *her* agent, pursuing *her* interests, not those of her family.

Autonomy and Advocacy

We must also rethink our conception of the patient. On one hand, if we continue to stress patient autonomy, we must recognize that this implies that patients have moral responsibilities. If, on the other hand, we do not want to burden patients with weighty moral responsibilities, we must abandon the ethic of patient autonomy.

Recognizing that moral responsibilities come with patient autonomy will require basic changes in the accepted meanings of both "autonomy" and "advocacy." Because medical ethics has ignored patient responsibilities, we have come to interpret "autonomy" in a sense very different from Kant's original use of the term. It has come to mean simply the patient's freedom or right to choose the treatment he believes is best for himself. But as Kant knew well, there

are many situations in which people can achieve autonomy and moral well-being only by sacrificing other important dimensions of their well-being, including health, happiness, even life itself. For autonomy is the *responsible* use of freedom and is therefore diminished whenever one ignores, evades, or slights one's responsibilities. Human dignity, Kant concluded, consists in our ability to refuse to compromise our autonomy to achieve the kinds of lives (or treatments) we want for ourselves.

If, then, I am morally empowered to make decisions about "my" medical treatment, I am also morally required to shoulder the responsibility of making very difficult moral decisions. The right course of action for me to take will not always be the one that promotes my own interests.

Some patients, motivated by a deep and abiding concern for the well-being of their families, will undoubtedly consider the interests of other family members. For these patients, the interests of their family are *part* of their interests. But not all patients will feel this way. And the interests of family members are not relevant *if* and *because* the patient wants to consider them; they are not relevant because they are *part* of the patient's interests. They are relevant *whether or not* the patient is inclined to consider them. Indeed, the *ethics* of patient decisions is most poignantly highlighted precisely when the patient is inclined to decide without considering the impact of his decision on the lives of the rest of his family.

Confronting patients with tough ethical choices may be part and parcel of treating them with respect as fully competent adults. We don't, after all, think it's right to stand silently by while other (healthy) adults ignore or shirk their moral responsibilities. If, however, we believe that most patients, gripped as they often are by the emotional crisis of serious illness, are not up to shouldering the responsibility of such decisions or should not be burdened with it, then I think we must simply abandon the ethic of patient autonomy. Patient autonomy would then be appropriate only when the various treatment options will affect only the patient's life.

The responsibilities of patients

Hastings Center Report. March/April 1990

imply that there is often a conflict between patient autonomy and the patient's interests (even as those interests are defined by the patient). And we will have to rethink our understanding of patient advocacy in light of this conflict: Does the patient advocate try to promote the patient's (self-defined) *interests*? Or does she promote the patient's *autonomy* even at the expense of those interests? Responsible patient advocates can hardly encourage patients to shirk their moral responsibilities. But can we really expect health care providers to promote patient autonomy when that means encouraging their patients to sacrifice health, happiness, sometimes even life itself?

If we could give an affirmative answer to this last question, we would obviously thereby create a third option for reinterpreting the role of the physician: The physician could maintain her traditional role as patient advocate without being morally required to refrain from making treatment decisions whenever interests of the patient's family are also at stake *if* patient advocacy were understood as promoting patient autonomy *and* patient autonomy were understood as the responsible use of freedom, not simply the right to choose the treatment one wants.

Much more attention needs to be paid to all of these issues. However, it should be clear that absolutely central features of our theories of medical ethics—our understanding of physician and patient, and thus of patient advocacy as well as patient dignity, and patient autonomy—have presupposed that the interests of family members should be irrelevant or should always take a back seat to the interests of the patient. Basic conceptual shifts are required once we acknowledge that this assumption is not warranted.

Who Should Decide?

Such basic conceptual shifts will necessarily have ramifications that will be felt throughout the field of medical ethics, for a host of new and very different issues are raised by the inclusion of family interests. Discussions of privacy and confidentiality, of withholding/withdrawing treat-

ment, and of surrogate decisionmaking will all have to be reconsidered in light of the interests of the family. Many individual treatment decisions will also be affected, becoming much more complicated than they already are. Here, I will only offer a few remarks about treatment decisions, organized around the central issue of who should decide.

There are at least five answers to the question of who should make treatment decisions in cases where important interests of other family members are also at stake: the patient, the family, the physician, an ethics committee, or the courts. The physician's role in treatment decisions has already been discussed. Resort to either the courts or to ethics committees for treatment decisions is too cumbersome and time-consuming for any but the most troubling cases. So I will focus here on the contrast between the patient and the family as appropriate decisionmakers. It is worth noting, though, that we need not arrive at one, uniform answer to cover all cases. On the contrary, each of the five options will undoubtedly have its place, depending on the particulars of the case at hand.

Should we still think of a patient as having the right to make decisions about "his" treatment? As we have seen, patient autonomy implies patient responsibilities. What, then, if the patient seems to be ignoring the impact of his treatment on his family? At the very least, responsible physicians must caution such patients against simply opting for treatments because they want them. Instead, physicians must speak of responsibilities and obligations. They must raise considerations of the quality of many lives, not just that of the patient. They must explain the distinction between making a decision and making it in a self-regarding manner. Thus, it will often be appropriate to make plain to patients the consequences of treatment decisions for their families and to urge them to consider these consequences in reaching a decision. And sometimes, no doubt, it will be appropriate for family members to present their cases to the patient in the hope that his decisions would be shaped by their appeals.

Nonetheless, we sometimes permit

people to make bad or irresponsible decisions and *excuse* those decisions because of various pressures they were under when they made their choices. Serious illness can undoubtedly be an extenuating circumstance, and perhaps we should allow some patients to make some self-regarding decisions, especially if they insist on doing so and the negative impact of their decisions on others is not too great.

Alternatively, if we doubt that most patients have the ability to make treatment decisions that are really fair to all concerned, or if we are not prepared to accept a policy that would assign patients the responsibility of doing so, we may conclude that they should not be empowered to make treatment decisions in which the lives of their family members will be dramatically affected. Indeed, even if the patient were completely fair in making the decision, the autonomy of other family members would have been systematically undercut by the fact that the patient alone decided.

Thus, we need to consider the autonomy of all members of the family, not just the patient's autonomy. Considerations of fairness and, paradoxically, of autonomy therefore indicate that the *family* should make the treatment decision, with all competent family members whose lives will be affected participating. Many such family conferences undoubtedly already take place. On this view, however, family conferences would often be morally *required*. And these conferences would not be limited to cases involving incompetent patients; cases involving competent patients would also often require family conferences.

Obviously, it would be completely unworkable for a physician to convene a family conference every time a medical decision might have some ramifications on the lives of family members. However, such discussion need not always take place in the presence of the physician; we can recognize that formal family conferences become more important as the impact of treatment decisions on members of the patient's family grows larger. Family conferences may thus be morally *required* only when the lives of family members would be

Hastings Center Report. March/April 1990

dramatically affected by treatment decisions.

Moreover, family discussion is often morally *desirable* even if not morally required. Desirable, sometimes, even for relatively minor treatment decisions: After the family has moved to a new town, should parents commit themselves to two-hour drives so that their teenage son can continue to be treated for his acne by the dermatologist he knows and whose results he trusts? Or should he seek treatment from a new dermatologist?

Some family conferences about treatment decisions would be characterized throughout by deep affection, mutual understanding, and abiding concern for the interests of others. Other conferences might begin in an atmosphere charged with antagonism, suspicion, and hostility but move toward greater understanding, reconciliation, and harmony within the family. Such conferences would be significant goods in themselves, as well as means to ethically better treatment decisions. They would leave all family members better able to go on with their lives.

Still, family conferences cannot be expected always to begin with or move toward affection, mutual understanding, and a concern for all. If we opt for joint treatment decisions when the lives of several are affected, we need to face the fact that family conferences will sometimes be bitter confrontations in which past hostilities, anger, and resentments will surface. Sometimes, too, the conflicts of interest between patient and family, and between one family member and another will be irresolvable, forcing families to invoke the harsh perspective of justice, divisive and antagonistic though that perspective may be. Those who favor family decisions when the whole family is affected will have to face the question of whether we really want to put the patient, already frightened and weakened by his illness, through the conflict and bitter confrontations that family conferences may sometimes precipitate.

We must also recognize that family members may be unable or unwilling to press or even state their own interests before a family member who

is ill. Such refusal may be admirable, even heroic; it is sometimes evidence of willingness to go "above and beyond the call of duty," even at great personal cost. But not always. Refusal to press one's own interests can also be a sign of inappropriate guilt, of a crushing sense of responsibility for the well-being of others, of acceptance of an inferior or dominated role within the family, or of lack of a sense of self-worth. All of these may well be mobilized by an illness in the family. Moreover, we must not minimize the power of the medical setting to subordinate nonmedical to medical interests and to emphasize the well-being of the patient at the expense of the well-being of others. Thus, it will often be not just the patient, but also other family members who will need an advocate if a family conference is to reach the decision that best balances the autonomy and interests of all concerned.

The existing theory of patient autonomy and also of proxy decisionmaking has been designed partly as a buttress against pressures from family members for both overtreatment and undertreatment of patients. The considerations I have been advancing will enable us to understand that sometimes what we've seen as undertreatment or overtreatment may not really be such. Both concepts will have to be redefined. Still, I do not wish to deny or minimize the problem of family members who demand inappropriate treatment. Treatment decisions are extremely difficult when important interests of the other members of the family are also at stake. The temptation of family members simply to demand the treatment that best suits *their* interests is often very real.

I do not believe, however, that the best safeguard against pressures from family members for inappropriate treatment is to issue morally inappropriate instructions to them in the hope that these instructions will prevent abuses. Asking a family member to pretend that her interests are somehow irrelevant often backfires. Rather, I think the best safeguard would be candidly to admit the moral relevance of the interests of other members of the family and then

to support the family through the excruciating process of trying to reach a decision that is fair to all concerned.

Acknowledging the interests of family members in medical treatment decisions thus forces basic changes at the level of ethical theory and in the moral practice of medicine. The sheer complexity of the issues raised might seem a sufficient reason to ignore family interests in favor of the much simpler ethic of absolute fidelity to the patient. But that would be the ostrich approach to the complexities of medical ethics. We must not abandon our patients' families to lives truncated by an over-simplified ethic, for that would be an unconscionable toll to exact to make our tasks as ethicists and moral physicians easier.

Reconstructing medical ethics in light of family interests would not be all pain and no gain for ethicists and physicians. Acknowledging family members' interests would bring benefits as well as burdens to medical practitioners, for the practice of medicine has rarely been as individualistic as codes and theories of medical ethics have advocated. Indeed, much of what now goes on in intensive care nurseries, pediatricians' offices, intensive care units, and long-term care institutions makes ethical sense *only* on the assumption that the interests of other members of the family are also to be considered.

Contemporary ethical theory and traditional codes of medical ethics can neither help nor support physicians, patients, and family members struggling to balance the patient's interests and the interests of others in the family. Our present ethical theory can only condemn as unethical any attempt to weigh in the interests of other family members. If we would acknowledge the moral relevance of the interests of the family we could perhaps develop an ethical theory that would guide and support physicians, patients, and families in the throes of agonizing moral decisions.

Acknowledgments

I wish to thank Mary Read English, Michael Lavin, Gary Smith, Joanne Lynn, and Larry Churchill for valuable suggestions.

10

[7]

Dworkin on Dementia
Elegant Theory, Questionable Policy

by Rebecca Dresser

When patients have progressive and incurable dementia, should their advance directives always be followed? Contra Dworkin, Dresser argues that when patients remain able to enjoy and participate in their lives, directives to hasten death should sometimes be disregarded.

I n his most recent book, *Life's Dominion: An Argument About Abortion, Euthanasia, and Individual Freedom,*[1] Ronald Dworkin offers a new way of interpreting disagreements over abortion and euthanasia. In doing so, he enriches and refines our understanding of three fundamental bioethical concepts: autonomy, beneficence, and sanctity of life. It is exciting that this eminent legal philosopher has turned his attention to bioethical issues. *Life's Dominion* is beautifully and persuasively written; its clear language and well-constructed arguments are especially welcome in this age of inaccessible, jargon-laden academic writing. *Life's Dominion* also is full of rich and provocative ideas; in this article, I address only Dworkin's remarks on euthanasia, although I will refer to his views on abortion when they are relevant to my analysis.

Professor Dworkin considers decisions to hasten death with respect to three groups: (1) competent and seriously ill people; (2) permanently unconscious people; and (3) conscious, but incompetent people, specifically, those with progressive and incurable dementia. My remarks focus on the third group, which I have addressed in previous work,[2] and which in my view poses the most difficult challenge for policymakers.

I present Dworkin's and my views as a debate over how we should think about Margo. Margo is described by Andrew Firlik, a medical student, in a *Journal of the American Medical Association* column called "A Piece of My Mind."[3] Firlik met Margo, who has Alzheimer disease, when he was enrolled in a gerontology elective. He began visiting her each day, and came to know something about her life with dementia.

Upon arriving at Margo's apartment (she lived at home with the help of an attendant), Firlik often found Margo reading; she told him

Rebecca Dresser is a professor in the School of Law and Center for Biomedical Ethics, School of Medicine, Case Western Reserve University, Cleveland, Ohio.

Rebecca Dresser, "Dworkin on Dementia: Elegant Theory, Questionable Policy," *Hastings Center Report* 25, no. 6 (1995): 32-38.

she especially enjoyed mysteries, but he noticed that "her place in the book jump[ed] randomly from day to day." "For Margo," Firlik wonders, "is reading always a mystery?" Margo never called her new friend by name, though she claimed she knew who he was and always seemed pleased to see him. She liked listening to music and was happy listening to the same song repeatedly, apparently relishing it as if hearing it for the first time. Whenever she heard a certain song, however, she smiled and told Firlik that it reminded her of her deceased husband. She painted, too, but like the other Alzheimer patients in her art therapy class, she created the same image day after day: "a drawing of four circles, in soft rosy colors, one inside the other."

The drawing enabled Firlik to understand something that previously had mystified him:

Despite her illness, or maybe somehow because of it, Margo is undeniably one of the happiest people I have known. There is something graceful about the degeneration her mind is undergoing, leaving her carefree, always cheerful. Do her problems, whatever she may perceive them to be, simply fail to make it to the worry centers of her brain? How

does Margo maintain her sense of self? When a person can no longer accumulate new memories as the old rapidly fade, what remains? Who is Margo?

Firlik surmises that the drawing represented Margo's expression of her mind, her identity, and that by repeating the drawing, she was reminding herself and others of that identity. The painting was Margo, "plain and contained, smiling in her peaceful, demented state."

In *Life's Dominion*, Dworkin considers Margo as a potential subject of his approach. In one variation, he asks us to suppose that

years ago, when fully competent, Margo had executed a formal document directing that if she should develop Alzheimer's disease . . . she should not receive treatment for any other serious, life-threatening disease she might contract. Or even that in that event she should be killed as soon and as painlessly as possible. (p. 226)

He presents an elegant and philosophically sophisticated argument for giving effect to her prior wishes, despite the value she appears to obtain from her life as an individual with dementia.

Hastings Center Report, November-December 1995

Dworkin's position emerges from his inquiry into the values of autonomy, beneficence, and sanctity of life. To understand their relevance to a case such as Margo's, he writes, we must first think about why we care about how we die. And to understand that phenomenon, we must understand why we care about how we live. Dworkin believes our lives are guided by the desire to advance two kinds of interests. *Experiential* interests are those we share to some degree with all sentient creatures. In Dworkin's words:

> We all do things because we like the experience of doing them: playing softball, perhaps, or cooking and eating well, or watching football, or seeing *Casablanca* for the twelfth time, or walking in the woods in October, or listening to *The Marriage of Figaro*, or sailing fast just off the wind, or just working hard at something. Pleasures like these are essential to a good life—a life with nothing that is marvelous only because of how it feels would be not pure but preposterous. (p. 201)

But Dworkin deems these interests less important than the second sort of interests we possess. Dworkin argues that we also seek to satisfy our *critical* interests, which are the hopes and aims that lend genuine meaning and coherence to our lives. We pursue projects such as establishing close friendships, achieving competence in our work, and raising children, not simply because we want the positive experiences they offer, but also because we believe we should want them, because our lives as a whole will be better if we take up these endeavors.

Dworkin admits that not everyone has a conscious sense of the interests they deem critical to their lives, but he thinks that "even people whose lives feel unplanned are nevertheless often guided by a sense of the general style of life they think appropriate, of what choices strike them as not only good at the moment but in character for them" (p. 202). In this tendency, Dworkin sees us aiming for the ideal of integrity, seeking to create a coherent narrative structure for the lives we lead.

Our critical interests explain why many of us care about how the final chapter of our lives turns out. Although some of this concern originates in the desire to avoid experiential burdens, as well as burdens on our families, much of it reflects the desire to escape dying under circumstances that are out of character with the prior stages of our lives. For most people, Dworkin writes, death has a "special, symbolic importance: they want their deaths, if possible, to express and in that way vividly to confirm the values they believe most important to their lives" (p. 211). And because critical interests are so personal and widely varied among individuals, each person must have the right to control the manner in which life reaches its conclusion. Accordingly, the state should refrain from imposing a "uniform, general view [of appropriate end-of-life-care] by way of sovereign law" (p. 213).

Dworkin builds on this hierarchy of human interests to defend his ideas about how autonomy and beneficence should apply to someone like Margo. First, he examines the generally accepted principle that we should in most circumstances honor the competent person's autonomous choice. One way to justify this principle is to claim that people generally know better than anyone else what best serves their interests; thus, their own choices are the best evidence we have of the decision that would most protect their welfare. Dworkin labels this the *evidentiary* view of autonomy. But Dworkin believes the better explanation for the respect we accord to individual choice lies in what he calls the *integrity* view of autonomy. In many instances, he contends, we grant freedom to people to act in ways that clearly conflict with their own best interests. We do this, he argues, because we want to let people "lead their lives out of a distinctive sense of their own character, a sense of what is important to them" (p. 224). The model once again assigns the greatest moral significance to the individual's critical interests, as opposed to the less important experiential interests that also contribute to a person's having a good life.

The integrity view of autonomy partially accounts for Dworkin's claim

that we should honor Margo's prior choice to end her life if she developed Alzheimer disease. In making this choice, she was exercising, in Dworkin's phrase, her "precedent autonomy" (p. 226). The evidentiary view of autonomy fails to supply support for deferring to the earlier decision, Dworkin observes, because "[p]eople are not the best judges of what their own best interests would be under circumstances they have never encountered and in which their preferences and desires may drastically have changed" (p. 226). He readily admits that Andrew Firlik and others evaluating Margo's life with dementia would perceive a conflict between her prior instructions and her current welfare. But the integrity view of autonomy furnishes compelling support for honoring Margo's advance directives. Margo's interest in living her life in character includes an interest in controlling the circumstances in which others should permit her life as an Alzheimer patient to continue. Limiting that control would in Dworkin's view be "an unacceptable form of moral paternalism" (p. 231).

Dworkin finds additional support for assigning priority to Margo's former instructions in the moral principle of beneficence. People who are incompetent to exercise autonomy have a right to beneficence from those entrusted to decide on their behalf. The best interests standard typically has been understood to require the decision that would best protect the incompetent individual's current welfare.[4] On this view, the standard would support some (though not necessarily all) life-extending decisions that depart from Margo's prior directives. But Dworkin invokes his concept of critical interests to construct a different best interests standard. Dworkin argues that Margo's critical interests persist, despite her current inability to appreciate them. Because critical interests have greater moral significance than the experiential interests Margo remains able to appreciate, and because "we must judge Margo's critical interests as she did when competent to do so" (p. 231), beneficence requires us to honor Margo's prior preferences for death. In Dworkin's view, far from providing

Hastings Center Report, November-December 1995

a reason to override Margo's directives, compassion counsels us to follow them, for it is compassion "toward the whole person" that underlies the duty of beneficence (p. 232).

To honor the narrative that is Margo's life, then, we must honor her earlier choices. A decision to disregard them would constitute unjustified paternalism and would lack mercy as well. Dworkin concedes that such a decision might be made for other reasons—because we "find ourselves unable to deny medical help to anyone who is conscious and does not reject it" (p. 232), or deem it "morally unforgiveable not to try to save the life of someone who plainly enjoys her life" (p. 228), or find it "beyond imagining that we should actually kill her" (p. 228), or "hate living in a community whose officials might make or license either of [Margo's] decisions" (pp. 228-29). Dworkin does not explicitly address whether these or other aspects of the state's interest in protecting life should influence legal policy governing how people like Margo are treated.

Dworkin pays much briefer attention to Margo's fate in the event that she did not explicitly register her preferences about future treatment. Most incompetent patients are currently in this category, for relatively few people complete formal advance treatment directives.[5] In this scenario, the competent Margo failed to declare her explicit wishes, and her family is asked to determine her fate. Dworkin suggests that her relatives may give voice to Margo's autonomy by judging what her choice would have been if she had thought about it, based on her character and personality. Moreover, similar evidence enables them to determine her best interests, for it is her critical interests that matter most in reaching this determination. If Margo's dementia set in before she explicitly indicated her preferences about future care, "the law should so far as possible leave decisions in the hands of [her] relatives or other people close to [her] whose sense of [her] best interests . . . is likely to be much sounder than some universal, theoretical, abstract judgment" produced through the political process (p. 213).

Life's Dominion helps to explain why the "death with dignity" movement has attracted such strong support in the United States. I have no doubt that many people share Dworkin's conviction that they ought to have the power to choose death over life in Margo's state. But I am far from convinced of the wisdom or morality of these proposals for dementia patients.

Advance Directives and Precedent Autonomy

First, an observation. Dworkin makes an impressive case that the power to control one's future as an incompetent patient is a precious freedom that our society should go to great lengths to protect. But how strongly do people actually value this freedom? Surveys show that a relatively small percentage of the U.S. population engages in end-of-life planning, and that many in that group simply designate a trusted relative or friend to make future treatment decisions, choosing not to issue specific instructions on future care.[6] Though this widespread failure to take advantage of the freedom to exercise precedent autonomy may be attributed to a lack of publicity or inadequate policy support for advance planning, it could also indicate that issuing explicit instructions to govern the final chapter of one's life is not a major priority for most people. If it is not, then we may question whether precedent autonomy and the critical interests it protects should be the dominant model for our policies on euthanasia for incompetent people.

Dworkin constructs a moral argument for giving effect to Margo's directives, but does not indicate how his position could be translated into policy. Consider how we might approach this task. We would want to devise procedures to ensure that people issuing such directives were competent, their actions voluntary, and their decisions informed. In other medical settings, we believe that a person's adequate understanding of the information relevant to treatment decisionmaking is a prerequisite to the exercise of true self-determination. We should take the same view of Margo's advance planning.

What would we want the competent Margo to understand before she chose death over life in the event of dementia? At a minimum, we would want her to understand that the experience of dementia differs among individuals, that for some it appears to be a persistently frightening and unhappy existence, but that most people with dementia do not exhibit the distress and misery we competent people tend to associate with the condition. I make no claims to expertise in this area, but my reading and discussions with clinicians, caregivers, and patients themselves suggest that the subjective experience of dementia is more positive than most of us would expect. Some caregivers and other commentators also note that patients' quality of life is substantially dependent on their social and physical environments, as opposed to the neurological condition itself.[7] Thus, the "tragedy" and "horror" of dementia is partially attributable to the ways in which others respond to people with this condition.

We also would want Margo to understand that Alzheimer disease is a progressive condition, and that options for forgoing life-sustaining interventions will arise at different points in the process. Dworkin writes that his ideas apply only to the late stages of Alzheimer disease, but he makes implementation of Margo's former wishes contingent on the mere development of the condition (pp. 219, 226). If we were designing policy, we would want to ensure that competent individuals making directives knew something about the general course of the illness and the points at which various capacities are lost. We would want them to be precise about the behavioral indications that should trigger the directive's implementation. We would want them to think about what their lives could be like at different stages of the disease, and about how invasive and effective various possible interventions might be. We would want to give them the opportunity to talk with physicians, caregivers, and individuals diagnosed with Alzheimer disease, and perhaps, to discuss their potential choices with a counselor.

The concern for education is one that applies to advance treatment di-

Hastings Center Report, November-December 1995

rectives generally, but one that is not widely recognized or addressed at the policy level. People complete advance directives in private, perhaps after discussion with relatives, physicians, or attorneys, but often with little understanding of the meaning or implications of their decisions. In one study of dialysis patients who had issued instructions on treatment in the event of advanced Alzheimer disease, a subsequent inquiry revealed that almost two-thirds of them wanted families and physicians to have some freedom to override the directives to protect their subsequent best interests.[8] The patients' failure to include this statement in their directives indicates that the instructions they recorded did not reflect their actual preferences. A survey of twenty-nine people participating in an advance care planning workshop found ten agreeing with both of the following inconsistent statements: "I would never want to be on a respirator in an intensive care unit"; and "If a short period of extremely intensive medical care could return me to near-normal condition, I would want it."[9] Meanwhile, some promoters of advance care planning have claimed that subjects can complete directives during interviews lasting fifteen minutes.[10]

We do not advance people's autonomy by giving effect to choices that originate in insufficient or mistaken information. Indeed, interference in such choices is often considered a form of justified paternalism. Moreover, advance planning for future dementia treatment is more complex than planning for other conditions, such as permanent unconsciousness. Before implementing directives to hasten death in the event of dementia, we should require people to exhibit a reasonable understanding of the choices they are making.[11]

Some shortcomings of advance planning are insurmountable, however. People exercising advance planning are denied knowledge of treatments and other relevant information that may emerge during the time between making a directive and giving it effect. Opportunities for clarifying misunderstandings are truncated, and decisionmakers are not asked to explain or defend their choices to the clinicians, relatives, and

friends whose care and concern may lead depressed or imprudent individuals to alter their wishes.[12] Moreover, the rigid adherence to advance planning Dworkin endorses leaves no room for the changes of heart that can lead us to deviate from our earlier choices. All of us are familiar with

---

We do not advance people's autonomy by giving effect to choices that originate in insufficient or mistaken information.

---

decisions we have later come to recognize as ill-suited to our subsequent situations. As Dworkin acknowledges, people may be mistaken about their future experiential interests as incompetent individuals. A policy of absolute adherence to advance directives means that we deny people like Margo the freedom we enjoy as competent people to change our decisions that conflict with our subsequent experiential interests.[13]

Personal identity theory, which addresses criteria for the persistence of a particular person over time, provides another basis for questioning precedent autonomy's proper moral and legal authority. In *Life's Dominion*, Dworkin assumes that Margo the dementia patient is the same person who issued the earlier requests to die, despite the drastic psychological alteration that has occurred. Indeed, the legitimacy of the precedent autonomy model absolutely depends on this view of personal identity. Another approach to personal identity would challenge this judgment, however. On this view, substantial memory loss and other psychological changes may produce a new person, whose connection to the earlier one could be less strong, indeed, could be no stronger than that between you and me.[14] Subscribers to this view of personal identity can argue that Margo's earlier choices lack moral authority to control what happens to Margo the dementia patient.

These shortcomings of the advance decisionmaking process are reasons to assign less moral authority to precedent autonomy than to contemporaneous autonomy. I note that Dworkin himself may believe in at least one limit on precedent autonomy in medical decisionmaking. He writes that people "who are repelled by the idea of living demented, totally dependent lives, speaking gibberish," ought to be permitted to issue advance directives "stipulating that if they become permanently and seriously demented, and then develop a serious illness, they should not be given medical treatment except to avoid pain" (p. 231). Would he oppose honoring a request to avoid all medical treatment, including pain-relieving measures, that was motivated by religious or philosophical concerns? The above remark suggests that he might give priority to Margo's existing experiential interests in avoiding pain over her prior exercise of precedent autonomy. In my view, this would be a justified limit on precedent autonomy, but I would add others as well.

Critical and Experiential Interests: Problems with the Model

What if Margo, like most other people, failed to exercise her precedent autonomy through making an advance directive? In this situation, her surrogate decisionmakers are to apply Dworkin's version of the best interests standard. Should they consider, first and foremost, the critical interests she had as a competent person? I believe not, for several reasons. First, Dworkin's approach to the best interests standard rests partially on the claim that people want their lives to have narrative coherence. Dworkin omits empirical support for this claim, and my own observations lead me to wonder about its accuracy. The people of the United States are a diverse group, holding many different world views. Do most people actually think as Dworkin says they do? If I were to play psychologist, my guess would be

that many people take life one day at a time. The goal of establishing a coherent narrative may be a less common life theme than the simple effort to accept and adjust to the changing natural and social circumstances that characterize a person's life. It also seems possible that people generally fail to draw a sharp line between experiential and critical interests, often choosing the critical projects Dworkin describes substantially because of the rewarding experiences they provide.

Suppose Margo left no indication of her prior wishes, but that people close to her believe it would be in her critical interests to die rather than live on in her current condition. Dworkin notes, but fails to address, the argument that "in the circumstances of dementia, critical interests become less important and experiential interests more so, so that fiduciaries may rightly ignore the former and concentrate on the latter" (p. 232). Happy and contented Margo will experience clear harm from the decision that purports to advance the critical interests she no longer cares about. This seems to me justification for a policy against active killing or withholding effective, nonburdensome treatments, such as antibiotics, from dementia patients whose lives offer them the sorts of pleasures and satisfactions Margo enjoys. Moreover, if clear evidence is lacking on Margo's own view of her critical interests, a decision to hasten her death might

actually conflict with the life narrative she envisioned for herself. Many empirical studies have shown that families often do not have a very good sense of their relatives' treatment preferences.[15] How will Margo's life narrative be improved by her family's decision to hasten death, if there is

no clear indication that she herself once took that view?

I also wonder about how to apply a best interests standard that assigns priority to the individual's critical interests. Dworkin writes that family members and other intimates applying this standard should decide based on their knowledge of "the shape and character of [the patient's] life and his own sense of integrity and critical interests" (p. 213). What sorts of life narratives would support a decision to end Margo's life? What picture of her critical interests might her family cite as justification for ending her life now? Perhaps Margo had been a famous legal philosopher whose intellectual pursuits were of utmost importance to her. This fact might tilt toward a decision to spare her from an existence in which she can only pretend to read. But what if she were also the mother of a mentally retarded child, whom she had cared for at home? What if she had enjoyed and valued this child's simple, experiential life, doing everything she could to protect and enhance it? How would this information affect the interpretation of her critical interests as they bear on her own life with dementia?

I am not sure whether Dworkin means to suggest that Margo's relatives should have complete discretion in evaluating considerations such as these. Would he permit anyone to challenge the legitimacy of a narrative

outcome chosen by her family? What if her closest friends believed that a different conclusion would be more consistent with the way she had constructed her life? And is there any room in Dworkin's scheme for surprise endings? Some of our greatest fictional characters evolve into figures having little resemblance to the persons we met in the novels' opening chapters. Are real-life characters such as the fiercely independent intellectual permitted to become people who appreciate simple experiential pleasures and accept their dependence on others?

Finally, is the goal of respecting individual differences actually met by Dworkin's best interests standard? Although Dworkin recognizes that some people believe their critical interests would be served by a decision to extend their lives as long as is medically possible (based on their pro-life values), at times he implies that such individuals are mistaken about their genuine critical interests, that in actuality no one's critical interests could be served by such a decision. For example, he writes that after the onset of dementia, nothing of value can be added to a person's life, because the person is no longer capable of engaging in the activities necessary to advance her critical interests (p. 230). A similar judgment is also evident in his discussion of an actual case of a brain-damaged patient who "did not seem to be in pain or unhappy," and "recognized familiar faces with apparent pleasure" (p. 233). A court-appointed guardian sought to have the patient's life-prolonging medication withheld, but the family was strongly opposed to this outcome, and a judge denied the guardian's request. In a remark that seems to conflict with his earlier support for family decisionmaking, Dworkin questions whether the family's choice was in the patient's best interests (p. 233). These comments lead me to wonder whether Dworkin's real aim is to defend an objective nontreatment standard that should be applied to all individuals with significant mental impairment, not just those whose advance directives or relatives support a decision to hasten death. If so, then he needs to provide additional argument for this more controversial position.

> We need community reflection on how we should think about people with dementia, including our possible future selves.

Hastings Center Report, November-December 1995

The State's Interest in Margo's Life

My final thoughts concern Dworkin's argument that the state has no legitimate reason to interfere with Margo's directives or her family's best interests judgment to end her life. A great deal of *Life's Dominion* addresses the intrinsic value of human life and the nature of the state's interest in protecting that value. Early in the book, Dworkin defends the familiar view that only conscious individuals can possess interests in not being destroyed or otherwise harmed. On this view, until the advent of sentience and other capacities, human fetuses lack interests of their own that would support a state policy restricting abortion. A policy that restricted abortion prior to this point would rest on what Dworkin calls a *detached* state interest in protecting human life. Conversely, a policy that restricts abortion after fetal sentience (which coincides roughly with viability) is supported by the state's *derivative* interest in valuing life, so called because it derives from the fetus's own interests (pp. 10-24, 168-70). Dworkin believes that detached state interests in ensuring respect for the value of life justify state prohibitions on abortion only after pregnant women are given a reasonable opportunity to terminate an unwanted pregnancy. Prior to this point, the law should permit women to make decisions about pregnancy according to their own views on how best to respect the value of life. After viability, however, when fetal neurological development is sufficiently advanced to make sentience possible, the state may severely limit access to abortion, based on its legitimate role in protecting creatures capable of having interests of their own (pp. 168-70).

Dworkin's analysis of abortion provides support, in my view, for a policy in which the state acts to protect the interests of conscious dementia patients like Margo. Although substantially impaired, Margo retains capacities for pleasure, enjoyment, interaction, relationships, and so forth. I believe her continued ability to participate in the life she is living furnishes a defensible basis for state limitations on the scope of her precedent autonomy, as well as on the choices her intimates make on her behalf. Con-

trary to Dworkin, I believe that such moral paternalism is justified when dementia patients have a quality of life comparable to Margo's. I am not arguing that all directives regarding dementia care should be overridden, nor that family choices should always be disregarded. I think directives and family choices should control in the vast majority of cases, for such decisions rarely are in clear conflict with the patient's contemporaneous interests. But I believe that state restriction is justified when a systematic evaluation by clinicians and others involved in patient care produces agreement that a minimally intrusive life-sustaining intervention is likely to preserve the life of someone as contented and active as Margo.

Many dementia patients do not fit Margo's profile. Some are barely conscious, others appear frightened, miserable, and unresponsive to efforts to mitigate their pain. Sometimes a proposed life-sustaining treatment will be invasive and immobilizing, inflicting extreme terror on patients unable to understand the reasons for their burdens. In such cases, it is entirely appropriate to question the justification for treatment, and often to withhold it, as long as the patient can be kept comfortable in its absence. This approach assumes that observers can accurately assess the experiential benefits and burdens of patients with neurological impairments and decreased ability to communicate. I believe that such assessments are often possible, and that there is room for a great deal of improvement in meeting this challenge.

I also believe that the special problems inherent in making an advance decision about active euthanasia justify a policy of refusing to implement such decisions, at the very least until we achieve legalization for competent patients without unacceptable rates of error and abuse.[16] I note as well the likely scarcity of health care professionals who would be willing to participate in decisions to withhold simple and effective treatments from someone in Margo's condition, much less to give her a lethal injection, even if this were permitted by law. Would Dworkin support a system that required physicians and nurses to compromise their own values and integ-

rity so that Margo's precedent autonomy and critical interests could be advanced? I seriously doubt that many health professionals would agree to implement his proposals regarding dementia patients whose lives are as happy as Margo's.

We need community reflection on how we should think about people with dementia, including our possible future selves. Dworkin's model reflects a common response to the condition: tragic, horrible, degrading, humiliating, to be avoided at all costs. But how much do social factors account for this tragedy? Two British scholars argue that though we regard dementia patients as "the problem," the patients

> are rather less of a problem than *we*. *They* are generally more authentic about what they are feeling and doing; many of the polite veneers of earlier life have been stripped away. *They* are clearly dependent on others, and usually come to accept that dependence; whereas many "normal" people, living under an ideology of extreme individualism, strenuously deny their dependency needs. *They* live largely in the present, because certain parts of their memory function have failed. *We* often find it very difficult to live in the present, suffering constant distraction; the sense of the present is often contaminated by regrets about the past and fears about the future.[17]

If we were to adopt an alternative to the common vision of dementia, we might ask ourselves what we could do, how we could alter our own responses so that people with dementia may find that life among us need not be so terrifying and frustrating. We might ask ourselves what sorts of environments, interactions, and relationships would enhance their lives.

Such a "disability perspective" on dementia offers a more compassionate, less rejecting approach to people with the condition than a model insisting that we should be permitted to order ourselves killed if this "saddest of the tragedies" (p. 218) should befall us. It supports as well a care and treatment policy centered on the conscious incompetent patient's sub-

Hastings Center Report, November-December 1995

jective reality; one that permits death when the experiential burdens of continued life are too heavy or the benefits too minimal, but seeks to delay death when the patient's subjective existence is as positive as Margo's appears to be. Their loss of higher-level intellectual capacities ought not to exclude people like Margo from the moral community nor from the law's protective reach, even when the threats to their well-being emanate from their own former preferences. Margo's connections to us remain sufficiently strong that we owe her our concern and respect in the present. Eventually, the decision to allow her to die will be morally defensible. It is too soon, however, to exclude her from our midst.

Acknowledgment

I presented an earlier version of this essay at the annual meeting of the Society for Health and Human Values, 8 October 1994, in Pittsburgh. I would like to thank Ronald Dworkin and Eric Rakowski for their comments on my analysis.

References

1. Ronald Dworkin, *Life's Dominion: An Argument About Abortion, Euthanasia, and Individual Freedom* (New York: Alfred A. Knopf, 1993).

2. See, for example, Rebecca Dresser, "Missing Persons: Legal Perceptions of Incompetent Patients," *Rutgers Law Review* 609 (1994): 636-47; Rebecca Dresser and Peter J. Whitehouse, "The Incompetent Patient on the Slippery Slope," *Hastings Center Report* 24, no. 4 (1994): 6-12; Rebecca Dresser, "Autonomy Revisited: The Limits of Anticipatory Choices," in *Dementia and Aging: Ethics, Values, and Policy Choices,* ed. Robert H. Binstock, Stephen G. Post, and Peter J. Whitehouse (Baltimore, Md.: Johns Hopkins University Press, 1992), pp. 71-85.

3. Andrew D. Firlik, "Margo's Logo," *JAMA* 265 (1991): 201.

4. See generally Dresser, "Missing Persons."

5. For a recent survey of the state of advance treatment decisionmaking in the U.S., see "Advance Care Planning: Priorities for Ethical and Empirical Research," Special Supplement, *Hastings Center Report* 24, no. 6 (1994).

6. See generally "Advance Care Planning." The failure of most persons to engage in formal end-of-life planning does not in itself contradict Dworkin's point that most people care about how they die. It does suggest, however, that people do not find the formal exercise of precedent autonomy to be a helpful or practical means of expressing their concerns about future life-sustaining treatment.

7. See generally Dresser, "Missing Persons," 681-91; Tom Kitwood and Kathleen Bredin, "Towards a Theory of Dementia Care: Personhood and Well-Being," *Ageing and Society* 12 (1992): 269-87.

8. Ashwini Sehgal et al., "How Strictly Do Dialysis Patients Want Their Advance Directives Followed?" *JAMA* 267 (1992): 59-63.

9. Lachlan Forrow, Edward Gogel, and Elizabeth Thomas, "Advance Directives for Medical Care" (letter), *NEJM* 325 (1991): 1255.

10. Linda L. Emanuel et al., "Advance Directives for Medical Care—A Case for Greater Use," *NEJM* 324 (1991): 889-95.

11. See Eric Rakowski, "The Sanctity of Human Life," *Yale Law Journal* 103 (1994): 2049, 2110-11.

12. See Allen Buchanan and Dan Brock, "Deciding for Others," in *The Ethics of Surrogate Decisionmaking* (Cambridge: Cambridge University Press, 1989), at 101-7 for discussion of these and other shortcomings of advance treatment decisionmaking.

13. See generally Rebecca Dresser and John A. Robertson, "Quality-of-Life and Non-Treatment Decisions for Incompetent Patients: A Critique of the Orthodox Approach," *Law, Medicine & Health Care* 17 (1989): 234-44.

14. See Derek Parfit, *Reasons and Persons* (New York: Oxford University Press, 1985), pp. 199-379.

15. See, e.g., Allison B. Seckler et al., "Substituted Judgment: How Accurate Are Proxy Predictions?" *Annals of Internal Medicine* 115 (1992): 92-98.

16. See generally Leslie P. Francis, "Advance Directives for Voluntary Euthanasia: A Volatile Combination?" *Journal of Medicine & Philosophy* 18 (1993): 297-322.

17. Kitwood and Bredin, "Towards a Theory of Dementia Care," 273-74.

[8]

SOUNDING BOARD

WHY SAYING NO TO PATIENTS IN THE UNITED STATES IS SO HARD

Cost Containment, Justice, and Provider Autonomy

Norman Daniels

IF cost-containment measures, such as the use of Medicare's diagnosis-related groups (DRGs), involved trimming only unnecessary health care services from public budgets, they would pose no moral problems. Instead, such measures lead physicians and hospitals to deny some possibly beneficial care, such as longer hospitalization or more diagnostic tests, to their own patients — that is, at the "micro" level.[1] Similarly, if the "macro" decision not to disseminate a new medical procedure, such as liver transplantation, resulted only in the avoidance of waste, then it would pose no moral problem. When is it morally justifiable to say no to beneficial care or useful procedures? And why is it especially difficult to justify saying no in the United States?

Justice and Rationing

Because of scarcity and the inevitable limitation of resources even in a wealthy society, justice — however we elucidate it — will require some no-saying at both the macro and micro levels of allocation. No plausible principles of justice will entitle an individual patient to every potentially beneficial treatment. Providing such treatment might consume resources to which another patient has a greater claim. Similarly, no class of patients is entitled to whatever new procedure offers them some benefit. New procedures have opportunity costs, consuming resources that could be used to produce other benefits, and other classes of patients may have a superior claim that would require resources to be invested in alternative ways.

How rationing works depends on which principles of justice apply to health care. For example, some people believe that health care is a commodity or service no more important than any other and that it should be distributed according to the ability to pay for it. For them, saying no to patients who cannot afford certain services (quite apart from whether income distribution is itself just or fair) is morally permissible. Indeed, providing such services to all might seem unfair to the patients who are required to pay.

In contrast, other theories of justice view health care as a social good of special moral importance. In one recent discussion,[2] health care was seen to derive its moral importance from its effect on the normal range of opportunities available in society. This range is reduced when disease or disability impairs normal functioning. Since we have social obligations to protect equal opportunity, we also have obligations to provide access, without financial or discriminatory barriers, to services that adequately protect and restore normal functioning. We must also weigh new technological advances against alternatives, to judge the overall effect of their introduction on equal opportunity. This gives a slightly new sense to the term "opportunity cost." As a result, people are entitled only to services that are part of a system that on the whole protects equal opportunity. Thus, even an egalitarian theory that holds health care as of special moral importance justifies sometimes saying no at both the macro and micro levels.

Saying No in the British National Health Service

Aaron and Schwartz have documented how beneficial services and procedures have had to be rationed within the British National Health Service, since its austerity budget allows only half the level of expenditures of the United States.[3] The British, for example, use less x-ray film, provide little treatment for metastatic solid tumors, and generally do not offer renal dialysis to the elderly. Saying no takes place at both macro and micro levels.

Rationing in Great Britain takes place under two constraints that do not operate at all in the United States. First, although the British say no to some beneficial care, they nevertheless provide universal access to high-quality health care. In contrast, over 10 percent of the population in the United States lacks insurance, and racial differences in access and health status persist.[4,5] Second, saying no takes place within a regionally centralized budget. Decisions about introducing new procedures involve weighing the net benefits of alternatives within a closed system. When a procedure is rationed, it is clear which resources are availa-

ble for alternative uses. When a procedure is widely used, it is clear which resources are unavailable for other uses. No such closed system constrains American decisions about the dissemination of technological advances except, on a small scale and in a derivative way, within some health maintenance organizations (HMOs).

These two constraints are crucial to justifying British rationing. The British practitioner who follows standard practice within the system does not order the more elaborate x-ray diagnosis that might be typical in the United States, possibly even despite the knowledge that additional information would be useful. Denying care can be justified as follows: Though the patient might benefit from the extra service, ordering it would be unfair to other patients in the system. The system provides equitable access to a full array of services that are fairly allocated according to professional judgments about which needs are most important. The salve of this rationale may not be what the practitioner uses to ease his or her qualms about denying beneficial treatment, but it is available.

A similar rationale is available at the macro level. If British planners believe alternative uses of resources will produce a better set of health outcomes than introducing coronary bypass surgery on a large scale, they will say no to a beneficial procedure. But they have available the following rationale: Though they would help one group of patients by introducing this procedure, its opportunity cost would be too high. They would have to deny other patients services that are more necessary. Saying yes instead of no would be unjust.

These justifications for saying no at both levels have a bearing on physician autonomy and on moral obligations to patients. Within the standards of practice determined by budget ceilings in the system, British practitioners remain autonomous in their clinical decision making. They are obliged to provide the best possible care for their patients within those limits. Their clinical judgments are not made "impure" by institutional profit incentives to deny care.

The claim made here is not that the British National Health Service is just, but that considerations of justice are explicit in its design and in decisions about the allocation of resources. Because justice has this role, British rationing can be defended on grounds of fairness. Of course, some no-saying, such as the denial of renal dialysis to elderly patients, may raise difficult questions of justice.[2] The issue here, however, is not the merits of each British decision, but the framework within which they are made.

Saying No in the United States

Cost-containment measures in the United States reward institutions, and in some cases practitioners, for delivering treatment at a lower cost. Hospitals that deliver treatment for less than the DRG rate pocket the difference. Hospital administrators therefore scrutinize the decisions of physicians to use resources,

1382 THE NEW ENGLAND JOURNAL OF MEDICINE May 22, 1986

pressuring some to deny beneficial care. Many cannot always act in their patients' best interests, and they fear worse effects if DRGs are extended to physicians' charges.[6] In some HMOs and preferred-provider organizations, there are financial incentives for the group to shave the costs of treatment — if necessary, by denying some beneficial care. In large HMOs, in which risks are widely shared, there may be no more denial of beneficial care than under fee-for-service reimbursement.[7] But in some capitation schemes, individual practitioners are financially penalized for ordering "extra" diagnostic tests, even if they think their patient needs them. More ominously, some hospital chains are offering physicians a share of the profits made in their hospitals from the early discharge of Medicare patients.

When economic incentives to physicians lead them to deny beneficial care, there is a direct threat to what may be called the ethic of agency. In general, granting physicians considerable autonomy in clinical decision making is necessary if they are to be effective as agents pursuing their patients' interests. The ethic of agency constrains this autonomy in ways that protect the patient, requiring that clinical decisions be competent, respectful of the patient's autonomy, respectful of the other rights of the patient (e.g., confidentiality), free from consideration of the physician's interests, and uninfluenced by judgments about the patient's worth. Incentives that reward physicians for denying beneficial care clearly risk violating the fourth-mentioned constraint, which, like the fifth, is intended to keep clinical decisions pure — that is, aimed at the patient's best interest.

Rationing need not violate the constraint that decisions must be free from consideration of the physician's interest. British practitioners are not rewarded financially for saying no to their patients. Because our cost-containment schemes give incentives to violate this constraint, however, they threaten the ethic of agency. Patients would be foolish to think the physician who benefits from saying no is any longer their agent. (Of course, patients in the United States traditionally have had to guard against unnecessary treatments, since reimbursement schemes provided incentives to overtreat.)

American physicians face a problem even when the only incentive for denying beneficial care is the hospital's, not theirs personally. For example, how can they justify sending a Medicare patient home earlier than advisable? Can they, like their British peers, claim that justice requires them to say no and that therefore they do no wrong to their patients?

American physicians cannot make this appeal to the justice of saying no. They have no assurance that the resources they save will be put to better use elsewhere in the health care system. Reducing a Medicare expenditure may mean only that there is less pressure on public budgets in general, and thus more opportunity to invest the savings in weapons. Even if the savings will be freed for use by other Medicare patients,

American physicians have no assurance that the resources will be used to meet the greater needs of other patients. The American health care system, unlike the British one, establishes no explicit priorities for the use of resources. In fact, the savings from saying no may be used to invest in a procedure that may never provide care of comparable importance to that the physician is denying the patient. In a for-profit hospital, the profit made by denying beneficial treatment may be returned to investors. In many cases, the physician can be quite sure that saying no to beneficial care will lead to greater harm than providing the care.

Saying no at the macro level in the United States involves similar difficulties. A hospital deciding whether or not to introduce a transplantation program competes with other medical centers. To remain competitive, its directors will want to introduce the new service. Moreover, they can point to the dramatic benefit the service offers. How can opponents of transplantation respond? They may (correctly) argue that it will divert resources from other projects — projects that are perhaps less glamorous, visible, and profitable but that nevertheless offer comparable medical benefits to an even larger class of patients. They insist that the opportunity costs of the new procedure are too great.

This argument about opportunity costs, so powerful in the British National Health Service, loses its force in the United States. The alternatives to the transplantation program may not constitute real options, at least in the climate of incentives that exists in America. Imagine someone advising the Humana Hospital Corporation, "Do not invest in artificial hearts, because you could do far more good if you established a prenatal maternal care program in the catchment area of your chain." Even if correct, this appeal to opportunity costs is unlikely to be persuasive, because Humana responds to the incentives society offers. Artificial hearts, not prenatal maternal-care programs, will keep its hospitals on the leading technological edge, and if they become popular, will bring far more lucrative reimbursements than the prevention of low-birth-weight morbidity and mortality. The for-profit Humana, like many nonprofit organizations, merely responded to existing incentives when it introduced a transplantation program during the early 1980s, at the same time prenatal care programs lost their federal funding. Similarly, cost-containment measures in some states led to the cutting of social and psychological services but left high-technology services untouched.[8] Unlike their British colleagues, American planners cannot say, "Justice requires that we forgo this procedure because the resources it requires will be better spent elsewhere in the system. It is fair to say no to this procedure because we can thereby provide more important treatments to other patients."

The failure of this justification at both the micro and macro levels in the United States has the same root cause. In our system, saying no to beneficial treatments or procedures carries no assurance that we are saying yes to even more beneficial ones. Our system is not closed; the opportunity costs of a treatment or procedure are not kept internal to it. Just as important, the system as a whole is not governed by a principle of distributive justice, appeal to which is made in decisions about disseminating technological advances. It is not closed under constraints of justice.

Some Consequences

Saying no to beneficial treatments or procedures in the United States is morally hard, because providers cannot appeal to the justice of their denial. In ideally just arrangements, and even in the British system, rationing beneficial care is nevertheless fair to all patients in general. Cost-containment measures in our system carry with them no such justification.

The absence of this rationale has important effects. It supports the feeling of many physicians that current measures interfere with their duty to act in their patients' best interests. Of course, physicians should not think that duty requires them to reject any resource limitations on patient care. But it is legitimate for physicians to hope they may act as their patients' advocate within the limits allowed by the just distribution of resources. Our cost-containment measures thus frustrate a legitimate expectation about what duty requires. Eroding this sense of duty will have a long-term destabilizing effect.

The absence of a rationale based on justice also affects patients. Resource constraints mean that each patient can legitimately expect only the treatments due him or her under a just or fair distribution of health care services. But if beneficial treatment is denied even when justice does not require or condone it, then the patient has reason to feel aggrieved. Patients will not trust providers who put their own economic gain above patient needs. They will be especially distrustful of schemes that allow doctors to profit by denying care. Conflicts between the interests of patients and those of physicians or hospitals are not a necessary feature of a just system of rationing care. The fact that such conflicts are central in our system will make patients suspect that there is no one to be trusted as their agent. In the absence of a concern for just distribution, our cost-containment measures may make patients seek the quite different justice afforded by tort litigation, further destabilizing the system.

Finally, these effects point to a deeper issue. Economic incentives such as those embedded in current cost-containment measures are not a substitute for social decisions about health care priorities and the just design of health care institutions. These incentives to providers, even if they do eliminate some unnecessary medical services, will not ensure that we will meet the needs of our aging population over the next several decades in a morally acceptable fashion or that we will make effective — and just — use of new procedures. These hard choices must be faced publicly and explicitly.

Supported by grants from the Retirement Research Foundation and the National Endowment of the Humanities.

This paper is based on the Truman Collins Memorial Lecture delivered to the Portland, Oregon, Academy of Medicine in December 1984.

Tufts University
Medford, MA 02155   NORMAN DANIELS, PH.D.

REFERENCES

1. Diagnosis-related groups (DRGs) and the Medicare program: implications for medical technology. Washington D.C.: U.S. Congress, 1983. (Office of Technology Assessment OTA-TM-H-17.)
2. Daniels N. Just health care. New York: Cambridge University Press, 1985.
3. Aaron HJ, Schwartz WB. The painful prescription: rationing hospital care. Washington D.C.: The Brookings Institution, 1984.
4. President's Commission for the Study of Ethical Problems in Medicine and Biomedical and Behavioral Research. Securing access to health care: ethical implications of differences in the accessibility of health services. Vol. 1. Washington D.C.: Government Printing Office, 1983.
5. Iglehart JK. Medical care of the poor — a growing problem. N Engl J Med 1985; 313:59-63.
6. Jencks SF, Dobson A. Strategies for reforming Medicare's physician payments: physician diagnosis-related groups and other approaches. N Engl J Med 1985; 312:1492-9.
7. Yelin EH, Henke CJ, Kramer JS, Nevitt MC, Shearn M, Epstein WV. A comparison of the treatment of rheumatoid arthritis in health maintenance organizations and fee-for-service practices. N Engl J Med 1985; 312:962-7.
8. Cromwell J, Kanak J. The effects of prospective reimbursement on hospital adoption and service sharing. Health Care Financ Rev 1982; 4:67.

Part II
Issues at the Outset of Life

[9]

Indicators of Humanhood:
A Tentative Profile of Man

It's time to spell out the "which" and "what" and "when"

by JOSEPH FLETCHER

Mark Twain complained that people are always talking about the weather but they never do anything about it. The same is true of the humanhood agenda. In biomedical ethics writers constantly say that we need to explicate humanness or humaneness, what it means to be a truly human being, but they never follow their admission of the need with an actual inventory or profile, no matter how tentatively offered. Yet this is what must be done, or at least attempted.

Synthetic concepts such as *human* and *man* and *person* require operational terms, spelling out the which and what and when. Only in that way can we get down to cases—to normative decisions. There are always some people who prefer to be visceral and affective in their moral choices, with no desire to have any rationale for what they do. But *ethics* is precisely the business of rational, critical reflection (encephalic and not merely visceral) about the problems of the moral

Dr. Joseph Fletcher is Visiting Professor of Medical Ethics at the University of Virginia School of Medicine. Excerpted from a paper presented at the National Conference on the Teaching of Medical Ethics, co-sponsored by the Institute and Columbia University College of Physicians and Surgeons.

agent—in biology and medicine as much as in law, government, education or anything else.

To that end, then, for the purposes of biomedical ethics, I am suggesting a "profile of man" in concrete and discrete terms. As only one man's reflection on man, it will no doubt invite adding and subtracting by others, but this is the road to be followed if we mean business. As a dog is said to "worry" a bone, let me worry out loud and on paper, hoping for some agreement and, at the least, consideration. There is space only to itemize it, not to enlarge upon it, but I have fifteen positive propositions and five negative propositions. Let me set them out, in no rank order at all, and as hardly more than a list of criteria or indicators, by simple title.

Positive Human Criteria

Minimal intelligence. Any individual of the species *homo sapiens* who falls below the I.Q. 40-mark in a standard Stanford-Binet test, amplified if you like by other tests, is questionably a person; below the 20-mark, not a person. *Homo* is indeed *sapiens*, in order to be *homo*. The *ratio*, in another turn of speech, is what makes a person of the *vita*. Mere biological life, before minimal intelligence is achieved or after it is lost irretrievably, is without personal status. This has

bearing, obviously, on decision making in gynecology, obstetrics and pediatrics, as well as in general surgery and medicine.

Self-awareness. Self-consciousness, as we know, is the quality we watch developing in a baby; we watch it with fascination and glee. Its essential role in personality development is a basic datum of psychology. Its existence or function in animals at or below the primate level is debatable; it is clearly absent in the lower vertebrates, as well as in the nonvertebrates. In psychotherapy non-self-awareness is pathological; in medicine, unconsciousness when it is incorrigible at once poses quality-of-life judgments—for example, in neurosurgical cases of irreversible damage to the brain cortex.

Self-control. If an individual is not only not controllable by others (unless by force) but not controllable by the individual himself or herself, a low level of life is reached about on a par with a paramecium. If the condition cannot be rectified medically, so that means-ends behavior is out of the question, the individual is not a person—not ethically, and certainly not in the eyes of the law—just as a fetus is not legally a person.

A sense of time. Time consciousness. By this is meant clock time or *chronos,* not timeliness or *kairos,* i.e., not the "fulness of time" or the pregnant moment (remember Paul Tillich?). A sense, that is, of the passage of time. A colleague of mine at the University of Virginia, Dr. Thomas Hunter, remarked recently, "Life is the allocation of time." We can disagree legitimately about how relatively important this indicator is, but it is hard to understand why anybody would minimize it or eliminate it as a trait of humanness.

A sense of futurity. How "truly human" is any man who cannot realize there is a time yet to come as well as the present? Subhuman animals do not look forward in time; they live only on what we might call visceral strivings, appetites. Philosophical anthropologies (one recalls William Temple's, for instance) commonly emphasize *purposiveness* as a key to humanness. Chesteron once remarked that we would never ask a puppy what manner of dog it wanted to be when it grows

Hastings Center Report

623 Warburton Avenue
Hastings-on-Hudson, NY 10706

Bruce Hilton, Editor

HASTINGS CENTER STAFF

Administration: Daniel Callahan, director; Willard Gaylin, president; Lyn Brydson, Leslie Hendricks
Behavior Control: Robert C. Neville, Helen Blatte, Raye Ann Gaskins
Genetics: Marc Lappe', Tabitha M. Powledge, Marguerite Robinson
Humanities: Peter Steinfels, Helen O'Sullivan
Information: Bruce Hilton, Martha Bush, Susan Travers
Population: Daniel Callahan, Robert M. Veatch, Sharmon Sollitto
Death: Robert M. Veatch, Rosalie Miller

up. The assertion here is that men are typically teleological, although certainly not eschatological.

A sense of the past. Memory. Unlike other animals, men as a species have reached a unique level of neurologic development, particularly the cerebrum and especially its neo-cortex. They are linked to the past by conscious recall—not only, as with subhuman animals, by conditioning and the reactivation of emotions (reactivated, that is, externally rather than autonomously). It is this trait, in particular, that makes man, alone among all species, a cultural instead of an instinctive creature. An existentialist focus on "nowness" truncates the nature of man.

The capability to relate to others. Inter-personal relationships, of the sexual-romantic and friendship kind, are of the greatest importance for the fulness of what we idealize as being truly personal. (Medical piety in the past has always held its professional ethics to be only a one-to-one, physician-patient obligation.) However, there are also the more diffuse and comprehensive social relations of our vocational, economic and political life. Aristotle's characterization of man as a social animal, *zoon politikon,* must surely figure prominently in the inventory. It is true that even insects live in social systems, but the cohesion of all subhuman societies is based on instinct. Man's society is based on culture—that is, on a conscious knowledge of the system and on the exercise in some real measure of either consent or opposition.

Concern for others. Some people may be skeptical about our capacity to care about others (what in Christian ethics is often distinguished from romance and friendship as "neighbor love" or "neighbor concern"). The extent to which this capacity is actually in play is debatable. But whether concern for others is disinterested or inspired by enlightened self-interest it seems plain that a conscious extra-ego orientation is a trait of the species; the absence of this ambience is a clinical indication of psychopathology.

Communication. Utter alienation or disconnection from others, if it is

It is a sense of the past which makes man, alone among species, a cultural creature

irreparable, is de-humanization. This is not so much a matter of not being disposed to receive and send "messages" as of the inability to do so. This criterion comes into question in patients who cannot hear, speak, feel or see others; it may come about as a result of mental or physical trauma, infection, genetic or congenital disorder, or from psychological causes. Completely and finally *isolated* individuals are subpersonal. The problem is perhaps most familiar in terminal illnesses and the clinical decision-making required.

Control of existence. It is of the nature of man that he is not helplessly subject to the blind workings of physical or physiological nature. He has only finite knowledge, freedom, and initiative, but what he has of it is real and effective. Invincible ignorance and total helplessness are the antithesis of humanness, and to the degree that a man lacks control he is not responsible, and to be irresponsible is to be subpersonal. This item in the agenda applies directly, for example, in psychiatric medicine, especially to severe cases of toxic and degenerative psychosis.

Curiosity. To be without affect, sunk in anomie, is to be not a person. Indifference is inhuman. Man is a learner and a knower as well as a tool maker and user. This raises a question, therefore, about demands to stop some kinds of biomedical inquiry. For example, an A.M.A. committee recently called a halt on *in vitro* reproduction and embryo transplants on the ground that they are dangerous. But dangerous ignorance is more dangerous than dangerous knowledge. It is dehumanizing to impose a moratorium on research. No doubt this issue arises, or will arise, in many other phases of medical education and practice.

Change and changeability. To the extent that an individual is unchangeable or opposed to change he denies the creativity of personal beings. It means not only the fact of biological and physiological change, which goes on as a condition of life, but the capacity and disposition for changing one's mind and conduct as well. Biologically, human beings are developmental: birth, life, health, and death are processes, not events, and are to be understood epigenetically, not episodically. All human existence is on a continuum, a matter of becoming. In this perspective, are we to regard potentials *als ob*, as if they were actual? I think not. The question arises prominently in abortion ethics.

Balance of rationality and feeling. To be "truly human," to be a wholesome *person*, one cannot be either Apollonian or Dionysian. As human beings we are not "coldly" rational or cerebral, nor are we merely creatures of feeling and intuition. It is a matter of being both, in different combinations from one individual to another. To be one rather than the other is to distort the *humanum*.

Idiosyncrasy. The human being is idiomorphous, a distinctive individual. As Helmut Schoeck has shown, even the function of envy in human behavior is entirely consistent with idiosyncrasy. To be a person is to have an identity, to be recognizable and callable by name. It is this criterion which lies behind the fear that to replicate individuals by so-called "cloning" would be to make "carbon copies" of the parent source and thus dehumanize the clone by denying it its individuality. One or two writers have even spoken of a "right" to a "unique genotype," and while such talk is ethically and scientifically questionable it nonetheless reflects a legitimate notion of something essential to an authentic person.

Neo-cortical function. In a way, this is the cardinal indicator, the one all the others are hinged upon. Before cerebration is in play, or with its end,

in the absence of the synthesizing function of the cerebral cortex, the *person* is non-existent. Such individuals are objects but not subjects. This is so no matter how many other spontaneous or artificially supported functions persist in the heart, lungs, neurologic and vascular systems. Such non-cerebral processes are not personal. Like the Harvard Medical School's *ad hoc* committee report on "brain death" the recent Kansas statute on defining death requires the absence of *brain* function. So do the guidelines recently adopted by the Italian Council of Ministers. But what is definitive in determining death is the loss of cerebration, not just of any or all brain function. Personal reality depends on cerebration and to be dead "humanly" speaking is to be ex-cerebral, no matter how long the *body* remains alive.

Negative Human Criteria

The five negative points I have can be put even more briefly than the 15 positive ones, although I am inclined to believe that they merit just as much critical scrutiny and elaboration.

Man is not non- or anti-artificial. As Gaylin says, men are characterized by technique, and for a human being to oppose technology is "self-hatred." We are often confused on this score, attitudinally. A "test tube baby," for example, although conceived and gestated *ex corpo*, would nonetheless be humanly reproduced and of human value. A baby made artificially, by deliberate and careful contrivance, would be more *human* than one resulting from sexual roulette—the reproductive mode of the subhuman species.

Man is not essentially parental. People can be fully personal without reproducing, as the religious vows of nuns, monks and celibate priests of the past have asserted, as the law has implied by refusing to annul marriages because of sterility, and as we see in the ethos-reversal of contemporary family and population control—and, more militantly, in the non-parental rhetoric of women's liberation and a growing rejection of the "baby trap".

Man is not essentially sexual. Sexuality, a broader and deeper phenomenon than sex, is of the fulness but not

of the essence of man. It is not even necessary to human species survival. I will not try here to indicate the psychological entailments of this negative proposition, but it is biologically apparent when we look at such non-sexual reproduction as cloning from somatic cells, and parthenogenetic reproduction by both androgenesis and gynogenesis. What light does this biology throw on the nature of man; what does a personistic view of man say about the ethics of such biology? (N.B. I do not refer here to personalism, which has more metaphysical freight than many of us want to carry.)

Man is not a bundle of rights. The notion of a human *nature* has served as

---

A test-tube baby would be more human than one resulting from sexual roulette

---

a conceptual bucket, to contain "human rights" and certain other *given* things, likè "original sin" and "the sense of oughtness" and "conscience." The idea behind this is that such things are objective, pre-existent phenomena, not contingent on biological or social relativities. People sometimes speak of rights to live, to die, to be healthy, to reproduce, and so on, as if they were absolute, eternal, intrinsic. But as the law makes plain, all rights are imperfect and may be set aside if human *need* requires it. We shall have to think through the relation of rights and needs, as it bears on clinical medicine's decision-making problems, as well as society's problems of health care delivery. One example: What is the "humane" policy if we should reach the point (I think we will) of deciding for or against compulsory birth control? Or, how are we to relate rights and needs if, to take only one example, an ethnic group protests against mass screening for sickle cell

Institute of Society, Ethics and the Life Sciences

Page 4

anemia? Or if after genetic counseling a couple elects to proceed with a predictably degenerate pregnancy?

Man is not a worshiper. Faith in supernatural realities and attempts to be in direct association with them are choices some human beings make and others do not. Mystique is not essential to being truly a person. Like sexuality, it may arguably be of the fulness of humanness but it is not of the essence. This negative proposition is required by our basic guideline, the premise that a viable biomedical ethics is humanistic, whatever reasons we may have for putting human wellbeing at the center of concern.

More Thinking

How are we to go about testing such criteria as these? And how are we to compare and combine the results of our criticism? How are we to rank order or give priority to the items in our man-hood profile? Which are only optimal, which are essential? What are the applications of these or other indicators to the normative decisions of biologists and physicians? In my own list, here, which factors can be eliminated, in whole or in part, without lowering individuals and patients below the personal line? I trust that by this time it is plain that I do not claim to have produced the pure gospel of humanness. I remain open to correction.

The "nature of man" question is of such depth and sensitivity that it is bound to raise controversy, and our task is to welcome the controversy but try to reduce it through analysis and synthesis. Said Heraclitus: "Opposition brings concord. Out of discord comes the fairest harmony. It is by disease that health is pleasant; by evil that good is pleasant; by hunger, satiety; by weariness, rest."

As a final note, I rather suspect that we are more apt to find good answers inductively and empirically, from medical science and the clinicians, than by the necessarily syllogistic reasoning of the humanities, which proceeds deductively from abstract premises. Syllogisms always contain their conclusions in their major or first premises. Divorced from the laboratory and the hospital, talk about what it means to be human could easily become inhumane.　　　●●

[10]

ARGUING FROM POTENTIAL*

STEPHEN BUCKLE

Introduction

One of the more common arguments employed in attempts to determine how we should treat the earliest forms of human life is the argument from potential. Typically, the argument holds that we should not interfere with, and perhaps should even assist,[1] the development of the human fertilised egg because it already possesses the potential to be a fully self-conscious being; to be, that is, not merely a biologically human being (a human object), but a human subject.[2] It is, potentially, just like us, so we cannot deny it any rights or other forms of protection that we accord ourselves. The argument holds that, although the fertilised egg is not just like us in possessing rationality, self-consciousness, etc, this is a difference which is not fundamental, because it is overcome in time through the normal course of events.[3] The fertilised egg is not 'just like us' only in the sense that it is not *yet* just like us. Therefore, the argument concludes, we should not interfere with its natural development towards being a rational, self-conscious being. On its strongest interpretation, the argument is thought to establish that we should treat a potential human subject as if it were already an actual human subject.

The argument has not been without its critics, and some of the criticisms will be considered in this paper. At least some of the criticisms, and the replies to them, give the impression that the argument's protagonists and critics are somewhat at cross-purposes. One aim of this paper is to help to show why that should be so. The central aim of the paper, however, is to

* This work was supported by an Australian National Health and Medical Research Council Special Initiative Grant to Professor J. Swan, Dr J. Funder, Ms B. Gaze and Dr H. Kuhse. My thanks to them, and also to Peter Singer and Richard Hare, for helpful comments on earlier versions of this paper.

provide an analysis of some distinct ways of arguing about potential, and the different senses of 'potential' on which they rely. Given the attractiveness of this sort of argument to so many who think about the moral issues raised by the sophisticated new technologies available for intervening in human development from the earliest stages of (biologically) human life, this is an important endeavour. To give an example of this kind of argument, and to illustrate its attractiveness across a broad spectrum, we shall begin by giving a brief account of the viewpoint arrived at by the majority of the Australian Senate Select Committee commissioned to examine the question of experimentation on human embryos.[4] (We shall below also consider the views expressed in the minority dissenting report of the same committee.)

The majority report of the Senate Select Committee identifies, as the 'correct query' at the centre of its enquiries, the question: What is the respect due to the human embryo? (2.40) It implicitly transforms this into the similar (but not identical) question: What features of the embryo (if any) command respect?[5] To this question it offers the following answer:

> It is in its orientation to the future that the Committee finds the feature of the embryo which commands such a degree of respect as to prohibit destructive non-therapeutic experimentation (3.6).

To the further question, What is this orientation, and why does it matter?, the report offers this answer:

> If, as is the view of the Committee, the embryo may be properly described as genetically new human life organised as a distinct entity oriented towards further development, then the stance and behaviour proper to adopt towards it would include not frustrating a process which commands respect because its thrust is towards the further development of a biologically individuated member of the human species (3.7).

Although the report does not specify exactly what it is for a being to 'command respect', its reasoning, and its conclusion, are clear enough. Given the embryo's orientation towards the future, and given that there are no sharp discontinuities in embryonic development—and therefore nothing which could 'bear the weight' of being a 'marker event' for distinguishing the different moral values of different stages of development (3.9)[6]—the report concludes thus:

In this situation prudence dictates that, until the contrary is demonstrated 'beyond reasonable doubt' (to use an expression well known in our community), the embryo of the human species should be regarded *as if it were a human subject* for the purposes of biomedical ethics (3.18). (Emphasis added.)

This, then is the viewpoint of the majority report. Despite the fact that it employs some novel terminology, it clearly appeals to a version of the argument from potential. As many versions of the argument from potential do, it concludes that we should treat some entity as if it were already something which it is not yet, and it reaches this conclusion by considering some feature(s) which the entity already possesses, and which will help it to become that sort of entity which it is not yet. In the terminology of the report, this feature is, in the embryo's case, called its 'orientation to the future', an orientation which reflects its organisation (3.6–7). As we shall see below, this way of putting the matter is not without its virtues. However, having provided an account of a recently advanced version of the argument from potential, we can now consider a very general (and very dismissive) response to the argument.

An Attempted Dismissal

The argument from potential can be characterised as holding that the entity's potential for acquiring morally significant characteristics is itself morally significant. Putting the matter this way, however, immediately seems to show a difficulty: the argument implicitly concedes that the entity possesses no morally significant characteristics other than its capacity to come to have them. But how can the capacity to develop morally significant characteristics be itself such a characteristic? Of course, it cannot, at this level of generality, be shown that this capacity cannot be such a characteristic, but it does seem as if we are being asked to regard the capacity to be a particular kind of thing as *itself* one such thing. But this seems patently false. The argument from potential seems, therefore, to depend on a fundamental confusion—on regarding the potential to possess a certain feature as itself such a feature. To take a concrete example, it apparently regards a potential person as a particular kind of person. But whatever a potential person is, it is *not* a person. (A child is a potential adult. Because it is a potential adult, it is not an actual adult. That is, it is not an adult.) So it seems the argument from potential confuses the capacity for developing certain features with their actual possession. If so, it is a failure.

It might be thought that this negative conclusion can be avoided by denying that capacity and actuality are confused in the argument. But it seems that denying the existence of confusion leaves us no better off. For if the potential to develop morally significant characteristics is *not* such a characteristic, why should it be heeded? That is, wouldn't the argument then reject precisely what it seeks to establish, by conceding that the entity in question possesses, as yet, no morally significant characteristics at all? Why, then, should one treat it as if it did? It seems that, on either version, the argument must fail.

It is not unusual for variants of this argument to be advanced against the argument from potential,[7] and there is no denying that it raises a number of awkward questions. However, two kinds of reasons can be offered for not being too quickly impressed. That is, there are two kinds of reasons which could be advanced in support of the view that, despite the dilemma just pointed out, the capacity to develop morally significant characteristics is indeed morally significant. They are, first, because it could be argued that it is precisely capacities, in particular the capacities of individuals, which *are* morally significant, that moral behaviour is a matter of respecting the capacities of other beings; and, secondly, that because present capacities are (in the ideal case) future actualities, and because it could be argued that moral behaviour is behaviour which regards the consequences of actions, then our moral obligations regard not merely present actualities but also future actualities, and therefore present potentialities.

Kinds Of Potential

The two kinds of reasons given above reflect two different kinds of moral theory.[8] It is thus not surprising, although it does not appear to have been noticed, that they also indicate two different interpretations of potentiality and the difference it makes. Briefly, the first reason holds that respect is due to an existing being because it possesses the capacity or power to develop into a being which is worthy of respect in its own right; and respect is due to such a being because it is *the very same being* as the later being into which it develops.[9] The already-existing being is a being which has the potential *to become*[10] a being worthy of respect in its own right. The second kind of reason focuses on future outcomes, and so accords moral significance to whatever has the potential *to produce* certain states of affairs. By focusing on different sorts of potential, the two kinds of reason also generate two distinct versions of the argument from potential. These will be given separate treatment below.

To avoid misunderstanding it is important to indicate how the two kinds of potential differ. Both are central cases of potential, in as much as both refer to a power in (the *potency* of) an object or group of objects. This is well worth mentioning, since a number of recent accounts of potential regard it purely as a provisional prediction about future actualities. John Harris's is a case in point. He says, for example:

> To say that the fertilised egg is a potential human being is just to say that if certain things happen to it (like implantation) and certain other things do not (like spontaneous abortion) it will eventually become a human being.[11]

Although it is true that we sometimes employ the notion of potential in this very broad sense, it is not true that it is this sense which is employed in potentiality arguments about how to treat early human life. This can be readily shown. In this very broad sense, potentiality is just possibility—whatever the entity in question can possibly become, or be transformed into, is its potential. An acorn is in this sense not merely a potential oak tree; it is also potential food, or humus, or whatever human ingenuity can make of it (for whatever purpose). In like manner, a foetus is not only a potential person, it is also a potential abortus, a potential experimental subject, even a potential meal for the dog. Because any entity has, in this very broad sense of the term, so many different potentials, and these potentials are concerned with states of affairs of sharply contrasting value, we can conclude that this sense is too undiscriminating to found, without further qualification, any *moral* argument.

This would be a comparatively uninteresting observation if the argument from potential were an argument, not about the moral significance of the mere possession of potential, but about fostering a particular potential at the expense of other potentials. The argument is not, however, typically (if ever) of this form. As the above quotations from the Tate majority report help to indicate—the report's concern for the potential of the early embryo is summed up in terms of the respect thought to be due to 'a distinct entity oriented towards further development'—the argument is typically couched in terms of allowing (whether this involves not interfering or actually assisting) a process to run its natural course, not in terms of selecting between different potentials. This is no accident. If the argument were to be understood as concerned with selecting between different potentials, this would presumably amount to its being concerned with selecting between different outcomes. As such, it would be a straightforwardly consequentialist argument. This is surely not the *intention*, at least, of most of those, including the Tate majority, who call on the argument; and their view that the argument is of quite a different colour finds some support in the fact that, if it were *simply* a consequentialist argument, then the notion of potentiality would be doing no crucial work. The argument could be rephrased without referring to potentiality at all. (There is, as has been indicated, a consequentialist version of the argument which depends on a narrower notion of potential. As a moral argument, however, its fate is not markedly different, as will be shown below.) So we can conclude that the argument from potential is typically presented as an argument about the moral significance of the mere possession of potential, and as such, if it is to be a viable argument, requires that potential cannot be understood simply as possibility.

It has already been pointed out that there *is* an available notion of potential which is appropriately narrower: the potential of an entity is its power to develop in certain ways, or to produce certain outcomes. It has also been claimed that this is the central meaning of the word 'potential'. This claim can be defended as follows. The use of 'potential' to mean possibility is most plausibly explained as the result either of broadening the conception of an entity's potency so that it includes the effects of that potency, or as a simple confusion of causes with their effects. Both of these alternatives reflect the fact that an entity's potency is related to its possibilities as cause is to effects: if an entity has a particular potency, then it has a particular possibility, or set of possibilities, which cannot be actualized except through the expression of that potency. It may be that, in some contexts, broadening the notion of potential may have its uses, and failing to discriminate between causes and their effects may not be harmful, but in the context of thinking about the status of early human life and the difference its potential might make shifts of this kind have greatly hindered enlightenment. I think it is not unfair to say that both advocates and critics of the potentiality argument are frequently not clear about what they understand potentiality to be, and that discussion of the argument has suffered from not distinguishing causes from their effects. (An example is provided below, in the discussion of the dissenting minority report.) As a result, discussion of the argument frequently seems to be at cross-purposes, or fails to scratch in the different places where potentiality has caused many moral consciences to itch.

Once it is recognized that the central meaning of 'potentiality' is that of an object's potency (the power it possesses in virtue of its specific constitution), and that arguments to moral value from potential invoke this central meaning, however unself-consciously, it can be seen that criticism of the argument from potential along lines of the kind employed by John Harris will not succeed. From the standpoint of the central, relevant, meaning of 'potential', Harris's account does confuse the effect with its cause. Judgements of potential, in this relevant sense, indeed *imply* predictions (with some saving clause) about future actualities, but not because judgements of potential are pro-visional or conditional claims about the future. Rather, they are attributions of a present power to an entity, a power which will or can have that future effect.[12]

It is also worth noticing that Harris takes for granted that some form of identity is preserved in his brief account of potentiality: the fertilised egg is a potential human subject if *it* will eventually become a human subject, not merely because it will cause, or help to cause, a human subject to come to exist. More will be said on identity below, but Harris's assumption here is worth noticing in order to indicate that the concern of this paper—with separating out two notions of potentiality according to whether or not some form of identity is preserved —is not merely arbitrary. Assumptions about identity are intimately connected with the employment of the notion of potentiality. In particular, expressions of the form 'X is a potential Y' differ from all other forms of expression about potential precisely in the fact that expressions of this form require that a relevant kind of identity is preserved. (It hardly needs pointing out that expressions of this form are very common when the potentiality of early forms of human life is discussed.)

The two types of potential already referred to can now be more profitably considered. The potential *to become* is the power possessed by an entity to undergo changes which are changes *to itself*, that is, to undergo growth or, better still, *development*. The potential *to become* can thus be called developmental potential. The process of actualizing the potential *to become* preserves some form of individual identity.[13] It is for this reason that the

potential *to become* is peculiarly appropriate to arguments which
are concerned to establish the importance of respecting the
capacities of a specific individual. The potential *to produce*
differs in precisely this respect—it does not require that any
form of identity be preserved; in fact, as we shall see, neither is
its application limited to individuals. It is therefore possible to
regard the potential *to become* as a special case of the potential *to
produce*, and the latter as potential *simpliciter*. But no matter of
substance depends on whether or not this particular course is
followed.

In the following two sections, the two kinds of potentiality
argument will be spelt out, and their implications determined.
It should be stressed that the value of these arguments will not
be considered; it will not be argued that the conclusions of
either are true (or false, for that matter). The strategy of these
sections is, more simply, to show what the arguments are, and
what they imply; in particular, it will be argued that the
arguments do not imply what the Tate majority report concludes. This obviously points up a problem with the report. But
it should be stressed that the following analysis, if correct, does
not show the majority report's conclusions to be wrong; rather,
it shows that its conclusions need different supports if they are
to be credible.

The 'Respect For Capacities Of Individuals' Argument

The first possible reason for holding that the capacity to
develop morally significant characteristics is itself morally
significant is that, according to one prominent kind of moral
theory, respect for certain capacities of other beings is precisely
the stuff of which morals is made. Of course, just *which*
capacities (and therefore also, just which other beings) do count
for moral status is the crucial matter to be answered before this
kind of approach can provide a concrete moral viewpoint. Most
commonly, theories of this kind focus on the interests of
sentient beings, thereby restricting the moral domain to such
beings. Much broader versions have been offered, however,
especially in recent times, with some environmentally concerned philosophers prepared to argue the case for trees or
even ecosystems. To include the human conceptus, a broad
version is certainly necessary. But it is not necessary, for the
purposes of this paper at least, to settle whether such a version
(let alone one that defends the case of trees, etc) is plausible. We

will be concerned only with what such a view, if plausible, implies. Therefore no attempt will be made to settle the question of what capacities *do* count, morally speaking; in what follows, I will speak indifferently of the capacities of other beings, and leave the proper account of these capacities to one side.

It is also worth noticing that respect for the capacities of other beings may take two forms: it may be interpreted to require merely not interfering with the (non-harmful) exercise of capacities, or it may take a stronger form, such that mere non-interference is not adequate; that, at least in some circumstances, positive assistance is required. The difference between these interpretations, especially in the context of debates about IVF, is an important one. For, although the weaker version finds wide support as a plausible and practicable moral principle, the stronger is equally widely regarded as too onerous to be morally obligatory, and too conducive to the erosion of civil liberties. (To say this is not, of course, to settle the question of their plausibility as moral principles—but that is too large a question to be adequately treated here.) It is the stronger version which must be established if this general principle is to have implications for the very possibility of *in vitro* research: not interfering with an embryo in a petri dish is no aid to its future survival. The notion of guardianship, to which the majority report appeals (see 3.34 and 3.44 in particular) requires the stronger of the two interpretations. However, even the weaker version is sufficient to prevent destructive non-therapeutic experimentation, so the conclusions reached by the majority do not depend on the specific interpretation of the principle.

For those moral viewpoints which regard the rights of individuals as the fundamental factors of moral significance, respect for the capacities of other beings is the core of moral behaviour. Rights are commonly explained in terms of the respect due to beings which possess interests, and interests in their turn reflect a set of capacities—whether to suffer harms, or to actively engage in pursuing certain goals or other courses of action. Since a potential being is a being with certain capacities, it is perhaps not surprising that the argument from potential is so frequently couched in terms of rights. In so doing the argument attempts to establish that the early embryo, in virtue of its developmental capacities, is a worthy object of respect because it is a being with the potential *to become* a human subject (in the sense given above).

It is necessary to employ these rather awkward formulations in order to make clear that this form of the argument from potential depends on identifying a particular being which is worthy of respect in virtue of what it has the potential *to become*. We must, on this version, be able to identify that individual which will itself come to be the human subject. This version of the argument, therefore, does not apply where such an identification is not possible—either because there is simply no such individual, or even because there is *not yet* such an individual. It is important to recognize this fact. It has a significant bearing on this, the individual respecting, version of the argument.

The argument from potential is commonly deployed to advance the claims of the fertilised egg as an entity worthy of respect because of its potential. The argument, thus deployed, is what has been described here as a 'respect for capacities' argument, and as such it discriminates sharply between the status of the fertilised egg and its progenitors, the unfertilised egg and sperm. It has been criticised for doing so. The objection runs as follows: if we can identify a particular sperm and the egg it will fertilise, why cannot we say of them that together they have much the same potential as the fertilised egg? After all, provided fertilisation is successfully achieved (and new IVF techniques may provide a high success rate in the laboratory), are they not (almost) as likely to generate a human subject as is the fertilised egg?[14] As far as likely outcomes are concerned, the objection is quite pertinent. However, the defender of the potentiality argument is likely to feel that such considerations miss the point; and the above exposition of the argument shows that this is indeed so. The potentiality argument, thus employed, is not about likely outcomes, nor even about outcomes at all—it is, rather, about respecting a being which is worthy of respect. Neither the sperm nor the egg are beings worthy of respect, on this view, because neither has the potential *to become* a human subject, even though both of course have the potential to help to produce a human subject. So this version of the potentiality argument appears to be justified in discriminating between the fertilised egg and its progenitors. (The possibility of parthenogenetic development of the unfertilised egg is a problem for this view, however. How serious a problem it is will not be considered here, since it involves complications which lead too wide of our main purpose.[15])

It might be objected at this point that, although the sperm and egg do not individually have the potential *to become* a

human subject, when considered together, they do. Arguing
thus requires that we allow that a potential entity need not be
composed only of a single object, and there seem to be reasons
for thinking this to be quite legitimate—we can justly speak of
the potential of an army, or of a sporting team, for example.[16]
Therefore, it might be argued, although separate objects, the
sperm and egg can be legitimately regarded as jointly constituting an entity with the potential *to become* a human subject.

The argument will not work, however, because it is misplaced.
As an argument about an entity which has the potential *to
produce*, it seems quite acceptable, and will be considered in the
next section. However, it will not do as an argument about the
potential *to become*. This is because the potential *to become* is that
potential which attaches only to distinct individuals which
preserve their identity over time. It therefore attaches only to
entities which, if they are composed of distinct parts, nevertheless can be classed as a distinct single individual. To satisfy
this condition, the several and distinct parts must in some way
constitute a complex *whole*. This is true of armies and, and to a
lesser extent, of sporting teams—although composed of discrete individuals, armies or sporting teams are (fighting or
sporting) *units*—they have a unity constituted by a specific
organization directed towards a particular end. (It should be
noted that what constitutes some group of objects as a complex
whole will, in all probability, vary in different cases. This
need not trouble us, however; the central question will always
be whether such a whole, however constituted, preserves
its identity through whatever changes it undergoes.) Consequently, armies and sporting teams can be understood to
possess the potential *to become* in all those contexts where they
are considered as complex wholes, that is, wherever they are
not being considered merely as a collection of discrete human
beings.

Where a collection of discrete entities is not organized into a
whole, there is no individual to possess the potential *to become*,
no individual which develops through the actualization of the
potential. So, where there is no unified whole, there is no
potential *to become*. No such restriction exists if we are considering the potential *to produce*. A mixture of gases, if it
includes hydrogen and oxygen, has the potential *to produce*
water, despite the fact that such a mixture has no organizational
unity. So, although it is possible to speak of the potential of
entities which are composed of a number of discrete objects
lacking in any unifying features, the potential in question is the

potential *to produce*. In contrast, it is only possible to speak of
entities having a potential *to become* where such entities are
complex wholes.

In the case of the sperm and egg, there is no complex unity,
no overarching organization. Such unity or organization arises
only with fertilisation (in fact, only with the completion of
the fertilisation process at syngamy). Prior to the event of
fertilisation, there are two organized, complex wholes — the
sperm and the (unfertilised) egg. So the sperm and the egg,
even when considered jointly, as a collectivity, fail to satisfy a
necessary condition for the possession of the potential *to become*;
therefore they do not possess that particular form of potential.
Although together they have the potential *to produce* a human
subject, they do not have the potential *to become* a human
subject.

The argument from potential, in its non-consequentialist
'respect for capacities' version, is that respect is due to a being
which has the potential *to become* a human subject, because of
that being's potential *to become* such a subject. The argument
therefore applies only when there exists a being with this
particular species of potential, and only *to* such a being. It does
not apply to any being, nor to any other kind of entity (unified
or not), which has the more general potential *to produce* a
human subject. Therefore it does not apply to the sperm and
egg, prior to fertilisation. It is, however, commonly understood
to apply to the fertilised egg, and, of course, to subsequent
stages of the development of the human infant.

This common understanding is not beyond criticism. For,
although it is certainly true that the fertilised egg stands at the
beginning of a process of development which ends (in the
normal case) in a human subject, this shows only that the
fertilised egg has the potential *to produce* a human subject. To
show that it also has the potential *to become* that subject it is
necessary to show that the fertilised egg is the same being
(albeit writ very small) as the human subject at the other end
of the developmental process. There are good reasons for
doubting whether this can be done, principally because the
fertilised egg cannot be identified as the same being as the
embryo proper, that is, it cannot be identified as the entity
which begins to develop at about the fourteenth day after
fertilisation (later developing arms, legs, etc), and which comes
to be sustained by the life-support system provided by the
uterus and placenta. The identification cannot be made (that is,
the embryo proper is not the same individual as the fertilised

egg, differing only in being at a later stage of development) because the changes that the fertilised egg undergoes are not changes through which it develops into, or itself becomes, the embryo proper. Rather, it undergoes a process of differentiation in which the various cells developed in the earliest stages after fertilisation take on a range of different functions, only one of which is the development of the embryo proper; and no one group of specialized cells can be singled out as the same individual as the fertilised egg.

This is perhaps not widely understood, so it is worth spelling out in some detail. The reproductive biologist Anne McLaren describes the process as follows:

> The first two weeks after fertilisation are essentially a period of preparation for the later development of the embryo. The fertilised egg divides once or twice a day for the first few days, to form a clump of cells which then spends about the next week burrowing into the wall of the woman's uterus. During this period of implantation, most of the cells become progressively committed to various tasks concerned with the protection and nourishment of the future embryo. Eventually they or their descendants form the placenta and the various other tissues that surround the embryo — chorionic villi, secondary yolk sac, primary mesoblast, amnion, allantois, and so forth.
>
> At the end of the period of implantation, there remain some cells not involved in any of these life-support systems. It is in this group of cells (the 'embryonic plate') that the so-called primitive streak appears, marking the place where the embryo itself finally begins to develop.[17]

The entity McLaren refers to here as 'the embryo' is what we have called 'the embryo proper'. It is not what the Tate Report refers to by its use of 'embryo', however — that is, the human conceptus from fertilisation onwards. The two entities are not the same, and McLaren rightly stresses the confusion that results from failing to recognize this:

> If this entity forming around the primitive streak is the embryo ... what are we to call the entire collection of cells derived from the fertilised egg, of which the embryo is a tiny subset? In recent years, we researchers have developed the bad habit of calling the whole set of cells, at each prior stage, the embryo as well. To the non-specialist this is confusing, just as it would be confusing persistently to refer to the [British] Shadow Cabinet as the Labour Party or vice versa.[18]

McLaren is quite correct, although she has, if anything, understated the point: it would be confusing to identify the Shadow Cabinet with the Opposition (Parliamentary) Party because, in any case other than a complete electoral disaster for the Opposition, it would simply be wrong to do so. The Shadow Cabinet is not the Opposition Party, even though it is part of, or comes from, that Party. Even though the Opposition Party can be said to produce the Shadow Cabinet, it is not itself the Shadow Cabinet. The two are distinct entities.

The same is true of the human conceptus after fertilisation and what we have called the embryo proper. The embryo proper is part of the organic system that develops from the fertilised egg, it comes from the fertilised egg, but it is not itself the same entity as the fertilised egg.[19]. The fertilised egg produces the embryo proper, but it is not itself the embryo proper. That is, the fertilised egg has the potential *to produce*, but not the potential *to become*, the embryo proper. But it is the potential *to become*, not the potential *to produce*, which is the kind of potential peculiar to individuals, and which is therefore the only kind of potential that can be plausibly regarded as capable of grounding whatever respect is due to an individual in virtue of its own capacities. Therefore the human conceptus, prior to the formation of the embryo proper, does not possess the kind of potential necessary for rendering respect for its capacities an appropriate response.[20]

But if the human conceptus prior to the formation of the embryo proper does not itself possess the potential *to become* a human subject, and therefore does not possess the kind of potential necessary for it to be accorded recognition as worthy of respect for its capacities, then the individual-respecting version of the argument from potential does not apply to the fertilised egg, or to subsequent stages prior to the formation of the embryo proper. As it stands, then, this version of the argument from potential does not establish the conclusion it is commonly thought to establish, the conclusion reached by the Tate Committee majority.

To conclude this section, it should also be observed that the moral significance of this version of the argument from potential has not been established, nor has it been denied. All that has been determined is where the argument applies, and where it does not. Therefore, to argue, as above, that this version of the argument provides no support for the conclusions of the majority report is not to argue that where the argument does apply, there it is morally decisive, or even significant. The discussion of this argument has concluded only that it cannot apply where there is no embryo proper; it has not concluded that where it does apply, there it is decisive. The special moral significance of this form of potential, and, therefore, of the embryo proper, remains to be settled.[21]

The Consequentialist Argument

The consequentialist version of the argument that the capacity to develop morally significant characteristics is itself morally significant is, fortunately, much less complicated than the 'respect for the capacities of individuals' version. As a result, it is also much easier to determine its implications. As already noted, this version of the argument focuses on the potential of an entity *to produce* morally significant states of affairs (commonly, but not necessarily, this state of affairs will be the existence of a future being), rather than on its potential *to become* a being of a certain kind.

On this version, then, tangled questions concerning whether or not there exists a being which will itself become the future being (mercifully) do not arise. For this reason, there is no important distinction to be drawn between the fertilised egg and the embryo proper. Both have the potential *to produce* a future human subject. (Whether they have the same such potential, or whether it is possible to accord degrees of potential *to produce*, will not be considered here.) So it may seem that this version of the argument is more promising as a support for the conclusions of the Tate majority report.

This, however, is not the case. For the majority report, the crucial distinction, as far as moral status is concerned, is between the fertilised egg on the one hand, and, on the other, the sperm and unfertilised egg. But, from a consequentialist standpoint, there is no crucial moral difference between the two states of affairs. This is so because the sperm and unfertilised egg, when considered jointly, also have the potential *to produce* a future human subject, even though that potential is not *activated* until fertilisation occurs. So this version of the argument does not establish a crucial difference in moral status between the fertilised egg and its biological forebears.

Does this mean that the consequentialist version of the argument must conclude that we ought not to interfere with, perhaps even encourage the conjunction of, any specific sperm and egg pair? This does not follow, because this version of the argument attaches moral significance to the potential *to produce* (that is, to the presently existing capacities), only derivatively. The central locus of moral value is here, as it is for all consequentialist arguments, not present potentialities but future realities. It is to what will be produced: that is, to the future human subject. The present potential (*to produce*) bears moral weight according to the moral weight of the possible future human subject. This means that, although it has genuine moral significance, this significance is not of the kind sought in the 'respect for capacities' version of the argument, but that significance necessary to figure in calculations concerning best outcomes.

So, in the end, this version of the argument from potential is best understood as one form of an argument about the moral significance of possible or future human subjects. As such, it is thus not unlike the argument from mere possibility considered above. Although it focuses on specific individuals, the moral weight of the argument rests on the value of possible future states of affairs; values which are ascertained by comparison with other possible futures. This point can be more fully explained as follows. If allowing a present embryo to develop will produce a future state that is less valuable than preventing the development of this embryo, and developing instead another, not yet conceived, embryo (for example, if the present one is suffering from a congenital defect, or if the parents or other appropriately placed parties are unable to care adequately for it), then a straightforward application of consequentialist principles requires that we follow the latter course. This course, however, attaches less moral significance to an actual being than to a merely possible one, because, in this case at least, the greater moral value is achieved thereby. What course should be followed, then, is not, on this view, determined by whether there is or is not an actually existing entity, but by determining the best outcome, regardless of whether this outcome is to be achieved by actual or merely possible entities.[22]

For the determined defender of the special moral significance of the potentiality *to produce*, there remains one possible recourse. Instead of accepting that the potential *to produce* is therefore of no special moral significance, being a feature of some, but not all, possible future human subjects, and therefore a feature of some, but not all, of the members of the relevant class of morally significant entities; one could cling to the special moral value of the potential *to produce* by arguing that this potential attaches not merely to actual, but also to possible, entities. But this is indeed a desperate move, and, in any case, reduces this form of potential to mere possibility quite unequivocally. It has little, if anything, to recommend it (save its indulgence in a fashionable vocabulary). It certainly makes no moral difference—as before, the moral course of action is determined by considering both actual and possible entities.

What all this means, as far as our practical purposes here are concerned, is that the consequentialist version of the potentiality (cum-possibility) argument has implications even more contrary to the conclusions of the majority report of the Tate Committee than the 'respect for capacities' version of the argument. For the consequentialist argument does not identify a point (a marker event) beyond which experimentation cannot be justified. This does not mean, it should be stressed, that it can be used to support experimentation willy-nilly. Far from it: what it means is that the justifiability of any particular research project is a matter of the perceivable costs and benefits likely to be achieved thereby, costs and benefits which will clearly include those to the developing foetus if it has reached a stage where it can be affected (and perhaps in other cases as well). Such projects will therefore justifiably involve more extensive experimentation on human embryos, provided the goals of such research are both sufficiently valuable and clearly achievable. Thus Dr Alan Trounson, in his submission to the Tate Committee, argued that 'if suddenly we get the answer to the whole of cancer or the whole of every debilitating disease by studying 200 28-day embryos', such study (presumably destructive) would be defensible (3.16). Dr Trounson's argument here is clearly inspired by consequentialist considerations, and his argument serves well to illustrate the sorts of arguments possible within a consequentialist framework.

The point here is not whether or not such arguments are compelling. It is, rather, to give an idea of where consequentialist arguments may lead; and to underline the fact of their divergence from the conclusions arrived at by the Tate Committee's majority report. So both versions of the argument from potential imply conclusions different from those arrived at by the majority report. If the report's conclusions are not to be abandoned, it is necessary to provide them with some foundation other than that of potentiality.

It is perhaps necessary to answer one possible complaint

244 STEPHEN BUCKLE

about the method employed in this discussion of the potentiality arguments. It is surely cheating, it might be objected, to
divide what is normally presented as one argument into two,
and then to show that the argument fails because neither half
of it gives the conclusion sought. Why cannot the argument be
understood as some combination of these two sorts of common
moral consideration (i.e. of consequences and respect for
individuals), and as such a combination come up with the
anticipated conclusion? The short answer to this objection is
that perhaps the best version of this type of argument would
indeed combine both sorts of consideration in some way, but
that it is very difficult to see how it could establish the claims of
the fertilised egg to possess the relevant potential in a way that
excluded both its antecedents and consequents. It is difficult to
see this because the combined argument would either recognize moral significance in the existence of the relevant kind of
individual, or it would not. But in the former case, there is no
good reason for thinking that the relevant individual could be
the fertilised egg rather than the embryo proper; and in the
latter, there is no reason for focusing on existing individuals at
all, and hence no reason for thinking that the fertilised egg
will come to carry any moral weight denied it by the consequentialist version of the argument already considered. So there
seems to be no reason for departing from the conclusions
already established.

The Dissenting Report

To this point, we have been concerned to show two possible
ways of construing the argument from potential, and to argue
that neither version establishes the moral distinctiveness of the
fertilised egg. In this section, we shall examine the report of the
dissenting minority of the Tate Committee, because they also
argue that, properly interpreted, considerations of potential do
not indicate any special status for the fertilised egg. It may be
thought, then, that this section will provide a defence of the
dissenting opinion. This is not so; although it will be argued
that a revised version of the argument of the minority report may bear fruit. As it stands, however, the minority
report provides a good example of one of the ways of arguing
about potential that this paper has shown to be inadequate.
Illustrating some of these inadequacies will be helpful, because doing so will serve to clarify the account of potential
offered in this paper, and to avoid some further pitfalls. It can

then be shown how a more viable reconstructed argument is possible.

The minority report advocates adoption of the marker event proposed by the Ethics Committee of the National Health and Medical Research Council of Australia—the stage of implantation in the uterus, a process which normally comes to completion around the fourteenth day after fertilisation. Although this is a different criterion to that implied by the individual-respecting version of the potentiality argument, it refers to a similar stage of development. (The embryo proper begins to form as the process of implantation reaches completion.) Further, the minority report's defence of this proposal depends on no new principles. Like the majority report, it too appeals to potential to ground its conclusions. In somewhat similar vein to the individual-respecting version of the argument already considered, the minority report argues that prior to the proposed marker event there is in fact no potential at all, and that therefore the argument from potential does not apply prior to this event. So, like the analysis of the argument from potential provided above, the minority report seeks not to discredit the argument from potential, but to show that, properly understood, the argument gives rise to conclusions quite different from those reached in the majority report.

In this attempt, however, the minority report fails, because it depends on an inadequate notion of potentiality. In terms of the account of potential offered in this paper, it confuses potential with the probability of that potential's actualization.[23] It identifies the potential of any entity with that entity's probable future. It holds, for example, that 'developmental potential is dependent on successful implantation, or at least the opportunity for this to occur' (D.26).[24] In the following discussion, this position will first be spelt out a little more fully. Then its weaknesses will be pointed out, and a contrast drawn with the account of potential provided in this paper.

The identification in the minority report of the potential of a being and its probable future is best illustrated by the following passage:

Any object or thing has an infinite number of possible future courses. For a non-sentient or inanimate thing, e.g. a rock, the particular future outcome that actually happens is determined by forces outside itself. An embryo is like a rock in this respect—it cannot make decisions for itself. Its future is decided by others. It has potential only in virtue of

246   STEPHEN BUCKLE

decisions by others about it. If there is a clearly defined
responsible party or parties their decisions determine the
embryo's potential and that becomes the embryo's potential
(D.20).

The inadequacies of this approach, even for the purposes of
the minority report, can be illustrated as follows. The argument
provides no support for the view that implantation in the
uterus is an event of moral significance, for even where such
implantation is the consequence of a specific decision to that
effect (as is so in the IVF case), new decisions can be made
concerning, and can therefore modify the potential of, the
embryo at any stage before it becomes capable of deciding for
itself. Given that even new-born infants lack the capacity to
choose for themselves, this account effectively denies potential
a role in governing the decisions we make about foetuses
(whatever their stage of development), and even of new-born
infants. In all such cases, the potential of the being could be
determined only by the decisions we make about it. The
minority report thus removes any guiding role for arguments
from potential. If, as the report seeks to establish, implantation
is to matter as an event of moral significance, it must be for
reasons other than the potential of the embryo.
    This is sufficient to show that the relevant notion of potential
has been lost. For the notion of potential employed in moral
arguments is not a mere free rider. The potential of a being is,
in all such arguments, advanced as a reason for acting in certain
ways rather than in others: it is not a consequence of such
actions. If we insist instead that potential is a power possessed
by a being, we can neatly capture this feature of such arguments. An everyday example will serve to show this. If a child is
declared to be a potential Mozart, this is a judgement about the
child's talent (one of the more common terms in which
potentiality judgements can be expressed). If the child's parents
decide to discontinue the piano lessons necessary for becoming
a Mozart, the child's potential is no more affected than is its
talent. Its potential is, however, a reason for the parents not to
discontinue the lessons. The lessons (and, indirectly, the
parents' decisions about them) are important because of the
potential they serve to realize; not because they constitute, or
even partially constitute, that potential. The minority report's
account of potential, and the anomalous results to which it gives
rise, can thus be construed as a confusion of causes with their
effects. It should therefore be rejected.

If we now return to the question of implantation, we can see that, on the account of potential provided in this paper, it is not potential but the likelihood that potential will be actualized that is dependent on the decision to implant. It is *because of* the potential of the entity that implantation is a crucial factor in its development. Acorns do not become potential oak trees when they are planted; rather, because they *are* potential oak trees, when they are planted they begin the journey towards being actual oak trees. As previously stressed, the potentiality of an entity is not what it will probably become, but the power it has to become something, whether or not that becoming is probable. An entity is a potential X if it has the power to become X; that is, if it will become X in virtue of the operation or expression of properties of its own, given circumstances conducive to the operation or expression of those properties.[25] If the relevant circumstances do not apply, then of course it will not become X, but this shows only that its potential will be frustrated (will not be actualized), not that it lacks such potential. The possibility of frustrating an entity's potential reflects the fact that being a potential X is not a sufficient condition for becoming an X.[26]

Finally, it has been shown that the minority report's account of potentiality is inadequate. However, this does not mean that the dissenting report must fail, despite the fact that its major conclusions—most notably, on the central role allotted to responsible decision-makers rather than on determination of the status of the conceptus (see D.126, for example)—reflect its account of potentiality. If anything, such recommendations can be defended rather more persuasively once the erroneous account of potentiality is set aside. This is so because the dissenting report's conclusions, or other conclusions not markedly dissimilar, can be rebuilt on more adequate grounds. Rebuilding thus is possible because this report implicitly rejects the individual-regarding version of the potentiality argument by focusing on decisions about the embryo rather than on questions of the embryo's own status. Its basic viewpoint can therefore be reasonably captured by some version of the consequentialist argument: it is perhaps best understood as an attempt to determine the scope, and proper bearers, of responsibilities for possible future human subjects. Thus understood, the dissenting report can be detached not only from its explicit dependence on a defective notion of potentiality but from any appeal to potentiality at all, as the account of the consequentialist version of the argument has shown. The

248   STEPHEN BUCKLE

dissenting viewpoint could then be reconstructed along the best available consequentialist lines.[27]

Concluding Remarks

This paper has attempted to distinguish between different ways of thinking about potential, and different ways of arguing from the senses thus distinguished. It has applied the results gained to the conclusions drawn from potentiality arguments by the Australian Senate Select Committee's report, *Human Embryo Experimentation In Australia*. It has been argued, firstly, that neither version of the argument supports the common belief that considerations of potentiality establish the special moral status of the fertilised egg, which is also the conclusion reached in the majority report. Secondly, it has been shown that an alternative employment of the argument in the dissenting report utilises a notion of potentiality which is seriously inadequate, but which can be reconstructed as a consequentialist argument from possibility.

If the general thrust of the discussion of potentiality in this paper is defensible, then the philosophical debate about arguments from potential is deficient in two related respects: the relevant notion of potentiality is frequently misunderstood, and, as a result, some fundamental differences of interpretation —reflecting deep-seated commitments to either deontological or consequentialist moral thinking—go unrecognized, thus serving to obscure the precise nature and source of the disagreement. It is perhaps too much to hope that this will actually help to settle those disagreements; but it should serve to illuminate some previously unrecognized strengths and weaknesses of the more common positions.

Centre for Human Bioethics
Monash University, Victoria, Australia

NOTES

1   This qualification can be understood in two ways: either as a denial of any moral difference between acts and omissions, or as a judgement about the degrees of stringency of our duties (we may have a stronger duty to do no harm than to do positive good).

2   This paper employs the term 'human subject' rather than some more common similar terms—such as 'person' or Michael Lockwood's use of 'human being' (see 'When Does A Life Begin?' in Lockwood (ed.) *Moral Dilemmas in Modern Medicine*, Oxford: Oxford University Press (1985),

ARGUING FROM POTENTIAL 249

pp.10–14). It (i.e. 'human subject') is a moral rather than a biological term, meaning a human organism of moral and therefore legal considerability. As such it is a content-free, or purely formal notion, and has been employed in later parts of this paper because it is conveniently agnostic about contentious issues.

3 There is a place for speaking of the *normal* course of events in contexts such as these, provided that the meaning, and the point, are both made clear. As Michael Tooley rightly points out, 'normal' cannot mean *statistically* normal. (See *Abortion and Infanticide*, Oxford: Clarendon Press (1983), section 6.1.) It must, rather, be understood in terms of biological normality, that is, in terms of the proper functioning of the relevant biological processes. (This path is indicated, but not pursued, in an unpublished paper by Michaelis Michael, 'The Moral Significance of Potential for Personhood'.) This point can be readily misunderstood. It is not that judgements of potential depend on distinguishing normal (or natural) environments from artificial ones. It is, rather, that potential can be frustrated or inhibited, and so depends on 'sympathetic', or at least non-inhibitory, environments in order to be expressed. The appeal to the normal (i.e., in this case, biologically functional) course of events must be understood to be an appeal to an environment which is assumed to be appropriately sympathetic. (An evolutionary account of natural environments as mutually adaptive systems could be called on to support the assumption.)

4 *Human Embryo Experimentation In Australia*, report of the Senate Select Committee On The Human Embryo Experimentation Bill 1985, chaired by Senator Michael Tate, Canberra: Australian Government Publishing Service (1986). This report will subsequently be referred to as the Tate Report; references in the text are to paragraph numbers in this report. It is also most important to recognize that the report employs the term 'embryo' to refer to the earliest stages of human life, including the just-fertilised egg, in contrast to much recent scientific practice. It will be argued below that this is regrettable.

5 The report thus equates the moral duties due to the embryo with the duties determined by establishing its 'moral status'. It is not uncommon for bioethical arguments of this sort to be interpreted as attempts to establish the moral status of the being or life in question, where a being's moral status is understood to be determined by its possession (or degree of possession) of morally relevant characteristics. (Most commonly, characteristics such as being sentient or self-conscious, or possessing interests, are advanced as morally relevant characteristics. It is not clear that the embryo possesses any of these, so, if the embryo is to have a moral status, this list must be expanded.)

Although it does not follow necessarily, it is also often assumed, on this approach, that moral behaviour is essentially a matter of respecting the moral status of other beings. Without doubt, this approach is frequently very fruitful. However, as an account of the nature of morality it suffers from some very definite shortcomings. For example, it is widely recognized that our moral duties include such things as providing appropriate burials, and burial ceremonies, for the dead. But this is either a duty to a corpse (which is entirely deficient in sentience, etc) or to a non-existent being (the person who has died). In neither case is there an existing being with a moral status which commands respect. If there is a genuine duty

250   STEPHEN BUCKLE

here, it cannot be because of the moral status of the being for whom the ceremonies are performed.

These matters are worth keeping in mind, because critics of the argument from potential seem frequently to assume that, if it can be shown that the argument does not establish the special moral status of the earliest forms of human life, then it is a failure. This does not necessarily follow. It may be that the argument can be interpreted as an implicit rejection of the adequacy of 'moral status' methods of moral thinking.

6 The conclusions of the majority report thus depend not merely on the argument from potential, but also on the view that fertilisation is the only decisive event in the course of the development of the human infant: from fertilisation until birth there are no other such events because the course of development is a continuous process. Presumably, it is being suggested here that, if the facts of development were otherwise (more disjointed?), other considerations could then come to override the fertilised egg's potential.

For all their widespread appeal, arguments of this kind are surprisingly weak. I have discussed some aspects in 'Biological Processes and Moral Events', *Journal of Medical Ethics* (forthcoming). For a more detailed discussion of relevant issues, see Bernard Williams, 'Which Slopes Are Slippery?', in Lockwood (ed.), *op. cit.*, pp.126–37; and 'Types of Moral Argument against Embryo Research', in The Ciba Foundation, *Human Embryo Research: Yes or No?*, London: Tavistock (1986), pp.185–94.

7 See, for example, John Harris, '*In Vitro* Fertilization: The Ethical Issues', *Philosophical Quarterly* 33 (1983), p.223: 'the fact that something will become x ... is not a good reason for treating it now as if it had become x'. However, in arguing thus Harris attaches too much importance to a particular formulation of the argument. To treat something in the same way as an x is not therefore to treat it as if it were an x (even though defenders of the argument, for example the Tate majority itself, sometimes think the argument either does or should establish the latter position).

8 For this reason this paper will not adjudicate on the two kinds of reasons. To attempt to do so would be to attempt to settle one fundamental problem of moral philosophy—the strengths and limitations of deontological and consequentialist considerations in moral thinking.

9 Although it is not, of course, a sufficient claim to establish this point, I think the insistence, by advocates of this version of the argument, that the fertilised egg is itself a human being is best interpreted in this light. At least, such claims rarely distinguish between the embryo's being biologically human and its claims as a member of the human moral community, and this is a gap which is most easily bridged if it is assumed that the embryo and the person into which (mishaps aside) it grows are one and the same. See, for example, the Sacred Congregation For The Doctrine Of The Faith, *Instruction on Respect for Human Life in its Origin and on the Dignity of Procreation*, Homebush, N.S.W.: St Paul Publications (1987), p.19:

> I.1 What respect is due to the human embryo taking into account his nature and identity?
> The human being must be respected—as a person—from the very first instant of his existence.

10 This terminology is introduced with some trepidation. There is a

common, broad, use of 'become' which means, roughly, *turn into*, and which therefore straddles precisely the gap I am marking out—because a being can be said to turn into some other being which is quite different (i.e. which is not 'the very same being'). Despite this problem, I have persevered with the term, mainly because the most obvious alternatives sound rather strained. In order to keep it clear that the term is employed with a distinctively narrow meaning, I have resorted to the rather unattractive stratagem of stressing it, and its companion term, whenever they appear in the text.

11 Harris, *op. cit.*

12 The power in question is, as the preceding discussion has implied, a causal power. This way of putting the matter will not, of course, recommend itself to advocates of regularity theories of causation, especially since, on that theory, it is events, rather than entities, which can be said to be causes. This difference helps us to see that the concept of an entity's potential reflects a philosophical perspective which has fallen on hard times. It is not, for all that, an indefensible position. One defence of this way of understanding objects in the world, as repositories of powers, is provided by R. Harré and E. H. Madden, *Causal Powers*, Oxford: Basil Blackwell (1975). The following quotation (pp.5–6) can serve as a brief summary of their position:

> The location of causal power or potency in things and materials need not be conceived as the attribution of occult and mysterious properties but can be given a quite unproblematic basis in the chemical, physical or genetic natures of the entities involved. The combining power or valency of a chemical atom is located in its electronic constitution and structure, and the power to resist shearing forces which a metal may have is located in its crystalline form. The re-emphasis upon the nature of things leads to a reintroduction of the concept of natural kind, exemplified in such ideas as the genotype of an organism or the subatomic structure of the atoms of an element.

One noteworthy feature of the Tate majority's notion of an entity *oriented towards* further development is that it appears to be an attempt to capture this sort of idea. An entity oriented towards X is, *ipso facto*, not purely passive. It is not an entity to which X merely happens, but is at least a contributory cause of the occurrence of X.

Harré and Madden contrast their view to what they call the 'Humean' view. However, although it is quite common to trace the regularity theory to Hume, it is not certain that he held to it. See, most notably, Norman Kemp Smith, *The Philosophy of David Hume*, London: Macmillan (1941), pp.91–2, and Barry Stroud, *Hume*, London: Routledge & Kegan Paul (1977), pp.88–92. The compatibility of the traditional interpretation of Hume with the arguments of Kemp Smith and his successors is defended by Tom L. Beauchamp and Alexander Rosenberg, *Hume and the Problem of Causation*, New York: Oxford University Press (1981), Ch.1.

13 The identity which is preserved in such cases is not *personal* identity, of course, since the embryo is not a person. Nor is it qualitative identity, since the actual being (of whatever kind) must possess qualities which the potential being lacks. It is, rather, what Parfit calls *numerical* identity—the potential and actual beings are identical in that they are the same single thing, albeit at different stages of development. For Parfit's discussion, see *Reasons and Persons*, Oxford: Clarendon Press (1984), ch.10.

252 STEPHEN BUCKLE

14 For a discussion of this question, see Helga Kuhse and Peter Singer, 'The Moral Status of the Embryo', in William Walters and Peter Singer (eds.), *Test-Tube Babies*, Melbourne: Oxford University Press (1982), pp.57–63.

15 Some of the problems raised by parthenogenesis are discussed by Peter Singer and Karen Dawson, 'IVF Technology and the Argument from Potential', *Philosophy and Public Affairs* (forthcoming).

16 See Singer and Dawson, *op. cit.*; also Brian Scarlett (with a response from Peter Singer and Helga Kuhse), 'The Moral Status of Embryos', *Journal of Medical Ethics*, 10 (1984), pp.79–81.

17 Anne McLaren, 'Why Study Early Human Development?', *New Scientist*, 24 April 1986, p.49.

18 *ibid.*

19 One way of avoiding this conclusion would be to argue that the extra-embryonic materials are external organs of the embryo which fulfil their purposes early in life, and are then discarded. The placenta, etc, could then be viewed as akin to a tadpole's gills, or (in the latter respect only) as like human milk teeth. This view is held by N. Tonti-Filippini and T. V. Daly, S.J., 'Experimenting with the Origins of Human Lives', a submission to the Tate committee. See *Senate Select Committee on the Human Embryo Experimentation Bill 1985* (Official Hansard Report), Canberra: Commonwealth Government Printer (1986), p.187.

   This is an argument well worth putting, but it is by no means conclusive. It seems most plausible with respect to the placenta, but rather less so with respect to the other extra-embryonic membranes. But even as an account of the placenta it is not without problems. The fact that the placenta has the same DNA as the developing embryo does not establish the conclusion, because this is also true of identical twins, which are clearly not (parts of) the same organism. A complete response to this view cannot be attempted here, because it would require a more detailed account of the earliest stages of (pre) embryonic development. Although it cannot be regarded as a complete answer, I think it is best to settle with claiming that this view becomes less plausible when we attend to the details of the earliest stages of development: for example, a particular object seems an unconvincing candidate as an organ of another entity if it begins to develop from material which is quite distinct from the material which forms the latter entity. The longer quotation from McLaren (above) helps to indicate this degree of separateness, but the point can be strengthened by considering the case of late twinning (at the time of formation of the primitive streak). Where twinning occurs at this late stage, there is no corresponding twinning of the extra-embryonic material, placenta included. The placenta thus behaves in such cases as an entity which is quite separate from the developing embryonic material. (It might be thought that this could be regarded as a case of a shared organ, as happens with Siamese twins, but the two cases are quite different. In the case of Siamese twins, there is an incomplete twinning of the embryonic material, generating two inter-dependent individuals; whereas the case under consideration does not involve a process which fails to reach completion, nor—without begging the question—can it be said to produce interdependence, even though it is certainly a case of *shared* dependence. But *every* set of embryonic twins display that kind of dependence.)

20 It should be noted here that it has not been shown that the potential *to become* does command the relevant kind of respect; only that, if potential

commands such respect, then that potential must be the potential *to become*.

21 In fact, if we were to follow the lead of Parfit, and conclude that our identity is not what matters (see Part Three of *Reasons and Persons*), the heavy reliance on identity in this version of the argument would suggest that, as a moral argument, its concern is quite misplaced. However, it is not the purpose of this paper to debate the pros and cons of Parfit's views.

22 This type of approach is characteristic of R. M. Hare's employment of potentiality arguments. Hare translates all talk of potential into questions of possibilities, and then uses this as a device not for respecting individuals, but for choosing between the claims of various possible persons in order to determine which embryos should be protected. See, most notably, 'Survival of the Weakest', in Samuel Gorovitz et al. (ed.), *Moral Problems in Medicine*, New Jersey: Prentice-Hall (1976), pp.364–9.

23 As such, it is rather similar to the equation of potentiality with possibility, at least in so far as both can be construed as confusing the cause with its effect.

24 The qualification added here indicates a degree of uncertainty about how tightly to constrain the criteria for possessing developmental potential. Since nothing of substance hangs on how tight the constraints are here (in either case the crucial role is accorded to the actions and decisions of adult agents), we can overlook any complications this qualification may introduce.

25 This means, incidentally, that where the powers of an entity can be changed by intervention, in those cases the potential can be changed. In the case of a fertilised egg, its powers, as already noted, reside in its DNA, particularly in its genes. So, although the minority report is wrong in thinking that implantation changes the fertilised egg's potential, it is not wrong in thinking that the potential of the egg can be changed by human action—for gene therapy, at least, is a way of changing the egg's potential. The same will hold, *mutatis mutandis*, for other sorts of entity. Suppose it becomes possible to change the DNA of chestnuts so that they, like acorns, develop into oak trees. The DNA-remodelled chestnuts will therefore be, like acorns, potential oak trees. All other (pristine) chestnuts, however, although they will indeed be possible oak trees, will not be potential oak trees. Only by having their DNA remodelled can they acquire that potential.

26 In this paragraph I have simplified exposition by considering only the potential *to become*; but the same relations hold for the potential *to produce*. Most importantly, having the potential to produce (an) X is not a sufficient condition for producing (an) X. I hope the terminology employed in this paper does not mislead with respect to this particular relation.

27 To confirmed deontologists, this would not appear to promise much. However, in cases which do not involve actual persons, it is worth asking whether the more common objections to consequentialist reasoning get any powerful grip. In such cases, the main objection to consequentialism appears to depend on the 'respect for capacities' version of the argument from potential, so an evaluation of that argument will play a crucial role in resolving this issue. For a strong presentation of the consequentialist case see Parfit's 'Rights, Interests, and Possible People', in Gorovitz, *op. cit.*, pp.369–75.

[11]

Why Potentiality Matters

JIM STONE
University of New Orleans
New Orleans, LA 70148
U.S.A.

Do fetuses have a right to life in virtue of the fact that they are potential adult human beings?[1] I take the claim that the fetus is a potential adult human being to come to this: if the fetus grows normally there will be an adult human animal that was once the fetus. Does this fact ground a claim to our care and protection? A great deal hangs on the answer to this question. The actual mental and physical capacities of a human fetus are inferior to those of adult creatures generally thought to lack a serious right to life (e.g., adult chickens), and the mere fact that a fetus belongs to *our* species in particular seems morally irrelevant. Consequently, a strong fetal claim to protection rises or falls with the appeal to the fetus's potentiality, for nothing else can justify it.

The appeal to fetal potentiality is often dismissed as implausible — what have a creature's potential properties to do with its present rights? — and because it is thought to lead to moral absurdities: won't we have to extend human rights to sperms, eggs, and clonable cells in virtue of their potentiality too? Further, some philosophers deny that the future entity which will have a right to life was ever a fetus. I will argue that the potentiality of the fetus grounds a strong claim to care and protection. In part I, I defend this thesis against the objec-

---

1 A note on terminology: By 'human being' I mean any animal which is a member of the species *homo sapiens*. A human baby is an animal which is a member of *homo sapiens*, when it is young, and a human fetus is an animal which is a member of *homo sapiens*, when it is still younger. The fetus is simply a very young human being: this much follows from modern biology and embryology. But it cuts no moral ice. The mere fact that a creature is a member of a particular species does not entail that it has (or lacks) a right to life. The question is: When and in virtue of what do members of the species *homo sapiens* (human beings) acquire a right to life? This doesn't answer itself.

tion that it leads to absurdity. In part II, I argue for its plausibility. Part III responds to objections derived from an appeal to the notion of *personhood* and the Psychological Criterion of personal identity.

I

The most popular objection to the appeal to potentiality is that it leads straight to absurdity. L.W. Sumner writes, 'But then if protection of life is to be extended back to fetuses, embryos, or zygotes in virtue of their potential, it must by parity of reasoning be extended back also to ova and spermatozoa in virtue of theirs.'[2] Sumner's *reductio* depends upon the assumption that a sperm or an egg is a potential adult human being. Is this true?

If we read the assumption as we did the claim about the fetus, we must say that a sperm or an egg is a potential adult human being only if, granting certain conditions, there will be an adult human animal which is identical to it. Suppose that a sperm penetrates an egg producing a zygote which in time becomes an adult human being. The sperm and the egg cannot *each* be identical to the adult human being they produce, for then, by the transitivity of identity, they are identical to each other, which is manifestly false. Can the adult human being be identical to just *one* of them? Whatever claim the sperm has to be identical to the adult animal it produces seems to be matched, hence cancelled, by that of the ovum, and vice versa. Further, if the adult human being is identical to the sperm, it follows (by the indiscernibility of identicals) that the animal which is now adult once fertilized an egg. This seems plainly false, though it is true that this animal once had only a few cells and was attached to the wall of a womb. Further, the sperm could have penetrated a different egg producing another zygote. But then, *if* the sperm is identical to the zygote it in fact produces (as it must be if it is to be identical to the adult the zygote produces), then (by parity of reasoning) the sperm would have been identical to this other zygote too. It follows (again by the indiscernibility of identicals) that the zygote the sperm actually produces *is* the zygote the sperm would have produced if it had penetrated a different egg. Plainly this is false. It follows that the sperm is not identical to the zygote it produces; but then it is not identical to the adult human animal either. The same reasoning applies to the egg.[3]

---

2 L.W. Sumner, *Abortion and Moral Theory* (Princeton, NJ: Princeton University Press 1981) 104

3 The embryo can produce different animals too: if the blastula divides it will pro-

The sperm and the egg cannot both be identical to the adult human being, nor can that creature be identical to just one of them. One possibility remains. We can maintain that the adult human being is identical to the composite or collection of the egg and the sperm; the two of them taken together constitute the earliest stage of the human animal, which exists before conception in a divided form. This leads to bizarre consequences. If the animal which becomes an adult human being existed before conception in a divided form, then it would have existed if it had never been conceived, for if a material thing exists at a time, it exists at that time no matter what happens at a later time. Further, it follows that this animal would have existed if the egg and sperm had found different partners. Given two sperms and two eggs we have four human animals, only two of which can survive their initial stages.[4] We are committed to the absurdity that the planet sustains billions of additional animals, each existing in a divided form from beginning to end, its cells having nothing to do with one another ever, and each cell part of countless other animals of the same kind. Plainly the human animal does not exist before conception: my body was once a fetus but never a sperm or an egg. Both the sperm and the egg can produce something which has the potential of becoming an adult human being, but neither the sperm nor the egg has that potential itself.

The assertion that the fetus is a potential adult human being, I maintain, comes to the claim that the fetus is identical to the adult human animal it will produce if it develops normally.[5] But this reading isn't

---

duce two animals, neither of which is identical to the animal it actually produces. But then doesn't the last argument show that the *embryo* isn't identical to the animal it actually produces? That argument depends upon the premiss 'If the sperm is identical to the zygote it in fact produces, then (by parity of reasoning) it would be identical to the zygote it would produce if it combined with a different egg'; plainly this premiss is true. But it is false that if the embryo is identical to the animal it actually produces, then (by parity of reasoning) it would be identical to the *animals* if would produce if it divided; one cannot be two. So the argument fails for the embryo.

4 We might try to blunt this point by denying that the human animal is an *animal* at its earliest stage: these four entities aren't animals though two will *become* animals if they survive. But this is entirely ad hoc: we shouldn't abandon the principle that animals form a natural kind (hence are animals throughout their careers) simply to avoid an inconvenient consequence of the claim that animals exist before conception. Further, we must deny that human animals were animals in their earliest stage *even though* they were living things composed of human cells – the sperm and the egg.

5 Note that 'fetus' refers to the animal which is at the fetal stage, not to the stage itself. 'Fetus' is like 'child' in 'This child will inherit a fortune when she is thirty.' The fetus can grow up, the fetal stage cannot.

forced upon us by the language of potentiality: we often say that something A is a potential B even though we know (or ought to) that A will not be identical to the B if a B is produced. A house, for example, is a potential pile of ashes, though it must cease to exist in order to produce them. A lump of bronze is a potential statue, though it isn't identical to any statue into which it is made because it precedes any such statue. Further, the lump of bronze is potentially *many* different statues. As we have seen, it follows that the bronze cannot be identical to the statue into which it is made, for then it would have been identical to these other statues if it had been made into them, hence the statue into which it is made would have been identical to these statues too. It seems sufficient for something A to be a potential B that A can be an element in a causal condition that produces a B and, further, the matter of A will be (or will at least help produce) the matter of the B. But then the sperm is a potential human being even though it will not be identical to the adult animal it produces.

We need to distinguish a strong from a weak reading of the claim that A is a potential B.[6] The weak reading requires only the two conditions I just stated; the strong reading adds the requirement that A will produce a B if A develops normally and the B so produced will be such that it was once A. The fetus satisfies the requirements for weak potentiality; if we maintain that *this* is sufficient to establish a right to life the *reductio* works, for the sperm and the egg are potential human beings on the weak reading too. But this is to attack a straw man. We ought to take the thesis as I initially construed it: the fact that the fetus will develop into an adult human being that was once that fetus (if the fetus develops normally) establishes the fetus's right to life. This claim is compatible with the fact that an egg and sperm have no rights at all.

But what is *normal* development? Talk of normal development for an entity belonging to a biological kind presupposes the existence of a developmental path determined primarily by the biological natures of members of the kind to which the entity belongs, a path which leads to their adult stage.[7] Further, talk of normal development presupposes

---

6 David B. Annis introduces the notion of 'direct potentiality' — in 'Abortion and the Potentiality Principle,' *The Southern Journal of Philosophy* **22** (1984) 155-63. 'Direct Potentiality' is wholly a matter of causal strength for Annis; it does not involve an identity condition. A distinction closer to the one I want is implicit in Roger Wertheimer's observation that '... people call the zygote a human life ... because it and it alone can claim to be the beginning of the spatiotemporal-causal chain of the physical object that is a human body...' (Roger Wertheimer, 'Understanding the Abortion Argument,' *Philosophy and Public Affairs* **1** [1971] 67-95, esp. 79).

7 A nature, we might say, is an inner principle a creature has from its beginning,

that the particular entity in question has a nature sufficient to be the primary determinant of its following a path which leads to the adult stage of members of its kind. If a zygote's genetic code is so damaged that it would have to be substantially created before it could be the primary determinant of a developmental path, the zygote is, as Aristotle might have put it, a zygote in name alone, and talk of its normal or abnormal development is idle. We may say then that a biological enti- ty develops normally if it follows to the end the developmental path primarily determined by its nature which leads to the adult stage of members of its kind. On this reading, normal development cannot be meaningfully predicated on something which lacks a nature sufficient to be the primary determinant of a developmental path. A sperm, for instance, lacks such a nature because its chromosomes can only be half of those of any future zygote; this is a second reason why it lacks the strong potentiality to become an adult human being.[8]

The thesis that strong potentiality grounds the fetus's right to life is also compatible with the fact that human cells which (suppose) might be cloned to produce a human body would have no rights. Supposing we could culture a liver cell to produce an embryo, that cell would not be identical to the resulting human being. For the cell ceases to exist upon fissioning: no substance can survive fissioning into duplicate sub- stances. Consequently, no cell the nature of which is to divide into duplicates can have strong potentiality.[9] If we could wave a magic wand

---

which primarily determines a developmental path leading to the creature's adult stage and which also primarily determines the creature's fundamental characteris- tics. A genetic code is a universal because it can have instances, as in the case of identical twins. We might call an instance of a genetic code a *genetic constitu- tion*. In higher animals we can identify a creature's nature with its genetic constitution.

8 A nature sufficient to be the primary determinant of a human developmental path is an *instance* of a human genetic code (what I called a *genetic constitution* in note 7). A genetic code is instantiated when the chromosomes of the sperm and the egg are united; a particular instance of a genetic code first exists at conception. Consequently the composite of the divided sperm and egg lacks a nature suffi- cient to be the primary determinant of a human developmental path.

9 Graeme Forbes observes that 'the zygote ceases to exist upon replication'; he con- cludes that we contradict Leibnitz's Law if we identify the zygote with the result- ing adult. (See Graeme Forbes, *The Metaphysics of Modality* [Oxford: Clarendon Press 1985] 135.) This seems right: one cannot be two. Consequently the zygote lacks strong potentiality. It is only after the first cleavage, about twenty-four hours after conception in a human fetus, that there is an organism which develops with- out fissioning (of course, its *cells* fission). The conclusion that no cell the nature of which is to divide into duplicates can have strong potentiality entails that par-

over a kitten so that it developed into a human being, the original kitten would lack strong potentiality. For if a kitten develops normally,
it will not produce a human animal. However, once the wand is waved
the resulting *embryo* satisfies the requirement for strong potentiality,
hence has a right to life.

II

I have defended the view that the fetus's potentiality grounds a right
to life against the charge that it leads to absurdities. Now I want to
argue for its plausibility. Why should strong potentiality matter morally? And why should the identity component make a moral difference?
To answer these questions I need to consider another: What is the
ground of interests? Joel Feinberg writes: 'Without awareness, expectation, belief, desire, aim, and purpose, a being can have no interests;
without interests he cannot be benefited; without the capacity to be
a beneficiary, he can have no rights.'[10] This theory leads to disturbing
and counter-intuitive consequences: we cannot harm a baby by killing her painlessly, for as the baby lacks the beliefs, expectations, aims,
and purposes required for her to desire to go on living, she has no
interest in continued life. Nor could a baby benefit from receiving lifesaving medical tretment, for example a transfusion or corrective heart
surgery. Feinberg observes that a child's *future* interests can be harmed
by bad treatment now − certainly we shouldn't let her go blind − but
if we refuse the transfusion, then she will have no future, hence no
future interests that we harm by allowing her to die. As interests are
necessary for rights, no infant has a right not to be killed. Even if the
heart surgery is free, a baby could have no more claim to it than a rock
or a tree.

· These conclusions conflict with the prevalent conviction that infants
have a claim to our care and protection, especially in matters of life
and death. Killing a child in her sleep seems an obvious harm, and
most people believe that the child with a defective heart is morally entitled to treatment if it is cheap and effective. If this conviction is not
misguided, infants must have benefits and interests which are not de-

---

thenogenesis, even if it became common, could not establish the strong potentiality of the unfertilized (or the self-fertilized) egg to become an adult human being.

10 Joel Feinberg, 'The Rights of Animals and Unborn Generations,' in Ernest Par-
    tridge, ed., *Responsibilities to Future Generations* (Buffalo, NY: Prometheus Books
    1981) 145

rived from present or future desires, beliefs, aims, and purposes. I think Feinberg is right in linking an animal's welfare to consciousness – the good which constitutes the animal's welfare must be a conscious good – but mistaken in concluding that an animal must consciously desire a welfare to have one. It is only required that the creature has a nature, the actualization of which involves some conscious good for that creature; then its welfare is the actualization of its nature, and anything which enables it to attain its welfare is a benefit. A human infant has a nature the actualization of which involves considerable conscious goods like self-awareness, social interactions, the possibility of moral stature; consequently it is in the interest of a human infant to grow up.

Nature, good, and identity are intimately related. An animal's nature determines a developmental path which guarantees identity, a path that produces the animal's adult stage.[11] In human animals, that stage involves the attainment of conscious goods, which are produced by the nature as it actualizes itself along an identity-preserving path that evolved because it produces those goods. Nature, good, and identity each determine the other, each is an aspect of the other; they are bound in a unity.[12] What the fetus *is* finally, is something that makes *itself* self-aware; that good is the fetus's good – this is its nature. Anything benefits from having the good which it is its nature to make for itself.

I submit that we have a prima facie duty to all creatures not to deprive them of the conscious goods which it is their nature to realize. As the good grows greater, our duty grows stronger and harder to override. Self-awareness, I believe, is greater than mere sentience; hence we have a powerful duty to protect and care for human infants as well as the infants of any species the adult members of which have self-awareness. As this duty is derived from interests which are derived

---

11 The fetus needn't cease to exist if he veers from the developmental path determined by his nature; still that path has a special status. For each creature, there is a set of developmental paths increasingly diverging from the path determined by the creature's genetic constitution. The more paths diverge, the more they are determined by factors other than his genetic constitution: for example, environmental interference or genetic change. The more a path is determined by factors other than his genetic constitution, the less likely it is to be a path which guarantees identity (a path *guarantees* identity when a creature which follows that path *must* survive). Hence the path determined by the creature's genetic constitution is the paradigm of a path which guarantees identity.

12 Note that this account of the relation between nature, good, and identity does not appeal to teleology. The adult stage is not construed as a *final cause* or goal, for the sake of which the organism develops.

from the biological natures of human infants, we have a duty to care
for and protect all human infants with a biological nature sufficient
to realize self-awareness. Now the duty to care for and protect is the
duty to look out for someone's interests, to do what benefits him. A
child's right to life is a *consequence* of his right to care and protection;
it is not fundamental. If a child will grow up, given our care and protection, he has a right to life, for continued life is necessary for the
actualization of his welfare.

But what if a child will not grow up no matter what we do? Suppose
the child is Andrew, a genetically normal infant born recently with only
a brain stem (a cyst covered Andrew's brain stem, preventing the rest
of the brain from forming).[13] A consequence of my view is that we have
as strong a duty to look out for Andrew's interests as we do for any
child's; for if Andrew follows to the end the developmental path
primarily determined by his nature, there will be a self-aware creature
that was once Andrew. But there is only one behaviour that counts
as looking out for Andrew's interests: giving him a treatment that enables his brain to grow. We have the same duty to give Andrew this
treatment if we find it as we have to give corrective surgery to a child
born in a coma on account of a heart defect; both will remain unconscious if untreated, both will become conscious and healthy if treated.
Unlike rocks and trees, Andrew has a welfare—there is a good for
Andrew—but as Andrew will never be conscious, he will never attain
it. Nothing we can do will enable Andrew to actualize his nature, hence
there is nothing we can actually do which benefits him, for Andrew
has no interest in a life he will never experience.[14] So, a biological nature sufficient to realize self-awareness, social interaction, and the possibility of moral stature grounds a right to care and protection, which
grounds a right to life for those children who, given care and protection, will grow up to be self-aware, interact with others, and have the

---

13 *New Orleans Times-Picayune/States Item* (Associated Press, Sept. 25, 1984), 23. The
brain stem provides Andrew with motor functions like breathing and swallow-
ing. I am supposing that Andrew is completely unconscious.

14 Andrew doesn't have a moral right to life, but we have good reasons to treat him
as if he does. For if we allow parents, doctors, or the state to cause Andrew's
death directly or by withholding medical care, we place all handicapped newborns in jeopardy. Indeed, they are already in jeopardy: mildly retarded newborns are sometimes starved to death in American hospitals when parents (often
advised by doctors) refuse the routine surgery that will enable them to eat. Further, we ought to protect Andrew for the sake of those wishing to adopt him—
twenty-four families tried to adopt Andrew and he was finally adopted by a nurse.

possibility of moral stature. This includes almost all retarded and hand-icapped newborns.[15]

Now we can answer the question: Why should strong potentiality matter morally? The fact that an infant has the strong potentiality of becoming an adult human being is the fact that if she follows to the end the developmental path primarily determined by her nature which leads to the adult stage of members of her kind, the infant will produce an adult human animal that was once the infant. This fact, conjoined with the fact that adult human animals are self-aware, entails that the infant has a nature, the actualization of which involves a great conscious good for the infant. This last fact, I have argued, grounds an interest in growing up and a claim to our care and protection; otherwise infants have no interest in growing up and no claim to our care and protection. If the strong potentiality of infants entails a fact that matters, strong potentiality matters. Further, we can see why the identity component of strong potentiality makes a moral difference. For if it is the nature of a creature merely to produce yet another creature which will have a conscious good, that first creature has no conscious good of its own, hence no welfare or rights. As the fetus is identical to the adult animal she produces and identical animals share their properties, the fetus will think, feel, and be self-aware if she develops normally. If we kill the fetus we deprive her of a welfare she would otherwise have realized for herself. The sperm and the egg, on the other hand, can never have these properties even though they can produce something which can. If we kill them there is no good of which they are deprived.

III

But is it true that the embryo, the fetus, and the baby one day can have the rich mental life that characterizes adult human beings? Is the being which will realize these goods the self-same creature as the fetus? Mary Anne Warren writes

---

15 What do we owe an infant with a (supposed) correctible genetic defect that will stop him from growing up? I can only sketch an answer here. If the defect *inhibits* the operation of a complete genetic constitution, the infant has strong potentiality and we ought to correct it. If the infant's genetic constitution is incomplete (e.g., he will not develop a liver), but there is still a developmental path of which it is the primary determinant, namely, the path he will take if we plug the genetic gap, he has strong potentiality and we ought to plug it. If the code is so incomplete that it cannot be the primary determinant of a path, the infant lacks strong potentiality. There *may* be a range of borderline cases.

For personal pronouns like "we" refer to people; we are essentially people if we are essentially anything at all. Therefore, if fetuses and gametes are not people, then we were never fetuses or gametes, though one might say that we emerged from them. The fetus which later *became* you was not *you* because you did not exist at that time…. So if it had been aborted nothing whatever would have been done to *you*, since you would never have existed.[16]

Warren's view is that the being which realizes self-awareness is a person; a person comes into being when it realizes self-awareness;[17] hence a person was never a fetus or an infant. It follows that the fetus, like the sperm, produces a numerically different entity which is the thing that thinks and feels, so the fetus has no welfare of its own.

We might say, following Locke, that a person is 'a thinking, intelligent being, that has reason and reflection, and can consider itself as itself, the same thinking thing in different times and places.'[18] Now I think it very strange to say that adult human animals are not self-aware, that these capacities are realized by yet another thing, so it seems reasonable and ontologically conservative to identify the beings which have reason, reflection, and self-awareness with human animals. That is, human animals which have reason, reflection, and self-awareness are persons.[19] But then, as the animals which exhibit these capacities existed before they had them and were once fetuses, persons existed before they were persons and were once fetuses. Persons aren't numerically different entities which fetuses produce, they are fetuses at a later stage of development; hence fetuses will be self-aware when they become persons. If I am identical to a person, it follows

---

16 Mary Anne Warren, 'Do Potential Persons Have Rights?' in Ernest Partridge, ed., *Responsibilities to Future Generations* (Buffalo, NY: Prometheus Books 1981) 264

17 Warren, 262. Also see p. 272, n.2. I am using 'self-awareness' as a place-marker for the conscious goods which characterize the lives of adult human beings. For Warren, self-awareness is one of a constellation of qualities (such as reason and communication), the absence of all of which precludes personhood.

18 John Locke, *Essay Concerning Human Understanding*, Ch. 27 in J. Perry, ed., *Personal Identity* (Berkeley, CA: University of California Press 1975) 39

19 Locke believes that identity conditions are determined by the idea we have of the entity in question (p. 37 in Perry); in particular, the idea of a person determines that personal identity consists in present consciousness and in memory. In fact, Locke's account of our idea of a person does *not* determine psychological identity conditions: nothing rules out the possibility that this thinking being is a *man*, that is, a living human animal, which can consider itself as itself in different times and places. Here the identity conditions for the sortal *man* do the work (person x at tl = person y at t10 if and only if x is the same man as y) and memory would not be a necessary condition for personal identity.

that there is a person and I have all of his properties. But this person existed before he was a person; indeed he was a fetus. Therefore I existed before I was a person and I was a fetus.[20] Therefore if I am identical to a person, then I am not essentially a person, for persons aren't essentially persons.[21]

Persons cannot be identical to self-aware animals if persons are numerically different from fetuses. Perhaps a person is to a human animal as the statue is to the lump of bronze. The lump of bronze preceded (and might survive) the statue, hence it is not identical to it. Nonetheless the statue is nothing more than the lump of bronze in a particular shape: the statue isn't ontologically extra, it is *constituted* by the lump of bronze. Given the lump of bronze in that shape, the statue cannot fail to exist. Where A is constituted by B, then, except for modal and temporal properties, A and B share all their properties; the statue has the weight, the location, the texture of the bronze. Further, A has its non-modal non-temporal properties *because* B has them.[22] The statue weighs 500 lbs because the lump of bronze has that property, not vice versa. These properties are parasitic on the properties of the bronze. So, if a person is constituted by a human animal they *both* have mental states, self-awareness, and so on; the person is nothing more than the human animal; it is a metaphysical epiphenomenon which owes its non-modal non-temporal properties to the properties of the human animal. Consequently, while the fetus isn't identical to the person who will think, feel, and be self-aware, the fetus *is* identical to the human animal which will think, feel, and be self-aware. So the animal which is a fetus will be self-aware even though it will never be a person.

If the animal which is a fetus is never to be self-aware, it must pro-

---

20 Consequently if that fetus had been aborted, *I* would have been aborted.

21 Suppose we identify a person with the *stage* of an animal during which it is self-aware (as opposed to the animal which is at that stage); then persons cannot exist before they are persons and they certainly were never fetuses. The trouble is that persons are substances (beings), not stages (temporal stretches) of substances. For example, persons are agents of actions and subjects of thoughts and feelings. A temporal stretch of an animal may *contain* actions and thoughts, but it is the animal, not the stage, that acts and feels. Further a whole person can exist at a point in time: I am all here now. But a whole stage cannot exist at a point in time: a temporal stretch cannot exist in its entirety at 10 AM.

22 I maintained earlier that a clonable cell ceases to exist upon fissioning, so it lacks strong potentiality. Consider the objection that the cell (C) *constitutes* a numerically distinct organism (O) which survives the demise of C and so has strong potentiality. My response is that if C *constitutes* O and C fissions, then O fissions, because C and O share all their non-modal non-temporal properties. Similarly, if the lump of bronze fissions, the statue fissions.

duce a numerically different entity from the adult human animal which, further, is ontologically extra, something which thinks and is self-aware though the human animal is not. But now persons are ontologically difficult. Shall we say they are immaterial substances that are the sole subjects of experience and somehow 'accompany' human animals through certain stages of their lives? Perhaps there is some materialist account of persons so that persons are the sole subjects of self-awareness and are ontologically extra to human animals. But on any account, we are beginning to pay a considerable personal price to deny that the fetus can one day be self-aware. *We* are turning out to be the sort of entities that tempt Ockham's Razor; it's not clear why we should pay it.

The conviction that persons are ontologically extra to human animals is sometimes motivated by the acceptance of the Psychological Criterion of personal identity: person X at t = person Y at t 10 if Y (and Y alone) is psychologically continuous with X. Even if Y can no longer remember X's experiences, no longer has his intentions, personality, and so on, still Y is psychologically continuous with X if he can remember someone (from the inside) who can remember X's experiences, and so on. The Psychological Criterion gains its plausibility from cases like this: We take Einstein and put him in John Perry's brain-zap machine.[23] Einstein's brain is wiped clean of neural traces; then we imprint the neural traces of Attila the Hun on Einstein's brain so that the individual who wakes up is psychologically continuous with Attila, whose body has just been destroyed. Many people believe the fellow in Einstein's body after the zap isn't Einstein; Einstein doesn't survive. Further, there is some plausibility to the claim that this fellow is Attila. But if a person is a human animal who is self-aware, then, as we have a self-aware animal after the zap which is identical to the self-aware animal that preceded it, we have the same person, so Einstein *does* survive. If psychological continuity is necessary for personal identity, persons aren't human animals that are self-aware.

Two comments seem relevant here: First, supposing the Psychological Criterion is correct, it only follows that persons aren't *identical* to human animals; it doesn't follow that they are ontologically extra to them. The mere fact that entities have different identity conditions doesn't compel us to say that one is something more than the other. The lump of bronze will constitute many different statues if it is re-cast, so no statue is identical to the lump; nonetheless, no statue is

---

23 John Perry, book review of Bernard Williams, *Problems of the Self: Philosophical Papers, 1956-1972*, in *The Journal of Philosophy* 73 (1976) 421.

extra to the lump either. Given the lump in the shape of a particular statue, that statue *must* exist. If the bronze in the statue is gradually replaced by gold, molecule by molecule (imagine a natural process analogous to petrification), the statue survives the lump of bronze. Nonetheless, the statue is nothing over and above the lump of bronze and (say) the lump of gold. There is no possible world in which the bronze and the gold have precisely *this* history and the statue fails to exist initially or fails to survive the lump of bronze.

Similarly, given the Psychological Criterion, there is no possible world in which my body has just the history it has in this world (including mental states realized) and I don't exist. The fact that this very animal could become a series of different people (multiple brain zaps) is compatible with all of them being constituted by this animal, as the different statues are merely constituted by the lump of bronze. Further, the fact that Attila survives his body and persists in Einstein's is consistent with his being *constituted* by one animal and later by another, as the statue is first constituted by the bronze and later by the gold. Indeed, given the Psychological Criterion, Attila cannot fail to exist in any world in which these bodies have the history they have in our story, nor can he fail to survive in Einstein's body in every one of these worlds in which (as in our story) the Psychological Criterion is satisfied.

Second, the Psychological Criterion is controversial. Some philosophers (most notably Bernard Williams) have the intuition that the fellow in Einstein's body after the zap is Einstein, who has been injured but not destroyed.[24] We can make the Psychological Criterion more controversial by considering what may plausibly be said to happen to the fellow in Einstein's body (the Attila personality) after the zap. As time passes the Attila personality grows more gentle and contemplative, with a growing interest in books and music. After all he has Einstein's brain. He discovers that he has a robust aptitude for mathematics and a fascination for hard science. Finally, the Attila personality enrolls in graduate school and begins to make important theoretical contributions to physics. The result is a personality markedly like Einstein's, not on account of psychological continuity (which has been severed), but because Einstein's biological nature tends to mold any personality that comes its way in certain directions.[25] Proponents

24 Bernard Williams, 'The Self and the Future' in Bernard Williams, *Problems of the Self* (Cambridge: Cambridge University Press 1973), 46-63

25 This is why I could have been stolen from my incubator, raised by gypsies, and still been me, though that life would be wholly psychologically discontinuous

of the Psychological Criterion assume that without psychological continuity there would be no marked resemblance between different stages
of a person's life; however, it seems likely that psychological resemblance owes as much to an enduring nature as it does to psychological
continuity.[26] This result robs the Psychological Criterion of intuitive force
and provides considerable support for the conclusion that Einstein has
survived after all and Attila has not. But then psychological continuity
is neither necessary nor sufficient for personal identity, and we can identify persons with self-aware animals that once were fetuses.

To conclude: Philosophers often dismiss the appeal to the fetus's
potentiality by enlisting a notion of potentiality so vague that everything
is potentially everything else. A cat *could* become a kangaroo given scientific advances or a wave of Merlin's wand; hence everything in nature
is a potential human being, most notably the sperm and the egg. However, a more sophisticated theory of potentiality avoids these absurdities, and it is time we quit attacking straw men. Also, many philosophers
are convinced that *mere* potentiality cannot be morally relevant. For a
creature's rights at time t depend upon her properties *at t*; properties
the creature has yet to actualize cannot matter. But strong potentiality
makes a difference to what a creature *is* at a time, even if the potentiality is never actualized: if the developmental path determined by a creature's genetic constitution leads to a conscious good for her, the creature
has an *actual* interest in growing up. It is true of her at t that growing
up is a benefit and not growing up a harm. A creature's present interests
are relevant to her rights; therefore potentiality matters.

----

from mine. The Psychological Criterion apparently entails that these lives would
belong to different people, for no psychological event in either life is caused by an
event in the other. (Supposing, on the other hand, I had been stolen at the age
of ten: some psychological events in that life, e.g., memories, *would* be caused by
events that are part of this one.) If we defend the Psychological Criterion by stipulating that psychologically discontinuous lives in different worlds belong to the same
person if they belong to the same animal, why shouldn't psychologically discontinuous lives lived serially by the same animal (the brain zap) belong to the same
person too? Or suppose I had merely been conceived a day later and that consequently no ensuing token mental event in my actual life. The Psychological Criterion
entails that my body would belong to someone else, a man with my parents, my
name, my friends, my profession, and so on.

26 There is considerable evidence that the same biological nature tends to create a
marked psychological resemblance between the lives of *different* people who share
it: studies of identical twins reared apart find striking correlations in brain wave
activity, IQ, personality, political slant, and recreational and intellectual interests,
compared to fraternal twins and the rest of the population. See David T. Lykken,
'Research with Twins: The Concept of Emergenesis,' *Psychophysiology* 19 (1982) 361-3.

According to some philosophers, the widespread conviction that we owe infants care and protection is a moral hallucination produced by enculturation. The Spartans, after all, practiced infanticide, and there are cultures today in which people try to collect insurance by throwing female infants beneath the wheels of automobiles. The truth is that healthy infants will not benefit from continued life, no matter how happy, and killing them painlessly is no harm.

My own view is that our conviction is a moral advance in the way that the recognition of the moral rights of blacks was an advance (though the practices of some contemporary cultures suggest that this too is an hallucination); surely killing healthy infants painlessly is a serious harm. But the infant's interest in continued life is as great as the harm of death; it must be grounded in strong potentiality, for nothing else can ground it. Strong potentiality generates the interests, harms, and benefits which entitle infants to care and protection; otherwise painless death is no harm. Fetuses are invisible and we have little concern for powerless creatures we know little about and never see, especially when killing them is convenient. Nonetheless, infants have strong potentiality before as well as after they are born; hence they have the same interests, and killing them is an equal harm. A human creature's moral right to life begins when he does.[27]

---

27 My thanks to *The Canadian Journal of Philosophy* and to my colleagues at The University of New Orleans for helpful comments on this paper.

[12]

Virtue Theory and Abortion

ROSALIND HURSTHOUSE

The sort of ethical theory derived from Aristotle, variously described as virtue ethics, virtue-based ethics, or neo-Aristotelianism, is becoming better known, and is now quite widely recognized as at least a possible rival to deontological and utilitarian theories. With recognition has come criticism, of varying quality. In this article I shall discuss nine separate criticisms that I have frequently encountered, most of which seem to me to betray an inadequate grasp either of the structure of virtue theory or of what would be involved in thinking about a real moral issue in its terms. In the first half I aim particularly to secure an understanding that will reveal that many of these criticisms are simply misplaced, and to articulate what I take to be the major criticism of virtue theory. I reject this criticism, but do not claim that it is necessarily misplaced. In the second half I aim to deepen that understanding and highlight the issues raised by the criticisms by illustrating what the theory looks like when it is applied to a particular issue, in this case, abortion.

Virtue Theory

Virtue theory can be laid out in a framework that reveals clearly some of the essential similarities and differences between it and some versions of deontological and utilitarian theories. I begin with a rough sketch of fa-

Versions of this article have been read to philosophy societies at University College, London, Rutgers University, and the Universities of Dundee, Edinburgh, Oxford, Swansea, and California–San Diego; at a conference of the Polish and British Academies in Cracow in 1988 on "Life, Death and the Law," and as a symposium paper at the Pacific Division of the American Philosophical Association in 1989. I am grateful to the many people who contributed to the discussions of it on these occasions, and particularly to Philippa Foot and Anne Jaap Jacobson for private discussion.

miliar versions of the latter two sorts of theory, not, of course, with the intention of suggesting that they exhaust the field, but on the assumption that their very familiarity will provide a helpful contrast with virtue theory. Suppose a deontological theory has basically the following framework. We begin with a premise providing a specification of right action:

P.1. An action is right iff it is in accordance with a moral rule or principle.

This is a purely formal specification, forging a link between the concepts of *right action* and *moral rule*, and gives one no guidance until one knows what a moral rule is. So the next thing the theory needs is a premise about that:

P.2. A moral rule is one that . . .

Historically, an acceptable completion of P.2 would have been

(i) is laid on us by God

or

(ii) is required by natural law.

In secular versions (not, of course, unconnected to God's being pure reason, and the universality of natural law) we get such completions as

(iii) is laid on us by reason

or

(iv) is required by rationality

or

(v) would command universal rational acceptance

or

(vi) would be the object of choice of all rational beings

and so on. Such a specification forges a second conceptual link, between the concepts of *moral rule* and *rationality*.

We have here the skeleton of a familiar version of a deontological theory, a skeleton that reveals that what is essential to any such version is the links between *right action*, *moral rule*, and *rationality*. That these form the basic structure can be seen particularly vividly if we lay out the familiar act-utilitarianism in such a way as to bring out the contrasts.

Act-utilitarianism begins with a premise that provides a specification of right action:

> P.1. An action is right iff it promotes the best consequences.

It thereby forges the link between the concepts of *right action* and *consequences*. It goes on to specify what the best consequences are in its second premise:

> P.2. The best consequences are those in which happiness is maximized.

It thereby forges the link between *consequences* and *happiness*.

Now let us consider what a skeletal virtue theory looks like. It begins with a specification of right action:

> P.1. An action is right iff it is what a virtuous agent would do in the circumstances.[1]

This, like the first premises of the other two sorts of theory, is a purely formal principle, giving one no guidance as to what to do, that forges the conceptual link between *right action* and *virtuous agent*. Like the other theories, it must, of course, go on to specify what the latter is. The first step toward this may appear quite trivial, but is needed to correct a prevailing tendency among many critics to define the virtuous agent as one who is disposed to act in accordance with a deontologist's moral rules.

> P.1a. A virtuous agent is one who acts virtuously, that is, one who has and exercises the virtues.

This subsidiary premise lays bare the fact that virtue theory aims to provide a nontrivial specification of the virtuous agent *via* a nontrivial specification of the virtues, which is given in its second premise:

---

1. It should be noted that this premise intentionally allows for the possibility that two virtuous agents, faced with the same choice in the same circumstances, may act differently. For example, one might opt for taking her father off the life-support machine and the other for leaving her father on it. The theory requires that neither agent thinks that what the other does is wrong (see note 4 below), but it explicitly allows that no action is uniquely right in such a case—both are right. It also intentionally allows for the possibility that in some circumstances—those into which no virtuous agent could have got herself— no action is right. I explore this premise at greater length in "Applying Virtue Ethics," forthcoming in a *festschrift* for Philippa Foot.

P.2. A virtue is a character trait a human being needs to flourish or live well.

This premise forges a conceptual link between *virtue* and *flourishing* (or *living well* or *eudaimonia*). And, just as deontology, in theory, then goes on to argue that each favored rule meets its specification, so virtue ethics, in theory, goes on to argue that each favored character trait meets its.

These are the bare bones of virtue theory. Following are five brief comments directed to some misconceived criticisms that should be cleared out of the way.

First, the theory does not have a peculiar weakness or problem in virtue of the fact that it involves the concept of *eudaimonia* (a standard criticism being that this concept is hopelessly obscure). Now no virtue theorist will pretend that the concept of human flourishing is an easy one to grasp. I will not even claim here (though I would elsewhere) that it is no more obscure than the concepts of *rationality* and *happiness*, since, if our vocabulary were more limited, we might, *faute de mieux*, call it (human) *rational happiness*, and thereby reveal that it has at least some of the difficulties of both. But virtue theory has never, so far as I know, been dismissed on the grounds of the *comparative* obscurity of this central concept; rather, the popular view is that it has a problem with this which deontology and utilitarianism in no way share. This, I think, is clearly false. Both *rationality* and *happiness*, as they figure in their respective theories, are rich and difficult concepts—hence all the disputes about the various tests for a rule's being an object of rational choice, and the disputes, dating back to Mill's introduction of the higher and lower pleasures, about what constitutes happiness.

Second, the theory is not trivially circular; it does not specify right action in terms of the virtuous agent and then immediately specify the virtuous agent in terms of right action. Rather, it specifies her in terms of the virtues, and then specifies these, not merely as dispositions to right action, but as the character traits (which are dispositions to feel and react as well as act in certain ways) required for *eudaimonia*.[2]

2. There is, of course, the further question of whether the theory eventually describes a larger circle and winds up relying on the concept of right action in its interpretation of *eudaimonia*. In denying that the theory is trivially circular, I do not pretend to answer this intricate question. It is certainly true that virtue theory does not claim that the correct conception of *eudaimonia* can be got from "an independent 'value-free' investigation of

Third, it does answer the question "What should I do?" as well as the question "What sort of person should I be?" (That is, it is not, as one of the catchphrases has it, concerned only with Being and not with Doing.)

Fourth, the theory does, to a certain extent, answer this question by coming up with rules or principles (contrary to the common claim that it does not come up with any rules or principles). Every virtue generates a positive instruction (act justly, kindly, courageously, honestly, etc.) and every vice a prohibition (do not act unjustly, cruelly, like a coward, dishonestly, etc.). So trying to decide what to do within the framework of virtue theory is not, as some people seem to imagine, necessarily a matter of taking one's favored candidate for a virtuous person and asking oneself, "What would they do in these circumstances?" (as if the raped fifteen-year-old girl might be supposed to say to herself, "Now would Socrates have an abortion if he were in my circumstances?" and as if someone who had never known or heard of anyone very virtuous were going to be left, according to the theory, with no way to decide what to do at all). The agent may instead ask herself, "If I were to do such and such now, would I be acting justly or unjustly (or neither), kindly or unkindly [and so on]?" I shall consider below the problem created by cases in which such a question apparently does not yield an answer to "What should I do?" (because, say, the alternatives are being unkind or being unjust); here my claim is only that it sometimes does—the agent may employ her concepts of the virtues and vices directly, rather than imagining what some hypothetical exemplar would do.

Fifth (a point that is implicit but should be made explicit), virtue theory is not committed to any sort of reductionism involving defining all of our moral concepts in terms of the virtuous agent. On the contrary, it relies on a lot of very significant moral concepts. Charity or benevolence, for instance, is the virtue whose concern is the *good* of others; that concept of *good* is related to the concept of *evil* or *harm,* and they are both related to the concepts of the *worthwhile,* the *advantageous,* and the *pleasant.* If I have the wrong conception of what is worthwhile and ad-

human nature" (John McDowell, "The Role of *Eudaimonia* in Aristotle's Ethics," in *Essays on Aristotle's Ethics,* ed. Amelie Rorty [Berkeley and Los Angeles: University of California Press, 1980]). The sort of training that is required for acquiring the correct conception no doubt involves being taught from early on such things as "Decent people do this sort of thing, not that" and "To do such and such is the mark of a depraved character" (cf. *Nicomachean Ethics* 1110a22). But whether this counts as relying on the concept of right (or wrong) action seems to me very unclear and requiring much discussion.

vantageous and pleasant, then I shall have the wrong conception of what is good for, and harmful to, myself and others, and, even with the best will in the world, will lack the virtue of charity, which involves getting all this right. (This point will be illustrated at some length in the second half of this article; I mention it here only in support of the fact that no virtue theorist who takes her inspiration from Aristotle would even contemplate aiming at reductionism.)[3]

Let me now, with equal brevity, run through two more standard criticisms of virtue theory (the sixth and seventh of my nine) to show that, though not entirely misplaced, they do not highlight problems peculiar to that theory but, rather, problems that are shared by familiar versions of deontology.

One common criticism is that we do not know which character traits are the virtues, or that this is open to much dispute, or particularly subject to the threat of moral skepticism or "pluralism"[4] or cultural relativism. But the parallel roles played by the second premises of both deontological and virtue theories reveal the way in which both sorts of theory share this problem. It is at the stage at which one tries to get the right conclusions to drop out of the bottom of one's theory that, *theoretically*, all the work has to be done. Rule deontologists know that they want to get "don't kill," "keep promises," "cherish your children," and so on as the rules that meet their specification, whatever it may be. They also know that any of these can be disputed, that some philosopher may claim, of any one of them, that it is reasonable to reject it, and that at least people claim that there has been, for each rule, some culture that

---

3. Cf. Bernard Williams' point in *Ethics and the Limits of Philosophy* (London: William Collins, 1985) that we need an enriched ethical vocabulary, not a cut-down one.

4. I put *pluralism* in scare quotes to serve as a warning that virtue theory is not incompatible with all forms of it. It allows for "competing conceptions" of *eudaimonia* and the worthwhile, for instance, in the sense that it allows for a plurality of flourishing lives—the theory need not follow Aristotle in specifying the life of contemplation as the only one that truly constitutes *eudaimonia* (if he does). But the conceptions "compete" only in the sense that, within a single flourishing life, not everything worthwhile can be fitted in; the theory does not allow that two people with a correct conception of *eudaimonia* can disagree over whether the way the other is living constitutes flourishing. Moreover, the theory is committed to the strong thesis that the same set of character traits is needed for *any* flourishing life; it will not allow that, for instance, soldiers need courage but wives and mothers do not, or that judges need justice but can live well despite lacking kindness. (This obviously is related to the point made in note 1 above.) For an interesting discussion of pluralism (different interpretations thereof) and virtue theory, see Douglas B. Rasmussen, "Liberalism and Natural End Ethics," *American Philosophical Quarterly* 27 (1990): 153–61.

rejected it. Similarly, the virtue theorists know that they want to get justice, charity, fidelity, courage, and so on as the character traits needed for *eudaimonia*; and they also know that any of these can be disputed, that some philosopher will say of any one of them that it is reasonable to reject it as a virtue, and that there is said to be, for each character trait, some culture that has thus rejected it.

This is a problem for both theories, and the virtue theorist certainly does not find it any harder to argue against moral skepticism, "pluralism," or cultural relativism than the deontologist. Each theory has to stick out its neck and say, in some cases, "This person/these people/other cultures are (or would be) in error," and find some grounds for saying this.

Another criticism (the seventh) often made is that virtue ethics has unresolvable conflict built into it. "It is common knowledge," it is said, "that the requirements of the virtues can conflict; charity may prompt me to end the frightful suffering of the person in my care by killing him, but justice bids me to stay my hand. To tell my brother that his wife is being unfaithful to him would be honest and loyal, but it would be kinder to keep quiet about it. So which should I do? In such cases, virtue ethics has nothing helpful to say." (This is one version of the problem, mentioned above, that considering whether a proposed action falls under a virtue or vice term does not always yield an answer to "What should I do?")

The obvious reply to this criticism is that rule deontology notoriously suffers from the same problem, arising not only from the fact that its rules can apparently conflict, but also from the fact that, at first blush, it appears that one and the same rule (e.g., preserve life) can yield contrary instructions in a particular case.[5] As before, I agree that this is a problem for virtue theory, but deny that it is a problem peculiar to it.

Finally, I want to articulate, and reject, what I take to be the major criticism of virtue theory. Perhaps because it is *the* major criticism, the reflection of a very general sort of disquiet about the theory, it is hard to state clearly—especially for someone who does not accept it—but it goes something like this.[6] My interlocutor says:

5. E.g., in Williams' Jim and Pedro case in J.J.C. Smart and Bernard Williams, *Utilitarianism: For and Against* (London: Cambridge University Press, 1973).

6. Intimations of this criticism constantly come up in discussion; the clearest statement of it I have found is by Onora O'Neill, in her review of Stephen Clark's *The Moral Status*

Virtue theory can't *get* us anywhere in real moral issues because it's bound to be all assertion and no argument. You admit that the best it can come up with in the way of action-guiding rules are the ones that rely on the virtue and vice concepts, such as "act charitably," "don't act cruelly," and so on; and, as if that weren't bad enough, you admit that these virtue concepts, such as charity, presuppose concepts such as the *good*, and the *worthwhile*, and so on. But that means that any virtue theorist who writes about real moral issues must rely on her audience's agreeing with her application of all these concepts, and hence accepting all the premises in which those applications are enshrined. But some other virtue theorist might take different premises about these matters, and come up with very different conclusions, and, within the terms of the theory, there is no way to distinguish between the two. While there is agreement, virtue theory can repeat conventional wisdom, preserve the status quo, but it can't get us anywhere in the way that a normative ethical theory is supposed to, namely, by providing rational grounds for acceptance of its practical conclusions.

My strategy will be to split this criticism into two: one (the eighth) addressed to the virtue theorist's employment of the virtue and vice concepts enshrined in her rules—act charitably, honestly, and so on—and the other (the ninth) addressed to her employment of concepts such as that of the *worthwhile*. Each objection, I shall maintain, implicitly appeals to a certain *condition of adequacy* on a normative moral theory, and in each case, I shall claim, the condition of adequacy, once made explicit, is utterly implausible.

It is true that when she discusses real moral issues, the virtue theorist has to assert that certain actions are honest, dishonest, or neither; charitable, uncharitable, or neither. And it is true that this is often a very difficult matter to decide; her rules are not always easy to apply. But this counts as a criticism of the theory only if we assume, as a condition of adequacy, that any adequate action-guiding theory must make the difficult business of knowing what to do if one is to act well easy, that it must provide clear guidance about what ought and ought not to be done which

of Animals, in *Journal of Philosophy* 77 (1980): 440–46. For a response I am much in sympathy with, see Cora Diamond, "Anything But Argument?" *Philosophical Investigations* 5 (1982): 23–41.

any reasonably clever adolescent could follow if she chose. But such a condition of adequacy is implausible. Acting rightly *is* difficult, and *does* call for much moral wisdom, and the relevant condition of adequacy, which virtue theory meets, is that it should have built into it an explanation of a truth expressed by Aristotle,[7] namely, that moral knowledge—unlike mathematical knowledge—cannot be acquired merely by attending lectures and is not characteristically to be found in people too young to have had much experience of life. There are youthful mathematical geniuses, but rarely, if ever, youthful moral geniuses, and this tells us something significant about the sort of knowledge that moral knowledge is. Virtue ethics builds this in straight off precisely by couching its rules in terms whose application may indeed call for the most delicate and sensitive judgment.

Here we may discern a slightly different version of the problem that there are cases in which applying the virtue and vice terms does not yield an answer to "What should I do?" Suppose someone "youthful in character," as Aristotle puts it, having applied the relevant terms, finds herself landed with what is, unbeknownst to her, a case not of real but of apparent conflict, arising from a misapplication of those terms. Then she will not be able to decide what to do unless she knows of a virtuous agent to look to for guidance. But her quandary is (*ex hypothesi*) the result of her lack of wisdom, and just what virtue theory expects. Someone hesitating over whether to reveal a hurtful truth, for example, thinking it would be kind but dishonest or unjust to lie, may need to realize, with respect to these particular circumstances, not that kindness is more (or less) important than honesty or justice, and not that honesty or justice sometimes requires one to act unkindly or cruelly, but that one does people no kindness by concealing this sort of truth from them, hurtful as it may be. This is the *type* of thing (I use it only as an example) that people with moral wisdom know about, involving the correct application of *kind*, and that people without such wisdom find difficult.

What about the virtue theorist's reliance on concepts such as that of the *worthwhile*? If such reliance is to count as a fault in the theory, what condition of adequacy is implicitly in play? It must be that any good normative theory should provide answers to questions about real moral issues whose truth is in no way determined by truths about what is worth-

7. Aristotle, *Nicomachean Ethics* 1142a12–16.

while, or what really matters in human life. Now although people are initially inclined to reject out of hand the claim that the practical conclusions of a normative moral theory have to be based on premises about what is truly worthwhile, the alternative, once it is made explicit, may look even more unacceptable. Consider what the condition of adequacy entails. If truths about what is worthwhile (or truly good, or serious, or about what matters in human life) do *not* have to be appealed to in order to answer questions about real moral issues, then I might sensibly seek guidance about what I ought to do from someone who had declared in advance that she knew nothing about such matters, or from someone who said that, although she had opinions about them, these were quite likely to be wrong but that this did not matter, because they would play no determining role in the advice she gave me.

I should emphasize that we are talking about real moral issues and real guidance; I want to know whether I should have an abortion, take my mother off the life-support machine, leave academic life and become a doctor in the Third World, give up my job with the firm that is using animals in its experiments, tell my father he has cancer. Would I go to someone who says she has *no* views about what is worthwhile in life? Or to someone who says that, as a matter of fact, she tends to think that the only thing that matters is having a good time, but has a normative theory that is consistent both with this view and with my own rather more puritanical one, which will yield the guidance I need?

I take it as a premise that this is absurd. The relevant condition of adequacy should be that the practical conclusions of a good normative theory *must* be in part determined by premises about what is worthwhile, important, and so on. Thus I reject this "major criticism" of virtue theory, that it cannot get us anywhere in the way that a normative moral theory is supposed to. According to my response, a normative theory that any clever adolescent can apply, or that reaches practical conclusions that are in no way determined by premises about what is truly worthwhile, serious, and so on, is guaranteed to be an inadequate theory.

Although I reject this criticism, I have not argued that it is misplaced and that it necessarily manifests a failure to understand what virtue theory is. My rejection is based on premises about what an adequate normative theory must be like—what sorts of concepts it must contain, and what sort of account it must give of moral knowledge—and thereby claims, implicitly, that the "major criticism" manifests a failure to understand what an *adequate normative theory* is. But, as a matter of fact, I think the criticism is often made by people who have no idea of what virtue theory looks like when applied to a real moral issue; they drastically underestimate the variety of ways in which the virtue and vice concepts, and the others, such as that of the *worthwhile*, figure in such discussion.

As promised, I now turn to an illustration of such discussion, applying virtue theory to abortion. Before I embark on this tendentious business, I should remind the reader of the aim of this discussion. I am not, in this article, trying to solve the problem of abortion; I am illustrating how virtue theory directs one to think about it. It might indeed be said that thinking about the problem in this way "solves" it by *dis*solving it, insofar as it leads one to the conclusion that there is no single right answer, but a variety of particular answers, and in what follows I am certainly trying to make that conclusion seem plausible. But, that granted, it should still be said that I am not trying to "solve the problems" in the practical sense of telling people that they should, or should not, do this or that if they are pregnant and contemplating abortion in these or those particular circumstances.

I do not assume, or expect, that all of my readers will agree with everything I am about to say. On the contrary, given the plausible assumption that some are morally wiser than I am, and some less so, the theory has built into it that we are bound to disagree on some points. For instance, we may well disagree about the particular application of some of the virtue and vice terms; and we may disagree about what is worthwhile or serious, worthless or trivial. But my aim is to make clear how these concepts figure in a discussion conducted in terms of virtue theory. What is at issue is whether these concepts are indeed the ones that should come in, that is, whether virtue theory should be criticized for employing them. The problem of abortion highlights this issue dramatically since virtue theory quite transforms the discussion of it.

ABORTION

As everyone knows, the morality of abortion is commonly discussed in relation to just two considerations: first, and predominantly, the status of the fetus and whether or not it is the sort of thing that may or may not be innocuously or justifiably killed; and second, and less predominantly (when, that is, the discussion concerns the *morality* of abortion rather than the question of permissible legislation in a just society), women's rights. If one thinks within this familiar framework, one may well be puzzled about what virtue theory, as such, could contribute. Some people assume the discussion will be conducted solely in terms of what the virtuous agent would or would not do (cf. the third, fourth, and fifth criticisms above). Others assume that only justice, or at most justice and charity,[8] will be applied to the issue, generating a discussion very similar to Judith Jarvis Thomson's.[9]

Now if this is the way the virtue theorist's discussion of abortion is imagined to be, no wonder people think little of it. It seems obvious in advance that in any such discussion there must be either a great deal of extremely tendentious application of the virtue terms *just, charitable,* and so on or a lot of rhetorical appeal to "this is what only the virtuous agent knows." But these are caricatures; they fail to appreciate the way in which virtue theory quite transforms the discussion of abortion by dismissing the two familiar dominating considerations as, in a way, fundamentally irrelevant. In what way or ways, I hope to make both clear and plausible.

Let us first consider women's rights. Let me emphasize again that we are discussing the *morality* of abortion, not the rights and wrongs of laws prohibiting or permitting it. If we suppose that women do have a moral right to do as they choose with their own bodies, or, more particularly, to terminate their pregnancies, then it may well follow that a *law* forbidding abortion would be unjust. Indeed, even if they have no such right, such a law might be, as things stand at the moment, unjust, or impractical, or inhumane: on this issue I have nothing to say in this article. But, putting all questions about the justice or injustice of laws to one side, and sup-

---

8. It seems likely that some people have been misled by Foot's discussion of euthanasia (through no fault of hers) into thinking that a virtue theorist's discussion of terminating human life will be conducted exclusively in terms of justice and charity (and the corresponding vice terms) (Philippa Foot, "Euthanasia," *Philosophy & Public Affairs* 6, no. 2 [Winter 1977]: 85–112). But the act-category *euthanasia* is a very special one, at least as defined in her article, since such an act must be done "for the sake of the one who is to die." Building a virtuous motivation into the specification of the act in this way immediately rules out the application of many other vice terms.

9. Judith Jarvis Thomson, "A Defense of Abortion," *Philosophy & Public Affairs* 1, no. 1 (Fall 1971): 47–66. One could indeed regard this article as proto–virtue theory (no doubt to the surprise of the author) if the concepts of callousness and kindness were allowed more weight.

posing only that women have such a moral right, *nothing* follows from this supposition about the morality of abortion, according to virtue theory, once it is noted (quite generally, not with particular reference to abortion) that in exercising a moral right I can do something cruel, or callous, or selfish, light-minded, self-righteous, stupid, inconsiderate, disloyal, dishonest—that is, act viciously.[10] Love and friendship do not survive their parties' constantly insisting on their rights, nor do people live well when they think that getting what they have a right to is of preeminent importance; they harm others, and they harm themselves. So whether women have a moral right to terminate their pregnancies is irrelevant within virtue theory, for it is irrelevant to the question "In having an abortion in these circumstances, would the agent be acting virtuously or viciously or neither?"

What about the consideration of the status of the fetus—what can virtue theory say about that? One might say that this issue is not in the province of *any* moral theory; it is a metaphysical question, and an extremely difficult one at that. Must virtue theory then wait upon metaphysics to come up with the answer?

At first sight it might seem so. For virtue is said to involve knowledge, and part of this knowledge consists in having the *right* attitude to things. "Right" here does not just mean "morally right" or "proper" or "nice" in the modern sense; it means "accurate, true." One cannot have the right or correct attitude to something if the attitude is based on or involves false beliefs. And this suggests that if the status of the fetus is relevant to the rightness or wrongness of abortion, its status must be known, as a truth, to the fully wise and virtuous person.

But the sort of wisdom that the fully virtuous person has is not supposed to be recondite; it does not call for fancy philosophical sophistication, and it does not depend upon, let alone wait upon, the discoveries of academic philosophers.[11] And this entails the following, rather startling,

10. One possible qualification: if one ties the concept of justice very closely to rights, then if women do have a moral right to terminate their pregnancies it *may* follow that in doing so they do not act unjustly. (Cf. Thomson, "A Defense of Abortion.") But it is debatable whether even that much follows.

11. This is an assumption of virtue theory, and I do not attempt to defend it here. An adequate discussion of it would require a separate article, since, although most moral philosophers would be chary of claiming that intellectual sophistication is a necessary condition of moral wisdom or virtue, most of us, from Plato onward, tend to write as if this were so. Sorting out which claims about moral knowledge are committed to this kind of elitism

conclusion: that the status of the fetus—that issue over which so much ink has been spilt—is, according to virtue theory, simply not relevant to the rightness or wrongness of abortion (within, that is, a secular morality).

Or rather, since that is clearly too radical a conclusion, it is in a sense relevant, but only in the sense that the familiar biological facts are relevant. By "the familiar biological facts" I mean the facts that most human societies are and have been familiar with—that, standardly (but not invariably), pregnancy occurs as the result of sexual intercourse, that it lasts about nine months, during which time the fetus grows and develops, that standardly it terminates in the birth of a living baby, and that this is how we all come to be.

It might be thought that this distinction—between the familiar biological facts and the status of the fetus—is a distinction without a difference. But this is not so. To attach relevance to the status of the fetus, in the sense in which virtue theory claims it is not relevant, is to be gripped by the conviction that we must go beyond the familiar biological facts, deriving some sort of conclusion from them, such as that the fetus has rights, or is not a person, or something similar. It is also to believe that this exhausts the relevance of the familiar biological facts, that all they are relevant to is the status of the fetus and whether or not it is the sort of thing that may or may not be killed.

These convictions, I suspect, are rooted in the desire to solve the problem of abortion by getting it to fall under some general rule such as "You ought not to kill anything with the right to life but may kill anything else." But they have resulted in what should surely strike any nonphilosopher as a most bizarre aspect of nearly all the current philosophical literature on abortion, namely, that, far from treating abortion as a unique moral problem, markedly unlike any other, nearly everything written on the status of the fetus and its bearing on the abortion issue would be consistent with the human reproductive facts' (to say nothing of family life) being totally different from what they are. Imagine that you are an alien extraterrestrial anthropologist who does not know that the human race is roughly 50 percent female and 50 percent male, or that our only (natural) form of reproduction involves heterosexual intercourse, vivipa-

---

and which can, albeit with difficulty, be reconciled with the idea that moral knowledge can be acquired by anyone who really wants it would be a major task.

rous birth, and the female's (and only the female's) being pregnant for nine months, or that females are capable of childbearing from late childhood to late middle age, or that childbearing is painful, dangerous, and emotionally charged—do you think you would pick up these facts from the hundreds of articles written on the status of the fetus? I am quite sure you would not. And that, I think, shows that the current philosophical literature on abortion has got badly out of touch with reality.

Now if we are using virtue theory, our first question is not "What do the familiar biological facts show—what can be derived from them about the status of the fetus?" but "How do these facts figure in the practical reasoning, actions and passions, thoughts and reactions, of the virtuous and the nonvirtuous? What is the mark of having the right attitude to these facts and what manifests having the wrong attitude to them?" This immediately makes essentially relevant not only all the facts about human reproduction I mentioned above, but a whole range of facts about our emotions in relation to them as well. I mean such facts as that human parents, both male and female, tend to care passionately about their offspring, and that family relationships are among the deepest and strongest in our lives—and, significantly, among the longest-lasting.

These facts make it obvious that pregnancy is not just one among many other physical conditions; and hence that anyone who genuinely believes that an abortion is comparable to a haircut or an appendectomy is mistaken.[12] The fact that the premature termination of a pregnancy is, in some sense, the cutting off of a new human life, and thereby, like the procreation of a new human life, connects with all our thoughts about human life and death, parenthood, and family relationships, must make it a serious matter. To disregard this fact about it, to think of abortion as

---

12. Mary Anne Warren, in "On the Moral and Legal Status of Abortion," *Monist* 57 (1973), sec. 1, says of the opponents of restrictive laws governing abortion that "their conviction (for the most part) is that abortion is not a *morally* serious and extremely unfortunate, even though sometimes justified, act, comparable to killing in self-defense or to letting the violinist die, but rather is closer to being a *morally neutral* act, like cutting one's hair" (italics mine). I would like to think that no one *genuinely* believes this. But certainly in discussion, particularly when arguing against restrictive laws or the suggestion that remorse over abortion might be appropriate, I have found that some people *say* they believe it (and often cite Warren's article, albeit inaccurately, despite its age). Those who allow that it is morally serious, and far from morally neutral, have to argue against restrictive laws, or the appropriateness of remorse, on a very different ground from that laid down by the premise "The fetus is just part of the woman's body (and she has a right to determine what happens to her body and should not feel guilt about anything she does to it)."

nothing but the killing of something that does not matter, or as nothing but the exercise of some right or rights one has, or as the incidental means to some desirable state of affairs, is to do something callous and light-minded, the sort of thing that no virtuous and wise person would do. It is to have the wrong attitude not only to fetuses, but more generally to human life and death, parenthood, and family relationships.

Although I say that the facts make this obvious, I know that this is one of my tendentious points. In partial support of it I note that even the most dedicated proponents of the view that deliberate abortion is just like an appendectomy or haircut rarely hold the same view of spontaneous abortion, that is, miscarriage. It is not so tendentious of me to claim that to react to people's grief over miscarriage by saying, or even thinking, "What a fuss about nothing!" would be callous and light-minded, whereas to try to laugh someone out of grief over an appendectomy scar or a botched haircut would not be. It is hard to give this point due prominence within act-centered theories, for the inconsistency is an inconsistency in attitude about the seriousness of loss of life, not in beliefs about which acts are right or wrong. Moreover, an act-centered theorist may say, "Well, there is nothing wrong with *thinking* 'What a fuss about nothing!' as long as you do not say it and hurt the person who is grieving. And besides, we cannot be held responsible for our thoughts, only for the intentional actions they give rise to." But the character traits that virtue theory emphasizes are not simply dispositions to intentional actions, but a seamless disposition to certain actions and passions, thoughts and reactions.

To say that the cutting off of a human life is always a matter of some seriousness, at any stage, is not to deny the relevance of gradual fetal development. Notwithstanding the well-worn point that clear boundary lines cannot be drawn, our emotions and attitudes regarding the fetus do change as it develops, and again when it is born, and indeed further as the baby grows. Abortion for shallow reasons in the later stages is much more shocking than abortion for the same reasons in the early stages in a way that matches the fact that deep grief over miscarriage in the later stages is more appropriate than it is over miscarriage in the earlier stages (when, that is, the grief is solely about the loss of *this* child, not about, as might be the case, the loss of one's only hope of having a child or of having one's husband's child). Imagine (or recall) a woman who already has children; she had not intended to have more, but finds herself unexpectedly pregnant. Though contrary to her plans, the pregnancy, once established as a fact, is welcomed—and then she loses the embryo almost immediately. If this were bemoaned as a tragedy, it would, I think, be a misapplication of the concept of what is tragic. But it may still properly be mourned as a loss. The grief is expressed in such terms as "I shall always wonder how she or he would have turned out" or "When I look at the others, I shall think, 'How different their lives would have been if this other one had been part of them.' " It would, I take it, be callous and light-minded to say, or think, "Well, she has already *got* four children; what's the problem?"; it would be neither, nor arrogantly intrusive in the case of a close friend, to try to correct prolonged mourning by saying, "I know it's sad, but it's not a tragedy; rejoice in the ones you have." The application of *tragic* becomes more appropriate as the fetus grows, for the mere fact that one has lived with it for longer, conscious of its existence, makes a difference. To shrug off an early abortion is understandable just because it is very hard to be fully conscious of the fetus's existence in the early stages and hence hard to appreciate that an early abortion is the destruction of life. It is particularly hard for the young and inexperienced to appreciate this, because appreciation of it usually comes only with experience.

I do not mean "with the experience of having an abortion" (though that may be part of it) but, quite generally, "with the experience of life." Many women who have borne children contrast their later pregnancies with their first successful one, saying that in the later ones they were conscious of a new life growing in them from very early on. And, more generally, as one reaches the age at which the next generation is coming up close behind one, the counterfactuals "If I, or she, had had an abortion, Alice, or Bob, would not have been born" acquire a significant application, which casts a new light on the conditionals "If I or Alice have an abortion then some Caroline or Bill will not be born."

The fact that pregnancy is not just one among many physical conditions does not mean that one can never regard it in that light without manifesting a vice. When women are in very poor physical health, or worn out from childbearing, or forced to do very physically demanding jobs, then they cannot be described as self-indulgent, callous, irresponsible, or light-minded if they seek abortions mainly with a view to avoiding pregnancy as the physical condition that it is. To go through with a pregnancy when one is utterly exhausted, or when one's job consists of crawling along tunnels hauling coal, as many women in the nineteenth century were obliged to do, is perhaps heroic, but people who do not achieve heroism are not necessarily vicious. That they can view the pregnancy only as eight months of misery, followed by hours if not days of agony and exhaustion, and abortion only as the blessed escape from this prospect, is entirely understandable and does not manifest any lack of serious respect for human life or a shallow attitude to motherhood. What it does show is that something is terribly amiss in the conditions of their lives, which make it so hard to recognize pregnancy and childbearing as the good that they can be.

In relation to this last point I should draw attention to the way in which virtue theory has a sort of built-in indexicality. Philosophers arguing against anything remotely resembling a belief in the sanctity of life (which the above claims clearly embody) frequently appeal to the existence of other communities in which abortion and infanticide are practiced. We should not automatically assume that it is impossible that some other communities could be morally inferior to our own; maybe some are, or have been, precisely insofar as their members are, typically, callous or light-minded or unjust. But in communities in which life is a great deal tougher for everyone than it is in ours, having the right attitude to human life and death, parenthood, and family relationships might well manifest itself in ways that are unlike ours. When it is essential to survival that most members of the community fend for themselves at a very young age or work during most of their waking hours, selective abortion or infanticide might be practiced either as a form of genuine euthanasia or for the sake of the community and not, I think, be thought callous or light-minded. But this does not make everything all right; as before, it shows that there is something amiss with the conditions of their lives, which are making it impossible for them to live really well.[13]

The foregoing discussion, insofar as it emphasizes the right attitude to human life and death, parallels to a certain extent those standard discussions of abortion that concentrate on it solely as an issue of killing. But it does not, as those discussions do, gloss over the fact, emphasized by those who discuss the morality of abortion in terms of women's rights, that abortion, wildly unlike any other form of killing, is the termination

---

13. For another example of the way in which "tough conditions" can make a difference to what is involved in having the right attitude to human life and death and family relationships, see the concluding sentences of Foot's "Euthanasia."

of a pregnancy, which is a condition of a woman's body and results in
her having a child if it is not aborted. This fact is given due recognition
not by appeal to women's rights but by emphasizing the relevance of the
familiar biological and psychological facts and their connection with having the right attitude to parenthood and family relationships. But it may
well be thought that failing to bring in women's rights still leaves some
important aspects of the problem of abortion untouched.

Speaking in terms of women's rights, people sometimes say things
like, "Well, it's her life you're talking about too, you know; she's got a
right to her own life, her own happiness." And the discussion stops there.
But in the context of virtue theory, given that we are particularly concerned with what constitutes a good human life, with what true happiness or *eudaimonia* is, this is no place to stop. We go on to ask, "And is
this life of hers a good one? Is she living well?"

If we are to go on to talk about good human lives, in the context of
abortion, we have to bring in our thoughts about the value of love and
family life, and our proper emotional development through a natural life
cycle. The familiar facts support the view that parenthood in general,
and motherhood and childbearing in particular, are intrinsically worthwhile, are among the things that can be correctly thought to be partially
constitutive of a flourishing human life.[14] If this is right, then a woman
who opts for not being a mother (at all, or again, or now) by opting for
abortion may thereby be manifesting a flawed grasp of what her life
should be, and be about—a grasp that is childish, or grossly materialistic,
or shortsighted, or shallow.

I said "*may* thereby": this *need* not be so. Consider, for instance, a
woman who has already had several children and fears that to have another will seriously affect her capacity to be a good mother to the ones
she has—she does not show a lack of appreciation of the intrinsic value
of being a parent by opting for abortion. Nor does a woman who has been
a good mother and is approaching the age at which she may be looking
forward to being a good grandmother. Nor does a woman who discovers
that her pregnancy may well kill her, and opts for abortion and adoption.
Nor, necessarily, does a woman who has decided to lead a life centered

---

14. I take this as a premise here, but argue for it in some detail in my *Beginning Lives*
(Oxford: Basil Blackwell, 1987). In this connection I also discuss adoption and the sense
in which it may be regarded as "second best," and the difficult question of whether the
good of parenthood may properly be sought, or indeed bought, by surrogacy.

around some other worthwhile activity or activities with which motherhood would compete.

People who are childless by choice are sometimes described as "irresponsible," or "selfish," or "refusing to grow up," or "not knowing what
life is about." But one can hold that having children is intrinsically
worthwhile without endorsing this, for we are, after all, in the happy position of there being more worthwhile things to do than can be fitted into
one lifetime. Parenthood, and motherhood in particular, even if granted
to be intrinsically worthwhile, undoubtedly take up a lot of one's adult
life, leaving no room for some other worthwhile pursuits. But some
women who choose abortion rather than have their first child, and some
men who encourage their partners to choose abortion, are not avoiding
parenthood for the sake of other worthwhile pursuits, but for the worthless one of "having a good time," or for the pursuit of some false vision
of the ideals of freedom or self-realization. And some others who say "I
am not ready for parenthood yet" are making some sort of mistake about
the extent to which one can manipulate the circumstances of one's life
so as to make it fulfill some dream that one has. Perhaps one's dream is
to have two perfect children, a girl and a boy, within a perfect marriage,
in financially secure circumstances, with an interesting job of one's own.
But to care too much about that dream, to demand of life that it give it
to one and act accordingly, may be both greedy and foolish, and is to run
the risk of missing out on happiness entirely. Not only may fate make
the dream impossible, or destroy it, but one's own attachment to it may
make it impossible. Good marriages, and the most promising children,
can be destroyed by just one adult's excessive demand for perfection.

Once again, this is not to deny that girls may quite properly say "I am
not ready for motherhood yet," especially in our society, and, far from
manifesting irresponsibility or light-mindedness, show an appropriate
modesty or humility, or a fearfulness that does not amount to cowardice.
However, even when the decision to have an abortion is the right decision—one that does not itself fall under a vice-related term and thereby
one that the perfectly virtuous could recommend—it does not follow that
there is no sense in which having the abortion is wrong, or guilt inappropriate. For, by virtue of the fact that a human life has been cut short,
some evil has probably been brought about,[15] and that circumstances

15. I say "some evil has probably been brought about" on the ground that (human) life

make the decision to bring about some evil the right decision will be a ground for guilt if getting into those circumstances in the first place itself manifested a flaw in character.

What "gets one into those circumstances" in the case of abortion is, except in the case of rape, one's sexual activity and one's choices, or the lack of them, about one's sexual partner and about contraception. The virtuous woman (which here of course does not mean simply "chaste woman" but "woman with the virtues") has such character traits as strength, independence, resoluteness, decisiveness, self-confidence, responsibility, serious-mindedness, and self-determination—and no one, I think, could deny that many women become pregnant in circumstances in which they cannot welcome or cannot face the thought of having *this* child precisely because they lack one or some of these character traits. So even in the cases where the decision to have an abortion is the right one, it can still be the reflection of a moral failing—not because the decision itself is weak or cowardly or irresolute or irresponsible or light-minded, but because lack of the requisite opposite of these failings landed one in the circumstances in the first place. Hence the common universalized claim that guilt and remorse are never appropriate emotions about an abortion is denied. They may be appropriate, and appropriately inculcated, even when the decision was the right one.

Another motivation for bringing women's rights into the discussion may be to attempt to correct the implication, carried by the killing-centered approach, that insofar as abortion is wrong, it is a wrong that only women do, or at least (given the preponderance of male doctors) that only women instigate. I do not myself believe that we can thus escape the fact that nature bears harder on women than it does on men,[16] but virtue theory can certainly correct many of the injustices that the emphasis on women's rights is rightly concerned about. With very little amendment, everything that has been said above applies to boys and men too. Although the abortion decision is, in a natural sense, the woman's decision, proper to her, boys and men are often party to it, for well

is (usually) a good and hence (human) death usually an evil. The exceptions would be (*a*) where death is actually a good or a benefit, because the baby that would come to be if the life were not cut short would be better off dead than alive, and (*b*) where death, though not a good, is not an evil either, because the life that would be led (e.g., in a state of permanent coma) would not be a good. (See Foot, "Euthanasia.")

16. I discuss this point at greater length in *Beginning Lives*.

or ill, and even when they are not, they are bound to have been party to the circumstances that brought it up. No less than girls and women, boys and men can, in their actions, manifest self-centeredness, callousness, and light-mindedness about life and parenthood in relation to abortion. They can be self-centered or courageous about the possibility of disability in their offspring; they need to reflect on their sexual activity and their choices, or the lack of them, about their sexual partner and contraception; they need to grow up and take responsibility for their own actions and life in relation to fatherhood. If it is true, as I maintain, that insofar as motherhood is intrinsically worthwhile, being a mother is an important purpose in women's lives, being a father (rather than a mere generator) is an important purpose in men's lives as well, and it is adolescent of men to turn a blind eye to this and pretend that they have many more important things to do.

CONCLUSION

Much more might be said, but I shall end the actual discussion of the problem of abortion here, and conclude by highlighting what I take to be its significant features. These hark back to many of the criticisms of virtue theory discussed earlier.

The discussion does not proceed simply by our trying to answer the question "Would a perfectly virtuous agent ever have an abortion and, if so, when?"; virtue theory is not limited to considering "Would Socrates have had an abortion if he were a raped, pregnant fifteen-year-old?" nor automatically stumped when we are considering circumstances into which no virtuous agent would have got herself. Instead, much of the discussion proceeds in the virtue- and vice-related terms whose application, in several cases, yields practical conclusions (cf. the third and fourth criticisms above). These terms are difficult to apply correctly, and anyone might challenge my application of any one of them. So, for example, I have claimed that some abortions, done for certain reasons, would be callous or light-minded; that others might indicate an appropriate modesty or humility; that others would reflect a greedy and foolish attitude to what one could expect out of life. Any of these examples may be disputed, but what is at issue is, should these difficult terms be there, or should the discussion be couched in terms that all clever adolescents can apply correctly? (Cf. the first half of the "major objection" above.)

Proceeding as it does in the virtue- and vice-related terms, the discussion thereby, inevitably, also contains claims about what is worthwhile, serious and important, good and evil, in our lives. So, for example, I claimed that parenthood is intrinsically worthwhile, and that having a good time was a worthless end (in life, not on individual occasions); that losing a fetus is always a serious matter (albeit not a tragedy in itself in the first trimester) whereas acquiring an appendectomy scar is a trivial one; that (human) death is an evil. Once again, these are difficult matters, and anyone might challenge any one of my claims. But what is at issue is, as before, should those difficult claims be there or can one reach practical conclusions about real moral issues that are in no way determined by premises about such matters? (Cf. the fifth criticism, and the second half of the "major criticism.")

The discussion also thereby, inevitably, contains claims about what life is like (e.g., my claim that love and friendship do not survive their parties' constantly insisting on their rights; or the claim that to demand perfection of life is to run the risk of missing out on happiness entirely). What is at issue is, should those disputable claims be there, or is our knowledge (or are our false opinions) about what life is like irrelevant to our understanding of real moral issues? (Cf. both halves of the "major criticism.")

Naturally, my own view is that all these concepts should be there in any discussion of real moral issues and that virtue theory, which uses all of them, is the right theory to apply to them. I do not pretend to have shown this. I realize that proponents of rival theories may say that, now that they have understood how virtue theory uses the range of concepts it draws on, they are more convinced than ever that such concepts should not figure in an adequate normative theory, because they are sectarian, or vague, or too particular, or improperly anthropocentric, and reinstate what I called the "major criticism." Or, finding many of the details of the discussion appropriate, they may agree that many, perhaps even all, of the concepts should figure, but argue that virtue theory gives an inaccurate account of the way the concepts fit together (and indeed of the concepts themselves) and that another theory provides a better account; that would be interesting to see. Moreover, I admitted that there were at least two problems for virtue theory: that it has to argue against moral skepticism, "pluralism," and cultural relativism, and that it has to find something to say about conflicting requirements of different virtues.

Proponents of rival theories might argue that their favored theory provides better solutions to these problems than virtue theory can. Indeed, they might criticize virtue theory for finding problems here at all. Anyone who argued for at least one of moral skepticism, "pluralism," or cultural relativism could presumably do so (provided their favored theory does not find a similar problem); and a utilitarian might say that benevolence is the only virtue and hence that virtue theory errs when it discusses even apparent conflicts between the requirements of benevolence and some other character trait such as honesty.

Defending virtue theory against all possible, or even likely, criticisms of it would be a lifelong task. As I said at the outset, in this article I aimed to defend the theory against some criticisms which I thought arose from an inadequate understanding of it, and to improve that understanding. If I have succeeded, we may hope for more comprehending criticisms of virtue theory than have appeared hitherto.

[13]

GOING TO THE ROOTS OF THE STEM CELL CONTROVERSY

SØREN HOLM

ABSTRACT

The purpose of this paper is to describe the scientific background to the current ethical and legislative debates about the generation and use of human stem cells, and to give an overview of the ethical issues underlying these debates.

The ethical issues discussed are 1) stem cells and the status of the embryo, 2) women as the sources of ova for stem cell production, 3) the use of ova from other species, 4) slippery slopes towards reproductive cloning, 5) the public presentation of stem cell research and 6) the evaluation of scientific uncertainty and its implications for public policy.

INTRODUCTION

The ability to produce and culture human embryonic stem cells has raised hopes for a range of new cell based therapies, but has at the same time created intense national and international debate.

The purpose of this paper is to describe the scientific background to the current ethical and legislative debates about the generation and use of human stem cells, and to give an overview of the ethical issues that are central to these debates. Because the paper is intended to be reasonably comprehensive the presentation and analysis of each individual argument must necessarily be rather brief.[1]

---

[1] One major topic has been left out of this paper because of space constraints. That is the question of intellectual and actual property rights in human stem cell lines and the techniques by which they are produced. This is a huge topic on its own, actualising all the issues of ownership of the human body, body parts and human genetic material.

494   SØREN HOLM

THE SCIENTIFIC BACKGROUND TO THE STEM CELL CONTROVERSY

Three partially independent scientific developments underlie the current debates about stem cell research. These are 1) the discovery of methods to derive and culture human embryonic stem cells, 2) the discovery of nuclear replacement techniques, and 3) the discovery of new and previously unsuspected potentialities of stem cells in the adult human body.

A stem cell is a non-differentiated cell that can divide and multiply in its undifferentiated state, but which can also give rise to more specialised differentiated cells. It has been known for a long time that adult human tissues contain stem cells that can replenish cells lost through normal wear and tear or through trauma or disease. This fact has been utilised as a basis for a number of different treatments including bone marrow and skin transplants.

It has also been known that cells from the inner cell mass of the early embryo are stem cells (since we know that they must necessarily be able to become every cell in the body during the development from embryo to adult individual), but no method existed by which these embryonic stem cells could be grown in culture in the laboratory in a way that preserved their stem cell character.

In 1998 researchers at the University of Wisconsin published a method for deriving and culturing human embryonic stem cells indefinitely.[2] This development made it possible to create stable human stem cell lines and generate (in principle) unlimited quantities of any particular embryonic stem cell, and thereby the possibility to 1) standardise research into human stem cells, and 2) create reproducible stem cell therapies.

Almost at the same time as the Wisconsin group developed the method for culturing human embryonic stem cells, a group at the Roslin Institute in Scotland developed methods for the cloning of adult mammals using nuclear replacement techniques.[3] The techniques basically work by removing a cell from an adult animal, and then taking the cell nucleus from the adult cell and placing it in an ovum from which the original nucleus

---

[2] J.A. Thomson, J. Itskovitz-Eldor, S.S. Shapiro, M.A. Waknitz, J.J. Swiergiel, V.S. Marshall, J.M. Jones. Embryonic stem cell lines derived from human blastocysts. *Science* 1998; 282: 1145–1147.

[3] I. Wilmut, A.E. Schnieke, J. McWhir, A.J. Kind, K.H. Campbell. Viable offspring derived from foetal and adult mammalian cells. *Nature* 1997; 385: 810–813.

GOING TO THE ROOTS OF THE STEM CELL CONTROVERSY   495

has been removed. This procedure reprogrammes the adult nucleus to an embryonic state and creates a cell that is more than 99% genetically identical with the original adult cell from which the nucleus was taken.[4] It is, however, not the ability to reproduce a fully-grown mammal by nuclear replacement that is of main interest to the stem cell debate. It is the combination of nuclear replacement techniques and embryonic stem cell culture. When these two techniques are combined it becomes possible to produce embryonic stem cells that are almost genetically identical to any given adult human being.

Research into the potentialities of the remaining stem cells in the adult human body has also progressed apace in recent years. Stem cells have been found in a number of tissues in which it was previously 'common knowledge' that they did not exist (e.g. neuronal stem cells in the brain),[5] many kinds of adult stem cells[6] have been cultured, and adult stem cells have been shown to be capable of transdifferentiation into different kinds of cells than the cells of the tissues in which they originated.[7] These discoveries have opened the possibility that adult stem cells may be used in a range of stem cell therapies far beyond what was thought possible.[8]

At present there are thus three main research programmes that are pursued in stem cell research: 1) research on adult stem cells, 2) research on embryonic stem cells from embryos

---

[4] The mitochondria in this cell come from the ovum, and contain their own genetic material. It is thus only if both nucleus and ovum come from the same woman that 100% genetic identity is achieved.

[5] C.B. Johanson, S. Momma, D.L. Clarke, M. Risling, U. Lendahl, J. Friesen. Identification of a neural stem cell in the adult mammalian central nervous system. *Cell* 1999; 96: 25–34.

[6] In this paper 'adult stem cell' will be used for any stem cell derived from a human being after birth.

[7] D.L. Clarke, C.B. Johansson, J. Wilbertz, B. Veress, E. Nilsson, H. Karlstrom, U. Lendahl, J. Friesen. Generalized potential of adult neural stem cells. *Science* 2000; 288: 1559–1561; P.A. Zuk, M. Zhu, H. Mizono, J. Huang, J.W. Futrell, A.J. Katz, P. Benhaim, H.P. Lorenz, M.H. Hedrick. Multilineage cells from human adipose tissue: implications for cell-based therapies. *Tissue Engineering* 2001; 7: 211–228.

[8] Two recent papers cast some doubt on these possibilites for transdifferentiation, but their validity and relevance is contested. N. Terada, T. Hamazaki, M. Oka, M. Hoki, D.M. Mastalerz, Y. Nakano, E.M. Meyer, L. Morel, B.E. Petersen, E.W. Scott. Bone marrow cells adopt the phenotype of other cells by spontaneous cell fusion. *Nature* 2002; 416: 542–545; Q-L. Ling, J. Nichols, E.P. Evans, A.G. Smith. Changing potency by spontaneous fusion. *Nature* 2002; 416: 545–548. N. Dewitt, J. Knight. Biologists question adult stem-cell versatility. *Nature* 2002; 416: 354.

496   SØREN HOLM

produced through IVF techniques, and 3) research on embryonic stem cells produced through nuclear replacement techniques.[9]

All three research programmes are directed at 1) increasing our knowledge about basic cell biology, 2) creating new therapies through stem cell culture and control of cell differentiation, and 3) producing commercially viable stem cell products either by the direct patenting of stem cell lines, or by combining stem cell technology with genetic engineering or other patentable interventions.

As we will see below, much of the discussion on stem cells is concerned with the ethical issues raised by each of these programmes, and with whether or not these ethical issues should influence decisions about regulation and/or funding of the research programmes.

THE EXPECTED BENEFITS FROM STEM CELL RESEARCH

Stem cell research is undoubtedly going to increase our knowledge about basic cell biology considerably, but this is not the benefit of stem cell research that excites most people. The really exciting thing about stem cell research is in the therapeutic potential of stem cells.

If we can develop methods to grow human stem cells in unlimited quantities, and if we can further learn how to control their differentiation, then a whole range of therapeutic possibilities becomes (theoretically) available.[10] The most immediate therapeutic gains are likely to be in the area of cell therapy. Many diseases are caused by, or accompanied by, loss of specific cell types. The lost cell types could be produced in the laboratory and later implanted to cure or alleviate the disease.

---

[9] The term 'research programme' is here used in the sense given to it by Lakatos, i.e. a group of concrete research endeavours kept together by a common core of relatively stable assumptions about the goals of research, the proper research methodologies and the most fruitful research topics. What distinguishes the three stem cell research programmes from each other is primarily different beliefs about what kind of stem cell is going to be the basis for the most progressive (i.e. productive in terms of scientific and commercial results) research. I. Lakatos. 1974. Falsification and the methodology of scientific research programmes. In *Criticism and the Growth of Knowledge*. I. Lakatos and A. Musgrave, eds. Cambridge. Cambridge University Press: 91–196.

[10] R.P. Lanza, J.P. Cibelli, M.D. West. Prospects for the use of nuclear transfer in human transplantation. *Nature Biotechnology* 1999; 17: 1171–1174; E. Fuchs, J.A. Segre. Stem Cells: A New Lease of Life. *Cell* 2000; 100: 143–155.

GOING TO THE ROOTS OF THE STEM CELL CONTROVERSY   497

Further into the future it may become possible to grow whole organs from stem cells and use these for transplantation, removing the need for organ donation; and even further into the future we may be able to use stem cells for rejuvenating therapies leading to an increased life-span.

The therapeutic potential of stem cells spans such a wide range of diseases and conditions that it will constitute a major medical breakthrough if only even a small percentage of the most likely uses (e.g. in the area of cell therapy) become a reality. Even if stem cell therapy turned out only to be effective in myocardial infarction it would still alleviate huge amounts of human suffering.

These very large, and very likely benefits of stem cell research indicate that prohibition of certain kinds of stem cell research needs strong justification. The ethical and regulatory debates have therefore concentrated on whether such justification can be found.

THE ETHICAL ISSUES

Stem cells and embryos

One of the main ethical issues discussed concerning stem cell research originates in the fact that embryonic stem cells have to be generated from embryos that are destroyed in the process. This means that stem cell research again raises the question of whether there are any ethical limits concerning the destruction of human embryos for research or therapeutic purposes, as well as the more fundamental question of the moral status of the human embryo. If human embryos have any moral status we need a good justification to destroy them, and the greater their moral status the more important or weighty the justification has to be.[11]

The question of the moral status of the embryo was not resolved during the abortion debate nor during the debates about various forms of assisted reproductive technologies. It is unlikely to be resolved during the current debates about stem cells, since no really new arguments seem to be forthcoming.[12]

---

[11] R.M. Doerflinger. The ethics of funding embryonic stem cell research: a Catholic viewpoint. *Kennedy Institute of Ethics Journal* 1999; 9: 137–150.

[12] L.H. Harris. Ethics and politics of embryo and stem cell research: Reinscribing the abortion debate. *Women's Health Issues* 2000; 10: 146–151; D.C. Wertz. Embryo and stem cell research in the USA: a political history. *TRENDS in Molecular Medicine* 2002; 8: 143–146.

498   SØREN HOLM

If one looks at the legislation about abortion and assisted reproductive technologies it is evident that no jurisdiction has legislation which is compatible with the view that human embryos are just things with no moral status, and that no jurisdiction has legislation compatible with the view that embryos have the same moral status as born human beings. Most legislations implicitly or explicitly adopt some kind of middle position, although it is often unclear to what extent this represents a considered view or whether it is the result of a political compromise.

The important question with regard to regulation or legislation therefore becomes how the use of embryos for stem cell research and therapy can be fitted into a legislative structure that either relies on a view that embryos have some moral value, or is a direct result of political compromise. Giving some moral status to embryos does not automatically rule out embryonic stem cell research, since it can be argued that the likely benefits in terms of reduction of human suffering and death in many cases outweigh the sacrifice of a (small?) number of human embryos.[13]

All of the ethical questions concerning the use of embryos would be by-passed if it became technically possible to produce cells equivalent to embryonic stem cells, without the creation of embryos. This could, for instance, be the case if other methods for re-programming nuclei from adult cells became available.

PPL Therapeutics PLC has claimed to have done this using bovine cells and is working towards doing it with human cells, but very few details have been released because of commercial concerns.[14]

The spare embryo

In arguments about the use of embryos for stem cell research the distinction between embryos produced for research and spare embryos left over after IVF and other forms of assisted reproduction has also been invoked. It has been argued that the use of spare embryos is less problematic than the use of embryos produced for research, and that at present the use of specifically produced embryos for stem cell research should not be allowed.[15] No new arguments to support or refute this

---

[13] G. McGee, A. Caplan. The ethics and politics of small sacrifices in stem cell research. *Kennedy Institute of Ethics Journal* 1999; 9: 151–158.

[14] PPL Therapeutics PLC. 2001. *Interim Report 2001*. Edinburgh. PPL Therapeutics PLC.

[15] See for instance the report from the American National Bioethics Advisory Commission. National Bioethics Advisory Commission. 1999. *Ethical*

GOING TO THE ROOTS OF THE STEM CELL CONTROVERSY 499

distinction have, however, been forthcoming in the stem cell debate.[16]

Women and the need for ova

If stem cells are to be produced from embryos that are not 'spare' after IVF, the ova for this production must come from women.[17] In the initial research phase the number of ova needed will be relatively small, but for stem cell therapy the number may become very large. If, for instance, a specific therapy is based on nuclear replacement from the intended recipient in order to ensure perfect immunological compatibility, at least one ovum will be needed for each patient (and probably more since the techniques for nuclear replacement are unlikely to become 100% effective any time soon).

This raises general problems concerning how we can ensure that the ova are obtained without coercion or exploitation of the ova donors, sellers or providers, but also more specific questions about how a new practice of non-reproduction related ova procurement would influence the status of women in society.

At an even more general level there is a connection to the debate about the rights and wrongs of the commodification of human body parts.[18]

Issues in Human Stem Cell Research. Rockville. NBAC. A number of jurisdictions have legislation concerning assisted reproductive technologies that allow research on spare embryos, but prohibit the creation of embryos for research purposes.

[16] On the cogency of the distinction see S. Holm. The spare embryo – A red herring in the embryo experimentation debate. *Health Care Analysis* 1993; 1: 63–66.

[17] Unless it is possible to use ova obtained from aborted foetuses, dead women, or ovaries removed as part of surgical interventions. The first two of these alternative sources of ova may in themselves raise ethical issues but these are beyond the scope of this paper.

[18] L.S. Cahill. Genetics, Commodification, and Social Justice in the Globalization Era. *Kennedy Institute of Ethics Journal* 2001; 11: 221–238; S. Holland. Contested Commodities at Both Ends of Life: Buying and Selling Gametes, Embryos, and Body Tissues. *Kennedy Institute of Ethics Journal* 2001; 11: 263–284; L. Andrews, D. Nelkin. 2001. *Body Bazaar: The Market for Human Tissue in the Biotechnology Age.* New York. Crown Publishers; M.J. Radin. 1996. *Contested Commodities.* Cambridge, MA. Harvard University Press; R. Macklin. 1996. What is Wrong with Commodification? In *New Ways of Making Babies: The Case of Egg Donation.* C.B. Cohen, ed. Bloomington. Indiana University Press: 106–121.

500   SØREN HOLM

Stem cells produced using ova from other species

One way of solving the problem of shortage of ova, and the potential ethical problems in using women as donors of ova for these purposes, is to use ova from other species (e.g. bovines) in the creation of stem cells by means of nuclear replacement techniques.

It is, as yet, unknown whether the use of ova from other species is technically possible, and if possible whether the stem cells produced would be functionally and immunologically equivalent to stem cells produced using human ova. The technique has been patented by the American firm Advanced Cell Technology, but there is still doubt in the scientific community whether it actually works.[19]

The additional ethical problems created by this different source of ova can, however, be argued to be small as long as the resulting embryos are only used for stem cell production and not for reproductive purposes.[20]

On some lines of argument the ethical problems may actually be less than if human ova are used, since it could be argued that the embryos produced are not really human embryos. If the moral status of human embryos is based in their being human, then the moral status of these 'less than human' embryos could be argued to be less important.

Slippery slopes towards reproductive cloning

A classical slippery slope argument has been prominent in the specific debate about whether the creation of stem cells by means of cell nuclear replacement techniques should be allowed. Opponents of this technique have claimed that allowing this would put us on a slippery slope towards reproductive cloning. The slope that is imagined is of a technical nature. If all the

---

[19] Advanced Cell Technology. *Advanced Cell Technology Announces Use of Nuclear Replacement Technology for Successful Generation of Human Embryonic Stem Cells.* Press Release November 12, 1998. Available at *http://www.advancedcell.com/ pr_11-12-1998.html* E. Marshall. Claim of human-cow embryo greeted with scepticism. *Science* 1998; 282: 1390–1391.

[20] There are two lines of argument seeing major ethical problems in the use of non-human ova. The first sees the technique in itself as a transgression of an important boundary line between human and animal. The second points to a possible slippery slope from the use of this technique for the production of stem cells, to a use for reproductive purposes.

GOING TO THE ROOTS OF THE STEM CELL CONTROVERSY 501

technical problems in the first steps of cell nuclear replacement techniques are solved succesfully then it becomes both easier and more tempting (because certain risks have been reduced) to try to use nuclear replacement techniques for reproductive cloning.

This is clearly not a problem if reproductive cloning does not raise any serious ethical problems because in that case there is no slope, slippery or not.[21]

If reproductive cloning is ethically problematic the question then becomes how to respond to the existence of the slope. The slope has to be taken seriously by politicians as a policy problem. Whatever the analysis of bioethicists as to the cogency of the belief that reproductive cloning is a serious ethical problem, there is no doubt that this belief is shared by many people and by many politicians.

The political reaction to the perceived slippery slope depends on whether it is seen as a possible threat to the positive development of stem cell research (as it is perceived by the government in the UK and a number of other European countries), or whether it is seen as a possible tool to justify the prohibition of stem cell research by nuclear replacement as part of a more comprehensive ban on all kinds of human cloning (as it is perceived by the government in the US).[22]

If the slope is seen as a possible threat to the acceptance of stem cell research the logical response is to legally prohibit human reproductive cloning, and to try to convince the public that such a prohibition will be effective.[23] Whether legal prohibition can be effective given the possibilities for international reproductive tourism to more permissive jurisdictions is, however, questionable.[24]

---

[21] The literature on the ethics of reproductive cloning is extensive. A range of views can be found in a thematic issue of the *Journal of Medical Ethics* 1999; 25(2), and in a thematic issue of the *Cambridge Quarterly of Health Care Ethics* 1998; 7(2).

[22] E. Check. Call for cloning ban splits UN. *Nature* 2002; 416: 3.

[23] This is the approach chosen by the governments of the UK, Denmark and the Netherlands among others. For an overview of European policies in this area see: L. Matthiessen. 2001. *Survey on opinions from National Ethics Committees or similar bodies, public debate and national legislation in relation to human embryonic stem cell research and use.* Bruxelles. European Commission Research Directorate-General.

[24] P.G. Wood. To what extent can the law control human cloning? *Medicine, Science & the Law,* 1999; 39: 5–10.

502   SØREN HOLM

The presentation of stem cell research – Promising too much too early?

The public presentation of the benefits of stem cell research has often been characterised by the promise of huge and immediate benefits. Like with many other scientific breakthroughs the public has been promised real benefits within 5–10 years, i.e. in this case significant stem cell therapies in routine clinical use.[25] Several years have now elapsed of the 5–10 years and the promised therapies are still not anywhere close to routine clinical use.[26] There are similarities to the initial enthusiastic presentation of gene therapy in the late 1980s and the later problems encountered, and some reason to fear that stem cell therapies will have an equally long trajectory between theoretical possibility and clinical practice. It is likely that many of the current sufferers from some of the conditions for which stem cell therapies have been promised will be long dead before the therapies actually arrive.[27]

It is clearly ethically problematic to raise false expectations in seriously ill people, and even more problematic if this is partly done from self-interest (e.g. to promote one's own research in the media). But the problem may go deeper because the optimistic predictions and the targeting of these predictions on certain groups of diseases also have a function in the political arena where public policy is decided. When gene therapy was initially promoted, and the public and political resistance overcome, gene therapy was promoted as a treatment for the unfortunate people suffering from genetic disorders. Gene therapy was put forward as their only hope of cure and alleviation. Today we do know however, that most gene therapy projects are not directed towards genetic disease, but towards the treatment of common diseases (partly for commercial reasons). The groups that were used as symbolic 'battering rams' to gain political and public acceptance of the gene therapy, have not yet benefited significantly from gene therapy, and many of the people having rarer forms of genetic disorders are unlikely ever to benefit.

---

[25] Anon. Taking stock of spin science. *Nature Biotechnology* 1998; 16: 1291.

[26] Given the time needed for basic research, clinical research and regulatory approval it is unlikely that any therapy using biological materials, and based on a truly novel therapeutic approach could move from initial discovery to clinical use in 5–10 years. See also R. Lovell-Badge. The future for stem cell research. *Nature* 2001; 14: 88–91.

[27] B. Albert. *Presentation to the All-Party Disablement Group* – July 25th 2000. Unpublished manuscript.

GOING TO THE ROOTS OF THE STEM CELL CONTROVERSY   503

Scientific uncertainty, ethical unease and the formulation of public policy

At the current point in time it is not known which (if any) of the three main lines of research described above is going to be most successful in terms of a) generating scientific knowledge about cell biology, and b) generating new stem cell based therapies for common diseases. That each is, at least at the moment, seen as a viable approach with regard to therapy is attested by the fact that many biotech firms have been founded aiming at exploiting each of the approaches.[28]

The question is important because it has been argued that there is no need to permit more ethically contentious ways of generating stem cells, if the same benefits can be realised using less contentious stem cells, either adult stem cells or stem cells from aborted foetuses.[29]

What factors could we use to decide whether one line of research is more promising than another?[30] One possibility is to think about what characteristics a stem cell should have in order to be therapeutically useful and then try to decide which of the research programmes is most likely to be able to lead to the production of such cells, and if more than one can produce the required cells, which one will progress fastest to the goal.[31] We do know (some of) the characteristics that the therapeutically optimal stem cell should display:

1. No immunological rejection
2. Immediate availability

---

[28] N. Axelsen. 2001. Commercial interests in stem cells. In *Nordic Committee on Bioethics. The Ethical Issues in Stem Cell Research.* Copenhagen. Nordic Council of Ministers: 79–80.

[29] J.R. Meyer. Human embryonic stem cells and respect for life. *Journal of Medical Ethics* 2000; 26: 166–170; V. Branick, M.T. Lysaught. Stem cell research: licit or complicit? Is a medical breakthrough based on embryonic and foetal tissue compatible with Catholic teaching? *Health Progress* 1999; 80: 37–42. This kind of reasoning also seems to underlie the National Bioethics Advisory Committee report *op. cit.* note 15, although it draws the line of contentiousness between the spare embryo and the embryo produced for research.

[30] Most of this debate has centred on the therapeutic uses of stem cells. With regard to the 'pure' scientific production of knowledge about cell biology it seems clear that each of the research programmes will produce at least some unique bits of knowledge, and that each of them must therefore be pursued if complete scientific knowledge is the goal.

[31] A difference in speed of development between two research programmes is important, even if they will both eventually lead to the same goal, since any delay in implementation of stem cell therapies entail costs in term of human suffering.

504   SØREN HOLM

3. Availability in large numbers
4. Controlled differentiation to desired cells
5. Controlled integration into existing tissues and biological niches leading to normal function
6. No other biological risks

From a theoretical point of view embryonic stem cells created by nuclear replacement should be able to fulfil most of these requirements. We know that they can become all types of cells, and we know that they are immunologically perfectly compatible. We are, however, not yet able to control their differentiation into all desired cell types, and there may be situations of acute organ or cell failure where we do not have the necessary time to grow a sufficient number of cells to initiate therapy in time.

Embryonic stem cells derived in other ways have the disadvantage of not being immunologically perfectly compatible, but they do, on the other hand, offer the advantage of being potentially immediately available from a stem cell bank in the necessary quantities. Adult stem cells are immunologically compatible, but it is still uncertain whether we can derive all types of cells from adult stem cells, and they may also not be available in sufficient quantities in acute cases.

No type of stem cell therefore fulfils all the criteria for a therapeutically optimal stem cell. How should we evaluate this evidence in order to decide what research programmes to pursue?

At approximately the same time, the American National Bioethics Advisory Commission and a British government expert group reviewed the evidence and came to two rather different conclusions. The National Bioethics Advisory Commission concluded that:

> Currently, we believe that cadaveric fetal tissue and embryos remaining after infertility treatments provide an adequate supply of research resources for federal research projects involving human embryos. Therefore, embryos created specifically for research purposes are not needed at the current time in order to conduct important research in this area.
> [...]
> We conclude that at this time, because other sources are likely to provide the cells needed for the preliminary stages of research, federal funding should not be provided to derive ES cells from SCNT. Nevertheless, the medical utility and

GOING TO THE ROOTS OF THE STEM CELL CONTROVERSY 505

scientific progress of this line of research should be monitored closely.[32]

Whereas the British Chief Medical Officer's Expert Group concluded that:

For some people, particularly those suffering from the diseases likely to benefit from the treatments that could be developed, the fact that research to create embryos by cell nuclear replacement is a necessary step to understanding how to reprogramme adult cells to produce compatible tissue provides sufficient ethical justification for allowing the research to proceed.[33]

What was a fact for one group of experts was clearly not a fact for the other. What is at play here is a different evaluation of the available scientific evidence, but possibly also a different approach to the decision of whether a line of research should be deemed 'necessary'. Is a particular line of research only necessary if it is the only way to get the knowledge we need for stem cell therapies, or is it necessary if scientific progress will otherwise be slowed down and will be much more costly, but will eventually lead to stem cell therapies any way even if this particular line of research is not pursued?[34]

The policy-maker is thus left with a very difficult problem. If we knew that adult stem cell research could deliver therapies for all the conditions where stem cell therapy seems to be a possibility, then there would be a straight forward policy argument for choosing only to support this ethically uncontentious research programme. If the same goal can be obtained in two ways, and if one of them is less contentious than the other it makes good political sense to choose the uncontentious one.[35] If on the other hand there was unequivocal certainty that research using embryonic stem cells was necessary for the development of stem cell therapies for one or more important diseases, a relatively

---

[32] National Bioethics Advisory Commission, *op.cit*, note 15, pp. 71–72.

[33] Chief Medical Officer's Expert Group. 2001. *Stem Cell Research: Medical Progress with Responsibility – A Report from the Chief Medical Officer's Expert Group Reviewing the Potential of Developments in Stem Cell Research and Cell Nuclear Replacement to Benefit Human Health.* London. Department of Health. p. 40.

[34] S. Holm. 2001. European and American ethical debates about stem cells – common underlying themes and some significant differences. In *Nordic Committee on Bioethics. The Ethical Issues in Stem Cell Research.* Copenhagen. Nordic Council of Ministers: 35–45.

[35] This might be the proper policy response even if it would lead to some delay in the development of treatments.

506   SØREN HOLM

strong consequentialist argument would offer itself based on a moral imperative to reduce human suffering, and this could be combined with appeals to consistency in those jurisdictions that already allow some kinds of embryo research.

Because there is scientific uncertainty each of these two lines of argument is, however, considerably weakened because an opponent can always point to uncertainty about the underlying empirical premises concerning whether embryonic stem cell research is necessary or not.

CONCLUSION

It should by now be evident that many of the most discussed ethical issues in connection with stem cell research are minor variants of issues that have been discussed in reproductive ethics since the beginning of modern bioethics in the late 1960s and early 1970s. Many arguments in the stem cell debate, for instance, merely re-iterate arguments for or against giving moral status to embryos, or arguments concerning the validity of the distinction between 'spare' embryos and embryos produced specifically for research. The underlying points of contention in these recycled arguments have not been resolved during the abortion debate, or during the debates about assisted reproductive technologies, and they are unlikely to be resolved now. Each side has arguments that it sees as compelling, but which the other side rejects utterly. It is probably this re-ignition of old debates that has added to the heat of the stem cell debates, because neither side can give ground without fearing a knock on effect on the political accommodations or compromises reached in the abortion and the assisted reproduction areas.

If we take all of these already well known debates into account it seems that there is a rough hierarchy of contentiousness ordering the different ways of producing human stem cells according to how many issues each raise. This would look something like the following (with the most contentious first):

Embryonic stem cells created by nuclear replacement
Embryonic stem cells from embryos created for research
Embryonic stem cells from spare embryos
Adult stem cells

This proposed hierarchy is not very illuminating for ethical analysis, but it may well influence public policy.

There are, however, also a few issues raised by the stem cell debate that are not as well worn. The most interesting of these

GOING TO THE ROOTS OF THE STEM CELL CONTROVERSY 507

are the questions surrounding how public policy should be formed in an area where there is 1) agreement about the value of the goal of a particular kind of research (i.e. the creation of effective stem cell therapies), 2) genuine scientific uncertainty about exactly what line of research is most likely to achieve this goal, and 3) disagreement about the ethical evaluation of some of these lines of research but not about others. This question is perhaps more a question of political or legal philosophy than a question of ethics, but it is nevertheless an issue that should be of interest to those bioethicists who want their elegant analyses transformed into public policy.

Søren Holm
Institute of Medicine, Law and Bioethics
University of Manchester
Manchester M13 9PT
UK
Soren.holm@man.ac.uk

[14]

"Goodbye Dolly?" The ethics of human cloning

John Harris   *The Institute of Medicine, Law and Bioethics, University of Manchester*

Abstract

The ethical implications of human clones have been much alluded to, but have seldom been examined with any rigour. This paper examines the possible uses and abuses of human cloning and draws out the principal ethical dimensions, both of what might be done and its meaning. The paper examines some of the major public and official responses to cloning by authorities such as President Clinton, the World Health Organisation, the European parliament, UNESCO, and others and reveals their inadequacies as foundations for a coherent public policy on human cloning. The paper ends by defending a conception of reproductive rights or "procreative autonomy" which shows human cloning to be not inconsistent with human rights and dignity.

The recent announcement of a birth[1] in the press heralds an event probably unparalleled for two millennia and has highlighted the impact of the genetic revolution on our lives and personal choices. More importantly perhaps, it raises questions about the legitimacy of the sorts of control individuals and society purport to exercise over something, which while it must sound portentous, is nothing less than human destiny. This birth, that of "Dolly", the cloned sheep, is also illustrative of the responsibilities of science and scientists to the communities in which they live and which they serve, and of the public anxiety that sensational scientific achievements sometimes provokes.

The ethical implications of human clones have been much alluded to, but have seldom been examined with any rigour. Here I will examine the possible uses and abuses of human cloning and draw out the principal ethical dimensions, both of what might be done and its meaning, and of public and official responses.

There are two rather different techniques available for cloning individuals. One is by nuclear substitution, the technique used to create Dolly, and the

other is by cell mass division or "embryo splitting". We'll start with cell mass division because this is the only technique for cloning that has, as yet, been used in humans.

Cell mass division

Although the technique of cloning embryos by cell mass division has, for some time been used extensively in animal models, it was used as a way of multiplying human embryos for the first time in October 1993 when Jerry Hall and Robert Stillman[2] at George Washington Medical Centre cloned human embryos by splitting early two- to eight-cell embryos into single embryo cells. Among other uses, cloning by cell mass division or embryo splitting could be used to provide a "twin" embryo for biopsy, permitting an embryo undamaged by invasive procedures to be available for implantation following the result of the biopsy on its twin, or to increase the number of embryos available for implantation in the treatment of infertility.[3] To what extent is such a practice unethical?

Individuals, multiples and genetic variation

Cloning does not produce identical copies of the same individual person. It can only produce identical copies of the same genotype. Our experience of identical twins demonstrates that each is a separate individual with his or her own character, preferences and so on. Although there is some evidence of striking similarities with respect to these factors in twins, there is no question but that each twin is a distinct individual, as independent and as free as is anyone else. To clone Bill Clinton is not to create multiple Presidents of the United States. Artificial clones do not raise any difficulties not raised by the phenomenon of "natural" twins. We do not feel apprehensive when natural twins are born, why should we when twins are deliberately created?

If the objection to cloning is to the creation of identical individuals separated in time, (because the twin embryos might be implanted in different cycles, perhaps even years apart), it is a weak one at best.

Key words

Cloning; Dolly; human dignity; procreative autonomy, human rights.

We should remember that such twins will be "identical" in the sense that they will each have the same genotype, but they will never (unlike some but by no means all natural monozygotic twins) be identical in the more familiar sense of looking identical at the same moment in time. If we think of expected similarities in character, tastes and so on, then the same is true. The further separated in time, the less likely they are to have similarities of *character* (the more different the environment, the more different environmental influence on individuality).

The significant ethical issue here is whether it would be morally defensible, by outlawing the creation of clones by cell mass division, to deny a woman the chance to have the child she desperately seeks. If this procedure would enable a woman to create a sufficient number of embryos to give her a reasonable chance of successfully implanting one or two of them, then the objections to it would have to be weighty indeed. If pre-implantation testing by cell biopsy might damage the embryo to be implanted, would it be defensible to prefer this to testing a clone, if technology permits such a clone to be created without damage, by separating a cell or two from the embryonic cell mass? If we assume each procedure to have been perfected and to be equally safe, we must ask what the ethical difference would be between taking a cell for cell biopsy and destroying it thereafter, and taking a cell to create a clone, and then destroying the clone? The answer can only be that destroying the cloned embryo would constitute a waste of human potential. But this same potential is wasted whenever an embryo is not implanted.

Nuclear substitution: the birth of Dolly

This technique involves (crudely described) deleting the nucleus of an egg cell and substituting the nucleus taken from the cell of another individual. This can be done using cells from an adult. The first viable offspring produced from fetal and adult mammalian cells was reported from an Edinburgh-based group in *Nature* on February 27, 1997.[4] The event caused an international sensation and was widely reported in the world press. President Clinton of the United States called for an investigation into the ethics of such procedures and announced a moratorium on public spending on human cloning; the British Nobel Prize winner, Joseph Rotblat, described it as science out of control, creating "a means of mass destruction",[5] and the German newspaper *Die Welt*, evoked the Third Reich, commenting: "The cloning of human beings would fit precisely into Adolph Hitler's world view".[6]

More sober commentators were similarly panicked into instant reaction. Dr Hiroshi Nakajima, Director General of the World Health Organisation said: "WHO considers the use of cloning for the replication of human individuals to be ethically unacceptable as it would violate some of the basic principles which govern medically assisted procreation. These include respect for the dignity of the human being and protection of the security of human genetic material".[7] The World Health Organisation followed up the line taken by Nakajima with a resolution of the Fiftieth World Health Assembly which saw fit to affirm "that the use of cloning for the replication of human individuals is ethically unacceptable and contrary to human integrity and morality".[8] Federico Mayor of UNESCO, equally quick off the mark, commented: "Human beings must not be cloned under any circumstances. Moreover, UNESCO's International Bioethics Committee (IBC), which has been reflecting on the ethics of scientific progress, has maintained that the human genome must be preserved as common heritage of humanity".[9]

The European parliament rushed through a resolution on cloning, the preamble of which asserted, (paragraph B):

"[T]he cloning of human beings . . . , cannot under any circumstances be justified or tolerated by any society, because it is a serious violation of fundamental human rights and is contrary to the principle of equality of human beings as it permits a eugenic and racist selection of the human race, it offends against human dignity and it requires experimentation on humans," And which went on to claim that, (clause 1) "each individual has a right to his or her own genetic identity and that human cloning is, and must continue to be, prohibited".[10]

These statements are, perhaps un-surprisingly, thin on argument and rationale; they appear to have been plucked from the air to justify an instant reaction. There are vague references to "human rights" or "basic principles" with little or no attempt to explain what these principles are, or to indicate how they might apply to cloning. The WHO statement, for example, refers to the basic principles which govern human reproduction and singles out "respect for the dignity of the human being" and "protection of the security of genetic material". How, we are entitled to ask, is the security of genetic material compromised? Is it less secure when inserted with precision by scientists, or when spread around with the characteristic negligence of the average human male?[11]

Human dignity

Appeals to human dignity, on the other hand, while universally attractive, are comprehensively vague and deserve separate attention. A first question to ask when the idea of human dignity is invoked is: whose dignity is attacked and how? Is it the duplication of a large part of the genome that is supposed to constitute the attack on human dignity? If so we might legitimately ask whether and how the dignity of a natural twin is threatened by the existence of her sister? The notion of human dignity is often also linked to Kantian ethics. A typical example, and one that attempts to provide some basis for objections to cloning based on human dignity, was Axel Kahn's invocation of this principle in his commentary on cloning in *Nature*.[12]

"The creation of human clones solely for spare cell lines would, from a philosophical point of view, be in obvious contradiction to the principle expressed by Emmanuel Kant: that of human dignity. This principle demands that an individual – and I would extend this to read human life – should never be thought of as a means, but always also as an end. Creating human life for the sole purpose of preparing therapeutic material would clearly not be for the dignity of the life created."

The Kantian principle, crudely invoked as it usually is without any qualification or gloss, is seldom helpful in medical or bio-science contexts. As formulated by Kahn, for example, it would outlaw blood transfusions The beneficiary of blood donation, neither knowing of, nor usually caring about, the anonymous donor uses the blood (and its' donor) simply as a means to her own ends. It would also outlaw abortions to protect the life or health of the mother.

Instrumentalization

This idea of using individuals as a means to the purposes of others is sometimes termed "instrumentalization". Applying this idea coherently or consistently is not easy! If someone wants to have children in order to continue their genetic line do they act instrumentally? Where, as is standard practice in *in vitro* fertilisation (IVF), spare embryos are created, are these embryos created instrumentally? If not how do they differ from embryos created by embryo splitting for use in assisted reproduction?[13]

Kahn responded in the journal *Nature* to these objections.[14] He reminds us, rightly, that Kant's famous principle states: "respect for human dignity requires that an individual is *never* used . . . *exclusively* as a means" and suggests that I have ignored the crucial use of the term "exclusively". I did not of course, and I'm happy with Kahn's reformulation of the principle. It is not that Kant's principle does not have powerful intuitive force, but that it is so vague and so open to selective interpretation and its scope for application is consequently so limited, that its utility as one of the "fundamental principles of modern bioethical thought", as Kahn describes it, is virtually zero.

Kahn himself rightly points out that debates concerning the moral status of the human embryo are debates about whether embryos fall within the *scope* of Kant's or indeed any other moral principles concerning persons; so the principle itself is not illuminating in this context. Applied to the creation of individuals which are, or will become autonomous, it has limited application. True the Kantian principle rules out slavery, but so do a range of other principles based on autonomy and rights. If you are interested in the ethics of creating people then, so long as existence is in the created individual's own best interests, and the individual will have the capacity for autonomy like any other, then the motives for which the individual was created are either morally irrelevant or subordinate to other moral considerations. So that even where, for example, a child is engendered exclusively to provide "a son and heir" (as so often in so many cultures) it is unclear how or whether Kant' principle applies. Either other motives are also attributed to the parent to square parental purposes with Kant, or the child's eventual autonomy, and its clear and substantial interest in or benefit from existence, take precedence over the comparatively trivial issue of parental motives. Either way the "fundamental principle of modern bioethical thought" is unhelpful and debates about whether or not an individual has been used *exclusively* as a means are sterile and usually irresolvable.

We noted earlier the possibility of using embryo splitting to allow genetic and other screening by embryo biopsy. One embryo could be tested and then destroyed to ascertain the health and genetic status of the remaining clones. Again, an objection often voiced to this is that it would violate the Kantian principle, and that "one twin would be destroyed for the sake of another".

This is a bizarre and misleading objection both to using cell mass division to create clones for screening purposes, and to creating clones by nuclear substitution to generate spare cell lines. It is surely ethically dubious to object to one embryo being sacrificed for the sake of another, but not to object to it being sacrificed for nothing. In *in vitro* fertilisation, for example, it is, in the United Kingdom, currently regarded as good practice to store spare embryos for future use by the mother or for disposal at her direction, either to other women who require donor embryos, or for research, or simply to be destroyed. It cannot be morally worse to use an embryo to provide information about its sibling, than to use it for more abstract research or simply to destroy it. If it is permissible to use early embryos for research or to destroy them, their use in genetic and other health testing is surely also permissible. The same would surely go for their use in creating cell lines for therapeutic purposes.

It is better to do good

A moral principle, that has at least as much intuitive force as that recommended by Kant, is that it is better to do some good than to do no good. It cannot, from the ethical point of view, be better or more moral to waste human material that could be used for therapeutic purposes, than to use it to do good. And I cannot but think that if it is right to *use* embryos for research or therapy then it is also right to *produce* them for such purposes.[15] Kant's prohibition does after all refer principally to use. Of course some will think that the embryo is a full member of the moral community with all the rights and protections possessed by Kant himself. While this is a tenable position, it is not one held by any society which permits abortion, post-coital contraception, or research with human embryos.

The UNESCO approach to cloning is scarcely more coherent than that of WHO; how does cloning affect "the preservation of the human genome as common heritage of humanity"? Does this mean that the human genome must be "preserved intact", that is without variation, or does it mean simply that it must not be "reproduced a-sexually"? Cloning cannot be said to impact on the variability of the human genome, it merely repeats one infinitely small part of it, a part that is repeated at a natural rate of about 3·5 per thousand births.[16]

Genetic variability

So many of the fears expressed about cloning, and indeed about genetic engineering more generally, invoke the idea of the effect on the gene pool or upon genetic variability or assert the sanctity of the human genome as a common resource or heritage. It is very difficult to understand what is allegedly at stake here. The issue of genetic variation need not detain us long. The numbers of twins produced by cloning will always be so small compared to the human gene pool in totality, that the effect on the variation of the human gene pool will be vanishingly small. We can say with confidence that the human genome and the human population were not threatened at the start of the present millennium in the year AD one, and yet the world population was then perhaps one per cent of what it is today. Natural species are usually said to be endangered when the population falls to about one thousand breeding individuals; by these standards fears for humankind and its genome may be said to have been somewhat exaggerated.[17]

The resolution of the European parliament goes into slightly more detail; having repeated the, now mandatory, waft in the direction of fundamental human rights and human dignity, it actually produces an argument. It suggests that cloning violates the principal of equality, "as it permits a eugenic and racist selection of the human race". Well, so does prenatal, and pre-implantation screening, not to mention egg donation, sperm donation, surrogacy, abortion and human preference in choice of sexual partner. The fact that a technique could be abused does not constitute an argument against the technique, unless there is no prospect of preventing the abuse or wrongful use. To ban cloning on the grounds that it might be used for racist purposes is tantamount to saying that sexual intercourse should be prohibited because it permits the possibility of rape.

Genetic identity

The second principle appealed to by the European parliament states, that "each individual has a right to his or her own genetic identity". Leaving aside the inevitable contribution of mitochondrial DNA,[18] we have seen that, as in the case of natural identical twins, genetic identity is not an essential component of personal identity[19] nor is it necessary for "individuality". Moreover, unless genetic identity is required either for personal identity, or for individuality, it is not clear why there should be a right to such a thing. But if there is, what are we to do about the rights of identical twins?

Suppose there came into being a life-threatening (or even disabling) condition that affected pregnant women and that there was an effective treatment, the only side effect of which was that it caused the embryo to divide, resulting in twins. Would the existence of the supposed right conjured up by the European parliament mean that the therapy should be outlawed? Suppose that an effective vaccine for HIV was developed which had the effect of doubling the natural twinning rate; would this be a violation of fundamental human rights? Are we to foreclose the possible benefits to be derived from human cloning on so flimsy a basis? We should recall that the natural occurrence of monozygotic (identical) twins is one in 270 pregnancies. This means that in the United Kingdom, with a population of about 58 million, over 200 thousand such pregnancies have occurred. How are we to regard human rights violations on such a grand scale?

A right to parents

The apparently overwhelming imperative to identify some right that is violated by human cloning sometimes expresses itself in the assertion of "a right to have two parents" or as "the right to be the product of the mixture of the genes of two individuals". These are on the face of it highly artificial and problematic rights – where have they sprung from, save from a desperate attempt to conjure some rights that have been violated by cloning? However, let's take them seriously for a moment and grant that they have some force. Are they necessarily violated by the nuclear transfer technique?

If the right to have two parents is understood to be the right to have two social parents, then it is of course only violated by cloning if the family identified as the one to rear the resulting child is a one-parent family. This is not of course necessarily any more likely a result of cloning, than of the use of any of the other new reproductive technologies (or indeed of sexual reproduction). Moreover if there is such a right, it is widely violated, creating countless "victims", and there is no significant evidence of any enduring harm from the violation of this supposed right. Indeed war widows throughout the world would find its assertion highly offensive.

If, on the other hand we interpret a right to two parents as the right to be the product of the mixture of the genes of two individuals, then the supposition that this right is violated when the nucleus of the cell of one individual is inserted into the de-nucleated egg of another, is false in the way this claim is usually understood. There is at least one sense in which a right expressed in this form might be violated by cloning, but not in any way which has force as an objection. Firstly it is false to think that the clone is the genetic child of the nucleus donor. It is not. The clone is the twin brother or sister of the nucleus donor and the genetic offspring of the nucleus donor's own parents. Thus this type of cloned individual is, and always must be, the genetic child of two separate genotypes, of two genetically different individuals, however often it is cloned or re-cloned.

Two parents good, three parents better

However, the supposed right to be the product of two separate individuals is perhaps violated by cloning in a novel way. The de-nucleated egg contains mitochondrial DNA – genes from the female whose egg it is. The inevitable presence of the mitochondrial genome of the egg donor, means that the genetic inheritance of clones is in fact richer than that of other individuals, richer in the sense of being more variously derived.[20] This can be important if the nucleus donor is subject to mitochondrial diseases inherited from his or her mother and wants a child genetically related to her that will be free of these diseases. How this affects alleged rights to particular combinations of "parents" is more difficult to imagine, and perhaps underlines the confused nature of such claims.

What good is cloning?

One major reason for developing cloning in animals is said to be[4] to permit the study of genetic diseases and indeed genetic development more generally. Whether or not there would be major advantages in human cloning by nuclear substitution is not yet clear. Certainly it would enable some infertile people to have children genetically related to them, it offers the prospect, as we have noted, of preventing some diseases caused by mitochondrial DNA, and could help "carriers" of X-linked and autosomal recessive disorders to have their own genetic children without risk of passing on the disease. It is also possible that cloning could be used for the creation of "spare parts" by for example, growing stem cells for

particular cell types from non-diseased parts of an adult.

Any attempt to use this technique in the United Kingdom, is widely thought to be illegal. Whether it would in fact be illegal might turn on whether it is plausible to regard such cloning as the product of "fertilisation". Apparently only fertilised embryos are covered by the *Human Fertilisation and Embryology Act 1990.*[21] The technique used in Edinburgh which involves deleting the nucleus of an unfertilised egg and then substituting a cell nucleus from an existing individual, by-passes what is normally considered to be fertilisation completely and may therefore turn out not to be covered by existing legislation. On the other hand, if as seems logical, we consider "fertilisation" as the moment when all forty-six chromosomes are present and the zygote is formed the problem does not arise.

The unease caused by Dolly's birth may be due to the fact that it was just such a technique that informed the plot of the film "The Boys from Brazil" in which Hitler's genotype was cloned to produce a fuehrer for the future. The prospect of limitless numbers of clones of Hitler is rightly disturbing. However, the numbers of clones that could be produced of any one genotype will, for the foreseeable future, be limited not by the number of copies that could be made of one genotype (using serial nuclear transfer techniques 470 copies of a single nuclear gene in cattle have been reported),[22] but by the availability of host human mothers.[23] Mass production in any democracy could therefore scarcely be envisaged. Moreover, the futility of any such attempt is obvious. Hitler's genotype might conceivably produce a "gonadically challenged" individual of limited stature, but reliability in producing an evil and vicious megalomaniac is far more problematic, for reasons already noted in our consideration of cloning by cell mass division.

Dolly collapses the divide between germ and somatic cells

There are some interesting implications of cloning by nuclear substitution (which have been clear since frogs were cloned by this method in the 1950s) which have not apparently been noticed.[24] There is currently a world-wide moratorium on manipulation of the human germ line, while therapeutic somatic line interventions are, in principal, permitted.[13] However, inserting the mature nucleus of an adult cell into a de-nucleated egg turns the cells thus formed into germ line cells. This has three important effects. First, it effectively eradicates the firm divide between germ line and somatic line nuclei because each adult cell nucleus is in principle "translatable" into a germ line cell nucleus by transferring its nucleus and creating a clone. Secondly, it permits somatic line modifications to human cells to become germ line modifications. Suppose you permanently insert a normal copy of the adenosine deaminase gene into the bone marrow cells of an individual suffering from severe combined immuno-deficiency (which affects the so called "bubble boy" who has to live in a protective bubble of clean air) with obvious beneficial therapeutic effects. This is a somatic line modification. If you then cloned a permanently genetically modified bone marrow cell from this individual, the modified genome would be passed to the clone and become part of his or her genome, transmissible to her offspring indefinitely through the germ line. Thus a benefit that would have perished with the original recipient and not been passed on for the protection of her children, can be conferred on subsequent generations by cloning.[25] The third effect is that it shows the oft asserted moral divide between germ line and somatic line therapy to be even more ludicrous than was previously supposed.[15]

Immortality?

Of course some vainglorious individuals might wish to have offspring not simply with their genes but with a matching genotype. However, there is no way that they could make such an individual a duplicate of themselves. So many years later the environmental influences would be radically different, and since every choice, however insignificant, causes a life-path to branch with unpredictable consequences, the holy grail of duplication would be doomed to remain a fruitless quest. We can conclude that people who would clone themselves would probably be foolish and ill-advised, but would they be immoral and would their attempts harm society or their children significantly?

Whether we should legislate to prevent people reproducing, not 23 but all 46 chromosomes, seems more problematic for reasons we have already examined, but we might have reason to be uncomfortable about the likely standards and effects of child-rearing by those who would clone themselves. Their attempts to mould their child in their own image would be likely to be more pronounced than the average. Whether they would likely be worse than so many people's attempts to duplicate race, religion and culture, which are widely accepted as respectable in the contemporary world, might well depend on the character and constitution of the genotype donor. Where identical twins occur naturally we might think of it as "horizontal twinning", where twins are created by nuclear substitution we have a sort of "vertical twinning". Although horizontal twins would be closer to one another in every way, we do not seem much disturbed by their natural occurrence. Why we should be disturbed either by artificial horizontal twinning or by vertical twinning (where differences between the twins would be greater) is entirely unclear.

Suppose a woman's only chance of having "her own" genetic child was by cloning herself; what are the strong arguments that should compel her to accept that it would be wrong to use nuclear substitution? We must assume that this cloning technique is safe, and that initial fears that individuals produced using nuclear substitution might age more rapidly have proved groundless.[26] We usually grant the so called "genetic imperative" as an important part of the right to found a family, of procreative autonomy.[27] The desire of people to have "their own" genetic children is widely accepted, and if we grant the legitimacy of genetic aspirations in so many cases, and the use of so many technologies to meet these aspirations,[28] we need appropriately serious and weighty reasons to deny them here.

It is perhaps salutary to remember that there is no necessary connection between phenomena, attitudes or actions that make us uneasy, or even those that disgust us, and those phenomena, attitudes, and actions that there are good reasons for judging unethical. Nor does it follow that those things we are confident *are* unethical must be prohibited by legislation or regulation.

We have looked at some of the objections to human cloning and found them less than plausible, we should now turn to one powerful argument that has recently been advanced in favour of a tolerant attitude to varieties of human reproduction.

Procreative autonomy

We have examined the arguments for and against permitting the cloning of human individuals. At the heart of these questions is the issue of whether or not people have rights to control their reproductive destiny and, so far as they can do so without violating the rights of others or threatening society, to choose their own procreative path. We have seen that it has been claimed that cloning violates principles of human dignity. We will conclude by briefly examining an approach which suggests rather that failing to permit cloning might violate principles of dignity.

The American philosopher and legal theorist, Ronald Dworkin has outlined the arguments for a right to what he calls "procreative autonomy" and has defined this right as "a right to control their own role in procreation unless the state has a compelling reason for denying them that control".[29] Arguably, freedom to clone one's own genes might also be defended as a dimension of procreative autonomy because so many people and agencies have been attracted by the idea of the special nature of genes and have linked the procreative imperative to the genetic imperative.

"The right of procreative autonomy follows from any competent interpretation of the due process clause and of the Supreme Court's past decisions applying it. . . . The First Amendment prohibits government from establishing any religion, and it guarantees all citizens free exercise of their own religion. The Fourteenth Amendment, which incorporates the First Amendment, imposes the same prohibition and same responsibility on states. These provisions also guarantee the right of procreative autonomy."[30]

The point is that the sorts of freedoms which freedom of religion guarantees, freedom to choose one's own way of life and live according to one's most deeply held beliefs are also at the heart of procreative choices. And Dworkin concludes:

"that no one may be prevented from influencing the shared moral environment, through his own private choices, tastes, opinions, and example, just because these tastes or opinions disgust those who have the power to shut him up or lock him up."[31]

Thus it may be that we should be prepared to accept both some degree of offence and some social disadvantages as a price we should be willing to pay in order to protect freedom of choice in matters of procreation and perhaps this applies to cloning as much as to more straightforward or usual procreative preferences.[32]

The nub of the argument is complex and abstract but it is worth stating at some length. I cannot improve upon Dworkin's formulation of it.

"The right of procreative autonomy has an important place . . . in Western political culture more generally. The most important feature of that culture is a belief in individual human dignity: that people have the moral right – and the moral responsibility – to confront the most fundamental questions about the meaning and value of their own lives for themselves, answering to their own consciences and convictions. . . . The principle of procreative autonomy, in a broad sense, is embedded in any genuinely democratic culture."[33]

In so far as decisions to reproduce in particular ways or even using particular technologies constitute decisions concerning central issues of value, then arguably the freedom to make them is guaranteed by the constitution (written or not) of any democratic society, unless the state has a compelling reason for denying its citizens that control. To establish such a compelling reason the state (or indeed a federation or union of states, such as the European Union for example) would have to show that more was at stake than the fact that a majority found the ideas disturbing or even disgusting.

As yet, in the case of human cloning, such compelling reasons have not been produced. Suggestions have been made, but have not been sustained, that human dignity may be compromised by the techniques of cloning. Dworkin's arguments suggest that human dignity and indeed democratic constitutions may be compromised by attempts to limit procreative autonomy, at least where greater values cannot be shown to be thereby threatened.

In the absence of compelling arguments against human cloning, we can bid Dolly a cautious "hello". We surely have sufficient reasons to permit experiments on human embryos to proceed, provided, as with any such experiments, the embryos are destroyed at an early stage.[34] While we wait to see whether the technique will ever be established as safe, we should consider the best ways to regulate its uptake until we are in a position to know what will emerge both by way of benefits and in terms of burdens.

Acknowledgements

This paper was presented to the *UNDP/WHO/World Bank Special Programme of Research, Development and Research Training in Human Reproduction* Scientific and Ethical Review Group Meeting, Geneva 25th April 1997 and to a hearing on cloning held by the *European parliament* in Brussels, 7th May 1997. I am grateful to participants at these events for many stimulating insights. I must also thank Justine Burley, Christopher Graham and Pedro Lowenstein for many constructive comments.

John Harris is Sir David Alliance Professor of Bioethics and Research Director of The Centre For Social Ethics and Policy, University of Manchester and a Director of The Institute of Medicine, Law and Bioethics.

References and notes

1 The arguments concerning human dignity are developed in my Cloning and human dignity in *The Cambridge Quarterly of Healthcare Ethics* [in press].The issues raised by cloning were discussed in a special issue of the *Kennedy Institute of Ethics Journal* 1994; **4**,3 and in my *Wonderwoman and Superman: the ethics of human biotechnology.* Oxford University Press, Oxford 1992, especially ch 1.

2 Human embryo cloning reported. *Science* 1993; **262:** 652–3.

3 Where few eggs can be successfully recovered or where only one embryo has been successfully fertilised, this method can multiply the embryos available for implantation to increase the chances of successful infertility treatment.

4 Wilmut I *et al.* Viable offspring derived from fetal and adult mammalian cells. *Nature* 1997; **385:** 810–13.

5 Arlidge J. *The Guardian* 1997 Feb 26: 6.

6 Radford T. *The Guardian* 1997 Feb 28: 1.

7 WHO press release (WHO/20 1997 Mar 11).

8 WHO document (WHA50.37 1997 May 14). Despite the findings of a meeting of the Scientific and Ethical Review Group (see **Acknowledgements**) which recommended that "the next step should be a thorough exploration and fuller discussion of the [issues]".

9 UNESCO press release No 97-29 1997 Feb 28.

360   *"Goodbye Dolly?" The ethics of human cloning*

10 The European parliament. Resolution on cloning. Motion dated March 11 1997. Passed March 13 1997.
11 Perhaps the sin of Onan was to compromise the security of his genetic material?
12 Kahn A. Clone mammals . . . clone man. *Nature* 1997; **386:** 119.
13 For use of the term and the idea of "instrumentalization" see: *Opinion of the group of advisers on the ethical implications of biotechnology to the European Commission No 9.* 1997 28 May. Rapporteur, Dr Anne McClaren.
14 Kahn A. Cloning, dignity and ethical revisionism. *Nature* 1997; **388:** 320. Harris J. Is cloning an attack on human dignity? *Nature* 1997; **387:** 754.
15 See my *Wonderwoman and Superman: the ethics of human biotechnology.* Oxford University press, Oxford 1992: ch 2.
16 It is unlikely that "artificial" cloning would ever approach such a rate on a global scale and we could, of course, use regulative mechanisms to prevent this without banning the process entirely. I take this figure of the rate of natural twinning from Moore KL and Persaud TVN. *The developing human* [5th ed]. Philadelphia: WB Saunders, 1993. The rate mentioned is 1 per 270 pregnancies.
17 Of course if *all* people were compulsorily sterilised and reproduced only by cloning, genetic variation would become fixed at current levels. This would halt the evolutionary process. How bad or good *this* would be could only be known if the course of future evolution and its effects could be accurately predicted.
18 Mitochondrial DNA individualises the genotype even of clones to some extent.
19 Although of course there would be implications for criminal justice since clones could not be differentiated by so called "genetic fingerprinting" techniques.
20 Unless of course the nucleus donor is also the egg donor.
21 Margaret Brazier alerted me to this possibility.
22 Apparently Alan Trounson's group in Melbourne Australia have recorded this result. *The Herald Sun* 1997 Mar 13.
23 What mad dictators might achieve is another matter; but such individuals are, almost by definition, impervious to moral argument and can therefore, for present purposes, be ignored.
24 Except by Pedro Lowenstein, who pointed them out to me.
25 These possibilities were pointed out to me by Pedro Lowenstein who is currently working on the implications for human gene therapy.
26 Science and technology: *The Economist* 1997 Mar 1: 101–4.
27 *Universal Declaration of Human Rights* (article 16). *European Convention on Human Rights* (article 12). These are vague protections and do not mention any particular ways of founding families.
28 These include the use of reproductive technologies such as surrogacy and Intra Cytoplasmic Sperm Injection (ICSI).
29 Dworkin R. *Life's dominion.* London: Harper Collins, 1993: 148.
30 See reference 28: 160.
31 Dworkin R. *Freedom's law.* Oxford: Oxford University Press, 1996: 237–8.
32 Ronald Dworkin has produced an elegant account of the way the price we should be willing to pay for freedom might or might not be traded off against the costs. See his *Taking rights seriously,* London: Duckworth, 1977: ch 10. And his *A matter of principle,* Cambridge, Mass: Harvard University Press, 1985: ch 17.
33 See reference 27: 166–7.
34 The blanket objection to experimentation on humans suggested by the European parliament resolution would dramatically change current practice on the use of spare or experimental human embryos.

Part III
Reproductive Ethics

[15]

Genetic Dilemmas and the Child's Right to an Open Future

by Dena S. Davis

Although deeply committed to the model of nondirective counseling, most genetic counselors enter the profession with certain assumptions about health and disability—for example, that it is preferable to be a hearing person than a deaf person. Thus, most genetic counselors are deeply troubled when parents with certain disabilities ask for assistance in having a child who shares their disability. This ethical challenge benefits little from viewing it as a conflict between beneficence and autonomy. The challenge is better recast as a conflict between parental autonomy and the child's future autonomy.

Dena S. Davis, "Genetic Dilemmas and the Child's Right to an Open Future," *Hastings Center Report* 27, no. 2 (1997): 7-15.

The profession of genetic counseling is strongly characterized by a respect for patient autonomy that is greater than in almost any other area of medicine. When moral challenges arise in the clinical practice of genetics, they tend to be understood as conflicts between the obligation to respect patient autonomy and other ethical norms, such as doing good and avoiding harm. Thus, a typical counseling dilemma exists when a person who has been tested and found to be carrying the gene for Tay-Sachs disease refuses to share that information with siblings and other relatives despite the clear benefits to them of having that knowledge, or when a family member declines to participate in a testing protocol necessary to help another member discover his or her genetic status.

This way of looking at moral issues in genetic counseling often leaves both the counselors and commentators frustrated, for two reasons. First, by elevating respect for patient autonomy above all other values, it may be difficult to give proper weight to other factors, such as human suffering. Second, by privileging patient autonomy and by defining the patient as the person or couple who has come for counseling, there seems no "space" in which to give proper attention to the moral claims of the future child who is the endpoint of many counseling interactions.

These difficulties have been highlighted of late by the surfacing of a new kind of genetic counseling request: parents with certain disabilities who seek help in trying to assure that they will have a child who shares their disability. The two reported instances are in families affected by achondroplasia (dwarfism) and by hereditary deafness. This essay will focus on deafness.

Such requests are understandably troubling to genetic counselors. Deeply committed to the principle of giving clients value-free information with which to make their own choices, most counselors nonetheless make certain assumptions about health and disability—for example, that it is preferable to be a hearing person rather than a deaf person. Thus, counselors typically talk of the "risk" of having a child with a particular genetic condition. Counselors may have learned (sometimes with great difficulty) to respect clients' decisions not to find out if their fetus has a certain condition or not to abort a fetus which carries a genetic disability. But to respect a parental value system that not only favors what most of us consider to be a disability, but actively expresses that preference by attempting to have a child with the condition, is "the ultimate test of nondirective counseling."[1]

To describe the challenge primarily as one that pits beneficence (concern for the child's quality of life) against autonomy (concern for the parents' right to decide about these matters) makes for obvious difficulties. These are two very different values, and comparing and weighing them invites the proverbial analogy of "apples and oranges." After all, the perennial critique of a principle-based ethics is that it offers few suggestions for ranking principles when duties conflict. Further, beneficence and respect for autonomy are values that will always exist in some tension within genetic counseling. For all the reasons I list below, counselors are committed to the primacy of patient autonomy and therefore to nondirective counseling. But surely, most or all of them are drawn to the field because they want to help people avoid or at least mitigate suffering.

Faced with the ethical challenge of parents who wish to ensure children who have a disability, I suggest a different way to look at this problem. Thinking this problem through in the way I suggest will shed light on some related topics in genetics as well, such as sex selection. I propose that, rather than conceiving this as a conflict between autonomy and beneficence, we recast it as a conflict between parental autonomy and the child's future autonomy: what Joel Feinberg has called "the child's right to an open future."

New Challenges

The Code of Ethics of the National Society of Genetic Counselors states that its members strive to:

• Respect their clients' beliefs, cultural traditions, inclinations, circumstances, and feelings.

• Enable their clients to make informed independent decisions, free of coercion, by providing or illuminating the necessary facts and clarifying the alternatives and anticipated consequences.[2]

Considering the uncertain and stochastic nature of genetic counseling, and especially in light of the difficulty physicians experience in sharing uncertainty with patients, it is remarkable that medical geneticists have hewed so strongly to an ethic of patient autonomy. This phenomenon can be explained by at least five factors: the desire to disassociate themselves as strongly as possible from the discredited eugenics movement;[3] an equally strong desire to avoid the label of "abortionist," a realistic fear if counselors are perceived as advocates for abortion of genetically damaged fetuses;[4] the fact that few treatments are available for genetic diseases (p. 29); an awareness of the intensely private nature of reproductive decisions; and the fact that genetic decisions can have major consequences for entire families.[5] As one counselor was quoted, "I am not going to be taking that baby home—they will."[6]

The commitment to patient autonomy faces new challenges with the advances arising from the Human Genome Project. The example of hereditary deafness is reported by Walter E. Nance, who writes:

It turns out that some deaf couples feel threatened by the prospect of having a hearing child and would actually prefer to have a deaf child. The knowledge that we will soon acquire [due to the Human Genome Project] will, of course, provide us with the technology that could be used to assist such couples in achieving their goals. This, in turn, could lead to the ultimate test of nondirective counseling. Does adherence to the concept of nondirective counseling actually require that we assist such a couple in terminating a pregnancy with a hearing child or is this nonsense?[7]

Several issues must be unpacked here. First, I question Nance's depiction of deaf parents as feeling "threatened" by the prospect of a hearing child. From Nance's own depiction of the deaf people he encounters, it is at least as likely that deaf parents feel that a deaf child would fit into their family better, especially if the parents themselves are "deaf of deaf" or if they already have one or more deaf children. Or perhaps the parents feel that Deafness (I use the capital "D," as Deaf people do, to signify Deafness as a culture) is an asset—tough at times but worthwhile in the end—like belonging to a racial or religious minority.

Second, I want to avoid the issue of abortion by discussing the issue of "deliberately producing a deaf child" as distinct from the question of achieving that end by aborting a hearing fetus. The latter topic is important, but it falls outside the purview of this paper. I will focus on the scenario where a deaf child is produced without recourse to abortion. We can imagine a situation in the near future where eggs or sperm can be scrutinized for the relevant trait before fertilization, or the present situation in which preimplantation genetic diagnosis after in vitro fertilization allows specialists to examine the genetic makeup of the very early embryo before it is implanted.

Imagine a Deaf couple approaching a genetic counselor. The couple's goals are to learn more about the cause(s) of their own deafness, and, if possible, to maximize the chance that any pregnancy they embark upon will result in a Deaf child. Let us suppose that the couple falls into the 50 percent of clients whose Deafness has a genetic origin.[8] The genetic counselor who adheres strictly to the tenets of client autonomy will respond by helping the couple to explore the ways in which they can achieve their goal: a Deaf baby. But as Nance's depiction of this scenario suggests, the counselor may well feel extremely uneasy about her role here. It is one thing to support a couple's decision to take their chances and "let Nature take its course," but to treat as a goal what is commonly considered to be a risk may be more pressure than the value-neutral ethos can bear. What is needed is a principled argument against such assistance. This refusal need not rise to a legal prohibition, but could become part of the ethical norms and standard of care for the counseling profession.[9]

The path I see out of this dilemma relies on two steps. First, we remind ourselves why client autonomy is such a powerful norm in genetic counseling. Clients come to genetic counselors with questions that are simultaneously of the greatest magnitude and of the greatest intimacy. Clients not only have the right to bring their own values to bear on these questions, but in the end they must do so because they—and their children—will live with the consequences. As the President's Commission said in its 1983 report on Screening and Counseling for Genetic Conditions:

The silence of the law on many areas of individual choice reflects the value this country places on pluralism. Nowhere is the need for freedom to pursue divergent conceptions of the good more deeply felt than in decisions concerning reproduction. It would be a cruel irony, therefore, if technological advances undertaken in the name of providing information to expand the range of individual choices resulted in unanticipated social pressures to pursue a particular course of action. Someone who feels compelled to undergo screening or to make particular reproductive choices at the urging of health care professionals or others or as a result of implicit social pressure is deprived of the choice-enhancing benefits of the new advances. The Commission recommends that those who counsel patients and those who educate the public about genetics should not only emphasize the importance of preserving choice but also do their utmost to safeguard the choices of those they serve.[10]

Now let us take this value of respect for autonomy and put it on both sides of the dilemma. Why is it morally problematic to seek to produce a child who is deaf? Being deaf does not cause one physical pain or shorten one's life span, two obvious conditions which it would be prima facie immoral to produce in another person. Deaf people might (or might not) be less happy on average than hearing people, but that is arguably a function of societal prejudice. The primary argument against deliberately seeking to produce deaf children is that it violates the child's own autonomy and narrows the scope of her choices when she grows up; in other words, it violates her right to an "open future."

The Child's Right to an Open Future

Joel Feinberg begins his discussion of children's rights by noticing that rights can ordinarily be divided into four kinds. First, there are rights that adults and children have in common (the right not to be killed, for example). Then, there are rights that are generally possessed only by children (or by "childlike" adults). These "dependency-rights," as Feinberg calls

them, derive from the child's dependence on others for such basics as food, shelter, and protection. Third, there are rights that can only be exercised by adults (or at least by children approaching adulthood), for example, the free exercise of religion. Finally, there are rights that Feinberg calls "rights-in-trust," rights which are to be "saved for the child until he is an adult." These rights can be violated by adults now, in ways that cut off the possibility that the child, when it achieves adulthood, can exercise them. A striking example is the right to reproduce. A young child cannot physically exercise that right, and a teenager might lack the legal and moral grounds on which to assert such a right. But clearly the child, when he or she attains adulthood, will have that right, and therefore the child now has the right not to be sterilized, so that the child may exercise that right in the future. Rights in this category include a long list: virtually all the important rights we believe adults have, but which must be protected now to be exercised later. Grouped together, they constitute what Feinberg calls "the child's right to an open future."[11]

Feinberg illustrates this concept with two examples. The first is that of the Jehovah's Witness child who needs a blood transfusion to save his life but whose parents object on religious grounds. In this case, the parents' right to act upon their religious beliefs and to raise their family within the religion of their choice conflicts with the child's right to live to adulthood and to make his own life-or-death decisions. As the Supreme Court said in another (and less defensible) case involving Jehovah's Witnesses:

Parents may be free to become martyrs themselves. But it does not follow that they are free in identical circumstances to make martyrs of their children before they have reached the age of full and legal discretion when they can make that decision for themselves.[12]

The second example is more controversial. In 1972, in a famous Supreme Court case, a group of Old Order Amish argued that they should be exempt from Wisconsin's requirement that all children attend school until they are either sixteen years old or graduate from high school.[13] The Amish didn't have to send their children to public school, of course; they were free to create a private school of their own liking. But they framed the issue in the starkest manner: to send their children to any school, past eighth grade, would be antithetical to their religion and their way of life, and might even result in the death of their culture.

> The primary argument against deliberately seeking to produce deaf children is that it violates the child's own autonomy and narrows the scope of her choices when she grows up.

The case was framed as a freedom of religion claim on the one hand, and the state's right to insist on an educated citizenry on the other. And within that frame, the Amish won. First, they were able to persuade the Court that sending their children to school after eighth grade would potentially destroy their community, because it

> takes them away from their community, physically and emotionally, during the crucial and formative adolescent period. During this period, the children must acquire Amish attitudes favoring manual work and self-reliance and the specific skills needed to perform the adult role of an Amish farmer or housewife. In the Amish belief higher learning tends to develop values they reject as influences that alienate man from God. (p. 211)

Second, the Amish argued that the state's concerns—that children be prepared to participate in the political and economic life of the state— did not apply in this case. The Court listened favorably to expert witnesses who explained that the Amish system of home-based vocational training— learning from your parent—worked well for that community, that the community itself was prosperous, and that few Amish were likely to end up unemployed. The Court said:

the value of all education must be assessed in terms of its capacity to prepare the child for life . . . It is one thing to say that compulsory education for a year or two beyond the eighth grade may be necessary when its goal is the preparation of the child for life in modern society as the majority live, but it is quite another if the goal of education can be viewed as the preparation of the child for life in the separated agrarian community that is the keystone of the Amish faith. (p. 222)

What only a few justices saw was that the children themselves were largely ignored in this argument. The Amish wanted to preserve their way of life. The state of Wisconsin wanted to make sure that its citizens could vote wisely and make a living. No justice squarely faced the question of whether the liberal democratic state owes all its citizens, especially children, a right to a basic education that can serve as a building block if the child decides later in life that she wishes to become an astronaut, a playwright, or perhaps to join the army. As we constantly hear from politicians and educators, without a high school diploma one's future is virtually closed. By denying them a high school education or its equivalent, parents are virtually ensuring that their children will remain housewives and agricultural laborers. Even if the children agree, is that a choice parents ought to be allowed to make for them?

From my perspective, the case was decided wrongly. If Wisconsin had good reasons for settling on high school graduation or age sixteen as

A liberal state must tolerate even those communities most unsympathetic to the liberal value of individual choice. However, this tolerance must exist within a limiting context.

the legal minimum to which children are entitled, then I think that the Amish children were entitled to that minimum as well, despite their parents' objections. In deciding the issue primarily on grounds that the Amish were not likely to create problems for the state if allowed to keep their children out of school, the Court reflected a rather minimalist form of liberalism. In fact, the abiding interest of this case for many political philosophers lies in the deep conflict it highlights between two different concepts of liberalism: commitment to autonomy and commitment to diversity. William Galston, for example, argues that:

A standard liberal view (or hope) is that these two principles go together and complement one another: the exercise of autonomy yields diversity, while the fact of diversity protects and nourishes autonomy. By contrast, my . . . view is that these principles do not always, perhaps even do not usually, cohere; that in practice they point in quite different directions in currently disputed areas such as education . . . Specifically: the decision to throw state power behind the promotion of individual autonomy can weaken or undermine individuals and groups that do not and cannot organize their affairs in accordance with that principle without undermining the deepest sources of their identity.[14]

Galston claims that "properly understood, liberalism is about the protection of diversity, not the valorization of choice . . . To place an ideal of autonomous choice . . . at the core of liberalism is in fact to narrow the range of possibilities available within liberal societies" (p. 523).

One can see this conflict quite sharply if one returns to the work of John Stuart Mill. On the one hand, there is probably no philosopher who gives more weight to the value of individual choice than does Mill. In *On Liberty*, he claims that the very measure of a human being is the extent to which he makes life choices for himself, free of societal pressure:

The human faculties of perception, judgment, discriminative feeling, mental activity, and even moral preference, are exercised only in making a choice. He who does anything because it is the custom makes no choice.[15]

Mill would abhor a situation like that of the Amish communities in *Yoder*, which unabashedly want to give their children as few choices as possible. But, on the other hand, it is clear from both common sense and from Mill's own statements that in order for people to have choices about the pattern of their lives (and to be inspired to create new patterns) there must be more than one type of community available to them. To quote Mill again, "There is no reason that all human existence should be constructed on some one or some small number of patterns"(p. 64). As we look at the last three centuries of American history, we see what an important role different community "patterns" have played, from the Shakers to the Mormons to Bronson Alcott's Fruitlands to the communal experiments of the 1960s. If those patterns are to exhibit the full range of human endeavor and experiment, they must include communities that are distinctly anti-liberal. Not only does the panoply of widely different communities enrich our culture, but it also provides a welcome for those who do not fit into the mainstream. As Mill says, "A man cannot get a coat or pair of shoes to fit him unless they are either made to his measure, or he has a whole warehouseful to choose from: and is it easier to fit him with a life than with a coat[?]" (p. 64). Some of us are geniuses who make our lives to "fit our measure," others are happy enough to fit into the mainstream, but for others, the availability of a "warehouseful" of choices increases the possibility of finding a good fit. And for some, a good fit means an authoritarian community based on tradition, where one is freed from the necessity of choice. Thus Galston is correct in pointing to the paradox: if the goal of a liberal democracy is to actively promote something like the greatest number of choices for the greatest number of individuals, this seems to entail hostility toward narrow-choice communities like the Amish. But if the Amish, because of that hostility, fail to flourish, there will be fewer choices available to all.

The compromise I promote is that a liberal state must tolerate even those communities most unsympathetic to the liberal value of individual choice. However, this tolerance must exist within a limiting context, which is the right of individuals to choose which communities they wish to join and to leave if they have a mind to. Even Galston begins with the presumption that society must "defend . . . the liberty not to be coerced into, or trapped within, ways of life. Accordingly, the state must safeguard the ability of individuals to shift allegiances and cross boundaries."[16] Thus, I argue that the autonomy of the individual is ethically prior to the autonomy of the group. Both ideals have powerful claims on us, but when group rights would extinguish the abilities of the individuals within them to make their own life choices, then the liberal state must support the individual against the group. This is especially crucial when the individual at issue is a child, who is particularly vulnerable to adult coercion and therefore has particular claims on our protection.

Unfortunately, it is precisely where children are concerned that groups are understandably most jealous of their prerogatives to guide and make decisions. The Amish are an example of a group guarding its ability to shape the lives of its children; Deaf parents wishing to ensure Deaf children are an example of families pursuing the same goals. Of course, groups and families ought to—in fact, they must—strive to shape the values and lives of the children in their care, not to do so leads to social and individual pathology. But when that shaping takes the form of a radically narrow range of choices available to the child when she grows up, when it impinges substantially on the child's right to an open future, then

liberalism requires us to intervene to support the child's future ability to make her own choices about which of the many diverse visions of life she wishes to embrace.

But I concede one problem with this point of view. As a liberal who believes that the state should not dictate notions of "the good life," Feinberg believes that the state must be neutral about the goals of education, skewing the question neither in favor of the Amish lifestyle nor in favor of the "modern," technological life most Americans accept. The goal of education is to allow the child to make up its own mind from the widest array of options; the best education is the one which gives the child the most open future. A neutral decision would assume only that education should equip the child with the knowledge and skills that will help him choose whichever sort of life best fits his native endowment and matured disposition. It should send him out into the adult world with as many open opportunities as possible, thus maximizing his chances for self-fulfillment.[17]

The problem here is that an education which gave a child this array of choices would quite possibly make it impossible for her to choose to remain Old Order Amish. Her "native endowment and matured disposition" might now have taken her away from the kind of personality and habits that would make Amish life pleasant. Even if she envies the peace, warmth, and security that a life of tradition offers, she may find it impossible to turn her back on "the world," and return to her lost innocence. To quote the Amish, she may have failed irreversibly to "acquire Amish attitudes" during "the crucial and formative adolescent period." This problem raises two issues. First, those of us who would make arguments based on the child's right to an open future need to be clear and appropriately humble about what we are offering. Insisting on a child's right to a high school education may open a future wider than she otherwise could have dreamed, but it also may foreclose one possible future: as

a contented member of the Amish community. Second, if the Amish are correct in saying that taking their children out of school at grade eight is crucial for the child's development into a member of the Amish community, then there is no "impartial" stance for the state to take. The state may well be impartial about whether the "better life" is to be found within or without the Amish community, but it cannot act in an impartial fashion. Both forcing the parents to send their children to school or exempting them from the requirement has likely consequences for the child's continued existence within the community when she grows up and is able to make a choice. Feinberg seeks to avoid this second problem by claiming that the neutral state would act to

> let all influences . . . work equally on the child, to open up all possibilities to him, without itself influencing him toward one or another of these. In that way, it can be hoped that the chief determining factor in the grown child's choice of a vocation and life-style will be his own governing values, talents, and propensities. (pp. 134-35)

The problem with this is that, as I understand the Amish way of life, being Amish is precisely not to make one's life choices on the basis of one's own "talents and propensities," but to subordinate those individual leanings to the traditions of the group. If one discovers within oneself a strong passion and talent for jazz dancing, one ought to suppress it, not nurture it.

Is Creating a Deaf Child a Moral Harm?

Now, as we return to the example of the couple who wish to ensure that they bear only deaf children, we have to confront two distinctly different issues. The first is, in what sense is it ever possible to do harm by giving birth to a child who would otherwise not have been born at all? The second is whether being deaf rather than hearing is in fact a harm.

The first issue has been well rehearsed elsewhere.[18] The problem is, how can it be said that one has harmed a child by bringing it into the world with a disability, when the only other choice was for the child not to have existed at all? In the case of a child whose life is arguably not worth living, one can say that life itself is a cruelty to the child. But when a child is born in less than ideal circumstances, or is partially disabled in ways that do not entail tremendous suffering, there seems no way to argue that the child herself has been harmed. This may appear to entail the conclusion, counter to our common moral sense, that therefore no harm has been done. "A wrong action must be bad for someone, but [a] choice to create [a] child with its handicap is bad for no one."[19]

All commentators agree that there is no purely logical way out of what Dan Brock calls the "wrongful handicap" conundrum (p. 272). However, most commentators also agree that one can still support a moral critique of the parents' decision. Bonnie Steinbock and Ron McClamrock argue for a principle of "parental responsibility" by which being a good parent entails refraining from bringing a child into the world when one cannot give it "even a decent chance at a good life."[20] Brock, following Parfit, distinguishes same person from same number choices. In same person choices, the same person exists in each of the alternative courses of action the agent chooses, but the person may exist more or less harmed. In same number choices, "the choice affects who, which child, will exist."[21] Brock claims that moral harms can exist in both instances, despite the fact that in same number choices the moral harm cannot be tied to a specific person. Brock generates the following principle:

> Individuals are morally required not to let any possible child . . . for whose welfare they are responsible

> Good parenthood requires a balance between having a child for our own sakes and being open to the moral reality that the child will exist for her own sake.

experience serious suffering or limited opportunity if they can act so that, without imposing substantial burdens or costs on themselves or others, any alternative possible child . . . for whose welfare they would be responsible will not experience serious suffering or limited opportunity. (pp. 272-73)

While agreeing with Brock, Steinbock, and others, I locate the moral harm differently, at least with respect to disabled persons wishing to reproduce in the form of a disabled child. Deliberately creating a child who will be forced irreversibly into the parents' notion of "the good life" violates the Kantian principle of treating each person as an end in herself and never as a means only. All parenthood exists as a balance between fulfillment of parental hopes and values and the individual flowering of the actual child in his or her own direction. The decision to have a child is never made for the sake of the child—for no child then exists. We choose to have children for myriad reasons, but before the child is conceived those reasons can only be self-regarding. The child is a means to our ends: a certain kind of joy and pride, continuing the family name, fulfilling religious or societal expectations, and so on. But morally the child is first and foremost an end in herself. Good parenthood requires a balance between having a child for our own sakes and being open to the moral reality that the child will exist for her own sake, with her own talents and weaknesses, propensities and interests, and with her own life to make. Parental practices that close exits virtually forever are insufficiently attentive to the child as end in herself. By closing off the child's right to an open future, they define the child as an entity who exists to fulfill parental hopes and dreams, not her own.

Having evaded the snares of the wrongful handicap conundrum, we must tackle the second problem: is being deaf a harm? At first glance, this might appear as a silly question. Ethically, we would certainly include destroying someone's hearing under

the rubric of "harm"; legally, one could undoubtedly receive compensation if one were rendered deaf through someone else's negligence. Many Deaf people, however, have recently been claiming that Deafness is better understood as a cultural identity than as a disability. Particularly in the wake of the Deaf President Now revolution at Gallaudet University in 1988, Deaf people have been asserting their claims not merely to equal access (through increased technology) but also to equal respect as a cultural minority. As one (hearing) reporter noted:

> So strong is the feeling of cultural solidarity that many deaf parents cheer on discovering that their baby is deaf. Pondering such a scene, a hearing person can experience a kind of vertigo. The surprise is not simply the unfamiliarity of the views; it is that, as in a surrealist painting, jarring notions are presented as if they were commonplace.[22]

From this perspective, the use of cochlear implants to enable deaf children to hear, or the abortion of deaf fetuses, is characterized as "genocide."[23] Deaf pride advocates point out that as Deaf people they lack the ability to hear, but they also have many positive gains: a cohesive community, a rich cultural heritage built around the various residential schools, a growing body of drama, poetry, and other artistic traditions, and, of course, what makes all this possible, American Sign Language.[24] Roslyn Rosen, the president of the National Association of the Deaf, is Deaf, the daughter of Deaf parents, and the mother of Deaf children. "I'm happy with who I am," she says, "and I don't want to be 'fixed.' Would an Italian-American rather be a WASP? In our society everyone agrees that whites have an easier time than blacks. But do you think a black person would undergo operations to become white?"[25]

On the other side of the argument is evidence that deafness is a very serious disability. Deaf people have incomes thirty to forty percent below the national average.[26] The state of education for the deaf is unacceptable by anyone's standards; the typical deaf student graduates from high school unable to read a newspaper.[27]

However, one could also point to the lower incomes and inadequate state of education among some racial and ethnic minorities in our country, a situation we do not (or at least ought not) try to ameliorate by eradicating minorities. Deaf advocates often cite the work of Nora Ellen Groce, whose oral history of Martha's Vineyard, *Everyone Here Spoke Sign Language*, tells a fascinating story. For over two hundred years, ending in the middle of the twentieth century, the Vineyard experienced a degree of hereditary deafness exponentially higher than that of the mainland. Although the number of deaf people was low in noncomparative terms (one in 155), the result was a community in which deaf people participated fully in the political and social life of the island, had an economic prosperity on par with their neighbors, and communicated easily with the hearing population, for "everyone here spoke sign language." So endemic was sign language for the general population of the island that hearing islanders often exploited its unique properties even in the absence of deaf people. Old-timers told Groce stories of spouses communicating through sign language when they were outdoors and did not want to raise their voices against the wind. Or men might turn away and finish a "dirty" joke in sign when a woman walked into the general store. At church, deaf parishioners gave their testimony in sign.

As one Deaf activist said, in a comment that could have been directly related to the Vineyard experience, "When Gorbachev visited the U.S., he used an interpreter to talk to the President. Was Gorbachev disabled?"[28] Further, one might argue that, since it is impossible to eradicate deafness completely even if that were a worthy goal, the cause of deaf equality is better served when parents who are proud to be Deaf deliberately have Deaf children who augment and strengthen the existing popula-

tion. Many of the problems that deaf people experience are the result of being born, without advance warning, to hearing parents. When there is no reason to anticipate the birth of a deaf child, it is often months or years before the child is correctly diagnosed. Meanwhile, she is growing up in a world devoid of language, unable even to communicate with her parents. When the diagnosis is made, her parents first must deal with the emotional shock, and then sort through the plethora of conflicting advice on how best to raise and educate their child. Most probably, they have never met anyone who is deaf. If they choose the route recommended by most Deaf activists and raise their child with sign language, it will take the parents years to learn the language. Meanwhile, their child has missed out on the crucial development of language at the developmentally appropriate time, a lack that is associated with poor reading skills and other problems later (p. 43).

Further, even the most accepting of hearing parents often feel locked in conflict with the Deaf community over who knows what is best for their child. If Deafness truly is a culture rather than a disability, then raising a deaf child is somewhat like white parents trying to raise a black child in contemporary America (with a background chorus of black activists telling them that they can't possibly make a good job of it!). Residential schools, for example, which can be part of the family culture for a Deaf couple, can be seen by hearing parents as Dickensian nightmares or, worse, as a "cultlike" experience in which their children will be lost to them forever.

By contrast, deaf children born to Deaf parents learn language (sign) at the same age as hearing children. They are welcomed into their families and inculcated into Deaf culture in the same way as any other children. Perhaps for these reasons, by all accounts the Deaf of Deaf are the acknowledged leaders of the Deaf Pride movement, and the academic crème de la crème. In evaluating the choice parents make who deliberately ensure

that they have Deaf children, we must remember that the statistics and descriptions of deaf life in America are largely reflective of the experience of deaf children born to hearing parents, who make up the vast majority of deaf people today.

But if Deafness is a culture rather than a disability, it is an exceedingly narrow one. One factor that does not seem clear is the extent to which children raised with American Sign Language as their first language ever will be completely comfortable with the written word. (Sign language itself has no written analogue and has a completely different grammatical structure from English.) At present, the conflicted and politicized state of education for the deaf, along with the many hours spent (some would say "wasted") on attempting to teach deaf children oral skills, makes it impossible to know what is to blame for the dismal reading and writing skills of the average deaf person. Some deaf children who are raised with sign language from birth do become skilled readers. But there is reason to question whether a deaf child may have very limited access to the wealth of literature, drama, and poetry that liberals would like to consider every child's birthright.

Although Deaf activists rightly show how many occupations are open to them with only minor technological adjustments, the range of occupations will always be inherently limited. It is not likely that the world will become as Martha's Vineyard, where everyone knew sign. A prelingually deafened person not only cannot hear, but in most instances cannot speak well enough to be understood. This narrow choice of vocation is not only a harm in its own sake but also is likely to continue to lead to lower standards of living. (Certainly one reason why the Vineyard deaf were as prosperous as their neighbors was that farming and fishing were just about the only occupations available.)

If Deafness is a culture rather than a disability, it is an exceedingly narrow one.

Either Way, A Moral Harm

If deafness is considered a disability, one that substantially narrows a child's career, marriage, and cultural options in the future, then deliberately creating a deaf child counts as a moral harm. If Deafness is considered a culture, as Deaf activists would have us agree, then deliberately creating a Deaf child who will have only very limited options to move outside of that culture, also counts as a moral harm. A decision, made before a child is even born, that confines her forever to a narrow group of people and a limited choice of careers, so violates the child's right to an open future that no genetic counseling team should acquiesce in it. The very value of autonomy that grounds the ethics of genetic counseling should preclude assisting parents in a project that so dramatically narrows the autonomy of the child to be.

Coda

Although I rest my case at this point, I want to sketch out some further ramifications of my argument. Are there other, less obvious, ways in which genetic knowledge and manipulation can interfere with the child's right to an open future?

The notion of the child's right to an open future can help in confronting the question of whether to test children for adult-onset genetic diseases, for example Huntington disease.[29] It is well known that the vast majority of adults at risk for Huntington disease choose not to be tested. However, it is not uncommon for parents to request that their children be tested; their goals may be to set their minds at rest, to plan for the future, and so on. On one account, parental authority to make medical decisions suggests that clinicans should accede to these requests (after proper counseling about possible risks). A better account, in my opinion, protects the child's right to an open future by preserving into adulthood his own choice to decide whether his life is better lived with that knowledge or without.[30]

Finally, a provocative argument can be made that sex selection can be deleterious to the child's right to an open future. I am ignoring here all the more obvious arguments against sex selection, even when accomplished without abortion. Rather, I suspect that parents who choose the sex of their offspring are more likely to have gender-specific expectations for those children, expectations that subtly limit the child's own individual flowering. The more we are able to control our children's characteristics (and the more time, energy, and money we invest in the outcome), the more invested we will become in our hopes and dreams for them. It is easy to sympathize with some of the reasons why parents might want to ensure a girl or boy. People who already have one or two children of one sex can hardly be faulted for wanting to "balance" their families by having one of each. And yet, this ought to be discouraged. If I spent a great deal of time and energy to get a boy in the hope of having a football player in the family, I think I would be less likely to accept it with good grace if the boy hated sports and spent all his spare time at the piano. If I insisted on having a girl because I believed that as a grandparent I would be more likely to have close contact with the children of a daughter than of a son, I think I would be find it much harder to raise a girl who saw motherhood as a choice rather than as a foregone conclusion. Parents whose preferences are compelling enough for them to take active steps to control the outcome, must, logically, be committed to certain strong gender-role expectations. If they want a girl that badly, whether they are hoping for a Miss America or the next Catherine McKinnon, they are likely to make it difficult for the actual child to resist their expectations and to follow her own bent.

ACKNOWLEDGMENTS

The author is grateful to the Cleveland-Marshall Fund for financial support while writing this article, and to Samuel Gorovitz, Eric Juengst, Thomas H. Murray, Lisa Parker, and Matthew Silliman for their comments on earlier drafts.

REFERENCES

1. Walter E. Nance, "Parables," in *Prescribing Our Future: Ethical Challenges in Genetic Counseling,* ed. Dianne M. Bartels, Bonnie S. LeRoy, and Arthur L. Caplan, (New York: Aldine De Gruyter, 1993), p. 92.

2. National Society of Genetic Counselors, Code of Ethics, reprinted in *Prescribing Our Future,* pp. 169-71.

3. James R. Sorenson, "Genetic Counseling: Values that have Mattered," *Prescribing Our Future,* p. 11; Arthur L. Caplan, "The Ethics of Genetic Counseling," *Prescribing Our Future,* p. 161.

4. Charles Bosk, "Workplace Ideology," *Prescribing Our Future,* pp. 27-28.

5. Dianne M. Bartels, "Preface," *Prescribing Our Future,* pp. ix-xiii.

6. Barbara Katz Rothman, *The Tentative Pregnancy: Prenatal Diagnosis and the Future of Motherhood* (New York: Viking Press, 1986), p. 41.

7. Nance, "Parables," p. 92.

8. D. Lindhout, P.G. Frets, and M.C. Niermeijer, "Approaches to Genetic Counseling," *Annals of the New York Academy of Sciences* 630 (1991): 223-29, at 224.

9. Jeffrey R. Botkin, "Fetal Privacy and Confidentiality," *Hastings Center Report* 25, no. 3 (1995): 32-39.

10. President's Commission for the Study of Ethical Problems in Biomedical and Behavioral Research, *Screening and Counseling for Genetic Conditions: A Report on the Ethical, Social, and Legal Implications of Genetic Screening, Counseling, and Education Programs* (Washington, D.C.: Government Printing Office, 1983), p. 56.

11. Joel Feinberg, "The Child's Right to an Open Future," in *Whose Child? Children's Rights, Parental Authority, and State Power,* ed. William Aiken and Hugh LaFollette (Totowa, N.J.: Littlefield, Adams & Co., 1980), pp. 124-53.

12. Prince v. Massachusetts, 321 U.S. 158 (1944), at 170.

13. Wisconsin v. Yoder, 406 U.S. 205 (1972).

14. William Galston, "Two Concepts of Liberalism," *Ethics* 105, no. 3 (1995): 516-34, at 521.

15. John Stuart Mill, *On Liberty* (New York: W. W. Norton, 1975), p. 55.

16. Galston, "Two Concepts of Liberalism," p. 522.

17. Feinberg, *The Child's Right,* pp. 134-35.

18. Cynthia Cohen, "'Give Me Children or I Shall Die!' New Reproductive Technologies and Harm to Children," *Hastings Center Report* 26, no. 2 (1996): 19-29.

19. Dan Brock, "The Non-Identity Problem and Genetic Harms," *Bioethics* 9, no. 3/4 (1995): 269-75, at 271.

20. Bonnie Steinbock and Ron Mc-Clamrock, "When Is Birth Unfair to the Child?" *Hastings Center Report* 24, no. 6 (1994): 15-21, at p. 17.

21. Brock, "The Non-Identity Problem," p. 272.

22. Edward Dolnick, "Deafness as Culture," *The Atlantic Monthly* 272/3 (1993): 37-53.

23. Amy Elizabeth Brusky, "Making Decisions for Deaf Children Regarding Cochlear Implants: The Legal Ramifications of Recognizing Deafness as a Culture Rather than a Disability," *Wisconsin Law Review* (1995): 235-70.

24. John B. Christiansen, "Sociological Implications of Hearing Loss," *Annals of the New York Academy of Science* 630 (1991): 230-35.

25. Dolnick, "Deafness as Culture," p. 38.

26. Nora Ellen Groce, *Everyone Here Spoke Sign Language: Hereditary Deafness on Martha's Vineyard* (Cambridge: Harvard University Press, 1985), p. 85.

27. Andrew Solomon, "Defiantly Deaf," *New York Times Magazine*, 28 August 1994: 40-45 et passim.

28. Dolnick, "Deafness as Culture," p. 43.

29. I am grateful to Thomas H. Murray and Ronald M. Green for bringing this topic to my attention.

30. "The Genetic Testing of Children," *Journal of Medical Genetics* 31 (1994): 785-97.

[16]

PROCREATIVE BENEFICENCE: WHY WE SHOULD SELECT THE BEST CHILDREN

JULIAN SAVULESCU

ABSTRACT

Eugenic selection of embryos is now possible by employing in vitro fertilization (IVF) and preimplantation genetic diagnosis (PGD). While PGD is currently being employed for the purposes of detecting chromosomal abnormalities or inherited genetic abnormalities, it could in principle be used to test any genetic trait such as hair colour or eye colour.

Genetic research is rapidly progressing into the genetic basis of complex traits like intelligence and a gene has been identified for criminal behaviour in one family. Once the decision to have IVF is made, PGD has few 'costs' to couples, and people would be more inclined to use it to select less serious medical traits, such as a lower risk of developing Alzheimer Disease, or even for non-medical traits. PGD has already been used to select embryos of a desired gender in the absence of any history of sex-linked genetic disease.

I will argue that: (1) some non-disease genes affect the likelihood of us leading the best life; (2) we have a reason to use information which is available about such genes in our reproductive decision-making; (3) couples should select embryos or fetuses which are most likely to have the best life, based on available genetic information, including information about non-disease genes. I will also argue that we should allow selection for non-disease genes even if this maintains or increases social inequality. I will focus on genes for intelligence and sex selection.

I will defend a principle which I call Procreative Beneficence: couples (or single reproducers) should select the child, of the possible children they could have, who is expected to have the best life, or at least as good a life as the others, based on the relevant, available information.

414   JULIAN SAVULESCU

INTRODUCTION

Imagine you are having in vitro fertilisation (IVF) and you produce four embryos. One is to be implanted. You are told that there is a genetic test for predisposition to scoring well on IQ tests (let's call this intelligence). If an embryo has gene subtypes (alleles) A, B there is a greater than 50% chance it will score more than 140 if given an ordinary education and upbringing. If it has subtypes C, D there is a much lower chance it will score over 140. Would you test the four embryos for these gene subtypes and use this information in selecting which embryo to implant?

Many people believe intelligence is a purely social construct and so it is unlikely to have a significant genetic cause. Others believe there are different sorts of intelligence, such as verbal intelligence, mathematical intelligence, musical ability and no such thing as general intelligence. Time will tell. There are several genetic research programs currently in place which seek to elucidate the genetic contribution to intelligence. This paper pertains to any results of this research even if it only describes a weak probabilistic relation between genes and intelligence, or a particular kind of intelligence.

Many people believe that research into the genetic contribution to intelligence should not be performed, and that if genetic tests which predict intelligence, or a range of intelligence, are ever developed, they should not be employed in reproductive decision-making. I will argue that we have a moral obligation to test for genetic contribution to non-disease states such as intelligence and to use this information in reproductive decision-making.

Imagine now you are invited to play the Wheel of Fortune. A giant wheel exists with marks on it from 0–$1,000,000, in $100 increments. The wheel is spun in a secret room. It stops randomly on an amount. That amount is put into Box A. The wheel is spun again. The amount which comes up is put into Box B. You can choose Box A or B. You are also told that, in addition to the sum already put in the boxes, if you choose B, a dice will be thrown and you will lose $100 if it comes up 6.

Which box should you choose?

The rational answer is Box A. Choosing genes for non-disease states is like playing the Wheel of Fortune. You should use all the available information and choose the option most likely to bring about the best outcome.

PROCREATIVE BENEFICENCE : THE MORAL OBLIGATION TO HAVE THE BEST CHILDREN

I will argue for a principle which I call Procreative Beneficence:

> couples (or single reproducers) should select the child, of the possible children they could have, who is expected to have the best life, or at least as good a life as the others, based on the relevant, available information.

I will argue that Procreative Beneficence implies couples should employ genetic tests for non-disease traits in selecting which child to bring into existence and that we should allow selection for non-disease genes in some cases even if this maintains or increases social inequality.

By 'should' in 'should choose', I mean 'have good reason to.' I will understand morality to require us to do what we have most reason to do. In the absence of some other reason for action, a person who has good reason to have the best child is morally required to have the best child.

Consider the following three situations involving normative judgements.

(1) 'You are 31. You will be at a higher risk of infertility and having a child with an abnormality if you delay child-bearing. But that has to be balanced against taking time out of your career now. That's only something you can weigh up.'
(2) 'You should stop smoking.'
(3) 'You must inform your partner that you are HIV positive or practise safe sex.'

The 'should' in 'should choose the best child' is that present in the second example. It implies that persuasion is justified, but not coercion, which would be justified in the third case. Yet the situation is different to the more morally neutral (1).

Definitions

A disease gene is a gene which causes a genetic disorder (e.g. cystic fibrosis) or predisposes to the development of disease (e.g. the genetic contribution to cancer or dementia). A non-disease gene is a gene which causes or predisposes to some physical or psychological state of the person which is not itself a disease state, e.g. height, intelligence, character (not in the sub-normal range).

416   JULIAN SAVULESCU

Selection

It is currently possible to select from a range of possible children
we could have. This is most frequently done by employing fetal
selection through prenatal testing and termination of pregnancy.
Selection of embryos is now possible by employing in vitro
fertilization and preimplantation genetic diagnosis (PGD). There
are currently no genetic tests available for non-disease states
except sex. However, if such tests become available in the future,
both PGD and prenatal testing could be used to select offspring
on the basis of non-disease genes. Selection of sex by PGD is now
undertaken in Sydney, Australia.[1] PGD will also lower the
threshold for couples to engage in selection since it has fewer
psychological sequelae than prenatal testing and abortion.

   In the future, it may be possible to select gametes according to
their genetic characteristics. This is currently possible for sex, where
methods have been developed to sort X and Y bearing sperm.[2]

Behavioural Genetics

Behavioural Genetics is a branch of genetics which seeks to
understand the contribution of genes to complex behaviour. The
scope of behavioural genetics is illustrated in Table 1.

AN ARGUMENT FOR PROCREATIVE BENEFICENCE

Consider the *Simple Case of Selection for Disease Genes*. A couple is
having IVF in an attempt to have a child. It produces two
embryos. A battery of tests for common diseases is performed.
Embryo A has no abnormalities on the tests performed. Embryo
B has no abnormalities on the tests performed except its genetic
profile reveals it has a predisposition to developing asthma.
Which embryo should be implanted?

   Embryo B has nothing to be said in its favour over A and
something against it. Embryo A should (on pain of irrationality)
be implanted. This is like choosing Box A in the Wheel of
Fortune analogy.

---

[1] J. Savulescu. Sex Selection – the case for. *Medical Journal of Australia* 1999;
171: 373–5.

[2] E.F. Fugger, S.H. Black, K. Keyvanfar, J.D. Schulman. Births of normal
daughters after Microsort sperm separation and intrauterine insemination, in-
vitro fertilization, or intracytoplasmic sperm injection. *Hum Reprod* 1998; 13:
2367–70.

PROCREATIVE BENEFICENCE   417

Table 1:   Behavioural Genetics

Aggression and criminal behaviour
Alcoholism
Anxiety and Anxiety disorders
Attention Deficit Hyperactivity Disorder (ADHD)
Antisocial personality disorder
Bipolar disorder
Homosexuality
Maternal Behaviour
Memory and intelligence
Neuroticism
Novelty Seeking
Schizophrenia
Substance Addiction

Why shouldn't we select the embryo with a predisposition to asthma? What is relevant about asthma is that it reduces quality of life. Attacks cause severe breathlessness and in extreme cases, death. Steroids may be required to treat it. These are among the most dangerous drugs which exist if taken long term. Asthma can be lifelong and require lifelong drug treatment. Ultimately it can leave the sufferer wheel chair bound with chronic obstructive airways disease. The morally relevant property of 'asthma' is that it is a state which reduces the well-being a person experiences.

Parfitian defence of voluntary procreative beneficence in the Simple Case

The following example, after Parfit,[3] supports Procreative Beneficence. A woman has rubella. If she conceives now, she will have a blind and deaf child. If she waits three months, she will conceive another different but healthy child. She should choose to wait until her rubella is passed.

Or consider the Nuclear Accident. A poor country does not have enough power to provide power to its citizens during an extremely cold winter. The government decides to open an old and unsafe nuclear reactor. Ample light and heating are then available. Citizens stay up later, and enjoy their lives much more. Several months later, the nuclear reactor melts down and large amounts of radiation are released into the environment. The

[3] D. Parfit. 1976. Rights, Interests and Possible People, in *Moral Problems in Medicine*, S. Gorovitz, et al, eds. Englewood Cliffs. Prentice Hall. D. Parfit. 1984. *Reasons and Persons*. Oxford. Clarendon Press: Part IV.

418   JULIAN SAVULESCU

only effect is that a large number of children are subsequently born with predispositions to early childhood malignancy.

The supply of heating and light has changed the lifestyle of this population. As a result of this change in lifestyle, people have conceived children at different times than they would have if there had been no heat or light, and their parents went to bed earlier. Thus, the children born after the nuclear accident would not have existed if the government had not switched to nuclear power. They have not been harmed by the switch to nuclear power and the subsequent accident (unless their lives are so bad they are worse than death). If we object to the Nuclear Accident (which most of us would), then we must appeal to some form of harmless wrong-doing. That is, we must claim that a wrong was done, but no one was harmed. We must appeal to something like the Principle of Procreative Beneficence.

An Objection to Procreative Beneficence in the Simple Case

The following objection to Procreative Beneficence is common.

> 'If you choose Embryo A (without a predisposition to asthma), you could be discarding someone like Mozart or an olympic swimmer. So there is no good reason to select A.'

It is true that by choosing A, you could be discarding a person like Mozart. But it is equally true that if you choose B, you could be discarding someone like Mozart without asthma. A and B are equally likely (on the information available) to be someone like Mozart (and B is more likely to have asthma).

Other Principles of Reproductive Decision-Making Applied to the Simple Case

The principle of Procreative Beneficence supports selecting the embryo without the genetic predisposition to asthma. That seems intuitively correct. How do other principles of reproductive decision-making apply to this example?

1. *Procreative Autonomy:* This principle claims that couples should be free to decide when and how to procreate, and what kind of children to have.[4] If this were the only decision-

---

[4] R. Dworkin. 1993. *Life's Dominion: An Argument about Abortion and Euthanasia.* London. Harper Collins; J. Harris. Goodbye Dolly? The ethics of human cloning. *Journal of Medical Ethics* 1997; 23: 353–60; J. Harris. 1998. Rights and Reproductive Choice, in *The Future of Reproduction,* J. Harris and S.

guiding principle, it would imply couples might have reason to choose the embryo with a predisposition to asthma, if for some reason they wanted that.

2. *Principle of Non-Directive Counselling:* According to this principle, doctors and genetic counsellors should only provide information about risk and options available to reduce that risk.[5] They should not give advice or other direction. Thus, if a couple wanted to transfer Embryo B, and they knew that it would have a predisposition to asthma, nothing more is to be said according to Non-Directive Counselling.

3. *The 'Best Interests of the Child' Principle:* Legislation in Australia and the United Kingdom related to reproduction gives great weight to consideration of the best interests of the child. For example, the Victorian Infertility Treatment Act 1995 states *'the welfare and interests of any person born or to be born as a result of a treatment procedure are paramount.'*[6] This principle is irrelevant to this choice. The couple could choose the embryo with the predisposition to asthma and still be doing everything possible in the interests of *that* child.

None of the alternative principles give appropriate direction in the Simple Case.

MOVING FROM DISEASE GENES TO NON-DISEASE GENES: WHAT IS THE 'BEST LIFE'?

It is not asthma (or disease) which is important, but its impact on a life in ways that matter which is important. People often trade length of life for non-health related well-being. Non-disease genes may prevent us from leading the best life.

By 'best life', I will understand the life with the most well-being. There are various theories of well-being: hedonistic, desire-fulfilment, objective list theories.[7] According to hedonistic theories, what matters is the quality of our experiences, for

Holm, eds. Oxford. Clarendon Press; J.A. Robertson. 1994. *Children of Choice: Freedom and the New Reproductive Technologies.* Princeton. Princeton University Press; C. Strong. 1997. *Ethics in reproductive and perinatal medicine.* New Haven. Yale University Press.

[5] J.A.F. Roberts. 1959. *An introduction to human genetics.* Oxford. OUP.

[6] The *Human Fertilization and Embryology Act 1990* in England requires that account be taken of the welfare of any child who will be born by assisted reproduction before issuing a licence for assistance (S.13(5)).

[7] Parfit, *op. cit.*, Appendix I, pp. 493–502; Griffin. 1986. *Well-Being.* Oxford. Clarendon Press.

420   JULIAN SAVULESCU

example, that we experience pleasure. According to desire-fulfilment theories, what matters is the degree to which our desires are satisfied. According to objective list theories, certain activities are good for people, such as achieving worthwhile things with your life, having dignity, having children and raising them, gaining knowledge of the world, developing one's talents, appreciating beautiful things, and so on.

On any of these theories, some non-disease genes will affect the likelihood that we will lead the best life. Imagine there is a gene which contributes significantly to a violent, explosive, uncontrollable temper, and that state causes people significant suffering. Violent outbursts lead a person to come in conflict with the law and fall out of important social relations. The loss of independence, dignity and important social relations are bad on any of the three accounts.

Buchanan et al. argue that what is important in a liberal democracy is providing people with general purpose means, i.e. those useful to any plan of life.[8] In this way we can allow people to form and act on their own conception of the good life. Examples of general purpose means are the ability to hear and see. But similarly the ability to concentrate, to engage with and be empathetic towards other human beings may be all purpose means. To the degree that genes contribute to these, we have reason to select those genes.

Consider another example. Memory (M) is the ability to remember important things when you want to. Imagine there is some genetic contribution to M: Six alleles (genes) contribute to M. IVF produces four embryos. Should we test for M profiles?

Does M relate to well-being? Having to go to the supermarket twice because you forgot the baby formula prevents you doing more worthwhile things. Failing to remember can have disastrous consequences. Indeed, forgetting the compass on a long bush walk can be fatal. There is, then, a positive obligation to test for M and select the embryo (other things being equal) with the best M profile.

Does being intelligent mean one is more likely to have a better life? At a folk intuitive level, it seems plausible that intelligence would promote well-being on any plausible account of well-being.

---

[8] A. Buchanan, D.W. Brock, N. Daniels, D. Wikler. 2000. *From Chance to Choice.* Cambridge. CUP: 167. Buchanan and colleagues argue in a parallel way for the permissibility of genetic manipulation (enhancement) to allow children to live the best life possible (Chapter Five). They do not consider selection in this context.

On a hedonistic account, the capacity to imagine alternative pleasures and remember the salient features of past experiences is important in choosing the best life. On a desire-fulfilment theory, intelligence is important to choosing means which will best satisfy one's ends. On an objective list account, intelligence would be important to gaining knowledge of the world, and developing rich social relations. Newson has reviewed the empirical literature relating intelligence to quality of life. Her synthesis of the empirical literature is that 'intelligence has a high instrumental value for persons in giving them a large amount of complexity with which to approach their everyday lives, and that it equips them with a tool which can lead to the provision of many other personal and social goods.'[9]

Socrates, in Plato's Philebus, concludes that the best life is a mixture of wisdom and pleasure. Wisdom includes thought, intelligence, knowledge and memory.[10] Intelligence is clearly a part of Plato's conception of the good life:

> without the power of calculation you could not even calculate that you will get enjoyment in the future; your life would be that not of a man, but of a sea-lung or one of those marine creatures whose bodies are confined by a shell.[11]

Choice of Means of Selecting

This argument extends in principle to selection of fetuses using prenatal testing and termination of affected pregnancy. However, selection by abortion has greater psychological harms than selection by PGD and these need to be considered. Gametic selection, if it is ever possible, will have the lowest psychological cost.

Objections to the Principle of Procreative Beneficence Applied to Non-Disease Genes

1. *Harm to the child:* One common objection to genetic selection for non-disease traits is that it results in harm to the child. There are various versions of this objection, which include the harm

[9] A. Newson. The value of intelligence and its implications for genetic research. *Fifth World Congress of Bioethics*, Imperial College, London, 21–24 September 2000.

[10] *Philebus* 21 C 1-12. A.E. Taylor's translation. 1972. Folkstone. Dawsons of Pall Mall: 21 D 11-3, E 1-3.

[11] *Philebus* 21 C 1-12.

422 JULIAN SAVULESCU

which arises from excessive and overbearing parental expectations, using the child as a means, and not treating it as an end, and closing off possible future options on the basis of the information provided (failing to respect the child's 'right to an open future').

There are a number of responses. Firstly, in some cases, it is possible to deny that the harms will be significant. Parents come to love the child whom they have (even a child with a serious disability). Moreover, some have argued that counselling can reduce excessive expectations.[12]

Secondly, we can accept some risk of a child experiencing some state of reduced well-being in cases of selection. One variant of the harm to child objection is: 'If you select embryo A, it might still get asthma, or worse, cancer, or have a much worse life than B, and you would be responsible.' Yet selection is immune to this objection (in a way which genetic manipulation is not).

Imagine you select Embryo A and it develops cancer (or severe asthma) in later life. You have not harmed A unless A's life is not worth living (hardly plausible) because A would not have existed if you had acted otherwise. A is not made worse off than A would otherwise have been, since without the selection, A would not have existed. Thus we can accept the possibility of a bad outcome, but not the probability of a very bad outcome. (Clearly, Procreative Beneficence demands that we not choose a child with a low predisposition to asthma but who is likely to have a high predisposition to cancer.)

This is different to genetic manipulation. Imagine you perform gene therapy to correct a predisposition to asthma and you cause a mutation which results in cancer later in life. You have harmed A: A is worse off in virtue of the genetic manipulation than A would have been if the manipulation had not been performed (assuming cancer is worse than asthma).

There is, then, an important distinction between:

- interventions which are genetic manipulations of a single gamete, embryo or fetus
- selection procedures (e.g. sex selection) which select from among a range of different gametes, embryos and fetuses.

2. *Inequality:* One objection to Procreative Beneficence is that it will maintain or increase inequality. For example, it is often argued that selection for sex, intelligence, favourable physical or

[12] J. Robertson. Preconception Sex Selection. *American Journal of Bioethics* 1:1 (Winter 2001).

psychological traits, etc. all contribute to inequality in society, and this is a reason not to attempt to select the best.

In the case of selection against disease genes, similar claims are made. For example, one version of the *Disability Discrimination Claim* maintains that prenatal testing for disabilities such as Down syndrome results in discrimination against those with those disabilities both by:

- the statement it makes about the worth of such lives
- the reduction in the numbers of people with this condition.

Even if the Disability Discrimination Claim were true, it would be a drastic step in favour of equality to inflict a higher risk of having a child with a disability on a couple (who do not want a child with a disability) to promote social equality.

Consider a hypothetical rubella epidemic. A rubella epidemic hits an isolated population. Embryos produced prior to the epidemic are not at an elevated risk of any abnormality but those produced during the epidemic are at an increased risk of deafness and blindness. Doctors should encourage women to use embryos which they have produced prior to the epidemic in preference to ones produced during the epidemic. The reason is that it is bad that blind and deaf children are born when sighted and hearing children could have been born in their place.

This does not necessarily imply that the lives of those who now live with disability are less deserving of respect and are less valuable. To attempt to prevent accidents which cause paraplegia is not to say that paraplegics are less deserving of respect. It is important to distinguish between disability and persons with disability. Selection reduces the former, but is silent on the value of the latter. There are better ways to make statements about the equality of people with disability (e.g., we could direct savings from selection against embryos/fetuses with genetic abnormalities to improving well-being of existing people with disabilities).

These arguments extend to selection for non-disease genes. It is not disease which is important but its impact on well-being. In so far as a non-disease gene such as a gene for intelligence impacts on a person's well-being, parents have a reason to select for it, even if inequality results.

This claim can have counter-intuitive implications. Imagine in a country women are severely discriminated against. They are abandoned as children, refused paid employment and serve as slaves to men. Procreative Beneficence implies that couples

424   JULIAN SAVULESCU

should test for sex, and should choose males as they are expected to have better lives in this society, even if this reinforces the discrimination against women.

There are several responses. Firstly, it is unlikely selection on a scale that contributes to inequality would promote well-being. Imagine that 50% of the population choose to select boys. This would result in three boys to every one girl. The life of a male in such a society would be intolerable.

Secondly, it is social institutional reform, not interference in reproduction, which should be promoted. What is wrong in such a society is the treatment of women, which should be addressed separately to reproductive decision-making. Reproduction should not become an instrument of social change, at least not mediated or motivated at a social level.

This also illustrates why Procreative Beneficence is different to eugenics. Eugenics is selective breeding to produce a better *population*. A *public interest* justification for interfering in reproduction is different from Procreative Beneficence which aims at producing the best child, of the possible children, a couple could have. That is an essentially private enterprise. It was the eugenics movement itself which sought to influence reproduction, through involuntary sterilisation, to promote social goods.

Thirdly, consider the case of blackmail. A company says it will only develop an encouraging drug for cystic fibrosis (CF) if there are more than 100, 000 people with CF. This would require stopping carrier testing for CF. Should the government stop carrier testing?

If there are other ways to fund this research (e.g., government funding), this should have priority. In virtually all cases of social inequality, there are other avenues to correct inequality than encouraging or forcing people to have children with disabilities or lives of restricted genetic opportunity.

LIMITS ON PROCREATIVE BENIFICENCE: PERSONAL CONCERN FOR EQUALITY OR SELF INTEREST

Consider the following cases. David and Dianne are dwarfs. They wish to use IVF and PGD to select a child with dwarfism because their house is set up for dwarfs. Sam and Susie live a society where discrimination against women is prevalent. They wish to have a girl to reduce this discrimination. These choices would not harm the child produced if selection is employed. Yet they conflict with the Principle of Procreative Beneficence.

We have here an irresolvable conflict of principles:

- personal commitment to equality, personal interests and Procreative Autonomy
- Procreative Beneficence.

Just as there are no simple answers to what should be done (from the perspective of ethics) when respect for personal autonomy conflicts with other principles such as beneficence or distributive justice, so too there are no simple answers to conflict between Procreative Autonomy and Procreative Beneficence.

For the purposes of public policy, there should be a presumption in favour of liberty in liberal democracies. So, ultimately, we should allow couples to make their own decisions about which child to have. Yet this does not imply that there are no normative principles to guide those choices. Procreative Beneficence is a valid principle, albeit one which must be balanced against others.

The implication of this is that those with disabilites should be allowed to select a child with disability, if they have a good reason. But the best option is that we correct discrimination in other ways, by correcting discriminatory social institutions. In this way, we can achieve both equality and a population whose members are living the best lives possible.

CONCLUSIONS

With respect to non-disease genes, we should provide:

- information (through PGD and prenatal testing)
- free choice of which child to have
- non-coercive advice as to which child will be expected to enter life with the best opportunity of having the best life.

Selection for non-disease genes which significantly impact on well-being is *morally required* (Procreative Beneficence). 'Morally required' implies moral persuasion but not coercion is justified.

If, in the end, couples wish to select a child who will have a lower chance of having the best life, they should be free to make such a choice. That should not prevent doctors from attempting to persuade them to have the best child they can. In some cases, persuasion will not be justified. If self-interest or concern to promote equality motivate a choice to select less than the best, then there may be no overall reason to attempt to dissuade a couple. But in cases in which couples do not want to use or obtain available information about genes which will affect well-

426   JULIAN SAVULESCU

being, and their desires are based on irrational fears (e.g., about interfering with nature or playing God), then doctors should try to persuade them to access and use such information in their reproductive decision-making.

Julian Savulescu
Director, Ethics Program
The Murdoch Children's Research Institute,
Royal Children's Hospital
Flemington Rd
Parkville
Melbourne
Victoria 3052
AUSTRALIA
savulesj@cryptic.rch.unimelb.edu.au

[17]

THE CASE AGAINST PERFECTION

*What's wrong with designer
children, bionic athletes, and genetic engineering*

BY MICHAEL J. SANDEL

Illustration by Guy Billout

.....

Breakthroughs in genetics present us with a promise and a predicament. The promise is that we may soon be able to treat and prevent a host of debilitating diseases. The predicament is that our newfound genetic knowledge may also enable us to manipulate our own nature—to enhance our muscles, memories, and moods; to choose the sex, height, and other genetic traits of our children; to make ourselves "better than well." When science moves faster than moral understanding, as it does today, men and women struggle to articulate their unease. In liberal societies they reach first for the language of autonomy, fairness, and individual rights. But this part of our moral vocabulary is ill equipped to address the hardest questions posed by genetic engineering. The genomic revolution has induced a kind of moral vertigo.

Consider cloning. The birth of Dolly the cloned sheep, in 1997, brought a torrent of concern about the prospect of cloned human beings. There are good medical reasons to worry. Most scientists agree that cloning is unsafe, likely to produce offspring with serious abnormalities. (Dolly recently died a premature death.) But suppose technology improved to the point where clones were at no greater risk than naturally conceived offspring. Would human cloning still be objectionable? Should our hesitation be moral as well as medical? What, exactly, is wrong with creating a child who is a genetic twin of one parent, or of an older sibling who has tragically died—or, for that matter, of an admired scientist, sports star, or celebrity?

Some say cloning is wrong because it violates the right to autonomy: by choosing a child's genetic makeup in advance, parents deny the child's right to an open future. A similar objection can be raised against any form of bioengineering that allows parents to select or reject genetic characteristics. According to this argument, genetic enhancements for musical talent, say, or athletic prowess, would point children toward particular

Michael J. Sandel teaches political philosophy at Harvard University, where he is the Anne T. and Robert M. Bass Professor of Government. He serves on the President's Council on Bioethics; this article reflects his personal views.

choices, and so designer children would never be fully free.

At first glance the autonomy argument seems to capture what is troubling about human cloning and other forms of genetic engineering. It is not persuasive, for two reasons. First, it wrongly implies that absent a designing parent, children are free to choose their characteristics for themselves. But none of us chooses his genetic inheritance. The alternative to a cloned or genetically enhanced child is not one whose future is unbound by particular talents but one at the mercy of the genetic lottery.

Second, even if a concern for autonomy explains some of our worries about made-to-order children, it cannot explain our moral hesitation about people who seek genetic remedies or enhancements for themselves. Gene therapy on somatic (that is, nonreproductive) cells, such as muscle cells and brain cells, repairs or replaces defective genes. The moral quandary arises when people use such therapy not to cure a disease but to reach beyond health, to enhance their physical or cognitive capacities, to lift themselves above the norm.

Like cosmetic surgery, genetic enhancement employs medical means for nonmedical ends—ends unrelated to curing or preventing disease or repairing injury. But unlike cosmetic surgery, genetic enhancement is more than skin-deep. If we are ambivalent about surgery or Botox injections for sagging chins and furrowed brows, we are all the more troubled by genetic engineering for stronger bodies, sharper memories, greater intelligence, and happier moods. The question is whether we are right to be troubled, and if so, on what grounds.

In order to grapple with the ethics of enhancement, we need to confront questions largely lost from view—questions about the moral status of nature, and about the proper stance of human beings toward the given world. Since these questions verge on theology, modern philosophers and political theorists tend to shrink from them. But our new powers of biotechnology make them unavoidable. To see why this is so, consider four examples already on the horizon: muscle enhancement, memory enhancement, growth-hormone treatment, and reproductive technologies that enable parents to choose the sex and some genetic traits of their children. In each case what began as an attempt to treat a disease or prevent a genetic disorder now beckons as an instrument of improvement and consumer choice.

Muscles. Everyone would welcome a gene therapy to alleviate muscular dystrophy and to reverse the debilitating muscle loss that comes with old age. But what if the same therapy were used to improve athletic performance? Researchers have developed a synthetic gene that, when injected into the muscle cells of mice, prevents and even reverses natural muscle deterioration. The gene not only repairs wasted or injured muscles but also strengthens healthy ones. This success bodes well for human applications. H. Lee Sweeney, of the University of Pennsylvania, who leads the research, hopes his discovery will cure the immobility that afflicts the elderly. But Sweeney's bulked-up mice have already attracted the attention of athletes seeking a competitive edge. Although the therapy is not yet approved for human use, the prospect of genetically enhanced weight lifters, home-run sluggers, linebackers, and sprinters is easy to imagine. The widespread use of steroids and other

In order to grapple with the ethics of enhancement, we need to confront questions largely lost from view— questions about the moral status of nature, and about the proper stance of human beings toward the given world.

performance-improving drugs in professional sports suggests that many athletes will be eager to avail themselves of genetic enhancement.

Suppose for the sake of argument that muscle-enhancing gene therapy, unlike steroids, turned out to be safe—or at least no riskier than a rigorous weight-training regimen. Would there be a reason to ban its use in sports? There is something unsettling about the image of genetically altered athletes lifting SUVs or hitting 650-foot home runs or running a three-minute mile. But what, exactly, is troubling about it? Is it simply that we find such superhuman spectacles too bizarre to contemplate? Or does our unease point to something of ethical significance?

It might be argued that a genetically enhanced athlete, like a drug-enhanced athlete, would have an unfair advantage over his unenhanced competitors. But the fairness argument against enhancement has a fatal flaw: it has always been the case that some athletes are better endowed genetically than others, and yet we do not consider this to undermine the fairness of competitive sports. From the standpoint

of fairness, enhanced genetic differences would be no worse than natural ones, assuming they were safe and made available to all. If genetic enhancement in sports is morally objectionable, it must be for reasons other than fairness.

Memory. Genetic enhancement is possible for brains as well as brawn. In the mid-1990s scientists managed to manipulate a memory-linked gene in fruit flies, creating flies with photographic memories. More recently researchers have produced smart mice by inserting extra copies of a memory-related gene into mouse embryos. The altered mice learn more quickly and remember things longer than normal mice. The extra copies were programmed to remain active even in old age, and the improvement was passed on to offspring.

Human memory is more complicated, but biotech companies, including Memory Pharmaceuticals, are in hot pursuit of memory-enhancing drugs, or "cognition enhancers," for human beings. The obvious market for such drugs consists of those who suffer from Alzheimer's and other serious memory disorders. The companies also have their sights on a bigger market: the 81 million Americans over fifty, who are beginning to encounter the memory loss that comes naturally with age. A drug that reversed age-related memory loss would be a bonanza for the pharmaceutical industry: a Viagra for the brain. Such use would straddle the line between remedy and enhancement. Unlike a treatment for Alzheimer's, it would cure no disease; but insofar as it restored capacities a person once possessed, it would have a remedial aspect. It could also have purely nonmedical uses: for example, by a lawyer cramming to memorize facts for an upcoming trial, or by a business executive eager to learn Mandarin on the eve of his departure for Shanghai.

Some who worry about the ethics of cognitive enhancement point to the danger of creating two classes of human beings: those with access to enhancement technologies, and those who must make do with their natural capacities. And if the enhancements could be passed down the generations, the two classes might eventually become subspecies—the enhanced and the merely natural. But worry about access ignores the moral status of enhancement itself. Is the scenario troubling because the unenhanced poor would be denied the benefits of bioengineering, or because the enhanced affluent would somehow be dehumanized? As with muscles, so with memory: the fundamental question is not how to ensure equal access to enhancement but whether we should aspire to it in the first place.

Height. Pediatricians already struggle with the ethics of enhancement when confronted by parents who want to make their children taller. Since the 1980s human growth hormone has been approved for children with a hormone deficiency that makes them much shorter than average. But the treatment also increases the height of healthy children.

Some parents of healthy children who are unhappy with their stature (typically boys) ask why it should make a difference whether a child is short because of a hormone deficiency or because his parents happen to be short. Whatever the cause, the social consequences are the same.

In the face of this argument some doctors began prescribing hormone treatments for children whose short stature was unrelated to any medical problem. By 1996 such "off-label" use accounted for 40 percent of human-growth-hormone prescriptions. Although it is legal to prescribe drugs for purposes not approved by the Food and Drug Administration, pharmaceutical companies cannot promote such use. Seeking to expand its market, Eli Lilly & Co. recently persuaded the FDA to approve its human growth hormone for healthy children whose projected adult height is in the bottom one percentile—under five feet three inches for boys and four feet eleven inches for girls. This concession raises a large question about the ethics of enhancement: If hormone treatments need not be limited to those with hormone deficiencies, why should they be available only to very short children? Why shouldn't all shorter-than-average children be able to seek treatment? And what about a child of average height who wants to be taller so that he can make the basketball team?

Some oppose height enhancement on the grounds that it is collectively self-defeating; as some become taller, others become shorter relative to the norm. Except in Lake Wobegon, not every child can be above average. As the unenhanced began to feel shorter, they, too, might seek treatment, leading to a hormonal arms race that left everyone worse off, especially those who couldn't afford to buy their way up from shortness.

But the arms-race objection is not decisive on its own. Like the fairness objection to bioengineered muscles and memory, it leaves unexamined the attitudes and dispositions that prompt the drive for enhancement. If we were bothered only by the injustice of adding shortness to the problems of the poor, we could remedy that unfairness by publicly subsidizing height enhancements. As for the relative height deprivation suffered by innocent bystanders, we could compensate them by taxing those who buy their way to greater height. The real question is whether we want to live in a society where parents feel compelled to spend a fortune to make perfectly healthy kids a few inches taller.

Sex selection. Perhaps the most inevitable nonmedical use of bioengineering is sex selection. For centuries parents have been trying to choose the sex of their children. Today biotech succeeds where folk remedies failed.

One technique for sex selection arose with prenatal tests using amniocentesis and ultrasound. These medical technologies were developed to detect genetic abnormalities such as spina bifida and Down syndrome. But they can also reveal the sex of the fetus—allowing for the abortion of a fetus of an undesired sex. Even among those who favor

abortion rights, few advocate abortion simply because the parents do not want a girl. Nevertheless, in traditional societies with a powerful cultural preference for boys, this practice has become widespread.

Sex selection need not involve abortion, however. For couples undergoing *in vitro* fertilization (IVF), it is possible to choose the sex of the child before the fertilized egg is implanted in the womb. One method makes use of pre-implantation genetic diagnosis (PGD), a procedure developed to screen for genetic diseases. Several eggs are fertilized in a petri dish and grown to the eight-cell stage (about three days). At that point the embryos are tested to determine their sex. Those of the desired sex are implanted; the others are typically discarded. Although few couples are likely to undergo the difficulty and expense of IVF simply to choose the sex of their child, embryo screening is a highly reliable means of sex selection. And as our genetic knowledge increases, it may be possible to use PGD to cull embryos carrying undesired genes, such as those associated with obesity, height, and skin color. The science-fiction movie *Gattaca* depicts a future in which parents routinely screen embryos for sex, height, immunity to disease, and even IQ. There is something troubling about the *Gattaca* scenario, but it is not easy to identify what exactly is wrong with screening embryos to choose the sex of our children.

One line of objection draws on arguments familiar from the abortion debate. Those who believe that an embryo is a person reject embryo screening for the same reasons they reject abortion. If an eight-cell embryo growing in a petri dish is morally equivalent to a fully developed human being, then discarding it is no better than aborting a fetus, and both practices are equivalent to infanticide. Whatever its merits, however, this "pro-life" objection is not an argument against sex selection as such.

The latest technology poses the question of sex selection unclouded by the matter of an embryo's moral status. The Genetics & IVF Institute, a for-profit infertility clinic in Fairfax, Virginia, now offers a sperm-sorting technique that makes it possible to choose the sex of one's child before it is conceived. X-bearing sperm, which produce girls, carry more DNA than Y-bearing sperm, which produce boys; a device called a flow cytometer can separate them. The process, called MicroSort, has a high rate of success.

If sex selection by sperm sorting is objectionable, it must be for reasons that go beyond the debate about the moral status of the embryo. One such reason is that sex selection is an instrument of sex discrimination—typically against girls, as illustrated by the chilling sex ratios in India and China. Some speculate that societies with substantially more men than women will be less stable, more violent, and more prone to crime or war. These are legitimate worries—but the sperm-sorting company has a clever way of addressing them. It offers MicroSort only to couples who want to choose the sex of a child for purposes of "family balancing." Those with more sons than daughters may choose a girl, and vice versa. But customers may not use the technology to stock up on children of the same sex, or even to choose the sex of their firstborn child. (So far the majority of MicroSort clients have chosen girls.) Under restrictions of this kind, do any ethical issues remain that should give us pause?

The case of MicroSort helps us isolate the moral objections that would persist if muscle-enhancement, memory-enhancement, and height-enhancement technologies were safe and available to all.

It is commonly said that genetic enhancements undermine our humanity by threatening our capacity to act freely, to succeed by our own efforts, and to consider ourselves responsible—worthy of praise or blame—for the things we do and for the way we are. It is one thing to hit seventy home runs as the result of disciplined training and effort, and something else, something less, to hit them with the help of steroids or genetically enhanced muscles. Of course, the roles of effort and enhancement will be a matter of degree. But as the role of enhancement increases, our admiration for the achievement fades—or, rather, our admiration for the achievement shifts from the player to his pharmacist. This suggests that our moral response to enhancement is a response to the diminished agency of the person whose achievement is enhanced.

Though there is much to be said for this argument, I do not think the main problem with enhancement and genetic engineering is that they undermine effort and erode human agency. The deeper danger is that they represent a kind of hyperagency—a Promethean aspiration to remake nature, including human nature, to serve our purposes and satisfy our desires. The problem is not the drift to mechanism but the drive to mastery. And what the drive to mastery misses and may even destroy is an appreciation of the gifted character of human powers and achievements.

To acknowledge the giftedness of life is to recognize that our talents and powers are not wholly our own doing, despite the effort we expend to develop and to exercise them. It is also to recognize that not everything in the world is open to whatever use we may desire or devise. Appreciating the gifted quality of life constrains the Promethean project and conduces to a certain humility. It is in part a religious sensibility. But its resonance reaches beyond religion.

It is difficult to account for what we admire about human activity and achievement without drawing upon some version of this idea. Consider two types of athletic achievement. We appreciate players like Pete Rose, who are not blessed with great natural gifts but who manage, through striving, grit, and determination, to excel in their sport. But we also admire players like Joe DiMaggio, who display natural gifts with grace and effortlessness. Now, suppose we learned that both players took performance-enhancing drugs. Whose turn to drugs would we find more deeply disillusioning? Which aspect of the athletic ideal—effort or gift—would be more deeply offended?

Some might say effort: the problem with drugs is that they provide a shortcut, a way to win without striving. But striving is not the point of sports; excellence is. And excellence consists at least partly in the display of natural talents and gifts that are no doing of the athlete who possesses them. This is an uncomfortable fact for democratic societies. We want to believe that success, in sports and in life, is something we earn, not something we inherit. Natural gifts, and the admiration they inspire, embarrass the meritocratic faith; they cast doubt on the conviction that praise and rewards flow from effort alone. In the face of this embarrassment we inflate the moral significance of striving, and depreciate giftedness. This distortion can be seen, for example, in network-television coverage of the Olympics, which focuses less on the feats the athletes perform than on heartrending stories of the hardships they have overcome and the struggles they have waged to triumph over an injury or a difficult upbringing or political turmoil in their native land.

But effort isn't everything. No one believes that a mediocre basketball player who works and trains even harder than Michael Jordan deserves greater acclaim or a bigger contract. The real problem with genetically altered athletes is that they corrupt athletic competition as a human activity that honors the cultivation and display of natural talents. From this standpoint, enhancement can be seen as the ultimate expression of the ethic of effort and willfulness—a kind of high-tech striving. The ethic of willfulness and the biotechnological powers it now enlists are arrayed against the claims of giftedness.

The ethic of giftedness, under siege in sports, persists in the practice of parenting. But here, too, bioengineering and genetic enhancement threaten to dislodge it. To appreciate children as gifts is to accept them as they come, not as objects of our design or products of our will or instruments of our ambition. Parental love is not contingent on the talents and attributes a child happens to have. We choose our friends and spouses at least partly on the basis of qualities we find attractive. But we do not choose our children. Their qualities are unpredictable, and even the most conscientious parents cannot be held wholly responsible for the kind of children they have. That is why parenthood, more than other human relationships, teaches what the theologian William F. May calls an "openness to the unbidden."

May's resonant phrase helps us see that the deepest moral objection to enhancement lies less in the perfection it seeks than in the human disposition it expresses and promotes. The problem is not that parents usurp the autonomy of a child they design. The problem lies in the hubris of the designing parents, in their drive to master the mystery of birth. Even if this disposition did not make parents tyrants to their children, it would disfigure the relation between parent and child, and deprive the parent of the humility and enlarged human sympathies that an openness to the unbidden can cultivate.

To appreciate children as gifts or blessings is not, of course, to be passive in the face of illness or disease. Medical intervention to cure or prevent illness or restore the injured to health does not desecrate nature but honors it. Healing sickness or injury does not override a child's natural capacities but permits them to flourish.

Nor does the sense of life as a gift mean that parents must shrink from shaping and directing the development of their child. Just as athletes and artists have an obligation to cultivate their talents, so parents have an obligation to cultivate their children, to help them discover and develop their talents and gifts. As May points out, parents give their children two kinds of love: accepting love and transforming love. Accepting love affirms the being of the child, whereas transforming love seeks the well-being of the child. Each aspect corrects the excesses of the other, he writes: "Attachment becomes too quietistic if it slackens into mere acceptance of the child as he is." Parents have a duty to promote their children's excellence.

These days, however, overly ambitious parents are prone to get carried away with transforming love—promoting and demanding all manner of accomplishments from their children, seeking perfection. "Parents find it difficult to maintain an equilibrium between the two sides of love," May observes. "Accepting love, without transforming love, slides into indulgence and finally neglect. Transforming love, without accepting love, badgers and finally rejects." May finds in these competing impulses a parallel with modern science: it, too, engages us in beholding the given world, studying and savoring it, and also in molding the world, transforming and perfecting it.

The mandate to mold our children, to cultivate and improve them, complicates the case against enhancement. We usually admire parents who seek the best for their children, who spare no effort to help them achieve happiness and success. Some parents confer advantages on their children by enrolling them in expensive schools, hiring private tutors, sending them to tennis camp, providing them with piano lessons, ballet lessons, swimming lessons, SAT-prep courses, and so on. If it is permissible and even admirable for parents to help their children in these ways, why isn't it equally admirable for parents to use whatever genetic technologies may emerge (provided they are safe) to enhance their children's intelligence, musical ability, or athletic prowess?

The defenders of enhancement are right to this extent: improving children through genetic engineering is similar in spirit to the heavily managed, high-pressure child-rearing that is now common. But this similarity does not

Improving children through genetic engineering is similar in spirit to the heavily managed child-rearing that is now common. But this similarity does not vindicate genetic enhancement. On the contrary, it highlights a problem with the trend toward hyperparenting.

vindicate genetic enhancement. On the contrary, it highlights a problem with the trend toward hyperparenting. One conspicuous example of this trend is sports-crazed parents bent on making champions of their children. Another is the frenzied drive of overbearing parents to mold and manage their children's academic careers.

As the pressure for performance increases, so does the need to help distractible children concentrate on the task at hand. This may be why diagnoses of attention deficit and hyperactivity disorder have increased so sharply. Lawrence Diller, a pediatrician and the author of *Running on Ritalin*, estimates that five to six percent of American children under eighteen (a total of four to five million kids) are currently prescribed Ritalin, Adderall, and other stimulants, the treatment of choice for ADHD. (Stimulants counteract hyperactivity by making it easier to focus and sustain attention.) The number of Ritalin prescriptions for children and adolescents has tripled over the past decade, but not all users suffer from attention disorders or hyperactivity. High school and college students have learned that prescription stimulants improve concentration for those with normal attention spans, and some buy or borrow their classmates' drugs to enhance their performance on the SAT or other exams. Since stimulants work for both medical and nonmedical purposes, they raise the same moral questions posed by other technologies of enhancement.

However those questions are resolved, the debate reveals the cultural distance we have traveled since the debate over marijuana, LSD, and other drugs a generation ago. Unlike the drugs of the 1960s and 1970s, Ritalin and Adderall are

not for checking out but for buckling down, not for beholding the world and taking it in but for molding the world and fitting in. We used to speak of nonmedical drug use as "recreational." That term no longer applies. The steroids and stimulants that figure in the enhancement debate are not a source of recreation but a bid for compliance—a way of answering a competitive society's demand to improve our performance and perfect our nature. This demand for performance and perfection animates the impulse to rail against the given. It is the deepest source of the moral trouble with enhancement.

Some see a clear line between genetic enhancement and other ways that people seek improvement in their children and themselves. Genetic manipulation seems somehow worse—more intrusive, more sinister—than other ways of enhancing performance and seeking success. But morally speaking, the difference is less significant than it seems. Bioengineering gives us reason to question the low-tech, high-pressure child-rearing practices we commonly accept. The hyperparenting familiar in our time represents an anxious excess of mastery and dominion that misses the sense of life as a gift. This draws it disturbingly close to eugenics.

The shadow of eugenics hangs over today's debates about genetic engineering and enhancement. Critics of genetic engineering argue that human cloning, enhancement, and the quest for designer children are nothing more than "privatized" or "free-market" eugenics. Defenders of enhancement reply that genetic choices freely made are not really eugenic—at least not in the pejorative sense. To remove the coercion, they argue, is to remove the very thing that makes eugenic policies repugnant.

Sorting out the lesson of eugenics is another way of wrestling with the ethics of enhancement. The Nazis gave eugenics a bad name. But what, precisely, was wrong with it? Was the old eugenics objectionable only insofar as it was coercive? Or is there something inherently wrong with the resolve to deliberately design our progeny's traits?

James Watson, the biologist who, with Francis Crick, discovered the structure of DNA, sees nothing wrong with genetic engineering and enhancement, provided they are freely chosen rather than state-imposed. And yet Watson's language contains more than a whiff of the old eugenic sensibility. "If you really are stupid, I would call that a disease," he recently told *The Times* of London. "The lower 10 percent who really have difficulty, even in elementary school, what's the cause of it? A lot of people would like to say, 'Well, poverty, things like that.' It probably isn't. So I'd like to get rid of that, to help the lower 10 percent." A few years ago Watson stirred controversy by saying that if a gene for homosexuality were discovered, a woman should be free to abort a fetus that carried it. When his remark provoked an uproar, he replied that he was not singling out gays but asserting a principle: women should be free to abort fetuses for any reason of genetic preference—for example, if the child would be dyslexic, or lacking musical talent, or too short to play basketball.

Watson's scenarios are clearly objectionable to those for whom all abortion is an unspeakable crime. But for those who do not subscribe to the pro-life position, these scenarios raise a hard question: If it is morally troubling to contemplate abortion to avoid a gay child or a dyslexic one, doesn't this suggest that something is wrong with acting on any eugenic preference, even when no state coercion is involved?

Consider the market in eggs and sperm. The advent of artificial insemination allows prospective parents to shop for gametes with the genetic traits they desire in their offspring. It is a less predictable way to design children than cloning or pre-implantation genetic screening, but it offers a good example of a procreative practice in which the old eugenics meets the new consumerism. A few years ago some Ivy League newspapers ran an ad seeking an egg from a woman who was at least five feet ten inches tall and athletic, had no major family medical problems, and had a combined SAT score of 1400 or above. The ad offered $50,000 for an egg from a donor with these traits. More recently a Web site was launched claiming to auction eggs from fashion models whose photos appeared on the site, at starting bids of $15,000 to $150,000.

On what grounds, if any, is the egg market morally objectionable? Since no one is forced to buy or sell, it cannot be wrong for reasons of coercion. Some might worry that hefty prices would exploit poor women by presenting them with an offer they couldn't refuse. But the designer eggs that fetch the highest prices are likely to be sought from the privileged, not the poor. If the market for premium eggs gives us moral qualms, this, too, shows that concerns about eugenics are not put to rest by freedom of choice.

A tale of two sperm banks helps explain why. The Repository for Germinal Choice, one of America's first sperm banks, was not a commercial enterprise. It was opened in 1980 by Robert Graham, a philanthropist dedicated to improving the world's "germ plasm" and counteracting the rise of "retrograde humans." His plan was to collect the sperm of Nobel Prize–winning scientists and make it available to women of high intelligence, in hopes of breeding supersmart babies. But Graham had trouble persuading Nobel laureates to donate their sperm for his bizarre scheme, and so settled for sperm from young scientists of high promise. His sperm bank closed in 1999.

In contrast, California Cryobank, one of the world's leading sperm banks, is a for-profit company with no overt eugenic mission. Cappy Rothman, M.D., a co-founder

of the firm, has nothing but disdain for Graham's eugenics, although the standards Cryobank imposes on the sperm it recruits are exacting. Cryobank has offices in Cambridge, Massachusetts, between Harvard and MIT, and in Palo Alto, California, near Stanford. It advertises for donors in campus newspapers (compensation up to $900 a month), and accepts less than five percent of the men who apply. Cryobank's marketing materials play up the prestigious source of its sperm. Its catalogue provides detailed information about the physical characteristics of each donor, along with his ethnic origin and college major. For an extra fee prospective customers can buy the results of a test that assesses the donor's temperament and character type. Rothman reports that Cryobank's ideal sperm donor is six feet tall, with brown eyes, blond hair, and dimples, and has a college degree—not because the company wants to propagate those traits, but because those are the traits his customers want: "If our customers wanted high school dropouts, we would give them high school dropouts."

Not everyone objects to marketing sperm. But anyone who is troubled by the eugenic aspect of the Nobel Prize sperm bank should be equally troubled by Cryobank, consumer-driven though it be. What, after all, is the moral difference between designing children according to an explicit eugenic purpose and designing children according to the dictates of the market? Whether the aim is to improve

Eugenics and genetic engineering represent the one-sided triumph of willfulness over giftedness, of dominion over reverence, of molding over beholding.

humanity's "germ plasm" or to cater to consumer preferences, both practices are eugenic insofar as both make children into products of deliberate design.

A number of political philosophers call for a new "liberal eugenics." They argue that a moral distinction can be drawn between the old eugenic policies and genetic enhancements that do not restrict the autonomy of the child. "While old-fashioned authoritarian eugenicists sought to produce citizens out of a single centrally designed mould," writes Nicholas Agar, "the distinguishing mark of the new liberal eugenics is state neutrality." Government may not tell parents what sort of children to design, and parents may engineer in their children only those traits that improve their capacities without biasing their choice of life plans. A recent text on genetics and justice, written by the bioethicists Allen Buchanan, Dan W. Brock, Norman Daniels, and Daniel Wikler, offers a similar view. The "bad reputation of eugenics," they write, is due to practices that "might be avoidable in a future eugenic program." The problem with the old eugenics was that its burdens fell disproportionately on the weak and the poor, who were unjustly sterilized and segregated. But provided that the benefits and burdens of genetic improvement are fairly distributed, these bioethicists argue, eugenic measures are unobjectionable and may even be morally required.

The libertarian philosopher Robert Nozick proposed a "genetic supermarket" that would enable parents to order children by design without imposing a single design on the society as a whole: "This supermarket system has the great virtue that it involves no centralized decision fixing the future human type(s)."

Even the leading philosopher of American liberalism, John Rawls, in his classic *A Theory of Justice* (1971), offered a brief endorsement of noncoercive eugenics. Even in a society that agrees to share the benefits and burdens of the genetic lottery, it is "in the interest of each to have greater

> ## In a social world that prizes mastery and control, parenthood is a school for humility. That we care deeply about our children and yet cannot choose the kind we want teaches parents to be open to the unbidden.

natural assets," Rawls wrote. "This enables him to pursue a preferred plan of life." The parties to the social contract "want to insure for their descendants the best genetic endowment (assuming their own to be fixed)." Eugenic policies are therefore not only permissible but required as a matter of justice. "Thus over time a society is to take steps at least to preserve the general level of natural abilities and to prevent the diffusion of serious defects."

But removing the coercion does not vindicate eugenics. The problem with eugenics and genetic engineering is that they represent the one-sided triumph of willfulness over giftedness, of dominion over reverence, of molding over beholding. Why, we may wonder, should we worry about this triumph? Why not shake off our unease about genetic enhancement as so much superstition? What would be lost if biotechnology dissolved our sense of giftedness?

From a religious standpoint the answer is clear: To believe that our talents and powers are wholly our own doing is to misunderstand our place in creation, to confuse our role with God's. Religion is not the only source of reasons to care about giftedness, however. The moral stakes can also be described in secular terms. If bioengineering made the myth of the "self-made man" come true, it would be difficult to view our talents as gifts for which we are indebted, rather than as achievements for which we are responsible. This would transform three key features of our moral landscape: humility, responsibility, and solidarity.

In a social world that prizes mastery and control, parenthood is a school for humility. That we care deeply about our children and yet cannot choose the kind we want teaches parents to be open to the unbidden. Such openness is a disposition worth affirming, not only within families but in the wider world as well. It invites us to abide the unexpected, to live with dissonance, to rein in the impulse to control. A *Gattaca*-like world in which parents became accustomed to specifying the sex and genetic traits of their children would be a world inhospitable to the unbidden, a gated community writ large. The awareness that our talents and abilities are not wholly our own doing restrains our tendency toward hubris.

Though some maintain that genetic enhancement erodes human agency by overriding effort, the real problem is the explosion, not the erosion, of responsibility. As humility gives way, responsibility expands to daunting proportions. We attribute less to chance and more to choice. Parents become responsible for choosing, or failing to choose, the right traits for their children. Athletes become responsible for acquiring, or failing to acquire, the talents that will help their teams win.

One of the blessings of seeing ourselves as creatures of nature, God, or fortune is that we are not wholly responsible for the way we are. The more we become masters of our genetic endowments, the greater the burden we bear for the talents we have and the way we perform. Today when a basketball player misses a rebound, his coach can blame him for being out of position. Tomorrow the coach may blame him for being too short. Even now the use of performance-enhancing drugs in professional sports is subtly transforming the expectations players have for one another; on some teams players who take the field free from amphetamines or other stimulants are criticized for "playing naked."

The more alive we are to the chanced nature of our lot, the more reason we have to share our fate with others. Consider insurance. Since people do not know whether or when various ills will befall them, they pool their risk by buying health insurance and life insurance. As life plays itself out, the healthy wind up subsidizing the unhealthy, and those who live to a ripe old age wind up subsidizing the families of those who die before their time. Even without a sense of mutual obligation, people pool their risks and resources and share one another's fate.

But insurance markets mimic solidarity only insofar as people do not know or control their own risk factors. Suppose genetic testing advanced to the point where it could reliably predict each person's medical future and life expectancy. Those confident of good health and long life would opt out of the pool, causing other people's premiums to skyrocket. The solidarity of insurance would disappear as those with good genes fled the actuarial company of those with bad ones.

The fear that insurance companies would use genetic

data to assess risks and set premiums recently led the Senate to vote to prohibit genetic discrimination in health insurance. But the bigger danger, admittedly more speculative, is that genetic enhancement, if routinely practiced, would make it harder to foster the moral sentiments that social solidarity requires.

Why, after all, do the successful owe anything to the least-advantaged members of society? The best answer to this question leans heavily on the notion of giftedness. The natural talents that enable the successful to flourish are not their own doing but, rather, their good fortune—a result of the genetic lottery. If our genetic endowments are gifts, rather than achievements for which we can claim credit, it is a mistake and a conceit to assume that we are entitled to the full measure of the bounty they reap in a market economy. We therefore have an obligation to share this bounty with those who, through no fault of their own, lack comparable gifts.

A lively sense of the contingency of our gifts—a consciousness that none of us is wholly responsible for his or her success—saves a meritocratic society from sliding into

One of the blessings of seeing ourselves as creatures of nature, God, or fortune is that we are not wholly responsible for the way we are. The more alive we are to the chanced nature of our lot, the more reason we have to share our fate with others. Genetic enhancement would make it harder to foster the moral sentiments that social solidarity requires.

the smug assumption that the rich are rich because they are more deserving than the poor. Without this, the successful would become even more likely than they are now to view themselves as self-made and self-sufficient, and hence wholly responsible for their success. Those at the bottom of society would be viewed not as disadvantaged, and thus worthy of a measure of compensation, but as simply unfit, and thus worthy of eugenic repair. The meritocracy, less chastened by chance, would become harder, less forgiving. As perfect genetic knowledge would end the simulacrum of solidarity in insurance markets, so perfect genetic control would erode the actual solidarity that arises when men and women reflect on the contingency of their talents and fortunes.

Thirty-five years ago Robert L. Sinsheimer, a molecular biologist at the California Institute of Technology, glimpsed the shape of things to come. In an article titled "The Prospect of Designed Genetic Change" he argued that freedom of choice would vindi-

cate the new genetics, and set it apart from the discredited eugenics of old.

> To implement the older eugenics ... would have required a massive social programme carried out over many generations. Such a programme could not have been initiated without the consent and co-operation of a major fraction of the population, and would have been continuously subject to social control. In contrast, the new eugenics could, at least in principle, be implemented on a quite individual basis, in one generation, and subject to no existing restrictions.

According to Sinsheimer, the new eugenics would be voluntary rather than coerced, and also more humane. Rather than segregating and eliminating the unfit, it would improve them. "The old eugenics would have required a continual selection for breeding of the fit, and a culling of the unfit," he wrote. "The new eugenics would permit in principle the conversion of all the unfit to the highest genetic level."

Sinsheimer's paean to genetic engineering caught the heady, Promethean self-image of the age. He wrote hopefully of rescuing "the losers in that chromosomal lottery that so firmly channels our human destinies," including not only those born with genetic defects but also "the 50,000,000 'normal' Americans with an IQ of less than 90." But he also saw that something bigger than improving on nature's "mindless, age-old throw of dice" was at stake. Implicit in technologies of genetic intervention was a more exalted place for human beings in the cosmos. "As we enlarge man's freedom, we diminish his constraints and that which he must accept as given," he wrote. Copernicus and Darwin had "demoted man from his bright glory at the focal point of the universe," but the new biology would restore his central role. In the mirror of our genetic knowledge we would see ourselves as more than a link in the chain of evolution: "We can be the agent of transition to a whole new pitch of evolution. This is a cosmic event."

There is something appealing, even intoxicating, about a vision of human freedom unfettered by the given. It may even be the case that the allure of that vision played a part in summoning the genomic age into being. It is often assumed that the powers of enhancement we now possess arose as an inadvertent by-product of biomedical progress—the genetic revolution came, so to speak, to cure disease, and stayed to tempt us with the prospect of enhancing our performance, designing our children, and perfecting our nature. That may have the story backwards. It is more plausible to view genetic engineering as the ultimate expression of our resolve to see ourselves astride the world, the masters of our nature. But that promise of mastery is flawed. It threatens to banish our appreciation of life as a gift, and to leave us with nothing to affirm or behold outside our own will. ◣

[18]

THE EXPLOITATION ARGUMENT AGAINST COMMERCIAL SURROGACY

STEPHEN WILKINSON

ABSTRACT

This paper discusses the exploitation argument against commercial surrogacy: the claim that commercial surrogacy is morally objectionable because it is exploitative. The following questions are addressed. First, what exactly does the exploitation argument amount to? Second, is commercial surrogacy in fact exploitative? Third, if it were exploitative, would this provide a sufficient reason to prohibit (or otherwise legislatively discourage) it? The focus throughout is on the exploitation of paid surrogates, although it is noted that other parties (e.g. 'commissioning parents') may also be the victims of exploitation.

It is argued that there are good reasons for believing that commercial surrogacy is often exploitative. However, even if we accept this, the exploitation argument for prohibiting (or otherwise legislatively discouraging) commercial surrogacy remains quite weak. One reason for this is that prohibition may well 'backfire' and lead to potential surrogates having to do other things that are more exploitative and/or more harmful than paid surrogacy. It is concluded therefore that those who oppose exploitation should (rather than attempting to stop particular practices like commercial surrogacy) concentrate on: (a) improving the conditions under which paid surrogates 'work'; and (b) changing the background conditions (in particular, the unequal distribution of power and wealth) which generate exploitative relationships.

I   OBJECTIONS TO COMMERCIAL SURROGACY

By 'commercial surrogacy', I mean: surrogacy arrangements in which a woman is paid a fee (not merely compensation) for carrying and giving birth to a foetus/child and for subsequently giving up that child (and all associated parental rights) to the

170   STEPHEN WILKINSON

'commissioning parent(s).' In some such cases, the surrogate mother is the 'genetic mother' because she is also the egg provider. This is termed 'partial' surrogacy, or 'straight' surrogacy. In others cases, the surrogate provides only 'gestational services' and the gametes are provided by others (often, but not necessarily, the commissioning parents). This is termed 'full' or 'host IVF' surrogacy.

As the following quotation makes clear, surrogate motherhood, especially the commercial variety, is a practice that some people regard as extremely morally objectionable:

> Surrogate motherhood has been described by its opponents not only as the buying and selling of children but as reproductive prostitution, reproductive slavery, the renting of a womb, incubatory servitude, the factory method of childbearing, and cutting up women into genitalia. The women who are surrogates are labelled paid breeders, biological entrepreneurs, breeder women, reproductive meat, interchangeable parts in the birth machinery, manufacturing plants, human incubators, incubators for men's sperm, a commodity in the reproductive marketplace, and prostitutes. Their husbands are seen . . . as pimps or cuckolds. The children conceived . . . have been called chattel or merchandise . . . [1]

Commercial surrogacy has been attacked in a variety of ways, but most of the arguments against it concern themselves primarily with one or more of the following: *harm* to surrogates, their children, or society as a whole; the *commodification* of surrogates, children, or women in general; and the *exploitation* of women, especially those who are poor or vulnerable in some other way.[2]

[1] L. Andrews. Surrogate Motherhood: the challenge for feminists. *Law Medicine and Health Care* 1988; 16: 74.

[2] These and similar arguments are all widely discussed in the literature. See for example: E. Anderson. Is Women's Labour a Commodity? *Philosophy and Public Affairs* 1990; 19; 71–92. G. Annas. Death without dignity for commercial surrogacy: the case of Baby M. *Hastings Center Report* 1988; 18; 21–24. R. Ber. Ethical Issues in Gestational Surrogacy. *Theoretical Medicine and Bioethics* 2000; 21; 153–169. R. Arneson. Commodification and Commercial Surrogacy. *Philosophy and Public Affairs* 1992; 21; 132–164. B. Brecher. Surrogacy and its Consequences: some misgivings. *Explorations in Knowledge* 1988; 15; 17–25. N. Duxbury. Do markets degrade? *Modern Law Review* 1996; 59; 331–356. N. Duxbury. Law, Markets and Valuation. *Brooklyn Law Review* 1995; 61; 657–701. C. Erin & J. Harris. Surrogacy. *Bailliere's Clinical Obstetrics and Gynaecology* 1991; 5; 611–635. J. Glover. 1989. *Fertility and the Family: the Glover Report on Reproduction Technologies to the European Commission*. London. Fourth Estates. J. Harris. 1985. *The Value of Life*. London. Routledge. M. Radin. Market Inalienability. *Harvard Law Review*

Because the 'harm and risk' objections to surrogacy depend largely (though not entirely) on various empirical issues (e.g. about just how psychologically damaging it is to be forced to give up a baby), those based on commodification and exploitation are the most philosophically interesting. This paper is concerned with just one of these, exploitation (and, as will become clear in a moment, with just one particular kind of exploitation).

The term 'exploitation' has more than one sense.[3] One of these is its *non-moral* sense:

> In the broadest sense, to exploit something, e.g. a natural resource, means to use it for a purpose. Such exploitation is morally neutral.[4]

In debates about surrogacy, though, 'exploitation' is normally used in one of its two *moral* senses. In the first of these (which I shall term 'wrongful use') exploitation is taken to be an evil because it amounts to *using a person (merely or solely) as a means*. This appears to be what the authors of the *Warnock Report* have in mind when they describe their exploitation-objection to commercial surrogacy:

> That people should treat others as a means to their own ends, however desirable the consequences, must always be liable to moral objection. Such treatment of one person by another becomes positively exploitative when financial interests are involved.[5]

'Wrongful use', then, refers to cases with the following structure: A treats B as if B has only *instrumental* value and does so wrong-

---

1987; 100; 1849–1937. D. Satz. Markets in Women's Reproductive Labour. *Philosophy and Public Affairs* 1992; 21; 107–131. A. Wertheimer. Two Questions About Surrogacy and Exploitation. *Philosophy and Public Affairs* 1992; 21; 71–92.

[3] In making this distinction, I am very much in line with philosophical orthodoxy, as identified and criticised by Wood: 'Most philosophers who reflect on the concept of exploitation tend to follow the practice of dictionaries, distinguishing a "non-moral" sense of "exploitation" from a "moral" sense, and taking the latter sense to involve the idea of making use of someone or something unjustly or unethically. Since they suppose that it is only the latter "pejorative" meaning of the term which interests social critics, they provide what I . . . call a "moralized" account of exploitation. That is, they suppose that the term "exploitation" (in the "pejorative" sense) already has wrongfulness built into its very meaning.' A. Wood. Exploitation. *Social Philosophy and Policy* 1995; 12: 137.

[4] J. Schwartz. What's wrong with exploitation? *Nous* 1995; 29: 176. See also: J. Feinberg. 1988. *Harmless Wrongdoing*. New York. Oxford University Press: 177.

[5] M. Warnock. 1985. *A Question of Life: the Warnock Report on Human Fertilisation and Embryology*. Oxford. Blackwell: para. 8.17.

172   STEPHEN WILKINSON

fully because B in fact has some other sort of value (normally, though not necessarily, as a person) which generates for B a right to respect and to (some level of) non-instrumental consideration and treatment.

'Exploitation', however, can also be used in a rather different (but nevertheless moral) sense to refer to what I shall call *unfair advantage exploitation*.[6] Although unfair advantage exploitation does inevitably involve A treating B as a means (though not necessarily *solely* as a means), its wrongness consists not in the fact that A *uses* B, but in the fact that she does so unjustly *and* under conditions which make it the case either that B does not consent, or that B's consent is not valid. Hence, one might argue that paying 'poverty wages' to people in areas of high unemployment is exploitative (in this sense) not because the workers are being *used* (since, after all, all workers are used), but because the wages paid are *unfairly* low and because the workers are in effect *forced* into their jobs (arguably invalidating their consent) by poverty and by lack of alternatives.

Those who wish to investigate the strength of the exploitation case against commercial surrogacy (and against any similar commercial practice[7]) are faced then with two distinct questions. First, does it involve *wrongful use?* Second, does it involve *unfair advantage exploitation?* My aim in this paper is to answer just the second of these, leaving the first for other papers.[8] I shall start by spelling out in more detail what exactly unfair advantage exploitation amounts to, before proceeding to argue that (given certain assumptions) there are good reasons for thinking that commercial surrogacy would involve exploitation of this sort. Finally, I argue that it does *not* follow from this that we ought to prohibit (or otherwise legislatively discourage) commercial surrogacy.

Because my main concern is with commercial surrogacy, 'surrogacy' should from henceforth be taken to mean 'commer-

---

[6] Harris makes a very similar distinction between 'two differing conceptions of the same concept of exploitation': one involving 'the idea of *wrongful* use', the other involving 'some disparity in the value of an exchange of goods or services.' See J. Harris. 1993. *Wonderwoman and Superman: the ethics of human biotechnology.* Oxford. Oxford University Press: 120.

[7] Although the sole concern of this paper is commercial surrogacy, much of the discussion will be relevant to other debates such as the one concerning organ sale.

[8] S. Wilkinson. Commodification arguments for the legal prohibition of organ sale. *Health Care Analysis* 2000; 8; 189–201. Reprinted in *Applied Ethics* (Volume 3: Ethical issues in medicine, technology and the life sciences II). R. Chadwick & D. Schroeder, eds. London: Routledge: 187–199. S. Wilkinson. 2003. *Bodies for Sale.* London. Routledge.

THE EXPLOITATION ARGUMENT   173

cial surrogacy' unless otherwise indicated; similarly, 'exploitation' should be taken to mean 'unfair advantage exploitation.'

II   THE NATURE OF EXPLOITATION

Wertheimer suggests that what is typically meant by 'exploitation' is that one party is taking 'unfair advantage' of another. This idea of 'unfair advantage' involves two elements: the 'dimension of value' and the 'dimension of choice.' The 'dimension of value' amounts to the claim that A exploits B only if B is harmed *or* treated unfairly as a result of the transaction; while the 'dimension of choice' means that 'A exploits B only when B's choice is somehow compromised.'[9] It seems to me that this analysis, in particular the idea that these two 'dimensions' (value and choice) are the essential features of exploitation, is fundamentally right.[10] I therefore propose the following partial analysis of exploitation.[11] A transaction between A and B amounts to A's exploiting B if and only if:

(a) the distribution of benefit and harm between A and B is (other things being equal) unjust (in A's favour); and,
(b) B does not validly consent.

My account differs from Wertheimer's in two main respects: one merely terminological, the other substantive. The first (terminological) difference is that I prefer to talk in terms of 'justice' and 'consent', rather than 'value' and 'choice', and so I shall from henceforth refer to (a) and (b) above as the *justice condition* and the *consent condition* respectively. The second (substantive) difference is that although he and I agree that the justice condition is necessary, we disagree about the consent condition, since while I view it also as necessary, he concludes that 'a defect in choice is not necessary but [merely] relevant.'[12]

The justice condition

According to the justice condition, A exploits B only if the distribution of benefits and harms between A and B is (other things

[9] Wertheimer, *op. cit.* note 2, p. 213.

[10] Wertheimer later rejects the view that a 'defect in choice' is an essential part of exploitation. Wertheimer, *op. cit.* note 2, p. 229.

[11] The correct account of exploitation is in fact much more complicated than this, although not in ways that affect the issues considered here. See: Wilkinson, *op. cit.* note 8, chapters 2 and 3.

[12] Wertheimer, *op. cit.* note 2, p. 229.

174 STEPHEN WILKINSON

being equal) unjust (in A's favour). This claim as it stands, though, is in need of clarification and explanation on a number of fronts.

Firstly, it should be noted that the justice condition is meant to be neutral with respect to particular accounts of distributive justice and therefore to be compatible with any such account. This does not however mean that the justice condition lacks content, for it does posit the existence of a close relationship between just distribution and exploitation. Given this, it follows that one's view about whether a particular activity is exploitative, and more generally one's view about how much exploitation there is in the world, will be largely determined by one's views on distributive justice. So if, for example, someone adopts a 'minimalist' (e.g. libertarian) account of justice, she is likely to think that there is relatively little exploitation around; but if someone adopts a strongly egalitarian account, then she is likely to see exploitation as a much more widespread phenomenon.

Secondly, the exploited party need not be harmed by the exploitation. Indeed, she may benefit from it. All that is required is that the transaction's effects on her welfare are *more negative* than justice dictates. In some cases, this will consist in her failing to benefit sufficiently; in others, it will consist in her being harmed too much. Hence, within the category 'exploitation', there is a distinction between *harmful* exploitation (where there is harm to the exploited party) and *mutually advantageous* exploitation (where both parties benefit).[13]

Finally, something should be said about the 'other things being equal' part of the justice condition. This amounts to an admission that although all exploitative transactions are unjust when considered in isolation, some may not be unjust 'all things considered', once 'external' factors (those outside the transaction itself) are taken into consideration. There may, for instance, be cases in which although A is exploiting B in the transaction under consideration, B (all things considered) *deserves* to be exploited by A either because of her past wrong actions with respect to A (and/or others), or because of the fact that B is presently exploiting A on other fronts.

The consent condition

People who are exploited are typically *under-rewarded* for something that they provide to the person or institution that exploits

---

[13] Wertheimer, *op. cit.* note 2, p. 229.

them. However, not all cases of under-reward are cases of exploitation. If someone very poor is forced to work in a factory for five pence per hour in order to avoid starvation for her family, then (if we allow certain economic assumptions) she is being both under-rewarded and exploited by her employer. If, on the other hand, a wealthy professional person agrees, entirely voluntarily, to spend a day working for charity for a 'token' five pence per hour then she is (probably) being under-rewarded but *not* exploited. The key difference between these two cases is the nature of the consent that each person gives. In the former case, the validity of the consent is questionable (since the only alternative to taking the underpaid job is starvation), but in the latter case the consent to underpayment is unproblematic. This is the thinking underpinning the *consent condition*, according to which A exploits B only if B's consent to the arrangement is invalid. In short, the consent condition allows us to distinguish cases of exploitation from non-exploitative cases in which an individual waives her rights to a fair share of the burdens/benefits.

Like the justice condition, the consent condition is neutral with respect to particular conceptions of valid consent, and furthermore, is compatible with the view that different standards of consent are applicable in different types of cases. Hence, the consent condition will only yield substantive results when allied to a particular account of valid consent. My own view, which will emerge later, is that the kinds of things that may invalidate a consent are those commonly discussed in the Bioethics literature, such as inadequate or misleading information, coercion, or compromised personal autonomy.

Both Wertheimer and Wood argue against my view that exploitation necessarily involves 'defective consent.' Consider, for instance, these cases from Wood:

> Someone who is propertyless and starving has a lot to gain by striking a deal with an employer who is willing to offer bare subsistence in exchange for long, hard labour under dangerous conditions – and a lot to lose (namely, life itself) if no such exploitative bargain is in the offing . . . A gambler who owes a large amount of money to ruthless and violent characters will be in desperate need of the loan shark who offers the needed funds at a usurious rate of interest; such a person will be more than willing under these conditions to consent to virtually any terms of payment.[14]

---

[14] Wood, *op. cit.* note 3, p. 149.

Wood's point here is that typical victims of exploitation (such as the starving person and the gambler) are likely to be all *too* willing to be exploited, because of the absence of less bad alternatives, and hence 'exploitation is often voluntary' and we ought not therefore to make the absence of consent part of our definition of exploitation.[15] This does seem to present a problem for my account, since both of Wood's cases appear to be fully voluntary cases of exploitation. We should bear in mind, however, that my proposed criterion is not *mere voluntariness*, but *valid consent*, which is a more demanding and more moralised standard.

One way of dealing with Wood's cases, is to argue that neither the starving person nor the gambler validly consent, because of their lack of acceptable alternatives. Although this seems initially intuitive, I would be reluctant to put too much weight on the idea that the lack of acceptable alternatives is in and of itself sufficient to invalidate a consent. There are a number of reasons for this. The first, a very general worry, is that it will be difficult, if not impossible, to specify non-arbitrarily what counts as a sufficient number of sufficiently good alternatives. Secondly, it would seem strange to say (as this proposal implies) that if someone were faced with an entirely free choice between X, which is extremely good, and Y, which is extremely bad, that that person could not validly consent to X because of the lack of acceptable alternatives. Thirdly, there are cases similar to the one described here by Wertheimer:

> If A (a physician) should say to B (a patient), 'You can choose to have this leg amputated or you will die', we do *not* say that B's decision to have his leg amputated is coerced because death is an unacceptable alternative. Rather, we seek B's informed consent to the procedure.[16]

It would be bizarre to rule out the possibility of valid consent here just because of the lack of acceptable alternatives. Therefore, taking these three points together, we can see that 'lack of acceptable alternatives' will not do the work required of it.

More promising is the idea that it is coercion that invalidates consent in Wood's cases. This looks straightforwardly plausible in the case of the gambler who is being threatened by 'ruthless and violent characters.' He is, we might say, coerced into taking the loan from the loan shark since the 'ruthless and violent characters' will harm him if he doesn't pay them, and (let's assume)

---

[15] Wood, *op. cit.* note 3, p. 148.
[16] Wertheimer, *op. cit.* note 2, p. 226.

getting money from the loan shark is his only means of doing so. So *de facto* they are coercing him into taking out the loan.

Wood's other case, the starving person, is rather harder to deal with, because it is not obvious that there is any coercion going on at all and, in order to deal with it, we shall need to tackle directly the question of what exactly coercion is. Once again, it seems to me that Wertheimer's analysis is fundamentally right:

> In general, A coerces B to do X if A proposes (threatens) to make B worse off with reference to some baseline condition unless B does X.[17]

What is interesting about this account is that coercion does not necessarily involve threatening to reduce someone's welfare-level over time (i.e. it does not necessarily involve making them less well off *than they are now*), but may (in certain circumstances) involve merely threatening not to benefit them in such a way that their level of welfare climbs to some other relevant baseline (though, as Wertheimer admits, 'specifying the appropriate baseline against which to measure the proposal can be problematic').[18] This allows for the possibility of what we might term *omissive coercion*, by which I mean – A omissively coerces B to do X if and only if:

(1) A has a duty to do Y for B; and
(2) A proposes/threatens *not* to do Y for B unless B does X.

Omissive coercion is presumably quite a widespread phenomenon. Imagine, for example, that an employee already deserves a pay-rise (based on past performance), but that the employer says that she won't get it unless she does further extra work. Surely, this is omissive coercion – a threat not to give her that to which she has a right. Alternatively, consider Nozick's drowning case:[19]

> A comes across B, who is drowning. A proposes to rescue B if B agrees to pay A $10,000. A and B know that there are no other potential rescuers.[20]

Many of us would want to say of this case that A *is* coercing B. However, A is not, in the standard sense, threatening to make B worse off (since she would have drowned anyway if A had not

[17] Wertheimer, *op. cit.* note 2, p. 225.
[18] Ibid.
[19] R. Nozick. 1969. Coercion. In *Philosophy Science and Method.* S. Morgenbesser, P. Suppes & M. White, eds. New York. St Martin's Press: 447.
[20] Wertheimer, *op. cit.* note 2, p. 226.

178   STEPHEN WILKINSON

turned up) but is rather threatening not to benefit her. So, if this is coercion at all, it is omissive coercion. What makes this a case of omissive coercion, as opposed to merely offering to benefit for a price, is the plausible background assumption that A has an independent duty to rescue B free of charge. The existence of this duty affects the relevant 'baseline' such that it is not *the level of welfare which B will have if A does nothing* but rather *the level of welfare which B will have if A acts on her relevant duties.* Hence, relative to this moralised baseline, A *is* threatening to make B worse off (i.e. worse off than the baseline) and so should be seen as coercing B.[21]

By now it will, I hope, have become clear what we should say about Wood's starving employee case. We should regard this as exploitation because the arrangement is unjust (since, *ex hypothesi*, the starving employee is underpaid) and because the validity of the worker's consent is in doubt, since (arguably) the employer is exercising *omissive coercion.* He probably has a duty to give her the money anyway, given that she is starving and that he is wealthy and close to hand, and so to insist that she works for the money is coercive. This case then looks similar to Nozick's 'drowning case' discussed above. Alternatively, we might think that it is not the employer who omissively coerces the starving person but rather society in general (or the State) since *it* has general welfare-duties towards this person and is, in effect, threatening her with starvation if she doesn't take on the poorly paid job. If so, then this would be a case of *third-party* omissive coercion, since the person doing the exploiting (the employer) is not the person doing the coercing.

In the light of these considerations, I conclude that an account of exploitation that includes the consent condition is to be preferred to one that does not. There are two reasons for this. First, the consent condition tracks an 'intuitive' distinction between exploitative and non-exploitative cases of underpayment (the latter being those cases in which there is truly valid consent). Second, it can deal well with problem cases like those provided by Wertheimer and Wood, chiefly by utilising the idea of coercion in the ways suggested above.

III   IS COMMERCIAL SURROGACY EXPLOITATIVE?

Some preliminaries

We are now in a position to address the question of whether commercial surrogacy involves the exploitation of surrogates and

---

[21] Or as Wertheimer puts it: 'A actually proposes to make B *worse off*... relative to what B has a *right* to expect from A'. Wertheimer, *op. cit.* note 2, p. 226.

THE EXPLOITATION ARGUMENT   179

if so, to what extent. Given the account of exploitation just offered, this question is reducible to the following two sub-questions:

(1) Is the distribution of benefit and harm between the commissioning parents and the surrogate unjust (other things being equal)?[22]
(2) Is the surrogate's consent invalid?

Surrogacy will be exploitative if and only if the answer to each of these sub-questions is 'yes.'

It is necessary first to make a number of preliminary points. First, my concern is solely with *commercial* surrogacy and so I shall deal only with arguments that seek to show that commercial surrogacy is *more exploitative* than the non-commercial variety; exploitation-objections to surrogacy-in-general will not therefore be considered. Second, I shall assume that a fairly clear distinction can be drawn between commercial and non-commercial surrogacy, while recognising that in reality things may be rather messier than this, chiefly because of the question of how to categorise 'compensation payments.'[23] Third, it should be noted that the claim that commercial surrogacy arrangements *could* be exploitative is obviously true, since almost any kind of commercial transaction *could* contain exploitative terms and conditions. The question then is not whether it *could* be exploitative but whether there are good reasons to believe that, because of some special feature of the practice, it is either *necessarily* exploitative or *very likely* to be exploitative.

Underpayment

One reason for regarding commercial surrogacy as exploitative is the idea that surrogate mothers are highly likely to be *underpaid*, both relative to the benefits accruing to the commissioning parents (which are presumed to be very great) and, more importantly, relative to the kind of risks to which the surrogate must subject herself. These risks may be physical, as noted by Warnock:

[22] For the sake of brevity, I shall focus just on the commissioning parents as potential exploiters. There are however other possible exploiters: e.g. agencies, or even surrogates themselves in certain circumstances.

[23] This kind of issue is one of the main concerns of the UK's 'Brazier Report.' See: M. Brazier, A. Campbell & S. Golombok. 1998. *Surrogacy: review for health ministers of current arrangements for payments and regulation.* London. The Stationary Office.

180   STEPHEN WILKINSON

. . . since there are some risks attached to pregnancy, no woman
ought to be asked to undertake pregnancy for another, in order
to earn money.[24]

Or psychological, as noted by Anderson:

Most surrogate mothers experience grief upon giving up their
children – in 10% of cases seriously enough to require therapy.[25]

There are, however, at least two reasons to think that the possibility of underpayment is not in fact sufficient to underpin an
exploitation-objection to commercial surrogacy.

The first is that, if underpayment is the problem, then why not
simply put in place regulations that would ensure a fair minimum
fee? As Wertheimer notes, it is rather surprising that those who
argue against commercial surrogacy on the grounds that it is
exploitative tend not to propose this:

. . . unlike other contexts in which it is uncontroversial that
exploitation can be eliminated or decreased by increasing the
compensation to the exploited party, it is rarely argued that
surrogacy would be less exploitative if the surrogate were paid
more. In fact, unpaid surrogacy is typically regarded as less
exploitative than paid surrogacy. Among the critics of surrogacy, higher pay is the dog that doesn't bark.[26]

The underpayment objection then seems not to work unless we
assume that there is some feature of surrogacy that makes it the
case that fair payment is not possible. If we conceive of commercial surrogacy as the provision of a service, then this seems implausible. However, if (as some would) we think of it as 'baby selling'
then, given the further assumption that babies are literally price-
less, perhaps the view that underpayment is unavoidable makes
some sense.[27] Alternatively, one might argue instead (and much

---

[24] Warnock, *op. cit.* note 5, para. 8.12.
[25] Anderson, *op. cit.* note 2, p. 238.
[26] Wertheimer, *op. cit.* note 2, p. 217.
[27] The view that commercial surrogacy is 'baby selling' is widespread and
appears, for example, in the 'Warnock Report': 'a surrogacy agreement is degrading to the child who is to be the outcome of it, since, for all practical purposes,
the child will have been bought for money'. Warnock, *op. cit.* note 5, para. 8.11.
   For discussions of whether or not commercial surrogacy is baby selling see
(e.g.): Andrews, *op. cit.* note 1. G. Annas. Baby M: babies (and justice) for sale.
Hastings Center Report 1987; 17; 13–15. R. Kornegay. Is Commercial Surrogacy
Baby-Selling? *Journal of Applied Philosophy* 1990; 7; 45–50. Wilkinson, *op. cit.* note
8, chapter 8.

more plausibly) that although fair payment is possible in principle, it is a practical impossibility because policy-makers would set the level too low, underestimating the true value of what the surrogate gives.

A second more serious problem with the underpayment objection, though, is the following. What we are looking for is some feature of commercial surrogacy in virtue of which it is more exploitative than unpaid surrogacy. The candidate under consideration is underpayment. However, if commercial surrogacy is underpaid then surely *a fortiori* so is unpaid surrogacy, which (by definition) involves no financial reward at all for the surrogate. This seems to me to be a decisive objection and leads me to the view that underpayment *per se* cannot be the basis of an exploitation-objection to commercial surrogacy (as opposed to surrogacy in general) since it is by definition better paid than the non-commercial variety. And so, if it is the case that commercial surrogacy is more exploitative than the non-commercial variety this must be on account of the effect that payment has on the quality of the consent given by the surrogate.[28]

Payment and consent

Why might one think that offering payment to surrogate mothers would compromise the validity of their consent? The main reason offered by critics is that paid surrogacy would attract extremely poor women, who were desperate for the money. Brecher, for example, suggests that if paid surrogacy was permitted:

> . . . a pool of surrogates could well be created on the model of working class prostitution; women would come to be imported from poor countries for the purpose of serving as surrogates . . .[29]

[28] Interestingly, this seems to be the view taken by the authors of the UK's 'Brazier report', who suggest that the main reason why payment generates exploitation is that it may constitute 'undue pressure': 'payment of a surrogate by a commissioning couple to bear a child for them creates a potentially exploitative situation . . . the absence of payment would reduce the likelihood of undue pressure being placed on the surrogate mother.' Brazier et al., *op. cit.* note 5, para. 5.16.

[29] B. Brecher. 1987. Liberal Individualism and the Moral Climate. In *Moral Philosophy and Contemporary Problems.* J. Evans, ed. Cambridge. Cambridge University Press: 195.

182   STEPHEN WILKINSON

Some writers have expressed doubts about this kind of claim.[30] However, let us for the present allow the assumption that paid surrogacy would attract extremely poor women to stand in order to see what, if anything, follows from it.

We should start by asking whether the consent of a desperately poor woman is more likely to be invalid than that of a rich woman and if so why. An intuitive answer to this is *yes*, because whereas the poor woman can in effect be *forced* to act as a surrogate (by her need for money), this is not true of the rich woman. The situation of the poor surrogate then is similar to that of the starving person described in Wood's example. Earlier, I concluded that that person is exploited because she is both underpaid and coerced. Might this also be true of the poor surrogate? More specifically (given that no-one is threatening to make her worse off in the standard sense) is she *omissively coerced* by anyone?

Given my earlier remarks about omissive coercion, this question depends crucially on whether anyone has a *duty* to improve her welfare without demanding anything in return – since the existence (or otherwise) of such duties will determine the relevant *welfare-baseline* with reference to which judgements about whether or not she is being *threatened* with being made 'worse off' (as opposed to merely being *offered* an additional option) should be made.

With this in mind it seems that paid surrogates may be the victims of omissive coercion in one of the following two ways. Either because:

(1) The commissioning parents have a duty to help her without demanding surrogacy services in return, but propose (threaten) not to act in accordance with this duty unless she provides surrogacy services.

Or because:

(2) Society in general (or, perhaps, the State) has a duty to ensure that she has a certain level of welfare, but makes it the case that she can only reach this level of welfare by selling surrogacy services.

The question of whether such duties in fact exist is far too complex and general to be dealt with here – apart from to say

---

[30] See, for example: R. Posner. The Ethics and Economics of Surrogate Motherhood. *Journal of Contemporary Health Law and Policy* 1989; 5: 21–29.

that (2) seems much more plausible than (1) (except perhaps in cases where the commissioning parents are *extremely* wealthy). What we can conclude, though, is that one's views about whether poor paid surrogates are coerced (and exploited) should be determined largely by one's more general views about the kinds of duties that society in general has towards the poor. More specifically, if one endorses what I shall call *the welfarist assumption* (which underpins (2) above) one should probably think that poorly paid surrogates are coerced and therefore (given certain other assumptions) exploited.

The reason for this is as follows. Given the welfarist assumption, society has an obligation to ensure that the prospective surrogate (SM) obtains a certain level of welfare (W) (insofar as this is practicable). Assume also that society both permits commercial surrogacy and makes it (or allows it to be) the case that becoming a surrogate is the only practicable way in which SM can obtain W. This amounts to what I earlier called omissive coercion because: (a) society has a free-standing duty to provide SM with W; and (b) society (perhaps not consciously or explicitly, but at least *in effect*) proposes or threatens *not* to provide SM with W unless she acts as a paid surrogate (or does something else which is worse). Given the existence of (enough) omissive coercion, SM's consent will be invalid. Therefore, (provided that she is also underpaid etc) she is exploited.

Interestingly, paid surrogacy, in this picture, turns out not to be fundamentally different from any other sort of employment and we could, for example, tell exactly the same story about poorly paid cleaning work, or factory work, or prostitution. What arguably makes surrogacy rather different from cleaning and factory work, though, is the thought that it is particularly harmful, especially psychologically, because of the close relationship between women and their offspring. Similar considerations apply to prostitution, given the (supposed) link between a person's sense of identity and her sexuality. And, because of this supposed harm, people tend to think both that surrogacy would not or cannot be justly rewarded, *and* that women are likely *only* to do it if they are coerced.[31]

---

[31] Harris makes a similar point about prostitution: 'Those who regard prostitution or surrogacy as exploitative *per se* . . . rely on . . . the hidden assumption that because no one would voluntarily choose to be a prostitute whatever the level of remuneration, the choice cannot be autonomous.' Harris, *op. cit.* note 6, p. 125.

IV LAW AND POLICY IMPLICATIONS

There are numerous legislative options available to policymakers. These include (in order of 'restrictiveness'):

(a) criminalising all forms of surrogacy (paid and unpaid) – i.e. making it an offence (paid or unpaid) to 'procure', and/or to 'supply', and/or to act as an intermediary;

(b) criminalising commercial surrogacy – by making it an offence (but only if done for money) to 'procure', and/or to 'supply', and/or to act as an intermediary;[32]

(c) not criminalising commercial surrogacy, but making surrogacy contracts unenforceable;

(d) allowing surrogacy contracts to be enforceable but only within a regulatory framework; and

(e) a more *laissez-faire* approach under which surrogacy contracts are governed only by the general principles of contract law (and other relevant general provisions).

The question that I want to address briefly in this closing section is how the view of exploitation and surrogacy developed earlier impacts on the justifiability or otherwise of options like those listed above.

The rather conditional ethical conclusion of this paper is that there are good reasons to view commercial surrogacy as exploita-

---

[32] Often, legislative attempts to prevent the commercialisation of surrogacy focus on intermediaries rather than on surrogates and commissioners. The UK's *Surrogacy Arrangements Act* 1985, for example, prevents surrogacy agencies from profiting from surrogacy arrangements without criminalising commercial surrogacy *per se*. Nonetheless, the ban on commercial agencies does make it much harder for British women to become paid surrogates and can therefore be viewed as 'legislative discouragement' of commercial surrogacy itself.

Freeman interestingly describes this legislation as 'an ill-considered and largely irrelevant panic measure', writing: 'There are few better modern examples of morally panicked legislation than the 1985 [Surrogacy Arrangements] Act (one MP said it 'rightly outlaw[ed] the hell and wickedness that exists in America – where women are exploited and handled in an undignified manner for gain).' M. Freeman. 1989. Is surrogacy exploitative? In *Legal Issues in Human Reproduction*. S. McLean, ed. Aldershot. Dartmouth: 165. M. Freeman. Does surrogacy have a future after Brazier? *Medical Law Review* 1999; 7: 2.

tive *provided that we accept a number of assumptions,* some of which
are highly controversial. The first assumption is that it would be
underpaid. The second is that it would attract large numbers of
poor women. And the third (the most controversial of the three)
is the 'welfarist assumption.' As suggested earlier, my own view is
that commercial surrogacy could be rendered non-exploitative by
regulations which guaranteed a generous minimum fee-level
(thereby eliminating the first assumption), but let us grant for
the sake of argument that such regulation is not, for whatever
reason, feasible. What then would be the implications for law and
public policy? More specifically, would it then follow that we ought
to adopt a relatively restrictive regulatory regime (for instance,
(a) or (b) above) in order to stop poor women from being
exploited?

There are two closely related reasons for answering 'no' to
this question. The first is *consistency*: would it not be inconsistent
to ban (or otherwise legislatively discourage) commercial surrogacy because it is exploitative whilst at the same time permitting
various other practices which are arguably just as exploitative (e.g.
some forms of prostitution or poorly paid cleaning or factory
work)? The second is the *welfare of prospective surrogates*: given that
they in reality have no other (or no better) way of gaining access
to the money that they need, is it really right to deprive them of
the opportunities that paid surrogacy may provide just in order
to stop them from being exploited? Of course, it would be much
better if they could be offered non-exploitative ways of earning
money, but (on the assumption that this is not going to happen
in the near future) ought we to harm them (by taking away
their chance to be paid surrogates) in order to save them from
exploitation?

None of this is meant to be a general argument for permitting
exploitation. On the contrary, I would like to see pay and conditions in these other sectors improved, through State action if necessary. What I do fail to see, though, is how banning (or otherwise
legislatively discouraging) commercial surrogacy helps much in
the fight against the exploitation of poor women, given that if
they can't be surrogates then they'll just have to do some (other)
job which is at least as bad or remain poor. The point is well-made
by Posner:

To someone who is desperately in need of $10,000, a court's
refusal to allow her to obtain it will seem a hypocritical token

186   STEPHEN WILKINSON

of concern for her plight, especially since the court has no power to alleviate that plight in some other way.[33]

So, even if commercial surrogacy does exploit poor women, permitting it may still be justified given that they need the money and are unlikely to get it in any other way, or could only otherwise get it in ways that were worse for them than undertaking to be a paid surrogate.[34]

We should conclude therefore that although permitting commercial surrogacy may allow poor women to be exploited, this is not a sufficient reason for prohibiting (or otherwise legislatively discouraging) it, because it is likely that they will be exploited anyway, and that this form of exploitation is less harmful than the alternatives. Ideally, though, we should seek to avoid the exploitation in other ways: by ensuring that surrogates are well paid and/or by providing them with other non-exploitative ways of earning money. And more generally, if our desire is to eliminate or reduce exploitation, we should focus not on prohibiting particular forms of exploitation, since this will (at best) simply move exploitation from one place to another, but should instead focus on changing the background conditions (in particular, the unequal distribution of power and wealth) that generate exploitative situations. The point is well made by John Harris:

> If we strongly object to the exploitation of the poor, as I do, then the therapy of choice is to remove the desperate nature of their poverty.[35]

Earlier I argued that there is a close relationship between the exploitation objection to commercial surrogacy and the welfarist assumption. More specifically, believers in the exploitation objection must make the welfarist assumption. Those who oppose commercial surrogacy on these grounds would therefore be well-advised to ensure that they act on their welfarist views in a consistent manner and, as well as attempting to prevent specific exploitings, attempt also to ensure that society acts in

[33] Posner, *op. cit.* note 30, p. 255.

[34] Laura Purdy notes that 'poor women now face substantial risks in the workplace. Even a superficial survey of the hazards in occupations available to poor women would give pause to those who would prohibit surrogacy on grounds of risk.' L. Purdy. Surrogate Mothering: exploitation or empowerment? *Bioethics* 1989; 3: 32.

[35] Harris, *op. cit.* note 6, p. 132.

accordance with its welfare duties to its most disadvantaged members.[36]

Stephen Wilkinson
Centre for Professional Ethics
Keele University
Keele ST5 5BG
UK
s.wilkinson@phil.keele.ac.uk

[36] I would like to thank Professor Anne Donchin and Professor Derek Morgan for their useful referees' comments. In addition, a number of people have provided helpful critiques of previous versions of this paper (and related material) spanning its 'evolution' over several years. These include Bob Brecher, Angus Dawson, Heather Draper, Eve Garrard, John Harris, David McNaughton, David Resnik, Sally Sheldon, and Adrian Walsh. This list however is almost certainly not complete and I apologise to anyone who I have inadvertently failed to mention.

Part IV
End-of-life Issues

[19]

PRESIDENTIAL ADDRESS: IS THE SANCTITY OF LIFE ETHIC TERMINALLY ILL?

PETER SINGER

ABSTRACT

Our growing technical capacity to keep human beings alive has brought the sanctity of life ethic to the point of collapse. The shift to a concept of brain death was already an implicit abandonment of the traditional ethic, though this has only recently become apparent. The 1993 decision of the British House of Lords in the case of Anthony Bland is an even more decisive shift towards an ethic that does not ask or seek to preserve human life as such, but only a life that is worth living. Once this shift has been completed and assimilated, we will no longer need the concept of brain death. Instead we can face directly the real ethical issue: when may doctors intentionally end the life of a patient?

I INTRODUCTION

It is surely no secret to anyone at this Congress that I have for a long time been a critic of the traditional sanctity of life ethic. So if I say that I believe that, after ruling our thoughts and our decisions about life and death for nearly two thousand years, the traditional sanctity of life ethic is at the point of collapse, some of you may think this is mere wishful thinking on my part. Consider, however, the following three signs of this impending collapse, which have taken place — coincidentally but perhaps appropriately enough — during the past two years in which I have had the honour of holding the office of President of the International Association of Bioethics.

- On February 4, 1993, in deciding the fate of a young man named Anthony Bland, Britain's highest court threw out many centuries of traditional law and medical ethics regarding the value of human life and the lawfulness of intentionally ending it.
- On November 30, 1993, the Netherlands parliament finally put into law the guidelines under which Dutch doctors have

328   IS THE SANCTITY OF LIFE ETHIC TERMINALLY ILL?

for some years been openly giving lethal injections to patients
who suffer unbearably without hope of improvement, and who
ask to be helped to die.

● On May 2, 1994, twelve Michigan jurors acquitted Dr Jack
Kevorkian of a charge of assisting Thomas Hyde to commit
suicide. Their refusal to convict Kevorkian was a major
victory for the cause of physician-assisted suicide, for it is hard
to imagine a clearer case of assisting suicide than this one.
Kevorkian freely admitted supplying the carbon monoxide
gas, tubing and a mask to Hyde, who had then used them to
end a life made unbearable by the rapidly progressing nerve
disorder ALS.

These three events are the surface tremors resulting from major
shifts deep in the bedrock of Western ethics. We are going through a
period of transition in our attitude to the sanctity of human life.
Such transitions cause confusion and division. Many factors are
involved in this shift, but today I shall focus on ways in which our
growing technical capacity to keep human beings alive has brought
out some implications of the sanctity of life ethic that — once we are
forced to face them squarely — we cannot accept. This will lead me
to suggest a way forward.

II   REVOLUTION BY STEALTH: THE REDEFINITION OF
DEATH

The acceptance of brain death — that is, the permanent loss of all
brain function — as a criterion of death has been widely regarded as
one of the great achievements of bioethics. It is one of the few issues
on which there has been virtual consensus; and it has made an
important difference in the way we treat people whose brains have
ceased to function. This change in the definition of death has meant
that warm, breathing, pulsating human beings are not given further
medical support. If their relatives consent (or in some countries, as
long as they have not registered a refusal of consent), their hearts
and other organs can be cut out of their bodies and given to
strangers. The change in our conception of death that excluded these
human beings from the moral community was among the first in a
series of dramatic changes in our view of life and death. Yet, in
sharp contrast to other changes in this area, it met with virtually no
opposition. How did this happen?

Everyone knows that the story of our modern definition of death
begins with "The Ad Hoc Committee of the Harvard Medical
School to Examine the Definition of Brain Death". What is not so

well known is the link between the work of this committee and Dr Christiaan Barnard's famous first transplantation of a human heart, in December 1967. Even before Barnard's sensational operation, Henry Beecher, chairman of a Harvard University committee that oversaw the ethics of experimentation on human beings, had written to Robert Ebert, Dean of the Harvard Medical School, suggesting that the Committee should consider some new questions. He had, he told the Dean, been speaking with Dr Joseph Murray, a surgeon at Massachusetts General Hospital and a pioneer in kidney transplantation. "Both Dr Murray and I", Beecher wrote, "think the time has come for a further consideration of the definition of death. Every major hospital has patients stacked up waiting for suitable donors."[1] Ebert did not respond immediately; but within a month of the news of the South African heart transplant, he set up, under Beecher's chairmanship, the group that was soon to become known as the Harvard Brain Death Committee.

The committee was made up mostly of members of the medical profession — ten of them, supplemented by a lawyer, an historian, and a theologian. It did its work rapidly, and published its report in the *Journal of the American Medical Association* in August 1968. The report was soon recognised as an authoritative document, and its criteria for the determination of death were adopted rapidly and widely, not only in the United States but, with some modification of the technical details, in most countries of the world. The report began with a remarkably clear statement of what the committee was doing and why it needed to be done:

Our primary purpose is to define irreversible coma as a new criterion for death. There are two reasons why there is a need for a definition: (1) Improvements in resuscitative and supportive measures have led to increased efforts to save those who are desperately injured. Sometimes these efforts have only a partial success so that the result is an individual whose heart continues to beat but whose brain is irreversibly damaged. The burden is great on patients who suffer permanent loss of intellect, on their families, on the hospitals, and on those in need of hospital beds already occupied by these comatose patients. (2) Obsolete criteria for the definition of death can lead to controversy in obtaining organs for transplantation.

[1] Henry Beecher to Robert Ebert, 30 October 1967. The letter is in the Henry Beecher Manuscripts at the Francis A. Countway Library of Medicine, Harvard University, and is quoted by David Rothman, *Strangers at the Bedside*, New York: Basic Books, 1991, pp. 160–1.

330   IS THE SANCTITY OF LIFE ETHIC TERMINALLY ILL?

To a reader familiar with bioethics in the 1990's, there are two striking aspects of this opening paragraph. The first is that the Harvard committee does not even attempt to argue that there is a need for a new definition of death because hospitals have a lot of patients in their wards who are really dead, but are being kept attached to respirators because the law does not recognise them as dead. Instead, with unusual frankness, the committee said that a new definition was needed because irreversibly comatose patients were a great burden, not only on themselves (why to be in an irreversible coma is a burden to the patient, the Committee did not say), but also to their families, hospitals, and patients waiting for beds. And then there was the problem of "controversy" about obtaining organs for transplantation.

   In fact, frank as the statement seems, in presenting its concern about this controversy, the Committee was still not being entirely candid. An earlier draft had been more open in stating that one reason for changing the definition of death was the "great need for tissues and organs of, among others, the patient whose cerebrum has been hopelessly destroyed, in order to restore those who are salvageable". When this draft was sent to Ebert, he advised Beecher to tone it down it because of its "unfortunate" connotation "that you wish to redefine death in order to make viable organs more readily available to persons requiring transplants".[2] The Harvard Brain Death Committee took Ebert's advice: it was doubtless more politic not to put things so bluntly. But Beecher himself made no secret of his own views. He was later to say, in an address to the American Association for the Advancement of Science:

> There is indeed a life-saving potential in the new definition, for, when accepted, it will lead to greater availability than formerly of essential organs in viable condition, for transplantation, and thus countless lives now inevitably lost will be saved. . .[3]

The second striking aspect of the Harvard committee's report is that it keeps referring to "irreversible coma" as the condition that it wishes to define as death. The committee also speaks of "permanent loss of intellect" and even says "we suggest that responsible medical opinion is ready to adopt new criteria for pronouncing death to have occurred in an individual sustaining irreversible coma as a result of permanent brain damage". Now "irreversible coma as a result of

---

[2] The first draft and Ebert's comment on it are both quoted by Rothman, *Strangers at the Bedside*, pp. 162 – 4. The documents are in the Beecher Manuscript collection.
   [3] Henry Beecher, "The New Definition of Death, Some Opposing Viewpoints", *International Journal of Clinical Pharmacology*, 5 (1971), pp. 120 – 121 (italics in original).

permanent brain damage" is by no means identical with the death of the whole brain. Permanent damage to the parts of the brain responsible for consciousness can also mean that a patient is in a "persistent vegetative state", a condition in which the brain stem and the central nervous system continue to function, but consciousness has been irreversibly lost. Even today, no legal system regards those in a persistent vegetative state as dead.

Admittedly, the Harvard committee report does go on to say, immediately following the paragraph quoted above: "*we are concerned here only with those comatose individuals who have no discernible central nervous system activity.*" But the reasons given by the committee for redefining death — the great burden on the patients, their families, the hospitals and the community, as well as the waste of organs needed for transplation — apply in every respect to *all* those who are irreversibly comatose, not only to those whose entire brain is dead. So it is worth asking: why did the committee limit its concern to those with no brain activity at all? One reason could be that there was at the time no reliable way of telling whether a coma was irreversible, unless the brain damage was so severe that there was no brain activity at all. Another could be that people whose whole brain is dead will stop breathing after they are taken off a respirator, and so will soon be dead by anyone's standard. People in a persistent vegetative state, on the other hand, may continue to breathe without mechanical assistance. To call for the undertakers to bury a "dead" patient who is still breathing would be a bit too much for anyone to swallow.

We all know that the redefinition of death proposed by the Harvard Brain Death Committee triumphed. By 1981, when the United States President's Commission for the Study of Ethical Problems in Medicine examined the issue, it could write of "the emergence of a medical consensus" around criteria very like those proposed by the Harvard committee.[4] Already, people whose brains had irreversibly ceased to function were considered legally dead in at least fifteen countries, and in more than half of the states of the United States. In some countries, including Britain, parliament had not even been involved in the change: the medical profession had simply adopted a new set of criteria on the basis of which doctors certified a patient dead.[5] This was truly a revolution without opposition.

---

[4] President's Commission for the Study of Ethical Problems in Medicine, *Defining Death: A Report on the Medical, Legal and Ethical Issues in the Determination of Death*, U.S. Government Printing Office, Washington,DC, 1981, pp. 24, 25.
[5] *Defining Death*, pp. 67, 72.

332   IS THE SANCTITY OF LIFE ETHIC TERMINALLY ILL?

The redefinition of death in terms of brain death went through so smoothly because it did not harm the brain-dead patients and it benefitted everyone else: the families of brain-dead patients, the hospitals, the transplant surgeons, people needing transplants, people who worried that they might one day need a transplant, people who feared that they might one day be kept on a respirator after their brain had died, taxpayers, and the government. The general public understood that if the brain has been destroyed, there can be no recovery of consciousness, and so there is no point in maintaining the body. Defining such people as dead was a convenient way around the problems of making their organs available for transplantation, and withdrawing treatment from them.

But does this way round the problems really work? On one level, it does. By the early 1990s as Sweden and Denmark, the last European nations to cling to the traditional standard, adopted brain death definitions of death, this verdict appeared to be confirmed. Among developed nations, only Japan was still holding out. But do people really think of the brain dead as *dead*? The Harvard Brain Death Committee itself couldn't quite swallow the implications of what it was recommending. As we have seen, it described patients whose brains have ceased to function as in an "irreversible coma" and said that being kept on a respirator was a burden to them. Dead people are not in a coma, they are dead, and nothing can be a burden to them any more.

Perhaps the lapses in the thinking of the Harvard committee can be pardoned because the concept of brain death was then so new. But twenty-five years later, little has changed. Only last year the *Miami Herald* ran a story headlined "Brain-Dead Woman Kept Alive in Hopes She'll Bear Child"; while after the same woman did bear her child, the *San Francisco Chronicle* reported: "Brain-Dead Woman Gives Birth, then Dies". Nor can we blame this entirely on the lamentable ignorance of the popular press. A study of doctors and nurses who work with brain dead patients at hospitals in Cleveland, Ohio, showed that one in three of them thought that people whose brains had died could be classified as dead because they were "irreversibly dying" or because they had an "unacceptable quality of life".[6]

Why do both journalists and members of the health care professions talk in a way that denies that brain death is really death?

[6] Stuart Youngner et al, " 'Brain Death' and Organ Retrieval: A Cross-sectional Survey of Knowledge and Concepts Among Health Professionals", *Journal of the American Medical Association*, 261 (1090) 2209.

One possible explanation is that even though people know that the brain dead are dead, it is just too difficult for them to abandon obsolete ways of thinking about death. Another possible explanation is that people have enough common sense to see that the brain dead are not really dead. I favour this second explanation. The brain death criterion of death is nothing other than a convenient fiction. It was proposed and accepted because it makes it possible for us to salvage organs that would otherwise be wasted, and to withdraw medical treatment when it is doing no good. On this basis, it might seem that, despite some fundamental weaknesses, the survival prospects of the concept of brain death are good. But there are two reasons why our present understanding of brain death is not stable. Advances in medical knowledge and technology are the driving factors.

To understand the first problem with the present concept of brain death, we have to recall that brain death is generally defined as the irreversible cessation of all functions of the brain.[7] In accordance with this definition, a standard set of tests are used by doctors to establish that all functions of the brain have irreversibly ceased. These tests are broadly in line with those recommended in 1968 by the Harvard Brain Death Committee, but they have been further refined and updated over the years in various countries. In the past ten years, however, as doctors have sought ways of managing brain dead patients, so that their organs (or in some cases, their pregnancies) could be sustained for a longer time, it has become apparent that even when the usual tests show that brain death has occurred, *some brain functions continue.* We think of the brain primarily as concerned with processing information through the senses and the nervous system, but the brain has other functions as well. One of these is to supply various hormones that help to regulate several bodily functions. We now know that some of these hormones continue to be supplied by the brains of most patients who, by the standard tests, are brain dead. Moreover, when brain dead patients are cut open in order to remove organs, their blood pressure may rise and their heartbeat quicken. These reactions mean that the brain is still carrying out some of its functions, regulating the

---

[7] See, for example, the United States Uniform Determination of Death Act. Note that the Harvard committee had referred to the absence of central nervous system "activity" rather than function. The use of the term "function" rather than "activity", makes the definition of brain death more permissive, because, as the United States President's Commission recognised (*Defining Death*, p. 74), electrical and metabolic activity may continue in cells or groups of cells after the organ has ceased to function. The Commission did not think that the continuation of this activity should prevent a declaration of death.

334   IS THE SANCTITY OF LIFE ETHIC TERMINALLY ILL?

responses of the body in various ways. As a result, the legal
definition of brain death, and current medical practice in certifying
brain dead people as dead, have come apart.[8]

It would be possible to bring medical practice into line with the
current definition of death in terms of the irreversible cessation of *all*
brain function. Doctors would then have to test for all brain
functions, including hormonal functions, before declaring someone
dead. This would mean that some people who are now declared
brain dead would be considered alive, and therefore would have to
continue to be supported on a respirator, at significant cost, both
financially and in terms of the extended distress of the family. Since
the tests are expensive to carry out and time consuming in
themselves, continued support would be necessary during the period
in which they are carried out, even if in the end the results showed
that the person had no brain function at all. In addition, during this
period, the person's organs would deteriorate, and may therefore
not be usable for transplantation. What gains would there be to
balance against these serious disadvantages? From the perspective of
an adherent of the sanctity of life ethic, of course, the gain is that we
are no longer killing people by cutting out their hearts while they are
still alive. If one really believed that the quality of a human life
makes no difference to the wrongness of ending that life, this would
end the discussion. There would be no ethical alternative. But it
would still be true that not a single person who was kept longer on a
respirator because of the need to test for hormonal brain functioning
would ever return to consciousness.

So if it is life with consciousness, rather than life itself, that we
value, then bringing medical practice into line with the definition of
death does not seem a good idea. It would be better to bring the
definition of brain death into line with current medical practice. But
once we move away from the idea of brain death as the irreversible
cessation of *all* brain functioning, what are we to put in its place?
Which functions of the brain will we take as marking the difference
between life and death, and why?

The most plausible answer is that the brain functions that really
matter are those related to consciousness. On this view, what we
really care about — and ought to care about — is *the person* rather

[8] Robert Truog, "Rethinking brain death", in K. Sanders and B. Moore, eds.,
Anencephalics, Infants and Brain Death Treatment Options and the Issue of Organ Donation,
Law Reform Commission of Victoria, Melbourne, 1991, pp. 62 – 74; Amir Halevy
and Baruch Brody, "Brain Death: Reconciling Definitions, Criteria and Tests",
Annals of Internal Medicine, 119:6 (1993) 519 – 525; Robert Veatch, "The Impending
Collapse of the Whole-Brain Definition of Death", *Hastings Center Report*, 23:4
(1993) 18 – 24.

than the body. Accordingly, it is the permanent cessation of function of the cerebral cortex, not of the whole brain, that should be taken as the criterion of death. Several reasons could be offered to justify this step. First, although the Harvard Brain Death Committee specified that its recommendations applied only to those who have "no discernible central nervous system activity", the arguments it put forward for its redefinition of death applied in every respect to patients who are permanently without any awareness, whether or not they have some brainstem function. This seems to have been no accident, for it reflected the view of the committee's chairman, Henry Beecher, who in his address to the American Association for the Advancement of Science, from which I have already quoted, said that what is essential to human nature is:

> . . . the individual's personality, his conscious life, his unique-
> ness, his capacity for remembering, judging, reasoning, acting,
> enjoying, worrying, and so on . . .[9]

As I have already said, when the Harvard Committee issued its report, the irreversible destruction of the parts of the brain associated with consciousness could not reliably be diagnosed if the brainstem was alive. Since then, however, the technology for obtaining images of soft tissues within the body has made enormous progress. Hence a major stumbling block to the acceptance of a higher brain definition of death has already been greatly diminished in its scope, and will soon disappear altogether.

Now that medical certainty on the irreversibility of loss of higher brain functions can be established in at least some cases, the inherent logic of pushing the definition of death one step further has already led, in the United States, to one Supreme Court judge suggesting that the law could consider a person who has irreversibly lost consciousness to be no longer alive. Here is Mr Justice Stevens, giving his judgment in the case of Nancy Cruzan, a woman who had been unconscious for eight years and whose guardians sought court permission to withdraw tube feeding of food and fluids so that she could die:

> But for patients like Nancy Cruzan, who have no consciousness
> and no chance of recovery, there is a serious question as to

---

[9] Henry Beecher, "The New Definition of Death, Some Opposing Views", unpublished paper presented at the meeting of the American Association for the Advancement of Science, December 1970, p. 4, quoted from Robert Veatch, *Death, Dying and the Biological Revolution*, New Haven: Yale University Press, 1976, p. 39.

whether the mere persistence of their bodies is "life", as that word
is commonly understood ... The State's unflagging determination
to perpetuate Nancy Cruzan's physical existence is comprehensible only as an effort to define life's meaning, not as an attempt
to preserve its sanctity ... In any event, absent some theological
abstraction, the idea of life is not conceived separately from the
idea of a living person.[10]

Admittedly, this was a dissenting judgment; the majority decided
the case on narrow constitutional grounds that are not relevant to
our concerns here, and what Stevens said has not become part of the
law of the United States. Nevertheless, dissenting judgments are
often a way of floating an idea that is "in the air" and may become
part of the majority view in a later decision. As medical opinion
increasingly comes to accept that we can reliably establish when
consciousness has been irreversibly lost, the pressure will become
more intense for medical practice to move to a definition of death
based on the death of the higher brain.

Yet there is a very fundamental flaw in the idea of moving to a
higher brain definition of death. If, as we have seen, people already
have difficulty in accepting that a warm body with a beating heart
on a respirator is really dead, how much more difficult would it be to
bury a "corpse" that is still breathing while the lid of the coffin is
nailed down? That is simply an absurdity. Something has gone
wrong. But what?

In my view, the trouble began with the move to brain death. The
Harvard Brain Death Committee was faced with two serious
problems. Patients in an utterly hopeless condition were attached to
respirators, and no-one dared to turn them off; and organs that
could be used to save lives were rendered useless by the delays
caused by waiting for the circulation of the blood in potential donors
to stop. The committee tried to solve both these problems by the
bold expedient of classifying as dead those whose brains had ceased
to have an discernible activity. The consequences of the redefinition
of death were so evidently desirable that it met with scarcely any
opposition, and was accepted almost universally. Nevertheless, it
was unsound from the start. Solving problems by redefinition rarely
works, and this case was no exception. We need to begin again, with
a different approach to the original problems, one which will break
out of the intellectual straight-jacket of the traditional belief that all
human life is of equal value. Until last year, it seemed difficult to
imagine how a different approach could ever be accepted. But last

---

[10]   *Cruzan v. Director, Missouri Department of Health* (1990) 110 S. Ct. pp. 2886–7.

year Britain's highest court took a major step toward just such a new approach.

III   REVOLUTION BY THE LAW LORDS: THE CASE OF ANTHONY BLAND

The revolution in British law regarding the sanctity of human life grew out of the tragedy at Hillsborough Football Stadium in Sheffield, in April 1989. Liverpool was playing Nottingham Forest in an FA Cup semi-final. As the match started, thousands of supporters were still trying to get into the ground. A fatal crush occurred against some fencing that had been erected to stop fans getting onto the playing field. Before order could be restored and the pressure relieved, 95 people had died in the worst disaster in British sporting history. Tony Bland, a 17-year-old Liverpool fan, was not killed, but his lungs were crushed by the pressure of the crowd around him, and his brain was deprived of oxygen. Taken to hospital, it was found that only his brain stem had survived. His cortex had been destroyed. Here is how Lord Justice Hoffmann was later to describe his condition:

> Since April 15 1989 Anthony Bland has been in persistent vegetative state. He lies in Airedale General Hospital in Keighley, fed liquid food by a pump through a tube passing through his nose and down the back of his throat into the stomach. His bladder is emptied through a catheter inserted through his penis, which from time to time has caused infections requiring dressing and antibiotic treatment. His stiffened joints have caused his limbs to be rigidly contracted so that his arms are tightly flexed across his chest and his legs unnaturally contorted. Reflex movements in the throat cause him to vomit and dribble. Of all this, and the presence of members of his family who take turns to visit him, Anthony Bland has no consciousness at all. The parts of his brain which provided him with consciousness have turned to fluid. The darkness and oblivion which descended at Hillsborough will never depart. His body is alive, but he has no life in the sense that even the most pitifully handicapped but conscious human being has a life. But the advances of modern medicine permit him to be kept in this state for years, even perhaps for decades.[11]

---

[11] *Airedale N.H.S. Trust v. Bland (C.A)* (19 Feburary 1993) 2 Weekly Law Reports, p. 350. Page numbers given without further identifying details in subsequent footnotes are to this report of the case.

338   IS THE SANCTITY OF LIFE ETHIC TERMINALLY ILL?

Whatever the advances of modern medicine might permit, neither Tony Bland's family, nor his doctors could see any benefit to him or to anyone else, in keeping him alive for decades. In Britain, as in many other countries, when everyone is in agreement in these situations it is quite common for the doctors simply to withdraw artificial feeding. The patient then dies within a week or two. In this case, however, the coroner in Sheffield was inquiring into the deaths caused by the Hillsborough disaster, and Dr Howe decided that he should notify the coroner of what he was intending to do. The coroner, while agreeing that Bland's continued existence could well be seen as entirely pointless, warned Dr Howe that he was running the risk of criminal charges — possibly even a charge of murder — if he intentionally ended Bland's life.

After the coroner's warning, the administrator of the hospital in which Bland was a patient applied to the Family Division of the High Court for declarations that the hospital might lawfully discontinue all life-sustaining treatment, including ventilation, and the provision of food and water by artificial means, and discontinue all medical treatment to Bland "except for the sole purpose of enabling Anthony Bland to end his life and to die peacefully with the greatest dignity and the least distress".

At the Family Division hearing a public law officer called the Official Solicitor was appointed guardian for Bland for the purposes of the hearing. The Official Solicitor did not deny that Bland had no awareness at all, and could never recover, but he nevertheless opposed what Dr Howe was planning to do, arguing that, legally, it was murder. Sir Stephen Brown, President of the Family Division, did not accept this view, and he made the requested declarations to the effect that all treatment might lawfully be stopped. The Official Solicitor appealed, but Brown's decision was upheld by the Court of Appeal. The Official Solicitor then appealed again, thus bringing the case before the House of Lords.

We can best appreciate the significance of what the House of Lords did in the case of Tony Bland by looking at what the United States Supreme Court would not do in the similar case of Nancy Cruzan. Like Bland, Cruzan was in a persistent vegetative state, without hope of recovery. Her parents went to court to get permission to remove her feeding tube. The Missouri Supreme Court refused, saying that since Nancy Cruzan was not competent to refuse life-sustaining treatment herself, and the state has an interest in preserving life, the court could only give permission for the withdrawal of life-sustaining treatment if there were clear and convincing evidence that this was what Cruzan would have wanted. No such evidence had been presented to the court. On appeal, the

United States Supreme Court upheld this judgment, ruling that the state of Missouri had a right to require clear and convincing evidence that Cruzan would have wanted to be allowed to die, before permitting doctors to take that step. (By a curious coincidence, that evidence was produced in court shortly after the Supreme Court decision, and Cruzan was allowed to die.)

The essential point here is that in America the courts have so far taken it for granted that life-support must be continued, *unless* there is evidence indicating that the patient would not have wished to be kept alive in the circumstances in which she now is. In contrast, the British courts were quite untroubled by the absence of any information about what Bland's wishes might have been. As Sir Thomas Bingham, Master of the Rolls of the Court of Appeal said in delivering his judgment:

> At no time before the disaster did Mr Bland give any indication of his wishes should he find himself in such a condition. It is not a topic most adolescents address.[12]

But the British courts did not therefore conclude that Bland must be treated until he died of old age. Instead, the British judges asked a different question: what is in the best interests of the patient?[13] In answer, they referred to the unanimous medical opinion that Bland was not aware of anything, and that there was no prospect of any improvement in his condition. Hence the treatment that was sustaining Bland's life brought him, as Sir Stephen Brown put in in the initial judgment in the case, "no therapeutical, medical, or other benefit".[14] In essence, the British courts held that when a patient is incapable of consenting to medical treatment, doctors are under no legal duty to continue treatment that does not benefit a patient. In addition, the judges agreed that the mere continuation of biological life is not, in the absence of any awareness or any hope of ever again becoming aware, a benefit to the patient.

On one level, the British approach is straightforward common sense. But it is common sense that breaks new legal ground. To see this, consider the following quotation from John Keown:

> Traditional medical ethics . . ., never asks whether the patient's *life* is worthwhile, for the notion of a worthless life is as alien to the Hippocratic tradition as it is to English criminal law, both of

---

[12] p. 333; the passage was quoted again by Lord Goff of Chieveley in his judgment in the House of Lords, p. 364.

[13] pp. 374, 386.

[14] p. 331.

340   IS THE SANCTITY OF LIFE ETHIC TERMINALLY ILL?

which subscribe to the principle of the sanctity of human life which holds that, because all lives are intrinsically valuable, it is always wrong intentionally to kill an innocent human being.[15]

As a statement of traditional medical ethics and traditional English criminal law, this is right. The significance of the *Bland* decision is that it openly embraces the previously alien idea of a worthless life. Sir Thomas Bingham, for example, said:

> Looking at the matter as objectively as I can, and doing my best to look at the matter through Mr Bland's eyes and not my own, I cannot conceive what benefit his continued existence could be thought to give him . . .[16]

When the case came before the House of Lords, their Lordships took the same view. Lord Keith of Kinkel discussed the difficulties of making a value judgment about the life of a "permanently insensate" being, and concluded cautiously that:

> It is, however, perhaps permissible to say that to an individual with no cognitive capacity whatever, and no prospect of ever recovering any such capacity in this world, it must be a matter of complete indifference whether he lives or dies.[17]

In a similar vein, Lord Mustill concluded that to withdraw life-support is not only legally, but also ethically justified, "since the continued treatment of Anthony Bland can no longer serve to maintain that combination of manifold characteristics which we call a personality".[18]

There can therefore be no doubt that with the decision in the Bland case, British law has abandoned the idea that life itself is a benefit to the person living it, irrespective of its quality. But that is not all that their lordships did in deciding Tony Bland's fate. The second novel aspect of their decision is that it was as plain as anything can be that the proposal to discontinue tube feeding was *intended* to bring about Bland's death. A majority of the judges in the House of Lords referred to the administrator's intention in very direct terms. Lord Browne-Wilkinson said:

> What is proposed in the present case is to adopt a course with the intention of bringing about Anthony Bland's death . . . the whole

---

[15] John Keown, "Courting Euthanasia? Tony Bland and the Law Lords", *Ethics & Medicine* 9:3 (1993) p. 36.
[16] p. 339.
[17] p. 361.
[18] p. 400.

purpose of stopping artificial feeding is to bring about the death of Anthony Bland.[19]

Lord Mustill was equally explicit:

> the proposed conduct has the aim for ... humane reasons of terminating the life of Anthony Bland by withholding from him the basic necessities of life.[20]

This marks a sharp contrast to what for many years was considered the definitive view of what a doctor may permissibly intend. Traditionally the law had held that while a doctor may knowingly do something that has the effect of shortening life, this must always be a mere side-effect of an action with a different purpose, for example, relieving pain. As Justice (later Lord) Devlin said in the celebrated trial of Dr John Bodkin Adams:

> ... it remains the fact, and it remains the law, that no doctor, nor any man, no more in the case of the dying than of the healthy, has the right deliberately to cut the thread of human life.[21]

In rewriting the law of murder regarding the question of intention, the British law lords have shown a clarity and forthrightness that should serve as a model to many others who try to muddle through difficult questions by having a little bit of both sides. There is no talk here of ordinary and extraordinary means of treatment, nor of what is directly intended and what is merely foreseen. Instead the judges declared that Bland's doctors were entitled to take a course of action that had Bland's death as its "whole purpose"; and they made this declaration on the basis of a judgment that prolonging Bland's life did not benefit him.

Granted, this very clarity forces on us a further question: does the decision allow doctors to kill their patients? On the basis of what we have seen so far, this conclusion seems inescapable. Their Lordships, however, did not think they were legalising euthanasia. They drew a distinction between ending life by actively doing something, and ending life by not providing treatment needed to sustain life. That distinction has long been discussed by philosophers and bioethicists, who debate whether it can make good sense to

---

[19] p. 383.

[20] p. 388.

[21] *R. v. Adams* (1959), quoted by Derek Morgan, "Letting babies die legally", *Institute of Medical Ethics Bulletin*, May 1989, p. 13. See also Patrick Devlin, *Easing the Passing: The Trial of Dr John Bodkin Adams*, London: Faber and Faber, 1986, pp. 171, 209.

342   IS THE SANCTITY OF LIFE ETHIC TERMINALLY ILL?

accept passive euthanasia while rejecting active euthanasia. In the *Bland* case, it is significant that while the Law Lords insist that in distinguishing between acts and omissions they are merely applying the law as it stands, they explicitly recognise that at this point law and ethics have come apart, and something needs to be done about it. Lord Browne-Wilkinson, for example, expressed the hope that Parliament would review the law. He then ended his judgment by admitting that he could not provide a moral basis for the legal decision he had reached! Lord Mustill was just as frank and even more uncomfortable about the state of the law, saying that the judgment, in which he had shared, "may only emphasise the distortions of a legal structure which is already both morally and intellectually misshapen".[22]

The law lords' problem was that they had inherited a legal framework that allowed them some room to manoevre, but not a great deal. Within that framework, they did what they could to reach a sensible decision in the case of Anthony Bland, and to point the law in a new direction that other judges could follow. In doing so, they recognised the moral incoherence of the position they were taking, but found themselves unable to do anything about it, beyond drawing the problem to the attention of parliament. They could hardly have done more to show clearly the need for a new approach to life-and-death decisions.

IV   CONCLUSION

What is the link between the problems we face in regard to the concept of brain death, and the decision reached by their Lordships in the case of Tony Bland? The link becomes clearer once we distinguish between three separate questions, often muddled in discussions of brain death and related issues:

1. When does a human being die?
2. When is it permissible for doctors intentionally to end the life of a patient?
3. When is it permissible to remove organs such as the heart from a human being for the purpose of transplantation to another human being?

Before 1968, in accordance with the traditional concept of death, the answer to the first question would have been: when the circulation of the blood stops permanently, with the consequent cessation of

[22]   pp. 388−9.

breathing, of a pulse, and so on.[23] The answer to the second question would then have been very simple: never. And the answer to the third question would have been equally plain: when the human being is dead.

The acceptance of the concept of brain death enabled us to hold constant the straightforward answers to questions two and three, while making what was presented as no more than a scientific updating of a concept of death rendered obsolete by technological advances in medicine. Thus no ethical question appeared to be at issue, but suddenly hearts could be removed from, and machines turned off on, a whole new group of human beings.

The *Bland* decision says nothing about questions 1 and 3, but dramatically changes the answer that British law gives to question 2. The simple "never" now becomes "when the patient's continued life is of no benefit to her": and if we ask when a patient's life is of no benefit to her, the answer is: "when the patient is irreversibly unconscious". If we accept this as a sound answer to question 2, however, we may well wish to give the same answer to question 3. Why not, after all? And if we now have answered both question 2 and question 3 by reference not to the death of the patient, but to the impossibility of the patient regaining consciousness, then question 1 suddenly becomes much less relevant to the concerns that the Harvard Brain Death Committee was trying to address. We could therefore abandon the redefinition of death that it pioneered, with all the problems that have now arisen for the brain death criterion. Nor would we feel any pressure to move a step further, to defining death in terms of the death of the higher brain, or cerebral cortex. Instead, we could, without causing any problems in the procurement of organs or the withdrawal of life-support, go back to the traditional conception of death in terms of the irreversible cessation of the circulation of the blood.[24]

Centre for Human Bioethics
Monash University

[23] For a statement of the traditional definition, see, for example, *Blacks Law Dictionary*, fourth edition, West Publishing Company, 1968.

[24] This address incorporates material subsequently published in my book *Rethinking Life and Death* (Text, Melbourne, 1994. St. Martin's Press, 1995).

[20]

A Modern Myth. That Letting Die is not the Intentional Causation of Death: some reflections on the trial and acquittal of Dr Leonard Arthur

HELGA KUHSE

ABSTRACT   *If a doctor kills a severely handicapped infant, he commits an act of murder; if he deliberately allows such an infant to die, he is said to engage in the proper practice of medicine. This is the view that emerged at the recent trial of Dr Leonard Arthur over the death of the infant John Pearson. However, the distinction between murder on the one hand and what are regarded as permissible lettings die on the other rests on the Moral Difference Myth, according to which deliberate lettings die in the practice of medicine are not instances of the intentional causation of death.*

I argue that a doctor who refrains from preventing a handicapped infant's death, causes that infant's death and does so intentionally. He commits an act of murder. But, I suggest, not all instances of the intentional causation of death are morally wrong. To the extent that they are not, killing rather than letting die will often be the preferable option because more economical of suffering. Hence what is required is the abolition of the Moral Difference Myth and legislation to the effect that those doctors who justifiably cause a patient's death—whether by an action or by an omission—commit no offence.

> Now I wonder if I could contrive one of those convenient stories we were talking about a few minutes ago, some magnificent myth that would in itself carry conviction to our whole community, including, if possible, the Guardians themselves.
> Socrates in Plato: *The Republic*

A 'magnificent myth', the Myth of Metals, lends credibility and stability to Plato's ideal state, the Republic. According to this myth, 'Mother Earth' is fashioning people differently—some have gold, others silver, bronze or iron inside them. Those with gold inside them are meant to rule; those with lesser metals, meant to be ruled. Moreover, the myth holds, gold will beget gold, silver will beget silver, and so on (although there is some room for exceptions). If believed, the myth is self-fulfilling and will become true: alleged differences 'in the nature of things' will be confirmed by social practices and fiction has become fact when, finally, the Guardians themselves believe that the myth is true [1].

We, too, have our myths. The 'magnificent myth' I am interested in is the myth that deliberate lettings die in the practice of medicine are, morally and legally, different from killings. Another way of stating this myth is to say that to deliberately allow someone to die is not intentionally to cause that person's death. This 'Moral Difference Myth' lends credibility and stability to our Ideal of the Sanctity of Human life.

Like Plato's Myth of Metals, our Moral Difference Myth is backed up by religious sanctions and has strong emotional appeal. It carries conviction with many conventional thinkers and is apparently accepted by the 'Guardians' themselves—at least that is the impression one gets when reading the summing-up by Mr Justice Farqhuarson of the recent trial of Dr Leonard Arthur for the attempted murder of John Pearson [2].

But social arrangements based on myths have their price. Plato sacrifices individual freedom and autonomy for the ideal of the Republic. We allow infants to suffer for the ideal of the Sanctity of Life. The price, in either case, may be too high.

Let me unfold the most recent re-statement of the Moral Difference Myth by beginning with a description of the happenings at Derby City Hospital in 1980, which led to the Leicester court case in 1981.

On Saturday, June 28 1980, at 7.55 am, Molly Pearson gave birth to a boy, John Pearson. The midwife immediately recognised Down's syndrome. This condition, also known as 'Mongolism', involves permanent mental retardation. Apart from Down's syndrome, the child appeared to be healthy. When told of the child's condition, the mother wept, and one sister heard Mrs Pearson say to her husband: "I don't want it, Duck".

Some four hours after the birth of John Pearson, Dr Leonard Arthur, a senior consultant paediatrician employed by the hospital, was called in to examine the baby in the presence of the baby's parents. Apart from the typical facial characteristics of Down's syndrome, there were no clinically detectable abnormalities, a fact recorded by Dr Arthur. While there is no account of the conversation that took place between the doctor and the parents (neither gave evidence at the subsequent trial), it appears that the parents rejected the baby on account of its being afflicted with Down's syndrome because Dr Arthur noted in the records: 'Parents do not wish baby to survive. Nursing care only".

Dr Arthur prescribed a narcotic analgesic, dihydrocodeine (DF 118), at a dosage of 5 mg, to be administered not less than every four hours 'as required'. The infant was given water, but no nourishment, and antibiotics were withheld when bronchopneumonia developed. John Pearson died at 5.10 am on Tuesday, the 1st of July, three days after his birth.

A member of the hospital staff reported the circumstances surrounding John Pearson's death to the right-to-life association 'Life', thereby initiating the events that led to Dr Arthur's prosecution. The original charge was murder, the prosecution claiming that

(1) Dr Arthur had ordered the administration of the drug DF 118 with the intention of bringing about the baby's death;
(2) the fact that Dr Arthur had ordered 'nursing care only' showed that he had intended the infant to die.

However, at an early stage during the trial it became apparent that the drug could not be proved to have caused the infant's death and Justice Farquharson reduced the charge to one of attempted murder because, as he put it, it had become "apparent that there was another possibility as to how that baby met his death, quite apart from anything that may or may not have been done by ... Dr Arthur" [3].

A long string of eminent physicians and paediatricians appeared for the accused, giving evidence of his high professional standing and confirming that what he had done was in accordance with their general practices.

On November 5 1981, two hours after retiring, the jury found Leonard Arthur not guilty of attempting to murder his patient, John Pearson.

Following Dr Arthur's acquittal, Nuala Scarisbrick, the Hon. Administrator of 'Life', commented:

> The verdict gives *carte blanche* to doctors to give treatment to patients who are unwanted or handicapped or both, that will result in their death. Now to be unwanted is to be guilty of a capital offence. [4]

The jury's verdict of 'not guilty' does not support Nuala Scarisbrick's conclusion about the present state of the law, because it is not clear that either the trial or the verdict has clarified the law at all. However, the case tells us something about contemporary social practices and the way in which the Moral Difference Myth helps to support the Ideal of the Sanctity of Life, an ideal which is violated by those practices.

The Sanctity of Life Ideal

Most of us believe that human life has some very special value and that it is wrong (at least *prima facie*) to kill other people. To the extent that we hold such beliefs, we subscribe to a cluster of principles that are central to discussions involving the value of life and the wrongness of killing. While the various ideas that life is valuable (or demands respect) are often impossibly vague and misleading [5], this is not the case in that particular area where medicine and legal theory overlap because here we encounter not mere respect for life, but the Ideal of the Sanctity of Life. According to this Ideal all innocent human life, irrespective of its quality or kind, is absolutely inviolable and equally valuable; innocent life must never intentionally be taken and must be preserved by those charged with its protection. (Henceforth the qualification 'innocent' will be taken as read, rather than repeated each time I refer to this doctrine.)

The basic idea that human life has 'sanctity' is deeply embedded in conventional thought. Moshe Tendler, a Professor of Talmudic Law, captures an important thrust of the Judaeo-Christian tradition when he comments:

> ... human life is of infinite value. This in turn means that a piece of infinity is also infinite and a person who has but a few moments to live is no less of value than a person who has 60 years to live ... a handicapped individual is a perfect specimen when viewed in an ethical context. The value is an absolute value. It is not relative to life expectancy, to state of health, or to usefulness to society. [6]

In the law, the sanctity of life is recognised in the prohibition of unlawful homicide, which retains its absolute force, irrespective of the quality or kind of life in question. As Justice Farquharson put it in his summing up:

> However serious the case may be, however much the disadvantage of a mongol ... no doctor has the right to kill it. Doctors are ... given no special powers to commit an act which causes death ... [7]

But the Sanctity of Life Ideal as it underlies the law does more than prohibit killing. It also imposes on doctors the duty to preserve the lives of their patients. Doctors not only have an obligation to refrain from killing, but also an obligation to prevent death, and this obligation extends to all patients equally. This is so because on the view we are discussing, all human lives are deemed equally valuable and hence equally worthy of protection. As one legal theorist puts it, it is a fundamental tenet of Anglo-American law that

24   *H. Kuhse*

> ... all human lives must be regarded as having an equal claim to preserva-
> tion simply because life is an irreducible value. Therefore the value of a
> particular life, over and above the value of life itself, may not be taken into
> account. [8]

This, then, is the Sanctity of Life Ideal: it holds that all human life is absolutely
inviolable and equally valuable; doctors must never take human life and they must
protect and prolong it when they can.

This Ideal was violated by Dr Leonard Arthur when he directed that John
Pearson receive large doses of the drug DF 118 and 'nursing care only'. It is also
violated by all those eminent paediatricians who, in giving evidence for the defence,
stated that they treat handicapped infants in their charge similarly: that they allow
handicapped infants to die if those infants are not wanted by their parents. But in
deliberately allowing handicapped infants to die, doctors are intentionally terminating human lives, and they are doing so on the basis of explicit or implicit quality-of-
life considerations. Excluding cases such as killings in war, legal executions and
killings in self-defence, the law regards the intentional termination of life as murder.
And yet, these doctors are not charged with murder and, as we know, Dr Arthur was
acquitted, even of attempted murder. Why? I suggest because the Moral Difference
Myth carries conviction with a large section of the community, including doctors
and some of the 'Guardians' themselves.

The Moral Difference Myth

According to the Moral Difference Myth, it is one thing deliberately to kill a patient
and quite another merely to let a patient die. Whereas the former is always
prohibited by the law and conventional morality as an act of murder, those believing
in the myth hold that the latter is not: there are times when a doctor may lawfully
allow a patient to die.

In his summing-up, Justice Farquharson drew a sharp distinction between murder
on the one hand and the mere 'setting of conditions' in which death may occur on
the other. While he agreed that the distinction is sometimes difficult to draw, he
pointed out that it is an important one in so far as it demarcates the line between
unlawful homicide and the proper practice of medicine. To illustrate the difference
to the jury, he gave the following four examples:

Example (1)

A Down's syndrome child is born with an intestinal obstruction. If the obstruction is
not removed, the child will die. Here, Justice Farquharson said, the surgeon might
say: "As this child is a mongol ... I do not propose to operate; I shall allow nature to
take its course". And, Justice Farquharson continued, "no-one could say that the
surgeon was committing an act of murder by declining to take a course which would
save the child".

Example (2)

A severely handicapped child, who is not otherwise going to die, is given a drug in
such amounts that the drug itself will cause death. If the doctor acts intentionally,

Justice Farquharson said, then "it would be open to the jury to say: yes, he was killing, he was murdering that child".

Example (3)

A patient is afflicted with terminal cancer and is suffering great pain. Increasing doses of pain-killing drugs are required to alleviate the patient's distress. The point will be reached where the pain-killing drug will cause the patient's death. This is a case, Justice Farquharson suggested, which "could never be murder. That was a proper practice of medicine".

Example (4)

A child, afflicted with an irreversible handicap and rejected by its mother contracts pneumonia. If, in this case, the doctor withheld antibiotics and "by a merciful dispensation of providence" the child died, then, Justice Farquharson suggested, "it would be very unlikely.. that you (or any other jury) would say that the doctor was committing murder" [9].

Thus, according to Justice Farquharson, not every doctor who allows a salvage-able infant to die is committing an act of murder. The distinction between 'murder' and the mere 'setting of conditions', Justice Farquharson said, is borne out by the distinction between examples (1), (3) and (4) on the one hand and example (2) on the other. What the jury had to decide was whether what Dr Arthur had done fell into the first or the second category: had he attempted to murder John Pearson, or had he merely set the conditions in which the baby's death could occur? [10]

On the basis of these comments and examples, it is difficult to imagine that many juries would have thought that Dr Arthur had murdered, or attempted to murder, John Pearson—for Justice Farquharson's comments imply that only positive acts directly intended to cause death (example 2) constitute murder and that neither deliberate lettings die (examples 1 and 4), nor positive acts not directly intended to cause death (example 3) fall into this category. But this, I suggest, is wrong. Or at least—since I am not a lawyer and hence am reluctant to correct a judge's interpretation of the law—if it is a correct statement of the law, then the law is based on the Moral Difference Myth. As such, it would be drawing a distinction where no significant difference exists.

The Intentional Causation of Death

During the trial of Dr Arthur, many reputable specialists were called in and testified that both the administration of large doses of analgesic narcotics and 'nursing care only' constitute a common and acceptable medical practice in cases of handicaps, such as Down's syndrome. However, whilst it is undoubtedly correct that treatment similar to that prescribed by Dr Arthur is widely *accepted* in paediatric medicine, this does not mean that it is *acceptable* under existing laws. Rather, such treatment constitutes an infringement of the Sanctity of Life Ideal underlying those laws.

In arguing for this view, I shall take as my starting point the legal prohibition of murder and suggest that not only 'direct' killings but also 'indirect' killings and deliberate lettings die fall into the category of murder. They fall into the category of murder, I shall argue, because they are all instances of the intentional causation of

26   *H. Kuhse*

death—and to intentionally cause the death of a patient is, other things being equal, to commit an act of murder. As a typical Crimes Act states:

> Murder shall be taken to have been committed where the act of the accused, or the things by him omitted to be done, causing the death charged, was done or omitted with reckless indifference to human life, or with intent to kill or inflict grievous bodily harm upon some person ... [11]

For our purposes, then, the key concepts are 'intention' and 'causation'. I shall deal with them in turn.

(a) *Intention*

Contrary to some ethical and theological theories, which attempt to draw a morally relevant distinction between what an agent 'directly' intends and what he merely foresees (or 'obliquely', or 'indirectly' intends), English law does not recognise the intention/foresight distinction. For legal purposes, the presumption is that "... everyone must be taken to intend that which is the natural consequence of his actions" [12]. This means that "[a] man can be guilty of murder although he did not intend to harm his victim, if he intended to do an act which a reasonable man would say was likely to cause death" [13]. In other words, intention is presumed to include not only those consequences which an agent directly intends to bring about as an end or as a means, but also those consequences which he only obliquely intends, or merely foresees [14]. The case of *R. V. Desmond and Others* will illustrate the point:

In 1868, two Irish Fenians were imprisoned. To liberate the prisoners, one of the accused, Barrett, dynamited the prison wall. Whilst the attempt to liberate the prisoners failed, the explosion killed some people living close by. Clearly, Barrett did not intend to kill or injure anyone, either as a means or as an end. However, Barrett was convicted on the grounds that he had foreseen those deaths. As Lord Coleridge summed it up at the time: it is murder "if a man did (an) act not with the purpose of taking life but with the knowledge or belief that life was likely to be sacrificed by it" [15].

It has been suggested that more recent judicial interpretations have thrown some doubt on the traditional view that foresight is sufficient for intention [16]. However, I will not here engage in legal exegesis. Whilst questions relating to individual judicial interpretations of the law are undoubtedly of great importance in some contexts, they are not of great importance to the philosophical points I wish to make in this paper. In the philosophical arena it is important to recognise that there are convincing reasons as to why the law has, in the past, treated foresight as sufficient for intention.

One of the main arguments for this presumption (the only one I will defend in this paper) is that *even if* an intrinsic moral difference were to exist between what an agent directly intends and what he foresees—a view I do not support—this moral difference would not be relevant to the question raised at the conviction stage: did the accused *cause* the death in question and is he *responsible*, as an agent, for what he has done. Let me elaborate.

If, according to the Sanctity of Life Ideal underlying the law, human life is both inviolable and valuable, then it follows that homicide is prohibited *because* it causes death, not because the victim's death was or was not a necessary part of the agent's plan or the reason for his action. Whilst what is or is not part of an agent's plan or the reason for his action, may be relevant to the question of *why* the agent did what he did and whether he ought to be blamed or punished for what he did (something that may be relevant at the sentencing stage), it is not relevant to the question of *what* he did—to the question of intentional action. When we ask, at the conviction stage, whether an agent has committed murder, we do not want to know whether what he has done was morally justifiable (as, perhaps, in some cases of euthanasia) but rather whether in doing what he did, he acted deliberately and freely (i.e. intentionally) and is thus responsible for what he chose to bring about [17].

The terminology of intention to cover both the directly intended and the foreseen, or obliquely intended, consequences of an action suggest's itself because of the close link between those things we do intentionally and our responsibility, as agents, for what we voluntarily and deliberately bring about. It seems that the following connection between an agent's intentional action and his responsibility applies: when an agent acts intentionally, what he intends is that he bring about a certain consequence. He desires, or wants, that consequence either for its own sake or as a means to a further end. If the consequence of an agent's intentional action thereby occurs, he brought it about intentionally. The term 'intentional' therefore denotes things done with the intention of doing them. But for an agent to have brought about a consequence intentionally, it is not necessary that he desired or wanted it. Rather, what seems to be necessary for intentional action is the concept of deliberate or voluntary choice: if an agent A in doing what he intends believes that he will inevitably or very likely bring about not only P but also Q, and if he could have refrained from doing as he intends, then A has brought about P and Q intentionally because he has deliberately and voluntarily chosen to do what he could have refrained from doing. Since we are preeminently responsible for our intentional doings, A is responsible not only for P but also for Q [18].

This means that both the intended and the foreseen consequences of an agent's action share a feature which any system, such as the law, concerned with assigning responsibility for prohibited consequences, must treat as crucial: that the agent could have refrained from bringing the prohibited consequence about, but that he nonetheless chose to bring it about [19]. But if this is correct, then it follows that many doctors are terminating life intentionally and are thus committing acts of murder. Take example (3) above, in which pain-killing drugs are administered in doses that cause death. This was presented by Justice Farquharson as an instance which "could never be murder" and which, he said, was an example of the proper practice of medicine. However, while it is true that the proper practice of medicine (or humanitarian concerns) would sometimes seem to require that a doctor does something which will cause a patient's foreseen death, this does not mean that the doctor is not then responsible for the death he brought about intentionally (that is, deliberately and voluntarily). If example (3) strikes many of us as one which could never be murder, this is so, I think, because we sometimes fail to distinguish between the questions of whether an agent was *justified* in bringing about a certain consequence, and whether he brought the consequence about *intentionally*. As Lord Edmund-Davies notes: "Killing both pain and patient may be good morals, but it is far from certain that it is good law" [20].

As far as the administration of the narcotic analgesic DF 118 is concerned, Dr Arthur handed a statement to the police, saying that "the [sole] intention . . . was to reduce any suffering on the part of the infant" [21]. What is clear, though, is that what Dr Arthur had directly intended (or *why* he did what he did), as distinct from *what* he intentionally brought about, is of little import when the question of murder

28   *H. Kuhse*

is at issue. Here the legal question is, simply, did the accused deliberately and voluntarily bring about death in a situation where he could have refrained from doing as he intended?

But murder ceased to be the issue when the defence was, early in the trial, able to show that the causal link between Dr Arthur's prescription of the drug DF 118 and the baby's death could not be established beyond reasonable doubt. Whilst the principal expert witness for the Crown, Professor Alan Usher, had certified that John Pearson had died of bronchial pneumonia which, he said, had been caused by the drug DF 118, subsequent histological evidence showed that there were abnormalities of the lungs, fibroelastosis of the heart and calcification of the brain. Although Professor Usher still insisted that the drug DF 118 had caused John Pearson's death, he also conceded that his initial evidence had been incomplete and inaccurate [22]. Since this raised doubts as to whether Dr Arthur's regime had caused the infant's death, Justice Farquharson withdrew the charge of murder and substituted for it the charge of attempted murder [23]. Following this, the question was no longer whether Dr Arthur had *caused* the death in question, but rather whether he *intended to cause* it. And with this, it seems, the emphasis moved more and more away from the largely objective criteria of intention and causation. The question became whether Dr Arthur had directly intended to cause the death in question and whether the treatment prescribed by the accused amounted in law to an 'attempt'.

There is no reason to doubt Dr Arthur's statement that all he (directly) intended to do, when prescribing the drug DF 118, was to 'reduce any suffering on the part of the infant" [24]. But since we know from Dr Arthur's records that he believed, at the time, that John Pearson was born healthy apart from his (painless) Down's syndrome, we must also ask 'what suffering was there to be reduced?'

The most plausible answer would appear to be: the suffering likely to arise from the policy of 'nursing care only', a policy which involved that the baby would not be fed and, if an infection developed, would not be treated. If the question as to why Dr Arthur had prescribed a narcotic analgesic to an apparently healthy infant had been raised, this could have led straight on to the second prong of the prosecution's initial charge of murder. This was that Dr Arthur's policy of non-treatment showed that he had intended the infant to die. Since the infant had in fact died (and may have died *because* it was not treated), the charge of murder might still have held good with regard to the charge of non-treatment. Even if doubts had arisen as to whether the drug DF 118 had caused pneumonia and John Pearson's subsequent death, John Pearson's death from pneumonia may still have been a consequence of Dr Arthur's intentional withholding of antibiotics. However, the question of whether intentional withholding of treatment, which results in a foreseen death, can ever be an instance of the intentional causation of death, or murder, was not examined at the trial. It was not examined because, as we know, by the time this question could have been raised, the charge had already been changed from 'murder' to 'attempted murder', where the issue had become whether Dr Arthur intended, and attempted, to cause death.

Whilst the question of whether a doctor can attempt to murder a patient by non-treatment could still have been raised in this context, it was not. It was not raised, partly because with the change in the charge there also came a subtle shift in emphasis; from the legal and inclusive notion of the *intentional causation* of death to the less inclusive subjective criterion of whether the accused did or did not *directly intend* to cause death when he embarked on the policy of non-treatment. But there was another reason as well: the Moral Difference Myth, which holds that killing in the practice of medicine is one thing and letting die quite another.

The Moral Difference Myth played an important role in the trial of Dr Leonard Arthur, because throughout the proceedings the view prevailed that it was, both morally and legally, permissible to allow handicapped infants to die. Only on the basis of this belief could Dr Arthur have been found not guilty of the attempted murder of John Pearson. For even if the jury believed Dr Arthur's statement to the police that when prescribing DF 118 he had intended to reduce suffering rather than to kill; and even if the jury (mistakenly) assumed that a direct intention to kill was necessary for an accused to be guilty of attempted murder; the jury would still have had to face the question of why there was likely to be any suffering to be reduced, and why the baby was not being fed in the normal manner and treated with antibiotics when it developed pneumonia. If the jury had asked these questions they would have had to conclude that the intention was that the baby should die. How then could anyone escape the conclusion that Dr Arthur was guilty of attempting to murder John Pearson? Only, it would seem, by taking the view that when a doctor lets a baby die, he does not cause its death and is not responsible for it. The baby dies, according to this view, from the disease or injury and not from what the doctor does [25].

It is this view I wish to challenge. It rests, as I will show, on an inadequate notion of causal agency and its connection with moral and legal responsibility.

(b) *Causation*

For the law, causation is of primary importance because unless it can be shown that a person has caused a certain consequence, such as death, that person cannot be held legally responsible for it. In the recent trial of Dr William Waddill (Jr), for example, a California Superior Court Judge told the jury: "You may not find the defendant guilty of murder unless you are satisfied that the defendant, by act or omission, was the proximate cause of the death of Baby Girl Weaver" [26].

This quotation suggests that omissions can be causes and that an agent can cause death not only by doing something but also by doing nothing. And, indeed, this is the case. The law holds agents not only responsible for the consequences of their intentional actions, but also for the consequences of at least some of their omissions.

Legal definitions of 'homicide' and 'murder' thus typically include reference to omissions as well as to positive acts. *Black's Law Dictionary*, for example, defines 'homicide' as "the killing of one human being by the procurement, or omission, of another" [27] and, as we saw above, the New South Wales (Australia) Crimes Act states that an agent can commit murder not only by an act but also by an omission [28].

Whilst the law thus recognises that omissions can be causes, this view was not considered at the trial of Dr Arthur. It was not considered because by the time this question could have been discussed, Professor Usher had already conceded that John Pearson was born with a number of previously undetected abnormalities. Because of these abnormalities, doubt had arisen as to whether John Pearson's death was caused by either an act of the accused (the administration of DF 118) or—our present concern—by Dr Arthur's omission to treat.

However, even if it could not be shown beyond reasonable doubt that Dr Arthur, by an act or an omission, caused John Pearson's death, it is clear that there are many instances in the practice of medicine where the causal link between a doctor's omission to treat and a patient's subsequent death is not in doubt. Example (1)—the Down's syndrome infant born with an intestinal obstruction—is a case in point. So is, other things being equal, example (4), where a handicapped infant is allowed to die of untreated pneumonia. These cases are cited by Justice Farquharson as instances of which 'no-one could say' that they constituted murder. However, for the following reasons I believe that they may well be murder.

That omissions can have consequences is most clearly seen when the act omitted to be done is one which is normally expected to be done. Indeed, it is in circumstances such as these that we quite unhesitatingly attribute the cause of the consequence to the act omitted. If a mother does not feed her infant and the infant dies, then we say that the mother's omission is the cause of the infant's death. Similarly, if a doctor refrains from giving, say, insulin to an otherwise healthy diabetic patient and the patient dies, then we say that the doctor's omission was the cause of the patient's death. We have certain expectations as to normal functioning, or the normal course of events, and if an agent deviates from them, then we cite his omission, or his failure to do what is expected, as the cause of a consequence, such as death.

Based on this notion of normal functioning, or the normal course of events, Hart and Honoré, in their now classical account of *Causation in the Law*, emphasise that not only actions but also negative states, static conditions and omissions can be causes:

> there is no convenient substitute for statements that the lack of the rain was the cause of the failure of the corn crop, the icy condition of the road was the cause of the accident, the failure of the signalman to pull the lever was the cause of the train smash. [29]

Thus, on Hart and Honoré's account, omissions become causes when what is omitted to be done deviates from normal expectations, normal functioning and normal conditions. As they put it:

> When things go wrong and we then ask for the cause, we ask this on the assumption that the environment persists unchanged, and something "has made the difference" between what normally happens in it and what happens on this occasion. [30]

On Hart and Honoré's view, then, the distinction between omissions that have causal status and those that do not, is expressed in terms of the distinction between 'causes' and 'conditions' which, in turn, is based on the difference between normal and abnormal functioning:

> ... and what is taken as normal for the purpose of the distinction between cause and mere conditions is very often an artefact of human habit, custom or convention. This is so because men have discovered that nature is not only sometimes harmful *if* we intervene, but it is also sometimes harmful *unless* we intervene, and have developed customary techniques, procedures and routines to counteract such harm. These have become a second 'nature' and so a second 'norm'. The effect of drought is regularly neutralized by governmental precautions in preserving water or food; disease is neutralized by inoculation; rain by the use of umbrellas. When such man-made conditions are established, deviations will be regarded as exceptional and so rank as the cause of harm. It is obvious that in such cases what is selected as the cause from the total set of conditions will often

be an omission which coincides with what is reprehensible by established standards of behaviour... [31]

Perhaps it is this difference between normal and abnormal functioning Justice Farquharson had in mind when he drew the distinction between unlawful murder and lawful lettings die in terms of the dichotomy between causing death on the one hand and the mere setting of conditions in which death may occur on the other [32]. For if it is a widely accepted practice in paediatric medicine to allow severely handicapped infants to die, then it might follow on Hart and Honoré's account that a doctor's refraining from preventing death is a mere background condition and not 'the cause' of an infant's death.

One thing did become abundantly clear during the trial: that many handicapped infants *are* deliberately being allowed to die. What is far less clear, though, is that a doctor's omission to treat is not, nonetheless, the cause of such an infant's death.

Let me begin by establishing what the policy of non-treatment or 'nursing care only' amounts to in such cases:

According to Sister Mahon, the midwife who delivered the baby, 'nursing care only' means "keeping the baby comfortable and feeding it with water..." For the houseman, Dr Fryatt, the term includes nourishment, but excludes treatment should an infection develop. And, again, for Sister Simcox it means the following:

> Nursing care only, if it appears on the sheet of the mother and the baby, the child goes to a different ward. The nurses would cherish him and remain in the ward until he died. If 'nursing care only' is prescribed, it depends on the context whether the patient survives, but in the cases of the severely deformed child, this has never happened in that hospital. [33]

As Justice Farquharson pointed out, while there was some disagreement as to what precisely the term 'nursing care only' amounted to, it was generally agreed that by the time the nurses were in fact looking after the child, it had developed pneumonia, "and by that stage... it was accepted that the child had reached the stage where, if infection overcame it, it was going to be left to die" [34].

So this is what I assume for the purposes of my subsequent discussion: that John Pearson was suffering from pneumonia, that antibiotics treatment was deliberately withheld, and that the infant's death from pneumonia was foreseen.

However, in this connection, we should also note the following: firstly, that in cases such as this, doctors are not powerlessly standing by as unsalvageable infants die, rather they *refrain* from preventing deaths that could quite easily be prevented. In other words, a doctor who refrains from preventing death has the ability and the opportunity to prevent the death, is aware of this and of the fact that were he not to refrain the infant would not die [35]. In examples (1) and (4), for example, the infants would not have died had the intestinal obstruction been removed in the first case, and had the second infant been treated with antibiotics. Similarly John Pearson: had he not been given excessive doses of the respiratory depressant DF 118 and been treated with antibiotics, we can assume that he would not have died of pneumonia when he did. Secondly, we should note that those involved in medical decision-making and interpretations of the law not only foresee (or 'obliquely' intend) that those untreated infants will die; they actually hope for, want or desire (and therefore 'directly' intend) those infants' early deaths.

Justice Farquharson thus spoke of the "realisation of hope" if a handicapped infant contracts an infection, and regarded it as a "merciful dispensation of providence'" if the child then dies of such an untreated infection [36]. Professor

Alexander Campbell, a witness for the defence, stated that he had, on a number of occasions, put an infant on 'nursing care only' with the intention that it should not survive [37]. A second witness, Dr Dunn, said that if he had been in charge of the treatment of John Pearson, he would have hoped that the infant "had contracted pneumonia . . . or had some defect . . ." He also stated that in cases such as this, food would be withheld "in the hope that complications would develop which would lead to death by natural causes" [38]. Yet another witness, Sir Douglas Black, President of the Royal College of Physicians, agreed with his colleagues. According to him, "it would be ethical to put (a handicapped and rejected child) upon a course of management that would end in its death . . . I say that it is ethical that a child suffering from Down's syndrome . . . should not survive" [39]. And a final witness, Dr Bluett, stated that if the parents decided that they did not want a child to survive, he would put that child on a regime like that prescribed by Dr Arthur, where "one hopes it would then contract an infection and die" [40].

It thus became quite clear during the trial that the practice of deliberately letting handicapped infants die is widespread in the medical community—moreover, it is endorsed by members of the community who are highly respected both in medical and non-medical circles. Whilst it is not impossible, Justice Farquharson pointed out, that such highly respected men were committing crimes, he imagined that the jury would "think long and hard before deciding that doctors of the eminence we have heard in presenting to you what medical ethics are . . . have evolved standards which amount to committing crime" [41].

And yet, a reasoned case can be offered for the claim that the standards which have evolved in medicine and that are apparently accepted by the general population [42] and the 'guardians' alike, are a direct infringement of the law of homicide. Refraining from preventing death is, in the cases we have discussed, always—I believe—an instance of the intentional causation of death. In other words, it is murder. To see why this is so, we need to return to the question of causation.

According to the analysis provided by Hart and Honoré, we can distinguish between 'the cause' of a consequence and the causal background conditions by relying on the distinction between normal and abnormal functioning. The authors point out that much of our interest in determining the cause of some outcome is prompted by something having gone wrong with the normal functioning of things. Thus, if we want to know why this house is now burning while normally it is not, we are asking 'what made the difference' between this house's not-burning and its burning, and it is this 'difference' that determines something's being the cause rather than a condition. Thus we would, in the present case, be satisfied in being told that the explosion of a kerosene lamp was the cause of the house's catching fire, while the presence of inflammable material and oxygen are merely conditions which exist in normal circumstances also. Frequently, as was already mentioned above, what will be selected as the cause of a consequence will be an omission because the notion of normal functioning often involves agents in performing certain actions, where failure to perform such actions will be a deviation from the norm. For example, we may ask: 'Why did the flowers die?', and the gardener's failure to water them will be cited as the cause. The gardener's omission would be the cause, according to Hart and Honoré, because it constituted "an abnormal failure of a normal condition" [43]. In other words, when certain man-made normal conditions are established, deviations from them will be regarded as exceptional and so rank as the cause of harm [44].

Hart and Honoré's analysis of negative causation—whilst correct in attributing causal status to some omissions—is ultimately too limited because we are causally (and morally) responsible not only for those omissions which constitute deviations from social norms and established practices, but for all significant refrainings. However, for reasons of space I will not here be able to argue for this view (although I have done so elsewhere [45])—nor will it be necessary for our present purposes. For our purposes Hart and Honoré's more limited notion of causation— widely accepted by legal theorists—will be quite sufficient to show that if doctors discriminatorily refrain from preventing *some* infant's deaths (the deaths of those who are handicapped and unwanted by their parents), then the doctors' omissions are 'the causes' for such infants' deaths. Moreover, in so far as those doctors either directly intend, or foresee, that the infants will die as a consequence of non-treatment, these are instances of the intentional causation of death, or murder.

This is so for the following reason: it is widely recognised that we can raise the question of causation in different causal contexts. Take the case of an infant born with Down's syndrome who develops pneumonia, is not treated with antibiotics and subsequently dies. What is 'the cause' of the infant's death?

If the question is raised in the context of handicapped infants who are not wanted by their parents and whom doctors therefore allow to die, a satisfactory answer would be that the cause of this particular infant's death was pneumonia. Here the causal field, or the normal background conditions, are given by the medical history of this untreated Down's syndrome infant. And it is against these causal background conditions that we are seeking to establish what "made the difference" between the time when death occurred and when it did not. In this context, the fact that the infant contracted pneumonia will allow us to differentiate between the time when the infant died and when it did not.

However, whilst the selection of such a restricted causal field will undoubtedly be relevant for the answering of certain questions, it is not a field which we may choose when we raise the question as to the cause of an infant's death in the context of the Sanctity of Life Ideal and the law. Since it is a fundamental tenet of the law that "all human lives must be regarded as having an equal claim to preservation" [46], the causal background conditions in this case are given by *all* the infants who contract pneumonia in the modern hospital setting. Since it is standard practice to prevent the death of all those infants who are not handicapped and are wanted by their parents, pneumonia may be the cause of death in relation to the former field of handicapped infants but cannot be the cause in relation to the latter field. It cannot be the cause in relation to the latter field since it is part of the description of that field, and being present throughout that field, it cannot differentiate one subregion from another [47].

What, then, is 'the cause' of an untreated Down's syndrome infant's death if pneumonia is ruled out as a possible cause? It is the same as in the case of an untreated non-handicapped infant. If a doctor deliberately refrained from prevent-ing such an infant's death, we would say that the doctor's failure to treat was the cause of that infant's death. Similarly in the case of Down's syndrome infants. If it can be shown that what differentiates those situations in which death occurs (or would have occured) is the doctor's failure to treat, then the doctor's omission is the causal factor that allows us to distinguish those situations in which death occurs from those in which it does not, and the doctor's failure to treat is identified as the causal factor that made, or would have made, the difference between an infant's dying and not-dying. Hence, the doctor's failure to treat is the cause of death [48].

In this connection, we do well to remind ourselves of the distinction drawn by

H.L.A. Hart between causal responsibility and liability responsibility, that is, between an agent being causally responsible for a consequence, and being liable, or having to answer for the consequences of one's actions or omissions [49]. Thus it would seem that only when an agent *refrains* from preventing death is he *prima facie* fully accountable for it, just as accountable or morally responsible as he would have been had he brought it about by a deliberate positive action.

Precisely what is to count as 'refraining' is a topic that needs further investigation; but for our purpose it is enough to note that when doctors like Dr Leonard Arthur and the witnesses who gave evidence at the trial leave a baby to die, they have the ability, the opportunity, and the awareness to make them fully accountable or morally responsible, just as accountable and responsible as they would be were they to administer a lethal injection.

Moreover, in cases of refraining from preventing death, doctors are not only morally, but also legally, accountable for a death they failed to prevent. It is true, moral responsibility and legal liability are not always coextensive. For example, if a stranger refrains from rescuing an infant drowning in a foot of water, he is morally responsible for the death, but not liable for legal conviction or punishment because, as H.L.A. Hart notes, refusing to aid those in danger is not generally considered a criminal offence in English law [50]. However, this situation is dramatically changed in the doctor/patient relationship. Here doctors must not only refrain from taking life, they must also preserve it when they can. This is so because a special relationship (recognised by the law) characterises the doctor/patient relationship. Thus it is widely agreed that a doctor is legally obligated to provide the 'necessaries of life' for those of his patients who are dependent on them [51]. Deliberately to withhold those 'necessaries of life' is the intentional causation of death by an omission. Legally such omissions have the same status as positive actions: if it is murder in one case, so it is—other things being equal—in the other.

Conclusion

Nothing in the above account suggests that it is morally wrong to let handicapped infants die if those infants are not wanted by their parents. Nor does anything I have said suggest that such a course of action would be right. Rather, the point of my argument has been to show that not only direct killings, but also 'indirect' killings and lettings die are cases of the intentional causation of death and thus an infringement of the Sanctity of Life Ideal and the law.

But the account has moral and legal implications: that we should abandon the convenient Moral Difference Myth which holds that letting a handicapped infant die is not an instance of the intentional causation of death or murder— and that we should reflect on a number of difficult ethical questions which have been present all along:

Does human life, irrespective of its quality or kind, have 'sanctity', i.e. is it equally valuable and inviolable and must it always be preserved by all available means; or should life and death decisions in the practice of medicine at least sometimes be based on quality-of-life considerations?

These are the fundamental questions that need to be answered first before we can arrive at morally defensible principles to instruct our life and death decisions. Whether we bring about another person's death by positive or negative means (or by killing or letting die) is ultimately but a question of method. From the moral and legal point of view, intentional killings and intentional lettings die are, other things being equal, the same.

However, the question of method is crucial in two other respects. It is crucial for the Sanctity of Life Ideal itself; and it may be crucial for the patient whose life is being terminated. Let me briefly deal with these two points in turn.

A consistent application of the Sanctity of Life Ideal leads to 'vitalism, the view that it is the doctor's duty to sustain his patient's life "even if it were decided that the patient were 'better off dead' " ' [52]. Whilst such a position is so patently inhumane that few of us would want to defend it, it is consistent with the Sanctity of Life Ideal's two tenets: that all human life is equally valuable and inviolable. The principle's inhumanity and its disregard for the interests of individual patients is the price one has to pay if this Ideal is to be followed consistently.

In the light of the obvious inhumanity of 'vitalism', it is not surprising that this position does not have many followers. However, this is where the Moral Difference Myth comes in, a myth which initially seems to rescue the Sanctity of Life Ideal from its objectionable link with vitalism; because the Moral Difference Myth holds that it is one thing to kill a patient and quite another to let a patient die. In other words, according to the Moral Difference Myth a doctor must never kill a patient, but there are times when he may refrain from preventing death.

Now, if my above arguments have been correct, this Moral Difference Myth cannot be sustained. But the widespread belief that it marks a morally and legally relevant distinction between killing and letting die superficially lends support to the Sanctity of Life Ideal. This support, however, is bought at a price. On the basis of the Moral Difference Myth, doctors choose letting die as their method of bringing about death, even though killing would, under the circumstances, often be the preferable option.

Let us simply assume, for the moment, that there are times when a doctor may refrain from preventing death because continued life is not in the patient's best interest. Let us also assume that case (1)—the Down's syndrome infant born with an intestinal obstruction—is such a case. Here the doctor says (in the words of Justice Farquharson): "As this child is a mongol ... I do not propose to operate; I shall allow nature to take its course". However, nature is not always kind. To see what happens when nature is allowed to take its course in a case like this, let us turn to the description one paediatric surgeon, Anthony Shaw, gives of the situation:

> When surgery is denied, the doctor must try to keep the infant from suffering while natural forces sap the baby's life away. As a surgeon whose natural inclination is to use the scalpel to fight off death, standing by and watching a salvageable baby die is the most emotionally exhausting experience I know. It is easy at a conference, in a theoretical discussion, to decide that such infants should be allowed to die. It is altogether different to stand by in the nursery and watch as dehydration and infection wither a tiny being over hours and days. It is a terrible ordeal for me and the hospital staff—much more so than for the parents who never set foot in the nursery. [53]

Letting die can thus be a terrible ordeal for all involved—not least for the infant for whose sake, we assume, doctors and parents are engaging in the practice of letting die in the first place. The tragedy is of course, that patients, relatives and medical staff undergo these ordeals on the basis of a distinction that is, in itself, morally and legally irrelevant: the distinction between killing and letting die.

36   *H. Kuhse*

However, whilst intentional killings and intentional lettings die are equivalent in so far as they are both instances of the intentional causation of death, it is clear that other extrinsic factors can make a moral difference. The point is this: whilst the administration of a lethal injection would bring a swift and painless death for the patient, letting die may be neither swift nor painless. In the much-discussed Johns Hopkins case (again involving a Down's syndrome infant with an intestinal obstruction), the dying process took 15 days [54]. The suffering involved in this is difficult to justify indeed, and it seems clear that in a case such as this a quick and painless injection would better serve the interests of the infant.

In the case of John Pearson, the letting die process took only three days. But even three days are too long if they involve those concerned in considerable unnecessary suffering. It is true, John Pearson may not have suffered as much as descriptions such as that provided by Anthony Shaw above might suggest. He was drugged with massive doses of the narcotic analgesic DF 118. However, the experience of the court proceedings and the continued belief in the Moral Difference Myth may make doctors more hesitant to administer sufficient doses of such drugs because their administration—in distinction to 'letting nature take its course'—may more easily be construed as an instance of the intentional causation of death. As a consequence, more infants may suffer for prolonged periods of time when the decision has been made to let them die. And whilst the Moral Difference Myth superficially holds the Sanctity of Life Ideal intact, the suffering of those infants is, I believe, too high a price to pay for this Ideal—an Ideal that might itself have to be questioned.

Just one final comment. Those parents and doctors who think that it is sometimes justifiable to bring about the death of a seriously handicapped infant are not moral monsters. It is clear that there are circumstances when death is the morally preferable option. So my complaint does not concern the moral dispositions of those who justifiably bring about the death of a seriously handicapped infant—it concerns the methods employed to bring those deaths about and the unarticulated and therefore frequently idiosyncratic criteria which inform life and death decisions in such cases. How can the situation be improved? By abolishing the Moral Difference Myth and recognising that deliberate lettings die are, both morally and legally, the same as deliberate killings—namely, instances of the intentional causation of death. Once this has been recognised, the real questions can be raised: under what circumstances may we intentionally cause the death of a handicapped infant; who should decide; and what is the most appropriate method of bringing death about? And if consensus can be reached on these issues, the next question, surely, must be this: how can we provide legal protection for those who do what it is sometimes right to do: intentionally cause the death of another human being? Thus what is required is not the creation of a new (and lesser) offence than that of unlawful homicide; rather, what is required is legislation to the effect that a doctor or parent who acts in accordance with accepted guidelines and brings about an infant's death commits *no* offence [55].

And with this, we return to the beginning. Once such legislation has been introduced and has become fact, the Moral Difference Myth will truly have been banished to the realm of fiction. It will be as embarassing for us to recount it as it was for Socrates to state his Myth of Metals: "... I don't know how I'm to find the courage or the words to do so" [56].

Acknowledgements

The article was written as part of a larger study on 'Life and Death Choices for

Defective Newborns', supported by the Australian Research Grants Scheme. I wish to thank the ARGS and Professor Peter Singer, Department of Philosophy, Monash University, for their support.

Correspondence: Helga Kuhse, Centre for Human Bioethics, Monash University, Clayton, Victoria 3168, Australia.

NOTES

[1] Plato: *The Republic,* Part Four (Book Three), 414–416.

[2] See Transcript of the Shorthand notes of the official court reporters Marten, Meredith & Co., Ltd, 36/38 Whitefriars Steet, London, EC4Y 8BJ, for the summing up by Justice Farquharson in *Regina v Leonard John Henry Arthur,* November 3, 4, 5 1981, at Leicester Court, Leicester/England (subsequently cited as 'Transcript').

[3] Ibid., p. 3.

[4] Quoted by GLOVER, JONATHAN (1982) Letting people die, *London Review of Books,* Vol. 4, No. 4, p. 3.

[5] See, for example, William K. Frankena's excellent exposition of this vagueness in 'The ethics of respect for life' in: BARKER, STEPHEN F. (Ed.) *Respect for Life in Medicine, Philosophy, and the Law,* pp. 24–62 (Baltimore, Johns Hopkins Press, 1977).

[6] Moshe Tendler, as cited by BRODY, HOWARD (1976) *Ethical Discussions in Medicine,* p. 66 (Boston, Little, Brown & Co.).

[7] Transcript, p. 16.

[8] KADISH, SANFORD H. (1977) Respect for life and regard for rights in the criminal law, in: BARKER, S.F. (Ed.) *Respect for Life . . ., op. cit.,* p. 72.

[9] The four examples are from pp. 18–19 of the Transcript.

[10] Transcript, pp. 19–20.

[11] The New South Wales (Australia) Crimes Act 1900, s.18 (1)(a); see also *Jowitt's Dictionary of English Law,* Vol. 1, 1977, entry under 'homicide' pp. 918–919.

[12] *Jowitt's Dictionary of English Law,* Vol. II, 1977, p. 1137.

[13] Ibid., p. 1212.

[14] Strictly speaking, the presumption that everyone must be taken to intend that which is the natural consequence of his actions would mean that an agent intentionally brings about not only the subjectively foreseen consequences of his action, but also those which were foreseeable (even though he may not have foreseen them). However, following the English Criminal Justice Act of 1967, a court or jury is not bound to take the latter view and may decide to include only the subjectively foreseen consequences under the legal notion of intention. The latter, less inclusive notion is sufficient for our purposes. I shall, therefore, leave moot such questions as gross unthinking negligence and extreme provocation (clearly relevant for the foreseeable/foreseen distinction) and merely assume that an agent is taken to intend the foreseen consequences of his/her action. (For a discussion of the notion of 'intention' see HART, H.L.A. (1968) (Ed.) Intention and punishment, in: HART, H.L.A. *Punishment and Responsibility Essays in the Philosophy of Law,* pp. 113–135 (Oxford, Clarendon Press).

[15] *The Times,* April 28 1868, as cited by H.L.A. Hart, ibid., p. 119.

[16] See KENNY, ANTHONY (1977) Intention and mens rea in murder, in: HACKER, P.M.S. & RAZ, J. (Eds) *Law, Morality and Society—Essays in Honour of H.L.A. Hart,* pp. 161–174 (Oxford, Clarendon Press). For a different view, see BALDWIN, THOMAS (1979) Foresight and responsibility, *Philosophy,* Vol. 54, No. 209, July, pp. 347–360.

[17] For a fuller discussion of the distinction between the permissibility of an action and its justifiability, see chapter III of my doctoral thesis: *The sanctity of life doctrine in medicine—a critique,* Monash University, 1983.

[18] For a more detailed defence of this view, see CHISHOLM, RODERICK M. (1970) The structure of intention, *The Journal of Philosophy,* Vol. 67, pp. 633–647.

[19] HART, H.L.A. (1968) Intention and punishment, *op. cit.,* makes a similar point but expresses it in terms of the connection between the control an agent has over bringing/not bringing a consequence about.

[20] DAVIES, LORD EDMUND (1977) On dying and dying well, *Proceedings of the Royal Society of Medicine,*

70, p. 73, as cited by MASON, J.K. & McCALL SMITH, R.A. (1983) *Law and Medical Ethics*, p. 179 (London, Butterworth).

[21] Transcript, p. 50.

[22] Ibid., pp. 45–46.

[23] Ibid., p. 43.

[24] Ibid., p. 50.

[25] See note [3].

[26] As cited by GREEN, O.H. (1980) Killing and letting die, *American Philosophical Quarterly*, 17, p. 195.

[27] *Black's Law Dictionary*, 4th ed. 1968, p. 867.

[28] See note [11].

[29] HART, H.L.A. & HONORÉ, A.M. (1959) *Causation in the Law*, pp. 28–29 (London, Oxford University Press). Hart and Honoré's account of negative causation has been criticised as being too limited. See, for example, HARRIS, JOHN (1980) *Violence and Responsibility*, pp. 37–42 (London, Routledge & Kegan Paul). See also note [45].

[30] HART, H.L.A. & HONORÉ, A.M. *Causation in the Law*, ibid., p. 34.

[31] Ibid., p. 35.

[32] Transcript, pp. 20–23.

[33] This and the preceding quotations are from pp. 34–35 of the Transcript.

[34] Ibid., p. 35.

[35] For a more extensive discussion of what it is for an agent to refrain from preventing a consequence, see, for example, GREEN, O.H. (1980) Killing and letting die, *op. cit.*, pp. 196–198.

[36] Transcript, p. 44.

[37] Ibid., p. 59.

[38] Ibid., pp. 69 and 73.

[39] Ibid., pp. 79–80.

[40] Ibid., p. 86.

[41] Ibid., p. 81.

[42] At the time of the trial, a Mori Opinion Poll showed that 86% of almost 2000 adults polled said that a doctor should not be found guilty of murder if, with the parents' agreement, 'he sees to it that a severely handicapped baby dies', *The Times*, November 10 1981).

[43] HART, H.L.A. & HONORÉ, A.M. (1959) *Causation in the Law*, *op. cit.*, p. 37.

[44] Ibid., p. 35.

[45] See chapter II of my PhD thesis: *The sanctity of life doctrine in medicine—a critique*, *op. cit.*

[46] See note [8].

[47] See, for example, MACKIE, J.L. (1975) Causes and conditions, in: SOSA, ERNEST (Ed.) *Causes and Conditionals*, pp. 15–38 (London, Oxford University Press).

[48] See also GRUZALSKI, BART (1981) Killing and letting die, *Mind*, 40, pp. 91–98.

[49] HART, H.L.A. (1968) Postscript: responsibility and retribution, in: HART, H.L.A. (Ed.) *Punishment and Responsibility*, *op. cit.*, pp. 212–230.

[50] Ibid., p. 217.

[51] See, for example, Introduction, in: STEINBOCK, BONNIE (Ed.) *Killing and Letting Die*, pp. 4–9 (Englewood Cliffs: Prentice Hall, 1980); LAW REFORM COMMISSION OF CANADA (1982) *Working Paper 28—Euthanasia Aiding Suicide and Cessation of Treatment*, pp. 19–20.

[52] KARNOFSKY, D.A. (1960) Why prolong the life of a patient with advanced cancer? *Cancer Journal for Clinicians*, 10, p. 9, see my Extraordinary means and the sanctity of life, *Journal of Medical Ethics*, 7, June 1981, pp. 74–82.

[53] As cited by RACHELS, JAMES (1979) Euthanasia, killing and letting die, in: LADD, JOHN (Ed.) *Ethical Issue-Relating to Life and Death*, p. 159 (Oxford University Press).

[54] DYCK, ARTHUR J. (1977) An alternative to the ethic of euthanasia, in: REISER, STANLEY JOEL, DYCK, ARTHUR J. & CURRAN, WILLIAM J. (Eds) *Ethics in Medicine—Historical Perspectives and Contemporary Concerns*, p. 534 (Cambridge, MIT Press).

[55] For such a proposal, see MASON, J.K. & McCALL SMITH, R.A. (1983) *Law and Medical Ethics*, *op. cit.*, pp. 81–89.

[56] Plato: *The Republic*, Part Four (Book Three), p. 414.

[21]

Euthanasia

The Way We Do It, the Way They Do It

Margaret Pabst Battin

Because we tend to be rather myopic in our discussions of death and dying, especially about the issues of active euthanasia and assisted suicide, it is valuable to place the question of how we go about dying in an international context. We do not always see that our own cultural norms may be quite different from those of other nations and that our background assumptions and actual practices differ dramatically—even when the countries in question are all developed industrial nations with similar cultural ancestries, religious traditions, and economic circumstances. I want to explore the three rather different approaches to end-of-life dilemmas prevalent in the United States, the Netherlands, and Germany—developments mirrored in Australia, Belgium, Switzerland, and elsewhere in the developed world— and consider how a society might think about which model of approach to dying is most appropriate for it.

Three Basic Models of Dying

The Netherlands, Germany, and the United States are all advanced industrial democracies. They all have sophisticated medical establishments and life expectancies over 75 years; their populations are all characterized by an increasing proportion of older persons. They are all in what has been called the fourth stage of the epidemiologic transition[1]—that stage of societal development in which it is no longer the case that the majority of the population dies of acute parasitic or infectious diseases, often with rapid, unpredictable onsets and sharp fatality curves (as

was true in earlier and less developed societies); rather, in modern industrial societies, the majority of a population—estimated in Europe at about 66–71%—dies
of degenerative diseases, especially delayed-degenerative diseases that are characterized by late, slow onset and extended decline.[2] This is the case throughout the
developed world. Accidents and suicide claim some, as do infectious diseases like
AIDS, pneumonia, and influenza, but most people in highly industrialized countries
die from heart disease (by no means always suddenly fatal); cancer; atherosclerosis;
chronic obstructive pulmonary disease; diabetes, liver, kidney, or other organ disease; or degenerative neurological disorders. In the developed world, we die not so
much from attack by outside diseases but from gradual disintegration. Thus, all
three of these modern industrial countries—the United States, the Netherlands, and
Germany—are alike in facing a common problem: how to deal with the characteristic new ways in which we die.

Dealing with Dying in the United States

In the United States, we have come to recognize that the maximal extension of
life-prolonging treatment in these late-life degenerative conditions is often inappropriate. Although we could keep the machines and tubes—the respirators, intravenous lines, feeding tubes—hooked up for extended periods, we recognize that this
is inhumane, pointless, and financially impossible. Instead, as a society we have
developed a number of mechanisms for dealing with these hopeless situations, all
of which involve withholding or withdrawing various forms of treatment.

Some mechanisms for withholding or withdrawing treatments are exercised by
the patient who is confronted by such a situation or who anticipates it. These
include refusal of treatment, the patient-executed do-not-resuscitate (DNR) order,
the living will, and the durable power of attorney. Others are mechanisms for
decision by second parties about a patient who is no longer competent or never
was competent, reflected in a long series of court cases from *Quinlan, Saikewicz,
Spring, Eichner, Barber, Bartling, Conroy, Brophy,* and the trio *Farrell, Peter,* and
Jobes to *Cruzan.* These cases delineate the precise circumstances under which it is
appropriate to withhold or withdraw various forms of therapy, including respiratory
support, chemotherapy, dialysis, antibiotics in intercurrent infections, and artificial
nutrition and hydration. Thus, during the past quarter-century, roughly since *Quinlan* (1976), the United States has developed an impressive body of case law and
state statutes that protects, permits, and facilitates the characteristic American strategy of dealing with end-of-life situations. These cases provide a framework for
withholding or withdrawing treatment when physicians and family members believe
there is no medical or moral point in going on. This has sometimes been termed
passive euthanasia; more often it is simply called *allowing to die.*

Indeed, "allowing to die" has become ubiquitous in the United States. For
example, a 1988 study found that of the 85% of deaths in the United States that
occurred in health-care institutions, including hospitals, nursing homes, and other
facilities, about 70% involved electively withholding some form of life-sustaining
treatment.[3] A 1989 study found that 85–90% of critical care professionals said they
were withholding or withdrawing life-sustaining treatments from patients who were

"deemed to have irreversible disease and are terminally ill."[4] A 1997 study of limits to life-sustaining care found that between 1987–88 and 1992–93, recommendations to withhold or withdraw life support prior to death increased from 51% to 90% in the intensive-care units studied.[5] Rates of withholding therapy such as ventilator support, surgery, and dialysis were found in yet another study to be substantial, and to increase with age.[6] A 1994/95 study of 167 intensive-care units—all the ICUs associated with U.S. training programs in critical care medicine or pulmonary and critical care medicine—found that in 75% of deaths, some form of care was withheld or withdrawn.[7] It has been estimated that 1.3 million American deaths a year follow decisions to withhold life support;[8] this is a majority of the just over 2 million American deaths per year.

In recent years, the legitimate use of withholding and withdrawing treatment has increasingly been understood to include practices likely or certain to result in death. The administration of escalating doses of morphine in a dying patient, which, it has been claimed, will depress respiration and so hasten death, is accepted under the (Catholic) principle of double effect, provided the medication is intended to relieve pain and merely foreseen but not intended to result in death; this practice is not considered killing or active hastening of death. The use of "terminal sedation," in which a patient dying in pain is sedated into unconsciousness while artificial nutrition and hydration are withheld, is also recognized as medically and legally acceptable; it too is understood as a form of "allowing to die," not active killing. With the single exception of Oregon, where physician-assisted suicide became legal in 1997,[9] withholding and withdrawing treatment and related forms of allowing to die are the only legally recognized ways we in the United States go about dealing with dying. A number of recent studies have shown that many physicians—in all states studied—do receive requests for assistance in suicide or active euthanasia and that a substantial number of these physicians have complied with one or more such requests; however, this more direct assistance in dying takes place entirely out of sight of the law. Except in Oregon, *allowing to die,* but not *causing to die,* has been the only legally protected alternative to maximal treatment legally recognized in the United States; it remains America's—and American medicine's—official posture in the face of death.

Dealing with Dying in the Netherlands

In the Netherlands, although the practice of withholding and withdrawing treatment is similar to that in the United States, voluntary active euthanasia and physician assistance in suicide are also available responses to end-of-life situations.[10] Active euthanasia, understood as the termination of the life of the patient at the patient's explicit and persistent request, is the more frequent form of directly assisted dying, and most discussion in the Netherlands has concerned it rather than assistance in suicide, though the conceptual difference is not regarded as great: many cases of what the Dutch term *euthanasia* involve initial self-administration of the lethal dose by the patient but procurement of death by the physician, and many cases of what is termed *physician-assisted suicide* involve completion of the lethal process by the physician if a self-administered drug does not prove fully effective. Although until

50   DILEMMAS ABOUT DYING

2002 they were still technically illegal under statutory law—and even with legalization remain an "exception" to those provisions of the Dutch Penal Code that
prohibit killing on request and intentional assistance in suicide—active euthanasia
and assistance in suicide have long been widely regarded as legal, or rather *gedoogd,* legally "tolerated," and have in fact been deemed justified (not only non-
punishable) by the courts when performed by a physician if certain conditions were
met. Voluntary active euthanasia (in the law, called "life-ending on request") and
physician-assisted suicide are now fully legal by statute under these guidelines.
Dutch law protects the physician who performs euthanasia or provides assistance
in suicide from prosecution for homicide if these guidelines, known as the conditions of "due care," are met.

Over the years, the guidelines have been stated in various ways. They contain
six central provisions:

1. That the patient's request be voluntary and well-considered
2. That the patient be undergoing or about to undergo intolerable suffering,
   that is, suffering that is lasting and unbearable
3. That all alternatives acceptable to the patient for relieving the suffering
   have been tried, and that in the patient's view there is no other reasonable
   solution
4. That the patient have full information about his or her situation and prospects
5. That the physician consult with a second physician who has examined the
   patient and whose judgment can be expected to be independent
6. That in performing euthanasia or assisting in suicide, the physician act
   with due care

Of these criteria, it is the first that is held to be central: euthanasia may be
performed only at the *voluntary* request of the patient. This criterion is also understood to require that the patient's request be a stable, enduring, reflective one—
not the product of a transitory impulse. Every attempt is to be made to rule out
depression, psychopathology, pressures from family members, unrealistic fears, and
other factors compromising voluntariness, though depression is not in itself understood to necessarily preclude such choice. Euthanasia may be performed *only* by
a physician, not by a nurse, family member, or other party.

In 1991, a comprehensive, nationwide study requested by the Dutch government, popularly known as the Remmelink Commission report, provided the first
objective data about the incidence of euthanasia and physician-assisted suicide.[11]
This study also provided information about other medical decisions at the end of
life, particularly withholding or withdrawal of treatment and the use of life-
shortening doses of opioids for the control of pain, as well as direct termination.
The Remmelink report was supplemented by a study focusing particularly carefully
on the characteristics of patients and the nature of their euthanasia requests.[12] Five
years later, the researchers from these two studies jointly conducted a major new
nationwide study replicating much of the previous Remmelink inquiry, providing
empirical data both about current practice in the Netherlands and change over a

five-year period.[13] A third replication of the nationwide study was published in 2003.[14]

About 140,000 people die in the Netherlands every year, and of these deaths, about 30% are sudden and unexpected, while the majority are predictable and foreseen, usually the result of degenerative illness comparatively late in life. Of the total deaths in the Netherlands, according to the 2001 data, about 20.2% involve decisions to withhold or withdraw treatment in situations where continuing treatment would probably have prolonged life; another 20.1% involve the "double effect" use of opioids to relieve pain but in dosages probably sufficient to shorten life. Only a small fraction of people who die do so by euthanasia—about 2.4%—and an even smaller fraction, 0.2%, do so by physician-assisted suicide. Of patients who do receive euthanasia or physician-assisted suicide, about 80 percent have cancer, while 3% have cardiovascular disease and 4% neurological disease, primarily ALS.

However, the 1990 Remmelink report had also revealed that another 0.8% of patients who died did so as the result of life-terminating procedures not technically called euthanasia, without explicit, current request. These cases, known as "the 1000 cases," unleashed highly exaggerated claims that patients were being killed against their wills. In fact, in about half of these cases, euthanasia had been previously discussed with the patient or the patient had expressed in a previous phase of the disease a wish for euthanasia if his or her suffering became unbearable ("Doctor, please don't let me suffer too long"); and in the other half, the patient was no longer competent and was near death, clearly suffering grievously although verbal contact had become impossible.[15] In 91% of these cases without explicit, current request, life was shortened by less than a week, and in 33% by less than a day.

Over the next decade, as revealed in the 1995 and 2003 nationwide studies, the proportion of cases of euthanasia rose slightly (associated, the authors conjectured, with the aging of the population and an increase in the proportion of deaths due to cancer, that condition in which euthanasia is most frequent); the proportion of cases of assisted suicide had remained about the same. The proportion of cases of life termination without current explicit request declined slightly to 0.7%, down from the notorious 1,000 to about 900. In 1990, a total of 2.9% of all deaths had involved euthanasia and related practices; by 2001 this total was about 3.7%.[16] In the early days of openly tolerated euthanasia, comparatively few cases were reported as required to the Public Prosecutor; there has been a dramatic gain since reporting procedures have been revised to require reporting to a review committee rather than to the police, and about 54% are now reported. However, there are no major differences between reported and unreported cases in terms of the patient's characteristics, clinical conditions, or reasons for the action.[17] Euthanasia is performed in about 1:25 of deaths that occur at home, about 1:75 of hospital deaths, and about 1:800 of nursing home deaths. The Netherlands has now established regional review committees for such cases and has initiated hospice-style pain management programs complete with 24-hour phone-in consultation services for physicians confronted by euthanasia requests.

Although euthanasia is thus not frequent, a small fraction of the total annual mortality, it is nevertheless a conspicuous option in terminal illness, well known to both physicians and the general public. There has been very widespread public discussion of the issues that arise with respect to euthanasia during the last quarter-century, and surveys of public opinion show that public support for a liberal euthanasia policy has been growing: from 40% in 1966 to 81% in 1988, then to about 90% by 2000. Doctors, too, support the practice, and although there has been a vocal opposition group, it has remained in the clear minority. Some 57% of Dutch physicians say that they have performed euthanasia or provided assistance in suicide, and an additional 30% say that although they have not actually done so, they can conceive of situations in which they would be prepared to do so. Ten percent say they would never perform it but would refer the patient to another physician. The proportion of physicians who say they not only would not do so themselves but would not refer a patient who requested it to a physician who would dropped from 4% in 1990 to 3% in 1995 to 1% in 2001. Thus, although many physicians who have performed euthanasia say that they would be most reluctant to do so again and that "only in the face of unbearable suffering and with no alternatives would they be prepared to take such action,"[18] all three nationwide studies have shown that the majority of Dutch physicians accept the practice. Surveying the changes over the 5-year period between 1990 and 1995, the authors of the nationwide study also commented that the data do not support claims of a slippery slope.[19] Work now in progress shows no such pattern either.[20]

In general, pain alone is not the basis for deciding upon euthanasia, since pain can, in most cases, be effectively treated. Only a third of Dutch physicians think that adequate pain control and terminal care make euthanasia redundant, and that number has been dropping. Rather, the "intolerable suffering" mentioned in the second criterion is understood to mean suffering that is intolerable in the patient's (rather than the physician's) view, and can include a fear of or unwillingness to endure *entluistering,* that gradual effacement and loss of personal identity that characterizes the end-stages of many terminal illnesses. In very exceptional circumstances, the Supreme Court ruled in the *Chabot* case of 1994, physician-assisted suicide may be justified for a patient with nonsomatic, psychiatric illness like intractable depression, but such cases are extremely rare and require heightened scrutiny.

In a year, about 35,000 patients seek reassurance from their physicians that they will be granted euthanasia if their suffering becomes severe; there are about 9,700 explicit requests, and about two-thirds of these are turned down, usually on the grounds that there is some other way of treating the patient's suffering. In 14% of cases in 1990, the denial was based on the presence of depression or psychiatric illness.

In the Netherlands, many hospitals now have protocols for the performance of euthanasia; these serve to ensure that the legal guidelines have been met. However, euthanasia is often practiced in the patient's home, typically by the general practitioner who is the patient's long-term family physician. Euthanasia is usually performed after aggressive hospital treatment has failed to arrest the patient's terminal illness; the patient has come home to die, and the family physician is prepared to ease this passing. Whether practiced at home or in the hospital, it is believed that euthanasia usually takes place in the presence of the family members, perhaps the visiting nurse, and often the patient's pastor or priest. Many doctors say that performing euthanasia is never easy but that it is something they believe a doctor ought to do for his or her patient when the patient genuinely wants it and nothing else can help.

Thus, in the Netherlands a patient who is facing the end of life has an option not openly practiced in the United States, except Oregon: to ask the physician to bring his or her life to an end. Although not everyone in the Netherlands does so—indeed, over 96% of people who die in a given year do not do so in this way—it is a choice legally recognized and widely understood.

Facing Death in Germany

In part because of its very painful history of Nazism, German medical culture has insisted that doctors should have no role in directly causing death. As in the other countries with advanced medical systems, withholding and withdrawing of care is widely used to avoid the unwanted or inappropriate prolongation of life when the patient is already dying, but there has been vigorous and nearly universal opposition in German public discourse to the notion of active euthanasia, at least in the horrific, politically motivated sense associated with Nazism. In the last few years, some Germans have begun to approve of euthanasia in the Dutch sense, based on the Greek root, *eu-thanatos,* or "good death," a voluntary choice by the patient for an easier death, but many Germans still associate euthanasia with the politically motivated exterminations by the Nazis and view the Dutch as stepping out on a dangerously slippery slope.

However, although under German law killing on request (including voluntary euthanasia) is illegal, German law has not prohibited assistance in suicide since the time of Frederick the Great (1742), provided the person is *tatherrschaftsfähig,* capable of exercising control over his or her actions, and also acting out of *freiverantwortliche Wille,* freely responsible choice. Doctors are prohibited from assistance in suicide not by law but by the policies and code of ethics of the Bundesärtzekammer, the German medical association.[21] Furthermore, any person, physician or otherwise, has a duty to rescue a person who is unconscious. Thus, medical assistance in suicide is limited, but it is possible for a family member or friend to assist in a person's suicide, for instance by providing a lethal drug, as long as the person is competent and acting freely and the assister does not remain with the person after unconsciousness sets in.

Taking advantage of this situation, a private organization, the Deutsche Gesellschaft für Humanes Sterben (DGHS), or German Society for Dying in Dignity, has developed; it provides support to its very extensive membership in many end-of-life matters, including choosing suicide as an alternative to terminal illness. Of course, not all Germans are members of this organization, and many are not sympathetic with its aims, yet the notion of self-directed ending of one's own life in terminal illness is widely understood as an option. Although since 1993 the DGHS has not itself supplied such information for legal reasons, it tells its members how to obtain the booklet "Departing Drugs," published in Scotland, and other information about ending life, if they request it, provided they have been a member for one year and have not received medical or psychotherapeutic treatment for depression or other psychiatric illness during the last three years. The information includes a list of prescription drugs, together with the specific dosages necessary for producing a certain, painless death. The DGHS does not itself sell or supply lethal drugs;[22] rather, it recommends that the member approach a physician for a prescription for the drug desired, asking, for example, for a barbiturate to help with sleep. If necessary, the DGHS has been willing to arrange for someone to obtain drugs from neighboring countries, including France, Italy, Spain, Portugal, and Greece, where they may be available without prescription. It also makes available the so-called Exit Bag, a plastic bag used with specific techniques for death by asphyxiation. The DGHS provides and trains family members in what it calls *Sterbebegleitung* (accompaniment in dying), which may take the form of simple presence with a person who is dying but may also involve direct assistance to a person who is committing suicide, up until unconsciousness sets in. The *Sterbebegleiter* is typically a layperson, not someone medically trained, and physicians play no role in assisting in these cases of suicide. Direct active *Sterbehilfe*—active euthanasia—is illegal under German law. But active indirect *Sterbehilfe,* understood as assistance in suicide, is not illegal, and the DGHS provides counseling in how a "death with dignity" may be achieved in this way.

To preclude suspicion by providing evidence of the person's intentions, the DGHS also provides a form—printed on a single sheet of distinctive purple paper— to be signed once when joining the organization, documenting that the person has reflected thoroughly on the possibility of "free death" *(Freitod)* or suicide in terminal illness as a way of releasing oneself from severe suffering, and expressing the intention to determine the time and character of one's own death. The person then signs this "free death directive" or "suicide decision declaration" *(Freitodverfügung)* again at the time of the suicide, leaving it beside the body as evidence that the act is not impetuous or coerced. The form also requests that, if the person is discovered before the suicide is complete, no rescue measures be undertaken. Because assisting suicide is not illegal in Germany (provided the person is competent and in control of his or her own will, and thus not already unconscious), there has been no legal risk for family members, the *Sterbebegleiter,* or others in reporting information about the methods and effectiveness of suicide attempts, and, at least in the past, the DGHS has encouraged its network of regional bureaus, located in major cities throughout the country, to facilitate feedback. On this basis it has regularly updated and revised the drug information provided. There has been no legal risk in remaining with the patient to assist him or her at the bedside—that is, at least until recent legal threats.

Open, legal assistance in suicide has been supported by a feature of the German language that makes it possible to conceptualize it in a comparatively benign way. While English, French, Spanish, and many other languages have just a single primary word for suicide, German has four: *Selbstmord, Selbsttötung, Suizid,* and *Freitod,* of which the latter has comparatively positive, even somewhat heroic connotations.[23] Thus German speakers can think about the deliberate termination of their lives in a linguistic way not easily available to speakers of other languages. The negatively rooted term *Selbstmord* ("self-murder") can be avoided; the comparatively neutral terms *Selbsttötung* ("self-killing") and *Suizid* ("suicide") can be used, and the positively rooted term *Freitod* ("free death") can be reinforced. The DGHS has frequently used *Freitod* rather than German's other, more negative terms to describe the practice with which it provides assistance.

No reliable figures are available about the number of suicides with which the DGHS has assisted, and, as in the Netherlands and Oregon, the actual frequency of directly assisted death is probably small: most Germans who die as a result of medical decision making, like most Dutch and most Americans, die as treatment is withheld or withdrawn or as opiates are administered in doses that foreseeably but not intentionally shorten life—that is, by being "allowed to die." Yet it is fair to say, both because of the legal differences and the different conceptual horizons of German-speakers, that the option of self-produced death outside the medical system is more clearly open in Germany than it has been in the Netherlands or the United States.

In recent years, the DGHS has decreased its emphasis on suicide, now thinking of it as a "last resort" when pain control is inadequate—and turned much of its attention to the development of other measures for protecting the rights of the terminally ill, measures already available in many other countries. It distributes newly legalized advance directives, including living wills and durable powers of attorney, as well as organ-donation documents. It provides information about pain control, palliative care, and Hospice. It offers information about suicide prevention. Yet, despite various legal threats, it remains steadfast in defense of the terminally ill patient's right to self-determination, including the right to suicide, and continues to be supportive of patients who make this choice.

To be sure, assisted suicide is not the only option open to terminally ill patients in Germany, and the choice may be infrequent. Reported suicide rates in Germany are only moderately higher than in the Netherlands or the United States, though there is reason to think that terminal-illness suicides in all countries are often reported as deaths from the underlying disease. Although there is political pressure from right-to-die organizations to change the law to permit voluntary active euthanasia in the way understood in the Netherlands, Germany is also seeing increasing emphasis on help in dying, like that offered by Hospice, that does not involve direct termination. Whatever the pressures, the DGHS is a conspicuous, widely known organization, and many Germans appear to be aware that assisted suicide is available and not illegal even if they do not use its services.

Objections to the Three Models of Dying

In response to the dilemmas raised by the new circumstances of death, in which the majority of people in the advanced industrial nations die after an extended period of terminal deterioration, different countries develop different practices. The United States, with the sole exception of Oregon, legally permits only withholding and withdrawal of treatment, "double effect" uses of high doses of opiates, and terminal sedation, all conceived of as "allowing to die." The Netherlands permits these but also permits voluntary active euthanasia and physician-assisted suicide. Germany rejects physician-performed euthanasia but, at least until recent legal threats, permits assisted suicide not assisted by a physician. These three serve as the principal types or models of response to end-of-life dilemmas in the developed world. To be sure, all of these practices are currently undergoing evolution, and in some ways they are becoming more alike: Germany is paying new attention to the rights of patients to execute advance directives and thus to have treatment withheld or withdrawn, and public surveys reveal considerable support for euthanasia in the Dutch sense, voluntary active aid-in-dying under careful controls. In the Netherlands, a 1995 policy statement of the Royal Dutch Medical Association expressed a careful preference for physician-assisted suicide over euthanasia, urging that physicians encourage patients who request euthanasia to administer the lethal dose themselves as a further protection for voluntary choice. And, in the United States, the Supreme Court's 1997 ruling that there is no constitutional right to physician-assisted suicide has been understood to countenance the emergence of a "laboratory of the states" in which individual states, following the example of Oregon, may in the future move to legalize physician-assisted suicide, though as of this writing no such further measures have yet succeeded. An attempt by U.S. Attorney General John Ashcroft to reinterpret the Controlled Substances Act to prohibit the use of scheduled drugs for the purpose of causing death and thus undercut Oregon's statute was rejected at the appellate level in 2004, though his further appeal may take the issue to the U.S. Supreme Court. Nevertheless, among these three countries that serve as the principal models of approaches to dying, there remain substantial differences, and while there are ethical and practical advantages to each approach, each approach also raises serious moral objections.

Objections to the German Practice

German law does not prohibit assisting suicide, but postwar German culture and the German physicians' code of ethics discourages physicians from taking an active role in causing death. This gives rise to distinctive moral problems. For one thing, if the physician is not permitted to assist in his or her patient's suicide, there may be little professional help or review provided for the patient's choice about suicide. If patients make such choices essentially outside the medical establishment, medical professionals may not be a position to detect or treat impaired judgment on the part of the patient, especially judgment impaired by depression. Similarly, if the patient must commit suicide assisted only by persons outside the medical profession, there are risks that the patient's diagnosis and prognosis will be inadequately confirmed, that the means chosen for suicide will be unreliable or inappropriately used, that the means used for suicide will fall into the hands of other persons, and that the patient will fail to recognize or be able to resist intrafamilial pressures and manipulation. While it now makes efforts to counter most of these objections, even the DGHS itself has been accused in the past of promoting rather than simply supporting choices of suicide. Finally, as the DGHS now emphasizes, assistance in suicide can be a freely chosen option only in a legal context that also protects the many other choices a patient may make—declining treatment, executing advance directives, seeking Hospice care—about how his or her life shall end.

Objections to the Dutch Practice

The Dutch practice of physician-performed active voluntary euthanasia and physician-assisted suicide also raises a number of ethical issues, many of which have been discussed vigorously both in the Dutch press and in commentary on the Dutch practices from abroad. For one thing, it is sometimes said that the availability of physician-assisted dying creates a disincentive for providing good terminal care. There is no evidence that this is the case; on the contrary, Peter Admiraal, the anesthesiologist who has been perhaps the Netherlands' most vocal defender of voluntary active euthanasia, insists that pain should rarely or never be the occasion for euthanasia, as pain (in contrast to suffering) is comparatively easily treated.[24] In fact, pain is the primary reason for the request in only about 5% of cases. Instead, it is a refusal to endure the final stages of deterioration, both mental and physical, that primarily motivates the majority of requests.

It is also sometimes said that active euthanasia violates the Hippocratic oath. The original Greek version of the oath does prohibit the physician from giving a deadly drug, even when asked for it; but the original version also prohibits the physician from performing surgery and from taking fees for teaching medicine, neither of which prohibitions has survived into contemporary medical practice. At issue is whether deliberately causing the death of one's patient—killing one's patient, some claim—can ever be part of the physician's role. "Doctors must not kill," opponents insist,[25] but Dutch physicians often say that they see performing euthanasia—where it is genuinely requested by the patient and nothing else can be done to relieve the patient's condition—as part of their duty to the patient, not as a violation of it. As the 1995 nationwide report commented, "a large majority of Dutch physicians consider euthanasia an exceptional but accepted part of medical practice."[26] Some Dutch do worry, however, that too many requests for euthanasia or assistance in suicide are refused—only about ⅓ of explicit requests are actually honored. One well-known Dutch commentator points to another, seemingly contrary concern: that some requests are made too early in a terminal course, even shortly after diagnosis, when with good palliative care the patient could live a substantial amount of time longer.[27] However, these are concerns about how euthanasia and physician-assisted suicide are practiced, not about whether they should be legal at all.

The Dutch are also often said to be a risk of starting down the slippery slope, that is, that the practice of voluntary active euthanasia for patients who meet the criteria will erode into practicing less-than-voluntary euthanasia on patients whose problems are not irremediable and perhaps by gradual degrees will develop into terminating the lives of people who are elderly, chronically ill, handicapped, mentally retarded, or otherwise regarded as undesirable. This risk is often expressed in vivid claims of widespread fear and wholesale slaughter—claims based on misinterpretation of the 1,000 cases of life-ending treatment without explicit, current request, claims that are often repeated in the right-to-life press in both the Netherlands and the United States. Work now in progress on the impact of legalized physician-assisted dying in the Netherlands and Oregon shows that these claims are simply not true: except for patients with AIDS, the rates of assisted dying show no evidence of disparate impact on ten groups of potentially vulnerable patients: the elderly, women, the uninsured (not applicable in the Netherlands, where all are insured), people with low educational status, the poor, racial minorities (except Asians in Oregon; data not available in the Netherlands), people with physical disabilities or chronic illness, mature minors, and people with psychiatric illness.[28] However, it is true that in recent years the Dutch have begun to agonize over the problems of the incompetent patient, the mentally ill patient, the newborn with serious deficits, and other patients who cannot make voluntary choices, though these are largely understood as issues about withholding or withdrawing treatment, not about direct termination.[29]

What is not often understood is that this new and acutely painful area of reflection for the Dutch—withholding and withdrawing treatment from incompetent patients—has already led in the United States to the emergence of a vast, highly developed body of law: namely, the long series of cases beginning with *Quinlan* and culminating in *Cruzan*. Americans have been discussing these issues for a long time and have developed a broad set of practices that are regarded as routine in withholding and withdrawing treatment from persons who are no longer or never were competent. The Dutch see Americans as much further out on the slippery slope than they are because Americans have already become accustomed to second-party choices that result in death for other people. Issues involving second-party choices are painful to the Dutch in a way they are not to Americans precisely because *voluntariness* is so central in the Dutch understanding of choices about dying. Concomitantly, the Dutch see the Americans' squeamishness about first-party choices—voluntary euthanasia, assisted suicide—as evidence that we are not genuinely committed to recognizing voluntary choice after all. For this reason, many Dutch commentators believe that the Americans are at a much greater risk of sliding down the slippery slope into involuntary killing than they are.

Objections to the American Practice

The German, Dutch, and American practices all occur within similar conditions—in industrialized nations with highly developed medical systems where a majority of the population die of illnesses exhibiting characteristically extended downhill courses—but the issues raised by the American response to this situation—relying on withholding and withdrawal of treatment—may be even more disturbing than those of the Dutch or the Germans. We Americans often assume that our approach is "safer" because, except in Oregon, it involves only letting someone die, not killing them; but it, too, raises very troubling questions.

The first of these issues is a function of the fact that withdrawing and especially withholding treatment are typically less conspicuous, less pronounced, less evident kinds of actions than direct killing, even though they can equally well lead to death. Decisions about nontreatment have an invisibility that decisions about directly causing death do not have, even though they may have the same result; hence there is a much wider range of occasions in which such decisions can be made. One can decline to treat a patient in many different ways, at many different times—by not providing oxygen, by not instituting dialysis, by not correcting electrolyte imbalances, and so on—all of which will cause the patient's death. Open medical killing also brings about death but is much more overt and conspicuous. Consequently, letting die offers many fewer protections. In contrast to the standard slippery-slope argument, which sees killing as riskier than letting die, the more realistic slippery-slope argument warns that because our culture relies primarily on decisions about nontreatment and practices like terminal sedation construed as "allowing to die," grave decisions about living or dying are not as open to scrutiny as they are under more direct life-terminating practices, hence are more open to abuse. Indeed, in the view of one influential commentator, the Supreme Court's 1997 decision in effect legalized active euthanasia, voluntary and nonvoluntary, in the form of terminal sedation, even as it rejected physician-assisted suicide.[30]

Second, reliance on withholding and withdrawal of treatment invites rationing in an extremely strong way, in part because of the comparative invisibility of these decisions. When a health-care provider does not offer a specific sort of care, it is not always possible to discern the motivation; the line between believing that it would not provide benefit to the patient and that it would not provide benefit worth the investment of resources in the patient can be very thin. This is a particular problem where health-care financing is decentralized, profit-oriented, and nonuniversal, as in the United States, and where rationing decisions without benefit of principle are not always available for easy review.

Third, relying on withholding and withdrawal of treatment can often be cruel. Even with Hospice or with skilled palliative care, it requires that the patient who is dying from one of the diseases that exhibits a characteristic extended, downhill course (as the majority of patients in the developed world all do) must, in effect, wait to die until the absence of a certain treatment will cause death. For instance, the cancer patient who forgoes chemotherapy or surgery does not simply die from this choice; he or she continues to endure the downhill course of the cancer until the tumor finally destroys some crucial bodily function or organ. The patient with ALS who decides in advance to decline respiratory support does not die at the time this choice is made but continues to endure increasing paralysis until breathing is impaired and suffocation occurs. Of course, attempts are made to try to ameliorate these situations by administering pain medication or symptom control at the time treatment is withheld—for instance, by using opiates and paralytics as a respirator is withdrawn—but these are all ways of disguising the fact that we are letting the disease kill the patient rather than directly bringing about death. But the ways diseases kill people can be far more cruel than the ways physicians kill patients when performing euthanasia or assisting in suicide.

End-of-Life Practices in Other Countries

In most of the developed world dying looks much the same. As in the United States, the Netherlands, and Germany, the other industrialized nations also have sophisticated medical establishments, enjoy extended life expectancies, and find themselves in the fourth stage of the epidemiological transition, in which the majority of their populations die of diseases with extended downhill courses. Dying takes place in much the same way in all these countries, though the exact frequency of withholding and withdrawing treatment, of double-effect use of opiates, and euthanasia and physician-assisted suicide varies among them. Indeed, new data is rapidly coming to light.

In Australia, a replication of the Remmelink Commission study originally performed in the Netherlands found that of deaths in Australia that involved a medical end-of-life decision, 28.6% involved withholding or withdrawing treatment; 30.9% involved the use of opiates under the principle of double effect, and 1.8% involved voluntary active euthanasia (including 0.1% physician-assisted suicide), though neither are legal.[31] But the study also found—this is the figure that produced considerable surprise—that some 3.5% of deaths involved termination of the patient's life without the patient's concurrent explicit request. This figure is five times as high as that in the Netherlands. In slightly more than a third of these cases (38%), there was some discussion with the patient, though not an explicit request for death to be hastened, and in virtually all of the rest, the doctor did not consider the patient competent or capable of making such a decision. In 0.5% of all deaths involving medical end-of-life decisions, doctors did not discuss the choice of hastening of death with the patient because they thought it was "clearly the best one for the patient" or that "discussion would have done more harm than good."[32]

A 2003 study of six European countries—Belgium, Denmark, Italy, the Netherlands, Sweden, and Switzerland—found that in all countries studied, about a third of deaths are sudden and unexpected; among the other two-thirds, the frequency of death following end-of-life decisions ranged from 23% in Italy to 51% in Switzerland. "Double-effect" deaths and direct termination without explicit current request were found everywhere. However, patients and relatives were more likely to be involved in decisionmaking where assistance in dying is legal and the frequency comparatively high—Switzerland and the Netherlands—and while rates of voluntary euthanasia were highest in the Netherlands, rates of euthanasia without current, explicit consent were higher in all five other countries. Rates of physician-assisted suicide were highest in Switzerland (0.36% of all deaths); 92% of such deaths involved the participation of a right-to-die organization.[33]

End-of-life practices in these and other developed countries tend to follow one of the three models explored here. For example, Canada's practices are much like those of the United States, in that it relies on withholding and withdrawing treatment and other forms of allowing to die, but, in the 1993 case, *Rodriquez v. British Columbia,* the Supreme Court of Canada narrowly rejected physician-assisted suicide. Australia's Northern Territory briefly legalized assisted dying in 1997, but the law was overturned after just four cases. The United Kingdom, the birthplace of the Hospice movement, stresses palliative care but also rejects physician-assisted suicide and active euthanasia. After the British courts rejected the poignant request of ALS patient Diane Pretty to be allowed to receive assistance in dying from her husband, she then traveled to Strasbourg to the European Court of Human Rights; early in 2002 it ruled that her human rights were not being violated and refused her request; she died not long thereafter. Late in 2001, Belgium legalized active euthanasia but not physician-assisted suicide; despite the latter, Belgium's law is patterned fairly closely after the Dutch law.

Switzerland has been particularly active in right-to-die issues. Like that of Germany, Switzerland's law does not criminalize assisted suicide, but unlike Germany, Switzerland does not impose a duty to rescue that makes medical assistance in suicide difficult. Rather, assisted suicide is not illegal if done without self-interest. Switzerland now has at least four right-to-die organizations, including Exit Deutsche Schweiz, Exit International, and Dignitas—in part analogues of Oregon's Compassion in Dying and the "Caring Friends" program of the Hemlock Society (now End-of-Life Choices)—and Germany's DGHS, that provide information, counseling, instruction, and personal guidance, as well as other support to terminally ill patients who choose suicide—or, as it is usually called in German-speaking Switzerland, where this is most common, *Freitod.* However, the Swiss groups are also able to provide such patients with an accompaniment team that consults with the patient to make sure that the choice of suicide is voluntary, secures a prescription from a physician for the lethal medication, and will deliver it to the person at a preappointed time. They also maintain "safe houses" where a person can go to die. These organizations encourage family members to be present when the patient takes the drug, if he or she still wants to use it, and Dignitas operates a safe house for patients traveling from abroad for this purpose. In general, the Swiss organizations provide extensive help to the patient who chooses this way of dying, though in keeping with Swiss law, they all insist that the patient take the drug himself or herself, either orally or (in an alternative permitted since 1997), through an intravenous line or feeding tube.[34] In Switzerland, as in Germany, assisted suicide is legal, but euthanasia is not. In 2002, about 500 people, approximately 0.4% of the 60,000 people in German-speaking Switzerland who died, died by assisted suicide.[35] Terminally ill Germans, Britons, and others now often travel to Switzerland to end their lives.

In contrast, practices in less developed countries look very, very different. In these countries, especially the least developed, background circumstances are different: life spans are significantly shorter, health-care systems are only primitively equipped and grossly underfunded, and many societies have not passed through to the fourth stage of the epidemiologic transition: in these countries, people die earlier, they are more likely to die of infectious and parasitic disease, including AIDS, and degenerative disease is more likely to be interrupted early by death from pneumonia, sepsis, malnutrition, and other factors in what would otherwise have been a long downhill course. Dying in the poorer countries continues to be different from dying in the richer countries, and the underlying ethical problem in the richer countries—what practices concerning the end of life to adopt when the majority of a population dies of late-life degenerative diseases with long downhill courses—is far less applicable in the less developed parts of the world.

The Problem: A Choice of Cultures

In the developed world, we see three sorts of models in the three countries just examined in detail. While much of medical practice in them is similar, they do

62   DILEMMAS ABOUT DYING

offer three quite different basic options in approaching death. All three of these options generate moral problems; none of them, nor any others we might devise, is free of moral difficulty. The question, then, is this: for a given society, which practices about dying are, morally and practically speaking, best?

It is not possible to answer this question in a less-than-ideal world without attention to the specific characteristics and deficiencies of the society in question. In asking which of these practices is best, we must ask which is best *for us.* That we currently employ one set of these options rather than others does not prove that it is best for us; the question is whether practices developed in other cultures or those not yet widespread in any culture would be better for our own culture than that which has so far developed here. Thus, it is necessary to consider the differences between our own society and these other societies in the developed world that have real bearing on which model of approach to dying we ought to adopt. This question can be asked by residents of any country or culture: which model of dying is best *for us?* I have been addressing this question from the point of view of an American, but the question could be asked by any member of any culture, anywhere.

First, notice that different cultures exhibit different degrees of closeness between physicians and patients—different patterns of contact and involvement. The German physician is sometimes said to be more distant and more authoritarian than the American physician; on the other hand, the Dutch physician is often said to be closer to his or her patients than either the American or the German physician. In the Netherlands, basic primary care is provided by the *huisarts,* the general practitioner or family physician, who typically lives in the neighborhood, makes house calls frequently, and maintains an office in his or her own home. This physician usually also provides care for the other members of the patient's family and will remain the family's physician throughout his or her practice. Thus, the patient for whom euthanasia becomes an issue—say, the terminal cancer patient who has been hospitalized in the past but who has returned home to die—will be cared for by the trusted family physician on a regular basis. Indeed, for a patient in severe distress, the physician, supported by the visiting nurse, may make house calls as often as once a day, twice a day, or even more frequently (after all, the physician's office is right in the neighborhood) and is in continuous contact with the family. In contrast, the traditional American institution of the family doctor who makes house calls has largely become a thing of the past, and although some patients who die at home have access to hospice services and receive house calls from their long-term physician, many have no such long-term care and receive most of it from staff at a clinic or from house staff rotating through the services of a hospital. Most Americans die in institutions, including hospitals and nursing homes; in the Netherlands, in contrast, the majority of people die at home. The degree of continuing contact that the patient can have with a familiar, trusted physician and the degree of institutionalization clearly influence the nature of the patient's dying and also play a role in whether physician-performed active euthanasia, assisted suicide, and/ or withholding and withdrawing treatment is appropriate.

Second, the United States has a much more volatile legal climate than either the Netherlands or Germany; its medical system is highly litigious, much more so than that of any other country in the world. Fears of malpractice actions or criminal prosecution color much of what physicians do in managing the dying of their patients. Americans also tend to develop public policy through court decisions and to assume that the existence of a policy puts an end to any moral issue. A delicate legal and moral balance over the issue of euthanasia, as has been the case in the Netherlands throughout the time it was understood as *gedoogd,* tolerated but not fully legal, would hardly be possible here.

Third, we in the United States have a very different financial climate in which to do our dying. Both the Netherlands and Germany, as well as virtually every other industrialized nation, have systems of national health insurance or national health care. Thus the patient is not directly responsible for the costs of treatment, and consequently the patient's choices about terminal care and/or euthanasia need not take personal financial considerations into account. Even for the patient who does have health insurance in the United States, many kinds of services are not covered, whereas the national health care or health insurance programs of many other countries provide multiple relevant services, including at-home physician care, home nursing care, home respite care, care in a nursing home or other long-term facility, dietician care, rehabilitation care, physical therapy, psychological counseling, and so on. The patient in the United States needs to attend to the financial aspects of dying in a way that patients in many other countries do not, and in this country both the patient's choices and the recommendations of the physician are very often shaped by financial considerations.

There are many other differences between the United States on the one hand and the Netherlands and Germany, with their different options for dying, on the other, including differences in degrees of paternalism in the medical establishment, in racism, sexism, and ageism in the general culture, and in awareness of a problematic historical past, especially Nazism. All of these cultural, institutional, social, and legal differences influence the appropriateness or inappropriateness of practices such as active euthanasia and assisted suicide. For instance, the Netherlands' tradition of close physician-patient contact, its comparative absence of malpractice-motivated medicine, and its provision of comprehensive health insurance, together with its comparative lack of racism and ageism and its experience in resistance to Nazism, suggest that this culture is able to permit the practice of voluntary active euthanasia, performed by physicians, as well as physician-assisted suicide, without risking abuse. On the other hand, it is sometimes said that Germany still does not trust its physicians, remembering the example of Nazi experimentation, and, given a comparatively authoritarian medical climate in which the contact between physician and patient is quite distanced, the population could not be comfortable with the practice of physician-performed active euthanasia or physician-assisted suicide. There, only a wholly patient-controlled response to terminal situations, as in non-physician-assisted suicide, is a reasonable and prudent practice.

But what about the United States? This is a country where (1) sustained contact with a personal physician has been decreasing, (2) the risk of malpractice action is perceived as substantial, (3) much medical care is not insured, (4) many medical decisions are financial decisions as well, (5) racism remains high, with racial and ethnic minorities tending to receive lower quality health care,[36] and (6) the public has not experienced direct contact with Nazism or similar totalitarian movements. Thus, the United States is in many respects an untrustworthy candidate for practicing active euthanasia. Given the pressures on individuals in an often atomized society, encouraging solo suicide, assisted if at all only by nonprofessionals, might well be open to considerable abuse too.

However, there are several additional differences between the United States and both the Netherlands and Germany that may seem peculiarly relevant here. First, American culture is more confrontational than many others, including Dutch culture. While the Netherlands prides itself rightly on a long tradition of rational discussion of public issues and on toleration of others' views and practices, the United States (and to some degree also Germany) tends to develop highly partisan, moralizing oppositional groups, especially over social issues like abortion. In general, this is a disadvantage, but in the case of euthanasia it may serve to alert the public to issues and possibilities it might not otherwise consider, especially the risks of abuse. Here the role of religious groups may be particularly strong, since in discouraging or prohibiting suicide and euthanasia (as many, though by no means all, religious groups do), they may invite their members to reinspect the reasons for such choices and encourage families, physicians, and health-care institutions to provide adequate, humane alternatives.

Second, though this may at first seem to be not only a peculiar but a trivial difference, it is Americans who are particularly given to self-analysis. This tendency not only is evident in the United States' high rate of utilization of counseling services, including religious counseling, psychological counseling, and psychiatry, but also is more clearly evident in its popular culture: its diet of soap operas, situation comedies, pop psychology books, and reality shows. It is here that the ordinary American absorbs models for analyzing his or her personal relationships and individual psychological characteristics. While, of course, things are changing rapidly and America's cultural tastes are widely exported, the fact remains that the ordinary American's cultural diet contains more in the way of professional and do-it-yourself amateur psychology and self-analysis than anyone else's. This long tradition of self-analysis may put Americans in a better position for certain kinds of end-of-life practices than many other cultures. Despite whatever other deficiencies U.S. society has, we live in a culture that encourages us to inspect our own motives, anticipate the impact of our actions on others, and scrutinize our own relationships with others, including our physicians. This disposition is of importance in euthanasia and assisted-suicide contexts because these are the kinds of fundamental choices about which one may have somewhat mixed motives, be subject to various interpersonal and situational pressures, and so on. If the voluntary character of choices about one's own dying is to be protected, it may be a good thing to inhabit a culture in which self-inspection of one's own mental habits and motives, not to mention those of one's family, physician, and others who might affect one's choices, is culturally encouraged. Counseling specifically addressed to end-of-life choices is not yet easily or openly available, especially if physician-assisted suicide is at issue—though some groups like Compassion in Dying and End-of-Life Choices (which merged in 2004 but later experienced some fission) now provide it—but I believe it will become more frequent in the future as people facing terminal illnesses characterized by long downhill, deteriorative courses consider how they want to die.

Finally, the United States population, varied as it is, is characterized by a kind of do-it-yourself ethic, an ethic that devalues reliance on others and encourages individual initiative and responsibility. (To be sure, this ethic is little in evidence in the series of court cases from *Quinlan* to *Cruzan*, but these were all cases about patients who had become or always were incapable of decisionmaking.) This ethic seems to be coupled with a sort of resistance to authority that perhaps also is basic to the American temperament, even in all its diversity. If this is really the case, Americans might be especially well served by end-of-life practices that emphasize self-reliance and resistance to authority.

These, of course, are mere conjectures about features of American culture relevant to the practice of euthanasia or assisted suicide. These are the features that one would want to reinforce should these practices become general, in part to minimize the effects of the negative influences. But, of course, these positive features will differ from one country and culture to another, just as the negative features do. In each country, a different architecture of antecedent assumptions and cultural features develops around end-of-life issues, and in each country the practices of euthanasia and assisted or physician-assisted suicide, if they are to be free from abuse, must be adapted to the culture in which they take place.

What, then, is appropriate for the United States' own cultural situation? Physician-performed euthanasia, even if not in itself morally wrong, is morally jeopardized where legal, time-related, and especially financial pressures on both patients and physicians are severe; thus, it is morally problematic in our culture in a way that it is not in the Netherlands. Solo suicide outside the institution of medicine (as in Germany) may be problematic in a country (like the United States) that has an increasingly alienated population, offers deteriorating and uneven social services, is increasingly racist and classist, and in other ways imposes unusual pressures on individuals, despite opportunities for self-analysis. Reliance only on withholding and withdrawing treatment and allowing to die (as in the United States) can be cruel, and its comparative invisibility invites erosion under cost-containment and other pressures. These are the three principal alternatives we have considered, but none of them seems wholly suited to our actual situation for dealing with the new fact that most of us die of extended-decline, deteriorative diseases.

Perhaps, however, there is one that would best suit the United States, certainly better than its current reliance on allowing to die, and better than the Netherlands' more direct physician involvement or Germany's practices entirely outside medicine. The "arm's-length" model of physician-assisted suicide—permitting physicians to supply their terminally ill patients who request it with the means for ending their own lives (as has become legal in Oregon)—still grants physicians some control over the circumstances in which this can happen (for example, only when the prognosis is genuinely grim and the alternatives for symptom control are poor) but leaves the fundamental decision about whether to use these means to the patient alone. It is up to the patient then—the independent, confrontational, self-analyzing, do-it-yourself, authority-resisting patient—and his or her advisors, including family members, clergy, the physician, and other health-care providers, to be clear about whether he or she really wants to use these means or not. Thus,

66   DILEMMAS ABOUT DYING

the physician is involved but not directly, and it is the patient's decision, although the patient is not making it alone. Thus also it is the patient who performs the action of bringing his or her own life to a close, though where the patient is physically incapable of doing so or where the process goes awry the physician must be allowed to intercede. We live in an imperfect world, but of the alternatives for facing death—which we all eventually must—I think that the practice of permitting this somewhat distanced though still medically supported form of physician-assisted suicide is the one most nearly suited to the current state of our own flawed society. This is a model not yet central in any of the three countries examined here—the Netherlands, Germany, or (except in Oregon) the United States, or any of the other industrialized nations with related practices—but it is the one, I think, that suits us best.

Notes

From *The Journal of Pain and Symptom Management* 6(5), July 1991, pp. 298–305. © 1991 U.S. Cancer Pain Relief Committee. Revised and updated multiple times by the author, most recently in March 2004 for Bruce N. Waller, ed., *Consider Ethics: Theory, Readings, and Contemporary Issues*, Pearson Education and Longman Publishing, forthcoming 2004. Updated again in June 2004.

1. S. J. Olshansky and A. B. Ault, "The Fourth Stage of the Epidemiological Transition: The Age of Delayed Degenerative Diseases," *Milbank Memorial Fund Quarterly Health and Society* 64 (1986): 355–91.

2. In a study of end-of-life decisionmaking in six European countries, about one-third of all deaths were found to have happened suddenly and unexpectedly, ranging from 29 percent in Italy to 34 percent in Belgium. See Agnes van der Heide, Luc Deliens, Karin Faisst, Tore Nilstun, Michael Norup, Eugenio Paci, Gerrit van der Wal, Paul J. van der Maas, on behalf of the EURELD consortium, "End-of-life decision-making in six European countries: Descriptive study," *Lancet* 361 (August 2, 2003), 345–50, table 2, p. 347.

3. S. Miles and C. Gomez, *Protocols for Elective Use of Life-Sustaining Treatment* (New York: Springer-Verlag, 1988).

4. C. L. Sprung, "Changing Attitudes and Practices in Forgoing Life-Sustaining Treatments," *JAMA* 262 (1990): 2213.

5. T. J. Prendergast and J.M. Luce, "Increasing Incidence of Withholding and Withdrawal of Life Support from the Critically Ill," *American Journal of Respiratory and Critical Care Medicine* 155, 1 (January 1997): 1–2.

6. M. B. Hamel, J. M. Teno, L. Goldman, J. Lynn, R. B. Davis, A. N. Galanos, N. Desbiens, A. F. Connors Jr., N. Wenger, R. S. Phillips. (SUPPORT investigators), "Patient Age and Decisions to Withhold Life-Sustaining Treatments from Seriously Ill, Hospitalized Adults," *Annals of Internal Medicine* 130, 2 (January 19, 1999): 116–25.

7. John M. Luce, "Withholding and Withdrawal of Life Support: Ethical, Legal, and Clinical Aspects," *New Horizons* 5, 1 (February 1997): 30–7.

8. *New York Times,* July 23, 1990, A13.

9. Accounts of the use of Oregon's Death with Dignity Act (Measure 16) begin with A. E. Chin, K. Hedberg, G. K. Higginson, and D. W. Fleming, "Legalized Physician-Assisted Suicide in Oregon—The First Year's Experience," *New England Journal of Medicine* 340 (1999): 577–83, and are updated annually in this journal and at the website of the Oregon Department of Human Services. The 171 cases of legal physician-assisted suicide that have

taken place in the first six years since it became legal in Oregon represent about one-tenth of one percent of the total deaths in Oregon.

10. For a fuller account, see my remarks in "A Dozen Caveats Concerning the Discussion of Euthanasia in the Netherlands," in my book *The Least Worst Death: Essays in Bioethics on the End of Life* (New York: Oxford University Press, 1994), 130–44; John Griffiths, Alex Bood, and Helen Weyers, *Euthanasia and Law in the Netherlands* (Amsterdam: Amsterdam University Press, 1998), and the three nationwide studies of end-of-life decisionmaking mentioned hereafter.

11. P. J. van der Maas, J.J.M. van Delden, and L. Pijnenborg, "Euthanasia and Other Medical Decisions Concerning the End of Life," published in full in English as a special issue of *Health Policy,* 22, 1–2 (1992), and, with C.W.N. Looman, in summary in *Lancet* 338 (1991): 669–74.

12. G. van der Wal, J.T.M. van Eijk, H.J.J. Leenen, and C. Spreeuwenberg, "Euthanasie en hulp bij zelfdoding door artsen in de thuissituatie," pts. 1 and 2, *Nederlands Tijdschrift voor Geneesekunde* 135 (1991): 1593–8, 1599–1604.

13. P. J. van der Maas, G. van der Wal, "Euthanasia, Physician-Assisted Suicide, and Other Medical Practices Involving the End of Life in the Netherlands, 1990–1995," *New England Journal of Medicine* 335 (1996): 1699–1705.

14. Bregje D. Onwuteaka-Philipsen, Agnes van der Heide, Dirk Koper, Ingeborg Keij-Deerenberg, Judith A. C. Rietjens, Mette Rurup, Astrid M. Vrakking, Jean Jacques Georges, Martien T. Muller, Gerrit van der Wal, and Paul J. van der Maas, "Euthanasia and Other End-of-Life Decisions in the Netherlands in 1990, 1995, and 2001," *Lancet* 362, (2003): 395–9. A full account is available in Gerrit van der Wal, Agnes van der Heide, Bregje D. Onwuteaka-Philipsen, Paul. J. van der Maas, *Medische besluitvorming aan het einde van het leven: De praktijk en de toetsingsprocedure euthanasie* (Utrecht: De Tijdstroom, 2003).

15. L. Pijnenborg, P.J.van der Maas, J.J.M. van Delden, C.W.N. Looman, "Life Terminating Acts without Explicit Request of Patient," *Lancet* 341 (1993): 1196–9.

16. Onwuteaka-Philipsen et al., "Euthanasia and Other End-of Life Decisions," 2003. These figures are an average of the results of the two principal parts of the 1990, 1995, and 2001 nationwide studies, the interview study, and the death-certificate study.

17. G. van der Wal, P. J. van der Maas, J. M. Bosma, B. D. Onwuteaka-Philipsen, D. L. Willems, I. Haverkate, P. J. Kostense, "Evaluation of the Notification Procedure for Physician-Assisted Death in the Netherlands," *New England Journal of Medicine* 335 (1996): 1706–11.

18. Van der Maas et al., "Euthanasia and other Medical Decisions Concerning the End of Life," 673.

19. Van der Maas et al., "Euthanasia, Physician-Assisted Suicide, and Other Medical Practices Involving the End of Life in the Netherlands, 1990–1995," p. 1705.

20. Margaret P. Battin, Agnes van der Heide, Linda Ganzini, and Gerrit van der Wal, "Legalized Physician-Assisted Dying in Oregon and the Netherlands: The Impact on Patients in Vulnerable Groups," in preparation.

21. Kurt Schobert, "Physician-Assisted Suicide in Germany and Switzerland, with Focus on Some Developments in Recent Years," manuscript in preparation, citing "Grundsätze der Bundesärztekammer zur ärztlichen Sterbebegleitung," in *Ethik in der Medizin,* ed., Urban Wiesing (Stuttgart: Gustav Fischer, 2002), 203–8.

22. That is, it no longer sells or supplies such drugs. A scandal in 1992–93 engulfed the original founder and president of the DGHS, Hans Hennig Atrott, who had been secretly providing some members with cyanide in exchange for substantial contributions; he was convicted of violating the drug laws and tax evasion, though not charged with or convicted of assisting suicides.

23. See my "Assisted Suicide: Can We Learn from Germany?" in *The Least Worst Death,* pp. 254–70.

24. P. Admiraal, "Euthanasia in a General Hospital," paper read at the Eighth World Congress of the International Federation of Right-to-Die Societies, Maastricht, the Netherlands, June 8, 1990.

25. See the editorial "Doctors Must Not Kill," *JAMA* 259 (1988): 2139–40, signed by Willard Gaylin, Leon R. Kass, Edmund D. Pellegrino, and Mark Siegler.

26. Van der Maas et al., "Euthanasia, Physician-Assisted Suicide, and Other Medical Practices," 1705.

27. Govert den Hartogh, personal communication.

28. Margaret P. Battin, Agnes van der Heide, Linda Ganzini, and Gerrit van der Wal, "Legalized Physician-Assisted Dying," in preparation.

29. H. ten Have, "Coma: Controversy and Consensus," *Newsletter of the European Society for Philosophy of Medicine and Health Care,* May 1990, 19–20.

30. David Orentlicher, "The Supreme Court and Terminal Sedation: Rejecting Assisted Suicide, Embracing Euthanasia," *Hastings Constitutional Law Quarterly* 24 (1997):947–68; see also *New England Journal of Medicine* 337 (1997): 1236–9.

31. Physician-assisted suicide was briefly legal in the Northern Territory of Australia in 1997, and four were performed before the law was overturned, but these cases did not occur during the study period.

32. Helga Kuhse, Peter Singer, Peter Baume, Malcolm Clark, and Maurice Rickard, "End-of-life Decisions in Australian Medical Practice," *Medical Journal of Australia* 166 (1997):191–6.

33. Van der Heide et al., "End-of-Life Decision-Making in Six European Countries, 345–50.

34. Georg Bosshard, Esther Ulrich, and Walter Bär, "748 Cases of Suicide Assisted by a Swiss Right-to-Die Organization," *Swiss Medical Weekly* 133 (2003): 310–7.

35. Swissinfo, June 19, 2003, citing a University of Zurich study. Available at: http:// www.swissinfo.org.

36. Institute of Medicine, *Unequal Treatment: Confronting Racial and Ethnic Disparities in Health Care* (Washington, D.C.: National Academy of Sciences, 2002).

[22]

"Culture of Life" Politics at the Bedside — The Case of Terri Schiavo

George J. Annas, J.D., M.P.H.

For the first time in the history of the United States, Congress met in a special emergency session on Sunday, March 20, to pass legislation aimed at the medical care of one patient — Terri Schiavo. President George W. Bush encouraged the legislation and flew back to Washington, D.C., from his vacation in Crawford, Texas, so that he could be on hand to sign it immediately. In a statement issued three days earlier, he said: "The case of Terri Schiavo raises complex issues. . . . Those who live at the mercy of others deserve our special care and concern. It should be our goal as a nation to build a culture of life, where all Americans are valued, welcomed, and protected — and that culture of life must extend to individuals with disabilities."[1]

The "culture of life" is a not-terribly-subtle reference to the antiabortion movement in the United States, which received significant encouragement in last year's presidential election. The movement may now view itself as strong enough to generate new laws to prevent human embryos from being created for research and to require that incompetent patients be kept alive with artificially delivered fluids and nutrition.

How did the U.S. Congress conclude that it was appropriate to attempt to reopen a case that had finally been concluded after more than seven years of litigation involving almost 20 judges? Has the country's culture changed so dramatically as to require a fundamental change in the law? Or do patients who cannot continue to live without artificially delivered fluids and nutrition pose previously unrecognized or novel questions of law and ethics?

The case of Terri Schiavo, a Florida woman who was in a persistent vegetative state and who died on March 31, was being played out as a public spectacle and a tragedy for her and her husband, Michael Schiavo. Mr. Schiavo's private feud with his wife's parents over the continued use of a feeding tube was taken to the media, the courts, the Florida legislature, Florida Governor Jeb Bush, the U.S.

Congress, and President Bush. Since Ms. Schiavo was in a medical and legal situation almost identical to those of two of the most well-known patients in medical jurisprudence, Karen Ann Quinlan and Nancy Cruzan, there must be something about cases like theirs that defies simple solutions, whether medical or legal. In this sense, the case of Terri Schiavo provides an opportunity to examine issues that most lawyers, bioethicists, and physicians believed were well settled — if not since the 1976 New Jersey Supreme Court decision in the case of Karen Quinlan, then at least since the 1990 U.S. Supreme Court decision in the case of Nancy Cruzan. Before reviewing Terri Schiavo's case, it is well worth reviewing the legal background information that was ignored by Congress and the president.

THE CASE OF KAREN QUINLAN

In 1976, the case of Karen Quinlan made international headlines when her parents sought the assistance of a judge to discontinue the use of a ventilator in their daughter, who was in a persistent vegetative state.[2] Ms. Quinlan's physicians had refused her parents' request to remove the ventilator because, they said, they feared that they might be held civilly or even criminally liable for her death. The New Jersey Supreme Court ruled that competent persons have a right to refuse life-sustaining treatment and that this right should not be lost when a person becomes incompetent. Since the court believed that the physicians were unwilling to withdraw the ventilator because of the fear of legal liability, not precepts of medical ethics, it devised a mechanism to grant the physicians prospective legal immunity for taking this action. Specifically, the New Jersey Supreme Court ruled that after a prognosis, confirmed by a hospital ethics committee, that there is "no reasonable possibility of a patient returning to a cognitive, sapient state," life-sustaining treatment can be removed and no one involved, including the physicians, can be held civilly or criminally responsible for the death.[2]

The publicity surrounding the Quinlan case motivated two independent developments: it encouraged states to enact "living will" legislation that provided legal immunity to physicians who honored patients' written "advance directives" specifying how they would want to be treated if they ever became incompetent; and it encouraged hospitals to establish ethics committees that could attempt to resolve similar treatment disputes without going to court.

THE CASE OF NANCY CRUZAN

Although *Quinlan* was widely followed, the New Jersey Supreme Court could make law only for New Jersey. When the U.S. Supreme Court decided the case of Nancy Cruzan in 1990, it made constitutional law for the entire country. Nancy Cruzan was a young woman in a persistent vegetative state caused by an accident; she was in physical circumstances essentially identical to those of Karen Quinlan, except that she was not dependent on a ventilator but rather, like Terri Schiavo, required only tube feeding to continue to live.[3] The Missouri Supreme Court had ruled that the tube feeding could be discontinued on the basis of Nancy's right of self-determination, but that only Nancy herself should be able to make this decision. Since she could not do so, tube feeding could be stopped only if those speaking for her, including her parents, could produce "clear and convincing" evidence that she would refuse tube feeding if she could speak for herself.[4]

The U.S. Supreme Court, in a five-to-four decision, agreed, saying that the state of Missouri had the authority to adopt this high standard of evidence (although no state was required to do so) because of the finality of a decision to terminate treatment.[3] In the words of the chief justice, Missouri was entitled to "err on the side of life." Six of the nine justices explicitly found that no legal distinction could be made between artificially delivered fluids and nutrition and other medical interventions, such as ventilator support; none of the other three justices found a constitutionally relevant distinction. This issue is not controversial as a matter of constitutional law: Americans have (and have always had) the legal right to refuse any medical intervention, including artificially delivered fluids and nutrition.

Supreme Court Justice Sandra Day O'Connor, in a concurring opinion (her vote decided the case), recognized that young people (such as Karen Quinlan, Nancy Cruzan, and now Terri Schiavo — all of whom were in their 20s at the time of their catastrophic injuries) do not generally put explicit treatment instructions in writing. She suggested that had Cruzan simply said something like "if I'm not able to make medical treatment decisions myself, I want my mother to make them," such a statement should be a constitutionally protected delegation of the authority to decide about her treatment.[3] O'Connor's opinion was the reason that the Cruzan case energized a movement — encouraging people to use the appropriate documents, such as health care proxy forms or assignments of durable power of attorney, to designate someone (usually called a health care proxy, or simply an agent) to make decisions for them if they are unable to make them themselves. All states authorize this delegation, and most states explicitly grant decision-making authority to a close relative — almost always to the spouse first — if the patient has not made a designation. Such laws are all to the good.

THE SCHIAVO CASE IN THE COURTS

Terri Schiavo had a cardiac arrest, perhaps because of a potassium imbalance, in 1990 (the year *Cruzan* was decided), when she was 27 years old. Until her death in 2005, she had lived in a persistent vegetative state in nursing homes, with constant vegetative care, being nourished and hydrated through tubes. In 1998, Michael Schiavo petitioned the court to decide whether to discontinue the tube feeding. Unlike *Quinlan* and *Cruzan*, however, the Schiavo case involved a family dispute: Ms. Schiavo's parents objected. A judge found that there was clear and convincing evidence that Terri Schiavo was in a permanent or persistent vegetative state and that, if she could make her own decision, she would choose to discontinue life-prolonging procedures. An appeals court affirmed the first judge's decision, and the Florida Supreme Court declined to review it.

Schiavo's parents returned to court, claiming that they had newly discovered evidence. After an additional appeal, the parents were permitted to challenge the original court findings on the basis of new evidence related to a new treatment that they believed might restore cognitive function. Five physicians were asked to examine Ms. Schiavo — two chosen by the husband, two by the parents, and one by the court. On the basis of their examinations and conclusions, the trial judge was persuad-

The NEW ENGLAND JOURNAL *of* MEDICINE

ed by the three experts who agreed that Schiavo was in a persistent vegetative state. The appeals court affirmed the original decision of the trial court judge

> Despite the irrefutable evidence that [Schiavo's] cerebral cortex has sustained irreparable injuries, we understand why a parent who had raised and nurtured a child from conception would hold out hope that some level of cognitive function remained. If Mrs. Schiavo were our own daughter, we could not hold to such faith.
>
> But in the end this case is not about the aspirations that loving parents have for their children. It is about Theresa Schiavo's right to make her own decision, independent of her parents and independent of her husband. . . . It may be unfortunate that when families cannot agree, the best forum we can offer for this private, personal decision is a public courtroom and the best decision-maker we can provide is a judge with no prior knowledge of the ward, but the law currently provides no better solution that adequately protects the interests of promoting the value of life.[5]

The Supreme Court of Florida again refused to hear an appeal.

Subsequently, the parents, with the vocal and organized support of conservative religious organizations, went to the state legislature seeking legislation requiring the reinsertion of Ms. Schiavo's feeding tube, which had been removed on the basis of the court decisions.[6,7] The legislature passed a new law (2003-418), often referred to as "Terri's Law," which gave Governor Jeb Bush the authority to order the feeding tube reinserted, and he did so. The law applied only to a patient who met the following criteria on October 15, 2003 — in other words, only to Terri Schiavo:

> (a) That patient has no written advance directive;
>
> (b) The court has found that patient to be in a persistent vegetative state;
>
> (c) That patient has had nutrition and hydration withheld; and

(d) A member of that patient's family has challenged the withholding of nutrition and hydration.

The constitutionality of this law was immediately challenged. In the fall of 2004, the Florida Supreme Court ruled that the law was unconstitutional because it violates the separation of powers — the division of the government into three branches (executive, legislative, and judicial), each with its own powers and responsibilities.[8] The doctrine states simply that no branch may encroach on the powers of another, and no branch may delegate to another branch its constitutionally assigned power. Specifically, the court held that for the legislature to pass a law that permits the executive to "interfere with the final judicial determination in a case" is "without question an invasion of the authority of the judicial branch."[8] In addition, the court found the law unconstitutional for an independent reason, because it "delegates legislative power to the governor" by giving the governor "unbridled discretion" to make a decision about a citizen's constitutional rights. In the court's words:

> If the Legislature with the assent of the Governor can do what was attempted here, the judicial branch would be subordinated to the final directive of the other branches. Also subordinated would be the rights of individuals, including the well established privacy right to self determination. . . . Vested rights could be stripped away based on popular clamor.[8]

In January 2005, the U.S. Supreme Court refused to hear an appeal brought by Governor Bush. Thereafter, the trial court judge ordered that the feeding tube be removed in 30 days (at 1 p.m., Friday, March 18) unless a higher court again intervened. The presiding judge, George W. Greer of the Pinellas County Circuit Court, was thereafter picketed and threatened with death; he has had to be accompanied by armed guards at all times.

Ms. Schiavo's parents, again with the aid of a variety of religious fundamentalist and "right to life" organizations, sought review in the appeals courts, a new statute in the state legislature, and finally, congressional intervention. Both the trial judge and the appeals courts refused to reopen the case on the basis of claims of new evidence (including the 2004 statement from Pope John Paul II regarding fluids and nutrition[9]) or the failure to appoint an independent lawyer for her at the original hearing. In Florida, the state legislature considered, and the House passed, new legislation aimed at restoring the feeding tube, but the Florida Senate — recognizing, I think, that this new legislation would be unconstitutional for the same reason as the previous legislation was — ultimately refused to approve the bill. Thereupon, an event unique in American politics occurred: after more than a week of discussion, and after formally declaring their Easter recess without action, Congress reconvened two days after the feeding tube was removed to consider emergency legislation designed to apply only to Terri Schiavo.

CONGRESS AT THE BEDSIDE

Under rules that permitted a few senators to act if no senator objected, the U.S. Senate adopted a bill entitled "For the relief of the parents of Theresa Marie Schiavo" on March 20, 2005. The House, a majority of whose members had to be present to vote, debated the same measure from 9 p.m. to midnight on the same day and passed it by a four-to-one margin shortly after midnight on March 21. The President then signed it into law. In substance, the new law (S. 686) provides that "the U.S. District Court for the Middle District of Florida shall have jurisdiction" to hear a suit "for the alleged violation of any right of Theresa Marie Schiavo under the Constitution or laws of the United States relating to the withholding or withdrawal of food, fluids, or medical treatment necessary to sustain her life." The parents "have standing" to bring the lawsuit (the federal court had previously refused to hear the case on the basis that the parents had no standing to bring it), and the court is instructed to "determine de novo any claim of a violation of any right of Theresa Marie Schiavo . . . notwithstanding any prior State court determination . . ." — that is, to pretend that no court has made any prior ruling in the case. The act is to provide no "precedent with respect to future legislation."

The brief debate on this bill in the House of Representatives (there were no hearings in either chamber and no debate at all in the U.S. Senate) was notable primarily for its uninformed and frenzied rhetoric. It was covered live on television by C-SPAN. The primary sponsor of the measure, Congressman Thomas DeLay (R-Tex.), for example, asserted that "She's not a vegetable, just handicapped like many millions of people walking around today. This has nothing to do with politics, and it's

disgusting for people to say that it does." Others echoed the sentiments of Senate majority leader and physician Bill Frist (R-Tenn.), who said that immediate action was imperative because "Terri Schiavo is being denied lifesaving fluids and nutrition as we speak."

Other physician-members of the House chimed in. Congressman Dave Weldon (R-Fla.) remarked that, on the basis of his 16 years of medical practice, he was able to conclude that Terri Schiavo is "not in a persistent vegetative state." Congressman Phil Gingrey (R-Ga.) agreed, saying "she's very much alive." Another physician, Congressman Joe Schwarz (R-Mich.), who was a head and neck surgeon for 27 years, opined that "she does have some cognitive ability" and asked, "How many other patients are there with feeding tubes? Should they be removed too?" Another physician-congressman, Tom Price (R-Ga.), thought the law was reasonable because there was "no living will in place" and the family and experts disagreed. The only physician who was troubled by Congress's public diagnosis and treatment of Terri Schiavo was James McDermott (D-Wash.), who chided his physician-colleagues for the poor medical practice of making a diagnosis without examining the patient.

Although he deferred to the medical expertise of his congressional colleagues with M.D. degrees, Congressman Barney Frank (D-Mass.) pointed out that the chamber was not filled with physicians. Frank said of the March 20 proceedings: "We're not doctors, we just play them on C-SPAN." The mantras of the debate were that in a life-or-death decision, we should err on the "side of life," that action should be taken to "prevent death by starvation" and ensure the "right to life," and that Congress should "protect the rights of disabled people."

The following day, U.S. District Court Judge James D. Whittemore issued a careful opinion denying the request of the parents for a temporary restraining order that would require the reinsertion of the feeding tube.[10] The judge concluded that the parents had failed to demonstrate "a substantial likelihood of success on the merits" of the case — a prerequisite for a temporary restraining order. Specifically, Judge Whittemore found that, as to the various due-process claims made, the case had been "exhaustively litigated"; that, throughout, all parties had been "represented by able counsel"; and that it was not clear how having an additional lawyer "appointed by the court [for Ms. Schiavo] would have reduced the risk of erroneous rulings." As to the allegation that the patient's First Amendment

The NEW ENGLAND JOURNAL *of* MEDICINE

rights to practice her religion had been violated by the state, the court held that there were no state actions involved at all, "because neither Defendant Schiavo nor Defendant Hospice are state actors."

Whittemore's decision was reasonable and consistent with settled law, and was, not suprisingly, upheld on appeal. The case of Terri Schiavo resulted in no changes in the law, nor were any good arguments made that legal changes were necessary. The religious right and congressional Republicans may nonetheless attempt to use this decision to their advantage. Despite the fact that Congress itself sent the case to federal court for determination, some Republicans have already begun to cite the ruling as yet another example of "legislating" by the courts. For they liken the action permitted — the withdrawal of a feeding tube — to unfavored activities, such as abortion and same-sex marriage, that courts have allowed to occur. All three activities, they argue, represent attacks on the "culture of life" and necessitate that the President appoint federal court judges who value life over liberty.

PROXY DECISION MAKERS, PERSISTENT VEGETATIVE STATES, AND DEATH

A vast majority of Americans would not want to be maintained in a persistent vegetative state by means of a feeding tube, like Terri Schiavo and Nancy Cruzan.[11] The intense publicity generated by this case will cause many to discuss this issue with their families and, I hope, to sign an advance directive. Such a directive, in the form of a living will or the designation of a health care proxy, would prevent court involvement in virtually all cases — although it might not have solved the problem in the Schiavo case, because the family members disagreed about Terri Schiavo's medical condition and the acceptability of removing the tube in any circumstances.

Despite the impression that may have been created by these three cases, and especially by the grandstanding in Congress, conflicts involving medical decision making for incompetent patients near the end of life are no longer primarily legal in nature, if they ever were. The law has been remarkably stable since *Quinlan* (which itself restated existing law): competent adults have the right to refuse any medical treatment, including life-sustaining treatment (which includes artificially delivered fluids and nutrition). Incompetent adults retain an interest in self-determination. Competent adults can execute an advance directive stating their wishes and designate a person to act on their behalf, and physicians

can honor these wishes. Physicians and health care agents should make treatment decisions consistent with what they believe the patient would want (the subjective standard). If the patient's desires cannot be ascertained, then treatment decisions should be based on the patient's best interests (what a reasonable person would most likely want in the same circumstances). This has, I believe, always been the law in the United States.[12]

Of course, legal forms or formalities cannot solve nonlegal problems. Decision making near the end of life is difficult and can exacerbate unresolved family feuds that then are played out at the patient's bedside and even in the media. Nonetheless, it is reasonable and responsible for all persons to designate health care agents to make treatment decisions for them when they are unable to make their own. After this recent congressional intervention, it also makes sense to specifically state one's wishes with respect to artificial fluids and hydration — and that one wants no politicians, even physician-politicians, involved in the process.

Most Americans will agree with a resolution that was overwhelmingly adopted by the California Medical Association on the same day that Congress passed the Schiavo law: "Resolved: That the California Medical Association expresses its outrage at Congress' interference with these medical decisions."

If there is disagreement between the physician and the family, or among family members, the involvement of outside experts, including consultants, ethics committees, risk managers, lawyers, and even courts, may become inevitable — at least if the patient survives long enough to permit such involvement. It is the long-lasting nature of the persistent vegetative state that results in its persistence in the courtrooms of the United States. There is (and should be) no special law regarding the refusal of treatment that is tailored to specific diseases or prognoses, and the persistent vegetative state is no exception.[13,14] Nor do feeding tubes have rights: people do. "Erring on the side of life" in this context often results in violating a person's body and human dignity in a way few would want for themselves. In such situations, erring on the side of liberty — specifically, the patient's right to decide on treatment — is more consistent with American values and our constitutional traditions. As the Massachusetts Supreme Judicial Court said in a 1977 case that raised the same legal question: "The constitutional right to privacy, as we conceive it, is an expression of the sanctity of individual free

LEGAL ISSUES IN MEDICINE

choice and self-determination as fundamental constituents of life. The value of life as so perceived is lessened not by a decision to refuse treatment, but by the failure to allow a competent human being the right of choice."[15]

From the Department of Health Law, Bioethics, and Human Rights, Boston University School of Public Health, Boston.

This article has been modified from the version that was published at www.nejm.org on March 22, 2005.

1. President's statement on Terri Schiavo. March 17, 2005. (Accessed March 31, 2005, at http://www.whitehouse.gov/news/releases/2005/03/20050317-7.html.)
2. In re Quinlan, 70 N.J.10, 355 A2d 647 (1976).
3. Cruzan v. Director, Missouri Dept. of Health, 497 U.S. 261 (1990).
4. Cruzan v. Harmon, 760 S.W.2d 408 (Mo. 1988).
5. In re Guardianship of Schiavo, 851 So. 2d 182 (Fla. 2d Dist. Ct. App. 2003).
6. Goodnough A. Victory in Florida feeding case emboldens the religious right. New York Times. October 24, 2005:A1.
7. Kirkpatrick DD, Stolberg SG. How family's cause reached the halls of Congress: networks of Christians rallied to case of Florida woman. New York Times. March 22, 2005:Al.
8. Bush v. Schiavo, 885 So.2d 321 (Fla. 2004).
9. Shannon TA, Walter JJ. Implications of the papal allocution on feeding tubes. Hastings Cent Rep 2004;34(4):18-20.
10. Schiavo ex rel. Schindler v. Schiavo, No. 8:05-CV-530-T-27TBM (M.D. Fla. Mar. 22, 2005) (slip opinion).
11. Eisenberg D. Lessons of the Schiavo battle. Time. April 4, 2005:23.
12. Annas GJ. The rights of hospital patients. New York: Discus Books, 1975:81-4.
13. *Idem.* The health care proxy and the living will. N Engl J Med 1991;324:1210-3.
14. The Multi-Society Task Force on PVS. Medical aspects of the persistent vegetative state. N Engl J Med 1994;330:1572-9. [Erratum, N Engl J Med 1995;333:130.]
15. Superintendent of Belchertown State School v. Saikewicz, 373 Mass. 728, 742, 370 N.E.2d 417 (Mass. 1977).

[23]

Death and the Value of Life*

Jeff McMahan

Among the services that philosophers have traditionally attempted to provide is the manufacture of arguments intended to show that death is not or cannot be bad for those to whom it happens. In the first section of this paper I will contend that the most influential of these arguments fails to establish the conclusions which its defenders have sought from it. I will then devote the bulk of the paper to developing an account of why it is that death can be bad for those who die. Finally, I will sketch an apparent paradox which threatens this account and conclude by proposing a way of dissolving the paradox.

I. THE EPICUREAN ARGUMENT

A. *The Existence Requirement and the Wide and Narrow Experience Requirements*

The argument I will consider derives from Epicurus.[1] Death, it is claimed, cannot be bad, or be a misfortune for the person who dies, for, when death occurs, there is no longer a subject to whom any misfortune can then be ascribed. This of course assumes, as I will assume throughout this paper, that death consists in the annihilation, or the ceasing to exist, of the person who dies.[2]

* I have been helped in writing this paper by comments on earlier drafts by Matthew Buncombe, William R. Carter, Gerald Dworkin, Dorothy Grover, Thomas Hurka, Gregory Kavka, Brian Pike, Alan Mattlage, Robert McKim, Richard Mohr, and Jan Narveson. And I am greatly indebted to David Brink, Hugh Chandler, Timothy McCarthy, Derek Parfit, and Steven Wagner for exceptionally helpful comments and discussion. For discussion both of certain aspects of the problem of death which are not addressed in this paper and of certain objections that might be raised to the arguments developed here, see chap. 1 of my book, *The Ethics of Killing* (Oxford: Basil Blackwell, 1989).

1. Epicurus, "Letter to Menoeceus," 124b–127a, in *Letters, Principal Doctrines, and Vatican Sayings*, ed. Russel M. Geer (Indianapolis: Bobbs-Merrill, 1964).

2. Strictly speaking, death is a biological phenomenon—something that happens to living organisms. Since I believe that persons are not identical with their organisms, I believe that persons can cease to exist in other ways than through death (e.g., a person will cease to exist if he loses consciousness irreversibly, and there are cases in which this is compatible with his organism's continuing to exist and even continuing to live); and, though this never in fact happens, it is in principle possible for persons to survive the deaths of their organisms. As things are, death is a sufficient condition of the ceasing to

Call this the Epicurean argument. It presupposes the following principle:

> *The Existence Requirement.*—A person can be the subject of some misfortune only if he exists at the time the misfortune occurs.[3]

The Epicurean argument should be distinguished from a similar argument which is based on a principle that Epicurus seems also to have held—namely, the principle that an event can be bad for a person only if he experiences it as bad. Call this principle the *Narrow Experience Requirement*. It implies that, while the prospect of death can be bad for a person if the anticipation of it disturbs him, death itself cannot be bad for him since, when it occurs, he will not experience it and, a fortiori, will not experience it as bad.

The Narrow Experience Requirement should in turn be distinguished from the *Wide Experience Requirement,* which holds that an event can be bad for someone only if it in some way affects or makes a difference to his conscious experience. The difference between the two principles is that, while the Narrow Requirement implies that death cannot be bad for the person who dies, the Wide Requirement does not. For, although one does not experience death, it does affect one's experience—by limiting or ending it.

Obviously, then, to sustain the belief that death can be bad for the person who dies one needs to reject only the Narrow and not the Wide Experience Requirement. Yet the two are frequently conflated, so that it is often assumed that one must reject the Wide Requirement as well. This is a natural mistake, since the rejection of the Wide Requirement entails the rejection of the Narrow Requirement. Moreover, although the rejection of the Narrow Requirement does not entail the rejection of the Wide Requirement, the main objections to the Narrow Requirement also apply with equal force to the Wide Requirement. For example, the hypothetical cases in which people who long to be loved and admired and believe that they are, when in fact they are ridiculed and despised behind their backs, constitute counterexamples to both requirements.[4]

In my view these counterexamples provide sufficient grounds for rejecting the Narrow Requirement. But I will not press the objection

---

exist of a person, but not a necessary condition. In this paper my concern is with the ceasing to exist of persons. But for convenience I will treat the death of a person as if it were equivalent to the ceasing to exist of a person.

3. The Existence Requirement does not, of course, require that the person exist when the cause of the misfortune occurs.

4. See, e.g., Thomas Nagel, "Death," in *Mortal Questions* (Cambridge: Cambridge University Press, 1979), p. 4; and James Rachels, *The End of Life: Euthanasia and Morality* (Oxford: Oxford University Press, 1986), pp. 46–48. An equally damaging objection to both Experience Requirements is that they have trouble accounting for the fact that experiential states such as happiness and unhappiness can be rational or irrational, appropriate or inappropriate. See Jeff McMahan, *The Ethics of Killing* (Oxford: Basil Blackwell, 1989), chap. 1.

here, since my target is instead the Epicurean argument. I mention the Narrow Requirement mainly to ensure that it is not confused with the Existence Requirement. To see how the two requirements diverge, consider the case of a person on holiday on a remote island. Back home, on Friday, his life's work collapses. But, because of the inaccessibility of the island, the bad news does not arrive until the following Monday. On the intervening Sunday, however, the man is killed by a shark; so he never learns that his life's work has come to nothing. While it is compatible with the Existence Requirement to suppose that he suffered a terrible misfortune when the collapse occurred, since he existed at the time, the Narrow Experience Requirement implies that this was not a misfortune for him since he was never aware of it. The Existence Requirement and the Narrow Experience Requirement are therefore quite different requirements, and the counterexamples that are often advanced against the latter leave the former, and therefore the Epicurean argument itself, entirely unscathed.

B. The Reconciliation Strategy

The obvious attraction of the Epicurean argument is that it is thought to have the welcome effect of undermining the idea that death is something to be feared. It is less often noticed, however, that, for the same reasons, the argument also threatens certain other commonsense beliefs that we are less eager to abandon—for example, that killing is wrong, that suicide can be rational or irrational, and so on. If we wish to salvage these latter beliefs, we must either reject the Epicurean argument or else show that the relevant beliefs are in fact compatible with the argument's conclusion. If we adopt the first option then obviously we will lose our ground for thinking that death should not be feared. I will argue that the most plausible way of pursuing the second option also has this consequence.

Though the two options are mutually exclusive, I will argue for them both. While I think the Epicurean argument should ultimately be rejected, the other option—which I will call the *reconciliation strategy*— is worth exploring as a fallback position in case the proposed reasons for rejecting the Epicurean argument prove unpersuasive.

Let us consider the reconciliation strategy first. It can be introduced by drawing on a comparison between death, or the ceasing to exist of a person, and the coming into existence of a person. It can be argued that, if a person's life would be worth living, then it would be good—not just impersonally, but good *for that person*—if he were to come into existence. The argument for this claim derives from the compelling commonsense view that it would be wrong, other things being equal, to bring a person into existence if his life could be expected to be utterly miserable. The most plausible explanation of why this would be wrong appeals to two claims: first, that to cause such a person to exist would be bad for that person, or would harm him; and second, that there is a general moral reason not to do what would be bad for people, or would harm them.

But, if to be caused to exist with a miserable life can be bad for a person, then it should also be the case that to be caused to exist with a life that is worth living can be good for a person.

To deny this—to accept that to be caused to exist can be bad for a person but to deny that it can be good for a person—would, in the absence of some explanation, be unacceptably ad hoc. And it is difficult to imagine what sort of explanation could be given for the claim that there is an asymmetry of this sort. Moreover, the moral implications of supposing that there is such an asymmetry are likely to be quite implausible. For example, if it were possible to harm but not to benefit people by bringing them into existence, then any decision to have a child would carry a risk of harming the child but would not involve a possibility of benefiting him. Thus there would always be a moral presumption against having children. But it seems clear that there is no general presumption of this sort. So it seems safe to assume that, if causing a person to exist can be bad for that person, then it can also be good for him. It is, of course, possible to deny both these claims, but then one would need to find an alternative explanation of the fact that it would be wrong to cause a miserable person to exist.[5]

The point that emerges from this that is relevant to the reconciliation strategy is that, if we bring a person into existence with a life that is worth living, there is no problem in locating the beneficiary. He is here before us, enjoying the goods of life. There is thus no obvious incompatibility between the claim that it can be good for a person to come into existence and the Existence Requirement. There is, moreover, a relevant parallel here between starting to exist and continuing to exist. You might have died five years ago. But you did not; instead you continued to exist. If your life has been worth living, then it was good for you to have continued to exist. There is no problem in this case in locating the subject of this good fortune: you are the beneficiary of your continued existence, and you clearly exist during the time when this good fortune occurs. Hence it is not obviously incompatible with the Existence Requirement to claim that your continuing to exist is a good thing for you.

The claim of the reconciliation strategy is that continuing to live can be good for a person even if, as the Existence Requirement implies, death would not be bad for him. There is, however, a way in which the Epicurean might try to establish that the claim that continuing to live

5. One alternative possible explanation appeals to the idea that it is wrong, other things being equal, to do what makes the outcome worse in impersonal terms by increasing the net amount of whatever it is that we regard as bad—suffering, for instance. Thus we might object to causing a miserable person to exist on the ground that this produces an uncompensated increase in the amount of suffering in the world. If we appeal to this alternative explanation, then we will be able to develop a way of reconciling the conclusion of the Epicurean argument with the various commonsense beliefs which it threatens that is analogous to the way developed in the text. The difference is that, according to the alternative account, death will be impersonally bad rather than what I call quasi-impersonally bad. (See n. 8 below.)

can be good is incompatible with the claim that death cannot be bad. This involves appealing to what has been called the "Comparative View." The Comparative View is the view that any judgment about what is good or bad for a person must be implicitly comparative in the following way. The judgment that an act or event is *good* for someone implies that, if there is no relevant alternative that would be equally good or better, then the relevant alternative or alternatives to that act must be *worse* for that person. Similarly, the claim that an act or event is *bad* for someone implies that, unless there is some relevant alternative that would be as bad or worse, then any relevant alternative must be *better* for that person.[6]

The conclusion of the Epicurean argument—that death is not bad for those who die—together with the Comparative View, implies that the alternative to death—namely, continuing to live—cannot be good. This implication, if allowed to stand, will defeat the reconciliation strategy. Thus to defend the reconciliation strategy, we must reject the Comparative View.

One objection to the Comparative View is that it seems to lead to paradoxes.[7] Consider some person who continues to exist. The Existence Requirement itself (which for the moment we are treating as a fixed point in the argument) provides no ground for denying that continuing to exist is good for this person. And if continuing to exist is good for the person, then, given the Comparative View, it follows that ceasing to exist would have been worse for him. But suppose now that the actual outcome is that the person dies. According to the Existence Requirement, this is not bad for the person. Given the Comparative View, it then follows that it would not have been good, or better, for the person had he in fact continued to exist. A similar paradox arises when we consider the alternatives of coming into existence and not coming into existence.

The Comparative View thus has conflicting implications depending, it may seem, on which outcome we suppose to be the actual one. The Epicurean may reply, however, that the paradoxes derive, not from the Comparative View itself, but from our failure to evaluate the outcomes consistently. If (he might argue) we think that ceasing to exist cannot be bad, then we must accept that continuing to exist cannot be good, and we cannot change our minds about this when the actual outcome is continued existence rather than death. If we consistently hold that neither coming to exist nor not coming to exist is either good or bad, and that neither continuing to exist nor ceasing to exist is either good or bad, then the Comparative View will not lead to paradoxes.

The paradoxes to which I have called attention do not, therefore, immediately undermine the Comparative View. They do, however, help

6. The Comparative View is both christened and advocated by Jan Narveson in "Future People and Us," in *Obligations to Future Generations,* ed. Richard Sikora and Brian Barry (Philadelphia: Temple University Press, 1978), p. 48.

7. Here I draw on the argument of my "Problems of Population Theory," *Ethics* 92 (1981): 104–5.

us to understand more clearly what is at issue here. The Epicurean starts with the Existence Requirement, infers that death cannot be bad for those who die, and then reasons via the Comparative View that continuing to exist cannot be good. The proponent of the reconciliation strategy starts with equal propriety with the claim that in most cases continuing to exist is good and then, seeing that an inconsistency arises when this claim is conjoined with both the Existence Requirement and the Comparative View, concludes that the Comparative View must be wrong. Thus to resolve this dispute, we must assess the relative plausibility of the Comparative Requirement and the claim that continuing to exist can be good.

As I suggested earlier, the claim that continuing to exist can be good is supported by the parallel between coming to exist and continuing to exist. I argued that it can be good for a person to come into existence and concluded that, if this is so, it can also be good for a person to continue in existence. This is, of course, a relatively weak case; no doubt more could be said. But for our purposes even a weak case will do. For there is no case for the Comparative View. The Comparative View takes a truth about standard cases of something being good or bad for a person and generalizes it, making it a necessary condition in all cases for something to be good or bad for a person. In standard cases, in which the person exists in both alternative outcomes, the Comparative View seems true as a matter of logic. But in the two nonstandard pairs of alternatives (coming to exist or not coming to exist and continuing to exist or ceasing to exist) in which the person exists in only one of the alternatives, there is no reason whatever to think that the Comparative View must be true. There is no reason to generalize from the standard to the nonstandard cases.

Since the Comparative View is without foundation in the two nonstandard cases, it should be rejected as a general necessary condition for something being good or bad for a person. The rejection of the view then allows us to reject the idea that never existing can be bad or worse for a person, while accepting that to come to exist can be good for a person. We can say that coming to exist can be good, even though it is not better than never existing—since the latter implies that never existing would be worse, which it would not be (at least if it were the actual outcome). This also allows us to concede the Epicurean claim that death is not bad for people, or worse for them than continuing to live, while at the same time accepting that continuing to live can be good for them. We can say that continuing to live can be a good thing for a person, though it is not better than dying. In short, we simply give up the comparative claims, while retaining the noncomparative ones. (If one insists on having a comparison, one could claim that, while never existing would not have been worse for me, it would not have been as good for me as existing has been, and similarly that, while dying would not be bad for me, it would not be as good for me as continuing to exist would be. These claims are true and unparadoxical, and therefore reinstate a comparative view of sorts, though not one which threatens the reconciliation strategy.)

Suppose we accept that continuing to live can be good for a person even if death would not be bad for him. We could then claim that death would be bad—not bad for the person who dies, but bad in a quasi-impersonal way.[8] It would be bad because it would exclude what would be good for a person—namely, continuing to exist. Death would be bad in the same way that it is bad if a person whose life would have been worth living fails to come into existence. In both cases something which would be good for a person fails to occur, though in both cases the nonoccurrence of the good is not bad for the person who would have experienced it, since the nonoccurrence of the good involves—indeed perhaps consists in—the nonexistence of the person.

If death can be bad in this quasi-impersonal way, then this provides a sufficient basis for the important beliefs that seem to presuppose that death can be bad for the person who dies. If, for example, death can be bad because it excludes what would have been good for a person, then this will provide a foundation for the belief that killing is wrong, the belief that it is not irrational to fear death, the belief that suicide can be irrational, and so on.[9] In this way these important commonsense beliefs can be reconciled with the Epicurean claim that death cannot be bad for those who die.

C. The Existence Requirement

Despite the apparent success of the reconciliation strategy, it may seem that a more satisfactory way of preserving the relevant range of commonsense beliefs would be simply to reject the Epicurean argument. And this argument can be challenged directly. Consider again the case of the person whose life's work collapses while he is on holiday on a remote island. Suppose we agree that the fact that his life's work has come to nothing is a misfortune for him.[10] On reflection, it seems hard to believe that it makes a difference to the misfortune he suffers whether the collapse of his life's work occurs shortly before he is killed or shortly afterward. Yet, according to the Existence Requirement, this difference in timing makes *all* the difference. If the collapse of his life's work occurs just before he dies, then, even though he never learns of it, he suffers a

---

8. I call the badness of death as it is here understood "quasi-impersonal" to distinguish it both from the badness of events that are bad because of their effects on people and from the badness of events which are bad in a fully impersonal way—that is, bad for reasons that are independent of considerations of effects on particular people.

9. One could appeal to a parallel reconciliation strategy to show that suicide can also be rational—e.g., in cases in which death would be quasi-impersonally good, excluding what would be bad for a person.

10. The Epicurean, it seems, can reject this claim only by appealing to the Narrow Experience Requirement. He cannot appeal to the Wide Requirement, since this is incompatible with the Existence Requirement.

terrible misfortune. If, on the other hand, it occurs just after he dies, he suffers no misfortune at all. If we find this hard to believe then we may be forced to reject the Existence Requirement.

Most of us, however, will be disposed to do this anyway. The example is probably superfluous, since most of us find death itself a sufficient counterexample. Apart from suffering great pain, it is hard to think of a clearer example than death of something that most people believe to be in most cases bad for the person to whom it happens. The Epicurean simply denies what most of us believe. Death, he claims, cannot be bad for us because when it occurs we will not exist at all. But that is precisely what we object to: that we will not exist when we might otherwise be enjoying the benefits of life.

Death differs from never existing in one crucial respect. Never existing is not something that ever happens to actual people. A fortiori, there are no actual people for whom never existing can be bad. But death always happens to actual people. It can deprive actual people of what would otherwise be good for them. The Existence Requirement stands in the way of our being able to conclude from this that death can be bad for the actual people to whom it happens. But what authority does this principle have to overturn an evaluative inference so fundamental and compelling as this? The conflict here is analogous to a type of conflict that commonly arises in moral theory. For all of us there are certain convictions which constitute more or less fixed points in the system of our moral beliefs. When a conviction of this sort clashes with the dictates of some moral theory, the challenge from the theory must be more rationally compelling than the conviction itself if the conviction is to be justifiably dislodged. Theories seldom satisfy this demand. In the present case, the Existence Requirement also lacks the requisite rational force. Indeed, it seems, like the Comparative View, to be a simple misgeneralization from standard cases to an importantly different nonstandard case. In most instances it is a necessary truth that a person must exist to be the subject of some misfortune: I cannot, for example, suffer the pain of a toothache unless I exist. But death is obviously a special case. To insist that it cannot be an evil because it does not meet a condition that most if not all other evils satisfy is tantamount to ruling it out as an evil simply because it has special features.

It is important to notice, however, that if we reject the Existence Requirement, we may get the claim that death can be bad for those who die as part of a larger package which includes claims about posthumous benefits and posthumous harms. Death, when it is an evil, is a privative evil. In itself it has no positive or negative features, so when it is bad this must be because of what it deprives us of. But many people believe that people who have ceased to exist may also be subject to positive evils and misfortunes—as when a person's life's work is unjustly despised or neglected after her death—as well as positive benefits, as when an artist's works achieve the recognition they deserve which they never received during her lifetime. It seems that the only way we can reject both the Existence Requirement and the idea that we can be posthumously harmed and benefited is to accept some view, such as hedonism, which incorporates the Wide Experience Requirement. If we are hedonists we can believe that death is bad for the person who dies because it deprives him of valuable mental states, but we can reject the notion of posthumous harms and benefits on the ground that a dead person's mental status can no longer be affected. If, however, we do not accept the Wide Experience Requirement, then the rejection of the Existence Requirement would seem to commit us to the idea that numerous events that occur after our deaths can be either good or bad for us, or in or against our interests.

II. THE BADNESS OF DEATH

Given, then, that death can be bad, either for the victim or in quasi-impersonal terms, how are we to understand the loss or deprivation involved in death? The correct general answer to this question would seem to be that given by Nagel, which is that death, when it is bad, is bad because it deprives us of possible future goods.[11] The apparent simplicity of this answer, however, conceals a host of difficult problems. This section will be devoted to exposing the nature of these problems and proposing solutions to them.

One such problem is implicit in the following remarks of Nagel's. "Countless possibilities for [an individual's] continued existence are imaginable, and we can clearly conceive of what it would be for him to go on existing indefinitely. However inevitable it is that this will not come about, its possibility is still that of the continuation of a good for him, if life is the good we take it to be. . . . Death, no matter how inevitable, is an abrupt cancellation of indefinitely extensive possible goods. . . . If there is no limit to the amount of life that it would be good to have, then it may be that a bad end is in store for us all."[12]

If, however, the goods that would be possible for us were it not for death are conceived of as potentially unlimited, then it may seem that there is nothing to prevent the conclusion that our losses in death are infinite. But then, if the loss involved in death is infinite, and if the badness of death consists in what it deprives us of, how can we explain the common and compelling belief that it is in general worse to die earlier rather than later—for example, that it is worse, or more tragic, when someone dies at thirty than it is when someone dies at eighty?

11. Nagel, pp. 7–10. If, as I suggested in Sec. I.C., there can be posthumous benefits, then death does not deprive us of all possibilities for good. It deprives us only of possibilities for goods of an active or experiential kind. This and other related points are made by Frances Myrna Kamm in her *Morality, Mortality* (Oxford: Oxford University Press, forthcoming), in a chapter entitled "Death and Later Goods."

12. Nagel, pp. 8 and 10.

A. What Death Deprives Us Of

What Nagel seems to be suggesting, in the passage quoted above, is that death is *always* bad for the person who dies relative to the possibilities for good that one could imagine his life containing had that life continued. What is unclear, however, is why one should think that a set of possibilities that are possible only in the sense of being imaginable constitutes a relevant alternative to death for purposes of comparison. Simply to point out that there is an imaginable possible future life that a person might have had if he had not died seems insufficient to show that he met with a bad end. For we can also imagine possible future lives that the person might have had which would not have been worth living, relative to which his death could be judged not to be bad, or even to be good. Since desirable future lives and undesirable future lives are all equally imaginable, there seems to be no more reason to judge the person's death to be bad than there is to judge it to be good. But unless there is some nonarbitrary way of selecting, from among the many imaginable lives the person might have had, the one which can be considered the relevant alternative to death for purposes of comparison, then Nagel's focus on what would have been imaginable in the absence of death provides no basis for the evaluation of an individual's death at all.

What is relevant in evaluating the badness of an individual's death is not what might have happened if he had not died, but what would in fact have happened. When we evaluate death relative to what would have happened in its absence, we find that it is clearly not the case that death is always infinitely bad because it deprives its victim of an "indefinitely extensive" set of possible goods. Rather, the possibilities for good of which a person is deprived by death are limited by the fact that, had he not died when and how he did, he would have been condemned by his biology and circumstances to die within a certain limited period of time thereafter. The relevant alternative to death for purposes of comparison is not continuing to live indefinitely, or forever, but living on for a limited period of time and then dying of some other cause. So, other things being equal, we measure the badness of death in terms of the quantity and quality of life that the victim would have enjoyed had he not died when and how he did. (I will later explain how other things might be relevantly unequal.)

This approach to determining the badness of death supports the common view that it is in general worse to die earlier rather than later.[13] As a rule, a person who dies at thirty would, had he not died, have en-

---

13. As his text makes clear, Nagel himself believes that it is normally worse to die earlier rather than later. It is not clear, however, how he thinks this can be rendered consistent with his belief that even those who die of extreme old age thereby suffer a loss of indefinite possibilities for good. In Sec. II.A.4., I will suggest a way of reconciling his various intuitions.

joyed more goods before meeting with death from some other cause than a person who dies at eighty. This approach also supports the view that most of us take in cases in which it seems that death is not a bad thing for the person who dies, or is even a good thing. These are cases in which we feel that suicide would be rational, or euthanasia justified. The reason why death is not bad in these cases is that, if the person were not to die, the life that he would subsequently have would not be worth living. If, however, we assume with Nagel that death should be evaluated relative to the possibilities for good that would be imaginable in its absence, then it seems that we should regard death as an evil even in these cases. This makes it difficult to see how those who take Nagel's view can find cases in which suicide would be rational or in which euthanasia would even be conceptually possible.

Let us call the account of the badness of death which I have sketched the "revised possible goods account." In order to be able to explain our intuitive beliefs about the comparative badness of different possible deaths, this account requires further refinement. The necessary additions and qualifications will be developed in the following five subsections.

1. *Counterfactual Conditionals and the Problem of Specifying the Antecedent.*—One problem which the possible goods account faces can best be introduced by means of an example. Consider the case of a thirty-year-old man who died today of cancer. Call him Mort. According to the possible goods account, our evaluation of Mort's death must be based on a counterfactual conditional claim to the effect that "such-and-such would have happened if. . . ." The natural candidate for the antecedent of the counterfactual is, of course, "if he had not died." But this is in fact hopelessly vague, for there are countless ways in which he might not have died. To imagine that his death did not occur we must imagine that its cause did not occur, or did not lead to its expected effect. Yet there are not only various ways of understanding what the cause of his death was, but there are also, for each way of conceiving of the cause of death, various ways in which it would have been possible for the cause not to have operated. Suppose, for example, that we say that the cancer was the cause of his death. Then to suppose that he might not have died is to suppose that he might have been cured of the cancer, or that he might never have been stricken with it in the first place, or that he might have lived on with it in a nonfatal form. In short, we must suppose that he might not have died from the cancer, but there are various ways in which this might have happened.

Suppose, on the other hand, that we want to be more specific in identifying the cause of Mort's death. We might then say that the cause of his death was the immediate mechanism by which his death was brought about—a hemorrhage, for example. (This is what a pathologist who knew of Mort's condition would want to know if he were to ask what the cause of death was.) If this is how we conceive of the cause of death, then to hypothesize that he might not have died is to suppose that *this* cause of death might not have operated.

Which of these various ways of spelling out the antecedent ("if he had not died at *t*") is the one on which we should base our evaluation of Mort's death? Certainly our choice of interpretation will make a difference to what our evaluation will be. For our estimation of what would have happened to Mort had he not died will depend on how we understand the circumstances of his not dying. If not dying would have involved being cured of the cancer, then it may be true that had he not died, he would have lived a long and prosperous life. Relative to that understanding of the antecedent, then, Mort's death can be regarded as a terrible tragedy. But suppose that his not dying is understood in such a way that it would have involved only the absence of the immediate mechanism of death (the hemorrhage). In that case we may suppose that, had he not died when he did, he would have lived on for only a short period of time until his death would have been brought about by some alternative mechanism associated with the cancer. Relative to this understanding of the antecedent, Mort's death was not tragic, and it may even have been a good thing (if, e.g., the brief future he would otherwise have had would have been filled with suffering).

Mort's case is in a way paradoxical, for there is both a clear sense in which it is true that his death today was not tragic—indeed, was perhaps on balance a good thing—as well as a clear sense in which his death was tragic. We can see now that each of these claims is true relative to certain ways of specifying the antecedent and false relative to others. His death today was perhaps a good thing relative to living on for a few days in agony, but it was bad relative to continued life free from cancer.

It seems unsatisfactory, however, to be left with a multiplicity of different and superficially conflicting evaluations of his death. What we want is a single, general, context-independent evaluation which tells us whether, all things considered, his death was good or bad, period. Our problem, then, is to find a method for picking out the single most general, context-independent way of understanding the idea that he might not have died. Let us call this *the problem of specifying the antecedent,* since what we are trying to do, in effect, is to assign precise and determinate content to the phrase "if he had not died . . . " in such a way that the completed conditional, if true, will provide the most general and context-independent assessment of what Mort has been deprived of, or has been spared, by his death.

How might we discover a method of specifying the antecedent in this and all other cases in which we seek a single overall evaluation of a person's death? I see no alternative but to propose various methods and test them against our intuitions by exploring their implications for a range of cases. Before proposing what seems a promising candidate, I will introduce some further cases which will not only help to illuminate the structure of the problem but will also serve as useful tests for assessing the plausibility of proposed methods.

2. *The Problem of Causal Overdetermination.* —There is a familiar problem in ethics, which is that it is often difficult to know how to evaluate an act which causes injury if, had the act not been done, some other cause would have operated around the same time to produce a relevantly similar injury to the same victim. Following Feinberg, I will say that these are cases in which injury to the victim is causally overdetermined.[14] A similar problem arises for the evaluation of death when death is causally overdetermined in this sense.

Consider the following case. Joe is twenty-nine and a half years old. Schmoe has just turned thirty. Both are run over by a bus as they step off the curb. Our initial reaction is to think of both deaths as terribly tragic, Joe's being perhaps slightly more tragic than Schmoe's because of his slightly younger age. But suppose that, while Schmoe was in robust good health, it is discovered during the autopsy that Joe had a silent, symptomless, but invariably fatal disease that would have killed him within two months had he not been mown down by the bus. Our response to the discovery of this fact is to revise our initial assessment of the badness of Joe's death. Joe's death now seems considerably less bad than it would have been had he not had the condition since, given the fact that he had the condition, all he lost in being hit by the bus was at most two months of further life. Our revised response is thus to think that Schmoe's death was the more tragic of the two, other things being equal, even though he was older than Joe.

The view that Joe lost only relatively little by dying in the accident is supported by the fact that it explains certain intuitions. Suppose that one knew about Joe's disease and that one was in a position to snatch either Joe or Schmoe, but not both, out of the path of the bus. It seems that it would be better to save Schmoe rather than Joe if other things, such as their importance to other people, were equal. The reason why it would be better to save Schmoe is simply that he would have more to lose by dying than Joe would.

This may seem straightforward. In fact it is not. When we learn the results of the autopsy, our inclination is to think that Joe's death was less bad than it initially seemed. But if we then report the results to Joe's grieving mother, it is very unlikely that she will find any grounds for consolation in the fact that he would soon have died anyway. She might reason as follows. Suppose that Joe had not been killed by the bus. Then he would have died sometime within the ensuing two months from the disease. What would we then have said of *that* death? If we were to ask

14. Joel Feinberg, "Wrongful Life and the Counterfactual Element in Harming," *Social Philosophy and Policy* 4, no. 1 (1986): 145–78. Normally the phrase "causal overdetermination" is reserved for cases in which two or more individually sufficient causes operate simultaneously to bring about some event.

what would have happened had he not then died from the disease, the answer could well be that he could have been expected to enjoy a long and fruitful life. In that case we would have said that his death from the disease was a terrible tragedy—a case of a young man cut down in his prime. But if death at so early an age from the disease would have been tragic, how can it be *less* bad when he is killed today by a bus at an even earlier age?

I will return to the question of Joe's misfortune in Section II.A.4. I want now to introduce another case—the case of a young officer in the cavalry who was killed in the charge of the Light Brigade. This officer was among the leaders of the charge and was shot quite early by a soldier named Ivan. Suppose that, had he not been shot by Ivan, he would have been killed within a few seconds by a bullet fired by Boris, who also had him within his sights. Our natural response to this case is to say that the officer's death was a grave misfortune, depriving him of many years of life. Yet it would seem that this case is like that of Joe in being a case in which death within a relatively short span of time is causally overdetermined. Thus, if we accept that Joe lost at most two months in being hit by the bus, should we not also conclude that in this case all the officer lost in being shot by Ivan was a few seconds of life, so that his death was hardly a misfortune at all?

Obviously we cannot accept this. Yet in the case of Joe it is *not* implausible to regard his death in the accident as considerably less bad than it would have been had there been no other cause of death which would soon have killed him if the bus had not. Is there some difference between the cases which explains our differing reactions to them? I think that there is and that examining that difference will point us toward a plausible resolution of the problem of specifying the antecedent.

3. *A Proposal.*—The solution I will offer to the problem of specifying the antecedent is based on a variant of the general analysis of the truth-value of counterfactuals associated with the work of David Lewis and Robert Stalnaker.[15] What the variants of this form of analysis have in common is the view that a counterfactual conditional is true if and only if the consequent is true in the possible world (or in all of the possible worlds) in which the antecedent is realized that is (or are) closest to the actual world, where closeness is determined by the application of some similarity metric. I will simply assume that some theory of this sort is true and that the version that I appeal to is a reasonable candidate for the best version. I will not try to defend or even to make explicit all the details of this version.[16] Indeed, as will soon become apparent, the proposal I will advance raises far more problems of metaphysics than there is

15. See Robert C. Stalnaker, "A Theory of Conditionals," *American Philosophical Quarterly*, monograph no. 2 (1968); and David Lewis, *Counterfactuals* (Princeton, N.J.: Princeton University Press, 1973).

16. I suspect, though I cannot prove this, that my proposal could be reformulated without significant loss in terms of other variants of the general theory of counterfactuals.

space to address here, so one should regard what follows as nothing more than a tentative sketch of a solution.

It is perhaps tempting to think that the solution to the problem of specifying the antecedent is given more or less directly by the Lewis-Stalnaker theory. One might think, for example, that we can identify the appropriate antecedent-world as the possible world in which the person does not die but which otherwise deviates minimally from the actual world (at least up to the time at which the person died in the actual world). This, however, would be a mistake. Return to the case of the cavalry officer. Suppose (what is not implausible) that the closest possible world in which the officer does not die from Ivan's bullet is one in which he is grazed by Ivan's bullet and then killed by Boris's bullet. In that case our answer to the question of what would have happened had the officer not died when and how he did will be that he would have lived for a few seconds, and then he would have been killed. This leads to the unacceptable conclusion that his actual death was hardly a misfortune at all.

In the case of the cavalry officer, as in the case of Mort, what we believe about what would have happened had he not died when and how he did depends on how we specify the cause of his death. If we single out the shot fired by Ivan as the cause and then ask what would have happened had that cause not operated (e.g., because Ivan's hand shook, or his gun jammed), we get the answer that the officer would soon have been killed by Boris. We might, however, identify the cause of the officer's death differently—for example, as his being shot in the charge. If we ask what would have happened had he not been shot in the charge, the answer may well be that he would subsequently have led a long and happy life. Of course, as in the case of Mort, these two claims about what would have happened lead to radically divergent evaluations of the officer's death.

The problem of specifying the antecedent, then, is a problem about identifying and delimiting the cause of death. In asking what would have happened had a certain person not died, we are asking what would have been the case had the cause of his death not operated. The many different ways of specifying the antecedent thus correspond to different ways in which the chain of causation leading to the person's death might have gone off course or been disrupted—different ways, in short, in which various individually or jointly necessary conditions of the person's death might not have occurred. The problem of specifying the antecedent, therefore, is the problem of determining which elements from the totality of causally relevant factors in the etiology of death we should imagine not occurring when, in order to obtain a single overall evaluation of the death, we imagine what would have been the case had the victim not died.

Return now to the comparison between the case of the officer and the case of Joe. An important difference between the two cases would seem to be that, while the two potential causes of the officer's death (the threat from Ivan and the threat from Boris) both seem to be parts of the same causal sequence, the two potential causes of Joe's death (the bus accident and the fatal condition) are not. Hence in the possible world in which the entire causal sequence containing the immediate cause of the officer's death is absent, there are no other causes of death lurking in the foreseeable future. But if in Joe's case we subtract the causal sequence leading to his death in the bus accident, we do not thereby remove the other cause of death—namely, the fatal condition.

What this suggests is that we can secure the intuitively correct counterfactual claims in these cases if our formula for specifying the antecedent is to subtract the entire causal sequence of which the immediate cause of death is a part. Thus, if the entire causal sequence leading to the officer's being shot by Ivan had not occurred, then he would presumably have gone on to lead a long and prosperous life; whereas if the entire causal sequence leading to Joe's being hit by the bus had not occurred, he would still have died within two months of the condition. Because of this, we may regard Joe's death as less tragic than that of the officer.

This formula, while promising, requires considerable tightening up. One problem, for example, is to give sufficient content to the notion of a causal sequence to allow for the individuation of causal sequences in the way that the formula requires. Here is one suggestion for dealing with this problem. Let us define the *transitive cause* of an event E as follows. If C is the immediate or proximate cause of E, then the transitive cause of E is the set of all the events that form part of the chain of causes leading to C. This set is understood to be both complete and closed, in the sense that all and only the members of the set satisfy the following condition: if C_i is a member of the set and C_j is a cause of C_i, then C_j is a member of the set. Given the notion of transitive cause, we can now state more precisely what it means to imagine a possible world in which the entire causal sequence containing a certain death is absent. To imagine such a world is simply to imagine a world which is like the actual world except that the entire transitive cause of the death is absent, along with those events for whose occurrence some element or elements of the transitive cause were a necessary condition given the laws of causation that hold in the actual world. So, for example, if we imagine that the transitive cause of the officer's being shot by Ivan did not occur, we must presumably imagine that the Crimean War did not occur, in which case the threat from Boris would not have occurred either.

It is important to notice that the plausibility of this suggestion depends on our distinguishing between the cause of some event and the causally relevant conditions of that event. The transitive cause of E, as I understand it, consists of a chain of causes (namely, the cause of the cause of the cause . . . of E) and not the set of all the causally relevant conditions of E. For example, the transitive cause of the officer's death presumably includes the occurrence of the battle and thus the occurrence of the war, but not the event of Ivan's birth, or the presence of oxygen in the air for Ivan to breathe, or even the fact that the officer was not wounded and sent home just prior to the battle—though all of these are causally necessary conditions of the officer's actual death. If the transitive cause of the officer's death were to include these and all the other causally relevant conditions of his death, the proposal I am putting forward would obviously be hopelessly implausible.[17]

Having sketched certain theories, concepts, and distinctions on which my proposed solution to the problem of specifying the antecedent is based, I am now in a position to state the proposal in full. Let t be the time at which some person died. Our overall, objective evaluation of how bad or good his death was for him will be based on a counterfactual claim about what would have happened to him if he had not died at t. Let the antecedent of the relevant counterfactual be "if the entire transitive cause of his death had not occurred. . . ." To complete the counterfactual, we consult the possible world in which the antecedent is realized which is closest to the actual world up to t.[18] In assessing comparative similarity, we give nomological similarity lexical priority over factual similarity. That is, we hold the laws of causation constant across possible worlds.[19] Then we simply let the future unfold in this world in accordance with the laws of causation that hold in the actual world, and see how the person fares. If, for example, in the closest world in which the antecedent is realized the person goes on to live a long and happy life subsequent to t, then it is true that if he had not died he would have lived a long and happy life. His death was then bad in rough proportion to the amount of good that his life would have contained. (If the future is causally underdetermined by the present, then he may fare differently in different possible futures which are all compatible with running the closest antecedent-world forward in accordance with the laws of causation. In that case, the sum of the goods that would have been causally possible for the person will presumably exceed the amount of good that would have been contained in any single future life. Thus, in attempting to calculate the losses that the person suffers through death, we should presumably weight each good that would have been causally possible for him according to how

17. I have no analysis of the distinction between cause and causal condition to offer, nor any view about whether the distinction marks a real difference or is simply context dependent. I here rely on our intuitive sense of what counts as a cause and what counts as a causal condition.

18. Lewis contends that there may be more than one closest possible world in which the antecedent is realized. I must ignore this complication here.

19. Unless, perhaps, we are forced to consider causally impossible worlds by the fact that the antecedent itself is causally impossible. (More on this later.) In insisting that we alter matters of fact before we alter the causal structure of the actual world, I am assuming a version of the similarity theory that many writers, including Lewis, would reject. For arguments in favor of banning miracles in closest antecedent-worlds, see Jonathan Bennett, "Counterfactuals and Temporal Direction," *Philosophical Review* 93 (1984): 57–91, esp. sec. 7.

probable its occurrence would have been had he lived. Again, however, there is no space to pursue this further complexity.)

This proposal provides what seem to be the intuitively correct answers in the cases we have considered so far. For example, it implies that the cavalry officer's death was tragic since, if the transitive cause of his death had never occurred, he would not have been threatened by either Ivan or Boris and so, we may assume, would have gone on to live a long and happy life. It also implies that Joe's death was significantly less bad than Schmoe's since, in the closest possible world in which the transitive cause of his death is absent, Joe would have lived on for at most two months; whereas, in Schmoe's case, removing the transitive cause of death would have left him with many years of life remaining. Finally, the proposal implies that Mort's death was a tragedy comparable to those suffered by the officer and by Schmoe, since the relevant counterfactual situation with which we compare his death is one in which he never contracts cancer in the first place.

It should be emphasized that these judgments represent only our most general, maximally context-independent evaluations of these deaths. As I noted earlier in introducing the problem of specifying the antecedent, there are many other possible evaluations of each of these deaths which are based on other imagined ways in which the causal chain leading to the death might have been interrupted so that the death would not have occurred. These alternative evaluations need not be mistaken. On the contrary, they can be quite important for certain purposes, such as guiding action at moments when, though it is not possible to prevent the entire transitive cause of some potential death, it nevertheless is possible to intervene in the causal chain in some other way. For example, the doctors may wish to know whether it would be in Mort's interests for them to avert the hemorrhage which they predict will occur unless he is given a certain medication. Whether it would be in or against his interests depends at least in part on whether his death from the hemorrhage would be good or bad for him at that time (i.e., relative to what would be in store for him if, in his present condition, his death from the hemorrhage were to be prevented). In making this decision, the doctors should be guided by their assessment of what Mort's life would be like in the closest possible world in which the causal chain which will otherwise lead to his death is broken or diverted at the point at which it is possible for them to intervene.

So evaluations of this sort need not be wrong, and indeed are indispensable in a variety of decision-making contexts. But, unlike the evaluations that issue from the application of the procedure outlined above, they are essentially context dependent. They can help to guide our action in relevant circumstances, but they do not tell us, for example, to what extent it is appropriate to feel pity for someone because he has died.

4. Deprivation of Future Goods and the Global Evaluation of Lives. — I have claimed that the proposal sketched above gives the right answer in the case of Joe, but earlier I raised doubts about whether it is really our intuition that his death was less tragic than that of Schmoe. Even when we discover that Joe suffered from the fatal condition, we, along with his mother, retain our sense that he has suffered a terrible misfortune. And in fact we are right. Our mistake is to identify this misfortune with the event of his death. For it remains true that the event of his death was not itself a grave misfortune for him, since at most it deprived him of only two months of life. Rather, his misfortune consists in his having been deprived of a future in which there would be possibilities for good. It is because the absence of future possibilities for good (at least of an active or experiential kind) was in this case overdetermined, in that it was guaranteed by the disease quite independently of the bus accident, that the misfortune is not ascribable to his death alone. It is instead ascribable to the fact that he was killed by the bus *together with* the fact that if he had not been killed by the bus he would have died soon of the disease. It is this which is the proper object of his mother's great grief.

It may, however, be objected to this that the misfortune which I claim that Joe suffered is one that befalls us all, so that in the end we are all equally unfortunate, equally deprived. Consider, for example, the case of a person who dies from extreme old age, at the biological limits of human life. Call this person Gerry. It seems that Gerry's case is, according to my view, relevantly like Joe's. His death within a short span of time is overdetermined. Suppose that he died of a heart attack. Even if the transitive cause of the heart attack had not occurred, Gerry would nevertheless have died soon of some other cause associated with the fragility of old age.[20] For this reason most of us readily concede that his death was not a great misfortune for him; we acknowledge, in this case, that very few goods would have been causally possible for him had he not died. But, an objector might claim, the fact that he would have had little to look forward to had he not died is, according to my view, itself a great misfortune—precisely the same misfortune which I have claimed that Joe suffered. But if Joe and Gerry both suffer this misfortune equally, and if neither one's death is particularly tragic, then it would seem that the problem raised in the passage from Nagel quoted in Section II— namely, that we all suffer infinite losses—has reemerged in a slightly altered form. For it now seems that, on my view, we all *do* suffer infinite losses, though these losses are not attributable to death alone. But if this is right, how can we explain our feeling that Joe has suffered a greater misfortune than Gerry and is more deserving of our pity?

One reply to this challenge might appeal to the idea that the failure to realize some good is less bad the less causally possible it was to realize

20. I assume that we may rule out counterfactual claims based on antecedent-worlds in which the aging process is arrested or reversed on the ground that any such world would be insufficiently similar to the actual world in terms of any plausible similarity metric to provide truth-conditions for a counterfactual.

that good.[21] If that were true, then Joe would be the more unfortunate of the two because future goods were causally more possible for him than for Gerry, for whom the absence of future goods was multiply overdetermined by a variety of potential causes of death as well as by aging, disease, and so forth. But in fact this hardly seems to matter. Even if the absence of future possibilities for good were equally overdetermined in the two cases (e.g., if there were twenty Murder Inc. hit men independently trying to kill Joe when he was hit by the bus), we would still grieve more for him and think him more unfortunate than Gerry.

There is a better reply. This reply begins by embracing the allegedly absurd view that Gerry suffers a serious misfortune. Indeed, it is compatible with the view that ultimately we *all* suffer a great misfortune—even those of us who live the longest, richest lives. This is not the best of all possible worlds. We are all subject to aging beyond maturity, disease, injury, death, and so on. Were it not for these various evils, each of us would enjoy the prospect of an indefinitely extensive succession of possible goods. Perhaps it is this fact that Nagel has in mind in the quotation cited earlier. If so, his mistake is to think that the deprivation of future possibilities for good that we all suffer is attributable to death when it is in fact overdetermined by a package of evils of which death is only one.

The fact that we all suffer this deprivation equally does not, however, imply that we are all equally unfortunate. Consider again the comparison between Joe and Gerry. Even if their losses are ultimately the same, their gains from life have not been. The explanation of why there is less reason to grieve for Gerry is simply that he has had a fair share of life. Relative to reasonable expectations, he has had a rich and full life. Joe's life, by contrast, has fallen short of what he could reasonably have expected to gain from life.

Even though those who gain more from life than most of us *do* suffer a misfortune when they die or when their lives become such that death, in the circumstances, would be good for them, they are nevertheless seldom to be pitied. Feelings such as pity have to be adjusted to normal or reasonable expectations. Consider the case of someone who badly wants to travel to distant parts of the universe. It would be a mistake to suppose that he suffers no misfortune in being unable to do what he most wants to do (something which we would all agree to be well worth doing if it were possible—i.e., his desire, though idle, is not frivolous). But the fact that his desire is frustrated does not evoke pity. This is because pity is appropriate only in cases in which a person is unable to fulfill reasonable expectations given the circumstances of human life.[22]

21. Compare Nagel, "Death," p. 9, where he appears to suggest that whether (and perhaps to what extent) the failure to realize some future good counts as a misfortune depends on how possible the relevant good is.

22. Our evaluation of a person's global good or ill fortune should thus be relativized to our perception of the norm for a certain sort of human life. This should not be confused with the common but nevertheless unacceptable idea that we should evaluate a person's

52   *Ethics   October 1988*

If we assume that there is a limit to the amount of good that any life can contain, then it is natural to conclude that there is a correlation between what a person gains from life and what he loses when possibilities for good cease to be available to him. But, when we assess our lives relative to the possibility of a desirable immortality (which is what we do when we measure the misfortune inflicted on us jointly by aging, disease, physical vulnerability, death, etc.), it ceases to be true that, if other things (such as the quality of life) are equal, then the more a person gains from life, the fewer his losses will be when deprived of future possibilities for good. Since this correlation breaks down in this case, it is not unreasonable to measure the comparative misfortune that a person suffers in being deprived of future possibilities for good in terms of the extent to which the deprivation limits his gains from life rather than in terms of the extent to which it increases his losses.

There is, however, an objection to this claim. Consider the case of two elderly men, Faust and his friend Fred. Both have had lives of roughly equal length and quality. Faust is approached by Mephistopheles and given the elixir of youth—in this case with no penalty to be paid later on. The elixir gives Faust the body of an eighteen-year-old. He then sets out joyously on a new life. But on the first day of this new life he and Fred are both run over by a bus. What should we say about this case? Both men suffer the misfortune of being deprived of future possibilities for good. Moreover, the limitation on their gains from life is the same in each case. Neither has gained more from life than the other. But surely Faust suffers a greater misfortune than Fred?

In fact Faust is no more unfortunate than Fred *in global terms*. It is true that Faust is killed just as he is about to embark on a second youth. What this means is that Faust's *death* is more tragic than Fred's. The event of his being hit by the bus is worse for Faust than being hit by the bus is for Fred. Thus if both Faust and Fred have been mortally injured by the bus and lie dying in their hospital beds, Faust will naturally feel greater bitterness about being hit by the bus than Fred will. It is often harder to bear the loss of some recently acquired good than it is never to acquire the good in the first place. But never to acquire some good is also a misfortune. So, just as Faust is unfortunate in having the benefits of the elixir snatched away from him, Fred is also unfortunate in never having been given the elixir.

I will now conclude this section by briefly considering one final problem case—a case which seems to pose a problem for any account of the badness of death. Suppose that there is a young woman who dies of a genetic condition that is both strongly incurable (in the sense that it is causally impossible to suppress its effects) and essential to her identity

---

death relative to the possibility of his living out a lifespan that is normal for persons in his society. Among the various objections to the latter idea is the fact that it seems to entail that death cannot be bad for those who have already lived longer than the normal lifespan.

(in that anyone born without the condition would not have been *her*). Call this woman Genette. If we ask what would have happened if the transitive cause of her death had not occurred, the answer seems to be that she would never have existed. The possible world in which the transitive cause is absent is therefore not one in which she fares better than she does in the actual world. So it may seem that we are forced to conclude that she suffers no misfortune in dying of the condition, nor indeed in having the condition. Yet many of us share Nagel's intuition that death can be a misfortune even when it is strongly impossible that it should not occur.

I will not defend a particular solution to this problem, but will simply outline three possible responses, all of which have a certain plausibility. The first response is just to accept that Genette's death is not a misfortune on the ground that she has had the longest life that she could have. The second response concedes that there are no possible worlds in which she lives longer but rejects the inference that her death was not bad for her. This response appeals to counterpart theory. It holds that the truth-conditions for claims about what would have happened had she not had the condition are provided by closest possible worlds containing the closest counterpart to Genette in whom the genetic defect is absent. The fact that this counterpart would not, strictly speaking, be *Genette* would not necessarily undermine the relevance of events in these worlds to evaluative claims about Genette's life. According to some versions of counterpart theory, such as Lewis's, a counterpart in some possible world is never identical with the original object in the actual world.

The third response involves two deviations from the proposal advanced earlier in Section II.A.3. The first is that we should ask, not what would have happened if the transitive cause of Genette's death had not occurred, but instead what would have happened if the effects of her condition had been suppressed. The second is that we should allow that the closest possible world in which that antecedent is realized may contain some violation of the laws of causation that hold in the actual world. We may perhaps plead necessity in both cases. For example, the justification for the second deviation might be that, while we must preserve the laws of causation wherever possible, we are simply forced to admit closest possible worlds containing causal impossibilities when we consider antecedents which are themselves causally impossible. Consider for example, the claim that, if the law of universal gravitation were an inverse cube law rather than an inverse square law, objects would then attract one another less strongly at great distances and more strongly at short distances. This claim seems true, though the possible world which provides its truth-conditions is causally impossible. Notice, furthermore, that unless we make this concession we will be unable to sustain my earlier claim that we all suffer a misfortune in being physically vulnerable, susceptible to disease, and so on. If we accept that we are unfortunate in being vulnerable to injury, on the ground that if we were not, our lives would be both longer and happier, then we should be able to make the analogous claim in Genette's case that she is unfortunate in suffering certain effects of her condition, among which we include the fact that it leads to premature death.

B. Death and the Degree of Psychological Connectedness

Let us turn now to one final problem for the possible goods account. In general our belief is that death is worse the earlier it occurs. This seems to be implied by the possible goods account. For it would seem that, the earlier death occurs, the greater are the losses which the victim suffers and, correspondingly, the fewer are the gains which he derives from life. But many people feel that there are instances in which an earlier death is not worse for the victim, even if the whole of the life that is lost would have been well worth living. They believe that death at, say, one month after conception, or one month after birth, is not worse, or more tragic, than death at, say, twenty, or forty. Rather, death at twenty, or forty, is in fact *worse* than death before birth, or perhaps even in early infancy. How can this view be explained?

I think it is best explained by appealing to the theory which holds that the criterion of personal identity over time is psychological continuity.[23] According to this theory, continuing to exist as the same person over time essentially involves the holding of certain psychological relations— such as that between an experience and the memory of it, or that between an intention and the later act that carries it out. This presupposes that it is a necessary condition of being a person *at all* that an entity should have at least some of the psychological states or characteristics that are the ingredients of these various relations. The theory is, moreover, reductionist. It holds that the existence of a person is ultimately reducible to the existence of a certain set of psychological events and the relations among them.

Since there is no mental life at all associated with a human fetus in the early stages of gestation, the fetus cannot be a person during this period. If, as I believe, personhood is an essential property, it follows that the fetus during this period cannot be the same individual as the person who would later exist if the fetus were to follow its natural path of development. Thus if a fetus dies early in its career, *it* suffers no loss at all. Since it has no mental life, its death cannot involve the loss of anything that is of value to it at that time; and the loss of the future life that its death involves is also no loss to it, since that life would not have

23. This theory is most persuasively developed in Derek Parfit's *Reasons and Persons* (Oxford: Oxford University Press, 1984), pt. 3. For the purposes of this paper I will assume that this theory is true. It is not, however, strictly necessary for my argument that we should accept this theory. While the claims that are essential to my argument—e.g., that it can be rational for a person to discount for diminished psychological connectedness—are probably best supported by this theory, they are in principle compatible with certain other theories. Hence one is not necessarily committed by the acceptance of my argument to any particular theory of personal identity.

been *its* life but would instead have belonged to the person.[24] Thus the reason why death at this early stage is not worse for the victim than death at age twenty is that death at this stage is not bad for the victim at all.

Later in the course of the development of a human fetus, when the rudiments of a mental life begin to appear, a person begins to develop. But the psychological attributes which are the constituent elements of personhood do not appear all at once, but instead appear gradually, so that the mental life that develops in association with the human organism becomes richer, more sophisticated, and more unified as the organism matures and develops. Since the existence of a person is nothing more than the existence of certain psychological states and their interrelations, and since the appearance of the states and relations that are constitutive of a person is a gradual process, the development or coming-into-existence of a person is also gradual.[25] It seems to follow that the existence of a person can be a matter of degree. During the period when the mental life associated with the developing organism remains relatively primitive, the person does not yet fully exist. What exists is only a potential or developing person—an entity in the process of becoming a person. Only when this sequence of mental activity reaches a certain level of complexity and sophistication does the person fully exist. There is, however, no determinate threshold of complexity and sophistication such that in passing the threshold the person suddenly achieves full existence. Rather, there is a period during which, while what exists is clearly at least a potential or developing person, it is indeterminate whether it has yet fully become a person.[26]

Let us suppose that even one month after the birth of the human organism the person is not yet fully realized. The one-month-old infant is still only a potential, or developing, person. If the infant dies, its losses will be less than those that a fully developed person normally suffers

24. It might be objected that, since my present physical organism is certainly the same organism as the fetus with which it is physically continuous, the claim that *I* am not identical with that fetus implies that I am not my physical organism. I accept this objection. Since I could cease to exist even if my organism were to continue to exist and indeed continue to live, it would seem that I cannot be identical with my organism. This, however, may be compatible with the claim that there is a further sense in which I am my organism. To borrow an old analogy, the sense in which I am my organism is the same sense in which a statue is the clay of which it is made. Just as the statue is constituted by the clay without being identical with it, so I consist of or am constituted by my organism without being identical with it. (These issues are ably discussed by W. R. Carter in "Do Zygotes Become People?" *Mind* 91 [1982]: 77–95, and in "Once and Future People," *American Philosophical Quarterly* 17 [1980]: 61–66; and by Warren Quinn in "Abortion: Identity and Loss," *Philosophy and Public Affairs* 13 [1984]: 24–54, though both of these writers defend a different position from that advocated here. I discuss the issue of the relation between persons and their organisms, as well as the other issues raised in this section, in considerable detail in chap. 2 of *The Ethics of Killing*.)

25. For a cogent defense of the view that persons, even if they are substances, come into existence gradually, see Quinn, pp. 33–40.

26. Compare Parfit, sec. 79.

through death. The future life that is lost when the infant dies would have been the life of a fully existing person, and hence it belonged only partially to the infant itself. This helps to explain why death in early infancy is not worse for the victim than, say, death at twenty. It is only after a person becomes fully real that death is normally worse for him the earlier in his life it occurs.

A different though closely related way of supporting the same conclusion appeals to a reductionist view about what matters in personal survival. Most of those who accept the psychological continuity theory of personal identity believe that identity is not what matters in personal survival. What matters is not that there should later exist someone who is *me* but instead that there should later be someone with whom I am sufficiently closely psychologically connected. Psychological connectedness, in other words, provides the principal basis for egoistic concern about the future.[27] Psychological connectedness, however, is a matter of degree. This suggests that the weaker the psychological connections between a person now and the same person later, the weaker his grounds will be now for egoistic concern about his later life.

Even if we suppose—what seems doubtful—that a one-month-old human being can be regarded as a fully real person, there will be few, if any, direct psychological connections between the person at one month and the person later in life. Hence our grounds for concern about the infant's future life for *its* sake will be correspondingly weak. If the infant dies, there is a sense in which *its* losses are less than those that an adult human being normally suffers through death, since the future it loses would have been less closely connected to it in the ways that provide grounds for egoistic concern—or perhaps, in this case, grounds for concern for its sake. (Of course, the infant's death may mean the loss of a glorious future life. But the only loss that matters significantly where the infant—qua infant—is concerned is the loss of those parts of its future life with which it would have been psychologically connected.)

C. The Revised Possible Goods Account

What this appeal to the theory of personal identity suggests is that the possible goods account, to be plausible, cannot assess the losses involved in death by simply summing up the goods that life would likely have contained were it not for death. These goods must instead be weighted in such a way that the loss through death of some future good will count

27. Ibid., chap. 12, esp. secs. 89 and 90. While psychological connectedness is what matters most, a simple argument suggests that psychological continuity also matters. Suppose that I am now psychologically connected with myself at t_1 but not with myself at t_2. Suppose that, because of the lack of any connections, I do not now have any direct concern about what happens to me at t_2. I nevertheless realize that at t_1 I will care about what happens to me at t_2, since at t_1 I will be connected to myself at t_2. Thus, since I now care about my interests at t_1, I now have an indirect reason for caring what happens to me at t_2, since what happens to me at t_2 will matter to me at t_1.

for more the closer the psychological connections would have been between the person as she was at the time of her death and as she would have been at the time at which she would have received or experienced the good.[28]

There are other ways in which the possible goods account can be revised or extended in order to be better harmonized with our common conception of the badness of death. It should, for example, make some provision for the importance of desire. While it seems implausible to suppose that one can fully account for the badness of death in terms of the fact that death frustrates so many of the victim's desires, it does seem to make a difference whether and to what extent the possible life which death prevents would have or might have contained experiences or activities that the victim actually cared about during his life.[29] So, for example, even if the possible life that is lost through death would have contained a rich variety of goods, and even if the victim would have cared about and valued these goods had he lived to experience them, his death may seem less tragic if these goods would have been ones that he cared little or nothing about while he was alive.

This might be partially explained in terms of the assumption that the change in values that would have been required for the person to come to appreciate the goods would have involved a weakening of psychological connectedness. But this is not a complete explanation. The desires and concerns a person has are important in assessing the badness of her death independently of the fact that desires and values are constituent elements in psychological connectedness. It is an important part of the explanation of the badness of death that death frustrates the victim's desires, retroactively condemns to futility her efforts to fulfill them, and generally renders many of her strivings vain and pointless.[30] In particular,

---

28. It might be argued that these implications of the theory of personal identity themselves imply that personal growth, evolution, and improvement are, in prospect at least, undesirable because they would involve a weakening of psychological connectedness and hence reduce the value to oneself now of goods that one might acquire or experience in the future. Two points may be made in reply. First, personal growth and improvement need not involve any weakening of psychological connectedness, since changes in one's character can occur in fulfillment of one's earlier desires and intentions. In these cases the relevant changes actually constitute psychological connections which bind the later person more closely to his earlier self. Thus a life in which there is substantial change and diversity will, if the diverse elements are connected by threads of desire and intention, be unified in a deeper and richer way than a life in which one's character remains static. Second, even in cases in which personal improvement simply *happens* to a person, and so may involve some weakening of psychological connectedness, it may still be desirable, all things considered. For the weakening of connectedness may be outweighed by the greater importance of, e.g., an enhancement of virtue or rationality.

29. On the claim that the badness of death can be explained solely in terms of the frustration of desire, see McMahan, *The Ethics of Killing*, chap. 1, and the references to other work, e.g. by Bernard Williams, cited there.

30. This point has been well expressed by Michael Lockwood, who writes, "Set against an ideal of human life as a meaningful whole, we can see that premature death can, as it

death is worse to the extent that sacrifices have been made for the future, or to the extent that there has been an *investment* in the future.

Let me now review the results so far of our examination of the badness of death. Death is bad for a person (or developing person) at any point in his life, provided that the life that is thereby lost would on balance have been worth living. Other things being equal, the badness of death is proportional to the quality and quantity of the goods of which the victim is deprived. But, in assessing the goods of which the victim is deprived, we must weight them both according to the extent to which they were desired by the victim and according to how closely psychologically connected the person would have been at the time of acquiring them to himself at (and perhaps prior to) the time at which he in fact died. A short but perhaps helpful way of summarizing these results would be to say that death is worse the greater the potential unity and coherence of the life it disrupts.

It is perhaps worth emphasizing, in concluding this section, that, while the degree of unity and psychological connectedness in a life is relevant to assessing the value of the life or the extent to which the life is worth living, even a high degree of unity and connectedness is not a sufficient condition for a life's being well worth living. For not only can a life be highly unified and yet be of a very low quality, but it can also be highly unified around projects or aspirations that are trivial, absurd, contemptible, vile, or even evil. Thus the account I have sketched of the badness of death, and the implied account of the goodness of continued life, is merely formal. It is an account (and only a partial account at that) of the *structure* of the good life, and thus is compatible with different conceptions of the *content* of the good life. A more complete account would have to provide criteria for evaluating the meaningfulness of the different ways of living even highly unified lives.

III. A PARADOX

As we have seen, the view I have developed implies that death at, say, thirty-five is normally worse than death at one month. This seems plausible, and coincides with our intuitions. For, when a person dies at thirty-five, the life she loses is normally one with which she would have been closely psychologically connected and in which she would have enjoyed many of the goods that she valued, desired, and strived for. But neither of these points is true in the case of the life that is lost when a person dies

---

were, make nonsense of much of what has gone before. Earlier actions, preparations, planning, whose entire purpose and rationale lay in their being directed towards some future goal, become, in the face of an untimely death, retrospectively pointless—bridges, so to speak, that terminate in mid-air, roads that lead nowhere" (Michael Lockwood, "Singer on Killing and the Preference for Life," *Inquiry* 22 [1979]: 167). This point, and the point about desire, reinforce the explanation developed in Sec. II.B of the view that death very early in life is not worse than death later in life.

at one month. It therefore seems plausible to say that a thirty-five-year-old normally stands to gain more from continuing to live than a one-month-old does, and that a thirty-five-year-old loses more through death. And this provides good grounds for thinking that death is worse at age thirty-five than it is at one month.

Let us suppose, however, that there is a newborn baby with a condition that, if untreated, will cause the baby to die at one month. The condition can be cured, but the treatment itself has the effect of making it inevitable that the person will die at the age of thirty-five. Should the baby's condition be treated? Most of us feel that, if the person's life could be expected to be worth living, then the baby ought to be treated. But this seems to indicate that we prefer for his sake that the person should die at thirty-five rather than at one month. But how can that be, given our earlier conclusion that death is worse at thirty-five than it is at one month?

We might say that to have more life that is worth living is always better than to have less, other things being equal. But that seems simply to restate the view that, if further life would be worth living, death is always worse the earlier it occurs. And that is what we have denied. We seem on the one hand to believe that death at thirty-five is worse, or more tragic, than death at one month. But now consideration of the case of the baby with the treatable condition leads us to believe that death *is* worse the earlier it occurs. We believe that it would be worse for this individual to die at one month than to die at thirty-five.

This paradox challenges the view about the badness of death that I have sketched because it seems to suggest that we feel compelled both to affirm and to deny the implications of that view. Is there a way in which the paradox might be dissolved? One suggestion might be that the paradox arises from our treating two different but superficially identical comparisons as if they were the same comparison. Consider, by way of analogy, the comparison between the following two choices. The first is a choice between death at a very early age—say at nine months after conception—and death at a much later age—say at thirty-five—for the *same person*. The second choice is between death at a very early age for one person and death at a much later age for *another* person. Both of these choices arise in a case in which a thirty-five-year-old woman who is nine months pregnant and will die unless a craniotomy is performed on the fetus. Suppose that, if the craniotomy is not performed, the baby will survive but, because of an inherited condition, will live to be only thirty-five. If we look just at the case of the fetus, we feel that it would clearly be worse for it to die now rather than at thirty-five. But if we compare the death of the mother now, at age thirty-five, with the death of the fetus now, most of us feel that the death of the mother would be the worse of the two.

While focusing on the case of the fetus alone might lead us to conclude that death at nine months after conception is worse than death at thirty-five, focusing on the comparison between the death of the fetus and the death of the mother tempts us to conclude that death at thirty-five is worse than death at nine months after conception. But, it might be argued, there is here only a surface paradox. For the terms of the two comparisons between death at nine months after conception and death at thirty-five are not the same. When we focus on the case of the fetus alone, we are comparing death at nine months with death at thirty-five rather than earlier, at nine months. In this case, therefore, choosing death at thirty-five would mean that the person would *gain* thirty-five years of life. But when we compare the death of the fetus with the death of the mother, we are comparing death at nine months rather than at thirty-five with death at thirty-five rather than much later, at the end of a full life. Death at thirty-five for the mother, unlike death at thirty-five for the person in the previous comparison, involves no gains. Hence it is not surprising that we get different answers in the two comparisons. Death at nine months *is* worse than death at thirty-five rather than at nine months; but it is *not* necessarily worse than death at thirty-five rather than at some much later time.

It may seem that the paradox as I stated it earlier trades on exactly the sort of confusion I have uncovered here. On the other hand, even here when we consider the case of the fetus alone we conclude that it would be worse for that individual to die at nine months after conception than to die at thirty-five, and this alone seems inconsistent with our earlier claim that prenatal death is less bad for the victim than death at thirty-five. To dissolve the paradox completely it seems that we must recognize that the comparative badness of different possible deaths does not necessarily determine which death it would be worse to suffer. While it is usually worse for a person to suffer a worse death (e.g., to die at forty rather than at fifty), the case of the fetus suggests that it can sometimes be better to suffer a worse death. Similarly, it can also be worse to have a less bad death—for example, when death becomes less bad for a person because the life that he would otherwise have had has now become less good than it might have been. In the latter case, the fact that his death has become less bad may seem a double misfortune.

But how, it might be asked, could it be better to suffer a worse death if the badness of death is simply a function of the deprivation which the victim suffers? How, in other words, can it be better to be deprived of more? The proper response to these questions is, it seems, to note that there are two ways of assessing the deprivation involved in death. My claims in Section II about the comparative badness of death in infancy and death in later life were relativized to persons-at-times. But the claims of this section, which seem to clash with those earlier claims, are of a different sort: they are claims about how death affects a life as a whole. The claim that death at thirty-five is worse than death in early infancy is a claim about the relative badness of death to persons at the time of death; while the claim that it is worse for a person to die in early infancy than at age thirty-five is a claim about the effect of death on the value of a person's life as a whole. Once we distinguish these two forms of evaluation, we can see that the two claims are in fact compatible and that there is no real paradox in the idea that it can be better for a person to suffer a worse death.

Part V
Professional Integrity and the Goals of Medicine

[24]

Reviving A Distinctive Medical Ethic

by Larry R. Churchill

Our culture is well on its way to reducing medical ethics to legal requirements, general citizen ethics, or personal values. A distinctive ethic for medicine provides critical distance and moral meaning for the profession and an enriched societal ethic.

Ethics is fundamentally a practical discipline, concerned with what we should do and how we should live, so beginning concretely may be wise. Consider the situation of a pediatrician who, in the course of a routine office visit, uncovers undeniable evidence of child abuse. What concerns me here is not whether the pediatrician should report this to the proper social service authorities, but what might motivate such an action. What are the rationales for reporting? I will consider four, though doubtless there are others.

A pediatrician could feel obligated to obey state statutes, so that if we were to ask, "Why are you reporting

Larry R. Churchill is professor and acting chair in the department of social medicine at the School of Medicine, University of North Carolina, Chapel Hill, NC. Earlier versions of this article were presented to the School of Medicine, University of Pittsburgh and as the 1988 Annual Oration to the Faculty Association, Society for Health and Human Values.

this case?," the response would be "Because it is the law...and I am obliged to obey the law." This might get morally more sophisticated in terms of a Kantian emphasis on not making exceptions of oneself in obedience to laws, or a utilitarian rationale for what consequences would ensue if abuse laws were ignored. The point is that the presence of the law provides moral justification for action.

Our pediatrician might report the abuse as a matter of general citizenship, appealing to citizens' responsibilities of general beneficence and to prevent harm where possible. Were we again to ask, "Why are you reporting?," the response might be couched in what are thought to be universally recognized goods, and in an impetus to act that any reasonable person would have. For example, "I'm merely doing what any right-thinking person would do." This too could be elaborated at great length in a series of justifications, but the point is that the basic motive to act is thought to spring from wells at which everyone drinks—a common ethic.

A third rationale might draw on personal, even idiosyncratic convictions, so that the question "Why report?" is answered by appeals to what one happens to believe, something peculiar to me. Here our pediatrician would be inclined to say "I just have to report this case, my conscience requires it. I couldn't live with myself if I kept quiet about it." One can well imagine this sort of rationale embellished with reference to religious authorities.

Frequently these sorts of rationales are taken to be private convictions that should generally be tolerated in a pluralistic society, where respect for difference constitutes a basic mode of our social interaction. Indeed, we sometimes tend to treat tolerance for pluralistic values as the very basis for society, so the appeal to personal moral beliefs is frequently a signal for others to stay clear—a conversation stopper, or a moral trump card. This kind of thinking is, of course, disastrous for ethics, but it is widely supported and even lauded by both liberals and libertarians. The basic point here is that this justification is warranted by individual moral judgment and its sanctity.

Finally, a fourth kind of rationale might appeal to professional ethics distinct from, though related to, an obligation to the law, a general citizen ethic, or a personal ethic. Professionals, especially doctors, have traditionally called upon canons of conduct peculiar to themselves, so that the response to "Why report?" is "Because I am obligated as a doctor to protect my patients from harm." The appeal here is to role-specific duties incurred precisely out of one's status and function as a physician, and its context is not just others, but *my patients,* persons who occupy a special, especially vulnerable position,

Hastings Center Report, May/June 1989

and with whom I have enacted special ties or bonds.

No doubt all these rationales—and perhaps others—filter through the moral sensibilities of pediatricians. They are not incompatible. But I have laid these out as options for a purpose. Imagine a moral sensibility devoid of a medical ethic *per se*, that is, in which the whole of a medical ethic is fundamentally reducible to legal requirements, general citizen ethics, or personal values. What would be lost? Are we tempted to say "Nothing"? Is what would be lost merely embellishment, an ornament like the fancy figures that used to adorn the hoods of expensive cars—a way of announcing status but having no real function?

If we think something *is* lost, do we know what? And why that something is important? Could we defend the presence of a distinctive professional ethic for medicine against egalitarian social currents, liberal philosophers, the Federal Trade Commission, Marxists, or anyone else who might challenge it? I pose the question sharply because we are, as a culture, well on our way to reducing professional ethics to these other moral modalities.

This process is unfortunate for doctors and patients alike. If it succeeds it will diminish the moral resources physicians need to do their job. I do not gainsay any of the other sources for ethics. I only argue that they are insufficient to nourish the moral sensibilities of doctors, and in the long run, to sustain the activity we now call medical practice.

How did we get to this point of not valuing a distinctive professional ethic? What are we losing if we no longer have such an ethic?

Moral Leveling and Relativism

Whether there ever was a robust professional ethic in medicine, it is clear that there was in the past aspiration for one. The paradigm is, of course, the Hippocratic Oath, which speaks not just to moral decisions but to the whole of the physician's life. It is an oath to be sworn, not principles to be convinced of cerebrally. It is particularized, it names deities who witness the swearing, and it evokes both a benediction and a malediction to underline its gravity. Currently, many graduating physicians at U.S. medical schools recite an oath claiming to be a revision of that of Hippocrates, which begins "I do solemnly swear by whatever I hold most sacred,"[1] implying either a plurality of sacred things among us, a gradation of the sacred into more/less, or, most cynically, that students do not know what they hold most sacred, but whatever it is, they will swear by it. What is noteworthy here is the dislocation of professional ethics from a commonly accepted moral framework, and the consequent "fill in the blank" quality to what authorizes professional convictions.

Bioethics teachers, like myself, have played a part in this diminution of confidence in a medical ethic. One of our favorite themes over the past fifteen or so years has been the elitism and arrogance of traditional medical ethics. The favorite example to cite is the line from the 1847 American Medical Association Code, taken from Sir Thomas Percival's writings, which enjoins physicians to "unite condescension with authority" in dealing with patients.[2] Most of us now view condescension with condescension, if not indignation.

Robert Veatch has been perhaps the most vocal of the critics who worry about the absence of general public grounding for medical ethics. "[T]he real problem," he says, "is the use of professional ethical standards rather than those rooted in some more universally accessible source of morality."[3] Veatch concludes that "a professionally generated ethic…makes no sense in theory or in practice." Many others have had similar worries.

The efforts of many teachers of bioethics over the past two decades to combat elitism and bring medical ethics into conversation with larger social norms should be seen as part of the great egalitarian emphasis of the mid-to-late-twentieth century. We are, as a society, nervous about power differences, even those that can benefit us. The result is a sense of moral leveling, in which the independent moral worth of all persons is affirmed, but in which also it is difficult to appeal to physicians' sense of themselves as special.

But something has been lost in this great moral leveling, where we are all equal, and all special, or all not special. What is lost is the importance of role-differentiated behavior and distinctive standards to guide that behavior. We do, and should, hold doctors to different and more stringent standards than farmers, postal clerks, or business people. The dean of a business school can say, as one recently did, that "Ethics is a floating crap game."[4] But the dean of a medical school cannot say that, at least not with the same glib self-assurance.

The critique of elitism in professional ethics has not resulted in a great egalitarian affirmation of values, but in a diminishment of the place and importance of values generally. This loss has been decried most recently by Alan Bloom.[5] What distresses Bloom is relativism—the facile acceptance of the proposition that any opinion is as good as any other, the view that what's true for me, is true for me, and that what's true for you is true for you.[6] This is illustrated in a *New Yorker* cartoon that shows the Prince of Darkness welcoming new arrivals into

Hell. "Welcome," he says, "you'll find that there's no right or wrong here—just whatever works for you." The insipid quality of moral relativism, its practical uselessness, is also manifest in another cartoon of entry into Hell. "The Far Side" shows a devil behind a counter with a computer terminal, processing entrants into Hell. The process looks something like an airport check-in counter. The devil meets each of the damned with the question: "Inferno or noninferno?" But he quickly follows: "Only kidding. It's all Inferno here. I just like to say that."

Modern medical students, mirroring the society from which they come, are largely anti-elitists, and adhere to high ideals of egalitarian tolerance for differences. But tolerance for differences is frequently mistaken for lack of difference, and too often *in*difference and relativism follow. On relativist grounds, any choice is as good as any other—whatever works for you. And so, there is no real choice to be made: "It's all Inferno here." On relativist grounds, we are left with the damnable conclusions that our opinions are always right, or wrong, and both, or perhaps neither. Choosing doesn't matter. So although I find Bloom's book strident, dyspeptic, and reactionary, he is concerned about something important, and something from which physicians and medical students are not exempt.

The consequences of this slippage from a noble egalitarian intent to moral relativism are many. The ones that concern me here are intellectual laziness and loss of orientation. Intellectual laziness results because in moral relativism there is nothing to be gained by deep, hard, prolonged, well-informed thought. Ill-informed, biased, and belittling opinions are just as good as well-informed and enlarging ones. The superficial ideology of relativist indifference excuses us from an essential task of ethics—critical reflection.

Loss of orientation results because relativism distracts our attention from the scene of moral choice, *viz.*, practice. But ethics is a practical discipline. Egalitarian motifs resulting in relativist postures draw attention from what doctors actually do, to focus on an ideology of anti-elitism. If we look, however, at what physicians do—the practice, for which an ethic is supposed to be some guide—it becomes clear that doctors do some extraordinary things. If they are to be able to do these things at all, never mind do them well, they need the morale, coherence, and guidance that a professional ethic provides.

I am not saying we should reaffirm the Hippocratic Oath, as Leon Kass thinks,[7] or reassert the old elitism, as the AMA occasionally seems to advocate.[8] Moral distinctiveness does not mean elitism. Moreover, by citing Bloom, even with disclaimers, I do not wish to be understood as sympathetic to the neoconservative moral and educational establishment, whose jeremiads on relativism are usually followed by nostalgic evocations for a lost golden age of universal, objective values and a sentimental communitarianism. The answer to a shallow egalitarianism of values is not a reassertion of the need for moral uniformity and objectivity. The answer, as I will argue later, is a deep egalitarianism—a real recognition of differences, an appreciation that we cannot be indifferent about differences, and that we can move beyond the spurious choice, frequently offered, between some all-embracing moral hierarchy and relativism.

I have no refutation for moral relativism. There really are no refutations, and the temptation to try only leads us in the wrong direction. Relativism, when honestly held and not put forward as cynicism from a disappointed absolutist, dies of its own weight. It is a luxury of theorists, for there are no practicing relativists, only theoretical ones—and ethics is a practical discipline. Why be concerned about relativism, if it dies of its own weight? Because if we are intellectually lazy we won't notice this theoretical corpse, we won't correlate theory and practice. Indeed, affirmations of relativism frequently serve as excuses from having to look at our practice. A vicious, self-confirmatory circle ensues, as a relativistic posture excuses us from taking any views seriously, including our own.

The Moral Distinctiveness of Medicine

What is lost if we don't have a distinctive ethic for medicine? Is our pediatrician any the worse for its absence? What things are provided by having a distinctive professional medical ethic?

One thing is critical distance—a perspective from which to view general, cultural, moral trends, the law, and one's personal convictions. A profession without its own distinctive moral convictions has nothing to profess. All that it does must be referred to and sanctioned by one of the three other sources for ethics. A profession with no distinctive moral tradition will be vulnerable to whatever currents are fashionable in religion, legal circles, or popular culture. A profession with no distinctive moral tradition will eventually lapse into dogma and succumb to whatever forces are most powerful, including now the forces of cost containment and "managed" care. By being part of a tradition—which is more than just what one happens to think—a physician can stand apart from these pressures to assess them. This is not to say that a medical ethic

Hastings Center Report, May/June 1989

can't be distorted, self-serving, or even harmful. But it is no more likely to be so than a legal, personal, or general social ethic.

Secondly, a distinctive medical ethic is necessary to tell both physicians and patients what the practice of medicine means.[9] An ethic is not just a nice addition, an optional adornment, but essential to what it means to have a profession, or be a professional, at all. Professionals without an ethic are merely technicians, who know how to perform work, but who have no capacity to say why their work has any larger meaning. To be a professional is to be existentially engaged in one's work *patterns*, that is, to see those patterns as constituting a source of nourishment for the self over time. This is, in the richest sense, to have a practice.[10]

The practice of a profession makes those who exercise it privy to a set of experiences that those who do not practice lack. The ethic peculiar to medicine becomes evident as it is practiced, and that ethic serves to interpret what the practice means. This, in turn, allows the persons engaged in the practice to continue it, to reflect upon it, to critique it, to be nourished by it, and, not least important, to pass it on. Ethics is not, then, just the "dos and don'ts" of right conduct, but a central point of orientation for professional life.

But a distinctive professional ethic does not benefit just doctors. What may surprise us—but shouldn't—is that when a distinctive ethic falters, the more general social ethic flounders as well. The effort to make doctors just like the rest of us morally didn't make all of us good citizens. Rather, it is part of a process that has resulted in a loss of confidence in any reliable moral standards at all. Ironically, rather than too much tolerance for pluralism, we have had too little. For a true tolerance should have made us appreciative of the special role of doctors, rather than made us passionate to mix them indistinguishably into a great, homogeneous moral soup. A special and an ordinary, a distinctive and a more general moral sensibility seem not to compete but to complement each other. We need them both. So the choice is not an either/or, but both, or nothing.

Now, one might gather that I am advocating a professional ethic for medicine that would be reliable because stable—in having a fixed content. Far from it. Traditions of ethics are best defined by their conflicts.[11] A tradition is in good working order when its members are actively engaged in debate about the central values. This is a picture, not of stasis and uniformity, but of incessant tension and only provisional agreement. Being a part of the tradition, or a member of the profession, is to be engaged in these debates.

Medicine is best defining and sustaining itself when, for example, it is debating the Baby Doe regulations, or whether to join in preparation for nuclear war, or participate in capital punishment, or prepaid, gatekeeper health financing schemes. Medicine is most threatened as a profession when it allows these debates to be settled in nonmoral terms, such as those of economics, or legal constraints, or even when it allows the moral debate on such issues to exclude the values intrinsic to medical practice.

I have been arguing against two extremes in interpreting the place and role of a medical ethic. One extreme says a medical ethic is unique and aboriginal, generated by physicians, and sets physicians apart from the rest of society. This view says, in effect, that in the face of special medical duties, usual ethical norms are suspended or overridden. The other extreme says that being a doctor is not relevant to how one makes moral decisions, that we are all the same morally and should all follow the same rules of a universally accessible, generic ethic. Professional duties must finally be grounded in rules and processes common to all.

Both positions have a point. Proponents of a special medical ethic are correct in their sense that professional roles give us moral definition. We cannot replace medical virtues with a generic, procedural ethic designed for "rational agents." Advocates of a universally accessible source of morality are correct in their criticism of the elitist forms that professional ethics have taken. However, the impediment to moving beyond these partial perspectives to a more appropriate medical ethic is not any particular item of medical moral traditions. Rather, the impediment is a meta-ethical requirement, an intellectual commitment about what ethics must be if it is to be conceptually satisfying. For the sake of convenience, not of complete adequacy, I will refer to this intellectual requirement as *verticality*.

The Problem of Verticality

Vertical thinking is the powerful tendency to arrange moral considerations into a single hierarchical order. The search for a grounding of moral choices, for grading actions and reasons for actions by the terms of a single, superordinate theoretical system, is one of the peculiarities of modern ethics. One prevalent mode of vertical ordering—a rationalist one we owe largely to Kant—goes like this: Actions are morally valued only if they follow from a choice, sanctioned by an enduring principle, which in turn is anchored in conceptual foundations,

Hastings Center Report. May/June 1989

what Kant called "the metaphysics of morals." Other thinkers, of course, recommend different sorts of hierarchies, anchored in sentiments, logic, conscience, custom, or revelation, rather than reason. So while the particulars of the hierarchy may vary, the idea that there must be some such vertical structure does not. The vision is of a moral life unified by *theoretical* coherence and consistency, a moral life vouchsafed by a permanent, neutral framework that will allow us to "touch bottom."

The drive for conceptual foundations has not always been a part of ethics. Aristotle, for example, believed that coherence and unity in moral life was an achievement of practice, highly contingent on factors beyond one's control and for which theory was only modestly useful.[12] The unfortunate result of the modern quest for theoretical unity is that it tends to treat practice in a Procrustean way, and see everything as deontological, or utilitarian, or Marxist, or Christian, or Hippocratic, and so on. These are not all "theories" in the same way, but they all serve as normative hierarchies.

The need for an all-embracing, unified moral framework is, again, the theoretician's need, not the moral actor's—what I called earlier an "intellectual requirement." The experience of moral actors (as opposed to the requirements of theory) indicates a variety of hierarchies, both among different persons, and even different hierarchies of thinking within a single agent, depending on the context. We should not assume that, by definition, pluralism is a problem. We are conditioned to think, I fear, that in the absence of some moral hierarchy, some grounding, some foundation common to all, we are impotent to discriminate good from evil, that our choice is a hierarchically ordered normative system, or the moral abyss of relativism. This is a spurious choice, spawned by theorizing in a vacuum.

Here, perhaps, a caveat is in order. For this is not an argument against all sorts of vertical thinking in ethics, only against the idea of a superordinate verticality that resolves all conflict. Conflict is resolved in practical judgments, not by possessing the right theory. And not all vertical approaches to ethical reasoning preclude pluralism. The difficulty arises when our investment in a theory tempts us to use it as an aegis against complexity, a way of ordering the variety and diversity of values evident in the living of life. Too often ethics is taught and talked about as competition among universal theories, and discussants are required to identify themselves and others as "deontologists," "rule-utilitarians," or "agapeists."

We are tempted to bandy these labels about because they allow us to assume the perspective of the moral judge, or *critic*. There is much to learn

> *The critique of elitism in professional ethics has not resulted in a great egalitarian affirmation of values, but in a diminishment of the place and importance of values generally.*

from the assumption of a different perspective, that of the moral *agent*. Moral agents or actors usually don't seek to ground actions in principles, and then in theories, but to ground *themselves*, that is, to orient the moral choices they make into the rest of their lives. They express a need to be able to live with themselves, to "feel right" about what they are doing. This is a complex process in which theories are useful as tools for probing, not as a priori norms. This process is not vertical structuring, but searching for "fit," trying on different alternative choices in the imagination, or in conversation, to see how they would work, like trying on a suit to see if it's the "right" size. The search for solid foundations, for unassailable grounds, for the right theory, will distract us from what persons in moral quandaries actually do, in favor of what theorists think they ought to do. More attention to how persons think and feel morally, as opposed to how a theory prescribes they ought to think and feel, would be salutary.

Theories are best understood as heuristic devices for moral reflection, not as guarantors of goodness or rightness. Disputes about the correct ethical theory (as some are given to read the history of moral philosophy) are in principle unresolvable. But such disputes are always resolvable in practice. Provisional and pragmatic resolution is possible because no theory seems to have enough heuristic power to explain all of the moral life, for each was devised to account for some particular facet of moral experience, and there are many facets. Theorists get into difficulty when they mistake mastery of one aspect of moral life for mastery of the whole.

Imagine a situation in which a person is inclined to forsake his duty. Kant would be of enormous help. Imagine a situation in which only a rigid sense of duty is considered and outcomes are ignored. John Stuart Mill is the answer. Another person neglects her conscience, another gives in to his sexual appetites, and yet another relates to her life as manager and controller. We would recommend that the first person study Butler, the second read Plato or perhaps St. Paul, and hold that the third would profit from Epictetus.

But when any of these moralists claim, or we claim for them, that their theory is *the* theory, capturing

Hastings Center Report, May/June 1989

the essence of morality, or the final justificatory mode against which all others are to be judged they become comical—caricatures of ethics. It is in this light that we should read the contested claims of legal, general, personal, and also professional ethics. My point is not that theory is unnecessary. Rather, my point is that we need multiple theories, and that we should be skeptical of the modern drive for an encompassing verticality, for it will homogenize moral experience.

Hierarchical assumptions also lead us to overestimate the place of rules and principles in moral thinking. A principle-dominated approach to ethics is the standard in late-twentieth-century America. Underscoring the image of verticality, an emphasis on principles portrays the basic task of ethics as one of ordering or "prioritizing"; this, however, neglects the importance of moral sentiments, the value of moral traditions, and the role of virtues. This neglect, in turn, has led us to ask the question about a distinctive professional ethic in a thin and unproductive way, *viz.,* "Do or should doctors justify their actions by appeal to the same rules as the rest of us?" or "Are there special principles of medical ethics?" A more productive question would be "Are there traditions that should inform the moral thinking of doctors in special ways?"; or "Should the moral sensibilities of doctors be turned and tuned to different nuances of situations than those of individuals who do not practice medicine?" Concern for the turning and tuning of moral sensibilities, however, is frequently dismissed as vague self-indulgence—a superficial stratum of the vertical hierarchy. So let me try to illustrate what I mean by a "moral sensibility" and how important a force it is in ethics.

Moral Sensibilities and Consonance

The moral sensibilities of persons can be compared to houses. Houses can look pretty much the same from the outside, especially if designed by like-minded architects and constructed by similar builders. So we might be tempted to say that such houses are about the same. But houses, like moral sensibilities have to be understood from within, as living space and not just architectural space, and on these terms, similar looking houses may be very different. Imagine one decorated in Scandinavian teak and another in Early American pine. Imagine that one house is a group home for troubled adolescents, while another is the residence of a bachelor and his widowed mother. Some houses have occupants, others are a residence, still others are "homes," in a variety of senses.

Just so, the differences between an ordinary

general ethic and a medical ethic may not be self-evident. We may not notice the differences if we merely ask "Do we all follow the same rules and principles?," since this is like asking "Are these houses the same?," where judgments about sameness are made from the architect's blueprints or the building inspector's manual. The difference between a general and a professional medical ethic is not the difference between a three-bedroom ranch and the Taj Mahal. It's more the difference between how residents in similar structures dwell in those structures, adapt them to their special needs, and make them "home."

Vertical ordering, in sum, tends to turn professional ethics and general ethics into competitors, as if one must be more basic, or more true, than the other. Vocal and musical metaphors are more fitting, for they enable us to talk of consonance or dissonance among professional norms, general cultural standards, personal values, and so on, implying a task of integration and harmonizing in which it is assumed that different voices will be in play. And the differences in these voices are not reducible to each other. Altos are not off-key sopranos. Moral differences are real differences, not alternative versions of the same thing. Medical ethics is not just a specialized version of general contract ethics, or covenantal ethics, or anything else.

Substituting consonance for verticality as a way of organizing moral discourse means a frank recognition of moral pluralism, both within individual lives and among different persons and groups in society. It also means giving up on the ideal of morality as necessarily unitary in nature, a single kind of thing, unified by a fundamental principle of ethics, a single foundation, an ultimate moral *Ursprach* from which all else can be derived and understood. As Lawrence Blum puts it, "there are irreducibly different and varied types of moral goodness."[13] Among other things this signals a thickness we must attend to in the moral activities of people. Theories that take account of this thickness, rather than flattening it out, will be superior to most we now work with. Claims to a distinctive professional ethic should be embraced, so long as those claims do not include assumptions of an acritical finality and are not preemptive of other forms or expressions of moral goodness.

Coda

Should there be a distinctive professional ethic for medicine? Yes. But my concern here is not to specify its contents. Moreover, I have no specific advice to give the pediatrician in the opening case. Except in extraordinary circumstances, it is clear

Hastings Center Report, May/June 1989

what duty would require. I have deliberately shaped the case so that the *what* would be (relatively) uncontroversial in order to focus on the *why*. Ethics is not just actions, but the mode of moral deliberation that gives meaning to those actions. It is the quality, depth, and character of that deliberation that will distinguish this pediatrician as a doctor—not just what she does, but *why* and *how* she does it. In contested or controversial actions it is access to the *why* and *how* that enables us to describe the actions at all.

The content of a medical ethic is very important. It is not, however, the job of moral philosophers to determine that content. Physicians (and patients) should map this terrain. Moral philosophers should worry more about how the topography is understood, and how the map is used. What the moral mapping of its practice will display or obscure will depend on the purposes and goals of medicine, and these are set through a complex nexus of forces involving the whole culture. The key thing to remember is that the map is not the territory. Every map both illuminates and distorts, and travelers will need several maps, not just one, for no one map can definitively and finally locate all the values involved.

The articulation of a distinctive medical ethic should steer clear of the old elitism and the new egalitarian universalism. It should distinguish physicians from the rest of us, but without assumptions of separateness, disrelatedness, or either superiority or inferiority. If medical ethics needs to be justified, it will be justified—or will not be—in terms of the practice of medicine, not because it fits a particular philosophical or political concept of "the good."

What will serve us well in the ongoing articulation and critique is both an intellectual and a moral virtue, not easy to encapsulate in a phrase. It is an agility of moral sensibility. Agility in our moral thinking is essential because of the nature of human moral experience: because moral unity, integrity, and coherence are achievements of practice, not primarily cognitive insights or achievements of theory; because many principles and virtues are needed for practice, not just a few rules; because we change, and grow (and unfortunately also wither) morally, rather than enjoy a steady state; because "the good" is protean, not captured in a single theory, and perhaps not capturable by the totality of all theories.

Stuart Hampshire puts it this way: "We have no pressing need for satisfactory total explanations of our conduct or our way of life. Our need is rather to construct and maintain a way of life of which we are not ashamed and which we shall not on reflection, regret or despise, and which we respect."[14]

References

[1] This revised Hippocratic Oath is apparently widely used. The earliest reference I can find is to its use at the Ohio State University School of Medicine, 1957.

[2] American Medical Association, *Code of Medical Ethics, 1847* (New York: H. Ludwig and Co., 1848). A good place to find the 1847 "Code" as well as subsequent codes and statements of principles is the appendix to Volume 4 of *The Encyclopedia of Bioethics*, Warren T. Reich, ed. (New York: The Free Press, 1978), 1737-46.

[3] Robert M. Veatch, *A Theory of Medical Ethics* (New York: Basic Books, 1981), 106.

[4] The Raleigh, NC, *News and Observer*, 20 March 1988, B-1.

[5] Alan Bloom, *The Closing of the American Mind* (New York: Simon and Schuster, 1987).

[6] For this portrait of relativism and the illustrations that follow I am indebted to John Churchill, "Liberal Education: Its End and Future," unpublished.

[7] See Leon Kass, *Toward a More Natural Science* (New York: The Free Press, 1985), 224-46.

[8] See, for example, the 1980 *Principles* adopted by the AMA House of Delegates at its annual meeting, July 22, 1980. A full statement can be found in *Medical Ethics*, Natalie Abrams and Michael Buckner, eds. (Cambridge, MA: MIT Press, 1983), 641-42.

[9] The notion of ethics as an interpretive tool for the social meaning of a profession is a very old one. One forceful modern exploration is that of Stanley Hauerwas in *Truthfulness and Tragedy* (Notre Dame, IN: University of Notre Dame Press, 1977), 184-202.

[10] Here I draw upon the concept of "practice" in its moral meaning as developed by Alasdair MacIntyre, *After Virtue* (Notre Dame, IN: University of Notre Dame Press, 1981), 169-89.

[11] Alasdair MacIntyre, *Whose Justice? Which Rationality?* (Notre Dame, IN: University of Notre Dame Press, 1988), especially at 370-88.

[12] See the brilliant work by the modern Aristotelian Martha Nussbaum, *The Fragility of Goodness* (Cambridge: Cambridge University Press, 1986), 318-42.

[13] Lawrence Blum, *Friendship, Altruism and Morality* (London: Routledge and Kegan Paul, 1980), 8.

[14] Stuart Hampshire, *Morality and Conflict* (Cambridge, MA: Harvard University Press, 1983), 168.

[25]

Neither for love nor money: why doctors must not kill

LEON R. KASS

I<small>S</small> THE profession of medicine ethically neutral? If so, whence shall we derive the moral norms or principles to govern its practices? If not, how are the norms of professional conduct related to the rest of what makes medicine a profession?

These difficult questions, now much discussed, are in fact very old, indeed as old as the beginnings of Western medicine. According to an ancient Greek myth, the goddess Athena procured two powerful drugs in the form of blood taken from the Gorgon Medusa, the blood drawn from her left side providing protection against death, that from her right side a deadly poison. According to one version of the myth, Athena gave to Asclepius, the revered founder of medicine, vials of both drugs; according to the other version, she gave him only the life-preserving drug, reserving the power of destruction for herself. There is force in both accounts: the first attests to

This article is dedicated to the memory of my father-in-law, Kalman Apfel, M.D., physician extraordinaire (1907-1988), and my mother-in-law, Polly Apfel (1911-1987), who exemplified even with her last breath the noblest possibilities of the human soul. Earlier versions of this essay were presented as lectures delivered for the Program in Ethics and the Professions, Harvard University, March 16, 1988, and for the Kennedy Institute of Ethics, Georgetown University, May 6, 1988.

the moral neutrality of medical means, and of technical power generally; the second shows that wisdom would constitute medicine an unqualifiedly benevolent—i.e., intrinsically ethical—art.

Today, we doubt that medicine is an intrinsically ethical activity, but we are quite certain that it can both help and harm. In fact, today, help and harm flow from the same vial. The same respirator that brings a man back from the edge of the grave also senselessly prolongs the life of an irreversibly comatose young woman. The same morphine that reverses the respiratory distress of pulmonary edema can, in higher doses, arrest respiration altogether. Whether they want to or not, doctors are able to kill—quickly, efficiently, surely. And what is more, it seems that they may soon be licensed and encouraged to do so.

Last year in Holland some 5,000 patients were intentionally put to death by their physicians, while authorities charged with enforcing the law against homicide agreed not to enforce it. Not satisfied with such hypocrisy, and eager to immunize physicians against possible prosecution, American advocates of active euthanasia are seeking legislative changes in several states that would legalize so-called mercy killing by physicians. A year ago the editor of the *Journal of the American Medical Association* published an outrageous (and perhaps fictitious) case of mercy killing, precisely to stir professional and public discussion of direct medical killing—perhaps, some have said, as a trial balloon.[1] So-called active euthanasia practiced by physicians seems to be an idea whose time has come. But, in my view, it is a bad idea whose time must not come—not now, not ever. This essay is in part an effort to support this conclusion. But it is also an attempt to explore the ethical character of the medical profession, using the question of killing by doctors as a probe. Accordingly, I will be considering these interrelated questions: What are the norms that all physicians, *as physicians*, should agree to observe, whatever their personal opinions? What is the basis of such a medical ethic? What does it say—and what should we think— about doctors intentionally killing?

Contemporary ethical approaches

The question about physicians killing is a special case of—but not thereby identical to—this general question: May or ought one kill people who ask to be killed? Among those who answer this gen-

---

[1] "It's Over, Debbie," *Journal of the American Medical Association*, 259: 272, January 8, 1988. See, in response, Willard Gaylin, Leon R. Kass, Edmund D. Pellegrino, Mark Siegler, "'Doctors Must Not Kill,'" *Journal of the American Medical Association*, 259: 2139-40, April 8, 1988.

eral question in the affirmative, two reasons are usually given. Because these reasons also reflect the two leading approaches to medical ethics today, they are especially worth noting. First is the reason of *freedom* or *autonomy*. Each person has a right to control his or her body and his or her life, including the end of it; some go so far as to assert a right to die, a strange claim in a liberal society, founded on the need to secure and defend the unalienable right to life. But strange or not, for patients with waning powers too weak to oppose potent life-prolonging technologies wielded by aggressive physicians, the claim based on choice, autonomy, and self-determination is certainly understandable. On this view, physicians (or others) are bound to acquiesce in demands not only for termination of treatment but also for intentional killing through poison, because the right to choose—freedom—must be respected, even more than life itself, and even when the physician would never recommend or concur in the choices made. When persons exercise their right to choose against their continuance as embodied beings, doctors must not only cease their ministrations to the body; as keepers of the vials of life and death, they are also morally bound actively to dispatch the embodied person, out of deference to the autonomous personal choice that is, in this view, most emphatically the patient to be served.

The second reason for killing the patient who asks for death has little to do with choice. Instead, death is to be directly and swiftly given because the patient's life is deemed no longer worth living, according to some substantive or "objective" measure. Unusually great pain or a terminal condition or an irreversible coma or advanced senility or extreme degradation is the disqualifying quality of life that pleads—choice or no choice—for merciful termination. Choice may enter indirectly to confirm the judgment: if the patient does not speak up, the doctor (or the relatives or some other proxy) may be asked to affirm that he would not himself choose—or that his patient, were he *able* to choose, *would* not choose—to remain alive with one or more of these stigmata. It is not his autonomy but rather the miserable and pitiable condition of his body or mind that justifies doing the patient in. Absent such substantial degradations, requests for assisted death would not be honored. Here the body itself offends and must be plucked out, from compassion or mercy, to be sure. Not the autonomous will of the patient, but the doctor's benevolent and compassionate love for suffering humanity justifies the humane act of mercy killing.

As I have indicated, these two reasons advanced to justify the killing of patients correspond to the two approaches to medical

ethics most prominent in the literature today: the school of autonomy and the school of general benevolence and compassion (or love).
Despite their differences, they are united in their opposition to the
belief that medicine is intrinsically a moral profession, with its own
immanent principles and standards of conduct that set limits on
what physicians may properly do. Each seeks to remedy the ethical
defect of a profession seen to be in itself *a*moral, technically competent but morally neutral.

For the first ethical school, morally neutral technique is morally
used only when it is used according to the wishes of the patient as
client or consumer. The implicit (and sometimes explicit) model of
the doctor-patient relationship is one of *contract*: the physician—a
highly competent hired syringe, as it were—sells his services on
demand, restrained only by the law (though he is free to refuse his
services if the patient is unwilling or unable to meet his fee). Here's
the deal: for the patient, autonomy and service; for the doctor,
money, graced by the pleasure of giving the patient what he wants.
If a patient wants to fix her nose or change his gender, determine
the sex of unborn children, or take euphoriant drugs just for kicks,
the physician can and will go to work—provided that the price is
right and that the contract is explicit about what happens if the cus-
tomer isn't satisfied.[2]

For the second ethical school, morally neutral technique is morally used only when it is used under the guidance of general benevolence or loving charity. Not the will of the patient, but the humane
and compassionate motive of the physician—not as physician but as
human being—makes the doctor's actions ethical. Here, too, there
can be strange requests and stranger deeds, but if they are done
from love, nothing can be wrong—again, providing the law is silent.
All acts—including killing the patient—done lovingly are licit, even
praiseworthy. Good and humane intentions can sanctify any deed.

In my opinion, each of these approaches should be rejected as a
basis for medical ethics. For one thing, neither can make sense of
some specific duties and restraints long thought absolutely inviolate
under the traditional medical ethic—e.g., the proscription against
having sex with patients. Must we now say that sex with patients is
permissible if the patient wants it and the price is right, or, alternatively, if the doctor is gentle and loving and has a good bedside
manner? Or do we glimpse in this absolute prohibition a deeper

---

[2] Of course, any physician with *personal* scruples against one or another of these
practices may "write" the relevant exclusions into the service contract he offers his
customers.

understanding of the medical vocation, which the prohibition both embodies and protects? Indeed, as I will now try to show, using the taboo against doctors killing patients, the medical profession has its own instrinsic ethic, which a physician true to his calling will not violate, either for love or for money.

Professing ethically

Let me propose a different way of thinking about medicine as a profession. Consider medicine not as a mixed marriage between its own value-neutral technique and some extrinsic moral principles, but as an inherently ethical activity, in which technique and conduct are both ordered in relation to an overarching good, the naturally given end of health. This once traditional view of medicine I have defended at length in four chapters of my book, *Toward a More Natural Science*.[3] Here I will present the conclusions without the arguments. It will suffice, for present purposes, if I can render this view plausible.

A profession, as etymology suggests, is an activity or occupation to which its practitioner publicly professes—that is, confesses—his devotion. Learning may, of course, be required of, and prestige may, of course, be granted to, the professional, but it is the profession's *goal* that calls, that learning serves, and that prestige honors. Each of the ways of life to which the various professionals profess their devotion must be a way of life worthy of such devotion—and so they all are. The teacher devotes himself to assisting the learning of the young, looking up to truth and wisdom; the lawyer (or the judge) devotes himself to rectifying injustice for his client (or for the parties before the court), looking up to what is lawful and right; the clergyman devotes himself to tending the souls of his parishioners, looking up to the sacred and the divine; and the physician devotes himself to healing the sick, looking up to health and wholeness.

Being a professional is thus more than being a technician. It is rooted in our moral nature; it is a matter not only of the mind and hand but also of the heart, not only of intellect and skill but also of character. For it is only as a being willing and able to devote himself to others and to serve some high good that a person makes a public profession of his way of life. To profess is an ethical act, and it makes the professional qua *professional* a moral being who prospectively affirms the moral nature of his activity.

---

[3] Leon R. Kass, M.D., *Toward a More Natural Science: Biology and Human Affairs*, New York: The Free Press, 1985; paperback, 1988. See Chapters Six to Nine.

Professing oneself a professional is an ethical act for many reasons. It is an articulate public act, not merely a private and silent choice—a confession before others who are one's witnesses. It freely promises continuing devotion, not merely announces present preferences, to a way of life, not just a way to a livelihood, a life of action, not only of thought. It serves some high good, which calls forth devotion because it is both good and high, but which requires such devotion because its service is most demanding and difficult, and thereby engages one's character, not merely one's mind and hands.

The good to which the medical profession is devoted is health, a naturally given although precarious standard or norm, characterized by "wholeness" and "well-working," toward which the living body moves on its own. Even the modern physician, despite his great technological prowess, is but an assistant to natural powers of self-healing. But health, though a goal tacitly sought and explicitly desired, is difficult to attain and preserve. It can be ours only provisionally and temporarily, for we are finite and frail. Medicine thus finds itself in between: the physician is called to serve the high and universal goal of health while also ministering to the needs and relieving the sufferings of the frail and particular patient. Moreover, the physician must respond not only to illness but also to its meaning for each individual, who, in addition to his symptoms, may suffer from self-concern—and often fear and shame—about weakness and vulnerability, neediness and dependence, loss of self-esteem, and the fragility of all that matters to him. Thus, the inner meaning of the art of medicine is derived from the pursuit of health and the care for the ill and suffering, guided by the self-conscious awareness, shared (even if only tacitly) by physician and patient alike, of the delicate and dialectical tension between wholeness and necessary decay.

When the activity of healing the sick is thus understood, we can discern certain virtues requisite for practicing medicine—among them, moderation and self-restraint, gravity, patience, sympathy, discretion, and prudence. We can also discern specific positive duties, addressed mainly to the patient's vulnerability and self-concern—including the demands for truthfulness, patient instruction, and encouragement. And, arguably, we can infer the importance of certain negative duties, formulable as absolute and unexceptionable rules. Among these, I submit, is this rule: Doctors must not kill. The rest of this essay attempts to defend this rule and to show its relation to the medical ethic, itself understood as growing out of the inner meaning of the medical vocation.

I confine my discussion solely to the question of direct, intentional killing of patients *by physicians*—so-called mercy killing. Though I confess myself opposed to such killing even by non-physicians, I am not arguing here against euthanasia per se. More importantly, I am not arguing against the cessation of medical treatment when such treatment merely prolongs painful or degraded dying, nor do I oppose the use of certain measures to relieve suffering that have, as an unavoidable consequence, an increased risk of death. Doctors may and must allow to die, even if they must not intentionally kill.

I appreciate the danger in offering arguments against killing: even at best, they are unlikely to be equal to the task. Most taboos operate immediately and directly, through horror and repugnance; discursive arguments against, say, incest or cannibalism can never yield the degree of certitude intuitively and emotionally felt by those who know such practices to be abominable, nor are they likely to persuade anyone who is morally blind. It is not obvious that any argument can demonstrate, once and for all, why murder is bad or why doctors must not kill. No friend of decency wants to imperil sound principles by attempting to argue, unsuccessfully, for their soundness. Yet we have no other choice. Some moral matters, once self-evident, are no longer self-evident to us. When physicians themselves—as in Holland—undertake to kill patients, with public support, intuition and revulsion have fallen asleep. Only argument, with all its limitations, can hope to reawaken them.

Assessing the consequences

Although the bulk of my argument will turn on my understanding of the special meaning of professing the art of healing, I begin with a more familiar mode of ethical analysis: assessing needs and benefits versus dangers and harms. To do this properly is a massive task. Here, I can do little more than raise a few of the relevant considerations. Still the best discussion of this topic is a now-classic essay by Yale Kamisar, written thirty years ago.[4] Kamisar makes vivid the difficulties in assuring that the choice for death will be *freely* made and adequately *informed*, the problems of physician error and abuse, the troubles for human relationships within families and between doctors and patients, the difficulty of preserving the bound-

---

[4] Yale Kamisar, "Some Non-Religious Views Against Proposed 'Mercy-Killing' Legislation," *Minnesota Law Review* 42: 969-1042 (May, 1958). Reprinted, with a new preface by Professor Kamisar, in "The Slide Toward Mercy Killing," *Child and Family Reprint Booklet Series*, 1987.

ary between voluntary and involuntary euthanasia, and the risks to the whole social order from weakening the absolute prohibition against taking innocent life. These considerations are, in my view, alone sufficient to rebut any attempt to weaken the taboo against medical killing; their relative importance for determining public policy far exceeds their relative importance in this essay. But here they serve also to point us to more profound reasons why doctors must not kill.

There is no question that fortune deals many people a very bad hand, not least at the end of life. All of us, I am sure, know or have known individuals whose last weeks, months, or even years were racked with pain and discomfort, degraded by dependency or loss of self-control, isolation or insensibility, or who lived in such reduced humanity that it cast a deep shadow over their entire lives, especially as remembered by the survivors. All who love them would wish to spare them such an end, and there is no doubt that an earlier death could do it. Against such a clear benefit, attested to by many a poignant and heartrending true story, it is difficult to argue, especially when the arguments are necessarily general and seemingly abstract. Still, in the aggregate, the adverse consequences —including real suffering—of being governed solely by mercy and compassion may far outweigh the aggregate benefits of relieving agonal or terminal distress.

The "need" for mercy killing

The first difficulty emerges when we try to gauge the so-called "need" or demand for medically assisted killing. This question, to be sure, is in part empirical. But evidence can be gathered only if the relevant categories of "euthanizable" people are clearly defined. Such definition is notoriously hard to accomplish—and it is not always honestly attempted. On careful inspection, we discover that if the category is precisely defined, the need for mercy killing seems greatly exaggerated, and if the category is loosely defined, the poisoners will be working overtime.

The category always mentioned first to justify mercy killing is the group of persons suffering from incurable and fatal illnesses, with intractable pain and with little time left to live but still fully aware, who freely request a release from their distress—e.g., people rapidly dying from disseminated cancer with bony metastases, unresponsive to chemotherapy. But as experts in pain control tell us, the number of such people with truly intractable and untreatable pain is in fact rather low. Adequate analgesia is apparently possible in the vast majority of cases, provided that the physician and patient are willing to use strong enough medicines in adequate doses and with proper timing.[5]

But, it will be pointed out, full analgesia induces drowsiness and blunts or distorts awareness. How can that be a desired outcome of treatment? Fair enough. But then the rationale for requesting death begins to shift from relieving experienced suffering to ending a life no longer valued by its bearer or, let us be frank, by the onlookers. If this becomes a sufficient basis to warrant mercy killing, now the category of euthanizable people cannot be limited to individuals with incurable or fatal painful illnesses with little time to live. Now persons in all sorts of greatly reduced and degraded conditions—from persistent vegetative state to quadriplegia, from severe depression to the condition that now most horrifies, Alzheimer's disease—might have equal claim to have their suffering mercifully halted. The trouble, of course, is that most of these people can no longer request for themselves the dose of poison. Moreover, it will be difficult—if not impossible—to develop the requisite calculus of degradation or to define the threshold necessary for ending life.

From voluntary to involuntary

Since it is so hard to describe precisely and "objectively" what kind and degree of pain, suffering, or bodily or mental impairment, and what degree of incurability or length of anticipated remaining life, could justify mercy killing, advocates repair (at least for the time being) to the principle of volition: the request for assistance in death is to be honored because it is freely made by the one whose life it is, and who, for one reason or another, cannot commit suicide alone. But this too is fraught with difficulty: How free or informed is a choice made under debilitated conditions? Can consent long in advance be sufficiently informed about all the particular circumstances that it is meant prospectively to cover? And, in any case, are not such choices easily and subtly manipulated, especially in the vulnerable? Kamisar is very perceptive on this subject:

> Is this the kind of choice, assuming that it can be made in a fixed and rational manner, that we want to offer a gravely ill person? Will we not sweep up, in the process, some who are not really tired of life, but think others are tired of them; some who do not really want to die, but who feel they should not live on, because to do so when there looms the legal alter-

---

[5] The inexplicable failure of many physicians to provide the proper—and available—relief of pain is surely part of the reason why some people now insist that physicians (instead) should give them death.

native of euthanasia is to do a selfish or a cowardly act? Will not some feel
an obligation to have themselves 'eliminated' in order that funds allocated
for their terminal care might be better used by their families or, financial
worries aside, in order to relieve their families of the emotional strain
involved?

Even were these problems soluble, the insistence on voluntariness as the justifying principle cannot be sustained. The enactment
of a law legalizing mercy killing on voluntary request will certainly
be challenged in the courts under the equal-protection clause of the
Fourteenth Amendment. The law, after all, will not legalize assistance to suicides in general, but only mercy killing. The change will
almost certainly occur not as an exception to the criminal law pro-
scribing homicide but as a new "treatment option," as part of a
right to "A Humane and Dignified Death."[6] Why, it will be argued,
should the comatose or the demented be denied such a right or such
a "treatment," just because they cannot claim it for themselves?
This line of reasoning has already led courts to allow substituted
judgment and proxy consent in termination-of-treatment cases since
Quinlan, the case that, Kamisar rightly says, first "badly smudged,
if it did not erase, the distinction between the right to choose one's
own death and the right to choose someone else's." When proxies
give their consent, they will do so on the basis not of autonomy but
of a substantive judgment—namely, that for these or those reasons,
the life in question is not worth living. Precisely because most of the
cases that are candidates for mercy killing are of this sort, the line
between voluntary and involuntary euthanasia cannot hold, and
will be effaced by the intermediate case of the mentally impaired or
comatose who are declared no longer willing to live because someone else wills that result for them. In fact, the more honest advocates of euthanasia openly admit that it is these nonvoluntary cases
that they especially hope to dispatch, and that their plea for *voluntary* euthanasia is just a first step. It is easy to see the trains of
abuses that are likely to follow the most innocent cases, especially
because the innocent cases cannot be precisely and neatly separated
from the rest.

Everyone is, of course, aware of the danger of abuses. So procedures are suggested to prevent their occurrence. But to provide
real safeguards against killing the unwilling or the only half-heartedly
willing, and to provide time for a change of mind, they must be

---

[6] This was the title of the recently proposed California voter initiative that barely
failed to gather enough signatures to appear on the November 1988 ballot. It will
almost certainly be back.

intrusive, cumbersome, and costly. As Kamisar points out, the scrupulous euthanasiasts seek a goal "which is *inherently inconsistent*: a procedure for death which *both* (1) provides ample safeguards against abuse and mistake; and (2) is 'quick' and 'easy' in operation." Whatever the procedure adopted, moreover, blanket immunity from lawsuits and criminal prosecution cannot be given in advance, especially because of ineradicable suspicions of coercion or engineered consent, and the likelihood of mixed motives and potential conflict, post mortem, among family members.

Damaging the doctor-patient relationship

Abuses and conflicts aside, legalized mercy killing by doctors will almost certainly damage the doctor-patient relationship. The patient's trust in the doctor's wholehearted devotion to the patient's best interests will be hard to sustain once doctors are licensed to kill. Imagine the scene: you are old, poor, in failing health, and alone in the world; you are brought to the city hospital with fractured ribs and pneumonia. The nurse or intern enters late at night with a syringe full of yellow stuff for your intravenous drip. How soundly will you sleep? It will not matter that your doctor has never yet put anyone to death; that he is legally entitled to do so—even if only in some well-circumscribed areas—will make a world of difference.

And it will make a world of psychic difference too for conscientious physicians. How easily will they be able to care wholeheartedly for patients when it is always possible to think of killing them as a "therapeutic option"? Shall it be penicillin and a respirator one more time, or perhaps just an overdose of morphine this time? Physicians get tired of treating patients who are hard to cure, who resist their best efforts, who are on their way down—"gorks," "gomers," and "vegetables" are only some of the less than affectionate names they receive from the house officers. Won't it be tempting to think that death is the best treatment for the little old lady "dumped" again on the emergency room by the nearby nursing home?

Even the most humane and conscientious physician psychologically needs protection against himself and his weaknesses, if he is to care fully for those who entrust themselves to him. A physician friend who worked many years in a hospice caring for dying patients explained it to me most convincingly: "Only because I knew that I could not and would not kill my patients was I able to enter most fully and intimately into caring for them as they lay dying." The psychological burden of the license to kill (not to speak of the brutalization of the physician-killers) could very well be an intolerably high price to pay for physician-assisted euthanasia, especially if it also leads to greater remoteness, aloofness, and indifference as defenses against the guilt associated with harming those we care for.

The point, however, is not merely psychological and consequentialist: it is also moral and essential. My friend's horror at the thought that he might be tempted to kill his patients, were he not enjoined from doing so, embodies a deep understanding of the medical ethic and its intrinsic limits. We move from assessing the consequences to looking at medicine itself.

The limits of medicine

Every activity can be distinguished, more or less easily, from other activities. Sometimes the boundaries are indistinct; it is not always easy, especially today, to distinguish some music from noise or some teaching from indoctrination. Medicine and healing are no different; it is sometimes hard to determine the boundaries, both with regard to ends and means. Is all cosmetic surgery healing? Are placebos—or food and water—drugs?

There is, of course, a temptation to finesse these questions of definition or to deny the existence of boundaries altogether: medicine *is* whatever doctors *do*, and doctors do whatever doctors *can*. Technique and power alone define the art. Put this way, we see the need for limits: Technique and power are ethically neutral, usable for both good and ill. The need for finding or setting limits to the use of power is especially important when the power is dangerous; it matters more that we know the proper limits on the use of medical power—or military power—than, say, the proper limits on the use of a paint brush or violin.

The beginning of ethics regarding power generally lies in naysaying. Small children coming into their powers must be taught restraint, both for their own good and for the good of others. The wise setting of boundaries is based on discerning the excesses to which the power, unrestrained, is prone. Applied to the professions, this principle would establish strict outer limits—indeed, inviolable taboos—against those "occupational hazards" to which each profession is especially prone. *Within* these outer limits, no fixed rules of conduct apply; instead, prudence—the wise judgment of the man on the spot—finds and adopts the best course of action in light of the circumstances. But the outer limits themselves are fixed, firm, and nonnegotiable.

What are those limits for medicine? At least three are set forth in the venerable Hippocratic Oath: no breach of confidentiality; no sexual relations with patients; no dispensing of deadly drugs.[7] These unqualified, self-imposed restrictions are readily understood in terms of the temptations to which the physician is most vulnerable, temptations in each case regarding an area of vulnerability and exposure that the practice of medicine requires of patients. Patients necessarily divulge and reveal private and intimate details of their personal lives; patients necessarily expose their naked bodies to the physician's objectifying gaze and investigating hands; patients necessarily entrust their very lives to the physician's skill, technique, and judgment. The exposure is, in all cases, one-sided and asymmetric: the doctor does not reveal his intimacies, display his nakedness, offer up his embodied life to the patient. The patient is vulnerable and exposed; the physician is neither, or, rather, his own vulnerabilities are not exposed to the patient. Mindful of the meaning of such nonmutual exposure, the physician voluntarily sets limits on his own conduct, pledging not to take advantage of or to violate the patient's intimacies, sexuality, or life itself.

The reason for these restraints is not just the asymmetry of power and the ever-present hazard of its abuse. The relationship between doctor and patient transforms the ordinary human meaning of exposure. Medical nakedness is not erotic nakedness; palpation is not caressing; frank speech is not shared intimacy and friendship; giving out diets and drugs is not hospitality. The physician necessarily objectifies, reduces, and analyzes, as he probes, pokes, and looks for latent clues and meanings, while curbing his own sentiments and interests, so as to make a diagnosis and find a remedy. The goal that constitutes the relationship requires the detachment of the physician and the asymmetry of exposure and communication, and legitimates the acquisition and exercise of power. Yet it also informs the limits on how the power should be used and the manner in which the patient should be treated.

The prohibition against killing patients rests also on a narrower ground, related not only to the meaning of the doctor-patient relationship, but also, once again, to the potentially deadly moral neutrality of medical technique—the problem of the two vials. For this reason, it stands as the *first* promise of self-restraint sworn to in the Hippocratic Oath, as medicine's primary taboo: "I will neither give

---

[7] For a fuller discussion of these prohibitions, both in relation to the Hippocratic Oath and to the meaning of the doctor-patient relationship, see my essays, "Is There a Medical Ethic? The Hippocratic Oath and the Sources of Ethical Medicine," and "Professing Ethically: The Place of Ethics in Defining Medicine," in *Toward a More Natural Science.*

a deadly drug to anybody if asked for it, nor will I make a suggestion to this effect. . . . In purity and holiness I will guard my life
and my art." In forswearing the giving of poison, the physician
recognizes and restrains the godlike power he wields over patients,
mindful that his drugs can both cure and kill. But in forswearing
the giving of poison *when asked for it*, the Hippocratic physician
rejects the view that the patient's choice for death can make killing
him right. For the physician, at least, human life in living bodies
commands respect and reverence—*by its very nature.* As its respectability does not depend upon human agreement or patient consent,
revocation of one's consent to live does not deprive one's living body
of respectability. The deepest ethical principle restraining the physician's power is not the autonomy or freedom of the patient; neither is it his own compassion or good intention. Rather, it is the dignity and mysterious power of human life itself, and, therefore, also
what the Oath calls the purity and holiness of the life and art to
which he has sworn devotion. A person can choose to be a physician, but he cannot choose what physicianship means.

The essence of medicine

One way to define medicine—or anything else—is to delimit its
boundaries, to draw the line separating medicine from non-
medicine, or its ethical from its unethical practice. Another way to
define medicine—or anything else—is to capture its center, to discern its essence. In the best case, the two kinds of definitions will be
related: the outer boundary will at least reflect, and will at best be
determined by, what is at the center. Some practices are beyond the
pale precisely because they contradict what is at the center.

To seek the center, one begins not with powers but with goals,
not with means but with ends. In the Hippocratic Oath, the physician states his goal this way: "I will apply dietetic measures *for the
benefit of the sick* according to my ability and judgment. I will
keep them from harm and injustice." In a more thorough explica-
tion of the Oath in my book, I have argued that this little paragraph,
properly unpacked, reveals the core of medicine. For example, the
emphasis on dietetics indicates that medicine is a cooperative rather
than a transformative art, and the physician an assistant to the immanent healing powers of the body. And because a body possessed
of reason is a body whose "possessor" may lead it astray through
ignorance or self-indulgence, the physician, as servant of the patient's
good, must teach, advise, and exhort to keep him from *self*-harm

and injustice. Here I focus only on the modest little phrase, "the benefit of the sick."

The physician as physician serves only the sick. He does not serve the relatives or the hospital or the national debt inflated due to Medicare costs. Thus he will never sacrifice the well-being of the sick to the convenience or pocketbook or feelings of the relatives or society. Moreover, the physician serves the sick not because they have rights or wants or claims, but because they are sick. The benefit needed by the sick qua sick is health. The healer works with and for those who need to be healed, in order to make them whole.

Healing is thus the central core of medicine: to heal, to make whole, is the doctor's primary business. The sick, the ill, the unwell present themselves to the physician in the hope that he can help them become well—or, rather, as well as they can become, some degree of well-ness being possible always, this side of death. The physician shares that goal; his training has been devoted to making it possible for him to serve it. Despite enormous changes in medical technique and institutional practice, despite enormous changes in nosology and therapeutics, the center of medicine has not changed: it is as true today as it was in the days of Hippocrates that the ill desire to be whole; that wholeness means a certain well-working of the enlivened body and its unimpaired powers to sense, think, feel, desire, move, and maintain itself; and that the relationship between the healer and the ill is constituted, essentially even if only tacitly, around the desire of both to promote the wholeness of the one who is ailing.

Human wholeness

The wholeness and well-working of a human being is, of course, a rather complicated matter, much more so than for our animal friends and relations. Because of our powers of mind, our partial emancipation from the rule of instinct, our self-consciousness, and the highly complex and varied ways of life we follow as individuals and as members of groups, health and fitness seem to mean different things to different people, or even to the same person at different times of life. Moreover, departures from health have varying importance depending on the way of life one follows. Yet not everything is relative and contextual; beneath the variable and cultural lies the constant and organic, the well-regulated, properly balanced, and fully empowered human body. Indeed, only the existence of this natural and universal subject makes possible the study of medicine. The cornerstone of medical education is the analytic study of the human body, *universally* considered: anatomy, physiology, biochemistry and molecular biology, genetics, microbiology, pathology, and pharmacology—all these sciences of somatic function, disorder, and remedy are the first business of medical schools, and they must be learned before one can hope to heal particular human beings.

But *human* wholeness goes beyond the kind of somatic wholeness abstractly and reductively studied by these various sciences. Whether or not doctors are sufficiently prepared by their training to recognize it, those who seek medical help in search of wholeness are not *to themselves* just bodies or organic machines. Each person intuitively knows himself to be a center of thoughts and desires, deeds and speeches, loves and hates, pleasures and pains, but a center whose workings are none other than the workings of his enlivened and mindful body. The patient presents himself to the physician, tacitly to be sure, as a psychophysical unity, as a *one*, not just as a body, but also not just as a separate disembodied entity that simply *has* or *owns* a body. The person and the body are self-identical. To be sure, the experience of psychophysical unity is often disturbed by illness, indeed, by bodily illness; it becomes hard to function as a unity if part of oneself is in revolt, is in pain, is debilitated. Yet the patient aspires to have the disturbance quieted, to restore the implicit feeling and functional fact of oneness with which we freely go about our business in the world. The sickness may be experienced largely as belonging to the body as something other; but the healing one wants is the wholeness of one's entire embodied being. Not the wholeness of *soma*, not the wholeness of *psyche*, but the wholeness of *anthropos* as a (puzzling) concretion of *soma-psyche* is the benefit sought by the sick. This human wholeness is what medicine is finally all about.

Wholeness and killing

Can wholeness and healing ever be compatible with intentionally killing the patient? Can one benefit the patient as a whole by making him dead? There is, of course, a logical difficulty: how can any good exist for a being that is not? "Better off dead" is logical nonsense—unless, of course, death is not death at all but instead a gateway to a new and better life beyond. But the error is more than logical: to intend and to act for someone's good requires his continued existence to receive the benefit.

Certain attempts to benefit may in fact turn out, unintentionally, to be lethal. Giving adequate morphine to control pain might induce respiratory depression leading to death. But the intent to relieve the pain of the living presupposes that the living still live to be relieved. This must be the starting point in discussing all medical benefits: no benefit without a beneficiary.

Against this view of healing the whole human being, someone will surely bring forth the hard cases: patients so ill-served by their bodies that they can no longer bear to live, bodies riddled with cancer and racked with pain, against which their "owners" protest in horror and from which they insist on being released. It is argued that it just isn't true that we are psychophysical unities; rather, we are some hard-to-specify duality (or multiplicity) of impersonal organic body plus supervening consciousness, what the professionals dub personhood: awareness, intellect, will. Cannot the person "in the body" speak up against the rest, and request death for "personal" reasons?

However sympathetically we listen to such requests, we must see them as incoherent. Strict person-body dualism cannot be sustained. "Personhood" is manifest on earth only in living bodies; our highest mental functions are held up by, and are inseparable from, lowly metabolism, respiration, circulation, excretion. There may be blood without consciousness, but there is never consciousness without blood. The body is the living ground of all so-called higher functions. Thus one who calls for death in the service of personhood is like a tree seeking to cut its roots for the sake of growing its highest fruit. No physician, devoted to the benefit of the sick, can serve the patient as person by denying and thwarting his personal embodiment.

To say it plainly, to bring nothingness is incompatible with serving wholeness: one cannot heal—or comfort—by making nil. The healer cannot annihilate if he is truly to heal. The boundary condition, "No deadly drugs," flows directly from the center, "Make whole."

Analogies

The reasonableness of this approach to medical ethics is supported by analogies with other professions. For example, we can clearly discover why suborning perjury and contempt of court are taboos for lawyers, why falsifying data is taboo for a scientist, or why violating the confessional is taboo for a priest, once we see the goals of these professions to be, respectively, justice under law, truth about nature, and purification of the soul before God. Let me expand two other analogies, somewhat closer to our topic.

Take the teacher. His business: to encourage, and to provide the occasion for, learning and understanding. Recognizing this central core, we see that the teacher ought never to oppose himself to the student's effort to learn, or even to his prospects for learning. This means, among other things, never ridiculing an honest effort, never crushing true curiosity or thoughtfulness; it also means opposing firmly the temptations that face students to scramble their minds through drugs. And even when the recalcitrant student refuses to make the effort, the teacher does not abandon his post, but continues to look for a way to arouse, to cajole, to inspire, to encourage. The teacher will perhaps not *pursue* the unwilling student, but as long as the student keeps coming to class, the true teacher will not participate in or assist him with his mental self-neglect.

Now consider the parent. These days only a fool would try to state precisely what the true business of a father or mother is, qua father or mother. Yet it must be something like protection, care, nurture, instruction, exhortation, chastisement, encouragement, and support, all in the service of the growth and development of a mature, healthy, competent, and decent adult, capable of an independent and responsible life of work and love and participation in community affairs—no easy task, especially now. What will the true parent do when teenagers rise in revolt and try to reject not only the teachings of their homes but even the parents themselves, when sons and daughters metaphorically kill their parents as parents by un-sonning and un-daughtering themselves? Should fathers acquiesce and willingly unfather themselves; should mothers stand against their life-work of rearing and abandon the child? Or does not the true parent "hang in there" in one way or another, despite the difficulty and sense of failure, and despite the need, perhaps, for great changes in his or her conduct? Does not the true parent refuse to surrender or to abandon the child, knowing that it would be deeply self-contradictory to deny the fact of one's parenthood, whatever the child may say or do? Again, one may freely choose or refuse to become a parent, but one cannot fully choose what parenthood means. The inner meaning of the work has claims on our hearts and minds, and sets boundaries on what we may do without self-contradiction and self-violation.

When medicine fails

Being a physician, teacher, or parent has a central inner meaning that characterizes it essentially, and that is independent both of the demands of the "clients" and of the benevolent motives of the practitioners. For a physician, to be sure, things go better when the patient is freely willing and the physician is virtuous and compassionate. But the physician's work centers on the goal of healing, and he is thereby bound not to behave in contradiction to that central goal.

But there is a difficulty. The central goal of medicine—health—is, in each case, a perishable good: inevitably, patients get irreversibly sick, patients degenerate, patients die. Unlike—at least on first glance—teaching or rearing the young, healing the sick is *in principle* a project that must at some point fail. And here is where all the trouble begins: How does one deal with "medical failure"? What does one seek when restoration of wholeness—or "much" wholeness—is by and large out of the question?

There is much that can and should be said on this topic, which is, after all, the root of the problems that give rise to the call for mercy killing. In my book I have argued for the primacy of easing pain and suffering, along with supporting and comforting speech, and, more to the point, the need to draw back from some efforts at prolongation of life that prolong or increase only the patient's pain, discomfort, and suffering. Although I am mindful of the dangers and aware of the impossibility of writing explicit rules for ceasing treatment—hence the need for prudence—considerations of the individual's health, activity, and state of mind must enter into decisions of *whether* and *how vigorously* to treat if the decision is indeed to be for the patient's good. Ceasing treatment and allowing death to occur when (and if) it will seem to be quite compatible with the respect that life itself commands for itself. For life is to be revered not only as manifested in physiological powers, but also as these powers are organized in the form of *a* life, with its beginning, middle, and end. Thus life can be revered not only in its preservation, but also in the manner in which we allow a given life to reach its terminus. For physicians to adhere to efforts at indefinite prolongation not only reduces them to slavish technicians without any intelligible goal, but also degrades and assaults the gravity and solemnity of a life in its close.

Ceasing medical intervention, allowing nature to take its course, differs fundamentally from mercy killing. For one thing, death does not necessarily follow the discontinuance of treatment; Karen Ann Quinlan lived more than ten years after the court allowed the "life-sustaining" respirator to be removed. Not the physician, but the underlying fatal illness becomes the true cause of death. More importantly morally, in ceasing treatment the physician need not *intend* the death of the patient, even when the death follows as a result of his omission. His intention should be to avoid useless and degrading medical *additions* to the already sad end of a life. In contrast, in active, direct mercy killing the physician must, necessarily and indubitably, intend *primarily* that the patient be made dead. And he must knowingly and indubitably cast himself in the role of the agent of death.

Being humane and being human

Yet one may still ask: Is killing the patient, even on request, compatible with respecting the life that is failing or nearing its close? Obviously, the euthanasia movement thinks it is. Yet one of the arguments most often advanced by proponents of mercy killing seems to me rather to prove the reverse. Why, it is argued, do we put animals out of their misery but insist on compelling fellow human beings to suffer to the bitter end? Why, if it is not a contradiction for the veterinarian, does the medical ethic absolutely rule out mercy killing? Is this not simply inhumane?

Perhaps inhumane, but not thereby inhuman. On the contrary, it is precisely because animals are not human that we must treat them (merely) humanely. We put dumb animals to sleep because they do not know that they are dying, because they can make nothing of their misery or mortality, and, therefore, because they cannot live deliberately—i.e., humanly—in the face of their own suffering or dying. They cannot live out a fitting end. Compassion for their weakness and dumbness is our only appropriate emotion, and given our responsibility for their care and well-being, we do the only humane thing we can. But when a conscious human being asks us for death, by that very action he displays the presence of something that precludes our regarding him as a dumb animal. Humanity is owed humanity, not humaneness. Humanity is owed the bolstering of the human, even or especially in its dying moments, in resistance to the temptation to ignore its presence in the sight of suffering.

What humanity needs most in the face of evils is courage, the ability to stand against fear and pain and thoughts of nothingness. The deaths we most admire are those of people who, knowing that they are dying, face the fact frontally and act accordingly: they set their affairs in order, they arrange what could be final meetings with their loved ones, and yet, with strength of soul and a small reservoir of hope, they continue to live and work and love as much as they can for as long as they can. Because such conclusions of life require courage, they call for our encouragement—and for the many small speeches and deeds that shore up the human spirit against despair and defeat.

Many doctors are in fact rather poor at this sort of encouragement. They tend to regard every dying or incurable patient as a failure, as if an earlier diagnosis or a more vigorous intervention might have avoided what is, in truth, an inevitable collapse. The enormous successes of medicine these past fifty years have made both doctors and laymen less prepared than ever to accept the fact of finitude. Doctors behave, not without some reason, as if they have godlike powers to revive the moribund; laymen expect an endless string of medical miracles. It is against this background that terminal illness or incurable disease appears as medical failure, an affront to medical pride. Physicians today are not likely to be agents of encouragement once their technique begins to fail.

It is, of course, partly for these reasons that doctors will be pressed to kill—and many of them will, alas, be willing. Having adopted a largely technical approach to healing, having medicalized so much of the end of life, doctors are being asked—often with thinly veiled anger—to provide a final technical solution for the evil of human finitude and for their own technical failure: If you cannot cure me, kill me. The last gasp of autonomy or cry for dignity is asserted against a medicalization and institutionalization of the end of life that robs the old and the incurable of most of their autonomy and dignity: intubated and electrified, with bizarre mechanical companions, helpless and regimented, once proud and independent people find themselves cast in the roles of passive, obedient, highly disciplined children. People who care for autonomy and dignity should try to reverse this dehumanization of the last stages of life, instead of giving dehumanization its final triumph by welcoming the desperate goodbye-to-all-that contained in one final plea for poison.

The present crisis that leads some to press for active euthanasia is really an opportunity to learn the limits of the medicalization of life and death and to recover an appreciation of living with and against mortality. It is an opportunity for physicians to recover an understanding that there remains a residual human wholeness—however precarious—that can be cared for even in the face of incurable and terminal illness. Should doctors cave in, should doctors become technical dispensers of death, they will not only be abandoning their posts, their patients, and their duty to care; they will set the worst sort of example for the community at large—teaching technicism and so-called humaneness where encouragement and humanity are both required and sorely lacking. On the other hand, should physicians hold fast, should they give back to Athena her deadly vial, should medicine recover the latent anthropological knowledge that alone can vindicate its venerable but now threatened practice, should doctors learn that finitude is no disgrace and that human wholeness can be cared for to the very end, medicine may serve not only the good of its patients, but also, by example, the failing moral health of modern times.

[26]

The debate over the ethics of physician-assisted death has suffered from inadequate analysis of professional integrity. Some who would permit it have tended to ignore professional integrity as a source of moral constraints on physician conduct. We contend that the attempt to ground its ethical appropriateness solely on the principles of respect for patient autonomy and relief of suffering fails to do justice to the internal values and norms of medicine, in accordance with which physicians ought to practice. The use of professional knowledge and skill to help a patient end his or her life can be justified only if professional integrity is not violated. However, some who oppose the practice as incompatible with medical norms employ too narrow or simplistic a conception of professional integrity.

Since so little has been written recently on the subject of professional integrity, we can in this paper do little more than introduce and apply some basic concepts; much more work would be necessary to develop a comprehensive theory of professional integrity in modern medicine. We aim to highlight some important features of the concept and to consider their bearing on the perplexing moral problem of physician-assisted death. We set the stage by examining briefly the related concept of personal integrity.

Personal Integrity

Martin Benjamin has provided some very useful observations about personal integrity and its moral importance in his recent study of integrity-preserving compromise. The root meaning of *integrity* refers to

Franklin G. Miller is an assistant professor in the Department of Medical Education, University of Virginia School of Medicine, Charlottesville; Howard Brody is a professor of family practice and philosophy and director of the Center for Ethics and Humanities in the Life Sciences, Michigan State University, East Lansing.

Franklin G. Miller and Howard Brody, "Professional Integrity and Physician-Assisted Death," *Hastings Center Report* 25, no. 3 (1995): 8-17.

Professional Integrity and Physician-Assisted Death

by Franklin G. Miller and Howard Brody

The practice of voluntary physician-assisted death as a last resort is compatible with doctors' duties to practice competently, to avoid harming patients unduly, to refrain from medical fraud, and to preserve patients' trust. It therefore does not violate physicians' professional integrity.

wholeness and intactness. Benjamin sees integrity as standing in a strong relationship to personal identity: "[Integrity] provides the structure for a unified, whole, and unalienated life. Those who through good fortune and personal effort are able to lead reasonably integrated lives generally enjoy a strong sense of personal identity." He suggests that the key elements of personal identity and personal integrity are the same: "(1) a reasonably coherent and relatively stable set of highly cherished values and principles; (2) verbal behavior expressing those values and principles; and (3) conduct embodying one's values and principles and consistent with what one says."[1] Thus, for me to have personal integrity at the most basic level requires that I believe in some values or principles, and that I both talk and act as I would be expected to if my thoughts and behavior were indeed guided by those values and principles.

Benjamin observes that integrity, though intimately connected with an individual's personal identity, has an important social dimension. He quotes Peter Winch: "To lack integrity is to act with the appearance of fulfilling a certain role but without the intention of shouldering the responsibilities to which the role commits one. If that, *per absurdum*, were

to become the rule, the whole concept of a social role would thereby collapse."[2] Benjamin adds that personal integrity is especially important in complex social organizations, such as health care settings, that cannot function without a great deal of interdependence and coordination. He might have further noted that when those organizations serve vulnerable individuals, who can benefit optimally from the encounter only if they are able to place a good deal of trust in the organization and its members, then integrity—both personal and professional—becomes absolutely critical, since lack of integrity undermines trust.

Benjamin treats integrity as primarily a formal principle; accordingly, it is a necessary but hardly sufficient condition for a morally praiseworthy life. If one's values and principles happen to be execrable, then acting consistently with them obviously will not make one virtuous. He goes on to describe various ways in which people might appear to be acting with integrity, while in fact their behavior is morally questionable. One problem arises from adhering to a narrow, simplistic framework of integrity. Benjamin describes this problem as one of emphasizing one aspect of integrity, consistency, over another equally important aspect, wholeness. A per-

Hastings Center Report, May-June 1995

son may act consistently on the basis of a single value, but this value may be quite insufficient to support or inform a complete life; one can behave consistently with it only by putting on blinders and radically restricting one's self-understanding and views of one's environment. A second problem arises from the challenges to integrity in a modern, pluralistic, rapidly developing society. To maintain integrity in the face of changing social and personal circumstances—for example, evolving conceptions of roles and responsibilities of spouses in the context of family life—one will have to modify one's values and principles, and how one talks and acts upon them, to some degree. If one modifies them too much, one will justly be accused of having lost one's moral grounding; but if one modifies them too little, then one will essentially have abandoned one's social role obligations. Benjamin notes that modern society poses a double threat to living a life of integrity: first, in a pluralistic culture, it is not at all clear what our core value commitments ought to be; and second, even once we have adopted some commitments, changing social circumstances tempt us with a bewildering number of ways to modify them.

Violating Integrity

Consideration of what it means to violate integrity can shed further light on this concept. When contemplating an act that would violate one's integrity, one is apt to say, "I can't do that!" Obviously, this does not mean that the act is physically impossible to perform. Nor does the person of integrity mean that to do the integrity-violating act would be too risky in view of the possible consequences: legal penalties, loss of reputation, etc. Rather, I can't do it because, knowing that it would be improper, unsuitable, or wrong (for anyone or for me), I could not live with myself, or maintain my self-respect, if I did it. For example, why did Socrates refuse the opportunity to leave Athens to escape the manifestly unjust death penalty awaiting him? He refused because it would have been contrary to his integrity as the philosophical gadfly of Athens and his loyalty to the scheme

of law under which he had lived and thrived. Being Socrates, it was unfitting to make a clandestine escape. Rather, it fit his sense of integrity to refuse to alter his mission in life and, accordingly, to submit to the unjust sentence of death.

The identity to which integrity is connected is not the sameness or continuity of personhood that makes one the same person from birth until death; nor is it sameness of personality or temperament. Integrity is tied to the moral identity of character. It involves a fit between character and conduct; therefore, it bridges being and doing. Persons of integrity shun conduct of various sorts because it does not fit with the sense of who they are. Professional integrity, which we discuss in the next section, also concerns character; but it relates to the moral identity of those who occupy a distinctive social role, in contrast to the full identity of persons, which characterizes their lives as a whole.

Professional Integrity

Discussions of integrity in the recent literature of biomedical ethics often lack any clear delineation of *professional* integrity. For example, while the fourth edition of Beauchamp and Childress's *Principles of Biomedical Ethics* contains a useful general account of the virtue of integrity and acknowledges its primary importance in health care ethics, integrity is not described in terms of the identity and normative commitments tied to the professional roles of physician, nurse, or other clinicians. "Our argument is that moral integrity in science, medicine, and health care should be understood primarily in terms of the principles, rules, and virtues that we have identified in the common morality."[3] We contend, however, that the common morality, shared by lay persons and professionals, does not provide a fully adequate framework for elucidating and assessing the moral responsibilities that are distinctive of physicians and other clinical professionals. In particular, at issue in the ethical problem of physician-assisted death is not only whether suicide and assistance in suicide can be morally justified. It is also morally significant to inquire whether it

ever can be permissible for a *physician* to assist in the death of a patient. In an adequate moral accounting of physician-assisted death, appeal to the internal morality of medicine and the virtue of professional integrity is needed to supplement appeal to the principles, rules, and virtues of our common morality. Beauchamp and Childress add that, "Of course, ours is not the only substantive moral framework for integrity in biomedical ethics, and we cannot wave away all other approaches" (p. 471). We develop here an alternative approach to integrity understood as a professional virtue of physicians, which is distinct from, but not in conflict with, the virtue of integrity in common morality.[4]

Like personal integrity, professional integrity shares a connection with the concept of identity. Professional integrity in medicine represents what it means normatively to be a physician; it encompasses the values, norms, and virtues that are distinctive and characteristic of physicians. Accordingly, the identity to which professional integrity corresponds is tied to a specific social role. The formation of an identity as a physician and commitment to the professional integrity of medicine, learned and internalized through medical education, are aptly described as professional *socialization*. Personal identity also presupposes a social context; it is formed in interaction with others. But personal identity in modern society is not essentially role-defined or role-specific. My personal identity is expressed in the variety of roles that I occupy and in the individual way that I perform them. Professional identity and integrity are much more strongly communally structured. While there remains some free scope for individuality in the practice of medicine, and a good physician may have a unique personal style, professional identity generally constrains individual expression in a way that personal identity does not.

We have arrived at the suggestion that a basic conception of the good of medicine and a core set of moral commitments of physicians can be identified, such that physicians of professional integrity can be expected to practice consistently in con-

Hastings Center Report, May-June 1995

formity with them. For example, we might agree that care, accuracy, and reliability in gathering data about the patient's illness is an absolutely essential feature of medical practice. We cannot conceive of someone who took no interest whatever in thorough clinical assessments, but who purported nonetheless to be a com-

many other ways besides being a physician, but only a physician can comprehend and experience the peculiar satisfaction that comes from making the correct diagnosis in those circumstances.

The two problems that Benjamin notes with maintaining personal integrity in a complex, changing world

---

A narrative account of how a profession has evolved over time remains a key mode of discovering elements of professional integrity.

---

petent physician, unless that person was a blatant charlatan. That leads us to the conclusion that falsifying a medical history or physical exam, for instance writing "ears normal" without even examining the ears, would count as a very basic violation of professional integrity.

This point can be made in a slightly different way. Benjamin (partly following Alasdair MacIntyre) insists that the unit of analysis for personal integrity is the complete human life; specifically, we look at human lives organized as narratives to reveal whether or not one's words and actions consistently manifest one's commitment to a set of core values and principles. A profession like medicine, unlike a person, does not have a discrete lifetime; but nonetheless a narrative account of how a profession has evolved over time remains a key mode of discovering elements of professional integrity. As part of that narrative, we routinely ask questions that relate to what sort of practice medicine is: what would count as virtuous or praiseworthy medical practice and as conduct of physicians that falls short of minimal expectations? Such questions point out for us the *internal goods* that make medicine the practice it is.[5] For example, unlike sifting through a puzzling set of signs and symptoms to make an accurate diagnosis, making money through successful medical practice is not an internal good. One can earn money in

also apply equally to professional integrity. First, physicians might misconstrue the requirement of professional integrity if they sacrifice wholeness to consistency. For example, a duty to prolong the life of the patient is certainly one of the general requirements of good medical practice. But one will contravene other important values if one holds that this duty is an *absolute* defining characteristic of medical integrity; such a misperception has led some physicians unethically to disregard patients' competent refusals of life-prolonging medical therapy. Second, the idea of a profession developing over time suggests that what counts as professional integrity should not be seen as absolutely fixed. Otherwise, physicians might hold so rigidly to a certain doctrine of professional integrity that they end up abrogating their social role responsibilities under changed conditions of medical practice. We shall argue that an absolute professional prohibition of physician-assisted death exemplifies this problem.

Integrity and Conscience

The close connection between integrity and conscience is reflected in the axiom of professional ethics that professionals are not obligated to perform acts that violate their consciences, even if the acts are not contrary to professional norms. A physician should not be required to sacri-

fice personal integrity in the practice of medicine. For example, abortion is not contrary to the norms of the medical profession, and physicians of integrity perform abortions for a variety of medical and nonmedical reasons. Physicians conscientiously opposed to abortion, however, are not obliged to compromise their personal integrity by performing abortions. If physician-assisted death becomes legalized and recognized by the medical profession as legitimate in some cases, physicians morally opposed to this practice would have a right to refuse to assist actively in bringing about the deaths of patients. Exercising integrity is not reducible to following conscience for two reasons. First, a person's integrity may involve commitment to nonmoral values, such as artistic creation and scholarship, which are passionately pursued but are not matters of conscience. Second, a person facing a moral dilemma is pulled by conflicting directives of conscience. When faced with such a conflict a person of integrity may lack any clear and certain conviction of conscience about what should be done. Considerable reflection, deliberation, consultation, and study may be required to arrive at a position which is considered reasonable. Analogous to a moral agent's internal conflict of conscience is professional conflict concerning practices that are subject to competing moral evaluations. Whether physicians should be permitted to assist actively in the deaths of suffering patients is an issue that calls for careful analysis of the professional integrity of physicians and a balancing of competing ethical considerations.

The Substantive Content of Professional Integrity

Benjamin treats integrity as a basically formal concept, since the lives, values, and sense of identity of persons of integrity may vary enormously. In the case of professional integrity, however, normative content can be specified, because the identity to which it corresponds consists of a distinctive and relatively stable social role. We offer the following as a brief overview of the substantive content of the professional integrity of modern

Hastings Center Report, May-June 1995

physicians. We attempt to elaborate some aspects of professional integrity in the subsequent discussion of physician-assisted death.

Reflection on medicine as a professional practice guides articulation of what professional integrity of physicians involves. Since medicine is a goal-directed practice, conduct that complies with (or violates) the professional integrity of physicians may be understood in terms of an ethical framework of ends and means. The acts of physicians of integrity must serve the proper ends or goals of medicine, and they must be ethically appropriate means to these ends in the light of the values and norms internal to the practice of medicine. As in the case of other skilled practices or arts, there is a conceptual and pragmatic fit between the goals and the means of medicine. The goals of medicine inform practitioners and theorists on the range of appropriate or inappropriate means of medical practice; and the understanding of the proper and improper means of medical practice elaborates the meaning of the goals of medicine.

Medicine is too complex to be oriented toward a single fundamental goal. We believe that most, if not all, legitimate medical practices can be encompassed by three goals: healing, promoting health, and helping patients achieve a peaceful and dignified death. Healing, broadly understood, includes interventions intended to save life, cure disease, repair injuries, restore impaired functioning or ameliorate dysfunction, help the patient cope with irreversible illness, and palliate pain and discomfort. Promoting health includes interventions intended to prevent disease or injury: consultations to encourage healthy behavior (including nutrition and exercise), vaccinations and prophylactic treatments, prenatal care and normal delivery of babies, and so on. Helping patients achieve a peaceful and dignified death may overlap with healing, since providing treatment intended to relieve suffering serves both goals. However, the third goal also includes activities that lie outside the scope of healing, such as helping patients plan for limiting treatment at the end of life and deciding for dying or incurably ill patients to forgo life-sustaining treatments that are more burdensome than beneficial. In addition, we shall argue that this third goal supports physician-assisted death as a last resort, provided that adequate safeguards are observed to assure that the patient makes a voluntary and informed choice and that the use of medical intervention to terminate life is not premature or unnecessary in view of available alternatives.

It might be objected that to cite helping patients achieve a peaceful death as a goal of medicine is an arbitrary and question-begging move, aimed solely at legitimating physician-assisted death. The objection is mistaken, however, since there is no necessary connection between affirming this goal and justifying the practice of voluntary physician-assisted death as a last resort. Daniel Callahan eloquently argues that contemporary medicine has neglected the goal of helping patients achieve a peaceful death.[6] Yet he remains a staunch opponent of physicians' direct involvement in patients' suicides.

Four basic duties of physicians govern ethically appropriate means of medical practice: (1) the duty to practice competently; (2) the duty to avoid disproportionate harm to patients in the effort to provide medical benefits; (3) the duty to refrain from fraudulent misrepresentation of medical knowledge and skills; and (4) the duty of fidelity to the therapeutic relationship with patients.

Competence is the first duty of physicians. The goals of medicine cannot be served unless physicians possess and exercise at least minimal standards of knowledge and skill. Competence includes the ability to communicate with and respond attentively to patients (and family) as well as possessing scientific knowledge, clinical judgment, and technical skill.

Since the power of medicine depends on interventions that invade the body or alter its functions, the maxim "Do no harm" fundamentally constrains medical practice. It is obvious, however, that the goals of medicine are often served by practices that produce harmful side effects or complications, as in chemotherapy for cancer. Therefore, this duty prescribes that physicians avoid producing harms to patients that are not balanced by the prospect of compensating benefits.

The duty of refraining from fraudulent misrepresentation enjoins physicians from unjustified departures from standard medical practice. It prohibits performing acts that pose as medical practice but conflict with the goals of medicine. Fraudulent misrepresentation is conceptually distinct from incompetence, though the two may overlap in particular cases. This distinction is evidenced by venality in medicine. A surgeon who performs unnecessary operations to boost his income may be technically competent. But besides violating the rule against disproportionate harm, he also fraudulently misrepresents the science and art of medicine, since the public may come to think, from his example, that surgery is necessary and proper in a much wider set of circumstances than it actually is.

The goals of medicine are pursued within the context of a therapeutic relationship between physician and patient. The generic duty of fidelity contains two component duties: the duty not to abuse the trust on which a therapeutic physician-patient relationship depends, and the duty not to abandon patients.

Medicine is a complex moral enterprise; it consists both of a body of technical knowledge and skills, and their application to specific sorts of human problems. Physicians can violate the integrity of medicine as a professional practice, then, in various ways: by perverting it to serve medically extraneous or antithetical ends (as in the conduct of Nazi doctors who performed forced sterilizations, engaged in brutal experiments, "euthanized" handicapped children and mental patients, and participated in the operation of the extermination camps[7]); by misrepresenting or debasing the body of knowledge itself; or by applying it in the wrong way or in the wrong circumstances, such as when much more harm than good is caused.

A physician who prescribes anabolic steroids for an athlete who wants to enhance his athletic performance violates professional integrity in a number of respects. Such practice serves no valid medical goals.

Hastings Center Report, May-June 1995

The patient may ultimately suffer complications that far outweigh any transitory advantage of increased athletic prowess, thus violating the duty of avoiding disproportionate harm. Also, medical practice is fraudulently misrepresented, because steroids are not medically indicated for the condition of the athlete. Moreover, this practice suggests that it is appropriate medical treatment to provide unfair advantages to one group of athletes by prescribing potentially harmful substances for them. This misrepresentation may be compounded if the mere fact that a *physician* is willing to prescribe steroids leads the credulous athlete, or others, to conclude that the risks are inconsequential. The patient may have given informed consent for steroid "treatment," but this is not sufficient to make it compatible with professional integrity. The physician is not a morally neutral technician available to do the bidding of patients.

We do not interpret professional integrity of physicians as coextensive with the whole of medical ethics. Ethical considerations of respect for patient autonomy, social utility, and justice lie outside the domain of professional integrity, which constitutes the internal morality of medicine.

Is Physician-Assisted Death Compatible with Professional Integrity?

A number of prominent physician-ethicists have argued that physician-assisted death is incompatible with the internal morality of medicine.[8] We agree that the professional integrity of physicians is at stake in ethical assessment of the practice. Doctors have a duty, grounded in the norms of professional integrity, not to kill or assist in the killing of patients. We contend, however, that this duty is not absolute, and that an exceptional practice of voluntary physician assistance as a last resort does not violate professional integrity.

Our argument proceeds in two steps. First, we will show that the practice is compatible with the goals of medicine. Second, after indicating how each of the norms of professional integrity, outlined above, supports a prima facie duty to refrain

from assisted suicide and active euthanasia, we will show that, on further analysis, each will permit cases of voluntary physician-assisted death in response to unrelievable suffering. Our aim is to show that this is allowed by professional integrity; accordingly, we offer a critique of a variety of arguments that conclude that physicians should be prohibited from practicing assisted death. Some proponents might argue that professional integrity in some cases *requires* a physician to assist in the death of a patient by prescribing or administering a lethal dose of medication, unless he or she is morally opposed to such assistance under all circumstances. We take no stand here on the duty to assist. In the face of traditional legal and moral prohibitions, it is a sufficiently daunting task to argue that such assistance is not incompatible with professional integrity. Furthermore, we urge caution in moving from the position that it is allowed in some cases to the position that it is required, since this practice should always be seen as problematic and justifiable only as a last resort.

The Goals of Medicine

If medicine is *essentially* a healing enterprise, then physicians should never help patients to die. Leon Kass argues that "being a physician, teacher, or parent has a central inner meaning that characterizes it essentially."[9] For Kass, the essence of medicine—its inner normative meaning and purpose—is healing, which physician-assisted death contravenes. In introducing the concept of professional integrity, we contended above that medicine is too complex to be captured by a single fundamental goal that defines the scope and limits of medical practice. Ludwig Wittgenstein pointed out the problems with such conceptual essentialism in his famous example of the concept of a game.[10] There is no essence of games: no necessary and sufficient conditions for an activity to qualify as a game. There are games of various sorts; and what unifies the class of games is a complex set of "family resemblances" between these various sorts of games. A similar point holds for the range of practices that fall

under the scope of clinical medicine. Although healing is a core goal of medicine, the concept of healing cannot be stretched to cover the full scope of legitimate medical practice. We argued instead that there is a plurality of goals of medicine, which includes healing, promoting health, and helping patients achieve a peaceful death.

The critical question is whether administering a lethal dose of medication can ever be a legitimate means of realizing the goal of helping patients achieve a peaceful death. When no healing interventions are appropriate for the condition of a patient who resolutely requests aid in ending his or her life because of intolerable suffering (in spite of careful consideration of comfort care alternatives), then resort to physician-assisted death may become, unfortunately, the best among the limited options available to achieve this important goal of medicine for this patient.

Kass argues that physicians, being concerned with the health of living, embodied human beings, must always refrain from this option. "For the physician, at least, human life in living bodies commands respect and reverence—*by its very nature*"(p. 38). Because the human organism is mortal, this respect is compatible with forgoing treatment when such treatment would be futile; however, it can never be compatible with interventions aimed at ending human life.

We agree with Kass that a norm of respect for the human body follows from the nature of medicine, but we dispute that this moral consideration rules out physician-assisted death. The moral force of physicians' respect for the human body is perhaps best illustrated by considering requests that they perform bodily mutilation. Suppose a modern Oedipus urges his physician to blind him—in a painless way, without otherwise endangering his health—because of his unwitting but terrible sins. Is the physician's reason for refusing simply that such a request would be regarded as deranged and therefore nonautonomous? There is an issue here of professional integrity: bodily mutilation on demand is not within the scope of what physicians properly do. And this consideration is logically

Hastings Center Report, May-June 1995

independent of concerns about the decisionmaking capacity of anyone who requests bodily mutilation. This is even more apparent in the case of requests for female circumcision, which are motivated by traditional cultural beliefs and attitudes and do not evidence mental derangement. Bodily mutilation violates professional integrity because it contravenes the goals of medicine. Furthermore, it harms patients without any compensating medical benefit, and it fraudulently misrepresents medical practice.

Kass seems to be arguing that physician-assisted death is akin to bodily mutilation. Indeed, it constitutes a greater violation than removing or damaging a functioning body part, since it causes the death of the organism as a whole. According to Kass, "Medicine violates the body only to heal it."[11] This statement, once again, reflects Kass's essentialism—that medicine serves only the goal of healing. If there are goals other than healing, then it may be legitimate for physicians to "violate" the body to serve another valid medical goal. Whereas no medical goal supports bodily mutilation, justified physician-assisted death is dedicated to helping a patient achieve a peaceful and dignified death when no other satisfactory option is available.

Consider the case of an eighty-five-year-old woman who has suffered a cascade of health problems and treatment complications that leave her incontinent, bedridden, and increasingly blind.[12] She is now in a nursing home—a fate she dreaded—with no prospect of recovery to independent living and doing those things she most values. She decides that she wants to die and asks her physician for help. Suppose that in response to this request her physician were to say, "I can't help you because I am bound as a physician to respect your body, and if I give you a lethal injection I will be destroying your body as a living organism." The patient might reply as follows: "My body is worse than useless to me, since it now brings me unbearable suffering, and there is no point in continuing to live, given my humiliating and dependent condition. I want you to do this for *me*, since the quality of my life has become in-

tolerable because of my diseased and debilitated body."

An absolute prohibition of physician-assisted death based on respect for the human body represents a mistaken view of medical priorities. Respect for the human body must be accompanied by respect for the per-

---

Some proponents might argue that professional integrity in some cases *requires* a physician to assist in the death of a patient by prescribing or administering a lethal dose of medication.

---

son whose body it is. The physician serves the patient via the body; however, in unfortunate circumstances the most appropriate service for the patient requires ending bodily life. Ultimately, respect for the person, who finds his or her continued existence intolerable, takes precedence over respect for the person's embodied life.

Competence

Standard measures of palliative care, encompassing thorough efforts to relieve pain and discomfort and supportive services to help patients cope with the process of dying, enable most patients to face death without unbearable suffering. Physician-assisted death constitutes incompetent medical practice insofar as palliative care, such as that provided within the context of hospice programs, is capable of relieving patients' suffering to a satisfactory degree.[13] To comply with a suffering patient's request for assistance in causing death without first carefully considering palliative care alternatives violates professional integrity.

Some hospice physicians and ethicists opposed to such assistance have argued that it always amounts to incompetent medical practice, because competent palliative care provided by well-trained hospice clinicians obviates the need to relieve suffering by lethal means.[14] We believe that clini-

cal experience fails to support this claim.[15] Not all patients can receive adequate relief of pain or suffering even under conditions of optimal palliative care.[16] Deep sedation to counteract refractory suffering is a possible option; however, this will not be satisfactory for patients who want to

remain alert without suffering intolerably.[17] Some patients may prefer to end their lives at home than to be hospitalized and persist in a sedated state pending death. Furthermore, it is not clear that relieving terminal suffering by inducing unconsciousness, which may hasten death, is morally superior to voluntary physician-assisted death.

Benefiting the Patient and Avoiding Harm

Killing can be seen as the ultimate harm, since ending a person's life deprives the victim of all future benefits and deprives others of that person's services and companionship. Accordingly, we recognize a duty binding on all persons not to kill and a right possessed by all persons not to be killed. In addition to being subject to this general prohibition against killing, physicians have a role-specific duty not to kill and indeed to preserve life. Furthermore, physicians are charged to avoid harms that are not compensated by proportionate benefits. How then can a physician ever be justified in administering lethal medication to a suffering patient?

Although death is prima facie harmful, it is clear that we do not always regard the occurrence of death as a harm. Deaths that bring a peaceful close to a full life may be regarded as merciful. Thus pneumonia was known as "the old man's friend." The growing power of medicine to stave off death has been accompanied by the ethical recognition that there are circumstances in which it is permissible, if not obligatory, to forgo life-sustaining interventions to allow the patient to die—thus suggesting that in those circumstances death counts as a lesser harm, or even as a benefit.

In contrast to forgoing treatment, physician-assisted death constitutes active intervention: the physician makes death happen, rather than allowing it to happen. Therefore, the practice conflicts more deeply with the duty to preserve life. Can it ever be beneficial, all things considered, for a suffering patient? Kass discerns a logical error in regarding it as benefiting a patient. "To intend and act for someone's good requires his continued existence to receive the benefit."[18] Although the idea that causing death can be beneficial may seem paradoxical, Kass's argument relies on too narrow a conception of benefits. If death is a liberation from unrelievable suffering, then it is a benefit. What removes an evil is a benefit, even if the benefit cannot be experienced. Furthermore, it is important not to ignore the benefit to incurably ill patients of knowing that there is a way out if suffering becomes unbearable.

Respect for professional integrity requires that physicians in performing assisted death must refrain from premature termination of life. If a reasonable quality of life remains available to the patient, with the help of comfort care, then assisted death is not appropriate, regardless of the wishes or requests of the patient. Certainly the patient and physician may differ in their respective assessments of the quality of life available to the patient. The patient's subjective appraisal of his or her situation must be considered carefully and discussed empathically. What is at stake, however, is not a solo act of suicide, which the patient may contemplate and execute without the assistance of a physician. When a physician is involved, a transaction occurs that must be negotiated between physician and patient. In entering into such a transaction the physician should be bound by professional integrity, which excludes physician assistance on demand. The physician is an independent moral agent, committed to the internal morality of medicine, not a tool at the command of the autonomous patient. The patient who wants the help of a physician to terminate his or her life should understand that such help is being sought from a professional clinician, who must be convinced that this course is the best option for the dire situation of this particular patient.[19]

A clear case of when requested death is not compatible with professional integrity was featured in a documentary on euthanasia in the Netherlands, aired 23 March 1993 on the Public Broadcasting System.[20] A forty-one-year-old man diagnosed with HIV, but not yet seriously ill, persuaded his reluctant physician to assist with suicide to avoid the future ravages of AIDS. We believe that the physician's action would be premature in such a case, because the patient, with the help of good medical care, probably can live at least a few years with a reasonable quality of life. To be sure, the patient may decide (not unreasonably) that his life is not worth living in view of what the future has in store. He remains free to undertake suicide on his own. The autonomy of the patient is not sufficient to justify physician-assisted death, which must accommodate respect for professional integrity.

Fraudulent Misrepresentation

Physicians who undertake unwarranted deviations from the standard of care fraudulently misrepresent medical practice; to provide procedures and treatments that are known to offer no benefit amounts to quackery. Professional integrity requires that physicians base their prescriptions for treatment on medical indications. Physician-assisted death is prima facie contrary to this norm of professional integrity, because it is never medically indicated in the sense that the medical condition of the patient warrants lethal "treatment." From a strictly medical perspective, no objective determination can be made that a dying patient needs active assistance from a physician.

To be sure, there are medical preconditions for the appropriateness of such assistance—as when the patient is suffering from a terminal illness or an incurable and debilitating condition and the patient's judgment is not clouded by treatable depression.[21] Physicians who offer assisted death without a careful assessment of the medical condition of the patient and discussion of available palliative care certainly fraudulently misrepresent medical practice. These medical preconditions, while necessary, are not, however, sufficient. The appropriateness of offering this assistance requires in addition the patient's subjective appraisal of his or her condition as intolerable and her or his determination to seek a swift and painless termination of life rather than to await natural death with the help of comfort care. Even then, as it is not medically indicated and involves killing, physician-assisted death lies outside standard medical practice.

If it is not medically indicated and departs from standard medical practice, how can it ever be considered appropriate? Respect for professional integrity does not rule out departures from standard medical practice. Clinical research, conducted by physicians, inherently departs from standard medical practice. It administers experimental treatments that are not proven or accepted as safe and effective, and tests procedures that are not intended for the medical benefit of research subjects. Clinical research is governed by federal regulations, including mandatory prior committee scrutiny by institutional review boards. The analogy to clinical research supports a case for formal regulation of physician-assisted death to assure that it is used only subject to stringent guidelines and safeguards.[22]

Trust

The integrity of medicine as a profession depends on trust. Vulnerability to the consequences of disease or injury and the prospect of death prompts persons to become patients by seeking the care of physicians. Trust makes it possible to assume the patient role, which involves permitting doctors to probe our bodies and submitting to the risks and burdens

Hastings Center Report, May-June 1995

of invasive procedures. Whereas our vulnerability as embodied persons gives rise to the need for trust in physicians, this very trust makes patients vulnerable. As Annette Baier points out, "Trust is accepted vulnerability to another's power to harm one, a power inseparable from the power to look after some aspect of one's good."[23] The trust that underwrites medicine reflects a double vulnerability of patients to physical and personal harm. To be a patient is to submit to the ills of the body and the treatment and care provided by clinicians.

Stanley Reiser aptly describes medicine as "this remarkable social institution whose members must daily prove themselves worthy of a crucial trust: that they will never take advantage of the vulnerability that is the hallmark of the patients who appear before them."[24] Patients trust physicians to use their skills to help, rather than to harm; for physicians have the power to produce the ultimate harm of wrongful death by virtue of their access to potentially lethal technology. The vulnerability of patients, the power of physicians, and the trust in physicians' professional integrity must not be abused by interventions that unjustly take (or risk) the lives of patients. Opponents of physician-assisted death commonly argue that legitimation of this practice would undermine trust.[25] How can persons trust doctors who have the socially sanctioned power to kill patients? If physicians possessed the unilateral authority to decide which patients "need" to be relieved of suffering through their help, then trust would be undermined. Yet if the practice is limited to competent patients who voluntarily request to terminate their lives and who are fully informed about available options of treatment and comfort care, physician-assisted death does not constitute an abuse of trust.

To be sure, suffering patients facing progressive disability, imminent death, or continued diminished quality of life and dependence on others are highly vulnerable. They are liable to distorted thinking, fear of pain and humiliation, and depressed mood. As a result, their autonomous decision-making may be impaired. In addition, dependent patients may feel pressured to end their lives to avoid burdening others. Sensitive and thorough discussion of the patient's situation and options for treatment and supportive care can help in discriminating between rational and irrational decisions to terminate life. Being vulnerable, such patients need protection and care. But they also need respect for their considered judgments regarding how to live and to die.

Patients who resolve to end their lives after due consideration and discussion waive their right not to be killed.[26] When the resolution is voluntary, the physician acts as the agent of the patient, not as the arbiter of death. The patient's voluntary request and informed authorization is a precondition for making the provision of lethal medication, from the patient's perspective, not a harm but a benefit. Thus the practice differs fundamentally from typical cases of criminal homicide, in which the person killed is an involuntary victim, and also from capital punishment, which we discuss below.

Abandonment

Physician-assisted death may be considered as abandonment of patients, particularly if it is performed without a careful and thorough assessment of the patient's condition and discussion of available alternatives. Adequate palliative care of the dying is hard work. It is much easier to get it over with quickly by offering "instant oblivion." Recognizing a duty not to kill or assist in the suicide of patients helps guard against a hasty decision in favor of putting an end to suffering by eliminating the patient. Nevertheless, an absolute prohibition of physician involvement in suicide risks abandoning patients to intolerable suffering against their will.

The norm of nonabandonment is relevant not only to whether physician-assisted death may be legitimate but also to how it should be performed. In his narrative of his patient "Diane," which is widely regarded as a paradigm case of justified physician-assisted death, Timothy Quill lamented the fact that Diane, after ingesting barbiturates, died alone: "I wonder whether Diane struggled in that last hour, and whether the Hemlock Society's way of death by suicide is the most benign. I wonder why Diane, who gave so much to so many of us, had to be alone for the last hour of her life."[27] Dying alone in this way raises two issues of abandonment. The physician-patient relationship is arbitrarily ruptured if fears of legal repercussions prevent the presence of the assisting physician at the time of death. Furthermore, there is a risk that the suffering patient may botch the suicide, thus losing control over the process of dying and possibly suffering unwanted medical interventions. If voluntary physician-assisted death as a last resort is a legitimate practice, then the norm of nonabandonment supports physician presence at this moment.

Physician Participation in Capital Punishment

It is instructive to contrast voluntary physician-assisted death with physician participation in capital punishment, in the light of professional integrity. We concur with the prevailing professional standard that considers it unethical for physicians to assist in the execution of convicted criminals.[28] Our stance is not based on a judgment that capital punishment is immoral. Whether or not it can be morally justified, physicians should not be involved as executioners. In capital punishment by lethal

---

> How can persons trust doctors who have the socially sanctioned power to kill patients?

Hastings Center Report, May-June 1995

injection, in which the physician operates as an agent of the state, the patient-centered focus of ethical medical practice is lacking.

Suppose, however, that a death-row prisoner has developed a relationship with a physician who provides health care for the inmates of the penal institution. If the prisoner requests that this physician administer a lethal injection in lieu of electrocution and the prison authorities do not oppose this request, is there any basis in professional integrity for the physician to refrain from participation in capital punishment?

Physician participation, though it may be more humane than the standard means of execution, violates professional integrity for a number of reasons. No medical goals are served by the physician-executioner. The act of execution by lethal injection is not a medical treatment or procedure. Typically, it is not initiated by a request for a physician's assistance and, even if such a request is made, the act of execution does not aim at responding effectively to the patient's medical condition. There may be no physician-patient relationship between the medical professional operating as executioner and the condemned criminal. And regardless of whether such a relationship is operative, execution by lethal injection obviously is not intended for the benefit of the prisoner. The prisoner would never have chosen the option of physician-inflicted death had it not been for the prior exercise of the state's coercive power in condemning the prisoner to die. In using his or her medical knowledge and skills to execute the prisoner, the physician does not serve the interests of the prisoner, but the interests of the state, which has determined that the prisoner's life must end.

Limits of the Argument

We have argued that the professional integrity of physicians grounds a prima facie duty to refrain from killing, or assisting in the killing of, patients. This prima facie duty may be overridden, however, in the situations of patients with intractable and intolerable suffering who voluntarily request to end their lives. Voluntary assistance in dying as a last resort is morally problematic but does not necessarily violate professional integrity. By contrast, an analysis of physician involvement in capital punishment fails to turn up any weighty countervailing considerations that can override the prima facie duty not to assist in a patient's death.

It is important to recognize the limitations of our argument in this essay. Professional integrity does not encompass the whole of medical ethics. Moral considerations other than the norms of professional integrity may be appealed to in favor of, or against, permitting a practice of limited physician-assisted death. We have argued elsewhere that an experimental public policy of legalizing the practice should be undertaken, subject to stringent regulatory safeguards to protect vulnerable patients and to preserve the professional integrity of physicians.[29] In this essay we have focused on the narrower question of whether the practice as a last resort can be compatible with the professional integrity of physicians. We believe that an affirmative answer to this question constitutes a necessary condition for legalization.

References

1. Martin Benjamin, *Splitting the Difference* (Lawrence: University Press of Kansas, 1990), pp. 52, 51.

2. Benjamin, *Splitting the Difference*, pp. 52-53.

3. Tom L. Beauchamp and James F. Childress, *Principles of Biomedical Ethics*, 4th ed. (New York: Oxford University Press, 1994), p. 471. The same criticism can be made with respect to the discussion of integrity in Baruch Brody's *Life and Death Decision Making* (New York: Oxford University Press, 1988), pp. 35-37 and 89-90.

4. In developing a conception of professional integrity of physicians we have been influenced by discussion of medical morality in the following sources: Edmund D. Pellegrino and David C. Thomasma, *A Philosophical Basis of Medical Practice* (New York: Oxford University Press, 1981), chap. 9, pp. 192-220; Leon R. Kass, *Toward a More Natural Science* (New York: The Free Press, 1985), chaps. 6-9, pp. 157-246; Charles Fried, *Medical Experimentation: Personal Integrity and Social Policy* (New York: Elsevier Publishing Co., 1974); John Ladd, "The Internal Morality of Medicine: An Essential Dimension of the Patient-Physician Relationship," in *The Clinical Encounter*, ed. Earl E. Shelp (Dordrecht, the Netherlands: D. Reidel, 1983), pp. 209-31; Charles L. Bosk, *Forgive and Remember* (Chicago: University of Chicago Press, 1979); and Joan Cassell, *Expected Miracles* (Philadelphia: Temple University Press, 1991).

5. The concept of a practice with internal goods and corresponding virtues is developed by Alasdair MacIntyre in *After Virtue*, 2nd ed. (Notre Dame, Ind.: University of Notre Dame Press, 1984), chap. 14, pp. 181-203.

6. Daniel Callahan, *The Troubled Dream of Life* (New York: Simon & Schuster, 1993).

7. Robert N. Proctor, *Racial Hygiene* (Cambridge: Harvard University Press, 1988).

8. Willard Gaylin, Leon R. Kass, Edmund D. Pellegrino, and Mark Siegler, "Doctors Must Not Kill," *JAMA* 259 (1988): 2139-40.

9. Leon R. Kass, "Neither for Love nor Money: Why Doctors Must Not Kill," *The Public Interest* 94 (1989): 40.

10. Ludwig Wittgenstein, *Philosophical Investigations*, 3rd ed. (New York: Macmillan, 1958), pp. 31-36.

11. Kass, *Toward a More Natural Science*, p. 198.

12. David M. Eddy, "A Conversation with My Mother," *JAMA* 272 (1994): 179-81.

13. Howard Brody, *The Healer's Power* (New Haven: Yale University Press, 1992), pp. 77-82.

14. David Cundiff, *Euthanasia Is Not the Answer* (Totowa, N.J.: Humana Press, 1992); Peter A. Singer and Mark Siegler, "Euthanasia—A Critique," *NEJM* 306 (1990): 1881-83.

15. Sidney Wanzer et al., "The Physician's Responsibility toward Hopelessly Ill Patients: A Second Look," *NEJM* 320 (1989): 844-49; Timothy E. Quill, *Death and Dignity* (New York: W.W. Norton, 1993), chap. 5; and Sherwin B. Nuland, *How We Die* (New York: Alfred A. Knopf, 1994).

16. Gregg A. Kasting, "The Nonnecessity of Euthanasia," in *Physician-Assisted Death*, ed. James M. Humber, Robert F. Almeder, and Gregg A. Kasting (Totowa, N.J.: Humana Press, 1994), pp. 25-45.

17. Nathan I. Cherny and Russell K. Portenoy, "Sedation in the Management of Refractory Symptoms: Guidelines for Evaluation and Treatment," *Journal of Palliative Care* 10, no. 2 (1994): 31-38.

18. Leon R. Kass, "Neither for Love nor Money," p. 40.

19. For descriptions of paradigm cases of physician-assisted death see Timothy E. Quill, "Death and Dignity: A Case of Individualized Decision Making," *NEJM* 324 (1991): 691-94; Franklin G. Miller, "Is

16

Hastings Center Report, May-June 1995

Active Killing of Patients Always Wrong?"
Journal of Clinical Ethics 2 (1991): 130-32;
and Lisa Belkin, "There's No Simple Suicide," *New York Times Magazine*, 14 November 1993.

20. William Goodman, "Euthanasia as
It Seems to Those Taking Part," *New York
Times*, 23 March 1993.

21. Timothy E. Quill, Christine K.
Cassel, and Diane E. Meier, "Care of the
Hopelessly Ill: Proposed Clinical Criteria
for Physician-Assisted Suicide," *NEJM* 327
(1992): 1384-88.

22. Franklin G. Miller and John C.
Fletcher, "The Case for Legalized Euthanasia," *Perspectives in Biology and Medicine*
36 (1993): 159-76.

23. Annette C. Baier, *Moral Prejudices*
(Cambridge: Harvard University Press,
1994), p. 153.

24. Stanley J. Reiser, "Science, Peda-
gogy, and the Transformation of Empathy
in Medicine," in *Empathy and the Practice of
Medicine*, ed. Howard M. Spiro et al. (New
Haven: Yale University Press, 1993), p.
130.

25. Edmund Pellegrino, "Doctors
Must Not Kill," *Journal of Clinical Ethics* 3
(1992): 95-102.

26. Brody, *Life and Death Decision Making*, pp. 24-26.

27. Quill, "Death and Dignity," p. 694.

28. Robert D. Truog and Troyen A.
Brennan, "Participation of Physicians in
Capital Punishment," *NEJM* 329 (1993):
1346-50; Council on Ethical and Judicial
Affairs, American Medical Association,
"Physician Participation in Capital Pun-
ishment," *JAMA* 270 (1993): 365-68.

29. Franklin G. Miller, Timothy E.
Quill, Howard Brody et al., "Regulating
Physician-Assisted Death," *NEJM* 331
(1994): 119-23.

17

[27]

DOING WHAT THE PATIENT ORDERS: MAINTAINING INTEGRITY IN THE DOCTOR-PATIENT RELATIONSHIP*

JEFFREY BLUSTEIN

INTRODUCTION

No profession has undergone as much scrutiny in the past several decades as that of medicine. Indeed, one might well argue that no profession has ever undergone so much change in so short a time. An essential part of this change has been the growing insistence that competent, adult patients have the right to decide about the course of their own medical treatment. However, the familiar and widely accepted principle of patient self-determination entails a corollary that has received little attention in the growing literature on the ethics of physician-patient relations: if patients are to direct the course of their own medical treatment, then physicians are at least sometimes to be guided in their actions on behalf of patients by values that are not, and may even be incompatible with, their own values. Unless it is supposed that it would be best if physicians were simply to accommodate any and all patient requests, a possibility I consider and reject in this paper, there are bound to be numerous instances of legitimate moral conflict between the preferences of physicians and patients. In this paper, I examine the implications of this sort of moral conflict from the standpoint of the integrity of the physician.

Critical to a proper appreciation of the significance of this conflict is a distinction that the literature on biomedical ethics has largely failed to draw: that between medical paternalism and physician integrity. Physicians who appeal to their integrity to justify acting or refraining from acting in certain ways are not necessarily adopting a paternalistic attitude toward their patients. But what is it that a person is appealing to when he or she appeals to integrity, and why should we be concerned about this? In the first section of this paper, I take up this question under the heading of "appeals to conscience" and examine the import of claims about maintaining self-integrity from both a phenomenological and a moral point of view. Though admittedly integrity can be possessed by the wicked no less than the good, it is not for this reason to be regarded as an utterly neutral character trait. Rather, I consider it to be an important virtue of a certain sort, one that, when combined with other valuable traits, provides an additional ground for admiration of the individual, Further, I reject the view espoused by some philosophers that concern for one's integrity is no more than a kind of moral egoism, a form of narcissistic self-indulgence. (It is perhaps because some such belief is tacitly shared by many that the topic of integrity has not received as much attention as it deserves, in the bioethics literature and elsewhere.) I hope to correct this misconception and to assign integrity an important place in the moral life.

Although the literature of biomedical ethics has not paid very much attention to the implicit potential for conflict between patient self-determination and physician integrity, in my experience physicians are well aware of it. One context in which it has arisen is New York State's Do-Not-Resuscitate (DNR) Law, which requires physicians to obtain the consent of the patient or appropriate surrogate prior to designating the patient a "no-code" concerning cardiopulmonary resuscitation (CPR). There is disagreement among legal commentators whether the law as written permits physicians to exercise their professional judgment in instances in which CPR would be futile. Whether rightly or not, many New York physicians to whom I have spoken regard this law as a threat to their integrity as physicians, which (many of them believe) does not permit them to undertake futile yet often painful measures. My purpose is not to enter the debate about the meaning of "futility", which has been much discussed elsewhere, but rather to explore the even more fundamental subject of physician integrity in the doctor-patient relationship.

1. APPEALS TO CONSCIENCE

I begin by clarifying the nature and significance of appeals to conscience. Though my discussion will focus on only one type of situation in which health care providers might make such appeals, viz. disputes between physicians and their patients, the analysis is intended to have wider relevance. It should also help us to better understand, for example, nurses' conscientious objection to following physicians' orders or physicians' conscientious objection to engaging in rationing at the bedside.

If doctors were merely the agents of their competent patients or

DOING WHAT THE PATIENT ORDERS 291

their incompetent patients' surrogates,[1] intermediaries between them and the health care delivery system whose only obligation is to carry out the wishes of their patients or surrogates, then physicians would have no right to refuse to honor the requests or demands of competent patients or surrogates for specific medical interventions.[2] Yet consider the following small sample of cases:

(a) A Catholic gynecologist's three-month pregnant patient requests an abortion, though the fetus does not directly threaten her life. The gynecologist refuses on the ground that his religious values forbid the taking of human life under these circumstances.

(b) The family of a patient suffering from metastatic cancer requests cardiac resuscitation in the event she arrests. Her physician refuses to honor this request on the ground that resuscitation under these circumstances is medically futile and would only subject the patient to needless pain and suffering.

(c) A Jehovah's Witness patient consents to cardiac surgery but refuses to give consent for blood transfusions, even if they should become necessary during the course of the surgery. The surgeon refuses to perform the procedure on these terms, claiming that the need for blood transfusions during surgery is a medical determination and that she will not be dictated to in matters of medical competence.

(d) A patient complains of recurring bifrontal headaches which, upon physcal examination, are diagnosed as tension headache. Nevertheless, he requests a CAT scan to rule out the possibility of a brain tumor. The physician refuses to order this marginally indicated procedure on the ground that scanning this patient would deprive another patient with a definable medical need of the opportunity to receive the test. As physicians in these cases conceive of their role, medical expertise should not merely be put at the disposal of patients or their surrogates.[3]

---

[1] The distinction between decision-making by competent patients and by their appropriate surrogates, important in other contexts, need not be dwelled on here. Since surrogate requests have no greater moral weight than those of competent patients, the argument from physician integrity concerning compliance with competent patients' requests has at least as much force with respect to the requests of surrogates.

[2] I am interested in physician integrity as a possible basis for refusing particular medical interventions. There may, of course, be other grounds for doing so (e.g. threat to the physician's health or life, larger social policy considerations) which can be discussed without raising the integrity issue.

[3] Though the problem of physician refusal of requested services has not been approached in a systematic way from the standpoint of physician integrity, this problem is receiving increasing attention in the bioethics literature. See, for example:

Physicians may refuse to accede to patient or surrogate requests or demands for various reasons. The refusal might be based on religious conviction (as in (a)); on a direct appeal to the moral principle to do no harm to one's patient (as in (b)); on one's conception of acceptable or good medical practice (as in (c)); on concern for the needs of other patients when a medical resource is in limited supply (as in (d)); or on some combination of these. But assuming that the physician is sincere in offering these reasons and is not just engaged in a process of rationalization, the refusal in each case is a principled one, motivated by ethical or other value considerations. It is not ad hoc or merely an expression of sentiment or preference, but reflects a more or less considered position that has definite implications for the physician's conduct in other similar situations. Nor are the physicians in these cases paternalistic, for they are not attempting to impose their conception of the patient's interests on the patient in the belief that this is for the patient's own good.

On the other hand, a physician might have no scruples about complying with patient or surrogate wishes. This may be because the physician subscribes to what Robert Veatch calls "the engineering model" of doctor-patient relationships, according to which the physician is only an applied scientist, a technician of the body, "who thinks he can just present all the facts and let the patient make the choices".[4] He accepts responsibility only for the skill, proficiency, and technique with which his interventions are performed, and divorces himself from consideration of the moral content of what he does. The physician, so conceived, is no more than "an engineer, a plumber making repairs, connecting tubes and flushing out clogged systems, with no questions asked".[5] However, this strategy of detachment involves either self-deception or a misunderstanding of the nature of agency, for one cannot block moral responsibility for one's professional activities merely by selectively focusing on the technical proficiency with which they are carried out. Alternatively, the physician might not refrain from placing his or her professional conduct within a framework of

---

Allan Brett and Laurence McCullough, "When Patients Request Specific Interventions", *NEJM*, 315, no. 21, November 20, 1986: 1347–1351; John Paris, Robert Crone, and Frank Reardon, "Physicians' Refusal of Requested Treatment: The Case of Baby L", *NEJM*, 322, no. 14, April 5, 1990: 1012–1015; Mark Siegler, "Physicians' Refusals of Patient Demands", in R. Bayer, A. Caplan, and N. Daniels, eds., *In Search of Equity: Health Needs and the Health Care System* New York: Plenum, 1983, pp.199–227.

[4] "Models for Ethical Medicine in a Revolutionary Age", in John Arras and Nancy Rhoden, eds. *Ethical Issues in Modern Medicine*, 3rd edition, Mountain View, California: Mayfield Publishing Co., 1989, p.52.

[5] Ibid., p.53.

DOING WHAT THE PATIENT ORDERS 293

moral value, but instead take the principled position that he or she is in all cases morally bound to respect the considered choice of the patient or the patient's surrogate. Such a physician has no doubt failed to understand both that physicians have other responsibilities as well and that the profession does not require violation of personal commitments to ethical or religious mandates. But at least he or she can no longer be said to be merely an amoral technician, indifferent to the moral implications of professional behavior.

In attempting to justify a physician's refusal to cooperate with the demands or requests of a patient or patient surrogate, we often invoke the notion of conscience. Thus, consider the languague used by one court in a Jehovah's Witness case of the sort described in (c) above:

> The patient voluntarily submitted himself to and insisted on medical treatment. At the same time, he sought to dictate a course of treatment to his physician which amounted to malpractice. The court held that under these circumstances, a physician cannot be required to ignore the mandates of his own conscience, even in the name of the exercise of religious freedom. A patient can knowingly refuse treatment, but he cannot demand mistreatment.[6]

Physicians also frequently appeal to conscience when they take a stand against complying with patient or surrogate choices. "I cannot in good conscience do what the patient or his family asks me to do", they may say, or "My conscience tells me that I should not do this". Such appeals, at least among otherwise basically decent persons, seem to add a certain moral gravity to refusals to facilitate patient or surrogate requests. But, we may wonder, what is a person actually claiming when he or she describes a refusal to perform a certain act as violative of conscience? Moreover, would anything of moral significance be lost if claims of the sort,

> I cannot do x with a clear conscience,

were replaced by straightforward claims about the wrongness of doing x?

According to the Oxford English Dictionary, one meaning of "conscience" is just "consciousness of right and wrong". When someone says that his conscience forbids him to do something, and uses the word in this way, he means that it would be wrong for him to do this, and if asked why, he will refer, not to some private voice within, but to the considerations that led him to make this decision. Imagine a physician reasoning as follows, for example:

As a physician, I am bound by the principle of nonmaleficence.

[6] United States v. George, 33 LW 2518, 1965.

294 JEFFREY BLUSTEIN

This principle directs me to do no harm to my patients. But if I honor this particular request of my patient, I will be violating this principle. To be sure, I am also bound by a principle of respect for patient self-determination. But either my patient has no right in this particular case to the requested procedure, or if he or she has a right, it is outweighed by my duty of nonmaleficence. Either way, I believe it would be wrong to facilitate my patient's request, and so I will not do it.

On one view – a view which I do not share – it would be redundant for the physician to add, "I would have a bad conscience if I did what the patient asks". Perhaps an individual who uses the language of conscience has the further thought that he or she will experience distress if the act in question is performed. But, it may be argued, anticipated distress cannot be a sufficient reason, or even *a* reason, for refraining from doing what the patient asks.

There is another objection to invoking conscience, more serious than the charge of redundancy, that has to do with the reflexive nature of appeals to conscience. According to this objection, thinking about prospective actions in terms of their relation to one's conscience can easily slide into treating a good conscience as an autonomous ideal in itself. Instead of impartially considering what it would be right or obligatory for me to do, and acting on the results of my deliberation, there is a very real danger that I will focus on *myself* and my feelings, and thus turn my attention away from the proper object of moral concern.[7] The question I should be asking is not how acting in a certain way will affect me, how it will affect my image of myself as a person of conscience, but whether it is right or wrong to so act. Appeals to conscience, in short, are liable to degenerate into a kind of idealized selfishness in which excessive self-preoccupation masquerades as moral conviction, and for this reason they should be condemned.

These criticisms, I believe, are unpersuasive. Appeals to conscience are not redundant. Properly used, conscience indicates a particular way of seeing moral and other normative demands, a mode of consciousness in which prospective actions are viewed in relation to one's self and character. When the notion of conscience is used in this way,

---

[7] This sort of criticism of appeals to conscience or integrity is made by: Jonathan Bennett, "Whatever the Consequences", in J. Thomson and G. Dworkin, eds. *Ethics*, New York: Harper and Row, 1968, and Jonathan Glover, "It Makes No Difference Whether or Not I Do It", *Proceedings of the Aristotelian Society*, Supplementary Volume 49, 1975, p.184. For a response, see Richard Norman, *Reasons for Action*, New York: Barnes and Noble, 1971, chapter 4, and Bernard Williams, "Utilitarianism and Moral Self-Indulgence", in H.D. Lewis, ed. *Contemporary British Philosophy 4*, London: Allen and Unwin, 1976.

moreover, appeals to conscience are compatible with a due regard for the rights and interests of others. Admittedly, the line between "conscience" and "moral egoism" is sometimes difficult to draw, but this is not enough to cast general doubt on the legitimacy of such appeals. The physician who appeals to conscience in refusing a patient's request, for example, may very well not be making the mistake of thinking that what makes it wrong to honor the request is his or her need to preserve a clear conscience, nor is the physician necessarily or even probably focused on self in any morally objectionable way. This is a perversion of the notion of conscience that consists in treating conscience itself as the standard of or source of right and wrong, and our understanding of the moral interest we take in ourselves and others would be seriously incomplete if, because of occasional abuses of this notion, we elected to use only a stripped-down normative vocabulary of rules, principles, duties, rights, and the like.

Persons are naturally reluctant to act against their consciences, and this reluctance can be explained in different ways. An individual might be reluctant to abandon a moral or religious viewpoint that he or she has grown up believing is correct and has expressed in his or her life over many years, even though, having achieved a more mature moral or religious understanding, that previous outlook now appears shallow, insensitive, or thoughtless. Since in this case adherence to the earlier view can be attributed to psychological inertia and lacks current normative support, the individual in question can act against conscience and believe his or her values justify doing so. More problematic, however, is the individual who decides to act against conscience despite the fact that there are no misgivings about the values expressed in its deliverances. The individual is sure that what conscience directs is the right or proper thing to do, but perhaps under pressure from his or her sympathies or other emotions, decides not to listen to it. In this case, the individual cannot believe him or herself to be justified, from a moral or religious point of view, in acting against conscience. Indeed, the decision is believed to be unjustified according to the values currently embraced. And the reluctance to take this step is explained by the pull of his or her moral or other principles.

In acting against one's conscience in this second sort of case, one violates one's own fundamental moral or religious convictions, personal standards that one sees as an important part of oneself and by which one is prepared to judge oneself. In so acting, one does not merely feel discomfort or disappointment, however intense: these feelings do not reach deeply enough to one's very self-conception. Nor does one merely feel regret: this seems a rather inadequate

296   JEFFREY BLUSTEIN

reaction under the circumstances. A person might also regret doing something that, in good conscience, he or she could not but do. (Consider the case of the teacher whose commitment to certain professional standards leaves her no choice but to fail a student, but who still regrets having to do so.) Rather, the painful feeling that accompanies acting against conscience is typically one of self-betrayal. One feels one has betrayed oneself because one violates a standard that is inescapably bound up with one's self-identity. And attendant on this self-betrayal is a loss of self-respect, for one judges one's worth in part in terms of how well one measures up to this standard. By contrast, there is no painful sense of self-betrayal or loss of self-respect in the first scenario, where, as we might say, the individual cannot in good conscience do what conscience dictates.

A person who acts against conscience and sincerely believes that what he or she does is wrong (not just wrong by societal standards or standards formerly accepted, but according to his or her present values), experiences inner conflict. The individual is, or takes him or herself to be, a person of principle, and feels guilt and/or shame for failure to follow the dictates of conscience. Of course, self-deception is always a possibility in these situations, since guilt and shame are painful emotions and persons can escape them if they manage to persuade themselves that their values actually permit the behavior in question. But this only preserves the semblance of inner harmony and circumvents the hard work of achieving genuine personal integration. The inner conflict can only be covered up by self-deception, not resolved.

A different course of action would be for one to use the conflict as an occasion for critical reflection on the content of one's conscience. Instead of living a divided life, the individual pays attention to those motivations that led him or her to violate conscience – sympathies, longings, fears, anxieties, etc. – and reconsiders the adequacy of his or her moral and other principles in light of them. It can then happen, Jonathan Bennett observes,

> that a certain moral principle becomes untenable – meaning literally that one cannot hold it any longer – because it conflicts intolerably with the pity or revulsion or whatever that one feels when one sees what the principle leads to.[8]

Those who deceive themselves about what they are doing may manage to escape the pain of a bad conscience. But conscience itself can change as a result of reflection on strong and persistent pressures

[8] "The Conscience of Huckleberry Finn", in Christina Hoff Sommers, ed. *Vice and Virtue in Everyday Life*, New York: Harcourt Brace Jovanovich, 1985, p.32.

that run counter to it, and if we take them seriously as checks on our principles, we may actually be able to repair our inner division.

It is tempting to say to the person who, by acting against conscience, betrays some principle that is constitutive of self-identity, "You owe it to yourself to try to repair your inner division". The language of "owing" suggests the special gravity of the problem: it is not just an unpleasant situation that the individual finds him or herself in and it is not just to bring the self greater happiness that the individual should work to resolve inner conflict. It is more like an instance of a moral duty we have to ourselves to lead personally integrated lives, to bring our actions and motivations into harmony with our principles. Or, alternatively, we speak of "owing" to make a point about the requirements of good character. Those who fail to take steps to prevent further deviations from principle or to remove themselves from situations in which such deviations are likely, or who resort to self-deception to evade acknowledging the discrepancy between their actions and principles, are lacking in this regard.

When we assert that a person owes it to him or herself to repair inner division, we are not expressing an interest in people doing what is right, though of course we do care about this too. Rather, we are expressing an interest, a moral interest, in an individual being a certain sort of person and taking him or herself seriously in a certain way. It is as if we are saying, "Your own integrity ought to matter to you. If you lack integrity, or if your integrity is incomplete, then you ought to face up to this with courage and honesty and make an effort to achieve personal integration". The fullest statement of our moral interest in ourselves and others is this: an interest in one's doing what is right as part of an integrated life.

It is in terms of this moral interest in personal integrity that I will understand the significance of appeals to conscience. Persons who claim that they cannot in good conscience do what they are asked or ordered to do are not necessarily asserting that integrity itself supplies them with the standard of right and wrong. Rather, they may be anticipating what will happen to self if they should not refuse, viz. they will be in a state of internal disharmony, and refuse partly because they value their own inner harmony.[9] Of course, in the absence of a humane sense of values, conscientiousness is hardly a virtue. But this does not entail that we are only concerned about persons doing what is right or avoiding what is wrong. For sometimes our good opinion of another partly derives from our recognition of the interest this person takes in and the importance he or she attaches to self-integrity.

[9] James Childress argues for this way of understanding the moral import of appeals to conscience in "Appeals to Conscience", *Ethics*, 89 (1979): 315–335.

298   JEFFREY BLUSTEIN

Our moral interest in people seeking after or maintaining personal integrity is reflected in (though not justified by) a common view about the following sort of situation. Suppose a patient requests a certain treatment from a physician that is not illegal, but that the physician judges it would be wrong or immoral to provide (case (a) above might serve as an example). Suppose also that the physician has good reason to believe that if he does not provide the service, the patient will go to another physician to receive it, perhaps to another physician who will not do as good a job. Does the first physician have any moral basis for refusing the patient's request? On the one hand, the former has good reason to believe that refusal will not prevent the wrong from being committed; he foresees that as a consequence of the refusal, the patient will go to someone else who will not refuse. Moreover, from the point of view of what the physician is asked to *do*, leaving out the fact that *he* will be the one who does it, he must admit that it is at least no worse for him to do it than for the second physician. Hence, it seems either to make no moral difference who does it or to be morally better if he does it. On the other hand, and here I come to the view alluded to at the start of this paragraph, it might be countered that this argument is defective precisely because it does not consider the action in relation to the agent, that is, the action-as-performed-by this particular physician. As performed by him, it would violate his inner harmony or integrity, and (we may suppose) it would not have this effect on the second physician. Looking at action in this agent-relative way, it now does seem to make a moral difference who honors the patient's request.

Suppose now that the first physician believes there is no moral difference, other things being equal, between performing an action which causes wrong and performing an action which one foresees will result in a wrongful reaction. Then he might not be able to invoke personal integrity to support refusal of services. For if he believes that other things are equal, that, for example, the wrong the second physician would do is as serious as the wrong he would do, and that the certainty of their occurring is the same, then his conscience would not tell him that it is worse to provide the service than to refuse to do so. If he judges that providing and refusing are both equally wrong, then whichever he does, he acts against his conscience and suffers a disruption of inner harmony. By contrast, I assume, as before, that the second physician has no moral qualms about providing the service and so would not act against conscience in doing so. Under these circumstances, it could be argued, it still makes a moral differerence which physician honors the patient's request (one acts against conscience in doing so, the other doesn't). Loss of integrity is a morally relevant factor even when, because of an individual's

DOING WHAT THE PATIENT ORDERS 299

moral beliefs, he or she finds him or herself in a moral bind, forced, as it were, to compromise integrity no matter what is done. And our moral interest in people's having moral integrity would be reflected in our judgement that it is a worse thing for the patient to have gone initially to the first physician rather than directly to the second. Whether the patient realizes it or not, the first would have been spared a genuine moral loss had the patient gone directly to the second.

I should now clarify my earlier remark about the essentially personal nature of conscience. To begin with, I do not mean that an individual must refrain from universalizing the moral standards that are determinative for his or her conscience. The individual may sometimes refrain, but need not. With respect to certain moral standards, viz. basic moral requirements, we do not expect the individual to apply them only to him or herself and to refrain from blaming or condemning others who fail to adhere to them. But conscience (distinguished here from the standards themselves) relates, in the first instance, only to one's own actions and not directly to the actions of others. Thus, we have no difficulty understanding a statement like "I would have a guilty conscience if I did this", but we require further information to make sense of something like, "I would have a guilty conscience if he did this". Perhaps the reason I would have a guilty conscience in this latter case is that I take myself to have a special responsibility for the behavior of this other person. But then what my conscience would trouble me about is the actions of the other insofar as they are due to *my* failure to discharge my responsibility, not the actions of the other person simpliciter. It is part of the logic of the concept of conscience that my conscience can only forbid *me* from acting in certain ways or instruct *me* to act in certain ways, not other people.

Conscience is also essentially personal in the sense that we have a special responsibility toward our own integrity. Earlier I claimed that we have a moral interest not only in people doing what is right but also in their taking their integrity seriously. The failure to do so, I suggested, might be thought of as a kind of failure to carry out a duty to oneself or as a failure to be responsible for oneself. The duty with respect to integrity, as I intend this to be understood, is not a duty to maximize the good of integrity, the number of instances of people preserving or achieving integrity, or to minimize the number of instances of people who do not do so. When the duty is construed in this impersonal way, it gives no special importance to the preservation or achievement of one's own integrity. Rather, the duty has a unique object, one's very own integrity, integrity relativized to the self. When we look at integrity from a personal point of view, we cannot say that it is a matter of indifference to the agent

300   JEFFREY BLUSTEIN

whose integrity is lost. For now the fact that my own integrity is
wrapped up with what I do is intrinsically relevant to how I should act.

We are not morally obligated to regard our lives, relationships,
and actions from a personal perspective: moral obligation does not
apply to this. But it is natural for us to do so, and moreover, the
realization of a range of important values would be foreclosed to us
if we did not do so. For example, love and deep friendship are only
possible if we do not place the well-being of particular others on the
same scale as the well-being of persons generally. The fact that some
person is *my* lover or *my* friend is taken by me as a good (though
not always sufficient) reason to favor him over a stranger or even
over my neighbor's lover or friend. This shows that we live our loves
and friendships from within the personal point of view. More
generally, much of what gives human life its preciousness and
significance is conditional on the adoption of a personal perspective
on the world and oneself. Love, friendship, and much else besides
would disappear from our lives if we chiefly lived from an impersonal
point of view.

I have argued in this section that conscientious refusal may be understood as motivated by a concern for one's integrity or wholeness and
that sometimes a physician may permissibly, even ought to, refuse
to accede to the request or demand of a patient or patient surrogate
on the ground that to do so would undermine his or her integrity.
It is important to inquire further whether the physician is correct
to think that his or her integrity would be undermined by acceding
to the request or demand. One may have misjudged the situation
one is in. Perhaps on further reflection one would realize that one's
values do not actually commit one to refuse to do what the patient
or surrogate wants. A conscientious physician would take this possiblity
seriously and would not rush to take cover, as it were, behind his
or her conscience.

I turn now to a closer examination of the question, how can a physician preserve self-integrity even as he or she modifies an initial principled stand against some course of action? I will be interested in
a particular aspect of this general problem, viz. whether a physician
can accept a compromise concerning a matter about which he or she
has strong moral convictions without sacrificing integrity.

2. THE PROBLEM OF COMPROMISE

Consider the case of a family that insists on what the physician believes
is medically inappropriate cardiopulmonary resuscitation for their
unconscious or incompetent relative. The physician does not see him
or herself as merely an extension of the will of the patient's family,

DOING WHAT THE PATIENT ORDERS 301

but has a basic professional/moral commitment not to provide futile treatment,[10] a commitment that, in some cases and this one in particular, runs counter to the wishes of the patient or patient surrogate. Is there any room for compromise here on the physician's part? That is, can the physician compromise on this matter without compromising his or her integrity?

It would be helpful at the outset to distinguish between genuine compromise with respect to one's principles or values and alteration of the principles/values themselves. For example, a physician who is unqualifiedly opposed to providing care that is believed to be medically inappropriate to the patient's condition might come to replace this principle with a narrower one that allows such care in certain cases where family members insist upon it. If the physician now accedes to the demands of a family for CPR, he or she may only be acting in accordance with the reformulated principle. It would still be important, in deciding whether the physician has managed to preserve integrity, to know more about why the position was changed: change of principle can itself indicate a failure to preserve one's integrity. But if the range of the principle has been restricted to accommodate family wishes in some situations, then questions about the need for or appropriateness of compromise to accommodate family wishes in those situations do not arise.

My interest is in compromise, and in the example I have chosen to discuss, the physician's opposition to inappropriate treatment is not qualified in the way specified. Must the physician, to preserve his or her integrity, regard any compromise with the family on this matter as unacceptable, as a kind of self-betrayal? Or is compromise compatible with, perhaps even required by, integrity? To answer this, we need to distinguish between different senses of integrity.

If integrity is thought of merely as fidelity to one's principles or commitments, then it may seem that any compromise on matters of principle means a loss of integrity. But in fact integrity is more complicated and demanding than this, for an individual may have several, equally important commitments and may be in a situation where strict adherence to each one of them is not possible. Under these circumstances, integrity demands something like doing the best one can with the plurality of values and principles one holds.

In the case of the physician, it is not implausible to suppose that conflict with the family brings a number of significant values to the fore. One of these, as already stated, has to do with the provision

---

[10] There are, admittedly, a number of important and difficult issues relating to the determination of medical futility, but given my aims in this paper, I believe I can safely pass over them.

302   JEFFREY BLUSTEIN

of treatment that offers nothing of significance for the patient's welfare
or interests. Another is compassion: the physician may believe that,
as a caring professional, he or she ought to help this family accept
the inevitable loss of a member and should give the patient's loved
ones time to adjust to it. Yet another is respect: though the physician
disagrees with family members over the correct way to proceed with
the patient, he or she may nevertheless appreciate their seriousness
and sincerity in the matter at hand and believe that the moral status
of the family's position ought to be acknowledged. Against the background of a plurality of central values, the physician might decide
that compromise with the family on the issue of resuscitation is the
best way to preserve self-integrity. For what compromise enables the
physician to do is accommodate the full range of major values that
are applicable to this situation. Moreover, these values are not only
important to the physician, as we have supposed. We recognize these
values as ones that a reasonable person might take to be of great
importance, and we grant integrity to the physician partly on this basis.

Though the physician in my example is unwavering in the belief
that when resuscitation is medically inappropriate it should not be
provided, and, in the absence of a demand for it, would not consider
attempting it, he or she might well decide that a compromise with
the family ought to be sought and accepted. For what one judges
ought to be done about a matter that is in dispute, leaving aside the
fact that there is a dispute, and what one judges ought to be done,
all things considered, are not always the same.[11] There is more to
be considered when an issue is in dispute than the issue itself. In
the case at hand, the physician might decide that compromise is best
because it involves only a partial abandonment of the commitment
not to provide inappropriate treatment at the same time that it shows
compassion for the family and respect for its moral sincerity and goodwill. But if one clearly judges, all things considered, that there ought
to be a compromise and acts accordingly, this hardly compromises
one's integrity.[12] On the contrary, what compromises one's integrity
is not acting in accordance with what one clearly judges one should
do, all things considered, but electing not to so act.

The features which justify compromise may underdetermine the
compromise in the sense that there may be a number of equally

[11] See Arthur Kuflik, "Morality and Compromise", in J. Pennock and J.
Chapman, eds., *Compromise in Ethics, Law, and Politics*, New York: New York
University Press, 1979, pp.48–52.

[12] Ibid., p.51. Also, my analysis of integrity and compromise resembles the
approach taken by Martin Benjamin in *Splitting the Difference: Compromise and Integrity
in Ethics and Politics*, Lawrence, Kansas: University Press of Kansas, 1990, pp.32–38,
121–123.

DOING WHAT THE PATIENT ORDERS 303

acceptable concessions an individual could make. The physician might meet the family half-way by agreeing to treat the patient for a specified period of time without a DNR order, with the understanding that an order will be written if the patient has not improved by the end of that time. In addition, resuscitation covers a range of interventions, including compression and defibrillation, drug support and fluid resuscitation. The physician might propose, as a reasonable compromise, a partial code in which only certain resuscitative measures are attempted – e.g. pharmacological support but no intubation. In each case, the physician's position on the patient's treatment has not changed. But it does not follow that a physician who takes this position can't make some limited concession to the family and preserve integrity. For a physician may have a number of moral concerns, no one of which is regarded as less central or well-grounded than the others, and may elect a compromise solution in order to reconcile a plurality of commitments.

A compromise on a matter of principle is not tantamount to a betrayal of principle, but there is no abstract formula that an individual can use to determine whether a particular compromise is integrity-preserving. Suffice it to say that an individual can maintain integrity only if in some significant sense he or she remains faithful to the principle being compromised. Further, I have argued for the justifiability of compromise in circumstances where a number of equally basic values or principles are engaged. But I do not disallow the possibility that an individual will be able to maintain integrity only if he or she refuses to compromise on a principle. If one of the values or principles at stake in a particular case is ranked significantly higher than the others in terms of importance, integrity-preserving compromise may not be possible. (The case of the Catholic gynecologist in section 1 may be an example of this.)

Compromise, as I have been thinking of it so far, belongs to the domain of interpersonal conflict. However, we also use the expression "compromise" in cases of conflict between personal and professional morality, as when we say that one's professional role can to some extent make it permissible, or even obligatory, to compromise one's substantive moral values, to do things (or refrain from doing things) that one would not normally, in a nonprofessional context, do (or refrain from doing). Here we are not thinking of compromise as a concession made within the context of conflict between at least two parties, but rather as something that takes place in connection with certain values or principles that one has because they are in conflict or tension with other values or principles one has. Because the latter is not a social enterprise, certain considerations that may be advanced to defend the moral acceptability of

304   JEFFREY BLUSTEIN

interpersonal compromise will not be relevant here. Thus, interpersonal compromise can be seen as a peculiarly liberal value grounded in respect for persons, but intrapersonal compromise cannot be justified in this way.

In our system, to take a non-medical example, it is widely held that the first duty of a lawyer is to advance the interests of his or her client. It is also commonly claimed that occupying this role makes one's situation morally different than it would otherwise have been because the role constitutes a sufficient reason for doing or not doing something that might otherwise be objectionable, even by one's own moral values. For example, legal ethics is said to require that lawyers keep the confidence of their clients and plead their defense even when they believe the clients are guilty.

One powerful argument in defense of a special role morality for lawyers is this: the legal system will end up doing more justice for more people if lawyers relatively single-mindedly pursue the interests of their clients in the way mandated by the role than if lawyers determine the shape of their professional obligations by consulting their individual substantive moral values.[13] An analogous argument can be made for physicians who, like lawyers, are entrusted with the care of vulnerable persons. Thus, it might be said, physicians should act as advocates of their patients and respect their confidences even when such behavior by others or by themselves in nonprofessional settings would be morally criticizable. A medical system that allows or requires physicians to attend to the needs of their patients in a relatively single-minded way leads to a morally better outcome overall.

A physician who holds that, as a professional, he or she is subject to a special morality, need not believe that he or she may or should do just *anything* to advance the interests of the patient. Indeed, a physician who took this view would have misunderstood what the role of physician either required or allowed. But there are times when a doctor's belief that he or she is allowed or required to depart from the requirements of common morality is well-founded and proper, and then compromising his or her ordinary moral values is compatible with the preservation of moral integrity.

In either sort of compromise, and whether it is integrity-preserving or not, one partially abandons or sets aside a principle or commitment, departs from a normative standpoint which one adopted before the circumstances of compromise arose and which is not completely relinquished even as the compromise is more or less reluctantly

[13] Richard Wasserstrom makes this argument in "Roles and Morality", in David Luban, ed., *The Good Lawyer: Lawyers' Roles and Lawyers' Ethics*, Totowa, N.J.: Rowman and Allanheld, 1984, pp.30–31.

accepted. To clarify the nature of compromise still further, I close this section with a brief discussion of another class of cases in contemporary health care ethics. Unlike those cited above, these are ones in which neither physicians nor their patients enter a morally unresolved situation with fixed views that are clearly in opposition to each other. For such cases, we need another model of physician-patient interaction than that of adversaries and another way of characterizing the process of reaching agreement than compromise. (I do not wish to suggest that the adversaries must be hostile to one another.)

A familiar example of this involves treatment decisions for severely impaired or anomalous newborns. Both the parents of such a newborn and the child's physician, I assume, agree on the ethical principle to govern this situation, viz. the best interests of the child. In many cases, of course, there would be no question that treatment is in the child's best interests. But there is lack of clarity, for parents and physician alike, about what the standard recommends when applied to the present case, for the case resists any straightforward application of normative standards. Because ethical ambiguity pervades this situation and none of the participants initially has any definite convictions about whether or not to treat the infant, the notion of reaching a compromise is out of place. Simply put, compromise is a way of coming to agreement with persons who are and remain wedded to a standpoint in conflict with one's own (or, alternatively, compromise is the product of this process), but here there is uncertainty rather than serious disagreement. On the other hand, the participants might be able to achieve a consensus on the treatment question and thereby find a solution that each can live with. For example, they might come to the following agreement: the physician will begin treatment for the infant and periodically reassess his or her probable prognosis, and the parents will stop treatment if there is a high probability the child will be so disabled that he or she will be unable to relate to others or the environment.

Compromise and consensus, not often distinguished, are nevertheless different ways of reaching mutually agreeable solutions to complex moral problems. In consensus decisionmaking processes, participants are not so divided on a case that a compromise between or with them has to be arranged. Rather, their posture is like that of colleagues who are engaged in a cooperative inquiry for some commonly acceptable operational solution.[14] Situations in which

---

[14] For more on consensus decisionmaking, see Jonathan Moreno, "Ethics by Committee: The Moral Authority of Consensus", *Journal of Medicine and Philosophy* 14, November 1988: 411–432; and "What Means This Consensus: Ethics Committees and Philosophic Tradition", *Journal of Clinical Ethics*: 38–43.

patient or surrogate demands for medical intervention collide with
the values or principles of the provider can be dealt with by
compromise, as long as the parties persist in holding to their respective positions, but these are not the conditions for building a consensus. Further, while both compromise-seeking and
consensus-seeking can be thought of as ways of showing respect for
the other person's seriousness and goodwill – and each derives at
least part of its moral value from this – they evince respect in different
ways. In compromise decisionmaking, at least one party, out of respect
for the other, is willing to make concessions and thus bear a share
of the burden of reaching a mutually acceptable solution. In consensus decisionmaking, by contrast, there is no burden that is borne,
no loss incurred (or at least no burden or loss of the same sort). Rather,
each party shows respect for the other by encouraging the other to
lend his or her insights to the clarification of a problematic situation
in an atmosphere of cooperative deliberation.

A willingness to compromise leads directly to questions about the
compromiser's integrity. There is a common opinion that people of
integrity just don't do this sort of thing (unless, perhaps, the cost
of not doing so is extreme), and while I have been at pains to show
why I do not share this view, there is certainly a problem here that
merits close attention: compromise needs to be defended against the
charge that it undermines integrity. But a willingness to work toward
consensus typically raises no such worries. Indeed, this seems innocent enough, from the point of view of integrity. Yet this judgment
is too hasty. For one can "sell out" by participating in a consensus
decisionmaking process or by agreeing to abide by a consensus solution no less than one can lose one's integrity by compromising.

3. PATIENT REFERRAL AND INTEGRITY PRESERVATION

I have maintained that physician integrity does not in every instance
require refusal of patient (or surrogate) requests for medical intervention to which the physician has serious ethical or religious objections.
Compromise, or meeting the other party halfway, so to speak, may be
a morally acceptable alternative and one that the physician can in good
conscience adopt. I now consider another possible response to situations in which the physician's moral or religious commitments conflict
with patient or surrogate choices: withdrawal from the case and transfer of the patient to another health care professional or institution.[15]

---

[15] There are few discussions in the philosophical literature of the moral issues
in professional referral. But see Michael D. Bayles, "A Problem of Clean Hands:
Refusals to Provide Professional Services," *Social Theory and Practice* 5, 1979: 165–181.

DOING WHAT THE PATIENT ORDERS 307

The argument for a right to withdraw is familiar. While the physician has a contract to provide care for and not abandon his or her patient, this contract does not extend to treatments or tests that go against the physician's moral or religious commitments. Since the physician cannot be compelled to act against conscience, in these cases he or she is morally permitted to refuse to provide the requested treatment or test. But this is not the end of the matter, for the physician is usually taken to have certain secondary obligations deriving from the duty to care. That is, the duty to care is still in effect even when one is morally justified in refusing to provide care oneself. To begin with, the physician should inform the patient or surrogate of his or her inability to continue to provide care and of the options that exist for transfer to another physician or institution. Then, if the patient or surrogate decides to transfer, the physician should assist in an orderly transfer of care. The standard view among physicians is that if they cannot provide a requested treatment based on their strongly held personal beliefs, they are morally (as well as legally) obligated to seek to find another physician who would provide the requested treatment, and if another physician is available and the patient is agreeable, assist in transferring care.

Referring patients to other physicians or institutions is an option that seems to preserve physican integrity. In arranging a transfer, the physician shows respect for the considered choices of the patient or the patient's surrogate and remains loyal to the patient, at the same time keeping his or her hands clean and conscience clear. Unlike compromise, how could any integrity objection be raised to patient referral?

I believe, however, that this strategy for coping with patient requests is not as morally unproblematic as most physicians seem to assume. If providing treatment T undermines physician A's integrity, why doesn't referring the patient to physician B for T (or seeking to find another physician who will provide T for the patient) do so as well? Is there a morally significant difference between providing treatment that one deems objectionable and transferring the patient to someone whom one believes will provide the same treatment? If both are equally damaging to physician integrity, and loss of integrity is a good and sufficient reason for a physician to refuse to honor a patient's request, then contrary to the popular view, he or she cannot have a moral obligation to refer the patient to another physician who will honor the request.

There might seem to be a difference if, borrowing a line from Bernard Williams, the value of integrity relates to the idea that "each of us is specially responsible for what *he* does, rather than for what

308   JEFFREY BLUSTEIN

other people do."[16] For then it might be thought that what the
physician is committed to is that *he* should not provide the treatment,
and since the physician is referring the patient to *another* caretaker,
he (the former) is not violating his commitment and so is retaining
his integrity. But surely the issue cannot be settled this easily.
Responsibility for an action is not only a matter of whether one does
the action oneself, but can encompass other people doing the action
when one has arranged for or persuaded them to do it. To think
otherwise, to deny responsibility for what others do simply because
one is not the immediate causal agent, raises a strong suspicion of
self-deception.

What we need to explore is what makes patient referrals integrity-
preserving when they are so and when continued treatment is
impossible as a matter of conscience or commitment to principle.
A number of possible explanations will be offered in the rest of this
section. To make the discussion somewhat less abstract, I focus on
the case of a terminally ill but still competent patient who has discussed his or her wishes to avoid a painful and undignified death
with friends and loved ones, who has rejected hospice care, and who
now seeks assistance from his or her physician in bringing about death.
If the physician cannot in good conscience help the patient commit
suicide, can the physician in good conscience refer the patient to
another physician who will help him or her do so? To argue, as before,
that since integrity relates only to what *he* does and he does not assist
in the suicide, his integrity remains intact and his hands are clean,
is unpersuasive. How else might we show that honoring a patient's
request oneself and referring the patient to another caregiver can
have different implications for physician integrity?

One approach looks to the nature of the physician's value
commitments. Consider the following argument in defense of patient
referral:

(I) Whereas, given my personal ethical and/or religious commitments, there is no choice for me but to refuse to assist in suicide,
I do not universalize my values. I feel other physicians may practice
as they wish and do not criticize them for helping patients commit
suicide. Since my opposition to assisted suicide is personal in this
way, I do nothing wrong or violative of my integrity if I transfer
my patient to another physician who does not share my convictions.

(I) seems to express the way many physicians think about the
morality of patient referral. However, there are problems with this
argument. First, even if we accept the point about not demanding

---

[16] J.J.C. Smart and Bernard Williams, *Utilitarianism For and Against*, Cambridge:
Cambridge University Press, 1973, p.99.

of other physicians what one demands of oneself, the referring physician should still have moral qualms about doing something that furthers what is, from his or her personal standpoint, impermissible. (It might be said in response that the physician only foresees that, as a result of referral, the patient will be assisted in committing suicide, and that whether integrity is maintained or lost depends only on what an agent intends to achieve. But this response fails, for one is just as responsible for all the reasonably foreseeable results of one's actions as for those results one has intended to achieve). Second, the refusal to universalize is troubling. For according to the standard philosophical account, a person who believes that it is morally wrong for him or her to do something is also committed to judging that it is morally wrong for anyone in exactly similar or relevantly similar circumstances to do likewise. From this it follows that if a physician believes it is wrong for him or her to assist in suicide but does not extend his or her judgment to another physician, the former must be able to point to some morally relevant difference between them. What's more, this morally relevant difference cannot consist in the bare fact that this other physician is a numerically distinct individual, nor can it consist only in the fact that this other physician happens to have no moral scruples about helping a patient commit suicide. Moral principles, it is held, differ from personal ideals in that, whereas one is not committed to judging others by the ideals one aspires to oneself, one must do so with respect to one's moral standards.[17]

This argument can be recast by returning to a distinction that was made earlier in the discussion of compromise, viz. between recognition of others as sincere and reflective moral agents and agreement with their moral principles or positions. The case for compatibility of physician integrity and patient referral would now be based not on the inappropriateness of universalizing one's values but rather on the realization that other responsible and reasonable individuals have a different opinion with regard to what the patient requests. Thus, I suppose the referring physician reasons in something like the following manner:

(II) My patient asks me to do something that I could only do by contravening my values, but I also recognize that there is widespread and thoughtful disagreement among physicians and in society at large about the propriety of physician-assisted suicide and that there are

---

[17] There is clearly much more that needs to be said about universalizability. The standard view, which has been challenged, is found in R.M. Hare, *Freedom and Reason*, New York: Oxford University Press, 1963. According to Hare, the "moral" ought must be applied to a class of individuals: moral judgments about what I ought to do have implications for what I must think others ought to do.

310   JEFFREY BLUSTEIN

other sincere and serious physicians who could do what the patient asks in good conscience. Though my patient and other physicians hold moral views opposed to my own and I remain confident of my own position, I believe their moral sincerity and seriousness in this matter should be acknowledged, and this is why I refer my patient to another physician who is likeminded with him or her.

It is important to note that the referring physician's degree of confidence in his or her position is not what the argument turns on here. While patient referral may be an acceptable alternative, from the standpoint of one's integrity, because it represents an admission that the matter at hand is so plagued by uncertainty that differences of opinion are within the realm of reason, this is not the basis of patient referral in (II). Rather, the basis is respect for the moral sincerity and intelligence of others, and this may ground patient referral even when the referring physician believes that others are clearly in the wrong. Being convinced that one is morally in the right, moreover, is perfectly compatible with being open to the possibility that additional considerations could at some time in the future lead one to adopt and act on the position of those who presently hold an opposing moral view.

The decision to transfer a patient to another physician is not necessarily a repudiation by the referring physician of his or her own position or even an admission of uncertainty about the correctness of that position. It may instead be an expression of values other than those that prevent the physician from complying with the patient's request. Something similar can be said about decisions by physicians affiliated with public medical institutions to transfer patients to the institution, when they cannot, as a matter of conscience, treat them themselves. Consider the following argument:

(III) I believe that it is not the business of public institutions in a liberal society such as mine to enforce specific, controversial moral or religious conceptions. While I have certain commitments or principles that make it impossible for me to honor the patient's request, I recognize that my views are contested, and I believe that the institution to which I belong must remain neutral with respect to contested moral and religious views. Transferring the patient to the institution can be justified on the basis of a distinction between the values to which I may appeal in the conduct of my own professional life and those to which I may appeal as a practitioner within a public institution.

I believe that the reasoning in (II) and (III) gives one good grounds for patient referral; more specifically, that it shows how referral of a patient whose request for medical intervention one cannot in good conscience honor can be integrity-preserving. But this only partially

DOING WHAT THE PATIENT ORDERS 311

captures the thinking of physicians on this matter. Often another sort of analysis altogether would be given if they were called upon to defend patient referral.

Sometimes a physician who considers refusing to treat a patient has good reason to believe that the patient can and will secure another physician to cooperate with his or her wishes. In this case, the following argument might be used:

(IV) It is true that if I advise a patient where he or she will find a likeminded physician, I am assisting someone in what I regard as wrongful conduct by providing a means to it. But, after all, if I just refuse to provide the requested services and to refer the patient to someone who will, there will be no decrease in the incidence of wrongful conduct. The same action is certain to occur in either event. Moreover, I can do some good for the patient if I assist in an orderly and timely transfer to a competent and agreeable physician. So, all things considered, it would be best if I arranged a transfer for my patient, and since I am doing what I believe is best, my integrity is maintained.

Such a physician reasons in a consequentialist manner, judging the alternatives before him or her in terms of which brings about the best state of affairs.

It may be noted, in response, that nothing said so far rules out the possibility that there will be no *increase* in the amount or seriousness of wrongdoing that is committed if the physician him or herself provides the service, and that in such cases the argument fails to show why the physician should transfer the patient rather than accede to the patient's wishes. But more could be said to make the argument in (IV) persuasive: since the physician happens to believe that he or she cannot in good conscience do what the patient requests, doing so would occasion guilt feelings that would interfere with good patient care. A consequentialist must take such feelings into account in arriving at the optimal course of action simply because they are among the givens of the physician's situation.

Even if a physician, reasoning in this way, does what is believed best on a particular occasion, we cannot automatically conclude that nothing has been done to cast doubt on his or her integrity. For it may be that the mode of moral analysis employed in this case is inconsistent with the principles used to resolve other morally problematic situations. But leaving this possiblility aside, there may be a more fundamental disagreement with a consequentialist approach to the problem of patient referral. Other physicians who are faced with patient requests that they cannot in good conscience honor may foresee that in some sense the same wrongful action will occur whether or not they refer their patients to other caregivers. That is, they may believe that, from an impersonal point of view, it makes no moral

312   JEFFREY BLUSTEIN

difference whether they refer the patient to another physician or simply withdraw from the case. But they may still think that their agency, and not just the amount of good or bad in the world, matters, morally speaking, and that the good they may do their patients by referring them to other caregivers does not outweigh their own involvement in the furtherance of wrongdoing. These persons will need another, nonconsequentialist, argument if they are to be convinced that their integrity is not damaged by patient referral, and (II) may appeal to them.

Finally, it may be thought that there is a simpler and more direct route to solving the problem of physician integrity and patient referral than I have so far suggested. It begins with the observation made at the start of this discussion, viz. that it is an essential part of the ethic of the medical profession that a physician not abandon a patient, and that when performing a procedure is not possible as a matter of conscience, this ethic requires referral to a physician who will per-form the procedure or at least the attempt to find such a physician. On entering the profession, the argument continues, an individual understands what is and is not expected of him or her and agrees to practice medicine according to the norms of the profession. Hence, there is an obligation of patient referral in cases where conscience does not permit performing the procedure oneself, and for this reason the physician's integrity is not damaged by patient referral. Even if in non professional contexts one believes there is no morally significant difference between cooperating with another's request to do something one believes is wrong and directing the other to a third party who will do the same thing, there is a duty to refer implicit in one's freely choosing to become a physician.

This argument is open to an obvious reply. Physicians who deny a duty to refer are saying, in effect, that they do not share the medi-cal profession's prevailing conception of itself. We would have good reason to decry this if they were advocating rejection of the profession's traditional ideals of service and adoption of a more self-centered view of the role of physician. But the denial by some physicians of a duty to refer cannot be discredited so easily if their position is based on concern for physician integrity. What is needed to convince them otherwise is not a simple appeal to the traditional ethic of patient advocacy, but an examination of the moral grounds of a professional obligation of patient referral.

In considering this matter more closely, it is clear that the duty of patient referral, as the medical profession conceives of it, is not unqualified. For it is understood that this duty is sensitive to the presence or lack of ethical consensus within the profession. For example, there is currently general agreement in the profession that physicians should not engage in active euthanasia of patients. If a patient requests this of his or her physician, the latter likely will both refuse to comply with the request and to refer the patient to another physician who will. Indeed, in this case the view of the profession is that there is no obligation to refer. The prevailing view, properly understood, seems to be that referral is obligatory when and only when the requested intervention is generally regarded within the profession as itself permissible. Moreover, from an ethical point of view, professional consensus is relevant to the problem of physician integrity and patient referral. If there is a consensus within the profession as a whole on the morality of some type of medical intervention, this strengthens the moral case either for or against referring patients to other physicians for receipt of that treatment. Given the profession's position on active euthanasia, it would certainly be difficult to show that patient referral for this purpose is compatible with the preservation of physician integrity. On the other hand, if a physician is asked to do something for a patient that the profession generally acknowledges is permissible but that this physician cannot as a matter of conscience do, patient referral seems to raise less of a problem for physician integrity.

In a third type of case, there is no stable consensus within the profession either allowing or prohibiting some medical intervention, no collective moral position to which the individual physician can turn. This may be the situation with physician-assisted suicide at the present time, and for thoughtful and conscientious physicians who cannot comply with patient requests, such cases are likely to be the most troubling.

4. CONCLUSION

Physicians' appeals to conscience, understood as fear of loss of integrity, should not be taken lightly. Integrity provides the basis for a unified, whole, and unalienated life, and its moral value, while dependent on the presence of other good traits in the agent, is not reducible to them. Moreover, as I noted in the introduction, I do not share the common view according to which physicians' appeals to their own consciences are to be dismissed out-of-hand as a form of paternalism. Such appeals are only paternalistic if the physician purports to be in a better position than the competent patient to make a moral judgment about what the patient should do. But a physician can consistently be concerned about his or her own integrity without claiming to know better than the patient what is in the patient's best interests.

Integrity is a virtue, albeit a formal one, and since appeals to conscience are linked to concerns about self-integrity, forcing people to

314 JEFFREY BLUSTEIN

act against their consciences is (prima facie) wrong. But is it possible for a person to agree to accommodate him or herself to the conflicting views and commitments of others without undermining self-integrity? On one view, "compromise" is a dirty word: any compromise on matters of principle constitutes a betrayal of principle and a loss of integrity. The conception of integrity I have proposed, however, allows for the possibility of integrity-preserving compromise. According to this conception, one acts with integrity when one takes into account the whole fabric of one's relevant moral principles and values, along with the weights one gives them, and does what one judges ought to be done, all things considered. Such a full moral assessment might lead one to decide that, under the circumstances, some form of compromise best expresses one's commitment to a number of different principles and values.

I have also considered the common practice of patient referral from the standpoint of physician integrity, and asked whether a physician who refuses to treat a patient as a matter of conscience can consistently refer the patient to another physician for the same treatment. This is an important question in light of the standard view, for if a physician cannot do so, then there is reason to question the consistency of a view which both allows physicians to withdraw from cases when their consciences would not permit them to do as their patients request *and* requires them to refer their patients to other physicians in such cases. In my view, there need be no conflict between physician integrity and patient referral, and in part for the same sort of reason that compromise does not necessarily damage one's integrity: in a dispute between physicians and their patients, there may be other values and principles at stake than the ones expressed in their conflicting positions, and a physician might well decide that referral in such a case is an appropriate response to a morally complex situation.

Mercy College, New York
Weiler Division, Montefiore Medical Center, Bronx, New York

* ACKNOWLEDGEMENTS

A late draft of this paper was read by Jonathan Adler, John Arras, Christopher Gowans, and Michael Stocker. The paper was also discussed by members of the Division of Humanities in Medicine Research Seminar at The State University of New York Health Science Center at Brooklyn. I thank all of these individuals for their constructive and illuminating comments. I owe a special debt of gratitude to Professor Jonathan Moreno from whose clinical experience and philosophical insight I benefited greatly during the writing of this article.

Part VI
Research Ethics

[28]

EQUIPOISE AND THE ETHICS OF CLINICAL RESEARCH

BENJAMIN FREEDMAN, PH.D.

Abstract The ethics of clinical research requires equipoise — a state of genuine uncertainty on the part of the clinical investigator regarding the comparative therapeutic merits of each arm in a trial. Should the investigator discover that one treatment is of superior therapeutic merit, he or she is ethically obliged to offer that treatment. The current understanding of this requirement, which entails that the investigator have no "treatment preference" throughout the course of the trial, presents nearly insuperable obstacles to the ethical commencement or completion of a controlled trial and may also contribute to the termination of trials because of the failure to enroll enough patients.

I suggest an alternative concept of equipoise, which would be based on present or imminent controversy in the clinical community over the preferred treatment. According to this concept of "clinical equipoise," the requirement is satisfied if there is genuine uncertainty within the expert medical community — not necessarily on the part of the individual investigator — about the preferred treatment. (N Engl J Med 1987; 317: 141-5.)

THERE is widespread agreement that ethics requires that each clinical trial begin with an honest null hypothesis.[1,2] In the simplest model, testing a new treatment B on a defined patient population P for which the current accepted treatment is A, it is necessary that the clinical investigator be in a state of genuine uncertainty regarding the comparative merits of treatments A and B for population P. If a physician knows that these treatments are not equivalent, ethics requires that the superior treatment be recommended. Following Fried, I call this state of uncertainty about the relative merits of A and B "equipoise."[3]

Equipoise is an ethically necessary condition in all cases of clinical research. In trials with several arms, equipoise must exist between all arms of the trial; otherwise the trial design should be modified to exclude the inferior treatment. If equipoise is disturbed during the course of a trial, the trial may need to be terminated and all subjects previously enrolled (as well as other patients within the relevant population) may have to be offered the superior treatment. It has been rigorously argued that a trial with a placebo is ethical only in investigating conditions for which there is no known treatment[2]; this argument reflects a special application of the requirement for equipoise. Although equipoise has commonly been discussed in the special context of the ethics of randomized clinical trials,[4,5] it is important to recognize it as an ethical condition of all controlled clinical trials, whether or not they are randomized, placebo-controlled, or blinded.

The recent increase in attention to the ethics of research with human subjects has highlighted problems associated with equipoise. Yet, as I shall attempt to show, contemporary literature, if anything, minimizes those difficulties. Moreover, there is evidence that concern on the part of investigators about failure to satisfy the requirements for equipoise can doom a trial

From the McGill Centre for Medicine, Ethics and Law, McGill University, Lady Meredith Bldg., 1110 Pine Ave. W., Montreal, PQ H3A 1A3, Canada, where reprint requests should be addressed to Dr. Freedman.

Supported in part by a research grant from the Social Sciences and Humanities Research Council of Canada.

as a result of the consequent failure to enroll a sufficient number of subjects.

The solutions that have been offered to date fail to resolve these problems in a way that would permit clinical trials to proceed. This paper argues that these problems are predicated on a faulty concept of equipoise itself. An alternative understanding of equipoise as an ethical requirement of clinical trials is proposed, and its implications are explored.

Many of the problems raised by the requirement for equipoise are familiar. Shaw and Chalmers have written that a clinician who "knows, or has good reason to believe," that one arm of the trial is superior may not ethically participate.[6] But the reasoning or preliminary results that prompt the trial (and that may themselves be ethically mandatory)[7] may jolt the investigator (if not his or her colleagues) out of equipoise before the trial begins. Even if the investigator is undecided between A and B in terms of gross measures such as mortality and morbidity, equipoise may be disturbed because evident differences in the quality of life (as in the case of two surgical approaches) tip the balance.[3-5,8] In either case, in saying "we do not know" whether A or B is better, the investigator may create a false impression in prospective subjects, who hear him or her as saying "no evidence leans either way," when the investigator means "no controlled study has yet had results that reach statistical significance."

Late in the study — when P values are between 0.05 and 0.06 — the moral issue of equipoise is most readily apparent,[9,10] but the same problem arises when the earliest comparative results are analyzed.[11] Within the closed statistical universe of the clinical trial, each result that demonstrates a difference between the arms of the trial contributes exactly as much to the statistical conclusion that a difference exists as does any other. The contribution of the last pair of cases in the trial is no greater than that of the first. If, therefore, equipoise is a condition that reflects equivalent evidence for alternative hypotheses, it is jeopardized by the first pair of cases as much as by the last. The investigator who is concerned about the ethics of recruitment after

Bioethics

142 THE NEW ENGLAND JOURNAL OF MEDICINE July 16, 1987

the penultimate pair must logically be concerned after the first pair as well.

Finally, these issues are more than a philosopher's nightmare. Considerable interest has been generated by a paper in which Taylor et al.[12] describe the termination of a trial of alternative treatments for breast cancer. The trial foundered on the problem of patient recruitment, and the investigators trace much of the difficulty in enrolling patients to the fact that the investigators were not in a state of equipoise regarding the arms of the trial. With the increase in concern about the ethics of research and with the increasing presence of this topic in the curricula of medical and graduate schools, instances of the type that Taylor and her colleagues describe are likely to become more common. The requirement for equipoise thus poses a practical threat to clinical research.

RESPONSES TO THE PROBLEMS OF EQUIPOISE

The problems described above apply to a broad class of clinical trials, at all stages of their development. Their resolution will need to be similarly comprehensive. However, the solutions that have so far been proposed address a portion of the difficulties, at best, and cannot be considered fully satisfactory.

Chalmers' approach to problems at the onset of a trial is to recommend that randomization begin with the very first subject.[11] If there are no preliminary, uncontrolled data in support of the experimental treatment B, equipoise regarding treatments A and B for the patient population P is not disturbed. There are several difficulties with this approach. Practically speaking, it is often necessary to establish details of administration, dosage, and so on, before a controlled trial begins, by means of uncontrolled trials in human subjects. In addition, as I have argued above, equipoise from the investigator's point of view is likely to be disturbed when the hypothesis is being formulated and a protocol is being prepared. It is then, before any subjects have been enrolled, that the information that the investigator has assembled makes the experimental treatment appear to be a reasonable gamble. Apart from these problems, initial randomization will not, as Chalmers recognizes, address disturbances of equipoise that occur in the course of a trial.

Data-monitoring committees have been proposed as a solution to problems arising in the course of the trial.[13] Such committees, operating independently of the investigators, are the only bodies with information concerning the trial's ongoing results. Since this knowledge is not available to the investigators, their equipoise is not disturbed. Although committees are useful in keeping the conduct of a trial free of bias, they cannot resolve the investigators' ethical difficulties. A clinician is not merely obliged to treat a patient on the basis of the information that he or she currently has, but is also required to discover information that would be relevant to treatment decisions. If interim results would disturb equipoise, the investigators are obliged to gather and use that information. Their

agreement to remain in ignorance of preliminary results would, by definition, be an unethical agreement, just as a failure to call up the laboratory to find out a patient's test results is unethical. Moreover, the use of a monitoring committee does not solve problems of equipoise that arise before and at the beginning of a trial.

Recognizing the broad problems with equipoise, three authors have proposed radical solutions. All three think that there is an irresolvable conflict between the requirement that a patient be offered the best treatment known (the principle underlying the requirement for equipoise) and the conduct of clinical trials; they therefore suggest that the "best treatment" requirement be weakened.

Schafer has argued that the concept of equipoise, and the associated notion of the best medical treatment, depends on the judgment of patients rather than of clinical investigators.[14] Although the equipoise of an investigator may be disturbed if he or she favors B over A, the ultimate choice of treatment is the patient's. Because the patient's values may restore equipoise, Schafer argues, it is ethical for the investigator to proceed with a trial when the patient consents. Schafer's strategy is directed toward trials that test treatments with known and divergent side effects and will probably not be useful in trials conducted to test efficacy or unknown side effects. This approach, moreover, confuses the ethics of competent medical practice with those of consent. If we assume that the investigator is a competent clinician, by saying that the investigator is out of equipoise, we have by Schafer's account said that in the investigator's professional judgment one treatment is therapeutically inferior — for that patient, in that condition, given the quality of life that can be achieved. Even if a patient would consent to an inferior treatment, it seems to me a violation of competent medical practice, and hence of ethics, to make the offer. Of course, complex issues may arise when a patient refuses what the physician considers the best treatment and demands instead an inferior treatment. Without settling that problem, however, we can reject Schafer's position. For Schafer claims that in order to continue to conduct clinical trials, it is ethical for the physician to offer (not merely accede to) inferior treatment.

Meier suggests that "most of us would be quite willing to forego a modest expected gain in the general interest of learning something of value."[15] He argues that we accept risks in everyday life to achieve a variety of benefits, including convenience and economy. In the same way, Meier states, it is acceptable to enroll subjects in clinical trials even though they may not receive the best treatment throughout the course of the trial. Schafer suggests an essentially similar approach.[5,14] According to this view, continued progress in medical knowledge through clinical trials requires an explicit abandonment of the doctor's fully patient-centered ethic.

These proposals seem to be frank counsels of desperation. They resolve the ethical problems of equipoise by abandoning the need for equipoise. In any event, would their approach allow clinical trials to be conducted? I think this may fairly be doubted. Although many people are presumably altruistic enough to forgo the best medical treatment in the interest of the progress of science, many are not. The numbers and proportions required to sustain the statistical validity of trial results suggest that in the absence of overwhelming altruism, the enrollment of satisfactory numbers of patients will not be possible. In particular, very ill patients, toward whom many of the most important clinical trials are directed, may be disinclined to be altruistic. Finally, as the study by Taylor et al.[12] reminds us, the problems of equipoise trouble investigators as well as patients. Even if patients are prepared to dispense with the best treatment, their physicians, for reasons of ethics and professionalism, may well not be willing to do so.

Marquis has suggested a third approach. "Perhaps what is needed is an ethics that will justify the conscription of subjects for medical research," he has written. "Nothing less seems to justify present practice."[4] Yet, although conscription might enable us to continue present practice, it would scarcely justify it. Moreover, the conscription of physician investigators, as well as subjects, would be necessary, because, as has been repeatedly argued, the problems of equipoise are as disturbing to clinicians as they are to subjects. Is any less radical and more plausible approach possible?

THEORETICAL EQUIPOISE VERSUS CLINICAL EQUIPOISE

The problems of equipoise examined above arise from a particular understanding of that concept, which I will term "theoretical equipoise." It is an understanding that is both conceptually odd and ethically irrelevant. Theoretical equipoise exists when, overall, the evidence on behalf of two alternative treatment regimens is exactly balanced. This evidence may be derived from a variety of sources, including data from the literature, uncontrolled experience, considerations of basic science and fundamental physiologic processes, and perhaps a "gut feeling" or "instinct" resulting from (or superimposed on) other considerations. The problems examined above arise from the principle that if theoretical equipoise is disturbed, the physician has, in Schafer's words, a "treatment preference" — let us say, favoring experimental treatment B. A trial testing A against B requires that some patients be enrolled in violation of this treatment preference.

Theoretical equipoise is overwhelmingly fragile; that is, it is disturbed by a slight accretion of evidence favoring one arm of the trial. In Chalmers' view, equipoise is disturbed when the odds that A will be more successful than B are anything other than 50 percent. It is therefore necessary to randomize treatment assignments beginning with the very first patient, lest equipoise be disturbed. We may say that theoretical equipoise is balanced on a knife's edge.

Theoretical equipoise is most appropriate to one-dimensional hypotheses and causes us to think in those terms. The null hypothesis must be sufficiently simple and "clean" to be finely balanced: Will A or B be superior in reducing mortality or shrinking tumors or lowering fevers in population P? Clinical choice is commonly more complex. The choice of A or B depends on some combination of effectiveness, consistency, minimal or relievable side effects, and other factors. On close examination, for example, it sometimes appears that even trials that purport to test a single hypothesis in fact involve a more complicated, portmanteau measure — e.g., the "therapeutic index" of A versus B. The formulation of the conditions of theoretical equipoise for such complex, multidimensional clinical hypotheses is tantamount to the formulation of a rigorous calculus of apples and oranges.

Theoretical equipoise is also highly sensitive to the vagaries of the investigator's attention and perception. Because of its fragility, theoretical equipoise is disturbed as soon as the investigator perceives a difference between the alternatives — whether or not any genuine difference exists. Prescott writes, for example, "It will be common at some stage in most trials for the survival curves to show visually different survivals," short of significance but "sufficient to raise ethical difficulties for the participants."[16] A visual difference, however, is purely an artifact of the research methods employed: when and by what means data are assembled and analyzed and what scale is adopted for the graphic presentation of data. Similarly, it is common for researchers to employ interval scales for phenomena that are recognized to be continuous by nature — e.g., five-point scales of pain or stages of tumor progression. These interval scales, which represent an arbitrary distortion of the available evidence to simplify research, may magnify the differences actually found, with a resulting disturbance of theoretical equipoise.

Finally, as described by several authors, theoretical equipoise is personal and idiosyncratic. It is disturbed when the clinician has, in Schafer's words, what "might even be labeled a bias or a hunch," a preference of a "merely intuitive nature."[14] The investigator who ignores such a hunch, by failing to advise the patient that because of it the investigator prefers B to A or by recommending A (or a chance of random assignment to A) to the patient, has violated the requirement for equipoise and its companion requirement to recommend the best medical treatment.

The problems with this concept of equipoise should be evident. To understand the alternative, preferable interpretation of equipoise, we need to recall the basic reason for conducting clinical trials: there is a current or imminent conflict in the clinical community over what treatment is preferred for patients in a defined population P. The standard treatment is A, but some evidence suggests that B will be superior (because of its effectiveness or its reduction of undesirable side effects, or for some other reason). (In the rare case when the first evidence of a novel therapy's superiority

144   THE NEW ENGLAND JOURNAL OF MEDICINE   July 16, 1987

would be entirely convincing to the clinical community, equipoise is already disturbed.) Or there is a split in the clinical community, with some clinicians favoring A and others favoring B. Each side recognizes that the opposing side has evidence to support its position, yet each still thinks that overall its own view is correct. There exists (or, in the case of a novel therapy, there may soon exist) an honest, professional disagreement among expert clinicians about the preferred treatment. A clinical trial is instituted with the aim of resolving this dispute.

At this point, a state of "clinical equipoise" exists. . There is no consensus within the expert clinical community about the comparative merits of the alternatives to be tested. We may state the formal conditions under which such a trial would be ethical as follows: at the start of the trial, there must be a state of clinical equipoise regarding the merits of the regimens to be tested, and the trial must be designed in such a way as to make it reasonable to expect that, if it is successfully concluded, clinical equipoise will be disturbed. In other words, the results of a successful clinical trial should be convincing enough to resolve the dispute among clinicians.

A state of clinical equipoise is consistent with a decided treatment preference on the part of the investigators. They must simply recognize that their less-favored treatment is preferred by colleagues whom they consider to be responsible and competent. Even if the interim results favor the preference of the investigators, treatment B, clinical equipoise persists as long as those results are too weak to influence the judgment of the community of clinicians, because of limited sample size, unresolved possibilities of side effects, or other factors. (This judgment can necessarily be made only by those who know the interim results — whether a data-monitoring committee or the investigators.)

At the point when the accumulated evidence in favor of B is so strong that the committee or investigators believe no open-minded clinician informed of the results would still favor A, clinical equipoise has been disturbed. This may occur well short of the original schedule for the termination of the trial, for unexpected reasons. (Therapeutic effects or side effects may be much stronger than anticipated, for example, or a definable subgroup within population P may be recognized for which the results demonstrably disturb clinical equipoise.) Because of the arbitrary character of human judgment and persuasion, some ethical problems regarding the termination of a trial will remain. Clinical equipoise will confine these problems to unusual or extreme cases, however, and will allow us to cast persistent problems in the proper terms. For example, in the face of a strong established trend, must we continue the trial because of others' blind fealty to an arbitrary statistical bench mark?

Clearly, clinical equipoise is a far weaker — and more common — condition than theoretical equipoise. Is it ethical to conduct a trial on the basis of clinical equipoise, when theoretical equipoise is disturbed?

Or, as Schafer and others have argued, is doing so a violation of the physician's obligation to provide patients with the best medical treatment?[4,5,14] Let us assume that the investigators have a decided preference for B but wish to conduct a trial on the grounds that clinical (not theoretical) equipoise exists. The ethics committee asks the investigators whether, if they or members of their families were within population P, they would not want to be treated with their preference, B? An affirmative answer is often thought to be fatal to the prospects for such a trial, yet the investigators answer in the affirmative. Would a trial satisfying this weaker form of equipoise be ethical?

I believe that it clearly is ethical. As Fried has emphasized,[3] competent (hence, ethical) medicine is social rather than individual in nature. Progress in medicine relies on progressive consensus within the medical and research communities. The ethics of medical practice grants no ethical or normative meaning to a treatment preference, however powerful, that is based on a hunch or on anything less than evidence publicly presented and convincing to the clinical community. Persons are licensed as physicians after they demonstrate the acquisition of this professionally validated knowledge, not after they reveal a superior capacity for guessing. Normative judgments of their behavior — e.g., malpractice actions — rely on a comparison with what is done by the community of medical practitioners. Failure to follow a "treatment preference" not shared by this community and not based on information that would convince it could not be the basis for an allegation of legal or ethical malpractice. As Fried states: "[T]he conception of what is good medicine is the product of a professional consensus." By definition, in a state of clinical equipoise, "good medicine" finds the choice between A and B indifferent.

In contrast to theoretical equipoise, clinical equipoise is robust. The ethical difficulties at the beginning and end of a trial are therefore largely alleviated. There remain difficulties about consent, but these too may be diminished. Instead of emphasizing the lack of evidence favoring one arm over another that is required by theoretical equipoise, clinical equipoise places the emphasis in informing the patient on the honest disagreement among expert clinicians. The fact that the investigator has a "treatment preference," if he or she does, could be disclosed; indeed, if the preference is a decided one, and based on something more than a hunch, it could be ethically mandatory to disclose it. At the same time, it would be emphasized that this preference is not shared by others. It is likely to be a matter of chance that the patient is being seen by a clinician with a preference for B over A, rather than by an equally competent clinician with the opposite preference.

Clinical equipoise does not depend on concealing relevant information from researchers and subjects, as does the use of independent data-monitoring committees. Rather, it allows investigators, in informing subjects, to distinguish appropriately among validated knowledge accepted by the clinical community, data on treatments that are promising but are not (or, for novel therapies, would not be) generally convincing, and mere hunches. Should informed patients decline to participate because they have chosen a specific clinician and trust his or her judgment — over and above the consensus in the professional community — that is no more than the patients' right. We do not conscript patients to serve as subjects in clinical trials.

THE IMPLICATIONS OF CLINICAL EQUIPOISE

The theory of clinical equipoise has been formulated as an alternative to some current views on the ethics of human research. At the same time, it corresponds closely to a preanalytic concept held by many in the research and regulatory communities. Clinical equipoise serves, then, as a rational formulation of the approach of many toward research ethics; it does not so much change things as explain why they are the way they are.

Nevertheless, the precision afforded by the theory of clinical equipoise does help to clarify or reformulate some aspects of research ethics; I will mention only two.

First, there is a recurrent debate about the ethical propriety of conducting clinical trials of discredited treatments, such as Laetrile.[17] Often, substantial political pressure to conduct such tests is brought to bear by adherents of quack therapies. The theory of clinical equipoise suggests that when there is no support for a treatment regimen within the expert clinical community, the first ethical requirement of a trial — clinical equipoise — is lacking; it would therefore be unethical to conduct such a trial.

Second, Feinstein has criticized the tendency of clinical investigators to narrow excessively the conditions and hypotheses of a trial in order to ensure the validity of its results.[18] This "fastidious" approach purchases scientific manageability at the expense of an inability to apply the results to the "messy" conditions of clinical practice. The theory of clinical equipoise adds some strength to this criticism. Overly "fastidious" trials, designed to resolve some theoretical

question, fail to satisfy the second ethical requirement of clinical research, since the special conditions of the trial will render it useless for influencing clinical decisions, even if it is successfully completed.

The most important result of the concept of clinical equipoise, however, might be to relieve the current crisis of confidence in the ethics of clinical trials. Equipoise, properly understood, remains an ethical condition for clinical trials. It is consistent with much current practice. Clinicians and philosophers alike have been premature in calling for desperate measures to resolve problems of equipoise.

I am indebted to Robert J. Levine, M.D., and to Harold Merskey, D.M., for their valuable suggestions.

REFERENCES

1. Levine RJ. Ethics and regulation of clinical research. 2nd ed. Baltimore: Urban & Schwarzenberg, 1986.
2. *Idem.* The use of placebos in randomized clinical trials. IRB: Rev Hum Subj Res 1985; 7(2):1-4.
3. Fried C. Medical experimentation: personal integrity and social policy. Amsterdam: North-Holland Publishing, 1974.
4. Marquis D. Leaving therapy to chance. Hastings Cent Rep 1983; 13(4):40-7.
5. Schafer A. The ethics of the randomized clinical trial. N Engl J Med 1982; 307:719-24.
6. Shaw LW, Chalmers TC. Ethics in cooperative clinical trials. Ann NY Acad Sci 1970; 169:487-95.
7. Hollenberg NK, Dzau VJ, Williams GH. Are uncontrolled clinical studies ever justified? N Engl J Med 1980; 303:1067.
8. Levine RJ, Lebacqz K. Some ethical considerations in clinical trials. Clin Pharmacol Ther 1979; 25:728-41.
9. Klimt CR, Canner PL. Terminating a long-term clinical trial. Clin Pharmacol Ther 1979; 25:641-6.
10. Veatch RM. Longitudinal studies, sequential designs and grant renewals: what to do with preliminary data. IRB: Rev Hum Subj Res 1979; 1(4):1-3.
11. Chalmers T. The ethics of randomization as a decision-making technique and the problem of informed consent. In: Beauchamp TL, Walters L, eds. Contemporary issues in bioethics. Encino, Calif.: Dickenson, 1978:426-9.
12. Taylor KM, Margolese RG, Soskolne CL. Physicians' reasons for not entering eligible patients in a randomized clinical trial of surgery for breast cancer. N Engl J Med 1984; 310:1363-7.
13. Chalmers TC. Invited remarks. Clin Pharmacol Ther 1979; 25:649-50.
14. Schafer A. The randomized clinical trial: for whose benefit? IRB: Rev Hum Subj Res 1985; 7(2):4-6.
15. Meier P. Terminating a trial — the ethical problem. Clin Pharmacol Ther 1979; 25:633-40.
16. Prescott RJ. Feedback of data to participants during clinical trials. In: Tagnon HJ, Staquet MJ, eds. Controversies in cancer: design of trials and treatment. New York: Masson Publishing, 1979:55-61.
17. Cowan DH. The ethics of clinical trials of ineffective therapy. IRB: Rev Hum Subj Res 1981; 3(5):10-1.
18. Feinstein AR. An additional basic science for clinical medicine. II. The limitations of randomized trials. Ann Intern Med 1983; 99:544-50.

[29]

INSTITUTING A RESEARCH ETHIC: CHILLING AND CAUTIONARY TALES[1]

PHILIP PETTIT

INTRODUCTION

The ethical review of research on human beings, and indeed the ethical review of broader ranges of human activity, is a growth industry. I want to look here at the ethical review of research on humans and raise some questions about the direction it is taking. I am pessimistic about where the institutions that we have set up are leading us and I want to sound a warning note and suggest some changes that are needed in the practice of ethical review.

It is easy to assume that with a policy as high-minded as the policy of reviewing research on human beings, the only difficulties will be the obstacles put in its way by recalcitrant and unreformed parties: by the special-interest groups affected. But this is not always true of high-minded policies and it is not true, in particular, of the policy of reviewing research. Ethical review is endangering valuable research on human beings and, moreover, it is endangering the very ethic that is needed to govern that research. And this is not anyone's fault, least of all the fault of any special-interest groups. The problem is that the process of ethical review has been driven by an institutional dynamic that is not in anyone's control and this dynamic is now driving us, willy nilly, on to some very stony ground.

My argument is developed in four sections. In the next section, section two, I look at a model of policy-making which identifies a reactive, institutional dynamic that lies at the origin of certain policy intitiatives. In the third section I argue that this model fits the appearance and development of the ethical review of human research, showing how the process of review has been motored by a dynamic of step-by-step reaction to chilling tales of abuse. In the fourth section I look at the predictions of the future development of ethical review that the extrapolation of that model yields. And then in the fifth and

---

[1] This is the text, slightly amended, of the Annual Lecture to the Academy of Social Sciences, in Australia, delivered in Canberra, Nov 1991.

90   PHILIP PETTIT

final section, I consider some lessons that the model has to teach. These lessons are cautionary in tone and they provide some balance for the chilling tales that I will have told earlier.

A MODEL OF POLICY DEVELOPMENT

In a seminal article on the growth of administrative government in the last century, Oliver MacDonagh developed an interesting model of why the British government sponsored the dramatic growth in regulative legislation and regulative agencies, especially in the period between 1825 and 1875.[2] The policy initiatives with which MacDonagh was concerned introduced a regulative machinery to govern matters as various as public health, factory employment of children, workplace safety procedures, the condition of prisons, and the ways in which people were treated on emigrant ships. He argued that we could generally find the same elements at work in the generation of policy in these different areas and that we could identify more or less the same stages in the evolution of such policy.

To simplify somewhat, there are four elements to which he directs us. In each case there is an evil to be dealt with by policy, usually an evil associated with the industrial revolution and the results of that revolution for the organisation of social life. Second, this evil is exposed, usually in the more or less sensational manner of the developing 19th century newspapers; the exposure of the evil may be triggered by some catastrophe or perhaps by the work of a private philanthropist or fortuitous observer. Third, the exposure of the evil leads to popular outrage; this outrage connects with the increasing humanitarian sentiments of people in 19th century Britain, sentiments in the light of which the evil appears as intolerable. Fourth, the popular outrage forces government to react by introducing legislative or administrative initiatives designed to cope with the evil; this reactiveness of government is due, no doubt, to the increasingly democratic character of 19th century British government.

Evil, exposure, outrage and reaction: these are the elements that play a crucial role in the MacDonagh model. The role they play becomes salient as we look at the different stages distinguished by MacDonagh in a typical process of evolution. I now describe those stages, though not exactly in the terms presented by MacDonagh himself.

In the first stage of evolution some evil is exposed, this leads to popular outrage and the government of the day responds by some change in the law.

[2] Oliver MacDonagh, 'The 19th century revolution in government: a reappraisal', *Historical Journal*, 1. 1958.

INSTITUTING A RESEARCH ETHIC   91

Once it was publicised sufficiently that, say, women on their hands and knees dragged trucks of coal through subterranean tunnels or that emigrants had starved to death at sea, or that children had been mutilated by unfenced machinery, these evils became 'intolerable'; and throughout and even before the Victorian years 'intolerability' was the master card. No wall of either doctrine or interest could permanently withstand that single trumpet cry, all the more so as governments grew ever more responsive to public sentiment, and public sentiment ever more humane. The demand for remedies was also, in a contemporary context, a demand for prohibitory enactments. Men's instinctive reaction was to legislate the evil out of existence.[3]

The first stage of evolution, described in this quotation, involves a popular scandal and a legislative response. The second stage identified by MacDonagh also involves a popular scandal, but one that is followed in this case by an adminstrative response. The scandal arises when, a number of years after the original legislation, it is discovered and revealed that the original evil remains more or less as it was. Again there is public outrage and again the government responds to this. But the response now is to appoint some individuals to look into the evil and to investigate how it may be remedied. The response, in short, is administrative rather than legislative.

If the first two stages are characterised by popular scandal, the next two are characterised by surprise on the part of the administrative experts appointed to look into the evil. At a third stage these experts come to realise that the original law was inadequate. They recommend amendments to the law, and they recommend a variety of administrative changes, usually involving a drift towards centralisation. The administrative changes require the systematic collecting of data on the problem, the appointment of officers required to monitor that information, and so on.

The fourth and last stage that we may identify in MacDonagh's evolutionary description involves a second phase of expert surprise: a surprise, this time, at discovering that even the amended law and amended administrative arrangements have not adequately coped with the original problem. The response now is to recognise that the problem cannot be eradicated by a single, once for all legislative or legislative-cum-administrative response. It requires the putting in place of a regulative bureaucracy, concerned with monitoring, reviewing and intervening in the activities where the original evil arose. The evolution is complete. We now have rule by officials and

---

[3] MacDonagh, 'The 19th century revolution in government . . .', p. 58.

92   PHILIP PETTIT

experts, we have the appearance of a new area of bureaucracy.

MacDonagh originally introduced this model of the growth of government as an alternative to the view that the changes were driven by an overarching, commonly accepted ideology such as utilitarianism. What he characterises is a reactive dynamic in the formation of public policy. He does not say, nor need we judge, whether the changes introduced in the 19th century made, in the end, for more good than harm. If we think that they were changes for the good, then we will say that MacDonagh describes an invisible hand whereby they emerged. If we think that they were for ill, then we will say that he describes an invisible backhand or, as it has also been called, an invisible foot. In either case we will say that he shows us how a certain novel set of arrangements, a novel order in things, came about without being designed by any individuals or organisations.

The reactive dynamic described by MacDonagh, or at least something fairly well analogous to it, can also be discerned in other areas. Consider the way in which contemporary governments in many different countries have been continually driven back towards law and order measures, in particular tough measures of imprisonment, despite the evidence that other measures may be more effective and cheaper. A crime of a certain sort is committed and receives a good deal of more or less sensational publicity. This creates public horror and outrage. The government is forced to respond to this outrage by showing itself to be tough on that sort of crime. But showing that it is tough on that sort of crime means showing that the relevant offenders are subjected to the harshest measures. No matter if those measures are not effective in the long run in containing the crime involved. The important point is that they present the government to the people in a manner that satisfies the outraged.

For a different example of the same sort of reactive dynamic at work, consider how social work agencies may be, and have been, driven to be very interventionist at taking children into care: taking them away from parents or guardians who are thought to pose some threat. Some child is left with its parents or guardians by a social worker, despite evidence of such a threat; some abuse of the child occurs; and then the offence receives more or less sensational publicity. The pattern should now be familiar. The public is scandalised and outraged. The government is forced to respond to this. And how can it respond other than by initiating an enquiry into the decision of the social worker, or some disciplining of that official? Hence a culture, even a routine, is established which furthers the taking of children into care, even though this may not be for the overall good of those children.

THE MODEL APPLIED

I would now like to show that the growth of the ethical review of research, in particular research on humans, has been driven by something like the reactive dynamic described in the last section. Biomedical and behavioural research enjoyed a huge growth in the late 19th century as the natural sciences extended their reach into human biology, and as the new sciences of human beings were developed on the model of natural science. By the turn of the century biomedical and behavioural research was a steadily growing, if not actually a boom, industry. Inevitably, the industry was bound to generate its scandals. And inevitably, those scandals were bound to elicit government responses.[4]

One of the first scandals occurred in 1916 when Udo J. Wile, Professor of Dermatology and Syphilogy at the University of Michigan, reported his research results in two major medical journals. Wile had inoculated rabbits with the treponenes that cause syphillis, which he had obtained by trephining the skulls of six insane patients with syphillis and by then taking a small sample of their brain. Antivivisectionists were alerted to the procedure and attacked the sampling of human brain tissue, arguing that animal vivisection had opened the way to this sort of abuse. The American Medical Association (AMA) defended experimentation and animal vivisection but criticised Wile's actions. An AMA committee recognised, however, that there was a need to establish guidelines of ethical research. One of its members, the Harvard physiologist, Walter B. Cannon, admitted:

> There is in this present flush of interest in clinical research, a danger that young men just entering upon it may lose their balance and become so interested in the pursuit of new knowledge that they forget their primary duty to serve the welfare of the person who has committed himself to their care.[5]

The abuse was not isolated: there were similar scandals in Germany in the 1920s. As a result of the scandals, guidelines for the ethical conduct of biomedical – and by extension behavioural – research came to be established. Usually they were voluntary guidelines. For example, the German medical profession issued guidelines in 1931, guidelines which superseded some earlier regulations introduced by the Prussian government in 1900.

---

[4] In this section I draw heavily for examples on Richard Gillespie, "Research on human subjects: An historical overview", *Bioethics News*, 8, no. 2, 1989, suppl. pp. 4–15, and I follow his descriptions of the examples closely, All otherwise unreferenced examples are described in this excellent overview and further references are provided there.

[5] Gillespie, "Research on human subjects". p. 7.

94 PHILIP PETTIT

The guidelines introduced as a response to this first phase of scandals focussed, as many later guidelines were to focus, on two major issues: that of whether the subjects of research had given their informed consent; and that of whether they were exposed to the risk of harm. Those two issues, together with the issue of whether data on research subjects are held under appropriate guarantees of confidentiality, have continued to dominate the ethics of research up to the present time. It is worth noting, for example, that according to a recent survey, the reason why Australian institutional ethics committees have sought modifications of human research proposals has had to do, in 95% of cases, with the form in which consent is sought.[6]

But the first appearance of guidelines was not, predictably, sufficient to block other scandals. The scandals in the second phase were much more dramatic. They were the scandals associated with the experimentation by Nazi doctors on inmates of concentration camps and by Japanese doctors on prisoners of war. The research explored the effects of chemical weapons, exposure to extreme heat and cold, and fatal infectious disease, among other matters. Revelations of the research at the Nuremberg trials created an international scandal.

The scandals were not limited to Germany and Japan. Some Nazi doctors tried to defend their action by compiling accounts of unethical research elsewhere, accounts that were shocking enough in their own right. In 1904 Colonel Strong, later Professor of Tropical Medicine at Harvard, had injected condemned criminals in Manila with live plague bacteria, apparently without getting their consent. Several years later he had induced experimental beri-beri in other condemned criminals, resulting in the painful death of one subject. And even during the Second World War, it transpired that there had been some ethically dubious, if sometimes defended, research. Illinois prison inmates had consented to participate in experiments on malaria, and had signed statements absolving the government of responsibility, but apparently had been induced to do so by payment and by the reduction of their sentences by Parole Board.

The Nuremberg Military Tribunal formulated a 10 point code for the judgment of Nazi doctors and we may see that code as a more or less internationally supported response to the second phase of scandal. The code was widely supported and it undoubtedly had an impact on the formation of an international code by the World Medical Association in 1962. That code was issued in 1964 as the Declaration of Helsinki and was revised in 1975.

---

[6] Paul McNeill, "The function and composition of institutional research ethics committees: preliminary reserach results", in Jill Hudson, ed., *Can Ethics be done by Committee?*, Centre for Human Bioethics, Monash University, 1988, p. 32.

INSTITUTING A RESEARCH ETHIC 95

It will come as no surprise that this second phase of code-making did not put a stop to scandals. We find an early, important scandal in the area of behavioural rather than biomedical research in 1955. That arose with the Wichita Jury Study, which was carried out in 1954 as a part of the University of Chicago jury project.[7] The enquiry was supported by the Ford Foundation but, without seeking the approval of the sponsor, the researchers persuaded local judges to grant permission for the recordings to be made of the deliberations of juries in a limited number of cases. Contrary to original intentions, an edited version of the deliberations of one of the juries was presented in 1955 at the annual conference of lawyers associated with the court circuit in which the cases had been heard. Thus the existence of the recordings became publicly known and this led to a public hearing by the internal security subcommittee of the Committee on the Judiciary attached to the United States Senate. The scandal did not lead to any response directed at research in general but it did cause a Bill to be passed in 1956 by both Houses of Congress, in which recording the deliberations of any federal jury was prohibited.

The most important scandals in this third phase of publicity broke in the early 1960s. In 1960 a survey commissioned by the National Institute of Health (NIH) reveal that only 9 of 52 responding institutions had formal guidelines for clinical research and only 16 had appropriate consent forms. And in 1962 it became public that an esteemed cancer researcher at the Sloan-Kettering Clinic in New York arranged for cancer cells to be injected into elderly patients, not suffering from cancer, at the Jewish Chronic Disease Hospital in Brooklyn. The patients did not sign consent forms, although it was said by the researchers that they gave verbal consent; however they were not told that they were to be injected with cancer cells. State Medical Board investigation led to two of the doctors being placed on probation.

But there was more to come. A report in 1964 noted that there were wide discrepancies between institutions and individual researchers in the United States as to what constituted acceptable professional conduct. And then in 1966 Henry Beecher of Harvard Medical School published a survey of ethical behaviour in clinical research in *The New England Journal of Medical Research*. By skimming the major journals containing articles on clinical research, he produced 50 examples of ethically dubious research on human subjects. Consent was mentioned in only two of these articles.

[7] For details on this study see John Barnes, *The Ethics of Enquiry in Social Science*, Oxford University Press, Delhi, 1977, pp. 22–23.

96   PHILIP PETTIT

Research included the withholding of effective treatment, in one
case resulting in the deaths of at least 23 patients from typhoid;
the injection of carbon dioxide during anasthaesia on patients undergoing minor surgery, until cardiac arrhythmias appeared; and the
induction of experimental hepatitis at an institution for mentally
defective children.[8]

This third wave of scandals led to more dramatic responses than
just the issuing of guidelines. As there was an escalation in
MacDonagh's story from legislative to administrative responses, so
in our story we see an escalation from the issuing of guidelines to
the establishment of review procedures. In 1966 the NIH required
all recipients of NIH and Public Health Service (PHS) grants in the
United States to have had their research proposal approved by an
ethics committee at their institution. This committee, so they required,
should have looked at the rights and welfare of the subjects, the sui-
tability of the methods used to secure informed consent and the risks
and potential benefits of the investigation. The move to committees
for the ethical review of research, as illustrated in this response, represented an important escalation in regulation. But naturally, as we
shall now see, it did not represent the final stage.

In 1972 a social worker associated with the PHS spoke to reporters
about a long running research project conducted by the PHS, a project
about which he had already raised questions internally. His revelations
caused a storm to break and ushered in a new stage of ethical
review.

The study on which the social worker reported had begun in the
1930s as a study of 400 men with syphillis in Alabama. The men
were poor, black, rural workers and were given periodic blood tests,
clinical examinations and autopsies upon their death. The aim was
to study the course of the disease and the subjects were not informed
they had syphillis, nor were they treated with any available therapy.
It was reported in medical journals and conferences from the 1930s
to the 1960s, but without anyone raising doubts about it. In response
to the questions raised by the social worker in 1966 and 1968, the
PHS set up a panel, much in accordance with the requirement for
review by a local ethics committee, but this panel recommended that
treatment continue to be withheld. It also argued that the men were
too uneducated to be able to give informed consent and that consent
should be obtained indirectly from local doctors. As it happened,
the local, mainly black doctors endorsed the continuation of the study

---

[8] Gillespie. "Research on human subjects: An historical overview" pp. 10–11.

INSTITUTING A RESEARCH ETHIC 97

and promised not to treat the men with any antibiotics.[9]

The revelations about the Tuskegee Study, as it came to be known, triggered important reactions and ushered in the era of mandatory ethical review. In 1974 Congress made institutional ethics committees – institutional review boards (IRBs), as they came to be called – mandatory in institutions receiving federal research grants and it established the National Commission for the Protection of Human Subjects of Biomedical and Behavioral Research. This Commission issued various reports and recommendations between 1974 and 1978 on various kinds of research and the NIH began conducting on-site inspections of IRBs to ensure that their membership, record-keeping and decisions met appropriate standards. IRBs were required to include members able to represent community attitudes, the law and professional standards, and to include at least one person from outside the local institution.

This wave of response must have been reinforced, and perhaps in part motivated, by the publication in 1973 of Bernard Barber's book *Research on Human Subjects*.[10] Barber conducted a survey in which he found that as many as 18% of researchers were permissive in their ethical decisions. He found that researchers were twice as likely to approve ethically dubious proposals if they involved socially disadvantaged patients. And he found that they were likely to adopt a professional persona that distanced them from the individuals studied.

The 1974 changes in the US left it unclear as to what range of research should be vetted by the institutional ethics committee. This ambiguity was clarified in 1979 when the Department of Health, Education and Welfare published proposed regulations that would have broadened the requirement for prior review to 'all disciplines that collect information about identifiable individuals, living or dead'.[11] Although that proposal was withdrawn in 1981, a bureaucratic manoeuvre meant that its effect remained in place. A model of institutional review was circulated to universities by the depart-

---

[9] This case will remind many readers of the case in the National Women's Hospital, Auckland where women suffering from cervical cancer were studied over an extended period, without being informed that they were suffering from that disease and without being treated for it according to the best contemporary standards. See Sandra Coney and Phillida Bunkle 'An Unfortunate Experiment', reprinted as a special supplement in *Bioethics News*, Vol. 8, No. 1, 1988.

[10] Russell Sage Publications, New York, 1973. See too Bernard Barber, "The ethics of experimentation with human subjects", *Scientific American*, 234, 1976, pp. 25–31.

[11] Edward L. Pattullo, 'Government regulation of the investigation of human subjects in social research', *Minerva*, 23, no.4, 1985, p. 521.

98   PHILIP PETTIT

ment, involving the application of relevant rules to all research on humans, and this was accepted without question by most universities.

> Thus a majority of universities have voluntarily adopted policies more restrictive than are required either by statute or by regulation as such. Some did so consciously: many, confused or fearful, thought it wise – or easier – to act as officials of the department clearly wished them to act.[12]

The pattern of scandal and response in the generation of ethical review is most clearly found in the USA. But, whether for analogous reasons, or reasons of imitation, the upshot of the pattern is to be found in many different countries. Thus we can see a sequence of initiatives in Australia that closely parallel the ones documented for the US. In 1966 the National Health and Medical Research Council (NH&MRC) issued the Helsinki guidelines as guidelines for the conduct of biomedical research. In 1976 it recommended the establishment of institutional ethics committees. In 1982 it established its own medical research ethics committee, a committee which required the vetting of any research it supported by the ethics committee of the home institution. And in 1985 the NH&MRC issued a guideline requiring that the institutional ethics committee in any institution where it supported research should review 'all research on humans', even research it did not support, even indeed research in nonmedical areas.[13]

The idea of the local institutional ethics committee was supported in the US by the NIH, because it did not want to issue a legalistic code; this is because of the difficulty of fitting such a code to all cases and because doctors and scientists were resistant to a degree of centralised control over their activities.[14] But the idea of having such a locally administered form of control may have had, and may continue to have, other attractions. I suspect that it appeals to government nowadays on at least two different grounds. First of all it goes with the popular culture of decentralisation. And secondly it enables government to pass the buck.

This last point can be illustrated with Australian examples. Case one. The Privacy Act 1988 (Commonwealth) is so strict that it would make much current research on human beings impossible. The Government has avoided that difficulty by identifying ethics

---

[12] Pattullo, 'Government regulation of the investigation of human subjects in social research', p. 529.

[13] For a discussion of this initiative see Peter Singer, 'Rats, patients and people: issues in the ethical regulation of research', Annual Lecture Academy of the Social Sciences in Australia, 1989, p. 6.

[14] Gillespie, "Research on human subjects: An historical overview", p 11.

committees as the bodies which should determine whether the public interest in a piece of research is great enough to warrant the breach of an information privacy principle. Case two. The Government has been under pressure from AIDS groups concerned that potentially beneficial drugs take too long to be approved by the government's therapeutic goods administration (TGA). The response of the government has been to allow local institutional ethics committees to approve the clinical trial of drugs on human beings without advice or approval from the TGA.[15] The local committee may of course refer a proposed trial to the TGA, thereby incurring the old delays (up to 60 days). But it does not have to do this; it may choose to expedite research, not referring the trial to the TGA, and bear the responsibility itself. On May 14, 1991 all institutional ethics committees received a letter from the National Health and Medical Research Council (NH&MRC) which contains a paragraph that underlines the extent to which the buck is being passed.

> These procedures have a considerable impact for institutional ethics committees particularly in relation to institutional liability which might need to be considered by boards or other governing bodies.

I have been describing the evolutionary process which has led us to the current procedures in the ethical review of research on human beings. I hope that the description is sufficient to bear out the point that here, as in so many other areas of policy-making, we see the operation of something like MacDonagh's reactive dynamic.

In MacDonagh's story the important elements were the existence of an evil, its exposure in the media, outrage at the evil exposed, and a government reaction designed to appease the outraged. In our story of the development of the ethical review of research the elements are of exactly the same kind. In MacDonagh's story the development which was driven by the interplay of those elements came in escalating waves; it began with a legislative response, moved to the appointment of administrators, then to the introduction of administrative routines, and finally it culminated in the establishment of a full-scale bureaucracy. In our story we see the same pattern of escalation in the successive waves of exposure, outrage and reaction. Initially the reaction is to institute guidelines for research, first voluntary, professional guidelines and then often guidelines imposed from without. Next the reaction escalates to requiring review by committee of any research that is funded by certain bodies. And finally

---

[15] See the document 'Clinical trials of drugs in Australia' issued in May 1991 by the Department of Community Services and Health, Canberra.

it culminates in the requirement of committee review for any research whatsoever.

THE MODEL EXTRAPOLATED

The MacDonagh model serves us well in making sense of how we have got to the present stage in the ethical review of research on humans. But now we must try to put the model to work in looking at where the evolutionary process is likely to lead us next. For we have no reason to believe that the process has played itself out; we have no reason to think that we have reached the stationary state in ethical review.

I am pessimistic about where the process will lead us: pessimistic, in the first place, about the effects it will have on the research practised, but pessimistic also about the effects it will have on the ethics of researchers. I will concentrate mainly on the effects which the process is likely to have on the research practised, only commenting briefly on the effects on research ethics. The reasons for my pessimism go back to certain considerations about the nature of ethics committees, and about the context in which they operate. These considerations combine to suggest that the reactive dynamic we have described may lead to a serious reduction in the current scope of research and to a substantial compromise of the ethic that currently governs research practice.

As we look at the context in which ethics committees operate, then there is one striking consideration that argues for pessimism. We can think of the context as one in which certain sorts of committee decisions and procedures are rewarded, and others punished. Looked at in that way, the striking thing about the context is that things are designed to elicit progressively more conservative postures and to drive out more liberal dispositions. The context is moulded in such a way that as time passes, ethics committees are bound to take on a more and more restrictive shape.

Consider an analogy which we mentioned already. Consider the context within which social workers operate in making decisions about whether to take children into care. The reactive dynamic operates there in such a way that we must expect social workers to be more and more cautious about leaving children with their parents, even if they believe that that is for the best overall. The reason is clear. Social workers get little credit for correct decisions, whether the decisions be cautious or liberal; the only relevant sanctions are the penalties that may follow on incorrect judgments. But the penalties for incorrect decisions are not even-handed. Social workers get little blame for any error they may make in taking a child into care; the child

INSTITUTING A RESEARCH ETHIC 101

may be worse off than it would have been at home but who is to tell? On the other side, social workers are liable to attract great blame, even public humiliation and dismissal, for any error they make in leaving a child with its parents; if the child is abused then, short even of newspaper coverage, they will suffer the wrath of their superiors. Little wonder if social workers should begin to become over-cautious and conservative.

As I view the context in which ethics committees work, the situation is very much the same. There are few rewards on offer for correct decisions; the focus, again, is on penalties for mistakes. But the penalties on offer for mistakes are not fairly distributed. Suppose an ethics committee makes a mistake in not allowing a particular research proposal to go ahead. Who is going to blame them? There may be a protest or two from the area of research in question but such protests are easily stilled with declarations about the public interest and, if necessary, with appeals to the Vice-Chancellor to protect the impartial referee against partisan attack. Suppose on the other hand that an ethics committee makes a mistake in allowing a questionable proposal to be pursued. There is always a possibility in such a case that the proposal will come to public attention, becoming a matter for media criticism and even a matter for the courts. And if that happens then the penalty on the ethics committee is going to be enormous.

The contexts of the social workers and the ethics committees have two features in common. One, they deploy lots of penalties and few rewards. And, two, the penalties on offer display a striking asymmetry. In each case there is little or no penalty for a false negative: for saying 'nay' to a proposal, when it deserves support. And in each case there is a potentially enormous penalty for a false positive: for saying 'yea' to a proposal, when it should have been blocked, or should apparently have been blocked. It does not require a great deal of reflection to realise how unsatisfactory this sort of situation is. As social workers tend to be driven towards over-cautious decisions, so I believe that ethics committees are likely to be driven more and more to adopt a conservative and restrictive profile. The incentive structure under which the committees operate is so seriously skewed that any other result would be miraculous. There is an invisible backhand in place which is designed to produce systematically inferior results.

This consideration about the context of ethics committees argues for a growing intrusiveness, even if there is no further wave of scandals. If there are further scandals, of course, then things are likely to happen even more quickly. Think about what will happen if some false positive, some decision judged to have been over-liberal, comes

102 PHILIP PETTIT

to light and causes a public outcry. The committee in question will be forced to revise its procedures in a manner that satisfies public outrage, whether or not the revision is really for the best. The revision required will affect every committee in the country, as the extra constraint is centrally imposed or is adopted by committees in a posture of preemptive surrender. And the constraint in question will be ratcheted into place, with little chance of ever coming under later review. The scenario hardly needs labouring.

This consideration about the context in which ethics committees operate is directly prompted by representing the development of ethical review in the MacDonagh model. Wherever the reactive dynamic has been established as a threat to relevant parties, even if it is not actually triggered by any further scandals, we will find the asymmetry of penalties attaching to false negatives and false positives. But this consideration about the context of ethics committees is bolstered by some further considerations too. If we turn now to the character of ethics committees themselves, then I believe that here also we find reasons for pessimism. I will mention two considerations that strike me as relevant.

A first consideration is that any ethics committee is more or less bound to be self-assertive: that no committee is likely to accept a rubber-stamping role. It is a universal experience that the individual members of committees, and indeed committees themselves as a whole, have a disposition to legitimate their presence by showing that they make a difference: to legitimate their presence, in effect, by making their presence felt. This tendency may yet have baneful effects on the ethical review of human research.

Imagine that the present arrangements for ethical review elicit a culture of self-criticism and self-regulation on the part of researchers. Imagine that, aware that certain expectations are in place, and aware that their proposals will be vetted by a local committee, researchers come to heel. They shape their practices to what, at present, most of us would find acceptable. They seek the informed consent of their subjects. They pursue projects where the promise of benefits clearly justifies the risk of harms. They ensure that any data on individuals is held under conditions of secure confidentiality. And so on. What then should we expect of the institutional ethics committee which reviews the proposals from such researchers? If the ethics committee is to be self-assertive, as I suspect it will tend to be, then I fear that it may begin to push for further and further changes in the practices of research. Otherwise it will have to accept that its role is mainly to rubber-stamp. And that is not a self-image that it is likely to espouse very readily.

But there is also a second feature of ethics committees, at least as currently constituted, that may support an intrusive disposition. This is the tendency of such committees to be, not only self-assertive, but also self-righteous. There are many reasonable research proposals which involve the adoption of procedures that are, in one respect or another, distasteful. The research may offend against a natural human sentiment, say in using foetal tissue in transplantation. The research may involve withholding treatment, or administering a placebo, to subjects who stand a somewhat better chance under the alternative therapy. And so on. In such a case it is bound to be hard for the members of an institutional ethics committee, in particular the lay members who may have little sense of the aggregate benefits involved, to endorse the research. On the other hand, it may not be clear to them that blocking the research can have disastrous consequences. After all, as they may implicitly or explicitly reason, the research in their particular institution is hardly likely to be the crucial contribution. Many institutions will be potentially involved in any area of research and the committee at each institution may hope that the research is done elsewhere. In other words, they may hope to free ride.

When I say that an institutional ethics committee is likely to be self-righteous, what I mean is that in such a case it is likely to move towards a posture of keeping its own hands clean, recoiling from the distasteful aspect of the research to be approved, and ignoring the possible loss associated with that decision. The members of the committee may baulk at the thought of allowing the use of foetal tissue or they may be horrified at the possibility of hastening the death of someone to whom a placebo is administered. The possibility can hardly be denied.

The self-assertiveness and self-righteousness of committees combine with the asymmetry of the context within which they operate – the asymmetry of the sanctions to which they are subject – to offer serious grounds for worry about the thrust behind current arrangements for the ethical review of research. The asymmetry of context means that there is little or no penalty for the false negative – for the excessively restrictive decision – and potentially a great penalty for the false positive: the adventurously liberal judgment. And the self-assertiveness and self-righteousness of committees means that there may actually be some rewards attached to false negatives. Every negative, true or false, enables the committee to put itself forward as a committee that is doing something, not just serving as a rubber stamp; and many a negative, true or false, will allow the committee to see itself as the righteous guardian of the weak and ignorant against the overweening pretensions of the researcher.

The prognosis that I offer, then, is bleak. It is bleak, even in the

104 PHILIP PETTIT

absence of any further scandals, and any further waves of outrage and reaction. The character of the ethics committees that we have set up, especially given the context in which we have placed them, is sufficient ground for predicting that those committees will grind away slowly into the agenda of behavioural and biomedical research.

What areas of research on humans look to be particularly vulnerable to erosion? It may be useful if I mention a number of types of research which are likely to come under pressure.

A good deal of human research, particularly biomedical research, involves some risk of harm to subjects. The risk may be very small, and the benefits promised by the research may be great, but the risk of harm is still there. Thus, a study conducted by the Survey Research Center of the Institute of Social Research of the University of Michigan in 1977 concluded that harmful effects occurred in 75 of 1,655 biomedical projects surveyed and in 4 of 729 behavioural science studies.[16] I fear that institutional committees may baulk more and more at the approval of research projects involving any risk of harm, however slight. I hope I am wrong about that but I do think that there are reasons for being pessimistic.

Many studies, both biomedical and behavioural, involve a further sort of risk also. This is a risk that, however secure the measures adopted, confidential information about individuals may still come to be released. For example, many studies may make individuals or corporations indentifiable to the shrewd eye of the investigative journalist. And many studies may be legally vulnerable, in the sense that the data collected may not prove to be protected by legal professional privilege; this was established in a recent case in Australia, where the original fieldwork notes of an anthropologist were held to be unprotected in the course of a hearing about a land claim.[17] As I think that committees may baulk at approving projects involving any risk of harm, so I fear that they may shrink from the approval of projects involving any risk of a breach of confidentiality.

A good deal of research on humans involves some invasion of privacy. It may involve access to records that are so extensive as to make it impossible to approach the individuals involved for their permission. It may involve just the observation of people in public places. But in any case I suspect that ethics committees may begin to worry about endorsing research that occasions such intrusions on privacy. Thus Edward Pattullo reports that the replication of bystander

[16] See Pattullo, 'Government regulation of the investigation of human subjects in social research', p. 530.

[17] See Don Rawson 'Ethics and the social sciences: the state of play in 1988', mimeo, *Academy of the Social Sciences in Australia*, University House, Canberra, 1988, p. 2.

experiments – these may involve simulating an accident in a public place, for example, to see how observers respond – has disappeared under the influence of ethical review.[18]

In this connection it may be worth mentioning one study that would certainly not be allowed under current practices. I mention this study, not necessarily because I think it ought to be allowed, but because it points towards the sort of invasion of privacy which ethics committees are likely to deplore. The study is described in Laud Humphrey's book *Tearoom Trade*.[19] Humphrey describes going to a public toilet frequented by homosexual men, pretending to be their lookout, and observing patterns in their behaviour in the course of this pretense. He traced some of the men through their car registration numbers, and later interviewed them, under the guise of conducting an anonymous public health survey. That research may have given us important information on the behaviour of male homosexuals and on their presentation in the wider non-homosexual community. I have little doubt, however, but that it would be blocked under current procedures.

Many people may not regret the fact that this sort of work has been inhibited by the development of ethics committees. But there are other, more urgent forms of research which the concern for privacy may also lead ethics committees to prevent. Norman Swan wrote as follows about an incident in 1988.

> Western Australia is one of the best places in the world for epidemiological research. The doyens of Australian epidemiology are in Perth. The NH&MRC funds an epidemiology unit in Perth. But they have had serious trouble getting their work past a lawyer on the university's ethics committee. He has dug his heels in over privacy. . . . The issue wasn't whether people would be harmed by the projects, whether they'd have bits of their brains chopped out or be asked to consume toxic tablets . . . no, the issue obsessing this ethics committee and the lawyer in particular was confidentiality. The research involved no human experimentation but the workers did need to use their world-leading system of linked hospital records which allows them to assess accurately the extent and patterns of cancer, heart disease and birth defects in the Western Australian population. The record linkage system is highly confidential using numbers rather than names with only limited

[18] Pattullo, 'Government regulation of the investigation of human subjects in social research', p. 531.

[19] Duckworth, London, 1970.

106   PHILIP PETTIT

access to the data. Yet even so this lawyer felt that privacy laws
were being broken.[20]

I have mentioned three types of research as vulnerable to future
review: research involving any risk of harm and research involving
any danger of a breach of confidentiality or privacy. A fourth area
in which I think that current research may prove vulnerable to the
escalation of review practice is the sort of research that involves withholding any information from subjects. Humphrey's study already
illustrates such research, for at the interview stage he deceived his
subjects into thinking that he was a public health investigator. Other
work in sociology and social psychology illustrates dramatically the
withholding of information. Indeed the two experiments that have
sometimes been described as the crucial experiments of the discipline, those associated with the names of Asch and Milgram, both
involved the deception of their subjects.[21] But we do not have to go
to behavioural research for examples of withholding information. The
use of placebos in biomedical research also involves such concealment. It is vital that the subject does not know that he is receiving
just a placebo. And it may be vital that he does not know even that
it is possible that he is receiving a placebo. I worry that institutional
ethics committees may yet become so invasive as to try to prohibit
even this type of concealment.

A fifth and last area of research that I think is vulnerable is research
on humans where the subject cannot give personal consent. I have
in mind research on children, on the mentally retarded and on the
mentally deranged. There has been great emphasis in recent times
on the rights of individuals in these categories. And I applaud that
emphasis for its effects in various areas of policy making. But one
effect it may have is to inhibit ethics committees about accepting that
research in such subjects can be approved by appropriate guardians.
I can see the possibility that committees will become more and more
loathe to allow such research.

In connection with these last two areas of research, something is
worth noting. This is that the original Nuremberg code appears to
have left no room for the withholding of information or the absence
of personal consent by the subjects of the research. The Helsinki code
does allow for the absence of personal consent but says nothing on

[20] Norman Swan 'Doctors, Lawyers and the Representatives of God: The 1988
Peter MacCallum Lecture', Melbourne. Quoted, with permission, from typescript.
[21] See Soloman Asch 'Effects of group pressure upon modification and distortion of judgments' in E.E. Maccoby, T.M. Newcomb, and E.L. Hartley, eds, *Readings in Social Psychology*, 3rd ed., Holt, New York, 1958 and Stanley Milgram *Obedience
to Authority*, Harper and Row, New York, 1974.

the withholding of information, as in the administration of placebos. These omissions may be significant. They may point to areas where there is going to be trouble ahead.

I have suggested that certain natural features of institutional ethics committees may lead those committees to intrude further on current research practice. In particular, I have indicated certain areas of research where we may expect committees to be more intrusive. I think that most of us would agree that it would be undesirable if these new forms of intrusion took place. Hence I see reason here for worrying about where the reactive dynamic that has been at the source of ethical review may yet take us.

But before leaving this section I must mention that there is also a second source of worry as to where the dynamic may take us. Not only may ethics committees come to intrude on current research in a way that is undesirable. It is also all too likely that, as they begin to intrude in this way, those committees will engender a culture of resistance among researchers, and that they may thereby undermine the existing commitments of researchers to ethical guidelines.

The scenario I have in mind is this. Researchers come to see ethics committees as over-assertive and over-righteous. They come to see them as putting a stop to research that may be of important benefit to humankind. In this situation, they may well come to scorn whatever restrictions are laid down for the research they are allowed to continue practicing. For example, they may come to be scornful of the informed consent requirements laid down by those committees. It is easy to see that researchers in hospitals, or in the anthropological field, may easily offend against regulations for seeking informed consent by excessive verbal persuasion, by glossing over various details, and so on. If researchers do come to lose a commitment to ethical guidelines, if they do come to be 'demoralised' this way, then I see a further reason for worrying about the trajectory along which we have looked. It may not only lead to a restriction of the research we currently tolerate. It may also lead to a restriction in the commitment of researchers to the ethic which currently prevails.

The point to stress here is that there is no regulation like self-regulation. There are so many areas where researchers on human beings may offend against ethical standards that the only hope of having research done in an ethical fashion is to have those researchers identify strongly with the desired ethical code. If ethics committees continue on the trajectory that I am plotting, then there is a serious danger that they may cause resentment and alienation on the part of the researchers, leading us towards a really sorry state of affairs. Indeed there is some evidence that this is happening already. Norman

108   PHILIP PETTIT

Swan reports as follows: 'in the course of my coverage of Australian and overseas medical research I'm coming across more and more researchers – decent people, not Dr Mengeles – who are fulminating against the practice of bioethics'.[22]

THE LESSONS

Where does this discussion leave us? I begin with the assumption that we certainly ought not to go back to the days where there was no ethical review. It is clear that there are great dangers in allowing the professional enthusiasm of researchers to go untempered by the need to satisfy ethical reviewers. But I add a further assumption to this starting one. I also assume that we want to put measures in place which will inhibit the drift that I predict in the extrapolation of my model. In this final section I want to mention some proposals which might help to block that drift.

One of the main problems identified in the discussion in the last section is the absence of rewards for the good decisions made by ethics committees and the asymmetry between the penalties attaching to questionable decisions: the false positives are likely to be harshly penalised, while the false negatives attract little or no punishment. There are a number of measures that might be taken to try to cope with this problem, although there is no sure-fire solution.

One measure I propose is the establishment of some appeals procedure whereby a researcher can gain a review of a negative decision made by an ethics committee. Such a procedure would help to redress the present balance in favour of researchers but it might also inhibit the ethics committee which is tending to become over-cautious. It would introduce the possibility of a penalty for the false negative: the penalty, to which any committee is likely to be sensitive, of having its judgment overturned. Of course, if an appeals procedure of this kind is to work then it would need to involve a different sort of body from the ethics committee itself: if it is a twin of that committee, then it is likely to mirror the decisions at the lower level, being subject to the same pressures. I suggest that the appeals body should involve two or three very senior people whose understanding of research, and whose commitment to a research ethic, is beyond doubt. It should involve the sort of people whom it would be difficult to recruit to the time-consuming labours of an ethics committee but who might well be willing to take part in a procedure involving the occasional appeal and review.

A second measure I propose is that each institution maintain and

---

[22] 'Doctors, Lawyers and the Representatives of God'.

publicise the record of its ethics committee in approving research and the record of the committee, where it has reservations, in negotiating a compromise with the researcher or researchers involved. I make this proposal in the hope of establishing a certain sort of reward for the committee that is not over-cautious and that goes to some trouble in facilitating research projects with which it initially finds some difficulties. Where the appeals procedure would help to establish a symmetry of penalties between false negatives and false positives, I hope that this measure would put some rewards in place for the committee that does not run too quickly to cover: the committee that really works at sponsoring ethically satisfactory research activity.

There is also a third proposal which comes naturally to mind in the light of our discussion of the context within which ethics committees operate. Not only can we try to manufacture the reward just mentioned, and not only can we try to introduce penalties for the false negative, we can also attempt to reduce the dimensions of the penalty that threatens any false positive, or any apparently false positive, decision. We can look at ways of protecting the members of ethics committees from media exposure and from litigation. I am unclear about how this end may be best achieved but I have no doubt that the goal is important. So long as ethics committee members remain vulnerable to exposure and litigation, they cannot be expected to pursue the task of ethical review in the responsible manner we would desire.

These three measures would help to cope with the problems generated by the context within which ethics committees operate. But what about problems generated by the character of ethics committees: generated, in particular, by their tendency to be self-assertive and self-righteous? Reflection on these problems motivates a number of further proposals.

First, I think it is important that ethical guidelines for the practice of each sort of human research should be established on a national or, even better, an international basis. These guidelines should be proposed by the researchers in each area but should be approved by bodies that involve not just professionals but also the representatives of other groups. There should be representatives from ethics committees; there should be representatives from consumer groups; and there should be representatives from governments. If such guidelines are in place then ethics committees are more likely to be well directed in their judgment of individual cases. They are more likely to see themselves as doing something more than rubber-stamping, even when they approve. And they are more likely to resist the self-righteous impulse.

Second, I think it is important that members of consumer move-

110   PHILIP PETTIT

ments, and perhaps representatives of government, be appointed to ethics committees. At the moment we have professional researchers on those committees who certainly will be sensitive to the potential aggregative benefits of research. But those professionals are set too starkly in contrast with the lay members of the committees, members who may tend to identify with individual subjects and be neglectful of potential aggregative effects. Professional researchers may not be persuasive in arguing for the benefits of research, as they can easily be cast as self-interested. The representatives of consumer movements and of government are likely to share an interest in aggregative effects, while lacking the self-interest of the professional researcher. They would help to temper any inclination on the part of lay members to over-identify with individual subjects, in righteous mode, and to prevent potentially important research.

Third, in order to guard against the self-assertiveness I described, I think it is important that ethics committees come to be concerned only with research projects that raise genuine difficulties. This being so, I think it is important that in each institution, perhaps on a national or international model, we should identify those sorts of research on humans that need not come before the committee. Peter Singer has suggested that we might describe such research as follows:

> Research that does not involve significant risk of harm to the subjects, and is carried out on the basis of informed consent, where researcher and research subject are in a position of equality.[23]

I do not say that that characterisation of exempted research is necessarily approporiate. But I do think that we should look for exemption on some such basis.

Finally, a simple measure that may be difficult to implement. It is often said that the only trustworthy politician is the reluctant politician. There may be something in the thought that the less inclined someone is to take a place on an ethics committee, the more inclined we should be to find a place for them. I think that it is important that we guard against the appointment of moral enthusiasts – or, for that matter, professional enthusiasts – on such committees. There is no end to the difficulties that such a busybody can cause. How to guard against this sort of appointee? There is no mechanical procedure that is sure to give the right result but it is important, at the least, that nominations for an institutional ethics committee are discussed by some body representing the different interests

---

[23] Singer, 'Rats, patients and people: issues in the ethical regulation of research', p. 22.

involved; it is important that nominations, in particular self-nominations, do not go through on the nod of an executive.

If the different measures I have mentioned were introduced, then I think that the future for research on human beings would look brighter than it does just now. But I also think that the future for a thriving research ethic would look better too. There would be less reason to fear the alienation and demoralisation of researchers that I mentioned earlier.

The two sets of recommendations presented so far bear on ethics committees themselves; they involve reshaping their context of operation and their inherent character. But it is important, not just that we reshape the context and the character of ethics committees; it is important also that we nurture a culture of research ethics that is independent of ethics committees. This is important, not just to contain the committees – not just to deprive them of a monopoly in the area of ethics – but also to nurture a reliable ethic of research and to reassure the community at large about the responsible attitudes of researchers. I see three measures that ought to be introduced.

First, all students of a behavioural or biomedical discipline ought to be educated in the ethics of research, and educated in particular by experts in their discipline, not just by outsiders. Philosophers might play a part in conducting appropriate ethics courses for students but I stress that members of the discipline itself ought to be involved in such a process of education. The students ought to be exposed to a discussion by professionals of the sorts of cases that they are likely to confront in research. They ought to be made aware of what, by current professional consensus, is acceptable behaviour.

Second, I believe it is important in each profession that there is a continuing discussion of the code that ought to bind researchers in the area and of the difficult kinds of cases which researchers confront. For example, there might be a special session at annual conferences, in which people raise difficult questions that have confronted them and discuss with their peers the sorts of response they ought to have taken.[24]

Finally, I think that each profession ought to establish procedures under which complaints may be heard against members of the profession and, if necessary, disciplinary action taken. If researchers in any area are to show that they take their own work seriously, then they must begin to institute such procedures.

In the earlier parts of this paper I described a reactive dynamic

[24] See in this connection Joan Cassell and Sue-Ellen Jacohs, eds. *Handbook on Ethical Issues in Anthropology*, American Anthropological Association, Washington, 1987.

112   PHILIP PETTIT

which has taken us to the present stage in the ethical review of human research and which, if left alone, is likely to carry us along a degenerating trajectory. In this section I have mentioned a number of measures that must be taken if that dynamic is to be contained, and if ethical review is to be conducted in a profitable manner. Unfortunately, no automatic mechanism will ensure that the measures I have described will be taken. Here we can only look to the professionals in the area, in particular the professional associations, to begin to think about what should be done. The point, for them, is not just to understand the world; the point is to begin to change it.[25]

Research School of Social Sciences,
Australian National University

[25] I have made use of suggestions received from John Braithwaite and Geoffrey Brennan and I am very grateful for their advice.

[30]

INDUCEMENT IN RESEARCH[1]

MARTIN WILKINSON AND ANDREW MOORE

ABSTRACT

Opposition to inducement payments for research subjects is an international orthodoxy amongst writers of ethics committee guidelines. We offer an argument in favour of these payments. We also critically evaluate the best arguments we can find or devise against such payments, and except in one very limited range of circumstances, we find these unconvincing.

The guidelines for many research ethics committees state that payment to subjects[2] should not be so high as to amount to an inducement. Here are some samples:

> [T]he participants' consent must be voluntary and not influenced by financial reward.[3]

> Volunteers may be paid for inconvenience and time spent, but such payment should not be so large as to be an inducement to participate.[4]

> The IRB [Institutional Review Board] should review both the amount of payment and the proposed method and timing of

[1] We are grateful to Jo Asscher, Andrew Brien, Alison Douglass, Tim Mulgan, Nicola Peart, Andrew Williams, the members of the Southern Regional Health Authority Ethics Committee (Otago), two referees, and participants in the University of Otago's Philosophy Department Seminar, Bioethics Research Centre Journals Club, and Bioethics Summer School 1996, for helpful comments.
[2] We prefer the term 'subjects' to 'participants'. The latter term is ambiguous between researchers and research subjects.
[3] Health Research Council of New Zealand (HRC), *Guidelines for Ethics Committees*, 6.3.2.1 (iii). The HRC Ethics Committee is the accrediting body for many ethics committees in New Zealand.
[4] National Health and Medical Research Council of Australia, *NHMRC Statement on human experimentation*, 1992, 13.

disbursement to assure that neither are coercive or present undue influence.[5]

Subjects may be paid for inconvenience and time spent, and should be reimbursed for expenses incurred, in connection with their participation in research; they may also receive free medical services. However, the payments should not be so large or the medical services so extensive as to induce prospective subjects to consent to participate in the research against their better judgement ('undue inducement').[6]

The quotations just given suggest that there is an international orthodoxy among writers of research ethics committee guidelines against inducement payments to subjects. We critically examine this orthodoxy in this paper, and our conclusions are generally sceptical and unorthodox.[7]

After setting out the scope of our inquiry, we raise in Section 1 some difficulties for the orthodoxy, and we present a *prima facie* argument that inducement is a good thing. Section 2 begins our critical examination of the orthodoxy, starting with the guideline writers' claim that inducement undermines voluntary decision-making and consent. Additionally, phrases in the guidelines such as 'against their better judgement' suggest that inducement is considered bad for subjects. In Section 3, we examine arguments that inducement leads subjects to act contrary to their own welfare. We group other objections to subject payments under the claim that they are exploitative, and the claim that they introduce bias into subject selection. We discuss arguments for these claims in Sections 4 and 5, respectively. Our paper limits itself to arguments for the orthodoxy which appeal to features of the individual research studies in which

---

[5] Food and Drug Administration, *FDA Information Sheet: Payment to Research Subjects, Rockville, United States, 1988.*

[6] Council for International Organizations of Medical Sciences, *International Ethical Guidelines for Biomedical Research Involving Human Subjects*, Guideline 4. The orthodoxy is very similar in Britain. See *Manual for Research Ethics Committees*, compiled by C. Foster, Centre of Medical Law and Ethics, Kings College, London, December 1994. Section II.49 of this document quotes numerous statements against inducement payments to research subjects from the guidelines of the Department of Health, the Royal College of Physicians, the General Medical Council, the Association of British Pharmaceutical Industries, the British Psychological Society, and the National Union of Students.

[7] It is hard to reconcile rejection of inducements with acceptance of payment for inconvenience, time spent, and out-of-pocket expenses, since these all increase the probability of participation. Perhaps the guideline writers rely on a distinction between due and undue inducement. If so, the rest of our discussion may be treated as an inquiry into whether there can be any undue inducement in research.

inducement payments are offered. We hope to address elsewhere arguments which make claims about the broader social and research consequences of these payments.

Research sponsors sometimes offer researchers cash inducements to recruit subjects, or to complete studies to specified standards. Important ethical issues arise about these practices, but they are not our topic here. Our question is whether researchers should be allowed by research review bodies, and by ethics committees in particular, to offer *cash inducements* to *competent* people to act as research subjects. From now on, we shall just call these payments 'inducements'. The focus on inducements sets aside difficult issues concerning invitations to participate in therapeutic research, which might in some cases also be inducements to subjects. We leave aside in-kind inducements too, such as offers of free treatment or reduced waiting time. We also leave aside payments to incompetent research subjects, because these raise substantial additional issues.[8] Most of our examples are medical in nature, but we do not intend our conclusions to be limited to medical research. Rather, they apply to all types of research which ethics committees are asked to approve. This includes research in medicine, nursing, psychiatry, psychology, education, social science, management studies, and so forth.

It might help if we indicate briefly at the outset why we find the anti-inducement orthodoxy peculiar. Given that people are allowed to volunteer to be research subjects for no pay, it seems odd to deny them the opportunity to volunteer for pay. Asymmetrical treatment of acting as a subject for no pay and acting as a subject for payment needs to be justified. This point is worth emphasising. A common picture of inducements is one in which people who are desperately short of money sign up for dangerous and dubious experiments. It is no part of our aim to justify inducement in these cases. We consider only research which ethics committees would allow to proceed, were the subjects not paid. Our question is this: if people are allowed to volunteer for no pay, why not for some pay?

1. A CASE FOR INDUCEMENT

Consider the following argument for allowing inducements. Some researchers would find it worthwhile to pay inducements in order to attract enough subjects. Those who would accept this reward would not do so unless it were worth it to them. As a result of offering the reward, the researchers get the subjects they want. As a result of

---

[8] We also leave aside the question of what should be done, in the context of inducement, when subjects wish to withdraw during a study.

participating, the subjects get the reward they want. Both are better off. No one is worse off. Inducement is thus a good thing.

This seems to us to be a good argument, which at least makes a *prima facie* case for inducement. It has the same structure as an argument justifying wages for work, or any other market transactions. Many people would not work if they were not paid; in that sense wages are inducements. Few people think that, as a result, it is wrong to offer wages. Those who do have concerns about the existing wage system usually object that wages are too *low*, not that they are too high, or that they are offered at all.

2.   INDUCEMENT AND CONSENT

Those who oppose inducements usually concede something like the *prima facie* case we have just made, but then claim that for some reason it does not constitute a persuasive case for inducements. The most prominent objection in ethics committee guidelines is that inducement is likely to invalidate informed consent, particularly when subjects are poor.

Ruth Faden and Tom Beauchamp imagine a case in which a woman in a low-paid job with five children desperately needs funds, which she can get in exchange for undergoing various risky and uncomfortable medical experiments.[9] They think that in this case the woman's autonomy is infringed upon. Paul McNeill tells us that his daughter was contemplating volunteering for drug trials, since she had run out of money. He sent her what she needed, apparently in part because he thought her consent invalidated by inducement.[10]

At first sight, the idea that inducement undermines consent is surprising. People receive inducements all the time to do things they otherwise would not do, such as parting with their goods or working under particular conditions for particular employers. There is no suggestion in the vast majority of these cases that their being paid undermines the voluntary nature of their actions. We shall argue that first appearances are correct. There is no good reason to think that inducements cause subjects to act non-voluntarily, or that they otherwise invalidate subject consent.

Freedom, autonomy, consent

There is some evidence that inducements cause an increase in the

[9] R. Faden and T. Beauchamp, *A History and Theory of Informed Consent*, New York: Oxford University Press, 1986, p. 358.

[10] P. McNeill, *The Ethics and Politics of Human Experimentation*, Cambridge: Cambridge University Press, 1993, p. 176.

proportion of poor subjects.[11] We think this evidence is inconclusive, but we concede it for the sake of argument. We argue, however, that this does not show that inducements would undermine the consent of even badly off subjects. Those who believe inducement does undermine consent must explain why this happens for research volunteers when it is not plausible that it happens in other cases of market transactions, such as when one desperately needs to sell some of one's property.

Desperate need is not sufficient to undermine consent. This point can be overlooked, if consent is thought to rest on freedom rather than autonomy. Skating over many complications, a person is autonomous when she decides what to do for herself. This requires her to have a sense of what she wants, which she cannot if, say, she is comatose. Furthermore, her autonomy would be undermined if others imposed their will on her. This could be done by manipulation or by coercion.

Freedom requires the presence of more than one acceptable option.[12] If one will starve unless one takes the only job available (pleasant or not) then one is unfree to refuse. We shall presently show that this does not rule out the morally important consent valued by ethics committees. Even if people are capable of consent, however, is it not morally important that they might be unfree to refuse inducements? It is, but on any view of freedom, denying people the option of taking inducements reduces their freedom, since it removes an option that they prefer to the alternatives.

Let us now make good our claim that desperate need — unfreedom — does not, in and of itself, undermine consent. Our argument depends on the doctrine of informed consent. If the sole alternative to death is some lifesaving treatment, then one is unfree to turn it down, but this does not rule out autonomous choice of the treatment. All the features of autonomous choice might be present: careful deliberation, correct understanding of the options, no manipulation, and so on. If informed consent is possible, despite the dire choice one faces, it cannot be because one is free to refuse the treatment. It must be because one can nonetheless act autonomously. We conclude that doctrines of informed consent aim to protect autonomy, not freedom.[13]

[11] See the evidence cited by McNeill, p. 176.

[12] The claim that freedom requires a plurality of acceptable options is controversial. For its denial, see H. Steiner, *An Essay on Rights*, Oxford: Blackwell, 1994, pp. 10–21. We adopt this controversial claim because it generates more difficulties for our argument than does its rejection.

[13] See, for example, Faden and Beauchamp, pp. 344–5 and, for exhaustive discussion of the subtleties, J. Feinberg, *Harm to Self*, New York: Oxford University Press, 1986.

378   MARTIN WILKINSON AND ANDREW MOORE

If consent protects autonomy rather than freedom, then it is a mistake to infer an absence of informed consent in those who cannot afford to turn down payments. The mere fact that they are badly off and have no acceptable alternative does not establish the absence of either autonomy or proper informed consent.

Coercive offers

If badly off people were in some way coerced into participating as subjects, then their autonomy would be infringed upon and their consent invalidated. Coercion is paradigmatically a case of the denial of autonomy, since it consists in the deliberate imposition of one person's will on another. However, coercion usually takes the form of threats, which restrict people's options. Inducements are offers, not threats, and they expand people's options.

Can there be coercive offers?[14] In our view, it is a necessary condition of an offer's being coercive that the offerer is also responsible for the bad circumstances of the offeree. For example, if we poison you and then offer to provide the only available antidote in exchange for your stamp collection, that is coercive. If you are poisoned in a way for which we are not responsible, and we make the same offer, that is not coercive.[15] Our argument here depends on the idea that coercion consists in the deliberate imposition of one person's will on another.

Let us re-examine our earlier case of the medical patient who gave uncoerced informed consent. With the exception of the lifesaving operation, this person's options were all unacceptable, but that did not make her consent coerced. Nor did the fact that her doctor was resonsible for her one acceptable option do so. If coercion requires the deliberate imposition of one person's will on another, and if making available the only acceptable option(s) is not sufficient for this, then coercive offers must involve something else. In our view, a person who makes a coercive offer must not only make available the victim's only acceptable option(s), but must also be responsible for at least one of the unacceptable options. Only then is the coercer responsible for the circumstances in which the victim has no choice but to surrender her or his will.

The argument we have just made has clear implications for consent in the context of inducement. As long as those making an offer are not responsible for the circumstances of the potential subjects, their offer is not coercive. A final empirical claim: researchers are very rarely

---

[14] For a summary of the large and rather baroque literature on coercive offers, see Feinberg, ch. 24.

[15] It might still be an exploitative offer. We discuss exploitation in Section 4.

responsible for the financial situation of subjects.[16] We conclude that inducement need not be coercive and that consent in this context to act as a research subject cannot be invalidated by the claim that it is the acceptance of a coercive offer.

We have argued in this section that it is implausible to think that inducement invalidates consent. One argument for the contrary view relies on the claim that desperate need invalidates consent. We argued that this is false. Another argument depends on the notion of a coercive offer. We argued that that notion is largely irrelevant to inducement in research. We have found no persuasive consent-based case against inducements.

3.   INDUCEMENT AND WELFARE

Can inducements be rejected on the grounds that they damage the welfare of potential subjects? The mutual gain argument offered above suggests that they cannot. Altruistic motives aside, why should people accept inducements unless they judge themselves better off for receiving them? In the absence of a good answer, we should expect inducements to enhance the welfare of subjects, not damage it. One might oppose this conclusion by claiming, paternalistically, that subjects choose against their own best interests. We discuss this claim below. But first we examine a non-paternalistic argument which holds that people benefit from not being in a position to accept inducements.

The non-paternalistic argument

The non-paternalistic argument claims that poor people are better off not having the freedom to participate in research for reward, because they could otherwise be forced to use that freedom against their interests. An analogy here could be the refusal to allow people the option to sell themselves into slavery. If people had that freedom then perhaps their creditors or others with power over them could force them to use it.

This argument is not paternalistic. It does not suppose that people need protection from themselves, or that we should restrict their autonomy to protect their autonomy. It holds instead that a denial of freedom is a way of helping people get what is better for them, because

---

[16] Faden and Beauchamp bizarrely overlook this point, and their own freedom/ autonomy distinction, in their confusing discussion of welcome and unwelcome offers. That discussion is an attempt to salvage their view that inducements undermine the autonomy of the poverty-stricken woman mentioned earlier. See their pp. 358–9.

380   MARTIN WILKINSON AND ANDREW MOORE

the loss of freedom gives them a bargaining advantage over those who
want them to act in a way that is worse for them. But it is difficult to
evaluate this argument. It points out a truth, namely that sometimes
it is prudent to want not to be free. But it is also sometimes perfectly
prudent to want to be free. The argument merely points out a general
disadvantage of freedom. If it succeeds in ruling out voluntary
slavery, that may be because slavery is so bad. But in general, being
a subject in research is not so bad, whether or not one is paid for it. It is
at least as good as engaging in risky work, for instance, which few seek
to prohibit. In short, the non-paternalistic argument against
inducement fails.

Paternalism

Consider the following paternalistic argument against inducement. If
offered inducement, there is a risk that some subjects would volunteer
against their best interests. If there is this risk, then inducement should
not be allowed. So it should not be allowed.

The first premise of the paternalistic argument is that if offered
inducement, there is a risk that some subjects would volunteer against
their best interests. They might do so if they underestimate the risks of
volunteering, overestimate the benefits of being paid, or volunteer
despite their accurate assessment that doing so is against their
interests. For purposes of the paternalistic argument, it does not
matter whether researchers or subjects are responsible for these
failures.[17]

It is a difficult empirical question whether or not subjects tend to
act imprudently. Ethics committees should certainly not simply infer
from the claim that it is imprudent for people in their own generally
comfortable middle-class circumstances to volunteer, to the
conclusion that it is imprudent for research subjects to volunteer. This
inference is particularly unreliable for poor people, for whom
volunteering might be a perfectly prudent use of their time, when
compared to their alternatives. Still, it is hard to deny that if offered
inducements, some subjects might volunteer against their own best
interests.

Consider now the second premise of the paternalistic argument, the
claim that if there is an inducement-generated risk of some subjects
volunteering against their best interests, then inducement should not
be allowed. A major initial problem for this claim is that there is also a

[17] In their discussion of the infamous Tuskegee syphilis experiment, Faden and
Beauchamp seem to suggest that the researchers used money as a blind to persuade
would-be subjects not to consider the matter properly. See their pp. 165, 356.

risk of some subjects volunteering against their best interests even if they are not paid. If it is not to yield a prohibition of all research involving human subjects, the paternalistic argument must consequently claim that, compared with a no-inducement regime, an inducement regime is one in which more people volunteer against their best interests, and/or people act more against their best interests, and these differences are enough to justify paternalistic intervention. Why should one believe these claims? The fact that some people who would not otherwise volunteer would do so if offered inducement does not establish these claims, for the introduction of pay might make volunteering worthwhile for those people. Without a much better defence of the claim we have outlined, the paternalistic argument against inducement is a non-starter.

There are, of course, also general ethical worries about the legitimacy of paternalism. In our view, even the strongest arguments for paternalism justify that approach to inducements only if the effects of subjects volunteering against their best interests would be *harmful*.[18] Being interviewed for a dull and badly thought out management project, for example, might not be worth the sum offered, contrary to what the subjects originally thought, but their mistake would not harm them. Another difficulty is that disallowing inducement to protect some people harms others who do not need protection and would like to be induced. To make paternalism acceptable, it would need to be shown that the benefits to those who might be harmed in the absence of paternalistic intervention have greater ethical importance than the benefits to those who will not.

The difficulties we have just outlined would face even a successful paternalistic argument. They suffice to show that not all inducement could be prohibited on paternalistic grounds. Many readers might want to go further, and hold that any paternalistic approach is entirely unjustified. But we think there probably are some defensible cases of paternalism, and that it is important to show in a more fine-grained way that these fail to establish a case against inducement.

One defence of the paternalistic argument proceeds by way of analogy from certain claims about the duties of doctors. It could be argued that doctors have a duty not to offer treatment if they think it is clearly against the interests of their patients, whatever the patients themselves think. Suppose, for example, that a patient mistakenly thinks only a major and dangerous operation can cure her condition, although a simple and entirely harmless pill would in fact do so. Some would argue that her doctor has a duty not to operate on her, whether or not there is a duty to tell her that it is possible to do so. By analogy,

---

[18] See Feinberg, pp. 118–121.

one might think ethics committees have a duty not to allow researchers to offer subjects the opportunity to make money out of research if they think it is clearly against their interests to do so, no matter what the subjects think.

The argument we have just sketched for the paternalistic duties of doctors might in itself be defensible. One reason is that patients sometimes want dangerous operations, and doctors have expertise on these matters which patients generally lack. Another reason is that in such cases, the doctor is likely to know a lot about the patient's relevant circumstances. Neither analogous claim seems to be true of ethics committees. Firstly, it is not easy to argue that there is danger to paid subjects, if there is no danger when subjects in those same studies are not paid.[19] Secondly, any justifiable medical paternalism is undertaken in the light of highly individualised information about the patient, but in general, ethics committees can have no such knowledge of individual subjects. We conclude that even if paternalism can be justified in the medical case, it does not follow that ethics committee paternalism is justified concerning inducement.

Friends of ethics committee paternalism about inducement might now move to a different analogy. There are cases in which the state paternalistically requires health insurance or retirement contributions from citizens. It does this not on the basis of knowledge about individuals, but on the basis of general knowledge that people tend imprudently to discount the future. Might ethics committees require researchers not to pay subjects for analogous reasons? We think not. It is uncontroversial that ill health and poverty in old age are bad, but it is controversial that paid participation in research is in itself bad. Secondly, the evidence that people imprudently discount the future is relevant to state paternalism about health and retirement funds but irrelevant to research, except in the very rare cases in which bad consequences of study participation are likely to occur long afterward. We know of no other evidence of imprudent general human dispositions which would make the case of inducement analogous to the case of state compulsion concerning health or retirement funding.

In sum, we have found no clear welfare-based case against inducement. The non-paternalistic argument is at best inconclusive, and the paternalistic argument faces major problems. We have found no convincing argument that research subjects are not the best judges of their interests in this setting, or that they will not act on those interests.

[19] For one special case in which this argument can perhaps be made, see Section 5.

4. INDUCEMENT AND EXPLOITATION

It is sometimes thought that paying poor people, and perhaps anyone, to act as research subjects is exploitative. The exact nature of this concern is unclear, mainly because the idea of exploitation is unclear.

On one account, people are exploited when they do not receive the full value of their labour product. We doubt that exploitation in this sense need be wrong.[20] But even if it is wrong, the solution in the case of research is to require bigger inducements, not to prohibit them. This variant of the argument from exploitation backfires on opponents of inducement.

Allen Wood has recently argued for the following alternative account of exploitation, which is well suited to our discussion:

> When people, or something about them, are its objects, exploitation consists in the exploiter's using something about the person for the exploiter's ends by playing on some weakness or vulnerability in that person.[21]

On Wood's account, an exploitative offer actually increases the exploitee's options, and also benefits that person, usually by more than it benefits the exploiter. Wood also argues that exploitation is not necessarily coercive, and that exploitees might well give their fully voluntary consent to it, and have acceptable alternatives.[22] Despite all this, he argues that exploitation is bad:

> Proper respect for others is violated when we treat their vulnerabilities as opportunities to advance our own interests or projects. It is degrading to have your weaknesses taken advantage of, and dishonorable to use the weaknesses of others for your ends.[23]

Let us accept Wood's account of the nature and moral badness of exploitation. Who might be exploited if inducement is allowed in research? The only plausible candidates are those who would not have volunteered but for the money and, within that group, those who need the money. Generalising somewhat, we shall call these people 'the poor'.[24]

---

[20] For valuable and sceptical discussion of the idea of exploitation as theft of labour product, see P. van Parijs, *Real Freedom For All* (Oxford, 1995), ch. 5; and G. Cohen, *Self-Ownership, Freedom, and Equality* (Cambridge, 1995), ch. 6.

[21] A. Wood, 'Exploitation', *Social Philosophy and Policy*, 1995, p. 147.

[22] Wood, pp. 147–9.

[23] Wood, pp. 150–1.

[24] Note that exploitation is avoided if the non-poor are the only subjects paid. This can be done by making poverty an exclusion criterion for research subjects. We assume, however, that this is objectionable on other grounds.

384   MARTIN WILKINSON AND ANDREW MOORE

An ethics committee might have agent-neutral concerns about the exploitation of subjects, and in particular, reasons which hold regardless of whether or not it participates itself in exploitation. The committee might in addition or alternatively have agent-relative concerns, and in particular, reasons concerning its own participation in exploitation. For example, committee approval of research protocols which involve exploitative inducements might be regarded as ethics committee participation in the exploitation of subjects.

The existence, nature, and strength of agent-relative and agent-neutral reasons are matters of controversy.[25] We shall sidestep these general issues, simply by assuming that reasons of both kinds exist, and by considering exploitation-based arguments of both sorts against inducement.

Consider the agent-neutral reasons an ethics committee might have to prevent exploitation of subjects, whoever the exploiter might be. Let us simply assume straight away that inducement of the poor to be research subjects is bad exploitation, and that ethics committees have agent-neutral reason to disallow it. Even given these assumptions, we still do not have a persuasive agent-neutral case against inducement. One reason arises from the fact that on Wood's account, exploitation is a pervasive feature of the social life of human beings. As he notes, it '. . . is endemic to all . . . transactions whose terms are significantly affected by the fact that the participants are in unequal bargaining positions'.[26] In virtually all their exchanges with people more powerful than themselves, including their alternatives to accepting inducement and their acceptance of invitations to be unpaid research subjects, the poor are exploited. Those who wish to make an agent-neutral argument from exploitation must consequently argue that exploitation comes in different amounts, and that there is more of it in inducement than in the alternatives open to the poor. As far as we know, they have yet to make any such case.

The following argument suggests that inducement is in fact less exploitative than are the alternatives open to the poor. Suppose the

---

[25] For a sample of the large literature on these topics, see T. Nagel, *The View From Nowhere*, New York and Oxford: Oxford University Press, 1986, especially ch. IX; S. Scheffler, *The Rejection of Consequentialism*, Oxford: Clarendon Press, 1982; D. Parfit, *Reasons and Persons*, Oxford: Clarendon Press, 1984, section 57; S. Kagan, *The Limits of Morality*, Oxford: Clarendon Press, 1989; J. Dancy, 'Agent-relativity — the very idea', in R. Frey and C. Morris (eds.), *Value, Welfare, and Morality*, New York and Cambridge: Cambridge University Press, 1993; and C. Korsgaard, 'The reasons we can share', in E. Paul and F. Miller (eds.) *Altruism*, New York and London: Cambridge University Press, 1993.

[26] Wood, p. 156.

amount of exploitation is a function of the extent to which the preferences of the exploitees are fulfilled. By hypothesis, paid subjects prefer this to any available alternative, otherwise they would not volunteer. If denied that option, they would have to do something they prefer less. On this measure of exploitation, they would therefore be even more exploited, and denying them the option of inducement would increase their exploitation. It follows that an ethics committee with agent-neutral reason to prevent exploitation of the poor has all-things-considered reason of this sort to allow inducement.

Furthermore, if ethics committees have agent-neutral reasons for action, these include not just reasons to prevent exploitation of subjects, but also reasons to promote subject freedom and welfare. As we argued above, both sorts of reasons support inducement. In short, considerations of exploitation do not generate any agent-neutral case against inducement, and considerations of subject freedom and welfare generate a case to allow it. Overall, then, there is an agent-neutral case in favour of inducement.

Turn now to the agent-relative argument from exploitation. Again, let us simply assume that ethics committees which allow inducement thereby participate in exploitation, and have agent-relative reason not to. It is in the nature of agent-relativity that this reason would be undefeated even if disallowing inducement were to result in greater exploitation of would-be subjects. We have assumed that there is such an agent-relative reason. This is something an opponent of inducement would need to argue, but even if there is such a reason, it makes no clear case specifically against inducement. One reason is that on Wood's account, it will often be bad exploitation to invite the poor to be research subjects, even without inducement. It follows that there is no distinctive objection to those invitations which are also inducements. Even if there is an agent-relative argument from exploitation which singles out inducements, the case is still not clear, for there are conflicting agent-relative reasons here. If ethics committees have agent-relative reasons for action, it is plausible that these include reasons to benefit subjects, and to facilitate their voluntary decisions. Yet ethics committees which disallow inducement thereby decide not to benefit subjects financially, and to rule out volunteering for pay.

In short, if ethics committees have agent-relative reasons for action, they have harm-related and freedom-related reasons of this sort to allow inducements, and exploitation-related reasons to disallow them. To make good their argument from exploitation, opponents of inducement must resolve this conflict among agent-relative reasons by showing that the exploitation-related reasons defeat those which concern the freedom and welfare of subjects.

In summary, an exploitation argument must show: (1) that ethics committees which allow inducement thereby participate in exploitation; (2) that this generates an agent-relative case specifically against inducement in research; (3) that this exploitation argument defeats opposing arguments from subject freedom and welfare; and (4) that it also defeats agent-neutral reasons of exploitation, freedom, and benefit, which largely favour inducement. An exploitation argument could in principle meet all these conditions, but we have yet to find any actual argument which does so, and we doubt that we will find one.

Those who are concerned about the exploitation of research subjects might understandably still feel troubled. It *is* appalling that someone should participate in unpleasant research because, for instance, she cannot pay her children's medical bills. The fact that some people are in these situations is appalling, but in our view, the fact that researchers offer these people inducements is not. The poor might well be in these situations as a result of fundamental social injustice, but ethics committee decisions will not make that go away. They must decide, against this background, whether or not to allow inducements. If they are concerned to help the poor, it is hard to see how denying them the option to make money through research helps. Even if they share instead Allen Wood's view that '*solidarity* with them [is] a far more vital achievement than any positive contribution to their welfare',[27] it is still hard to see how denying the poor the option to make money through research achieves even that goal.

5.   SUBJECT SELECTION BIAS

According to the argument from subject selection bias, if inducements are allowed in research, this will undermine the science and consequently the ethics of these studies. A more formal version of the argument is this: (1) inducements bias subject selection, (2) biased subject selection makes for bad science, (3) bad science is always ethically bad science, and (4) ethics committees should not allow ethically bad science; therefore, (5) ethics committees should not allow inducements.

In our view, the argument from subject selection bias is not persuasive. To begin with, there is an important scope problem with (1), the claim that inducements bias subject selection. It is plausible that this sometimes happens, but it is also plausible that inducements sometimes reduce or prevent bias. This happens whenever relevant individuals or groups will not agree to be subjects unless they are paid.

[27] Wood, p. 153.

We conclude that since (1) is false of some inducements, it cannot ground a general argument against them. Subject selection bias consequently has to be looked at case by case.

Premise (2) of the argument claims that biased subject selection makes for bad science. This claim inherits the scope problem of premise (1), and adds a further problem of the same sort. Subject selection bias is hard to eliminate altogether, and in general, scientists should look for the least biased method amongst the feasible and scientifically worthwhile alternatives. Even if inducement always introduces selection bias, this does not show that it always or even usually generates bad science. Roughly speaking, the addition of inducements to a subject selection method turns good science into bad only if there is a scientifically worthwhile and feasible alternative study design which is free of inducements, and which generates less bias.

Finally, consider (3), the claim that bad science is always ethically bad science. The standard justification for this is that research always imposes costs on subjects, and these are unjustified unless the science of the study is good. We agree that research always imposes costs on subjects, though these are often small. We also agree that these costs should be justified. One attempt to do so points out that subjects voluntarily incur these costs. It is plausible, however, that some subjects volunteer only because they think they are doing something worthwhile. If the science is poor, and subjects are not paid, then they are not doing anything worthwhile. If they are paid, however, this offsets their costs, and if they are paid enough, participation will actually be a benefit to them overall, even if the science is bad. Any residual concern about the voluntariness of participation of subjects who wish only to be involved in *scientifically* worthwhile studies can be met by requiring researchers whose studies do not meet this standard to state this on their subject information sheet.

To sum up: if subjects are sufficiently well paid, then bad science imposes no net cost on them. Nor need the voluntariness of their participation be compromised.[28] Bad science can thus be ethically acceptable, especially when subjects are adequately paid for their part in it.

Three premises of the argument from subject selection bias are false, at least if they are taken to have the broad scope they need to make a general case against inducements. We conclude that the argument as a whole fails.

[28] One further argument for the inference from bad science to bad ethics appeals to the waste of researcher time and money it involves. This issue need trouble only researchers themselves, and their funding bodies.

388   MARTIN WILKINSON AND ANDREW MOORE

Biased subject selection can nevertheless generate serious ethical problems in one sort of case. We call this the excluded subject case. The worry is that pay might induce the participation of financially hard-pressed people who are ineligible to participate under a study's exclusion criteria. Consider, for example, a poor person with a heart condition which would exclude her from a pharmaceutical study, who is tempted to deny its existence so she can secure the $100 fee for subjects, and thus feed her children. It seems that any ethics committee which allows inducement makes excluded participation in her sort of case more likely than it would otherwise be. Serious injury or even death to one or more subjects might result. Legal liability and damage to the study's science might also result, but we shall assume that these are issues primarily for researchers, their sponsors and their employers, rather than for ethics committees.

Not all excluded subjects cases are ethically worrying. For example, studies with no harm-related exclusion criteria are not a concern. Where there is at least one harm-related exclusion criterion, ethics committees should determine whether adequate methods are available, independent of subject self-report, for checking subject eligibility. If such methods are available, ethics committees should simply require researchers to use them. No prohibition on inducement is needed.

That leaves studies with at least one harm-related exclusion criterion, and no adequate independent method for researchers to check potential subjects against it. Ethics committees should probably not allow these studies to proceed at all. If they are allowed to proceed, on condition that they do not involve inducement, then excluded subjects might still participate at significant risk to themselves. They might do so because they are ignorant of their own excluded conditions, because they overlook or misunderstand harm-related exclusion criteria, or because they are disposed to please researchers and to believe they always want volunteers. Opponents of inducement must argue that ethics committees take an acceptable risk when they approve studies without inducement, but with at least one harm-related exclusion criterion against which researchers have no adequate independent method to check potential subjects. They must also argue that the addition of inducement turns these acceptably risky studies into unacceptably risky studies. As far as we know, opponents of inducement have not argued for these claims. We do not insist that the required arguments cannot be made. We conclude merely that at most, there is a very narrow range of excluded subject cases in which ethics committees should disallow inducements.

6. CONCLUSION

We have argued that there is an international orthodoxy opposed to inducement payments for research subjects, and we have presented a *prima facie* case against this orthodoxy. In examining arguments for the orthodoxy, we concentrated on those which appeal to features of the individual research studies in which inducements are offered, and we considered the strongest case we could find or devise. No argument for the orthodoxy based on consent or welfare was persuasive. Nor were any of the arguments from exploitation. That left only arguments from subject selection bias, and here, at most one quite narrow set of circumstances presented difficulties for inducement. With this single possible exception, then, we have found the arguments against inducement in research to be unpersuasive.

Department of Political Studies   *Department of Philosophy*
University of Auckland   *University of Otago*

[31]

UNETHICAL TRIALS OF INTERVENTIONS TO REDUCE PERINATAL TRANSMISSION OF THE HUMAN IMMUNODEFICIENCY VIRUS IN DEVELOPING COUNTRIES

P. Lurie and S.M. Wolfe

IT has been almost three years since the *Journal*[1] published the results of AIDS Clinical Trials Group (ACTG) Study 076, the first randomized, controlled trial in which an intervention was proved to reduce the incidence of human immunodeficiency virus (HIV) infection. The antiretroviral drug zidovudine, administered orally to HIV-positive pregnant women in the United States and France, administered intravenously during labor, and subsequently administered to the newborn infants, reduced the incidence of HIV infection by two thirds.[2] The regimen can save the life of one of every seven infants born to HIV-infected women.

Because of these findings, the study was terminated at the first interim analysis and within two months after the results had been announced, the Public Health Service had convened a meeting and concluded that the ACTG 076 regimen should be recommended for all HIV-positive pregnant women without substantial prior exposure to zidovudine and should be considered for other HIV-positive pregnant women on a case-by-case basis.[3] The standard of care for HIV-positive pregnant women thus became the ACTG 076 regimen.

In the United States, three recent studies of clinical practice report that the use of the ACTG 076 regimen is associated with decreases of 50 percent or more in perinatal HIV transmission.[4-6] But in developing countries, especially in Asia and sub-Saharan Africa, where it is projected that by the year 2000, 6 million pregnant women will be infected with HIV,[7] the potential of the ACTG 076 regimen remains unrealized primarily because of the drug's exorbitant cost in most countries.

Clearly, a regimen that is less expensive than ACTG 076 but as effective is desirable, in both developing and industrialized countries. But there has been uncertainty about what research design to use in the search for a less expensive regimen. In June 1994, the World Health Organization (WHO) convened a group in Geneva to assess the agenda for research on perinatal HIV transmission in the wake of ACTG 076. The group, which included no ethicists, concluded, "Placebo-controlled trials offer the best option for a rapid and scientifically valid assessment of alternative antiretroviral drug regimens to prevent [perinatal] transmission of HIV."[8] This unpublished document has been widely cited as justification for subsequent trials in developing countries. In our view, most of these trials are unethical and will lead to hundreds of preventable HIV infections in infants.

Primarily on the basis of documents obtained from the Centers for Disease Control and Prevention (CDC), we have identified 18 randomized, controlled trials of interventions to prevent perinatal HIV transmission that either began to enroll patients after the ACTG 076 study was completed or have not yet begun to enroll patients. The studies are designed to evaluate a variety of interventions: antiretroviral drugs such as zidovudine (usually in regimens that are less expensive or complex than the ACTG 076 regimen), vitamin A and its derivatives, intrapartum vaginal washing, and HIV immune globulin, a form of immunotherapy. These trials involve a total of more than 17,000 women.

In the two studies being performed in the United States, the patients in all the study groups have unrestricted access to zidovudine or other antiretroviral drugs. In 15 of the 16 trials in developing countries, however, some or all of the patients are not provided with antiretroviral drugs. Nine of the 15 studies being conducted outside the United States are funded by the U.S. government through the CDC or the National Institutes of Health (NIH), 5 are funded by other governments, and 1 is funded by the United Nations AIDS Program. The studies are being conducted in Côte d'Ivoire, Uganda, Tanzania, South Africa, Malawi, Thailand, Ethiopia, Burkina Faso, Zimbabwe, Kenya, and the Dominican Republic. These 15 studies clearly violate recent guidelines designed specifically to address ethical issues pertaining to studies in developing countries. According to these guidelines, "The ethical standards applied should be no less exacting than they would be in the case of research carried out in [the sponsoring] country."[9] In addition, U.S. regulations governing studies performed with federal funds domestically or abroad specify that research procedures must "not unnecessarily expose subjects to risk."[10]

The 16th study is noteworthy both as a model of an ethically conducted study attempting to identify less expensive antiretroviral regimens and as an indication of how strong the placebo-controlled trial orthodoxy is. In 1994, Marc Lallemant, a researcher at the Harvard School of Public Health, applied for NIH funding for an equivalency study in Thailand in which three shorter zidovudine regimens were to be compared with a regimen similar to that used in the ACTG 076 study. An equivalency study is typically conducted when a particular regimen has already been proved effective and one is interested in determining whether a second regimen is about as effective but less toxic or expensive.[11] The NIH study section repeatedly put pressure on Lallemant and the Harvard School of Public Health to conduct a

The New England Journal of Medicine

placebo-controlled trial instead, prompting the director of Harvard's human subjects committee to reply, "The conduct of a placebo-controlled trial for [zidovudine] in pregnant women in Thailand would be unethical and unacceptable, since an active-controlled trial is feasible."[12] The NIH eventually relented, and the study is now under way. Since the nine studies of antiretroviral drugs have attracted the most attention, we focus on them in this article.

ASKING THE WRONG RESEARCH QUESTION

There are numerous areas of agreement between those conducting or defending these placebo-controlled studies in developing countries and those opposing such trials. The two sides agree that perinatal HIV transmission is a grave problem meriting concerted international attention; that the ACTG 076 trial was a major breakthrough in perinatal HIV prevention; that there is a role for research on this topic in developing countries; that identifying less expensive, similarly effective interventions would be of enormous benefit, given the limited resources for medical care in most developing countries; and that randomized studies can help identify such interventions.

The sole point of disagreement is the best comparison group to use in assessing the effectiveness of less-expensive interventions once an effective intervention has been identified. The researchers conducting the placebo-controlled trials assert that such trials represent the only appropriate research design, implying that they answer the question, "Is the shorter regimen better than nothing?" We take the more optimistic view that, given the findings of ACTG 076 and other clinical information, researchers are quite capable of designing a shorter antiretroviral regimen that is approximately as effective as the ACTG 076 regimen. The proposal for the Harvard study in Thailand states the research question clearly: "Can we reduce the duration of prophylactic [zidovudine] treatment without increasing the risk of perinatal transmission of HIV, that is, without compromising the demonstrated efficacy of the standard ACTG 076 [zidovudine] regimen?"[13] We believe that such equivalency studies of alternative antiretroviral regimens will provide even more useful results than placebo-controlled trials, without the deaths of hundreds of newborns that are inevitable if placebo groups are used.

At a recent congressional hearing on research ethics, NIH director Harold Varmus was asked how the Department of Health and Human Services could be funding both a placebo-controlled trial (through the CDC) and a non–placebo-controlled equivalency study (through the NIH) in Thailand. Dr. Varmus conceded that placebo-controlled studies are "not the only way to achieve results."[14] If the research can be satisfactorily conducted in more than one way, why not select the approach that minimizes loss of life?

INADEQUATE ANALYSIS OF DATA FROM ACTG 076 AND OTHER SOURCES

The NIH, CDC, WHO, and the researchers conducting the studies we consider unethical argue that differences in the duration and route of administration of antiretroviral agents in the shorter regimens, as compared with the ACTG 076 regimen, justify the use of a placebo group.[15-18] Given that ACTG 076 was a well-conducted, randomized, controlled trial, it is disturbing that the rich data available from the study were not adequately used by the group assembled by WHO in June 1994, which recommended placebo-controlled trials after ACTG 076, or by the investigators of the 15 studies we consider unethical.

In fact, the ACTG 076 investigators conducted a subgroup analysis to identify an appropriate period for prepartum administration of zidovudine. The approximate median duration of prepartum treatment was 12 weeks. In a comparison of treatment for 12 weeks or less (average, 7) with treatment for more than 12 weeks (average, 17), there was no univariate association between the duration of treatment and its effect in reducing perinatal HIV transmission (P = 0.99) (Gelber R: personal communication). This analysis is somewhat limited by the number of infected infants and its post hoc nature. However, when combined with information such as the fact that in non–breast-feeding populations an estimated 65 percent of cases of perinatal HIV infection are transmitted during delivery and 95 percent of the remaining cases are transmitted within two months of delivery,[19] the analysis *suggests* that the shorter regimens may be equally effective. This finding should have been explored in later studies by randomly assigning women to longer or shorter treatment regimens.

What about the argument that the use of the oral route for intrapartum administration of zidovudine in the present trials (as opposed to the intravenous route in ACTG 076) justifies the use of a placebo? In its protocols for its two studies in Thailand and Côte d'Ivoire, the CDC acknowledged that previous "pharmacokinetic modelling data suggest that [zidovudine] serum levels obtained with this [oral] dose will be similar to levels obtained with an intravenous infusion."[20]

Thus, on the basis of the ACTG 076 data, knowledge about the timing of perinatal transmission, and pharmacokinetic data, the researchers should have had every reason to believe that well-designed shorter regimens would be more effective than placebo. These findings seriously disturb the equipoise (uncertainty over the likely study result) necessary to justify a placebo-controlled trial on ethical grounds.[21]

DEFINING PLACEBO AS THE STANDARD OF CARE IN DEVELOPING COUNTRIES

Some officials and researchers have defended the use of placebo-controlled studies in developing countries by arguing that the subjects are treated at least according to the standard of care in these countries, which consists of unproven regimens or no treatment at all. This assertion reveals a fundamental misunderstanding of the concept of the standard of care. In developing countries, the standard of care (in this case, not providing zidovudine to HIV-positive pregnant women) is not based on a consideration of alternative treatments or previous clinical data, but is instead an economically determined policy of governments that cannot afford the prices set by drug companies. We agree with the Council for International Organizations of Medical Sciences that researchers working in developing countries have an ethical responsibility to provide treatment that conforms to the standard of care in the sponsoring country, when possible.[9] An exception would be a standard of care that required an exorbitant expenditure, such as the cost of building a coronary care unit. Since zidovudine is usually made available free of charge by the manufacturer for use in clinical trials, excessive cost is not a factor in this case. Acceptance of a standard of care that does not conform to the standard in the sponsoring country results in a double standard in research. Such a double standard, which permits research designs that are unacceptable in the sponsoring country, creates an incentive to use as research subjects those with the least access to health care.

What are the potential implications of accepting such a double standard? Researchers might inject live malaria parasites into HIV-positive subjects in China in order to study the effect on the progression of HIV infection, even though the study protocol had been rejected in the United States and Mexico. Or researchers might randomly assign malnourished San (bushmen) to receive vitamin-fortified or standard bread. One might also justify trials of HIV vaccines in which the subjects were not provided with condoms or state-of-the-art counseling about safe sex by arguing that they are not customarily provided in the developing countries in question. These are not simply hypothetical worst-case scenarios; the first two studies have already been performed,[22,23] and the third has been proposed and criticized.[24]

Annas and Grodin recently commented on the characterization and justification of placebos as a standard of care: "'Nothing' is a description of what happens; 'standard of care' is a normative standard of effective medical treatment, whether or not it is provided to a particular community."[25]

JUSTIFYING PLACEBO-CONTROLLED TRIALS BY CLAIMING THEY ARE MORE RAPID

Researchers have also sought to justify placebo-controlled trials by arguing that they require fewer subjects than equivalency studies and can therefore be completed more rapidly. Because equivalency studies are simply concerned with excluding alternative interventions that fall below some preestablished level of efficacy (as opposed to establishing which intervention is superior), it is customary to use one-sided statistical testing in such studies.[11] The numbers of women needed for a placebo-controlled trial and an equivalency study are similar.[26] In a placebo-controlled trial of a short course of zidovudine, with rates of perinatal HIV transmission of 25 percent in the placebo group and 15 percent in the zidovudine group, an alpha level of 0.05 (two-sided), and a beta level of 0.2, 500 subjects would be needed. An equivalency study with a transmission rate of 10 percent in the group receiving the ACTG 076 regimen, a difference in efficacy of 6 percent (above the 10 percent), an alpha level of 0.05 (one-sided), and a beta level of 0.2 would require 620 subjects (McCarthy W: personal communication).

TOWARD A SINGLE INTERNATIONAL STANDARD OF ETHICAL RESEARCH

Researchers assume greater ethical responsibilities when they enroll subjects in clinical studies, a precept acknowledged by Varmus recently when he insisted that all subjects in an NIH-sponsored needle-exchange trial be offered hepatitis B vaccine.[27] Residents of impoverished, postcolonial countries, the majority of whom are people of color, must be protected from potential exploitation in research. Otherwise, the abominable state of health care in these countries can be used to justify studies that could never pass ethical muster in the sponsoring country.

With the increasing globalization of trade, government research dollars becoming scarce, and more attention being paid to the hazards posed by "emerging infections" to the residents of industrialized countries, it is likely that studies in developing countries will increase. It is time to develop standards of research that preclude the kinds of double standards evident in these trials. In an editorial published nine years ago in the *Journal*, Marcia Angell stated, "Human subjects in any part of the world should be protected by an irreducible set of ethical standards."[28] Tragically, for the hundreds of infants who have needlessly contracted HIV infection in the perinatal-transmission studies that have already been completed, any such protection will have come too late.

PETER LURIE, M.D., M.P.H.
SIDNEY M. WOLFE, M.D.
Public Citizen's Health Research Group
Washington, DC 20009

REFERENCES

1. Connor EM, Sperling RS, Gelber R, et al. Reduction of maternal–infant transmission of human immunodeficiency virus type 1 with zidovudine treatment. N Engl J Med 1994;331:1173-80.

The New England Journal of Medicine

2. Sperling RS, Shapiro DE, Coombs RW, et al. Maternal viral load, zido-vudine treatment, and the risk of transmission of human immunodeficiency virus type 1 from mother to infant. N Engl J Med 1996;335:1621-9.

3. Recommendations of the U.S. Public Health Service Task Force on the use of zidovudine to reduce perinatal transmission of human immunodeficiency virus. MMWR Morb Mortal Wkly Rep 1994;43(RR-11):1-20.

4. Fiscus SA, Adimora AA, Schoenbach VJ, et al. Perinatal HIV infection and the effect of zidovudine therapy on transmission in rural and urban counties. JAMA 1996;275:1483-8.

5. Cooper E, Diaz C, Pitt J, et al. Impact of ACTG 076: use of zidovudine during pregnancy and changes in the rate of HIV vertical transmission. In: Program and abstracts of the Third Conference on Retroviruses and Opportunistic Infections, Washington, D.C., January 28–February 1, 1996. Washington, D.C.: Infectious Diseases Society of America, 1996:57.

6. Simonds RJ, Nesheim S, Matheson P, et al. Declining mother to child HIV transmission following perinatal ZDV recommendations. Presented at the 11th International Conference on AIDS, Vancouver, Canada, July 7–12, 1996. abstract.

7. Scarlatti G. Paediatric HIV infection. Lancet 1996;348:863-8.

8. Recommendations from the meeting on mother-to-infant transmission of HIV by use of antiretrovirals, Geneva, World Health Organization, June 23–25, 1994.

9. World Health Organization. International ethical guidelines for biomedical research involving human subjects. Geneva: Council for International Organizations of Medical Sciences, 1993.

10. 45 CFR 46.111(a)(1).

11. Testing equivalence of two binomial proportions. In: Machin D, Campbell MJ. Statistical tables for the design of clinical trials. Oxford, England: Blackwell Scientific, 1987:35-53.

12. Brennan TA. Letter to Gilbert Meier, NIH Division of Research Ethics, December 28, 1994.

13. Lallemant M, Vithayasai V. A short ZDV course to prevent perinatal HIV in Thailand. Boston: Harvard School of Public Health, April 28, 1995.

14. Varmus H. Testimony before the Subcommittee on Human Resources, Committee on Government Reform and Oversight, U.S. House of Representatives, May 8, 1997.

15. Draft talking points: responding to Public Citizen press conference. Press release of the National Institutes of Health, April 22, 1997.

16. Questions and answers: CDC studies of AZT to prevent mother-to-child HIV transmission in developing countries. Press release of the Centers for Disease Control and Prevention, Atlanta. (undated document.)

17. Questions and answers on the UNAIDS sponsored trials for the prevention of mother-to-child transmission: background brief to assist in responding to issues raised by the public and the media. Press release of the United Nations AIDS Program. (undated document.)

18. Halsey NA, Meinert CL, Ruff AJ, et al. Letter to Harold Varmus, Director of National Institutes of Health. Baltimore: Johns Hopkins University, May 6, 1997.

19. Wiktor SZ, Ehounou E. A randomized placebo-controlled intervention study to evaluate the safety and effectiveness of oral zidovudine administered in late pregnancy to reduce the incidence of mother-to-child transmission of HIV-1 in Abidjan, Cote D'Ivoire. Atlanta: Centers for Disease Control and Prevention. (undated document.)

20. Rouzioux C, Costagliola D, Burgard M, et al. Timing of mother-to-child HIV-1 transmission depends on maternal status. AIDS 1993;7:Suppl 2:S49-S52.

21. Freedman B. Equipoise and the ethics of clinical research. N Engl J Med 1987;317:141-5.

22. Heimlich HJ, Chen XP, Xiao BQ, et al. CD4 response in HIV-positive patients treated with malaria therapy. Presented at the 11th International Conference on AIDS, Vancouver, B.C., July 7–12, 1996. abstract.

23. Bishop WB, Laubscher I, Labadarios D, Rehder P, Louw ME, Fellingham SA. Effect of vitamin-enriched bread on the vitamin status of an isolated rural community — a controlled clinical trial. S Afr Med J 1996;86:Suppl:458-62.

24. Lurie P, Bishaw M, Chesney MA, et al. Ethical, behavioral, and social aspects of HIV vaccine trials in developing countries. JAMA 1994;271:295-301.

25. Annas G, Grodin M. An apology is not enough. Boston Globe. May 18, 1997:C1-C2.

26. Freedman B, Weijer C, Glass KC. Placebo orthodoxy in clinical research. I. Empirical and methodological myths. J Law Med Ethics 1996;24:243-51.

27. Varmus H. Comments at the meeting of the Advisory Committee to the Director of the National Institutes of Health, December 12, 1996.

28. Angell M. Ethical imperialism? Ethics in international collaborative clinical research. N Engl J Med 1988;319:1081-3.

[32]

Moral Standards for Research in Developing Countries

From "Reasonable Availability" to "Fair Benefits"

by THE PARTICIPANTS IN THE 2001 CONFERENCE ON
ETHICAL ASPECTS OF RESEARCH IN DEVELOPING COUNTRIES

Commentators have argued that when research conducted in a developing country shows an intervention to be effective, the intervention must be made "reasonably available" to the host population after the trial. But this standard is sometimes too stringent, and sometimes too lenient. It offers a benefit, but not necessarily a *fair* benefit.

Over the last decade, clinical research conducted by sponsors and researchers from developed countries in developing countries has grown very controversial.[1] The perinatal HIV transmission studies that were sponsored by the National Institutes of Health and the Centers for Disease Control and conducted in Southeast Asia and Africa inflamed this controversy and focused it on the standard of care—that is, on whether treatments tested in developing countries should be compared to the treatments provided locally or to the best interventions available anywhere.[2] Since then, this debate has expanded to include concerns about informed consent.

A subject that has received less discussion but is potentially even more important is the requirement that any drugs proven effective in the trial be made available to the host population after the trial.[3] There seems to be general agreement that "reasonable availability" is necessary in order to ensure that the subject population is not exploited.

This consensus is mistaken, however. A "fair benefits" framework offers a more reliable and justifiable way to avoid exploitation. In this paper we develop the argument for the fair benefits framework in detail and compare the two approaches in a specific case—the trail of hepatitis A vaccine in Thailand.

Current Views on the Reasonable Availability Requirement

The idea of making interventions reasonably available was emphasized in the *International*

The participants in the 2001 Conference on Ethical Aspects of Research in Developing Countries, "Moral Standards for Research in Developing Countries: From 'Reasonable Availability' to 'Fair Benefits,'" *Hastings Center Report* 34, no. 3 (2004): 17-27.

Ethical Guidelines issued in 1993 by the Council for International Organizations of Medical Sciences (CIOMS), and it was reiterated in the 2002 revision in Guideline 10 and its commentary.

As a general rule, the sponsoring agency should agree in advance of the research that any product developed through such research will be made reasonably available to the inhabitants of the host community or country at the completion of successful testing. Exceptions to this general requirement should be justified and agreed to by all concerned parties before the research begins.[4]

Four issues have generated disagreement. First, how strong or explicit should the commitment to provide the drug or vaccine be at the initiation of the research trial? CIOMS required an explicit, contract-like mechanism, agreed to before the trial, and it assigns this responsibility to the sponsors of research. The Declaration of Helsinki's 2000 revision endorses a less stringent guarantee that does not require availability of interventions to be "ensured" "in advance."[5] Several other ethical guidelines suggest "discussion in advance" but do not require formal, prior agreements.[6] Conversely, some commentators insist that the CIOMS guarantee is "not strong or specific enough."[7] For instance, the chair and executive director of the U.S. National Bioethics Advisory Commission (NBAC) contended:

If the intervention being tested is not likely to be affordable in the

host country or if the health care infrastructure cannot support its proper distribution and use, it is unethical to ask persons in that country to participate in the research, since they will not enjoy any of its potential benefits.[8]

To address these concerns, others advocate that research in developing countries ethically requires a formal and explicit prior agreement that "includes identified funding" and specifies improvements necessary in the "country's health care delivery capabilities."[9]

The second area of disagreement has concerned who is responsible for ensuring reasonable availability. Are sponsors responsible, as the original CIOMS guideline called for? Does responsibility rest with host country governments? Or international aid organizations? The third area of disagreement focuses on what it means for drugs to be made reasonable available. Does it require that the drug or vaccine be free, subsidized, or at market prices?

Finally, to whom should interventions be made reasonably available? Should they be restricted to participants in the research study? Should they include the village or tribe from which individual participants were enrolled? Or the whole country in which the research was conducted?

The Justification of Reasonable Availability

Why is reasonable availability thought to be a requirement for ethical research in developing countries? Research uses participants to develop generalizable knowledge that can improve health and health care for others.[10] The potential for exploitation of individual participants enrolled in research as well as communities that support and bear the burdens of research is inherent in every research trial. Historically, favorable risk-benefit ratios, informed consent, and respect for enrolled participants have been the primary

mechanisms for minimizing the potential exploitation of individual research participants.[11] In developed countries, exploitation of populations has been a less significant concern because there is a process, albeit an imperfect one, for ensuring that interventions proven effective through clinical research are introduced into the health care system and benefit the general population.[12] In contrast, the potential for exploitation is acute in research trials in developing countries. Target populations may lack access to regular health care, political power, and an understanding of research. Hence, they may be exposed to the risks of research with few tangible benefits. The benefits of research—access to new effective drugs and vaccines—may be predominantly for people in developed countries with profits to the pharmaceutical industry. Many consider this scenario the quintessential case of exploitation.[13]

Supporters deem that reasonable availability is necessary to prevent such exploitation of communities. As one group of commentators put it:

[I]n order for research to be ethically conducted [in a developing country] it must offer the potential of actual benefit to the inhabitants of that developing country. . . . [F]or underdeveloped communities to derive potential benefit from research, they must have access to the *fruits* of such research.[14] (emphasis added)

Or as the commentary to the 2002 CIOMS Guideline 10 put it:

[I]f the knowledge gained from the research in such a country [with limited resources] is used primarily for the benefit of populations that can afford the tested product, the research may rightly be characterized as exploitative and, therefore, unethical.[15]

What Is Exploitation?

Even though it seems initially plausible, there are a number of problems with making reasonable availability a necessary ethical requirement for multinational research in developing countries. The most important problem is that the reasonable availability requirement embodies a mistaken conception of exploitation and therefore offers wrong solution to the problem of exploitation.

There are numerous ways of harming other individuals, only one of which is exploitation. Oppression, coercion, assault, deception, betrayal, and discrimination are all distinct ways of harming people. They are frequently all conflated and confused with exploitation.[16] One reason for distinguishing these different wrongs is that they require very different remedies. Addressing coercion requires removing threats, and addressing deception requires full disclosure, yet removing threats and requiring full disclosure will not necessarily prevent exploitation.

What is exploitation? In the useful analysis developed by Alan Wertheimer, Party A exploits party B when B receives an unfair level of benefits as a result of B's interactions with A.[17] Whether B's benefits are fair depends upon the burdens that B bears as part of the interaction and the benefits that A and others receive as a result of B's participation in the interaction. If B runs his car into a snow bank and A offers to tow him out but only at the cost of $200— when the normal and fair price for the tow is $75—then A exploits B.

Wertheimer's conception of exploitation is distinct from the conventional idea that exploitation entails the "use" of someone else for one's own benefit. There are many problems with this familiar conception. Most importantly, if exploitation is made to depend only on instrumental use of another person, then almost all human interactions are exploitative. We constantly and necessarily use other people.[18] In the example above, not only does A exploit B, but B also exploits A, because B uses A to get his car out of the snow bank. Sometimes the word "exploit" refers to a *neutral* use—as when we say that a person exploited the minerals or his own strength. However, in discussions of research, especially but not exclusively when the research occurs in developing countries, exploitation is never neutral; it is always a moral wrong. Consequently, we do not need to mark out all cases of use. We need only to identify those that are morally problematic.[19]

The Wertheimerian conception of exploitation also departs from the commonly cited Kantian conception. As Allan Buchanan characterizes the Kantian conception, "To exploit a person involves the *harmful, merely instrumental utilization* of him or his capacities, for one's own advantage or for the sake of one's own ends."[20] The Kantian conception of exploitation seems to expand beyond use to include a separate harm. But in the case of exploitation, what is this "other harm"? For a Kantian, *to exploit* must mean to use in a way that the other person could not consent to, a way that undermines their autonomy.[21] However in many cases, people consent—with full knowledge and without threats—and yet we think they are exploited. People in developing countries could consent to being on a research study after full informed consent and still be exploited. Similarly, snow bank-bound B seems exploited even if he consents to being towed out for $200. Thus the Kantian conception seems mistaken in fusing exploitation with inadequate consent.

In any event, the reasonable availability requirement is not grounded in Kantian claims about use and violation of autonomy. Rather, it is aimed at ensuring that people have access to the interventions that they helped to demonstrate were effective. It is related to the benefits people receive from participating in a research study, not to their autonomy in consent. Consequently, whatever the merits of the Kantian conception of exploitation, it seems irrelevant to deciding whether making the trial intervention reasonably available can prevent exploitation. In contrast, the Wertheimerian view, which locates the core moral issue inherent in ex-

> **Exploitation is about "how much," not "what," each party receives. The key issue is fairness in the level of benefits. An unequal distribution of benefits may be fair if there are differences in the burdens and contributions of each party.**

ploitation in the fair level of benefits each party of an interaction receives, captures the ethical concern underlying the reasonable availability requirement.

In determining whether exploitation has occurred in any case, the Wertheimerian conception gives us at least six important considerations to bear in mind. First, exploitation is a micro-level concern. Exploitation is about harms from discrete interactions, rather than about the larger social justice of the distribution of background rights and resources. Certainly macro-level distributions of resources can influence exploitation, but the actual exploitation is distinct. Furthermore, while past events may lead people to feel and claim that they have been exploited, whether exploitation occurred does not depend either on their feelings or on historical injustices. Exploitation is about the fairness of an individual exchange. Indeed, as we shall note below, exploitation can happen even in a just society, and it can fail to occur even when there is gross inequality between the parties. As Wertheimer argues:

[W]hile the background conditions shape our existence, the primary experiences occur at the micro level. Exploitation matters to people. People who can accept an unjust set of aggregate resources with considerable equanimity will recoil when they feel exploited in an individual or local transaction. . . . Furthermore, micro-level exploitation is not as closely linked to macro-level injustice as might be thought. Even in a reasonably just society, people will find themselves in situations [that] will give rise to allegations of exploitation.[22]

The reasonable availability requirement recognizes the possibility of exploitation associated with a particular study, and it does not require ensuring the just distribution of all rights and resources or a just international social order. This is more than just a pragmatic point; it reflects the deep experience that exploitation is transactional.

Second, because exploitation is about interactions at a micro level, between researcher and community, it can occur only once an interaction is initiated. In this sense, the obligations to avoid exploitation are obligations that coexist with initiating an interaction.

Third, exploitation is about "how much," not "what," each party receives. The key issue is fairness in the level of benefits. Moreover, exploitation depends upon fairness, not "equalness." An unequal distribution of benefits may be fair if there are differences in the burdens and contributions of each party. Fairness in the distribution of benefits is common to both Wertheimer's theory of exploitation and Rawls's theory of justice, but the notion of fairness important for exploitation is not Rawlsian. They differ in that Rawls addresses macro- and Wertheimer micro-level distributions of benefits. The Rawlsian conception of fairness addresses the dis-

tribution of rights, liberties, and resources for the basic structure of society within which individual transactions occur.[23] In other words, Rawlsian fairness is about constitutional arrangements, taxes, and opportunities. Rawls's conception has often but wrongly been applied to micro level decisions, where it usually issues in implausible and indefensible recommendations. Fairness in individual interactions, which is the concern of exploitation, is based on ideal market transactions.[24] Thus a fair distribution of benefits at the micro-level is based on the level of benefits that would occur in a market transaction devoid of fraud, deception, or force, in which the parties have full information. While this is always idealized—in just the way that economic theory is idealized—it is the powerful ideal informing the notion of fairness of micro-level transactions. This notion of fairness is also relative: just as fair price in a market is based on comparability, so too is the determination of fair benefits based on comparisons to the level of benefits received by other parties interacting in similar circumstances.

Fourth, that one party is vulnerable may make exploitation more likely, but does not inherently entail exploitation. Since exploitation involves the distribution of benefits and burdens, vulnerability is neither necessary nor sufficient for its occurrence. The status of the parties is irrelevant in determining whether exploitation has occurred. If the exchange is fair to both parties, then no one is exploited, regardless of whether one party is poor, uneducated, or otherwise vulnerable and disadvantaged. In the case of snow-bound B, if A charges B $75 for towing the car out, then B is not exploited even though B is vulnerable.

Fifth, since exploitation is about the fairness of micro-level interactions, the key question is the level of benefits provided to the parties who interact. Determining whether exploitation has occurred does not involve weighing the benefits received

by people who do not participate in the interaction.

Finally, because fairness depends on idealized market transactions, determining when exploitation occurs—when the level of benefits is unfair—will require interpretation. As with the application of legal principles and constitutional provisions, the inevitability of interpretation means that reasonable people can and will disagree. But such interpretation and controversy does not invalidate either judicial or moral judgments.

Problems with the Reasonable Availability Requirement

The fundamental problem with the reasonable availability standard is that it guarantees a benefit—the proven intervention—but not a *fair level* of benefits, and therefore it does not necessarily prevent exploitation. Reasonable availability focuses on *what*—the products of research—but exploitation requires addressing *how much*—the level of benefit. For some research in which either the subjects would be exposed to great risks or the sponsor stands to gain enormously, reasonable availability might be inadequate and unfair. Conversely, for very low- or no-risk research in which the population would obtain other benefits, or in which the benefits to the sponsor are minimal, requiring the sponsor to make a product reasonably available could be excessive and unfair.

There are also other problems with the reasonable availability standard. First, it embodies a very narrow notion of benefits. It suggests that only one type of benefit—a proven intervention—can justify participation in clinical research. But a population in a developing country could consider a diverse range of other benefits from research, including the training of health care or research personnel, the construction of health care facilities and other physical infrastructure, and the provision of public health measures and health services beyond those required as part of the research trial. The reasonable availability standard ignores such benefits, and hence cannot reliably determine when exploitation has occurred.

Second, at least as originally formulated by CIOMS, the reasonable availability standard applies to only a narrow range of clinical research—successful Phase III testing of interventions.[25] It does not apply to Phase I and II drug and vaccine testing, or to genetic, epidemiology, and natural history research, which are all necessary and common types of research in developing countries but may be conducted years or decades before any intervention is proven safe and effective. Consequently, either the reasonable availability requirement suggests that Phase I and II studies cannot be ethically conducted in developing countries—a position articulated in the original CIOMS guidelines but widely repudiated—or there is no ethical requirement to provide benefits to the population when conducting such early phase research, or reasonable availability is not the only way to provide benefits from a clinical research study.

To address this gap, CIOMS altered the reasonable availability requirement in 2002:

Before undertaking research in a population or community with limited resources, the sponsor and the investigator must make every effort to ensure that. . . any intervention or product developed, or *knowledge generated*, will be made reasonably available for the benefit of that population or community.[26] (emphasis added)

According to CIOMS some knowledge alone may constitute a fair level of benefits for some non-Phase III studies. But in many non-Phase III studies, it may not match either the risks to subjects or the benefits to others. Indeed, the requirement could permit pharmaceutically sponsored Phase I and II testing of drugs in developing countries while shifting Phase III testing and sales to developed countries as long as data from the early studies are provided to the developing countries. This modification to encompass non-Phase III studies might actually invite *more* exploitation of developing countries.

Third, even in Phase III studies, the reasonable availability requirement provides an *uncertain* benefit to the population, since it makes benefit depend on whether the trial is a "successful testing" of a new product. If there is true clinical equipoise at the beginning of Phase III trials conducted in developing countries, then the new intervention should be proven more effective in only about half of the trials.[27] Consequently, reliance on reasonable availability alone to provide benefits implies that the host country will receive sufficient benefits from half or fewer of all Phase III studies.

Fourth, assuring reasonable availability does not avert the potential for undue inducement of a deprived population. One worry about research in developing countries is that collateral benefits will be escalated to induce the population to enroll in excessively risky research. If the population lacks access to public health measures, routine vaccines, medications for common ailments, and even trained health care personnel, then providing these services as part of a research study might induce them to consent to the project despite its risks, and despite the fact that it disproportionately benefits people in developed countries.[28] Similarly, guaranteeing reasonable availability to a safe and effective drug or vaccine after a study could also function as an undue inducement if the population lacks basic health care.

Fifth, it is beyond the authority of researchers and even of many sponsors of research to guarantee reasonable availability. Clinical researchers and even some sponsors in developed countries, such as the NIH and Medical Research Council, do not control drug approval processes in their own countries, much less in other countries. Similarly they do not control budgets for health ministries or foreign aid to implement research results, and may be, by law, prevented from providing assistance with implementation of research results. At best, they can generate data to inform the deliberations of ministers of health, aid officials, international funding organizations, and relevant others, and then try to persuade those parties to implement effective interventions.

Further, because most Phase III trials take years to conduct, policymakers in developing countries and aid agencies may resist agreements to provide an intervention before they know how beneficial it is, the logistical requirements for implementing and distributing it, and how it compares to other potential interventions. Such cautiousness seems reasonable given the scarce resources available for health delivery.

Sixth, requiring reasonable availability tacitly suggests that the population cannot make its own, autonomous decisions about what benefits are worth the risks of a research trial. In many cases the resources expended on making a drug or vaccine available could be directed to other benefits instead, which the host community might actually prefer. Disregarding the community's view about what constitutes appropriate benefits for them—insisting that a population must benefit in a specific manner—implies a kind of paternalism.

> Requiring a prior agreement to supply a proven product at the end of a successful trial can become a "golden handcuff," constraining rather than benefiting the population.

Finally, requiring a prior agreement to supply a proven product at the end of a successful trial can become a "golden handcuff," constraining rather than benefiting the population. If there is a prior agreement to receive a specific drug or vaccine, rather than cash or some other transferable commodity, the prior agreement commits the population to using the specific intervention tested in the trial. (Pharmaceutical companies are likely to provide their own product directly and avoid agreements in which they are required to provide the product of a competitor.) Yet if other, more effective or desirable interventions are developed, the population is unlikely to have the resources to obtain those interventions. Hence prior agreements can actually limit access of the population to appropriate interventions.

Because of these difficulties, the reasonable availability requirement is recognized more in the breech than in

African and three Western countries—Egypt, Ghana, Kenya, Malawi, Mali, Nigeria, Tanzania, Uganda, Norway, the United Kingdom, and the United States—who participated in the 2001 Conference on Ethical Aspects of Research in Developing Countries (EARD). (See the attached list.) As an alternative to reasonable availability, this group proposes the "fair benefits framework."[29]

The fair benefits framework supplements the usual conditions for the ethical conduct of research trials, such as independent review by an institutional review board or research ethics committee and individual informed consent.[30] In particular, it relies on three background principles that are widely accepted as requirements for ethical research. First, the research should have social value: it should address a health problem of the developing country population. Second, the subjects should be selected fairly: the scientific objectives of the research it-

search participants and the population from both the conduct and results of the research. These benefits can be of three types: (1) benefits to research participants during the research; (2) benefits to the population during the research; or (3) benefits to the participants and population after completion of the research. It is not necessary to provide each of these types of benefits; the ethical imperative based on the conception of exploitation is only for a fair level of benefits. It would seem fair that as the burdens and risks of the research increase, the benefits should also increase. Similarly, as the benefits to the sponsors, researchers, and others outside the population increase, the benefits to the host population should also increase.

Because the aim of the fair benefits framework is to avoid exploitation, the population at risk for exploitation is the relevant group to receive benefits and determine their fairness. Indeed, determination of whether the distribution of benefits is fair depends on the level of benefits received by those members of the community who actually participate in the research, for it is they who bear the burdens of the interaction. However, each benefit does not have to accrue solely to the research participants; a benefit could be directed instead to the entire community. For instance, capacity development or enhanced training in ethics review would be provided to the community, and then benefit the participants indirectly. The important question is how much the participants will benefit from these measures.

In addition, the community will likely bear some burdens and impositions of the research because its health care personnel are recruited to staff the research teams, and its physical facilities and social networks are utilized to conduct the study. Thus, to avoid exploitation, consideration of the benefits for the larger community may also be required. However, since exploitation is a characteristic of micro-level transactions, there is no

The fair benefits framework relies on three background principles: the research should have social value, subjects should be selected fairly, and the research must have a favorable risk-benefit ratio.

its fulfillment; consequently much effort has been devoted to identifying and justifying exceptions.

The Fair Benefits Framework

Certainly, targeted populations in developing countries ought to benefit when clinical research is performed in their communities. Making the results of the research available is one way to provide benefits to a population, but it is not the only way. Hence it is not a necessary condition for ethical research in developing countries, and it should not be imposed unless the developing countries have themselves affirmed it.

This was the consensus of the clinical researchers, bioethicists, and IRB chairs and members from eight

self, not poverty or vulnerability, must provide a strong justification for conducting the research in a specific population. The subjects might be selected, for example, because the population has a high incidence of the disease being studied or of the transmission rates of infection necessary to evaluate a vaccine. Third, the research must have a favorable risk-benefit ratio: benefits to participants must outweigh the risks, or the net risks must be acceptably low.

To these widely accepted principles, the fair benefits framework adds three further principles, which are specified by fourteen benchmarks (see the table):

Principle 1: Fair Benefits. There should be a comprehensive delineation of tangible benefits to the re-justification for including everybody in an entire region or country in the distribution of benefits (nor in the decisionmaking that is required by the next principle) unless the whole region or country is involved in bearing the burdens of the research and at risk for exploitation.

Principle 2: Collaborative Partnership. The population being asked to enroll determines whether a particular array of benefits is sufficient and fair. Currently, there is no shared international standard of fairness; reasonable people disagree.[31] More importantly, only the host population can determine the value of the benefits for itself. Outsiders are likely to be poorly informed about the health, social, and economic context in which the research is being conducted, and they are unlikely to fully appreciate the importance of the proposed benefits to the population.

Furthermore, the population's choice to participate must be free and uncoerced; refusing to participate in the research study must be a realistic option. While there can be controversy about who speaks for the population being asked to enroll, this is a problem that is not unique to the fair benefits framework. Even—or especially—in democratic processes, unanimity of decisions cannot be the standard; disagreement is inherent. But how consensus is determined in the absence of an electoral process is a complex question in democratic theory beyond the scope of this article.

Principle 3: Transparency. Fairness is relative, since it is determined by comparisons with similar interactions. Therefore transparency—like the full information requirement for ideal market transactions—allows comparisons with similar transactions. A population in a developing country is likely to be at a distinct disadvantage relative to the sponsors from the developed country in determining whether a proposed level of benefits is fair. To address these concerns, a publicly accessible repository of all benefits agreements should be established and operated by an inde-

TABLE 1: The Fair Benefits Framework

Principles	Benchmarks for determining whether the principle is honored.
Fair benefits	• **Benefits to participants during the research** 1) **Health improvement:** Health services that are essential to the conduct of the research will improve the health of the participants. 2) **Collateral health services:** Health services beyond those essential to the conduct of the research are provided to the participants. • **Benefits to participants and population during the research** 3) **Collateral health services:** Additional health care services are provided to the population. 4) **Public Health Measures:** There are additional public health measures provided to the population. 5) **Employment and economic activity:** The research project provides jobs for the local population and stimulates the local economy. • **Benefits to population after the research** 6) **Availability of the intervention:** If proven effective, the intervention should be made available to the population. 7) **Capacity development:** There are improvements in health care physical infrastructure, training of health care and research personnel, or training of health personnel in research ethics. 8) **Public health measures:** Additional public health measures provided to the population will have a lasting benefit.[OK?] 9) **Long-term collaboration:** The particular research trial is part of a long-term research collaboration with the population. 10) **Financial rewards:** There is a plan to share fairly with the population the financial rewards or intellectual property rights related to the intervention being evaluated.
Collaborative partnership	1) **Free, uncoerced decisionmaking:** The population is capable of making a free, uncoerced decision: it can refuse participation in the research. 2) **Population support:** When it has understood the nature of the research trial, the risks and benefits to individual subjects, and the benefits to the population, the population decides that it wants the research to proceed.
Transparency	1) **Central repository of benefits agreements:** An independent body creates a publicly accessible repository of all formal and informal benefits agreements. 2) **Community consultation:** Forums with populations that may be invited to participate in research, informing them about previous benefits agreements.

pendent body, such as the World Health Organization. A central repository permits independent assessment of the fairness of benefits agreements by populations, researchers, governments, and others, such as nongovernmental organizations. There could also be a series of community consultations to make populations in developing countries aware of the terms of the agreements reached in other research projects. Such information will facilitate the development of "case law" standards of fairness that evolve out of a number of agreements.

Together with the three background conditions, these three new principles of the fair benefits framework ensure that: (1) the population

States), SmithKline Beecham Biologicals, and Thailand's Ministry of Public Health. Initially, there was a randomized, double-blind Phase II study involving 300 children, primarily family members of physicians and nurses at the Kamphaeng Phet provincial hospital. After a demonstration of safety and of an antibody response that neutralizes hepatitis A, a randomized, double blind Phase III study with a hepatitis B vaccine control involving 40,000 children, one to sixteen years old, was initiated to assess protection against hepatitis A infection.

The study was conducted in Thailand for several reasons. First, there were increasingly common episodes of hepatitis A infection during adoles-

tion at no cost. In addition, SmithKline Beecham Biologicals made no commitment to provide free Havrix to Thailand. However, the company did commit to provide the vaccine to all research participants effective and to pursue Havrix registration in Thailand, enabling the vaccine to be sold in the private market. While there was no promise about what the prices would be for the private market, SmithKline Beecham Biologicals had previously utilized tiered pricing on vaccines. Registration and distribution would enable the Ministry of Public Health to use Havrix to control hepatitis A outbreaks at schools and other institutions. Nevertheless, at the start of the trial, all collaborators recognized that the largest market for Havrix would be travelers from developed countries.

Was the Havrix study ethical? Although all the study participants ultimately received hepatitis A and B vaccines, the study did not fulfill the reasonable availability requirement. There was no prior agreement to provide the vaccine to everyone in Kamphaeng Phet province, and since most Thais would not be able to afford the vaccine, committing to registering and selling it on the private market does not seem to "reasonably available." Thus, by this standard, the trial seems to be unethical.

Did the Havrix study provide fair benefits? The dissent focused not on whether the vaccine would be made available, but on a broad range of burdens and benefits.

has been selected for good scientific reasons, (2) the research poses few net risks to the research participants, (3) there are sufficient benefits to the participants and population, (4) the population is not subject to a coercive choice, (5) the population freely determines whether to participate and whether the level of benefits is fair given the risks of the research, and (6) there is an opportunity for comparative assessments of the fairness of the benefit agreements.

Application to the Hepatitis A Vaccine Case

We can compare the reasonable availability requirement with the fair benefits framework in the case of Havrix, an inactivated hepatitis A vaccine that was tested in 1990 among school children from Kamphaeng Phet province in northern Thailand.[32] The study was a collaboration of the Walter Reed Army Institute of Research (in the United

cence and adulthood, including hepatitis A outbreaks, such as at the National Police Academy in 1988. Second, while hepatitis A transmission was focal, there was a sufficiently high transmission rate—119 per 100,000 population—in rural areas to assess vaccine efficacy. Third, the area had been the site of a prior Japanese encephalitis vaccine study.[33] Ultimately, the Japanese encephalitis vaccine was registered in Thailand in 1988 and included in the Thai mandatory immunization policy in 1992.

Prior to the Phase III study, there was no formal agreement to make Havrix widely available in Thailand. Due to competing vaccination priorities (especially for implementation of hepatitis B vaccine), the cost of a newly developed hepatitis A vaccine, and the available health care budget in Thailand, it was unlikely that Havrix would be included in the foreseeable future in Thailand's national immunization program, in which vaccines are provided to the popula-

The fair benefits framework, however, requires a more multifaceted assessment. First, the study seemed to fulfill the background requirements of social value, fair subject selection, and favorable risk-benefit ratio. Hepatitis A was a significant health problem in northern Thailand and recognized as such by the Thai Ministry of Public Health. Although the population in Kamphaeng Phet province was poor, the epidemiology of hepatitis A provided an independent scientific rationale for site selection. The preliminary data indicated that the candidate vaccine had an excellent safety profile and probable protective efficacy, suggesting a highly favorable risk-benefit ratio for participants.

The benefits of the Havrix trial were of several sorts. By design, all 40,000 children in the trial received both hepatitis A and B vaccines. In addition, regional medical services were augmented. The research team contracted with the community pubic health workers to examine all enrolled children absent from school at their homes, to provide necessary care, and, if appropriate, to arrange transfer to the district or provincial hospital.

There were also benefits for the provincial population. Public health stations throughout Kamphaeng Phet province that lacked adequate refrigeration to store vaccines, medicines, and blood specimens received new refrigerators. Similarly, rural health stations lacking reliable access to the existing FM wireless network link with the provincial hospital's consultants were joined to the network. In the six schools that had hepatitis A outbreaks during the study, the research team

arranged for inspection of the schools and identification of deficiencies in toilet, hand-washing facilities, and water storage contributing to the outbreak. At each school, the researchers contracted and paid to have recommended improvements implemented. In addition, public health workers were provided with unlimited stocks of disposable syringes and needles, as well as training on measures to reduce the incidence of blood-borne diseases. Hepatitis B vaccinations were provid-

---

The participants in the 2001 Conference on Ethical Aspects of Research in Developing Countries

Egypt
Maged El Setouhy
Department of Community, Environmental, and Occupational Medicine
Ain Shams University

Ghana
Tsiri Agbenyega
Department of Physiology
University of Science and Technology
School of Medical Sciences

Francis Anto
Navrongo Health Research Centre
Ministry of Health

Christine Alexandra Clerk
Navrongo Health Research Centre
Ministry of Health

Kwadwo A. Koram
Noguchi Memorial Institute for Medical Research
University of Ghana

Kenya
Michael English
Centre for Geographic Medicine Research - Coast
Kenya Medical Research Institute &
Wellcome Trust Research Laboratories

Rashid Juma
Center for Clinical Research
Kenya Medical Research Institute

Catherine Molyneux
Centre for Geographic Medicine Research - Coast
Kenya Medical Research Institute &
Wellcome Trust Research Laboratories

Norbert Peshu
Centre for Geographic Medicine Research - Coast
Kenya Medical Research Institute (KEMRI)

Malawi
Newton Kumwenda
University of Malawi College of Medicine

Joseph Mfutso-Bengu
Department of Community Health
University of Malawi College of Medicine

Malcolm Molyneux
Director, Malawi-Liverpool-Wellcome Trust Research Programme
University of Malawi College of Medicine

Terrie Taylor
University of Malawi College of Medicine
Blantyre, Malawi and
Department of Internal Medicine
College of Osteopathic Medicine

Mali
Doumbia Aissata Diarra
Department of Pharmacy and Dentistry

Saïbou Maiga
Department of Pharmacy and Dentistry
University of Mali

Mamadou Sylla
Department of Pharmacy and Dentistry
University of Mali

Dione Youssouf
Eglise Protestante Bamako Coura

Nigeria
Catherine Olufunke Falade
Post-Graduate Institute for Medical Research and Training
University of Ibadan College of Medicine

Segun Gbadegesin
Department of Philosophy
Howard University

Norway
Reidar Lie
Department of Philosophy
University of Bergen

Tanzania
Ferdinand Mugusi
Department of Internal Medicine
Muhimbili University College of Health Sciences

David Ngassapa
Department of Anatomy
Muhimbili University College of Health Sciences

Uganda
Julius Ecuru
Uganda National Council for Science and Technology

Ambrose Talisuna
Resource Centre
Ministry of Health

United States
Ezekiel Emanuel
Department of Clinical Bioethics
National Institutes of Health

Christine Grady
Department of Clinical Bioethics
National Institutes of Health

Elizabeth Higgs
Parisitology and International Programs
National Institutes of Health, NIAID, DMID

Christopher Plowe
Malaria Section, Center for Vaccine Development
University of Maryland School of Medicine

Jeremy Sugarman
Center for the Study of Medical Ethics and Humanities
Duke University Medical Center

David Wendler
Department of Clicical Bioethics
National Institutes of Health

---

ed to all interested government personnel working on the trial, including approximately 2,500 teachers, public health workers, nurses, technicians, and physicians. Since deaths of enrolled research participants were tracked and investigated, the research team identified motor vehicle accidents, especially pedestrians struck by cars, as a major cause of mortality in the province and recommended corrective measures.[34] Finally, the training of Thai researchers and experience in conducting the Havrix trial may have facilitated subsequent research trials, including the current HIV vaccine trials in Thailand.

Regarding the principle of collaborative partnership, there were extensive consultations in Kamphaeng Phet province prior to initiating and conducting the trial. The provincial governor, medical officer, education secretary, and hospital director provided comments before granting their approval. In each of the 146 participating communities, researchers made public presentations about the study and held briefings for interested parents and teachers. Each school appointed a teacher to maintain a liaison with the research team. Parental and community support appeared to be related to the provision of hepatitis B vaccine to all participants, since hepatitis was seen as a major health problem and the children lacked access to the vaccine.

Furthermore, the protocol was reviewed by the Thai Ministry of Public Health's National Ethical Review Committee, as well as by two IRBs in the United States. The Ministry of Public Health appointed an independent committee composed of thirteen senior physicians and ministry officials to monitor the safety and efficacy of the trial. And rejecting the trial appeared to be a genuine option; certainly those Thai scientists who tried hard to prevent it, including by lobbying the National Ethics Review Committee, seemed to think so.

At the time of this trial, there was no central repository of benefits agreements to fulfill the transparency principle. However, the measures taken to benefit the population, including provision of the hepatitis A and B vaccines and registration of Havrix in Thailand, were discussed with the Ministry of Public Health and provincial officials and published.

Did the Havrix study provide fair benefits? Clearly some in Thailand thought not. They argued that the trial did not address a pressing health need in a manner appropriate to the country; instead, they held, it addressed a health interest of the U.S. army. Second, some have alleged there was insufficient technology transfer. In particular, no training was provided to Thai researchers to conduct testing for the antibody to hepatitis A or to develop other laboratory skills. Third, it was claimed that inadequate respect was accorded to Thai researchers, as none were among the study's principal investigators and none were named in the original protocol (they were simply referred to as "Thai researchers"). Only after protests were they individually identified. The American investigators claim vehemently that this charge is inaccurate. A prominent vaccine researcher summarized the sentiment against Thai participation:

Journalists in the country have accused the government and medical community of a national betrayal in allowing Thai children to be exploited. . . . The role of Thailand in rounding up its children for immunization was hardly seen as a meaningful partnership in this research aim. In private, government ministers agreed with this, but the sway of international politics and money was too persuasive.[35]

Many others argued that the benefits to the population of Kamphaeng Phet province were sufficient, especially given the minimal risk of the study. Still others are uncertain. In their view, the level of benefits were not clearly inadequate, but more long-term benefits could have been provided to the community depending on the level of the sponsors' benefits—in this case, SmithKline Beecham's profits from vaccine sales. To address the uncertainty of how much a company might benefit from drug or vaccine sales, some propose profit-sharing agreements that provide benefits to the community related to the actual profits.

Universal agreement is a naïve and unrealistic goal. The goal is only a consensus in the population to be enrolled in the trial. Consensus on the appropriateness of a research study acknowledges that some disagreement is not only possible but likely, and even a sign of a healthy partnership.[36] In this trial, the national ministry, the provincial governmental and health officials, and the Kamphaeng Phet population seemed supportive.

Further, the dissent focused not on whether the vaccine would be made available to the population if it were proven effective, but on the level of a broad range of burdens and benefits, both to the community and to the sponsors. It is precisely this sort of broad, nuanced, and realistic assessment of the community's interests that is permitted and promoted by the fair benefits framework. Rather than making any one type of benefit into a moral litmus test, the fair benefits framework takes into account all of the various ways the community might benefit from the research.

Acknowledgements

We thank Dean Robin Broadhead, of Malawi, and Dan Brock and Jack Killen for support and critical reviews of the manuscript. We thank Bruce Innis of SmithKline Beecham and Thai clinical researchers who prefer to remain anonymous for discussing the Havrix case with us and providing many substantive details.

References

1. M. Barry, "Ethical Considerations of Human Investigation in Developing Countries: the AIDS Dilemma," *NEJM* 319 (1988) 1083-86; M. Angell, "Ethical Imperialism? Ethics in International Collaborative Clinical Research," *NEJM* 319 (1988): 1081-83; N.A. Christakas, "The Ethical Design of an AIDS Vaccine Trial in Africa,"

Hastings Center Report 18, no. 3 (1988): 31-37.

2. P. Lurie and S.M. Wolfe, "Unethical Trials of Interventions to Reduce Perinatal Transmission of the Human Immunodeficiency Virus in Developing Countries," *NEJM* 337 (1997): 853-56; M. Angell, "The Ethics of Clinical Research in the Third World," *NEJM* 337 (1997): 847-49; H. Varmus and D. Satcher, "Ethical Complexities of Conducting Research in Developing Countries," *NEJM* 337 (1997): 1003-1005; R. Crouch and J. Arras, "AZT Trials and Tribulations," *Hastings Center Report* 28, no. 6 (1998): 26-34; C. Grady, "Science in the Service of Healing," *Hastings Center Report* 28, no. 6 (1998): 34-38; R.J. Levine, "The 'Best Proven Therapeutic Method' Standard in Clinical Trials in Technologically Developing Countries," *IRB* 20 (1998): 5-9; B.R. Bloom, "The Highest Attainable Standard: Ethical Issues in AIDS Vaccines," *Science* 279 (1998): 186-88.

3. World Medical Association. Declaration of Helsinki, 2000 at www.wma.net/e/policy12-c_e.html; Council for International Organizations of Medical Science, *International Ethical Guidelines for Biomedical Research Involving Human Subjects* (Geneva: CIOMS, 1993); P. Wilmshurst, "Scientific Imperialism: If They Won't Benefit from the Findings, Poor People in the Developing World Shouldn't be Used in Research," *BMJ* 314 (1997): 840-41; P.E. Cleaton-Jones, "An Ethical Dilemma: Availability of Anti-retroviral Therapy after Clinical Trials with HIV Infected Patients are Ended," *BMJ* 314 (1997): 887-88.

4. CIOMS, *International Ethical Guidelines*, 1993.

5. World Medical Association Declaration of Helsinki.

6. Medical Research Council of the United Kingdom, *Interim Guidelines—Research Involving Human Participants in Developing Societies: Ethical Guidelines for MRC-sponsored Studies* (London: MRC, 1999); Joint United National Programme on HIV/AIDS (UNAIDS), *Ethical Considerations in HIV Preventive Vaccine Research* (Geneva: UNAIDS, 2000); National Consensus Conference, *Guidelines for the Conduct of Health Research Involving Human Subjects in Uganda* (Kampala, Uganda: National Consensus Conference, 1997); Medical Research Council of South Africa, *Guidelines on Ethics for Medical Research* (South Africa: Medical Research Council, 1993).

7. L.H. Glantz et al., "Research in Developing Countries: Taking 'Benefit' Seriously," *Hastings Center Report* 28, no. 6 (1998): 38-42; G.J. Annas and M.A. Grodin, "Human Rights and Maternal-Fetal HIV Transmission Prevention Trials in Africa,"

American Journal of Public Health 88 (1998): 560-63.

8. H.T. Shapiro and E.M. Meslin, "Ethical Issues in the Design and Conduct of Clinical Trials in Developing Countries," *NEJM* 345 (2001): 139-42. See also National Bioethics Advisory Commission, *Ethical and Policy Issues in International Research: Clinical Trials in Developing Countries* (Washington D.C.: U.S. Government Printing Office, 2001).

9. Annas and Grodin, "Human Rights and Maternal-Fetal HIV Transmission Prevention Trials in Africa."

10. E.J. Emanuel, D. Wendler, and C. Grady, "What Makes Clinical Research Ethical?" *JAMA* 283 (2000): 2701-711; E.J. Emanuel et al., "What Makes Clinical Research in Developing Countries Ethical? The Benchmarks of Ethical Research," *Journal of Infectious Diseases* 189 (2004): 930-37.

11. Ibid.; R.J. Levine, *Ethical and Regulatory Aspects of Clinical Research*, 2nd Edition (New Haven, Conn.: Yale University Press, 1988).

12. N. Black, "Evidence based policy: proceed with care," *BMJ* 323 (2001): 275-79.

13. Wilmshurst, "Scientific Imperialism," and National Consensus Conference, *Guidelines for the Conduct of Health Research Involving Human Subjects in Uganda*; L.H. Glantz et al., "Research in Developing Countries: Taking 'Benefit' Seriously;" G.J. Annas and M.A. Grodin, "Human Rights and Maternal-Fetal HIV Transmission Prevention Trials in Africa."

14. Glantz et al., "Research in Developing Countries."

15. CIOMS, *International Ethical Guidelines for Biomedical Research Involving Human Subjects*, 2nd edition (Geneva: CIOMS, 2002).

16. A. Wertheimer, *Exploitation* (Princeton, N.J.: Princeton University Press, 1999), chapter 1; N.A. Christakis, "The Ethical Design of an AIDS Vaccine Trial in Africa," *Hastings Center Report* 28 (1998): 31-37.

17. Wertheimer, *Exploitation*.

18. A. W. Wood, "Exploitation," *Social Philosophy and Policy* 12 (1995): 135-58.

19. Wertheimer, *Exploitation*.

20. Buchanan, *Ethics, Efficiency and the Market*, p.87.

21. C. Korsgaard, "The Reasons We Can Share: An Attack on the Distinction Between Agent-relative and Agent-neutral Values," in *Creating the Kingdom of Ends* (New York: Cambridge University Press, 1996).

22. Wertheimer, *Exploitation*.

23. J. Rawls, *A Theory of Justice*, 2nd edition (Cambridge, Mass.: Harvard University Press, DATE).

24. Wertheimer, *Exploitation*.

25. CIOMS, *International Ethical Guidelines for Biomedical Research Involving Human Subjects*.

26. CIOMS, *International Ethical Guidelines for Biomedical Research Involving Human Subjects*, 2nd edition.

27. I. Chalmers, "What is the Prior Probability of a Proposed New Treatment being Superior to Established Treatments?" *BMJ* 314 (1997): 74-75; B. Djulbegovic et al., "The Uncertainty Principle and Industry-Sponsored Research," *Lancet* 356 (2000): 635-38.

28. NBAC, *Ethical and Policy Issues in International Research*.

29. Participants in the 2001 Conference on Ethical Aspects of Research in Developing Countries,"Fair Benefits from Research in Developing Countries," *Science* 298 (2002): 2133-34.

30. Emanuel, Wendler, and Grady, "What Makes Clinical Research Ethical?" and Levine, *Ethical and Regulatory Aspects of Clinical Research*; J. Rawls, *The Law of Peoples* (Cambridge, Mass.: Harvard University Press, 1999).

31. T. Pogge, *World Poverty and Human Rights* (Cambridge, U.K.: Polity Press, 2002), chapters 1 and 4.

32. B.I. Innis et al. "Protection against Hepatitis A by an Inactivated Vaccine," *JAMA* 271 (1994): 1328-34.

33. C. Hoke et al., "Protection against Japanese Encephalitis by Inactivated Vaccines," *NEJM* 319 (1988): 608-614.

34. C.A. Kozik et al., "Causes of Death and Unintentional Injury among School Children in Thailand," *Southeast Asian Journal of Tropical Medicine and Public Health* 30 (1999): 129-35.

35. "Interview with Prof Natth," *Good Clinical Practice Journal* 6, no. 6 (1999): 11.

36. A. Gutmann and D. Thompson, *Democracy and Disagreement* (Cambridge, Mass.: Harvard University Press, 1996).

Part VII
Ethics and the
Pharmaceutical Industry

[33]

HUMAN RIGHTS AND GLOBAL HEALTH: A RESEARCH PROGRAM

THOMAS W. POGGE

Abstract: One-third of all human lives end in early death from poverty-related causes. Most of these premature deaths are avoidable through global institutional reforms that would eradicate extreme poverty. Many are also avoidable through global health-system reform that would make medical knowledge freely available as a global public good. The rules should be redesigned so that the development of any new drug is rewarded in proportion to its impact on the global disease burden (not through monopoly rents). This reform would bring drug prices down worldwide close to their marginal cost of production and would powerfully stimulate pharmaceutical research into currently neglected diseases concentrated among the poor. Its feasibility shows that the existing medical-patent regime (trade-related aspects of intellectual property rights—TRIPS—as supplemented by bilateral agreements) is severely unjust—and its imposition a human-rights violation on account of the avoidable mortality and morbidity it foreseeably produces.

Keywords: diseases, drugs, health, human rights, incentives, justice, medicine, patents, pharmaceutical research, poverty, public goods, TRIPS.

1

Some eighteen million human beings die prematurely each year from medical conditions we can cure—this is equivalent to fifty thousand avoidable deaths per day, or one-third of all human deaths.[1] Hundreds of millions more suffer grievously from these conditions.[2] The lives of additional hundreds of millions are shattered by severe illnesses or

---

[1] In 2002, there were fifty-seven million human deaths. Among the main avoidable causes of death were (with death tolls in thousands): respiratory infections (3,963—mainly pneumonia), HIV/AIDS (2,777), perinatal conditions (2,462), diarrhea (1,798), tuberculosis (1,566), malaria (1,272), childhood diseases (1,124—mainly measles), maternal conditions (510), malnutrition (485), sexually transmitted diseases (180), menengitis (173), hepatitis (157), and tropical diseases (129). See WHO 2004b, annex table 2; cf. also FAO 1999 and UNICEF 2002.

[2] Such morbidity is due to the conditions listed in the preceding footnote as well as to a variety of other communicable diseases, including dengue fever, leprosy, trypanosomiasis

premature deaths in their family. And these medical problems also put a great strain on the economies of many poor countries, thereby perpetuating their poverty, which in turn contributes to the ill health of their populations.

This huge incidence of mortality and morbidity is not randomly distributed. For a variety of social reasons, females are significantly overrepresented among those suffering severe ill health (UNDP 2003, 310–30; UNIFEM 2001). Being especially vulnerable and helpless, children under the age of five are also overrepresented, accounting for about two-thirds of the death toll (USDA 1999, iii). But the most significant causal determinant is poverty: Nearly all the avoidable mortality and morbidity occurs in the poor countries (WHO 2004b, annex table 2), particularly among their poorer inhabitants.

There are different ways of attacking this problem. One approach, exemplified in much of my previous work, focuses on the eradication of severe poverty. In the world as it is, consumption by the poorest 44 percent of humankind, those living below the World Bank's "US$2/day" benchmark (1993 purchasing power), accounts for approximately 1.3 percent of the global social product. If all 2,736 million currently below it were instead living right at the US$2/day threshold, their consumption would still amount to only 2.2 percent of the global social product.[3] But they would then be much better able to gain access to things that help the rest of us ward off ill health, such as adequate nutrition, safe drinking water, adequate clothing and shelter, basic sanitation, mosquito nets in malaria-infested regions, and so on.[4]

Another way of addressing the huge mortality and morbidity rates is through ensuring improved access to medical treatments—preventive (like vaccines) or remedial. This way is exemplified in the research to be sketched here. The two ways of addressing the problem are complementary: Just as the eradication of severe poverty would greatly reduce the

---

(sleeping sickness and Chagas disease), onchocerciasis (river blindness), leishmaniasis, Buruli ulcer, lymphatic filariasis, and schistosomiasis (bilharzia). See Gwatkin and Guillot 1999.

[3] According to the World Bank's (flawed) estimate, there are 2,736 million people worldwide living below the "$2/day" international poverty line, which means that their daily consumption falls below the purchasing power of US$2.16 in the United States in 1993 (www.worldbank.org/research/povmonitor). This threshold is today equivalent to the purchasing power of about US$1,000 per person per year and, at current exchange rates, amounts to somewhere between US$120 and US$480 (depending on the poor-country currency in question). According to the World Bank's researchers, these global poor live, on average, 42 percent below the $2/day poverty line (Chen and Ravallion 2004 tables 3 and 6, dividing the poverty-gap index by the headcount index). See Pogge 2004, 395 nn. 15–16, for additional references and detailed calculations supporting my estimates.

[4] Among the global poor, some 800 million are undernourished, 1,000 million lack access to safe water, 2,400 million lack access to basic sanitation (UNDP 2003, 87, 9, 6); more than 880 million lack access to basic health services (UNDP 1999, 22); approximately 1,000 million have no adequate shelter and 2,000 million no electricity (UNDP 1998, 49).

global disease burden, so improved access to essential medicines would greatly reduce severe poverty by enhancing the ability of the poor to work, and to organize themselves, for their own economic advancement.

Exemplifying the latter approach, this essay outlines how one crucial obstacle to a dramatic reduction in the global disease burden can be removed by giving medical innovators stable and reliable financial incentives to address the medical conditions of the poor. My aim is to develop a concrete, feasible, and politically realistic plan for reforming current national and global rules for incentivizing the search for new essential drugs. If adopted, this plan would not add much to the overall cost of global health-care spending. In fact, on any plausible accounting, which would take note of the huge economic losses caused by the present global disease burden, the reform would actually save money. Moreover, it would distribute the cost of global health-care spending more fairly across countries, across generations, and between those lucky enough to enjoy good health and the unlucky ones suffering from serious medical conditions.

The decision about whether and how to implement such a plan obviously rests with national parliaments and international organizations, such as the World Trade Organization (WTO) and the World Health Organization (WHO). But these decision makers could benefit from an exploration of the more promising reform options together with a full assessment of their comparative advantages and disadvantages, resulting in a specific reform recommendation.

2

The existing rules for incentivizing pharmaceutical research are morally deeply problematic. This fact, long understood among international health experts, has come to be more widely recognized in the wake of the AIDS crisis, especially in Africa, where the vital needs of poor patients are pitted against the need of pharmaceutical companies to recoup their research-and-development investments (Barnard 2002). Still, this wider recognition does not easily translate into political reform. Some believe (like Churchill about democracy) that the present regime is the lesser evil in comparison to its alternatives that have any chance of implementation. And others, more friendly to reform, disagree about what the flaws of the present system are exactly and have put forward a wide range of alternative reform ideas. What is needed now is a careful comparative exploration of the various reforms that have been proposed by academics, nongovernmental organizations (NGOs), and politicians as well as in the media, with the aim of formulating and justifying a specific alternative that is clearly superior to the present regime.

Filling this gap requires economic expertise. But it also, and centrally, requires moral reflection. From an economist standpoint, health care is a commodity like many others in the service sector (for example, haircuts and car repairs) and, from that standpoint, the creation of effective new medical treatments is an intellectual achievement like many others (for example, the creation of new music or software). From a moral stand-point, however, there is a world of difference between poor people lacking access to haircuts and poor people avoidably lacking access to treatment for serious medical conditions—and also a world of difference in importance between the aim of encouraging the creation of new music and the aim of encouraging the creation of new essential drugs.

We need to develop and defend a moral standard that can ground the assessment of the current patent regime (trade-related aspects of intellec-tual property rights, or TRIPS, as supplemented by a growing number of bilateral agreements that the United States has been pressing upon its trading partners) against the various ideas for reforming it and can guide the formulation of a specific reform plan as well as organize the argument in its favor. To be useful as a policy option for decision makers, and as a clear focal point for advocacy, media discussions, and the general public, this must be a detailed and specific reform plan fully informed by the relevant facts and insights from science, statistics, medicine, economics, law, and (moral and political) philosophy.

In addition, this plan must be politically feasible and realistic. To be *feasible* it must, once implemented, generate its own support from governments, pharmaceutical companies, and the general public (taking these three key constituencies as they would be under the reformed regime). To be *realistic*, the plan must possess moral and prudential appeal for governments, pharmaceutical companies, and the general public (taking these three constituencies as they are now, under the existing regime). A reform plan that is not incentive compatible in these two ways is destined to remain a philosopher's pipe dream.

3

Bringing new, safe and effective life-saving medications to market is hugely expensive, as inventor firms must pay for the research and development of new drugs as well as for elaborate testing and the subsequent approval process.[5] In addition, newly developed medical treatments often turn out to be unsafe or not effective enough, to have bad side effects, or to fail getting government approval for some other reason, which may lead to the loss of the entire investment.

---

[5] This point may be controversial to some extent. It has been asserted that pharmaceu-tical companies wildly overstate their financial and intellectual contributions to drug development and that most basic research is funded by governments and universities and then made available to the pharmaceutical industry for free. See Consumer Project on Technology (www.cptech.org/ip/health/econ/rndcosts.html) and UNDP 2001, ch. 5.

THOMAS W. POGGE

Given such large investment costs and risks, very little innovative pharmaceutical research would take place in a free-market system. The reason is that an innovator would bear the full cost of its failures but would be unable to profit from its successes because competitors would copy or retro-engineer its invention (effectively free riding on its effort) and then drive down the price close to the marginal cost of production. This is a classic instance of market failure leading to a collectively irrational (Pareto-suboptimal) outcome in which medical innovation is undersupplied by the market.

The classic solution, also enshrined in the TRIPS regime (adopted under WTO auspices in the Uruguay Round), corrects this market failure through patent rules that grant inventor firms a temporary monopoly on their inventions, typically for twenty years from the time of filing a patent application. With competitors barred from copying and selling any newly invented drug during this period, the inventor firm can sell it at the profit-maximizing monopoly price well above, and often very far above, its marginal cost of production.[6] In this way, the inventor firm can recoup its research and overhead expenses plus some of the cost of its other research efforts that failed to bear fruit.

This solution corrects the market failure (undersupply of medical innovation), but its monopoly feature creates another. During the patent's duration, the profit-maximizing sale price of the invented medicine will be far above its marginal cost of production. This large differential is collectively irrational by impeding many mutually beneficial transactions between the inventor firm and potential buyers who are unwilling or unable to pay the monopoly price but are willing and able to pay substantially more than the marginal cost of production. If modified rules could facilitate these potential transactions, then many patients would benefit—and so would the drug companies, as they would book additional profitable sales and typically also, through economies of scale, reduce their marginal cost of production. Such a reform would not merely avoid a sizable economic loss for the national and global economies. It would also avoid countless premature deaths and much severe suffering worldwide that the present patent regime engenders by blocking mutually advantageous sales of essential medicines.

There are two basic reform strategies for avoiding this second market failure associated with monopoly pricing powers. I will refer to these as the differential-pricing and public-good strategies, respectively. The *differential-pricing strategy* comes in different variants. One would have inventor firms themselves offer their proprietary drugs to different

---

[6] The inventor firm can also sell permissions to produce its invention. Paying a hefty licensing fee to the inventor firm, the producer must charge a price well above, often very far above, its marginal cost of production. In this case, too, the second market failure I go on to discuss in the text arises, though it does so somewhat differently.

customers at different prices, thereby realizing a large profit margin from sales to the more affluent without renouncing sales to poorer buyers at a lower margin. Another variant is the right of governments, recognized under TRIPS rules, to issue compulsory licenses for inventions that are urgently needed in a public emergency. Exercising this right, a government can force down the price of a patented invention by compelling the patent holder to license it to other producers for a set percentage (typically below 10 percent) of the latter's sales revenues. The United States claims this right under 28 USC 1498, particularly for cases where the licensed producer is an agency of, or contractor for, the government,[7] but has been reluctant to invoke the right in the case of pharmaceuticals, presumably to avoid setting an international precedent detrimental to its pharmaceutical industry. Thus, during the anthrax scare of 2001, the United States preferred to pressure Bayer into supplying its patented drug CIPRO for US$0.90 per pill (versus a wholesale price of US$4.67) over purchasing generic versions from Polish or Indian suppliers. Canada invoked compulsory licensing in this case but backed down under pressure four days later (www.cptech.org/ip/health/cl/cipro/). It has often been suggested that poor countries should assert their compulsory licensing rights to cope with their public-health crises, particularly the AIDS pandemic.

Differential-pricing solutions are generally unworkable unless the different categories of buyers can be prevented from knowing about, or from trading with, one another. In the real world, if the drug were sold at a lower price to some, then many buyers who would otherwise be willing and able to pay the higher price would find a way to buy at the lower price. Selling expensive drugs more cheaply in poor developing countries, for example, would create strong incentives to divert (for example, smuggle) this drug back into the more affluent countries, leading to relative losses in the latter markets that outweigh the gains in the former. Anticipating such net losses through diversion, inventor firms typically do not themselves try to overcome the second market failure through differential pricing, resist pressures to do so, and fight attempts to impose compulsory licensing upon them. As a result, differential pricing has not gained much of a foothold, and many poor patients who would be willing and able to purchase the drug at a price well above the marginal cost of production are excluded from this drug because they cannot afford the much higher monopoly price (Kanavos et al. 2004). While such exclusion is acceptable for other categories of intellectual property (for example, software, films, and music), it is morally highly problematic in the case of essential medicines.

---

[7] See www4.law.cornell.edu/uscode/28/1498.html. This right has been litigated in various important cases, producing licensing fees as low as 1 percent in the case of the Williams patent held by Hughes Aircraft Corporation (for details, see www.cptech.org/ip/health/cl/us-1498.html).

To be sure, insofar as a government does succeed, against heavy pressure from pharmaceutical companies and often their home governments, in exercising its right to issue compulsory licenses, any net losses due to diversion are simply forced upon the patent holders. But such compulsory licensing, especially if it were to become more common, brings back the first market failure of undersupply: Pharmaceutical companies will tend to spend less on the quest for essential drugs when the uncertainty of success is compounded by the additional unpredictability of whether and to what extent they will be allowed to recoup their investments through undisturbed use of their monopoly pricing powers.

4

In light of these serious problems, I doubt that the differential-pricing strategy can yield a plan for reform that would constitute a substantial improvement over the present regime. So I am proceeding, for now, on the assumption that an exploration of the *public-good strategy* is more promising, that is, more likely to lead to the formulation of a reform plan that would avoid the main defects of the present monopoly-patent regime while preserving most of its important benefits. The great difficulty to be overcome lies in devising the best possible reform plan within this much larger domain of the public-good strategy.

We may think of such a reform plan as consisting of three components. First, the results of any successful effort to develop (research, test, and obtain regulatory approval for) a new essential drug are to be provided as a public good that all pharmaceutical companies may use free of charge. This reform would eliminate the second market failure (associated with monopoly pricing powers) by allowing competition to bring the prices of new essential drugs down close to their marginal cost of production. Implemented in only one country or a few countries, this reform would engender problems like those we have found to attend differential-pricing solutions: Cheaper drugs produced in countries where drug development is treated as a public good would seep back into countries adhering to the monopoly-patent regime, undermining research incentives in the latter countries. The reform should therefore be global in scope, just as the rules of the current TRIPS regime are. The first reform component, then, is that results of successful efforts to develop new essential drugs are to be provided as public goods that all pharmaceutical companies anywhere may use free of charge.

Implemented in isolation, this first reform component would destroy incentives for pharmaceutical research. This effect is avoided by the second component, which is that, similar to the current regime, inventor firms should be entitled to take out a multiyear patent on any essential medicines they invent but, during the life of the patent, should be rewarded, out of public funds, in proportion to the impact of their invention on the global disease burden. This reform component would reorient the incentives of such firms in highly desirable ways: Any inventor firm would have incentives to sell its innovative treatments cheaply (often even below their marginal cost of production) in order to help get its drugs to even very poor people who need them. Such a firm would have incentives also to see to it that patients are fully instructed in the proper use of its drugs (dosage, compliance, and so on), in order to ensure that, through wide and effective deployment, they have as great an impact on the global disease burden as possible.[8] Rather than ignore poor countries as unlucrative markets, inventor firms would moreover have incentives to work together toward improving the heath systems of these countries in order to enhance the impact of their inventions there. In addition, any inventor firm would have reason to encourage and support efforts by cheap generic producers (already well established in India, Brazil, and South Africa, for example) to copy its drugs, because such copying would further increase the number of users and hence the invention's favorable impact on the global disease burden. In all these ways, the reform would align and harmonize the interests of inventor firms with those of patients and the generic drug producers—interests that, under the current regime, are diametrically opposed.[9] The reform would also align the moral and prudential interests of the inventor firms who, under the present regime, are forced to choose between recouping their investments in the search for essential drugs and preventing avoidable suffering and deaths.

This second component of a plausible public-good strategy realizes yet one further tremendous advantage over the status quo: Under the current regime, inventor firms have incentives to try to develop a new medical treatment only if the expected value of the temporary monopoly pricing power they might gain, discounted by the probability of failure, is greater than the full development and patenting costs. They have no incentives, then, to try to develop treatments that few people have a need for and treatments needed by people who are unable to afford them at a price far above the marginal cost of production. The former category contains treatments for many so-called orphan diseases that affect only small

---

[8] The absence of such incentives under the present rules gravely undermines the effectiveness of drugs delivered into poor regions, even when these drugs are donated (cf. UNDP 2001, 101).

[9] This opposition was displayed most dramatically when a coalition of thirty-one pharmaceutical companies went to court in South Africa in order to prevent their inventions from being reproduced by local generic producers and sold cheaply to desperate patients whose life depended on such affordable access to these retroviral drugs. In April 2001, the attempted lawsuit collapsed under a barrage of worldwide public criticism (see Barnard 2002).

THOMAS W. POGGE

numbers of patients. The latter category contains many diseases mainly affecting the poor, for which treatments priced far above the marginal cost of production could be sold only in small quantities. It may be acceptable that no one is developing software demanded only by a few and that no one is producing music valued only by the very poor. But it is morally problematic that no treatments are developed for rare diseases, and it is extremely problematic, morally, that so few treatments are developed for medical conditions that cause most of the premature deaths and suffering in the world today.

Even if common talk of the 10/90 gap[10] is now an overstatement, the problem is certainly real: Malaria, pneumonia, diarrhea, and tuberculosis, which together account for 21 percent of the global disease burden, receive 0.31 percent of all public and private funds devoted to health research (GFHR 2004, 122). And diseases confined to the tropics tend to be the most neglected: Of the 1,393 new drugs approved between 1975 and 1999, only thirteen were specifically indicated for tropical diseases and five out of these thirteen actually emerged from veterinary research (Trouiller et al. 2001; Drugs for Neglected Diseases Working Group 2001, 11).

Rewarding pharmaceutical research on the basis of its impact on the global disease burden would attract inventor firms toward medical conditions whose adverse effects on humankind can be reduced most cost effectively. This reorientation would greatly mitigate the problem of neglected diseases that overwhelmingly affect the poor. And it would open new profitable research opportunities for pharmaceutical companies.

One might worry that the second component of the reform would also *reduce* incentives to develop treatments for medical conditions that, though they add little to the global disease burden (on any plausible conception thereof), affluent patients are willing to pay a lot to avoid. But this worry can be addressed, at least in part, by limiting the application of the reform plan to *essential* drugs, that is, to medicines for diseases that destroy human lives. Drugs for other medical conditions, such as hair loss, acne, and impotence, for example, can remain under the existing regime with no loss in incentives or rewards.

Incorporating this distinction between essential and nonessential drugs into the reform plan raises the specter of political battles over how this distinction is to be defined and of legal battles over how some particular invention should be classified. These dangers could be averted by allowing inventor firms to classify their inventions as they wish and then designing the rewards in such a way that these firms will themselves choose to

---

[10] "Only 10 percent of global health research is devoted to conditions that account for 90 percent of the global disease burden" (Drugs for Neglected Diseases Working Group 2001, 10; cf. GFHR 2000, 2002, 2004).

register under the reform rules any inventions that stand to make a real difference to the global disease burden. Such freedom of choice would also greatly facilitate a smooth and rapid phasing in of the new rules, as there would be no disappointment of the legitimate expectations of firms that have undertaken research for the sake of gaining a conventional patent. The reform plan should be *attractive* for pharmaceutical companies by winning them new lucrative opportunities for research into currently neglected diseases without significant losses in the lucrative research opportunities they now enjoy—and by restoring their moral stature as benefactors of humankind.

This second reform component requires a way of funding the planned incentives for developing new essential medicines, which might cost some US$45–90 billion annually on a global scale.[11] The third component of the reform plan is then to develop a fair, feasible, and politically realistic allocation of these costs, as well as compelling arguments in support of this allocation.

5

While the general approach as outlined may seem plausible enough, the great intellectual challenge is to specify it concretely in a way that shows it to be both feasible and politically realistic. This is an extremely complex undertaking that involves a formidable array of multiply interdependent tasks and subtasks. Here one main task, associated with the second component, concerns the design of the planned incentives. This requires a suitable measure of the global disease burden and ways of assessing the contributions that various new medical treatments are making to its reduction. When two or more different medicines are alternative treatments for the same disease, then the reward corresponding to their aggregate impact must be allocated among their respective inventors on the basis of each medicine's market share and effectiveness.

---

[11] The precise amount each year would depend on how successful innovative treatments would be in decimating the global disease burden. My estimate in the text is thus necessarily tentative and speculative, meant to provide a rough orientation and thus to illustrate the order of magnitude and hence the degree of realism of the reform. My estimate derives from current corporate spending on pharmaceutical research, which is reckoned to have been US$30.5 billion in 1998, the latest year for which I have found a credible figure (GFHR 2004, 112). This suggests that the current figure is around US$40 billion. Only part of this money is spent toward developing *essential* drugs. But the reformed rules would stimulate substantially greater spending on pharmaceutical research toward developing new essential drugs (especially for heretofore neglected diseases). Such outlays might well exceed corporate expenditures on *all* pharmaceutical research under the existing rules. The rewards offered under the reformed rules must not merely match but also substantially exceed these outlays, because pharmaceutical companies will brave the risks and uncertainties of an expensive and protracted research effort only if its expected return substantially exceeds its cost.

THOMAS W. POGGE

More complex is the case (exemplified in the fight against HIV, tuberculosis, and malaria) of "drug cocktails" that combine various drugs that frequently have been developed by different companies. Here the reform plan must formulate clear and transparent rules for distributing the overall reward, based on the impact of the drug cocktail, among the inventors of the drugs it contains. And it must also include specific rules for the phase-in period so as not to discourage ongoing research efforts motivated by the existing patent rules. It is of crucial importance that all these rules be clear and transparent, lest they add to the inevitable risks and uncertainties that complicate the work of inventor firms and sometimes discourage them from important research efforts. This task requires expertise in medicine, statistics, economics, and legal regulation.

Another main task, associated with the third component, concerns the design of rules for allocating the cost of the incentives as well as the formulation of good arguments in favor of this allocation. Effective implementation of the reform requires that much of its cost be borne by the developed countries, which, with 16 percent of the world's population, control about 81 percent of the global social product (World Bank 2004, 253). This is feasible even if these countries, after retargeting existing subsidies to the pharmaceutical industry in accordance with the reformed rules, still had to shoulder around US$70 billion in new expenditures.[12] This amount, after all, is only 0.27 percent of the aggregate gross national income of the high-income countries, or US$70 for each of their residents.[13] To make this planned spending increase realistic, the taxpayers and politicians of the high-income countries need to be given compelling reasons for supporting it.

The plan can be supported by prudential considerations. For one thing, the taxpayers of the more affluent countries gain a substantial benefit for themselves in the form of lower drug prices. Under the current regime, affluent persons in need of essential drugs pay high prices for them, either directly or through their contributions to commercial insurance companies. Under the projected scheme, the prices of such drugs would be much lower, and their consumers, even the richest, would thus save money on drugs and/or insurance premiums. To be sure, such a shifting of costs, within affluent countries, from patients to taxpayers would benefit less-healthy citizens at the expense of the healthier ones. But such a mild mitigation of the effects of luck is actually morally appealing—not least because even those fortunate persons who never or rarely need to take advantage of recent medical advances still benefit from

[12] This figure is in line with the estimates made by the WHO Commission on Macroeconomics and Health (chaired by Jeffrey Sachs), according to which some eight million deaths could be prevented each year in the developing world through providing real access to medical care at a cost of about US$60 billion annually (WHO 2001).

[13] See World Bank 2004, 253, for the aggregate gross national income and the aggregate population of the high-income countries.

pharmaceutical research that affords them the peace of mind derived from knowing that, should they ever become seriously ill, they would have access to cutting-edge medical knowledge and treatments.

A second prudential argument is that, by giving poor populations a free ride on the pharmaceutical research conducted for the benefit of citizens in the affluent countries, we are building goodwill toward ourselves in the developing world by demonstrating in a tangible way our concern for the horrendous public-health problems these populations are facing. This argument has a moral twin: In light of the extent of avoidable mortality and morbidity in the developing world, the case for giving the poor a free ride is morally compelling.

These last twin arguments have wider application. The reform plan would not merely encourage the same sort of pharmaceutical research differently but would also expand the range of medical conditions for which inventor firms would seek solutions. Under the current regime, these firms understandably show little interest in tropical diseases, for example, because, even if they could develop successful treatments, they would not be able to make much money from selling or licensing them. Under the alternative regime I suggest we design, inventor firms could make lots of money by developing such treatments, whose potential impact on the global disease burden is enormous. Measles, malaria, and tuberculosis each kill well over a million people per year, mostly children, and pneumonia kills more than these three combined. New drugs could dramatically reduce the impact of these diseases.

But, it may be asked, why should we citizens of the high-income countries support a rule change that benefits *others* (poor people in the developing world) at our expense? Viewed narrowly, underwriting such incentives for research into widespread but currently neglected diseases might seem to be a dead loss for the affluent countries.

Taking a larger view, however, important gains are readily apparent: The reform would create top-flight medical-research jobs in the developed countries. It would enable us to respond more effectively to public-health emergencies and problems in the future by earning us more rapidly increasing medical knowledge combined with a stronger and more diversified arsenal of medical interventions. In addition, better human health around the world would reduce the threat we face from invasive diseases. The recent SARS outbreak illustrates the last two points: Dangerous diseases can rapidly transit from poor-country settings into cities in the industrialized world (as happened in Toronto); and the current neglect of the medical needs of poor populations leaves us unprepared to deal with such problems when we are suddenly confronted with them. Slowing population growth and bringing enormous reductions in avoidable suffering and deaths worldwide, the reform would further-more be vastly more cost effective and also be vastly better received by people in the poor countries than similarly expensive humanitarian

interventions we have undertaken in recent years and the huge, unrepay-
able loans our governments and their international financial institutions
tend to extended to (often corrupt and oppressive) rulers and elites in the
developing countries. Last, but not least, there is the important moral and
social benefit of working with others, nationally and internationally,
toward overcoming the morally preeminent problem of our age, which is
the horrendous, poverty-induced and largely avoidable morbidity and
mortality in the developing world.

6

In the remainder of this essay, I will further underscore the moral urgency
of the task of dramatically lessening the global burden of disease by
formulating it in human-rights terms. We are used to relating human
rights to the conduct of individual and collective agents—such as prison
guards, generals, corporations, and governments, whose conduct may be
criticized for failing to safeguard the human rights of persons falling
within their domain of responsibility. And their conduct may also be
criticized (typically more severely) for actively violating the human rights
of persons. In the former case, such agents stand accused of failing to
fulfill positive responsibilities they have toward specific persons by not
taking reasonable steps toward ensuring these persons have secure access
to the objects of their human rights.[14] In the latter case, such agents stand
accused of violating negative responsibilities they have toward all human
beings by actively depriving some persons of secure access to the objects
of some of their human rights.

Social (paradigmatically: legal) rules, too, can be criticized in human-
rights terms. This is clearest when such rules explicitly mandate or
authorize conduct that violates human rights, as with laws authorizing
the enslavement of blacks and mandating the forcible return of fugitive
slaves. Such laws violated the human rights of blacks. And those who
participated in imposing such laws, even if they did not themselves own
slaves, violated their negative responsibilities by helping to deprive blacks
of secure access to the objects of their human rights.

Even social rules that do not explicitly mandate or authorize conduct
that violates human rights may still violate human rights. This is most
clearly the case with economic rules that avoidably produce massive
extreme poverty or even famine, as exemplified by the economic regimes
of feudal France and Russia, the economic rules Britain imposed on

---

[14] Here the *object* of a human right is whatever this human right is a right to—adequate
nutrition, for example, or physical integrity. And what matters is *secure access* to such
objects, rather than these objects themselves, because an institutional order is not morally
problematic merely because some of its participants are choosing to fast or to compete in
boxing matches. For a more elaborate statement of my understanding of human rights, see
Pogge 2002a, 2002b.

Ireland and India (causing the Irish potato famine of 1846 to 1850 and the great Bengal famines of 1770 and 1942 to 1945), and the economic regimes temporarily imposed in the Soviet Union and China (the "Great Leap Forward"), which led to massive famines from 1930 to 1933 and 1959 to 1962, respectively.

The assertion that the mentioned economic regimes violated human rights crucially presupposes the claim that the horrendous deprivations and famines in question were in part *due to* those regimes and would have been—partly or wholly—avoided if a suitably modified regime had been in place instead. If this presupposition holds, the economic regimes mentioned were indeed in violation of human rights.

Here it may be objected that a just economic order should be immune from criticism on human-rights grounds: If a laissez-faire libertarian or communist or feudal economic order is what justice requires, then it is right that such an order should be upheld, even if doing so avoidably leads to deprivations on a massive scale.

The flaw in this objection is obvious. The objection assumes that the justice of an economic order is independent of how this order affects the fulfillment of human rights. But human rights are the core values of our moral and political discourse, central to how justice is conceived in the modern world. Social rules that avoidably deprive large numbers of persons of secure access to the objects of their human rights are, for this reason alone, unjust (assuming again that these deprivations are avoidable, wholly or in part, through suitably modified rules). In the era of human rights, then, social rules are in good part judged by their effects on the fulfillment of human rights. To be just, such rules must not violate human rights, that is, they must afford human beings secure access to the objects of their human rights insofar as this is reasonably possible.

When social rules violate human rights without explicitly mandating or authorizing conduct that violates human rights, then those who participate in upholding these rules may not be human-rights violators. They are not violators of human rights when they are sincerely and on the basis of the best available evidence convinced that the social rules they are upholding do not violate human rights (that is, that these rules contribute to the realization of human rights insofar as this is reasonably possible). Participation in the imposition of social rules constitutes a human-rights violation only when these rules *foreseeably* and avoidably deprive human beings of secure access to the objects of their human rights—when the imposers of the rule could and should have known that these rules fail to realize human rights insofar as this is reasonably possible, could and should have known that there are feasible and practicable reforms of these rules through which a substantial portion of existing deprivations could be avoided.

Much of the account I have just given is suggested by Article 28 of the 1948 *Universal Declaration of Human Rights*:

> Everyone is entitled to a social and international order in which the rights and freedoms set forth in this Declaration can be fully realized. (*UDHR*, Article 28; cf. also Article 22)

Three points are worth noting about this article. First, its peculiar status. As its reference to "the rights and freedoms set forth in this Declaration" indicates, Article 28 does not add a further right to the list but rather addresses the concept of a human right, says something about what a human right is. It is then consistent with any substantive account of what human rights there are—even while it significantly affects the meaning of any human rights postulated in the other articles of this *Universal Declaration*: They all are to be understood as claims on the institutional order of any comprehensive social system.

Second, this idea about how the human rights postulated in the *Universal Declaration* are to be understood fits well with what I have just outlined—with how human rights can figure centrally in the critical examination of social rules. In fact, we can achieve perfect congruence through four plausible interpretive conjectures:

(1) Alternative institutional orders that do not satisfy the require- ment of Article 28 can be ranked by how close they come to enabling the full realization of human rights: Social systems ought to be structured so that human rights can be realized in them as fully as possible.

(2) How fully human rights *can* be realized under some institutional order is measured by how fully these human rights generally are, or (in the case of a hypothetical institutional order) generally would be, realized in it.

(3) An institutional order *realizes* a human right insofar as (and fully if and only if) this human right is *fulfilled* for the persons upon whom this order is imposed.

(4) A human right is fulfilled for some person if and only if this person enjoys *secure access to the object of this human right*.

Taking these four conjectures together, Article 28 should be read as holding that the moral quality, or justice, of any institutional order depends primarily on its success in affording all its participants secure access to the objects of their human rights: Any institutional order is to be assessed and reformed principally by reference to its relative impact on the realization of the human rights of those on whom it is imposed.[15]

The third noteworthy feature of Article 28 is its explicit reference to the international order. When we reflect on social rules, we tend to think of the institutional (and more specifically legal) rules of a territorial state

---

[15] "*Relative* impact," because a comparative judgment is needed about how much more or less fully human rights are realized in this institutional order than they would be realized in its feasible alternatives.

first and foremost. Less familiar, but no less important in the modern world, are the rules of the international institutional order, whose design profoundly affects the fulfillment of human rights, especially in the poorer and weaker countries. Recognizing this point, Article 28 requires that the rules of the international order be shaped, insofar as this is reasonably possible, so as to afford human beings everywhere secure access to the objects of their human rights.

In the world as it is, some eighteen million human beings die each year from poverty-related causes, mostly from communicable diseases that could easily be averted or cured. Insofar as these deaths and the immense suffering of those still surviving these diseases are avoidable, their victims are deprived of some of the objects of their human rights—for example, of their "right to a standard of living adequate for the health and well-being of himself and of his family, including food, clothing, housing and medical care and necessary social services" (*UDHR*, Article 25; cf. *ICESCR*, Articles 11–12).

If these victims are so deprived, then who or what is depriving them, violating their human rights? Several factors, national and global, substantially contribute to the deprivations they suffer. As I have been arguing, one important such factor is the way pharmaceutical research into drugs and vaccines is incentivized under the current rules of the TRIPS Agreement as supplemented by various bilateral agreements the United States has been pursuing.

With this background, we can look once more at the question of why we citizens of the high-income countries should support a reform of the global health system that benefits others (poor people in the developing world) at our expense. The landholders of feudal France or Russia could have asked likewise. And the answers are closely analogous: We ought to support such a reform, even if it involves significant opportunity costs for us, because it is necessary for rendering minimally just (in the explicated sense of "realizing human rights insofar as this is reasonably possible") the rules of the world economy considered as one scheme. Minimal justice in this sense is compatible with these rules being designed by, and with their greatly and disproportionately benefiting, the governments and corporations of the developed countries. However, minimal justice is not compatible with these rules being designed so that they result in a much higher incidence of extreme poverty and in much higher mortality and morbidity from curable diseases than would be reasonably avoidable.

7

Against this line of argument, it may be objected that accession to the TRIPS Agreement (and the whole WTO Treaty) is voluntary. Since the poor countries have themselves signed on to the rules as they are, the imposition of these rules cannot be a violation of their human rights. *Volenti non fit iniuria* (to the willing, no wrong is done).

There are at least four distinct responses to this objection, each of which seems sufficient to refute it.

First, appeal to consent can defeat the charge of rights violation only if the rights in question are alienable and, more specifically, can be waived by consent. Yet, on the usual understanding of human rights, they cannot be so waived: Persons cannot waive their human rights to personal freedom, political participation, freedom of expression, or freedom from torture. (Persons can promise, through a religious vow perhaps, to serve another, to refrain from voting, or to keep quiet. But, wherever human rights are respected, such promises are legally unenforceable and thus do not succeed in waiving the right in question.) There are various reasons for conceiving human rights in this way: A person changes over time, and her later self has a vital interest in being able to avoid truly horrific burdens her earlier self had risked or incurred. Moreover, the option of placing such burdens on one's future self is likely to be disadvantageous even to the earlier self by encouraging predators seeking to elicit a waiver from this earlier self through manipulation of her or of her circumstances (for example, by getting her into a life-threatening situation from which one then offers to rescue her at the price of her permanent enslavement). Finally, waivers of human rights impose considerable burdens on third parties who will be (more or less directly) confronted with the resulting suffering of people enslaved or tortured or starving.

Second, an appeal to consent blocks the complaint of those now lacking secure access to the objects of (some of) their human rights only insofar as they have *themselves* consented to the regime that perpetuates their deprivation. Yet, most of those who are endangered by diseases or are severely impoverished live in countries that are not meaningfully democratic, and consent to the present global economic order by their rulers thus cannot be counted as consent by their subjects. For example, in 1995 Nigeria's accession to the WTO was effected by its brutal military dictator Sani Abacha, Myanmar's by the notorious SLORC junta (the State Law and Order Restoration Council), Indonesia's by the kleptocrat Suharto, and Zimbabwe's by Robert Mugabe and, two years later, Zaire's (since renamed the Congo) by Mobutu Sese Seko.

Third, consent to a very burdensome global regime can have justificatory force only if it was not impelled by the threat of even greater burdens. Thus, your consent cannot justify your enslavement when your consent was your only escape from continued torture or, indeed, from an accidental drowning. An appeal to consent thus blocks a complaint by the poor against the present global economic order only if, at the time of consenting, they had an alternative option that would have given them secure access to the objects of their human rights. Yet, the populations of most poor WTO member states would have suffered even more if they had remained outside the regime. These people would still have been subject to coercively enforced global rules preventing them from offering their products in the more affluent countries or from migrating there. Thus, even the unreal case of a poor country's population voting with full information and unanimously for WTO accession does not exemplify appropriate consent if the severely deprived within this population were only given a choice between the deprivations they now endure and the even greater deprivations they would have had to endure outside the WTO.[16]

Fourth, an appeal to consent cannot justify the severe impoverishment of children who are greatly overrepresented among those suffering severe poverty and account for about two-thirds of all deaths from poverty-related causes (thirty-four thousand daily).[17] The claim that the present global economic order foreseeably and avoidably violates the human rights of *children* cannot be blocked by any conceivable appeal to consent.

8

Participation in the imposition of social rules constitutes a human-rights violation only when these rules *foreseeably* and avoidably deprive human beings of secure access to the object of their human rights—only when the imposers of the rules could and should have known that these rules fail to realize human rights insofar as this is reasonably possible, could and should have known that there are feasible and practicable reforms of these rules through which a substantial portion of existing deprivations can be avoided. I think this condition is fulfilled in the world today. The governments and citizens of the high-income countries could and should know that most of the current premature mortality and morbidity is avoidable through feasible and modest reforms, such as the global health-system reform outlined here. Still, with the suffering of the poor far away and invisible, powerful psychological tendencies and economic incentives suppress such knowledge through a constant barrage of rationalizations and deceptions. It may be possible to break through this barrage with a concrete plan for a feasible and realistic institutional reform that would help extend the benefits of the enormous technological and economic

---

[16] I am not disputing that joining the WTO was better for most poor states, and even for their poor citizens, than staying out. But this claim cannot defend the WTO regime (though it is often so used): Analogously, one could defend the fascist order briefly established in Europe by pointing out that countries cooperating with Hitler and Mussolini did better than countries opposing that order.

[17] USDA 1999, iii. The U.S. government mentions this fact while arguing that the developed countries should *not* follow the U.N. Food and Agriculture Organization's proposal to increase development assistance for agriculture by $6 billion annually, that $2.6 billion is ample. See ibid., appendix A.

gains of the previous century to that other half of humankind currently still largely excluded from them.

Centre for Applied Philosophy and Public Ethics
Australian National University
LPO Box 8260
Canberra, ACT 2601
Australia
tp6@columbia.edu

Bibliography

Anand, S. 2002. "The Concern for Equity in Health." *Journal of Epidemiology and Community Health* 56, no. 7:485–87.

Attaran, A., K. I. Barnes, C. Curtis, U. d'Alessandro, C. I. Fanello, M. R. Galinski, et al. 2004. "WHO, the Global Fund, and Medical Malpractice in Malaria Treatment." *Lancet* 363, no. 9404:237–40.

Attaran, A., and L. Gillespie-White. 2001. "Do Patents for Antiretroviral Drugs Constrain Access to AIDS Treatment in Africa?" *Journal of the American Medical Association* 286, no. 15:1886–92.

Balasubramaniam, K. 2001. "Equitable Pricing, Affordability and Access to Essential Drugs in Developing Countries: Consumers Perspective." WHO/WTO Secretariat Workshop on Differential Pricing and Financing of Essential Drugs. www.wto.org/english/tratop_e/trips_e/hosbjor_presentations_e/35balasubramaniam_e.pdf.

Banta, H. D. 2001. "Worldwide Interest in Global Access to Drugs." *Journal of the American Medical Association* 285, no. 22:2844–46.

Barnard, D. 2002. "In the High Court of South Africa, Case No. 4138/98: The Global Politics of Access to Low-Cost AIDS Drugs in Poor Countries." *Kennedy Institute of Ethics Journal* 12, no 2:159–74.

Barry, C., and K. Raworth. 2002. "Access to Medicines and the Rhetoric of Responsibility." *Ethics and International Affairs* 16, no. 2:57–70.

Barton, J. H. 2001. Differentiated Pricing of Patented Products." Commission on Macroeconomics and Health Working Paper Series, Work Group 4, Paper 2. www.cmhealth.org/docs/wg4_paper2.pdf.

Beitz, C. R. 1979. *Political Theory and International Relations*. Princeton: Princeton University Press.

———. 1981. "Economic Rights and Distributive Justice in Developing Societies." *World Politics* 33, no. 3:321–46.

Beitz, C. R. et al., eds. 1985. *International Ethics*. Princeton: Princeton University Press.

Black, R. E., S. S. Morris, and J. Bryce. 2003. "Where and Why Are 10 Million Children Dying Every Year?" *Lancet* 361, no. 9376:2226–34.

Boelaert, M., L. Lynen, W. van Damme, R. Colebunders, E. Goemaere, A. V. Kaninda, et al. 2000. "Do Patents Prevent Access to Drugs for

HIV in Developing Countries?" *Journal of the American Medical Association* 287, no. 7:840–43. Also available at www.accessmed msf. org / prod / publications.asp?scntid = 21520031747452&contentty pe = PARA&.

Canadian Medical Association Journal. 2003. "Patently Necessary: Improving Global Access to Essential Medicines" (editorial). *Canadian Medical Association Journal* 169, no. 12:1257.

Chatterjee, D. K., ed. 2004. *The Ethics of Assistance: Morality and the Distant Needy*. Cambridge: Cambridge University Press.

Chen, S., and M. Ravallion. 2001. "How Did the World's Poorest Fare in the 1990s?" *Review of Income and Wealth* 47:283–300.

———. 2004. "How Have the World's Poorest Fared since the Early 1980s?" World Bank Policy Research Working Paper 3341. http:// econ.worldbank.org/files/36297_wps3341.pdf.

Claeson, M., J. De Beyer, P. Jha, and R. Feachem. 1996. "The World Bank's Perspective on Global Health." *Current Issues in Public Health* 2, nos. 5–6:264–69.

Cohen, J. C., and P. Illingworth. 2004. "The Dilemma of Intellectual Property Rights for Pharmaceuticals: The Tension Between Ensuring Access of the Poor to Medicines and Committing to International Agreements." *Developing World Bioethics* 3, no. 1:27–48.

Corbett, E. L., C. J. Watt, N. Walker, D. Maher, B. G. Williams, M. C. Raviglione, et al. 2003. "The Growing Burden of Tuberculosis: Global Trends and Interactions with the HIV Epidemic." *Archive of Internal Medicine* 163, no. 9:1009–21.

Cornia, G. A., R. Jolly, and F. Stewart, eds. 1987. *Adjustment with a Human Face: Protecting the Vulnerable and Promoting Growth*. 2 volumes. Oxford: Clarendon Press.

Correa, C. 2000. *Intellectual Property Rights, the WTO and Developing Countries: The TRIPs Agreement and Policy Options*. London: Zed Books.

Crocker, D. A., and T. Linden, eds. 1998. *Ethics of Consumption: The Good Life, Justice, and Global Stewardship*. Lanham, Md.: Rowman and Littlefield.

Daniels, N. 1985. *Just Health Care*. Cambridge: Cambridge University Press.

Danzon, P. M. 2003. "Differential Pricing for Pharmaceuticals: Reconciling Access, R&D, and Patents." *International Journal of Health Care Finance and Economics* 3:183–205.

Dasgupta, P. 1993. *An Inquiry into Well-Being and Destitution*. Oxford: Oxford University Press.

De Greiff, P., and C. Cronin, eds. 2002. *Global Justice and Transnational Politics*. Cambridge, Mass.: MIT Press.

Deaton, A. 2003. "How to Monitor Poverty for the Millennium Development Goals." *Journal of Human Development* 4:353–78.

Denicolo, V., and L. A. Franzoni. 2003. "The Contract Theory of Patents." *International Review of Law and Economics* 23, no. 4:365–80.

Diamond, J. 1999. *Guns, Germs, and Steel: The Fates of Human Societies.* New York: Norton.

Dreze, J., and A. K. Sen. 1995. *India: Economic Development and Social Opportunity.* Delhi: Oxford University Press.

Drugs for Neglected Diseases Working Group. 2001. *Fatal Imbalance: The Crisis in Research and Development for Drugs for Neglected Diseases.* Geneva: Médecins Sans Frontières Access to Essential Medicines Campaign and the Drugs for Neglected Diseases Working Group. Also available at www.msf.org/source/access/2001/fatal/fatal.pdf.

Dworkin, R. 1993. "Justice in the Distribution of Health Care." *McGill Law Journal* 38, no. 4:883–98.

Eichengreen, B., J. Tobin, and C. Wyplosz. 1995. "Two Cases for Sand in the Wheels of International Finance." *Economic Journal* 105, no. 127:162–72.

Elster, J., and J. Roemer, eds. 1991. *Interpersonal Comparisons of Well-Being.* Cambridge: Cambridge University Press.

Evans, R. G., M. L. Barer, and T. R. Marmor. 1994. *Why Are Some People Healthy and Others Not?: The Determinants of Health of Populations.* Hawthorne, N.Y.: Aldine de Gruyter.

Evans, T., M. Whitehead, F. Diderichsen, A. Bhuiya, and M. Wirth. 2001. *Challenging Inequities in Health: From Ethics to Action.* New York: Oxford University Press.

FAO (Food and Agriculture Organization of the United Nations). 1999. *The State of Food Insecurity in the World 1999.* www.fao.org/news/1999/img/sofi99-e.pdf.

Farmer, P. 1999. *Infections and Inequalities: The Modern Plagues.* Berkeley: University of California Press.

———. 2003. *Pathologies of Power: Health, Human Rights, and the New War on the Poor.* Berkeley: University of California Press.

Finger, J. M., and P. Schuler. 1999. "Implementation of Uruguay Round Commitments: The Development Challenge." World Bank Research Working Paper 2215. http://econ.worldbank.org/docs/941.pdf.

Friedman, M. A., H. den Besten, and A. Attaran. 2003. "Out-Licensing: A Practical Approach for Improvement of Access to Medicines in Poor Countries." *Lancet* 361, no. 9354:341–44.

Fukuda Parr, S., and A. K. Shiva Kumar, eds. 2003. *Readings in Human Development: Concepts, Measures, and Policies for a Development Paradigm.* New Delhi: Oxford University Press.

GFHR (Global Forum for Health Research). 2000. *The 10/90 Report on Health Research 2000.* Geneva: Global Forum for Health Research. Also available at http://mim.nih.gov/english/news/global forum.html.

————. 2002. *The 10/90 Report on Health Research 2001–2002*. Geneva: Global Forum for Health Research.

————. 2004. *The 10/90 Report on Health Research 2003–2004*. Geneva: Global Forum for Health Research. Also available at www.globalfor umhealth.org/pages/index.asp.

Goodin, R. E. 1988. "What Is So Special about Our Fellow Countrymen?" *Ethics* 98:663–86.

————, ed. 1996. *The Theory of Institutional Design*. Cambridge: Cambridge University Press.

Gupta, R., J. Y. Kim, M. A. Espinal, J. M. Caudron, B. Pecoul, P. E. Farmer, et al. 2001. "Public Health: Responding to Market Failures in Tuberculosis Control." *Science* 293, no. 5532:1049–51.

Gwatkin, D. R., and M. Guillot. 1999. *The Burden of Disease among the Global Poor: Current Situation, Future Trends, and Implications for Strategy*. Washington, D.C., and Geneva: The World Bank and the Global Forum for Health Research.

Gwatkin, D. R. 2000. "Health Inequalities and the Health of the Poor: What Do We Know? What Can We Do?" *Bulletin of the World Health Organization* 78:3–15. Also available at www.who.int/bulletin/tableof contents/2000/vol.78no.1.html.

Hurrell, A., and N. Woods, eds., 1999. *Inequality, Globalisation and World Politics*. Oxford: Oxford University Press.

ICESCR (*International Covenant on Economic, Social, and Cultural Rights*). 1966. Available at www.unhchr.ch/html/menu3/b/a_cescr. htm.

ILO (International Labour Organisation). 2002. *A Future without Child Labour*. Geneva: International Labour Office. Also available at www.ilo.org/public/english/standards/decl/publ/reports/report3. htm.

Jha, P., A. Mills, K. Hanson, L. Kumaranayake, L. Conteh, C. Kurowski, et al. 2002. "Improving the Health of the Global Poor." *Science* 295, no. 5562:2036–39.

Juma, C. 1999. "Intellectual Property Rights and Globalization: Implications for Developing Countries." Science, Technology and Innovation Discussion Paper No. 4, Harvard Center for International Development, www2.cid.harvard.edu/cidbiotech/dp/discuss4.pdf.

Kagan, S. 1989. *The Limits of Morality*. Oxford: Oxford University Press.

Kamm, F. M. 1993, 1996. *Morality, Mortality*. 2 volumes. Oxford: Oxford University Press.

Kanavos, P., J. Costa-i-Font, S. Merkur, and M. Gemmill. 2004. "The Economic Impact of Pharmaceutical Parallel Trade in European Union Member States: A Stakeholders Analysis." London School of Economics and Political Science Working Paper. www.lse.ac.uk/col lections/LSEHealthAndSocialCare/pdf/Workingpapers/Paper.pdf.

Kaul, I., P. Conceicao, K. Coulven, and K. Mendoza. 1999. *Providing Global Public Goods: Managing Globalization*. Oxford: Oxford University Press.

Kaul, I., I. Grunberg, M. Stern, and M. A. Stern. 2003. *Global Public Goods: International Cooperation in the 21st Century*. Oxford: Oxford University Press.

Kawachi, I., B. P. Kennedy, and R. G. Wilkinson. 1999. *The Society and Population Health Reader: Income Inequality and Health*. New York: New Press.

Kessel, E., S. Chattopadhyay, and B. Pecoul. 1999. "Access to Essential Drugs in Poor Countries." *Journal of the American Medical Association* 282, no. 7:630–31.

Keusch, G. T., and R. A. Nugent. 2002. "The Role of Intellectual Property and Licensing in Promoting Research in International Health: Perspectives from a Public Sector Biomedical Research Agency." Commission on Macroeconomics and Health Working Paper Series, Work Group 2, Paper 7. www3.who.int/whosis/cmh/cmh_papers/e/pdf/wg2_paper06.pdf.

Kim, J. Y., J. V. Millen, A. Irwin, and J. Gershman. 2000. *Dying for Growth: Global Inequality and the Health of the Poor*. Monroe, Me.: Common Courage Press.

Kindermans, J., and F. Matthys. 2001. "Introductory Note: The Access to Essential Medicines Campaign." *Tropical Medicine and International Health* 6, 11:955–56.

Kremer, M. 2001. "Public Policies to Stimulate the Development of Vaccines and Drugs for Neglected Diseases." Commission on Macroeconomics and Health Working Paper Series, Work Group 2, Paper 8. www.cmhealth.org/docs/wg2_paper8.pdf.

Landes, D. 1998. *The Wealth and Poverty of Nations: Why Some Are So Rich and Some So Poor*. New York: Norton.

Lanjouw, J. O. 2001. "A Proposal to Use Patent Law to Lower Drug Prices in Developing Countries." Commission on Macroeconomics and Health Working Paper Series, Work Group 2, Paper 11. www.cmhealth.org/docs/wg2_paper11.pdf.

———. 2002a. "A New Global Patent Regime for Diseases: U.S. and International Legal Issues." *Harvard Journal of Law and Technology* 16, no. 1:85–124.

———. 2002b. "Beyond TRIPS: A New Global Patent Regime." *Policy Brief No. 3*. Washington, D.C.: Center for Global Development.

———. 2003a. "A Proposed Solution to the TRIPS Debate over Pharmaceuticals." *Technological Innovation and Intellectual Property Newsletter* 2003, no. 3. Also available at http://www.researchoninnovation.org/tiip/index.htm.

———. 2003b. "Intellectual Property and the Availability of Pharmaceuticals in Poor Countries. In *National Bureau of Economic Research*

Innovation Policy and the Economy, vol. 3. Cambridge, Mass.: MIT Press.

Loff, B. 2002. "World Trade Organization Wrestles with Access to Cheap Drugs Solution." *Lancet* 360, no. 9346:1670.

Milanovic, B. 2002. "True World Income Distribution, 1988 and 1993: First Calculation Based on Household Surveys Alone." *Economic Journal* 112:51–92. Also available at www.blackwellpublishers.co.uk/specialarticles/ecoj50673.pdf.

Miller, D. 2001. "Distributing Responsibilities." *Journal of Political Philosophy* 9, no. 4:453–71.

MSF (Médecins Sans Frontières). 2001. *Fatal Imbalance: The Crisis in Research and Development for Drugs for Neglected Diseases*. Geneva: Médecins Sans Frontières.

Murphy, L. 2000. *Moral Demands in Non-Ideal Theory*. Oxford: Oxford University Press.

Musgrave, R. A., and A. T. Peacock, eds. 1958. *Classics in the Theory of Public Finance*. London: Macmillan.

Nagel, T. 1977. "Poverty and Food: Why Charity Is Not Enough." In *Food Policy: The Responsibility of the United States in Life and Death Choices*, edited by P. Brown and H. Shue, 54–62. New York: The Free Press.

———. 1991. *Equality and Partiality*. Oxford: Oxford University Press.

Nussbaum, M. C. (with respondents). 1996. *For Love of Country: Debating the Limits of Patriotism*. Boston: Beacon Press.

———. 2000. *Women and Human Development: The Capabilities Approach*. Cambridge: Cambridge University Press.

———. 2001. *Women and Human Development*. Cambridge: Cambridge University Press.

Nussbaum, M. C., and J. Glover, eds. 1995. *Women, Culture, and Development: A Study of Human Capabilities*. Oxford: Oxford University Press.

Nussbaum, M. C., and A. K. Sen, eds. 1993. *The Quality of Life*. Oxford: Oxford University Press.

Okin, S. 1989. *Justice, Gender, and the Family*. New York: Basic Books.

———. 1986. *Faces of Hunger*. London: Allen and Unwin.

———. 1974. "Lifeboat Earth." *Philosophy and Public Affairs* 4: 273–92.

Orbinski, J. 2001. "Health, Equity and Trade: A Failure in Global Governance." In *The Role of the World Trade Organization in Global Governance*, edited by G. Sampson, 223–41. Tokyo: United Nations University Press.

Parfit, D. 1984. *Reasons and Persons*. Oxford: Oxford University Press.

Pecoul, B. 1999. "Access to Essential Drugs in Poor Countries—Reply." *Journal of the American Medical Association* 282, no. 7:631.

Pecoul, B., P. Chirac, P. Trouiller, and J. Pinel. 1999. "Access to Essential Drugs in Poor Countries—A Lost Battle?" *Journal of the American Medical Association* 281, no. 4:361–67.

Pennock, J. R., and J. W. Chapman, eds. 1981. *Human Rights*. New York: New York University Press.

———. 1982. *Ethics, Economics, and the Law*. New York: New York University Press.

Pogge, T. W. 1989. *Realizing Rawls*. Ithaca: Cornell University Press.

———, ed. 2001. *Global Justice*. Oxford: Blackwell.

———. 2002a. *World Poverty and Human Rights: Cosmopolitan Responsibilities and Reforms*. Cambridge: Polity Press.

———. 2002b. "Human Rights and Human Responsibilities." In *Global Justice and Transnational Politics*, edited by P. de Greiff and C. Cronin, 151–95. Cambridge, Mass.: MIT Press.

———. 2004. "The First U.N. Millennium Development Goal." *Journal of Human Development* 5, no. 3:377–97.

———. Forthcoming. "Relational Conceptions of Justice: Responsibilities for Health Outcomes." In *Health, Ethics, and Equity*, edited by S. Anand, F. Peter, and A. K. Sen, 135–62. Oxford: Oxford University Press.

Pogge, T. W., and S. G. Reddy. 2003. "Unknown: The Extent, Distribution, and Trend of Global Income Poverty." Available at www.social analysis.org.

Ramsey, S. 2001. "No Closure in Sight for the 10/90 Health-Research Gap." *Lancet* 358:1348.

Rawls, J. 1996. *Political Liberalism*. New York: Columbia University Press. Original published in 1993.

———. 1999a. *A Theory of Justice*. Cambridge, Mass.: Harvard University Press. Original published in 1971.

———. 1999b. *The Law of Peoples*. Cambridge, Mass.: Harvard University Press.

———. 2001. *Justice as Fairness: A Brief Restatement*. Cambridge, Mass.: Harvard University Press.

Reddy, S. G., and T. W. Pogge. Forthcoming. "How *Not* to Count the Poor." Forthcoming in an anthology edited by S. Anand and J. Stiglitz. Also available at www.socialanalysis.org

Roemer, J. 1996. *Theories of Distributive Justice*. Cambridge, Mass.: Harvard University Press.

Rome Declaration on World Food Security. 1996, www.fao.org/wfs/.

Rorty, R. 1996. "Who Are We?: Moral Universalism and Economic Triage." *Diogenes* 173:5–15.

Ruggie, J. G. 1998. *Constructing the World Polity*. London: Routledge.

Sachs, J., and P. Malaney. 2002. "The Economic and Social Burden of Malaria." *Nature* 415, no. 6872:680–85.

Scanlon, T. M. 1998. *What We Owe to Each Other*. Cambridge, Mass.: Harvard University Press.

Scheffler, S. 2001. *Boundaries and Allegiances*. Oxford: Oxford University Press.

Scherer, F. M., and J. Watal. 2001. "Post-TRIPS Options for Access to Patented Medicines in Developing Countries." Commission on Macroeconomics and Health Working Paper Series, Work Group 4, Paper 1. www.cmhealth.org/docs/wg4_paper1.pdf.

Schüklenk, U. 2001. "Affordable Access to Essential Medication in Developing Countries: Conflicts Between Ethical and Economic Imperatives." *Journal of Medicine and Philosophy* 27, no. 2:179–95.

Sen, A. K. 1981. *Poverty and Famines*. Oxford: Oxford University Press.

———. 1982. *Choice, Welfare and Measurement*. Cambridge: Cambridge University Press.

———. 1984. *Resources, Values, and Development*. Cambridge, Mass.: Harvard University Press.

———. 1987. *The Standard of Living*. Cambridge: Cambridge University Press.

———. 1992. *Inequality Reexamined*. Cambridge, Mass.: Harvard University Press.

———. 1999. *Commodities and Capabilities*. Delhi: Oxford University Press. Original published in 1985.

———. 2000. *Development as Freedom*. New York: Anchor Books.

Sen, A. K., and B. Williams, eds. 1982. *Utilitarianism and Beyond*. Cambridge: Cambridge University Press.

Shue, H. 1996. *Basic Rights: Subsistence, Affluence, and U.S. Foreign Policy*. Princeton: Princeton University Press. Original published in 1980.

Singer, P. 1972. "Famine, Affluence and Morality." *Philosophy and Public Affairs* 1, no. 3:229–43.

———. 1993. *Practical Ethics*. 2nd edition. Cambridge: Cambridge University Press.

———. 2002. *One World: The Ethics of Globalization*. New Haven: Yale University Press.

Smith, A. 1976. *The Wealth of Nations*. Oxford: Clarendon Press. Original published in 1776.

———. 1982. *A Theory of the Moral Sentiments*. Indianapolis: Liberty Classics. Original published in 1759.

Smith, R., R. Beaglehole, D. Woodward, and N. Drager. 2003. *Global Public Goods for Health: Health, Economic, and Public Health Perspectives*. Oxford: Oxford University Press.

Stansfield, S. K., M. Harper, G. Lamb, and J. Lob-Levyt. 2002. "Innovative Financing of International Public Goods for Health." Commission on Macroeconomics and Health Working Paper Series,

Work Group 2, Paper 22. www.who.int/macrohealth/infocentre/pre sentations/en/2wg2_paper22Stansfield.pdf.

Stiglitz, J. 2002. *Globalization and Its Discontents*. Harmondsworth: Penguin.

Townsend, P., N. Davidson, and M. Whitehead. 1990. *Inequalities in Health: The Black Report and the Health Divide*. London: Penguin.

Trouiller, P., P. Olliaro, E. Torreele, J. Orbinski, R. Laing, and N. Ford. 2002. "Drug Development for Neglected Diseases: A Deficient Market and a Public-Health Policy Failure." *Lancet* 359, no. 9324:2188–94. Also available at www.accessmed-msf.org/prod/publications.asp?scn tid = 2592002174315&contenttype = PARA&.

Trouiller, P., E. Torreele, P. Olliaro, N. White, S. Foster, D. Wirth, et al. 2001. "Drugs for Neglected Diseases: A Failure of the Market and a Public Health Failure?" *Tropical Medicine and International Health* 6, no. 11:945–51.

UDHR (Universal Declaration of Human Rights), approved and proclaimed by the General Assembly of the United Nations on December 10, 1948, as Resolution 217 A (III).

U.N. Millennium Declaration, General Assembly Resolution 55/2, 2000, www.un.org/millennium/declaration/ares552e.htm.

UNCTAD (United Nations Conference on Trade and Development). 1999. *Trade and Development Report 1999*. New York: U.N. Publications. Also available at http://r0.unctad.org/en/pub/ps1tdr99.htm.

UNDP (United Nations Development Programme). 1998. *Human Development Report 1998*. New York: Oxford University Press.

———. 1999. *Human Development Report 1999*. New York: Oxford University Press.

———. 2001. *Human Development Report 2001*. New York: Oxford University Press. Also available at www.undp.org/hdr2001/.

———. 2003. *Human Development Report 2003*. New York: Oxford University Press. Also available at www.undp.org/hdr2003/.

UNICEF (United Nations Children's Fund). 2002. *The State of the World's Children 2002*. New York: UNICEF. Also available at www.unicef.org/sowc02/pdf/sowc2002-eng-full.pdf.

UNIFEM (United Nations Development Fund for Women). 2001. "Eradicating Women's Poverty," www.unifem.undp.org/ ec_pov.htm.

USDA (United States Department of Agriculture). 1999. *U.S. Action Plan on Food Security*. Washington, D.C.: USDA. Also available at www.fas.usda.gov/icd/summit/usactplan.pdf.

Velasquez, G., and P. Boulet. 1999. "Essential Drugs in the New International Economic Environment." *Bulletin of the World Health Organization* 77, no. 3:288–92.

Wallerstein, I. 1984. *The Politics of the World Economy*. Cambridge: Cambridge University Press.

Watal, J. 2000. "Access to Essential Medicines in Developing Countries: Does the WTO TRIPS Agreement Hinder It?" Science, Technology, and Innovation Discussion Paper No. 8, Harvard Center for Interna tional Development. www2.cid.harvard.edu/cidbiotech/dp/discus sion8. pdf.

WHO (World Health Organisation). 2000. *WHO Medicines Strategy: Framework for Action in Essential Drugs and Medicines Policy 2000– 2003*. Geneva: WHO Publications.

———. 2001. *Macroeconomics and Health: Investing in Health for Economic Development: Report of the Commission on Macroeconomics and Health*. Geneva: WHO Publications. Also available at www.cmhealth. org/www.cid.harvard.edu/cidcmh/CMHReport.pdf.

———. 2003. *World Health Report 2003: Shaping the Future*. Geneva: WHO Publications.

———. 2004a. *Medicines and the Idea of Essential Drugs (EDM)*. Geneva: WHO Publications. Also available at www.who.int/medicines/ rationale.shtml.

———. 2004b. *The World Health Report 2004*. Geneva: WHO Publications. Also available at www.who.int/whr/2004.

WHO and WTO (World Trade Organisation). 2002. *WTO Agreements and Public Health: A Joint Report of the World Health Organisation (WHO) and the Secretariat of the World Trade Organisation (WTO)*. Geneva: Secretariat of the WTO.

Wilkinson, R. G., ed. 1986. *Class and Health: Research and Longitudinal Data*. London: Tavistock.

Wilkinson, R. G. 1996. *Unhealthy Societies: The Afflictions of Inequality*. London: Routledge.

WIPO (World Intellectual Property Organization). 2000. *Patent Protection and Access to HIV/AIDS Pharmaceuticals in Sub-Saharan Africa*. Washington, D.C.: International Intellectual Property Institute.

Woodward, D. 2001. "Trade Barriers and Prices of Essential Health-Sector Inputs." Commission on Macroeconomics and Health Working Paper Series, Work Group 4, Paper 9. www.cmhealth.org/docs/ wg4_paper9.pdf.

World Bank. 1993. *World Development Report 1993: Investing in Health*. New York: Oxford University Press.

———. 2004. *World Development Report 2004*. New York: Oxford University Press.

WTO (World Trade Organization). "TRIPs and Pharmaceutical Patents, Fact Sheet." www.wto.org/english/tratop_e/trips_e/factsheet_phar m00_e.htm.

———. "Pharmaceutical Patents and the TRIPs Agreement." www.wto. org/english/tratop_e/trips_e/pharma_ato186_e.htm.

[34]

Biomedical conflicts of interest: a defence of the sequestration thesis—learning from the cases of Nancy Olivieri and David Healy

A Schafer

....

Correspondence to:
Professor Arthur Schafer,
Centre for Professional and
Applied Ethics, University
of Manitoba, 220 Dysart
Road, Winnipeg,
Manitoba, Canada
R3T 2M8;
Schafer@cc.umanitoba.ca

September 2003
....

No discussion of academic freedom, research integrity, and patient safety could begin with a more disquieting pair of case studies than those of Nancy Olivieri and David Healy. The cumulative impact of the Olivieri and Healy affairs has caused serious self examination within the biomedical research community. The first part of the essay analyses these recent academic scandals. The two case studies are then placed in their historical context—that context being the transformation of the norms of science through increasingly close ties between research universities and the corporate world. After a literature survey of the ways in which corporate sponsorship has biased the results of clinical drug trials, two different strategies to mitigate this problem are identified and assessed: a regulatory approach, which focuses on managing risks associated with industry funding of university research, and a more radical approach, the sequestration thesis, which counsels the outright elimination of corporate sponsorship. The reformist approach is criticised and the radical approach defended.

The leading individual roles in this diptych are taken by two internationally eminent medical researchers, haematologist Nancy Olivieri and psychiatrist David Healy. The institutional players include one research intensive university (the University of Toronto) and two affiliated research intensive teaching hospitals (the Hospital for Sick Children, referred to as "Sick Kids" or "Sick Kids Hospital" and the Centre for Addiction and Mental Health, referred to as "CAMH"). The cast of supporting characters is large. On one side are senior hospital administrators and medical faculty deans, together with hospital and university presidents and boards of directors. On the other side is to be found a small group of medical scientists, supported primarily by the Canadian Association of University Teachers (CAUT).

Not coincidentally, the Olivieri and Healy scandals share in common a number of key elements:

- Wealthy and powerful drug companies hover in the background of both, and sometimes occupy a good deal of the foreground, as well: Apotex in the case of Olivieri, Eli Lilly in the case of Healy.
- These drug companies not only fund university and hospital researchers, they are also major donors to the institutions within which researchers carry out their clinical studies.
- Neither Apotex nor Eli Lilly was happy to have adverse information about their drugs publicised.
- Both Olivieri and Healy personally experienced serious negative consequences from their willingness to speak publicly about potential dangers to patients.
- Each of them appealed for assistance, unavailingly, to the senior administrators of the University of Toronto and its Faculty of Medicine. Although there had been a changeover of university presidents and medical faculty deans in the interval between these two scandals, personnel changes made very little difference to the university's official response.
- In both scandals, university and hospital officials failed to recognise that there had been a fundamental violation of

the principle of academic freedom at the affiliated hospitals.
- In both cases, the whistleblowing physicians found themselves removed from their positions: Olivieri was fired from her position as director of the Hemoglobinopathy Research Program at Sick Kids' Hospital; Healy's employment contract with both CAMH and the University of Toronto's Department of Psychiatry was terminated.
- Both hospitals and the university denied strenuously that these "firings" were in any way related to the whistleblowing.
- Damaging rumours were circulated among Olivieri's colleagues, including allegations that she was scientifically incompetent, guilty of stealing money from her research grants, unethical in her patient care and sleeping with some of the scientists who looked favourably on her research findings[1]; damaging rumours were circulated about Healy that he was a bad clinician, and both a racist, and a member of a cult known as Scientology. A journalist who telephoned me for an interview at the height of the Healy controversy asked whether I knew that Healy was a prominent Scientologist. Her previous interviewee had been a hospital spokesperson who was circulating that piece of disinformation among the media, presumably in an effort to discredit Dr Healy.
- The perpetrators of these false but damaging accusations against Olivieri and Healy mostly preferred to remain anonymous.

Two of the world's most respected blood researchers, David Nathan of Harvard and David Weatherall of Oxford, writing in *The New England Journal of Medicine*, describe the Olivieri affair as a "debacle ...complicated by personal animosity, poor administrative judgment, and bad behaviour among academic colleagues".[2] However, the authors pointedly caution the biological research community not to dismiss the affair as a mere aberration since, they suggest, there is "growing evidence that things may not be much better, albeit less bizarre, elsewhere" (Nathan DG, *et al*,[2] p 1370). Nathan and Weatherall identify close partnerships between universities and the pharmaceutical industry as a crucial factor in generating such moral crises, both at the University of Toronto and elsewhere.

Surprisingly, however, Drs Nathan and Weatherall conclude their *NEJM* commentary with an apparent endorsement of scientific commercialisation:

> We now have the potential to enter one of the most productive periods of biomedical research, the success of which will depend to no small degree on an increasingly close partnership between universities and industry. (Nathan DG, et al,[2] p 1370)

Since commercialisation of university research is the very process which Nathan and Weatherall themselves identify as responsible for having undermined university integrity in the Olivieri affair, the reader is entitled to feel nonplussed. This apparent disconnection between analysis and prescription, puzzling as it may seem to an outsider, reflects a developing consensus within the biomedical research community. The consensus view, strongly promoted by editors of several leading general medical journals, holds that there is nothing inherently wrong or improper about the connubial relationship between universities and industry, so long as the union is properly regulated and managed.

Steven Lewis and his fellow authors of "Dancing with the porcupine"[3] also fall within the developing consensus and, once again, the reader is presented with a perceptive analysis of the problems generated by academic industrial collaborations, oddly combined with an anaemic prescription concerning how best to deal with such problems. Thus, Lewis *et al* recognise that the basic commitment of universities diverges sharply from the basic commitment of corporations: "The duty of universities is to seek truth. The duty of pharmaceutical companies is to make money for their shareholders." They go on to describe at least some university/industry partnerships as "an unholy alliance whereby researchers and universities become handmaidens of industry" (Lewis S, et al,[3] p 783). Nevertheless, when it comes to answering the question: "What is to be done?" the authors hasten to reassure the scientific community: "We are not asking academic researchers to forswear all interactions with industry. We are merely proposing rules for exercising due diligence to protect the essence of academic inquiry" (Lewis s, et al,[3] p 783).

The Porcupine authors adopt the view that it is OK to dance with porcupines if one does so carefully. By analogy, it is OK for scientists and universities to partner with industry, so long as precautions are taken. The suggestion is that if the right regulatory framework is created then the behaviour of industry will "improve voluntarily," "enlightened companies" will adopt "honourable codes of conduct," and cynicism toward industry sponsorship of research will no longer be warranted (Lewis S, et al,[3] p 783).

Readers of a mildly sceptical disposition may wonder, however, whether "due diligence" is the proper response to an "unholy" alliance between institutions each of which has a fundamentally different and potentially contradictory mission. If the threat to research integrity and patient safety is as serious as the available evidence suggests (see below), then the danger posed to universities and hospitals by commercial partnerships might be better compared to swimming with sharks than to dancing with porcupines. Granted, those who wish to dance with porcupines must exercise extreme caution in order to avoid painful skin punctures, but those who swim with sharks may find that they have become little more than shark bait. To avoid such a

cruel fate for our leading universities and their researchers, it might be necessary to decline the swimming invitation altogether. Returning to the porcupine metaphor: there are some dances which it might be better to sit out if one values one's integrity.

Proponents of university/industry partnerships may argue, on the contrary, that instead of business values undermining the integrity of university research, the values of the academy might, instead, elevate morally the conduct of business. Steven Lewis, for example, claims that the involvement of universities in the commercialisation of research has the potential, if accompanied by hardnosed management of the relationship and an acknowledgement of possible dangers, "to keep corporations honest, to ensure that a wider perspective is brought to bear, to create products that might otherwise not see the light of day in a purely private sector milieu" (S Lewis, personal communication, 2003). One must concede that there is no logical impossibility attaching to the hypothesis that the marriage between universities and the corporate sector could produce a "levelling up" rather than a "levelling down" effect. Theoretically, university/industry partnerships might help to produce the "soulful corporation" extolled in some business ethics textbooks. Practically speaking, however, the available evidence shows many cases in which the partnership has had a corrosive effect upon universities and researchers. Evidence to show the opposite effect—the transformation of corporations in an altruistic direction—seems rather thin on the ground. This may not be a decisive objection, however, since the absence of evidence showing the existence of the alleged beneficent effect of university/industry partnerships on the commercial partner could be attributable to the fact that no one has thought fit to investigate this question, or to the practical difficulties of doing so. How would one ascertain whether or not altruistic uplift actually occurs, let alone quantify it? (This argument was suggested to me by Steven Lewis.)

The argument presented in this paper concludes that the deep malaise in our research universities, exposed in its most acute form by the Olivieri and Healy cases, is not likely to be resolved adequately through the kind of risk management strategies currently advocated by the new consensus. If one is determined to protect core university values of research integrity and academic freedom then reformist measures such as (a) disclosure of conflicts of interest and (b) regulation of contracts between researchers and companies, are not likely to do the job. Instead, there needs to be something close to an outright prohibition on the much vaunted "partnerships" between university researchers, on the one hand, and the pharmaceutical industry, on the other.

What follows next is a discussion and analysis of some issues raised by the Olivieri and Healy cases, respectively.

NANCY OLIVIERI AND THE HOSPITAL FOR SICK CHILDREN

Accounts of the Olivieri/Apotex/Sick Kids Hospital/University of Toronto controversy have multiplied and divided to the point where they would now overfill the shelves of a reasonably sized library. The "Naimark report" (1998),[4] commissioned by the Hospital for Sick Children, took several hundred pages to document its claim that if anyone was at fault in this sorry tale it was Dr Nancy Olivieri. No criticism is directed toward either the hospital or the university for their failure to support Olivieri's academic freedom.

Significant parts of the testimony on which Naimark based his findings were later shown to be incorrect.[5] It took some time, however, for the historical record to be authoritatively established and, in the interim, because of the adverse findings of the Naimark report, Olivieri was charged with "research misconduct" and was thereupon referred, amidst great publicity, first to the medical advisory committee of her own hospital, and subsequently to the College of Physicians and Surgeons of Ontario. Olivieri's patient care was then thoroughly scrutinised by the college. When the Ontario College Committee of Inquiry finally reported, it exonerated her of all charges, and found her conduct to have been exemplary. Unfortunately for Olivieri, the highly publicised referral to the college, together with repeated attempts to dismiss her, forced her to endure years of public humiliation before the charges of unprofessional conduct were exposed as baseless.

Serious doubts about the objectivity of the Naimark inquiry were raised as soon as it was established, and doubts about the accuracy of its report surfaced almost immediately after its publication. Naimark was appointed unilaterally by the hospital, over the objections of Olivieri and her supporters. The latter favoured an investigation conducted by a panel whose composition both sides could accept as impartial and objective. After a good deal of public controversy, the hospital decided to allow Naimark, at the midway point of his inquiry, to recruit two additional panel members; but Olivieri was allowed no input as to their identity. She and her supporters boycotted the entire proceedings as a public demonstration of their lack of confidence in the process by which the inquiry chair and his two fellow panellists were chosen. Evidence that the Naimark report's authors had relied on false, misleading, and heavily biased information led to the launch of a second inquiry, this time commissioned by the Canadian Association of University Teachers.[5] Thompson and his co-authors insisted that they operate independently of CAUT and insisted also that their report be published without alteration. The Canadian Association of University Teachers accepted these conditions. This inquiry was able to draw on much information unavailable to Naimark, and the 540 page report it published, known as the Thompson report, reached conclusions very different from those of Naimark. Here are a few of their findings, all taken from page 29 of the Thompson report:

> Apotex issued more legal warnings to deter Dr Olivieri from communicating this second unexpected risk of L1 to anyone. However, she was legally and ethically obligated to communicate the risk to those taking, or prescribing the drug as there were potential safety implications for patients, and she fulfilled these obligations despite the legal warnings.
> Apotex acted against the public interest in issuing legal warnings to Dr Olivieri to deter her from communicating about risks of L1. None of the legal warnings have been rescinded.
> Apotex's legal warnings violated Dr Olivieri's academic freedom.
> The Hospital for Sick Children and the University of Toronto did not provide effective support either for Dr Olivieri and her rights, or for the principles of research and clinical ethics, and of academic freedom, during the first two and a half years of this controversy. After the controversy became public in 1998, the university stated publicly that it had provided effective support for Dr Olivieri's academic freedom, but this was not true.
> The Hospital for Sick Children and the University of Toronto did not provide effective support either for Dr Olivieri and her rights, or for the principles of research and clinical ethics, and of academic freedom, during the first two and a half years of this controversy. (Thompson J, et al,[5] p 29)

Not surprisingly, given the intensely polarised atmosphere in which this dispute was played out, Naimark responded to the Thompson report's findings by flatly refusing to concede that his own report was seriously deficient.

Naimark and the two academics with whom he collaborated on his report then attempted to rebut some of the CAUT report's findings,[6] and the authors of the CAUT report have, in turn, challenged Naimark's evidence and arguments.[7] Fortunately, at least for those who prefer clarity to confusion, the report of the Ontario College of Physicians and Surgeons, settled many of these disputed matters by authoritatively clearing Olivieri of the charges made against her by Naimark and by the medical advisory council of Sick Kids Hospital.[8] The college's findings were "authoritative" in a legal sense, because it has legislative authority in such disciplinary matters. They were also widely seen as "above the battle", which gave their findings a kind of moral authority. But their jurisdiction was limited, and they could not adjudicate many of the important issues. By exonerating Olivieri and praising her professional conduct, the Ontario college report made it much more likely that Sick Kids Hospital and the University of Toronto would finally move towards a settlement with Olivieri and her scientific supporters. Such a settlement was reached in the autumn of 2002, a mere six years after the conflict became a national and international *cause célèbre*.

The reports and counter-reports, arguments, and rebuttals, have all been widely splashed on the internet and in the mass media. As well, news reports of the affair, together with editorials and commentaries, have appeared in many leading medical journals, including the *New England Journal of Medicine*, the *Lancet*, *Nature*, *Science*, the *Journal of the American Medical Association*, and the *Canadian Medical Association Journal*. The *Canadian Medical Association Journal* published a concise review of both the Naimark and Thompson reports.[9] Hundreds, probably thousands of articles on the scandal have appeared in the Canadian and international press. Lawsuits have proliferated almost as rapidly. News stories and documentaries on radio and television have filled the airwaves. British novelist John le Carré published a novel based loosely on the facts of the Olivieri case,[10] and Hollywood producers are rumoured to be interested in turning this drama into a blockbuster movie.

Yet, despite the apparent complexity of the facts and circumstances surrounding the scandal, the Canadian public almost immediately understood the gist of the underlying ethical issues. With seeming indifference to the campaign of vilification against Olivieri—a campaign which questioned her scientific competence, her ethics, her personality, and even her sanity—both the scientific community and the general public appeared intuitively to understand that when Olivieri spoke out publicly about perceived dangers to her patients, she was acting in a manner consistent with the highest traditions of her profession. This subjective judgment about popular perceptions of the scandal is based upon reports and commentaries in medical/scientific journals, and supported by an unscientific survey of letters to the editor and callers to open line radio shows in Canada.

In short, notwithstanding the proliferation of competing reports, the rights and wrongs of the Olivieri/Apotex dispute are not so very complicated or difficult to comprehend. Indeed, they can be encapsulated in a few sentences. (1) Once Dr Olivieri came to believe, based on scientifically credible preliminary evidence, that the experimental treatment she was administering might cause unanticipated harm to some of her patients/research subjects, she was duty bound to disclose those risks. (The risks of harm were discovered by serial liver biopsy, but actual harm, were it to occur, would be expected to occur very gradually over a period of many years.) (2) Olivieri's university and her hospital had a corollary duty to support her request for assistance in this exercise of academic freedom and in the performance of her obligations as a physician and a researcher. Their failure to provide this support in an effective manner raises important questions about the way in which society funds biomedical research institutions and biomedical research.

Every version of the Hippocratic Oath, from ancient times down to the present day, has had, as its leading principle, some version of the maxim that "the life and health of my patient will be my first consideration". Thus, whether or not Dr Olivieri is ultimately proven to have been correct in her negative interpretation of the preliminary scientific data, once her data indicated the possibility of unanticipated harm, she was morally obliged to inform her patients of this risk. Writing in the *New England Journal of Medicine*, two blood science researchers, David G Nathan, of Harvard's Dana-Farber Cancer Institute and David J Weatherall, of Oxford University, comment that: "a]s of this writing, the safety and efficacy of deferiprone have not been established". They suggest that it takes years of careful monitoring before the effectiveness of any iron chelator is clinically established; but they then go on to remark that: "Suffice it to say, when the dispute began, Olivieri had good reason to believe that deferiprone was neither safe nor effective" (Nathan DG, *et* al,[7] p 17). (Since Apotex discontinued the clinical trial prematurely, no conclusive scientific evidence exists, and the scientific aspect of the controversy remains unresolved.)

One important qualification should be appended to this claim. Given that the stakes were high, both for the patients/research subjects and for the drug company, Olivieri had an obligation to exercise due diligence by consulting qualified colleagues about her interpretation. This she did, and they supported her concerns. (Apotex, however, most definitely did not agree with Olivieri's interpretation of her data, and the company was supported in its favourable interpretation by a number of scientists receiving financial support from them.) It would then be the responsibility of patients to weigh the hoped for benefits against the possible risks of harm. Respect for the value of patient autonomy clearly requires that those patients who are also research subjects be given all materially relevant information in order to enable them to decide whether they wish to continue participating in a clinical trial. It should go without saying that the information to which patients are morally and legally entitled includes information about risks of harm which comes to light during the course of a clinical trial.

Olivieri also had ancillary obligations to report any newly discovered risks to the research ethics board of her hospital and to share her findings with other researchers, both at scientific meetings and in peer reviewed journals. Only in this way could her colleagues, worldwide, test and assess her conclusions and properly inform their own thalassaemia patients of newly discovered potential risks. In every case, Dr Olivieri behaved in the manner required by her professional obligations, though she, and the core group of colleagues who supported her, paid a heavy career and personal price for doing her/their duty. Dr Brenda Gallie, Dr Helen Chan, Dr Peter Durie, and Dr John Dick were all colleagues of Olivieri at the Hospital for Sick Children. All supported Olivieri in her struggles with Apotex, Sick Kids Hospital, and the University of Toronto, despite serious risks of harm to their own careers.[8] It is difficult not to empathise with Olivieri when she laments: "It should not be so hard to protect children at Sick Kids Hospital". This sentence was quoted by a colleague and supporter of Olivieri, Dr Paul Ranalli, in a letter published by the *Globe and Mail*, headed "Courage under fire".[11]

It is true, of course, that Apotex had a legal contract with Dr Olivieri, which was signed in 1995. That contract contained a confidentiality provision—one that prohibited her from disclosure "to any third party" of data from her Apotex sponsored clinical trial of the drug deferiprone, without the express permission of the company, for a period of three years after the termination of the trial. The non-disclosure clause of the LA–01 contract between Olivieri and Apotex reads as follows:

> All information whether or not obtained or generated by the investigators during the term of this agreement and for a period of one year thereafter, shall be and remain secret and confidential and shall not be disclosed in any manner to any third party, except to an appropriate regulatory agency for the purposes of obtaining regulatory approval to manufacture, use or sell L1 unless the information has been previously disclosed to the public with the consent of Apotex. The investigator shall not submit any information for publication without the prior written approval of Apotex.

This clause, it should be noted, does not specifically list "patients", but they would clearly appear to be covered under the phrase "any third party". Olivieri claims, supported by tapes of telephone conversations with Apotex, that Apotex threatened repeatedly to sue her if she breached the confidentiality clause of the contract, and that they warned her not to disclose her concerns to patients and others.

At the time Olivieri signed the contract such non-disclosure provisions were common. Olivieri readily admits that she failed to appreciate the potential significance of that contract, and concedes that she should never have signed it. The University of Toronto admits that it was guilty of an institutional oversight by permitting its researchers to agree to such terms, and the university subsequently took steps to preclude repetition by any of its faculty.

Because Apotex refused, repeatedly, to give permission for disclosure, Olivieri might have been found legally liable for significant damages arising out of her disclosure of risks to her patients and colleagues.

Since the protection of human life is, other things being equal, a higher value than respect for the sanctity of contracts, it is possible that the legal system would have "thrown out of court" any lawsuit for breach of contract brought by Apotex against Olivieri, as being against public policy and, hence, unenforceable. For our purposes, it matters little whether the non-disclosure provision of the contract Olivieri signed with Apotex would have been found by the courts to be nugatory. Nor, for our purposes, does it matter much whether the information Olivieri disclosed to patients and colleagues was information actually covered by the terms of the confidentiality agreement she signed—an issue also in dispute. Even if Nancy Olivieri were *legally* bound to keep confidential all information about the risks of deferiprone, she was *morally* obliged to disclose that information to her patients and to her colleagues worldwide. It could be argued, of course, that one has a moral obligation to keep the contracts one signs. This moral obligation is prima facie, however, rather than absolute, and should surely be over-ridden where the lives and health of patients are at stake.

Apotex did not agree with Olivieri's interpretation of her data and they refused her request to disclose these risks to her patients. They also threatened to take legal action against her if she were to violate the non-disclosure clause of the contract. Olivieri proceeded anyway, in the face of these threats, to disclose her findings, and some time after these events, the company did take legal action against her. On 24 May 1996—for example, Apotex wrote to Olivieri that it was terminating both of the clinical trials she was conducting for them, and warned her not to disclose information "in any manner to any third party except with the prior written consent of Apotex", and warned further that it would "vigorously pursue all legal remedies in the event that there is any breach of these obligations" (Thompson J, *et al*,[5] p 143). Just prior to their suing her, she sued them for defamation.

According to one standard account of heroism, the hero is a person who acts far beyond the call of duty. By this test, Olivieri's actions would not count as heroic. She only did that which it was her duty to do. But there is another account of heroism according to which the hero is a person who does her duty, at great risk to her own self interest, when most others would resist from fear. Olivieri relates a story about her personal fears. Sitting in a restaurant with her scientific collaborator, Dr Garry Brittenham, she raised the concern with him that if they were to break their contract with Apotex by disclosing to patients the risks they had newly discovered, Apotex might act on its threats to sue, and the enormous costs of fighting such a lawsuit could mean that they would each lose their homes. Brittenham replied: "Red wine or white?" At that moment, Olivieri reports, it became obvious to her that there was no decision to make concerning whether or not to disclose. They had to disclose the risks. Better, therefore, to concentrate on those matters that still required a decision, such as the colour of the wine they were to consume with their dinner (*The Current*, CBC radio interview, 2 Mar 02).

Apotex is currently suing Olivieri for damages, claiming that she defamed both the company and their drug (deferiprone). Olivieri is suing Apotex for defamation. For the benefit of those who have had the good fortune never to be involved in a legal action of this sort, it is perhaps worth noting that the costs of defending such an action (at least in North America and England) tend to be ruinously expensive; hence, utterly beyond the means of any except the wealthiest individuals. When Olivieri turned to her hospital and university for financial and other help in the face of intimidating threats of legal action against her, they provided little effective assistance (Thompson J, *et al*,[5] p 29). Instead, both the University of Toronto and the Hospital for Sick Children "took actions that were harmful to Dr Olivieri's interests and professional reputation, and disrupted her work" (Thompson J, *et al*,[5] p 32). In their public pronouncements about the case, none of the senior administrators of the university, the medical faculty, or the hospital gave any sign that they recognised that the case was one involving a serious issue of academic freedom. They justified their official "tread lightly" policy in part by characterising the conflict as a "scientific dispute", to be resolved primarily between the parties themselves. Some University of Toronto officials did make efforts, behind the scenes, to promote a settlement between Olivieri and Apotex but, as the Thompson report found, the support which they offered was "not effective".[5]

It was discovered during this period of conflict and controversy that the University of Toronto was negotiating for a twenty million dollar donation from Apotex (with additional millions promised for its affiliated hospitals). Some were led to speculate that the university's failure to recognise and support Olivieri's academic freedom might not have been unconnected to its eagerness to secure financial support from Apotex for the university's proposed molecular medicine building project. Indeed, it was subsequently revealed that the university's then president had gone so far as to lobby the Government of Canada on behalf of Apotex. In a private letter to the Prime Minister of Canada, President Robert Prichard stated that the government's proposed changes to drug patent regulations would adversely affect Apotex's revenues and could thereby jeopardise the

building of the university's new medical research centre. President Prichard was unsuccessful in persuading the federal government to change its drug patent laws, but his action demonstrated the lengths to which the university was prepared to go in appeasing the company or promoting its interests. When Prichard's conduct became public knowledge, he apologised to the executive committee of the university for acting inappropriately in this matter (Thompson J, *et al*,[5] p 13).

This embarrassing episode illustrates the dangers that can ensue from university reliance upon industry "philanthropy". When career success for university/hospital presidents and deans is measured in significant part by their ability to raise vast sums of money from corporate donors, such fundraising can easily become a dominating priority. In North America, top university and hospital officials are now required to ride two horses: their fundraiser's horse and, simultaneously, their academic horse (as guardians of core university values). Unfortunately, those who attempt to ride two horses can come to grief when, as sometimes happens, the horses pull in opposite directions. Perhaps it is time for a radical rethinking of the competing role responsibilities of top university and hospital officials.

The word "philanthropy" is placed above in warning quotes, not to suggest that big pharma never behaves in a genuinely philanthropic manner but, rather, to flag the point that when corporate donors make substantial donations they often expect to gain substantial influence. Indeed, it is the legally mandated duty of corporate executives and board members to act in the "best interests" of the corporation, which is commonly interpreted to mean that they have a legal duty to maximise overall profitability. Corporate donations to universities are typically viewed, at least in part, as an investment. This, in turn, raises the questions (to which an answer is supplied later): What exactly is being bought by such investments? What exactly is being sold?

DAVID HEALY AND THE CENTRE FOR ADDICTION AND MENTAL HEALTH

In December of 2000, while the Olivieri affair was still capturing attention, both within and without the University of Toronto, a second major scandal, also raising basic issues of academic freedom and patient safety, was brewing at the same university.

Some months previously, the Centre for Addiction and Mental Health had hired Dr David Healy to become the new director of its Mood and Anxiety Disorders Clinic. After accepting their offer and the offer of a joint appointment in the university's Department of Psychiatry, Healy notified his employer in Wales of his intention to resign, and prepared to move his family to Canada to take up this new appointment. Then, Healy's career plans came dramatically unstuck.

On 30th November 2002, some months before his new appointment was officially scheduled to begin, Healy made a conference presentation at CAMH. (The symposium, called "Looking Back, Looking Ahead", was held to mark the 75th anniversary of the university Department of Psychiatry, as well as the 150th anniversary of the Queen Street Mental Health Service.) In this lecture, which he subsequently delivered at Cornell, and in Paris, Minneapolis, and Cambridge, Healy raised the question of whether the drug Prozac, manufactured by Eli Lilly, might be responsible for increasing the risk of suicide among certain kinds of patients. This issue was by no means the principal theme of Healy's talk, but the potential link of Prozac to patient suicides, and the call for further research on this matter, was almost certainly regarded by CAMH officials as the most controversial part of Healy's presentation. Healy reports that his talk was well received in all the places where he presented it, and it is noteworthy that the audience at the CAMH conference honoured his lecture with the highest rating for content.[12] Despite this fact, senior administrators of CAMH were not well pleased. Within 24 hours of the talk they were trying to contact him. Within a week he received an email unilaterally rescinding their offer of employment.

Why was David Healy's employment terminated so precipitately by both the Centre for Addiction and Mental Health and the university Department of Psychiatry? No one disputes that Healy is an internationally distinguished psychiatrist and researcher. The university and CAMH recruited him with enthusiasm and persistence. Since he was unhired almost immediately after he gave his conference lecture at CAMH, the inference is inescapable that his contract for employment was cancelled because of the contents of his lecture that day. In this lecture, Healy expressed the view, referred to above, that the antidepressant drug Prozac might cause some patients to commit suicide. Although Healy did not condemn Prozac outright, he did advocate caution on the part of doctors who prescribe this drug, and he called for further research into possible adverse side effects. He was also critical of the practice whereby drug companies are engaged in ghostwriting some of the therapeutic literature.

Some time prior to Healy's conference presentation, Eli Lilly had donated 1.5 million dollars to CAMH, and a new wing of the hospital, built with their financial assistance, was scheduled to have its official opening soon after. There is no evidence that Eli Lilly attempted to have Dr Healy fired from his new appointment at CAMH. The incident raises legitimate questions, however, about whether those involved with rescinding his contract offer were affected, consciously or unconsciously, by the relationship between CAMH and Eli Lilly.

In this connection, it is worth noting that six months before Healy delivered his fateful presentation at CAMH, he had published an article on Prozac in the biomedical ethics journal, the *Hastings Center Report*.[12] In this article, Healy developed several of the themes which later became controversial at the University of Toronto, namely suicide and Prozac, and ghostwriting of scientific articles by drug companies. Eli Lilly, which had hitherto been the largest annual private donor to the Hastings Center, publisher of the *Hastings Center Report*, subsequently withdrew its financial support for the centre.[13]

The administrations of both the University of Toronto and CAMH claim that the unhiring of Dr Healy had nothing to do with academic freedom. Instead, they contend, his lecture gave rise to "clinical concerns" and revealed that he would be a "bad fit" with his new colleagues. It may be worth quoting a key paragraph from the email which the University of Toronto sent to Healy by way of explaining their decision to rescind his contract:

> Essentially, we believe that it is not a good fit between you and the role as leader of an academic program in mood and anxiety disorders at the centre. While you are held in high regard as a scholar of the history of modern psychiatry, we do not feel your approach is compatible with the goals for development of the academic and clinical resource that we have. This view was solidified by your recent appearance at the centre in the context of an academic lecture. (Healy D,[12] p 6)

University of Toronto officials later denied that Healy was unhired because of fears on their part that if Dr Healy were allowed to take up his position drug companies might be reluctant in future to donate money to or fund research at the

centre. Notwithstanding their strenuous denials, however, many people understood the above quoted words to mean "… the university was worried about the risk to the financial inflows to the department from pharmaceutical company sources" (Healy D,[12] p 6).

In September 2001, an international group of physicians published an open letter to the president of the University of Toronto, in which they protested against what they termed the "maltreatment" of Dr Healy. In their open letter they concluded: "To have sullied Dr Healy's reputation by withdrawing the job offer is an affront to the standards of free speech and academic freedom". The signatories, who included two Nobel Prize winners, chose not to focus on the possible involvement of a drug company in university affairs, but they nevertheless insisted that the central issue in the case was the failure of the University of Toronto and CAMH to uphold "the standards of open discussion and frank exchange in university life".[14] That is, the issue was essentially one of academic freedom.

The university's official response to the concerns expressed by this international group of scholars was dismissive: they (the protesting scholars) were ill informed outsiders, unaware of all the pertinent information. University of Toronto spokespeople went even further in their defence of the unhiring of Dr Healy by suggesting that his publicly expressed concerns were dangerously irresponsible. On the University of Toronto's website, Healy's warnings about the potential hazards of Prozac were compared to the "fool" who cries "fire" in a crowded theatre.[15] To this accusation, Healy responds: "But what if there is a fire in the theatre?" (Healy D,[12] p 11) It is worth bearing in mind that Prozac or other drugs of its class, known as SSRIs, are often prescribed to healthy patients with problems in living. If, as Healy believes the evidence indicates, some of these healthy patients become suicidal because of their ingestion of SSRI type drugs, then a failure to warn them and their physicians of this potential side effect would be grossly irresponsible.

The argument underlying such an analogy is, presumably, that Healy's warnings (of possible adverse side effects from taking Prozac)[16 18] might deter some depressive patients from using Prozac or other SSRI drugs and this, in turn, might result in their committing suicide. In other words, the university's position seems to be that when the values of clinical care clash with the values of science, the former should trump the latter. The problem with this argument, however, is that if valid it proves too much. It proves that researchers ought never to warn patients of potentially harmful side effects lest some patients thereupon forgo an effective medication.

This manifestation of an approach often labelled "physician paternalism" would be morally objectionable because it would usurp the patient's right to give informed consent to treatment. How can patients weigh and balance the benefits and harms of treatment options (including the option of not taking any antidepressant medication) if evidence about potential harms is deliberately withheld from them? There is by now a vast literature, both legal and ethical, in which the near universal consensus of philosophers and jurists is that competent adult patients have a fundamental right to give informed consent to treatment. In practice, this means that research scientists must make the results of their research public, so that physicians can adequately inform their patients about potential risks. The duty to warn would seem, then, to be a fundamental obligation of every research scientist. Both Healy and Olivieri were alerting patients and the scientific community to the need for further research into potentially serious adverse consequences of the drugs they were investigating. For either to have remained silent about their preliminary adverse data would surely have been a violation of their legal, as well as their moral, duty.

Interestingly, on 10 June 2003, the Medicines and Healthcare Products Regulatory Agency |MHRA| of the UK issued a caution to physicians that Seroxat (Paxil) was "contra-indicated" in children under 18 for the treatment of major depressive disorder. Potential side effects include dramatically increased risk of "potentially suicidal behaviour". (G Duff, personal communication, 2003). Thus, it seems that recent evidence further confirms the wisdom of Healy's warnings about drugs of the SSRI category. Sadly, his scrupulous caution appears to have cost him his job at the University of Toronto.

A short time after the university's dismissive rejection of the open letter, described above, Dr Healy initiated what might have been the first legal action in the English speaking world based, in part, on the alleged tort of violating academic freedom. ("Alleged" because until there is a legal precedent in which the courts find that such a tort exists, one cannot be sure of its validity.) A settlement was subsequently negotiated, which included the appointment of Healy as visiting professor in the Department of the History of Medicine (with unrestricted academic freedom to speak out publicly about any of the issues). The appointment as visiting professor of the history of medicine is for one week a year during each of the following three years. He was not permitted, however, to assume the position for which he had originally been hired, as director of the Mood Disorders and Anxiety Clinic of CAMH.

David Healy, himself, feels little doubt about the most important lesson to be learned from his experience at CAMH, and he insists that it is the same lesson that should be learned from the experience of Nancy Olivieri at Sick Kids Hospital: "What is involved is a contrast between the values of science and the values of business" (Healy D,[12] p 11). Although the Thompson report dealt only with the Olivieri case, the Thompson authors, like Healy, conclude that the problem is system wide: "...T]he safety of research subjects in clinical trials and the integrity of the research project are more important than corporate interests" (Thompson J, *et al*,[3] p 17). Nathan and Weatherall, in their *NEJM* commentary on the Olivieri case reach a similar conclusion,[2] as does Somerville writing in *Nature*,[19] and as do the authors of the *CMAJ* article "Dancing with porcupines".[3] Together, the Healy and Olivieri cases have forced both the university community and the wider public to confront the ways in which university/industry partnerships can imperil the fundamental values of academic freedom, research integrity, and patient safety.

Before we attempt to analyse potential cures for what appears—from evidence presented below—to be a systemic malaise affecting research universities and hospitals worldwide, it will be useful to step back one or two paces, in an effort to gain some historical perspective.

ANCIENT HISTORY: WHERE WE CAME FROM

In 1961, ex President Dwight Eisenhower warned his compatriots of the dangers posed to American society by the rise of what he called "the military/industrial complex". At that historical juncture ties between the American military and the arms industry had become so intimate and extensive that Eisenhower—by no means a Marxist revolutionary—felt compelled to speak publicly of his fears for the future of American democracy.

It is not implausible to speculate that were Eisenhower alive today, he might be tempted to issue a comparable warning against "the scientific/industrial complex". The dramatically increased role of for profit corporations in the funding of medical and life sciences research is, arguably, a trend that threatens to undermine both the traditional values of science and the public's trust in our research universities and teaching hospitals. Although this discussion will focus primarily on medical research, the argument advanced could easily be reiterated about research in such diverse fields of study as agriculture and economics. If respected researchers, such as Olivieri and Healy, can experience persecution from their own hospitals and universities for disclosing potential risks to patients, then which other researchers will be brave enough to speak out in a manner likely to attract industry disapprobation?

The fundamental ethos of contemporary scientific research has evolved so rapidly during the past few decades that it would scarcely count as hyperbole were one to describe the process as a "revolution", or perhaps as a "commercial revolution". To offer but one example from a vast range of possible examples outside biomedicine, one recent report describes how the British government is subsidising the oil and gas industry's profits to the tune of about 40 million pounds every year through the "capture" of some of Britain's most respected academic institutions. The report outlines how Britain's universities and colleges are being co-opted into directing their research and training for the benefit of the fossil fuel industry, with potentially devastating long term effects on the environment. Although no branch of inquiry, from agriculture to climate change, has escaped the revolution, the change has been more dramatic in the field of biomedicine than in any other area of university research.

Like most other complex human endeavours, the scientific enterprise has always been norm governed. A classic elaboration of those norms is to be found in the work of Robert Merton.[20] The picture of scientific culture painted by Merton features several key elements: "universalism," "communism," "disinterestedness," and "organised skepticism". Loosely translated, Merton is claiming that within the scientific community (a) the soundness of scientific research is judged by impersonal criteria; (b) research findings are treated as open and shared rather than secretive or proprietary; (c) researchers are motivated by the pursuit of truth, rather than by financial or career self advancement, and (d) research findings are accepted only after a rigorous process of testing.

Congressional testimony of Dr Jonathan King, Professor of Biology, Massachusetts Institute of Technology, nicely encapsulates and echoes the spirit of science as formulated by Mertonians:

> The openness, the free exchange of ideas and information, the free exchange of strains of protein, of techniques, have been a critical component in the creativity and productivity of the biomedical research community....
> This freedom of communication stemmed from the fact that all of the investigators shared the same professional canon: the increase of knowledge of health and disease for the benefit of the citizenry....

The above excerpt was taken from *Commercialization of Academic Biomedical Research* (hearing before the subcommittee on investigations and oversight and the subcommittee on science, research and technology of the House Committee on Science and Technology, 97th congress, first session, 1981, 62–63, as cited by R P Merges.[1]

These cultural norms of traditional science are meant, in part, to be descriptive of the actual practice of members of the scientific community, but they are also partly "aspirational". That is, they establish goals or ideals from which actual practice may sometimes fall short.

It would be naïve to deny that previous generations of scientists were sometimes reluctant to share their ideas, in case a colleague might "steal" them. "Pure" motives, such as intellectual curiosity or the welfare of humankind, were inevitably admixed with such "impure" motives as personal status and career advancement.[1] Thus, well before the currently prevailing trend towards commercialisation of scientific research, the free sharing of scientific ideas, information, and materials was sometimes honoured in the breach. Members of the scientific community have never been total strangers to such less than elevated motivations as the desire to scoop the competition or win promotion and honours.

Still, even if one concedes that the Golden Age of "science in the public interest" was never quite as pure or golden as some romantics might like to imagine, it seems undeniable that the enormous increase of corporate research funding for university and hospital scientists, over the past half century, has contributed to a profound transformation of the culture of biomedical science.

The recent history of Johns Hopkins University serves as a paradigm case to illustrate what is happening at many North American and British universities. Johns Hopkins, which can plausibly claim to have been America's first pure research university, has only recently embraced commercialisation. Sadly, it compensates for being late to the commercial game with its current unbridled enthusiasm for the entrepreneurial model. From its Quaker origins (1876) until just a few years ago, the ethos prevailing at Hopkins was explicitly antibusiness. Patents were simply not sought on the many important discoveries originating at the university. In 1933 the faculty actually voted, formally, against a proposal that the medical school adopt a policy of owning patents. This Hopkins decision to reject close commercial ties, both for the university and for its researchers, was taken at a time when the anticommercial spirit was still common among elite American research universities. Stanford University and the Massachusetts Institute of Technology were both business friendly; Harvard was not.

William R Brody, who became Hopkins's president in 1997, provided much of the impetus towards shifting the university's ethos in a more entrepreneurial direction. President Brody was certainly aware that the promotion of university/industry partnerships posed a "minefield of potential conflicts". He nevertheless insisted that "[t]o move your research forward, you've got to do partnerships with industry".[2] The former vice dean of research at the medical school, Dr Bart Chernow, asserts with unselfconscious pride that Hopkins has become "one of the biggest biotech companies in the world". A few decades earlier, such an utterance would have been received as a shameful admission rather than a prideful boast. Some Hopkins administrators, such as former Vice Dean David Blake, now go so far as to argue that researchers become more productive when they own a large financial stake in the company sponsoring their work: "No conflict, no interest".

Hopkins's researchers and the university itself stand to make millions upon millions of dollars from their ownership of shares in the companies with whom the university has entered commercial agreements. Such arrangements can now be found at many leading American universities. They appear to have become the new norm. A few examples: Stanford University and the University of California, San Francisco, split $270 million in income from a single genetics invention. Michigan State University earned more than $160 million from sales of two anticancer drugs. In its anticommercial phase, Johns Hopkins University declined an opportunity to patent a DNA testing method, from which a Bethesda, Maryland, company subsequently earned $100 million.[3] For

any university to turn its back on moneymaking opportunities of this magnitude requires a willingness to forgo a source of enormous potential income, in the certain knowledge that such income will flow, instead, to other, less scrupulous, competitors. Derek Bok, former president of Harvard University, introduces a somewhat cautionary, note, however: "Most universities have not earned much money from royalties; the odds of making anything substantial from patenting a new discovery are extremely small".[4]

This background helps us to understand how it has come to pass that Johns Hopkins University, historically disdainful of the corrupting potential of commercialised research, is now a marketplace "leader" among universities. Hopkins officials confidently answer those who warn that "the market is corrupting" with the rejoinder: any threat to research objectivity resulting from financial conflicts of interest can be managed by careful regulations. To discourage potential abuse, Hopkins requires that scientists who are engaged in drug trials disclose their financial ties. This contrasts with the somewhat stricter approach taken at Harvard Medical School, which also requires disclosure but which, in addition, does not permit its researchers to have more than a maximum of $20 000 invested in the company sponsoring their research.

Critics might argue that even the comparatively stern standards prevailing at Harvard are nevertheless unacceptably permissive of financial conflicts of interest. Harvard administrators reply by publicly expressing concern that if Harvard does not move further in the direction of wide open for business universities, such as Johns Hopkins, it will continue to lose some of its best researchers to competitors with more permissive ethical standards. The expression "race to the ethical bottom" might have been coined for just such situations.

The list of indictments which traditionalists raise against the new model entrepreneurial university is already long, and seems to be lengthening rapidly. Critics fear that widescale commercial funding has already produced an erosion of cooperation and community among biomedical researchers. Instead of an easy sharing of knowledge and reagents, one finds something approximating to a quasiHobbesian war of each (laboratory) against all (others). Instead of concern above all for the safety of research subjects and the integrity of research findings, one finds shabby compromises of both these foundational values. Instead of jealously protecting academic freedom and intellectual openness, university administrations become hospitable to censorship and nondisclosure.

Because commercialised research responds primarily to "effective demand" (that is, demand backed by money) in the marketplace, it has also the potential to produce a different kind of challenge to basic social values, as illustrated by the history of the drug eflornithine. Eflornithine was originally developed by the Aventis drug company as a possible treatment for cancer. It proved to be ineffective as an anticancer agent, but highly effective as a cure for sleeping sickness. Unfortunately, the victims of sleeping sickness were mostly people living in the Third World, too poor to bring effective demand to the marketplace. Since the drug could not make a profit, however beneficial (in this case, lifesaving) its results, Aventis discontinued making it. Serendipitously, however, the drug was later discovered to be an effective depilatory, and since there is a robust market in wealthy Western nations for products to remove facial hair, the drug is back in production and is now also being made available at little or no cost to treat sleeping sickness in poor countries.[5] The twists and turns of the eflornithine story illustrate but one of the many ways in which society's decision to allow the research and development agenda for new drugs to be dominated by commercial considerations can produce morally perverse consequences.

In sum, the critics of corporate funding argue that if biomedical research continues to be absorbed within the profit seeking ethos of the marketplace, the norms of commerce may swamp both the traditional norms of science and the best interests of the wider community; the disinterested pursuit of knowledge may give way to the entrepreneurial pursuit of financial self interest, and universities and hospitals may forfeit the public trust without which they cannot function. This is a serious charge sheet, and there is a growing body of evidence to support the conclusion that the traditional norms of science ought to be placed, forthwith, on the Endangered Species List. What follows is a sampling of that evidence.

CORPORATE FINANCING OF MEDICAL RESEARCH IN NORTH AMERICA: A BRIEF OVERVIEW

As the United States emerged from the second world war, the funding of scientific research became a top national priority. A report prepared for President Harry Truman, by Vannevar Bush, director of the wartime Office of Scientific Research and Development, argued that the advancement of scientific knowledge through massive spending on research was necessary for America's health, prosperity, and security and that, in consequence, government funding of scientific research ought to enjoy the highest priority.[25]

The fifties and sixties in America were a golden age for government funding of basic scientific research, with most funds dispersed through the National Institutes of Health (NIH). Scientists enjoyed a high degree of research independence and were comparatively free from commercial pressure to produce short term results. During this period, less than five per cent of university research funding came from private industry. Thus, direct interaction between academic scientists, on the one hand, and for profit corporations, on the other, was rather limited. By the late seventies, however, academic science came to be viewed by both industry and government as a potentially powerful commercial weapon in an increasingly competitive world economy. Laws were passed to strengthen intellectual property rights. With the passage of the Bayh-Dole Act (1980), which permitted American universities and university researchers to patent discoveries resulting from federally funded research, the academic world moved very rapidly toward the world of business. That same year, 1980, also saw some important judicial decisions supporting patent protection for bioengineered molecules.[26] In the fifteen year period between 1974 and the early 1990s, corporate support for academic biomedical research increased from less than five million dollars to hundreds of millions.[27] By the beginning of the new millennium, for profit companies were providing financial support for 70 per cent of clinical drug trials.[28]

So called "strategic alliances" between universities and the pharmaceutical industry flourished, in part because of the perception that federal research funds were declining—which turned out to be true in Canada, though untrue in the US. The corollary fear was that lost federal funds could only be replaced by the private sector. In addition, as American scholar Sheldon Krimsky notes, there were also technological developments that helped to promote such partnerships: "... I]n biosciences you can now go from the lab to commerce very quickly because of gene splicing".[29] This technological development in the life sciences, sometimes referred to as "the genomics revolution", had the effect of blurring the distinction between "pure" and "applied" research.

For these reasons, large scale "scientific entrepreneurship" moved, almost in one fell swoop, from being an oxymoron to

becoming the prevailing norm on university campuses across America. The pharmaceutical industry became the major source of grants for researchers carrying out clinical trials and a major financial contributor to medical schools and universities, via donations of capital and equipment. Even medical journal editors had reason to feel gratitude for the generosity of the pharmaceutical industry, which began to provide significant financial subsidies via the purchase of advertisements and special supplements to the main journal. Scientific articles appearing in these corporate financed sections of academic medical journals, although signed by otherwise reputable researchers, would often be ghostwritten by company employees. No good data are currently available about the percentage of articles, whether in the peer reviewed sections of journals or in non-peer reviewed supplements, which are ghostwritten. Understandably, neither the ghostwriters, who are paid between $10 000 and $20 000 per article, nor the authors who allow their names to appear on these articles, are anxious to have their identities revealed. The practice of ghostwriting appears to be not uncommon, according to an investigative report done for the CBC TV programme *Marketplace* (*Marketplace*, CBC TV, 25 Mar 03). "Authors" would often not even have access to the raw data on which their "findings" were based. Unlike the rest of the journal's content, such supplementary articles would not be peer reviewed (Healy D, unpublished ms: *Shaping the intimate influences on the experience of everyday nerves*). The industry hopes, presumably, that by placing their supplements within the covers of prestigious journals, these industry funded studies will parasitically acquire scientific legitimacy. Status by association could then be exploited by drug company salespeople ("reps") when marketing their products to the large number of "docs" whose busy clinical practices leave them short of time to check on the *bona fides* of published studies.

The story in Canada follows a similar trajectory, though with a time lag of about ten years. Sometime around the late eighties, the Canadian federal government came to view multinational drug companies as a major vehicle for promoting economic growth. Despite consumer fears of rising drug costs, patent protection was extended. The pharmaceutical industry promised, as its *quid pro quo* for this extension, that it would increase its spending on Canadian drug research. By the 1990s, despite fears of government retrenchment, American government spending on drug research was actually doubling. At the same time, Canadian governments decided to battle rising national debt and deficits by cutting and freezing grants for medical research. Canadian researchers were thus caught in a squeeze between (a) the rising costs of medical research and (b) their stagnant or shrinking research grants from government. Salvation, of a kind, was provided by industrial sponsorship.

Canadian biomedical researchers shared the excitement of their American colleagues at the prospect of participating in major scientific discoveries. Canada's leading research universities and their affiliated teaching hospitals shared with their American counterparts an aspiration toward research excellence. In order, however, to achieve national or, better still, international research standing, universities and research hospital required massive new funds, funds sufficient both to build and equip first rate laboratories and to attract and keep top notch researchers. Thus, since Canadian governments, federal and provincial, seemed unable or unwilling to provide needed research funding, universities and hospitals felt themselves compelled to go, virtually cap in hand, to the pharmaceutical industry.

In these circumstances, it is not surprising that leading universities and teaching hospitals made a conscious decision to devote the time and energy necessary to build and sustain the good will of drug company executives. The case for diligently pursuing corporate sponsorships is made vividly by Michael Strofolino, President of Sick Kids Hospital at the height of the Olivieri scandal: "Our goal is to be the best hospital in the world, to be number 1. How do we do it? Do we close down commercialism? Do you think the federal government is going to give us the money? Do you think we're going to get scientists to come up to Canada in an environment like that?"[1] For Strofolino, but also for many other hospital and university presidents and deans, commercialising university research by marketing universities to wealthy corporations was the best way, perhaps the only realistic way, to obtain the hundreds of millions of dollars needed to achieve research excellence. This commercial "imperative" has grown, if anything, more pressing over time.

Hence the current popularity of what have come to be called university/industry "partnerships". As suggested above, the beneficiaries are not just biomedical researchers, casting about for research funding. Cash starved universities and hospitals themselves stand to make considerable fortunes by cultivating joint ventures with private industry. Corporate funding has become crucial to the business plans of many North American universities. It has provided universities and their affiliated research hospitals with the resources they need to strive for excellence. When new drugs are discovered and patented the university can then collect its share of what will sometimes prove to be a veritable "gold mine". Johns Hopkins University again provides us with some prime examples:

> Hopkins ... permitted physicians to do human testing of tiny Magnetic Resonance Imaging devices that they had invented—instruments being developed by a company that the doctors and Hopkins partly own. A Hopkins neurologist recently tested a drug that could earn millions for Hopkins, some of its leading scientists and a company closely tied to both.

For this reason, university presidents and deans are often chosen, at least partly, on the basis of their attractiveness to potential corporate donors. The national and international league table of universities assigns its top places to those most successful at raising the vast sums of private money necessary to hire the best researchers and provide them with the best laboratories, the best equipment, and the most doctoral and postdoctoral students, in order to produce the best and most profitable research.

These developments, increasingly prevalent at North American research universities, have led critics to accuse the entrepreneurial university of institutional conflict of interest. One study reports that approximately two thirds of academic institutions hold equity in "start up" businesses that sponsor research performed at their university.[30] When academic institutions have become businesses, seeking to commercialise and profit from their inhouse research discoveries, can the public still look to them as sources of objective scholarly information?[31]

The death of eighteen year old Jesse Gelsinger, who had altruistically volunteered to participate as a research subject in an industry sponsored gene therapy trial, focused attention on the issue of whether individual and institutional financial conflicts of interest were responsible for undermining the protection of research subjects.[32] The US government's Food and Drug Administration (FDA) has charged the clinical researchers involved in the Gelsinger case with inadequately informing him of the risks entailed by this trial and also with a conflict between their financial interest in a gene therapy

technology company and their duty to protect the safety of research subjects. The most troubling question raised by the Gelsinger case, one which has not yet been properly answered, is: how can universities and hospitals assure the public that they will rigorously and impartially oversee the ethics of research carried out by their scientists when both the researchers and the institutions have acquired a significant financial stake in the outcome of the research? Answers to this question will be explored below, under the heading of "conflict of interest".

THE ETHICS AND PRAGMATICS OF INDUSTRY SUPPORT FOR UNIVERSITY BIOMEDICAL RESEARCH

One of the most influential studies of how researchers' objectivity might be compromised by drug industry sponsorship appeared in The *New England Journal of Medicine*, in January of 1998.[33] Stelfox and colleagues set out to examine published articles on the safety of calcium channel antagonists. Their goal was to answer the question: to what extent does industry support of medical research influence the research findings of investigators? For the purposes of this study, Stelfox divided authors according to their relationships with pharmaceutical companies and then, independently, classified their research findings on the safety issue as "supportive", "critical", or "neutral". The conclusion reached by Stelfox *et al* must be of serious concern to every supporter of industry university partnerships: "Our results demonstrate a strong association between authors' published positions on the safety of calcium channel antagonists and their financial relationships with pharmaceutical manufacturers."[33]

It may be worth spelling out just how influential drug company sponsorship appears to have been: "Ninety six per cent of supportive authors had financial relationships with the manufacturers of calcium channel antagonists, as compared with 60 per cent of the neutral authors and 37 per cent of the critical authors."[33] A caveat is required here. The Stelfox study needs be interpreted with care. Were authors first funded by companies making calcium channel blockers, after which they wrote favourably about the product, or did they first write favourably about the product and only then receive financial support from the companies? Since the Stelfox authors were unable to determine the time line, this question cannot be answered conclusively. Interestingly, even researchers who had financial ties with manufacturers of competing products were significantly less critical of the drugs being tested than authors who had no ties to industry. In other words, scientists who are funded by the pharmaceutical industry produce studies which tend to be more favourable to new drugs than those whose funding is industry independent even when the new drug being tested is produced by a rival company.

In a more recent study, Bekelman and colleagues have attempted a comprehensive synthesis of evidence relating to biomedical conflicts of interest.[34] According to their data, over a period of roughly two decades (January 1980 to October 2002), approximately one fourth of investigators were found to have industry affiliations, and roughly two thirds of academic institutions were found to hold equity in start ups that sponsor research performed at the same institution. By combining data from articles examining 1140 studies, Bekelman found that "industry sponsored studies were significantly more likely to reach conclusions that were favourable to the sponsor than were non-industry studies".[34] Thus, Bekelman's findings are consistent with those of Stelfox. The Bekelman study also found that industry sponsorship was associated with restrictions on publication and data sharing. Bekelman *et al* conclude: "Financial relationships among industry, scientific investigators and academic institutions are widespread. Conflicts of interest arising from these ties can influence biomedical research in important ways."[34]

Lexchin and colleagues have also done a comprehensive meta-analysis of what is currently known about the alleged tendency of drug company sponsorship to produce biased research results.[35] They conclude that "there is some kind of systematic bias to the outcome of published research funded by the pharmaceutical industry":

> Research sponsored by the drug industry was more likely to produce results favouring the product made by the company sponsoring the research than studies funded by other sources. The results apply across a wide range of disease states, drugs and drug classes, over at least two decades and regardless of the type of research being assessed—pharmacoeconomic studies, clinical trials, or meta-analyses of clinical trials.[35]

Although it seems intuitively obvious that "he who pays the piper calls the tune", there are several different and competing hypotheses, each of which may explain why it is the case that when a pharmaceutical company pays for the clinical trial of its new drug, the results are more likely to be favourable to that drug than when the funding is industry independent. (1) It is possible that the pharmaceutical companies are highly skilful at picking "winner" drugs; or (2) industry sponsored trials might be of low quality (thereby exaggerating treatment benefits); or (3) drug company sponsored research might produced biased results (whether consciously or subconsciously) because it chooses inappropriate comparator agents, or, finally, (4) publication bias might be an important factor.

Lexchin *et al* argue that there is no empirical evidence to support the first two hypotheses. Bekelman agrees, citing four studies, each of which demonstrates empirically that industry preferentially supports trial designs that favour the new drug being tested (thereby refuting the first hypothesis).[34 36] The second hypothesis blends into the third to the extent that the allegedly poor quality of the studies is attributable to the use of inappropriate control therapies. The third hypothesis is potentially important, Lexchin and Bekelman both acknowledge, but Lexchin argues that it requires further investigation. By contrast, the hypothesis of publication bias seems well supported, both by a number of studies done specifically on the issue of publication bias, and also by a number of high profile cases—for example, Apotex/Olivieri and Knoll; Boots Pharmaceutical/Betty Dong—in which drug companies have attempted to prevent researchers from publishing studies unfavourable to their products. See also a paper by P A Rochon, *et al*,[37] and one by E Shenk.[38] The phrase "publication bias" seems to originate with a 1980 *JAMA* article by Smith.[39] It is employed to describe a "tendency on the parts of investigators, reviewers or editors to submit or accept manuscripts for publication based upon the direction or strength of the study findings".[40] There is now a considerable body of evidence in support of the hypothesis that when the results of a clinical trial are unfavourable to the new drug being tested, the researchers often decide not to publish (in order not to alienate the good will of their sponsors), or the company may decide that the researchers will not be allowed to publish (as happened in the Olivieri/Apotex case), or journal editors may decide they are uninterested in publishing studies which have produced negative results. Another caveat. Publication bias certainly exists, but there is as yet, no published research (as distinguished from anecdotal reports) which distinguishes carefully among the possible causes of the bias. What can be said with confidence, however, is that when publication bias

occurs, the effect is to deprive clinicians and patients alike of some part of the materially relevant evidence needed for them to make good treatment decisions.

Publication bias is sometimes referred to, colloquially, as "the file drawer effect". Suppose that there are twenty studies done of some new drug; and suppose that of those twenty studies, six are positive and fourteen are negative. Suppose, further, that as a direct or indirect result of company influence, twelve of the negative studies are not published (that is, they are banished to the file drawer), while *every* positive study is published, celebrated even. Those physicians who then attempt conscientiously to review the literature would find six positive but only two negative studies. (I owe this way of explaining the issue to Dr Paul Ranalli.) The new drug would be hailed as a medical breakthrough and would rapidly become part of standard therapy. This is not science, however, so much as marketing through censorship or self censorship. If the much touted movement towards "evidence based medicine" is to mean anything, then physicians need unbiased data on the clinical effectiveness, toxicity, convenience, and cost of new drugs compared with available alternatives.[41] Because of the phenomenon of publication bias, what passes for good scientific evidence may be simply a mirage.

The findings of Bekelman and Lexchin clearly call into question the integrity of company funded research.[34 35] Since company funded research has become preponderant, in both Canada and the US, the clear implication is that the integrity problem is both systemic and serious. Evidence for this claim is provided by both Statistics Canada and the Office of Technology Assessment in the USA.[42 43]

As noted above, when clinicians consult a drug study to help them in their treatment decisions, they are generally seeking objective information about the comparative effectiveness, toxicity, and cost of the new drug compared to available alternatives. Bero and Rennie clearly summarise some of the reasons why clinicians often do not find such vital information in the current literature:

> Many examples of published drug studies fail to fill this need. Clinicians too often see studies that favourably compare the new drug with a second rate alternative, studies that compare doses of drugs that favour the new product, studies that test the new drug on the wrong subjects, studies that are too small to test hypotheses, and studies with unsupported conclusions.[41]

Bleak as this picture may be, reality is sometimes bleaker still:

> Even well designed studies can be poorly conducted, and biases that favour the sponsor's product can be introduced by protocol violations, failure to keep proper records, or failure to submit accurate data to the journal for publication.[41]

This last mentioned danger is illustrated by the way in which drug manufacturer Pharmacia was able to elicit a favourable editorial in *JAMA* for its blockbuster arthritis drug Celebrex, in the summer of 2000.

Celebrex was tested over a period of twelve months in a Pharmacia sponsored study. The study showed, based on data from the first six months of the trial, that this new drug was associated with lower rates of stomach and intestinal ulcers than two older and much less expensive drugs. To his subsequent chagrin, arthritis expert M Michael Wolfe did not discover until *after* his favourable appraisal of Celebrex was published in *JAMA* that the company possessed an additional six months of data. When the full year's data—to which Wolfe was not given timely access—were taken into account, the Celebrex advantage at the six month point had virtually disappeared. Dr Wolfe was, understandably, furious. *JAMA*'s editor, Catherine DeAngelis lamented: "I am disheartened to hear that they had those data at the time they submitted [the manuscript] to us."[44]

All of the *JAMA* Celebrex study's authors were either employees of the sponsoring drug company, Pharmacia, or paid consultants of the company. More worrying, at least for those who still believe that the public can reliably trust to the integrity of university researchers, is the fact that half of the study's 16 authors were medical faculty at eight different medical schools.

With its trust in the integrity of the biomedical science community somewhat dented, if not entirely shattered, *JAMA* now requires a statement, signed by an author who is not employed by the sponsoring company, in which responsibility is taken "for the integrity of the data and the accuracy of the data analyses".[44] Although Pharmacia continues to claim that Celebrex has a superior safety profile, the US government Food and Drug Administration's arthritis advisory committee concluded, based on the full year's data, that Celebrex offers no proven safety advantage, compared to the two older drugs, in reducing the risk of ulcer complications.

Bero and Rennie conclude that the pharmaceutical industry must take some responsibility for the poor quality of published drug studies, but their exhortation to the industry to show educational leadership is somewhat undercut by their own observation that "the pharmaceutical industry has little incentive to conduct and publish the type of drug study that the practising clinician needs most".[41] The same conclusion is reached by P A Dieppe, *et al.*[45] One may be forgiven for doubting whether manufacturers of new and expensive drugs would often be keen to fund studies the purpose of which is to determine whether inexpensive, off patent drugs could replace profitable single source products. All the more reason why the public should not hold its breath waiting for the pharmaceutical industry to fund studies into the curative powers of vitamins, broccoli, or regular exercise, since none of these treatment modalities lends itself as readily as prescription drugs to commercial exploitation. In other words, despite what Bero and Rennie have to say, the pharmaceutical industry is not likely to adopt with enthusiasm any educational role which threatens to weaken its bottom line. If the public needs good quality drug studies— and clearly it does—then the public may have to reconsider whether it can afford to rely on industry funding of biomedical research.

BIOMEDICAL CONFLICTS OF INTEREST

A proper understanding of "conflict of interest" is essential for a clear understanding of why corporate sponsorship of university research is ethically troubling. Denis Thompson's formulation, which has become more or less standard in the biomedical literature, defines a conflict of interest as "a set of conditions in which professional judgment concerning a primary interest (such as a patient's welfare or the validity of research) tends to be unduly influenced by a secondary interest (such as financial gain)".[46] Since Thompson's use of the term "interest" to describe a physician's duty to her patient is both idiosyncratic and potentially misleading, the following definition seems preferable:

A person is in a conflict of interest situation if she is in a relationship with another in which she has a moral obligation to exercise her judgment in that other's service and, at the same time, she has an interest tending to interfere with the proper exercise of judgment in that relationship.[47]

"Judgment" refers to intelligent activity requiring more than mechanical rule following. "Interest" refers to personal financial benefit or family interest or any special influence or loyalty which could undermine the performance of one's duty to exercise one's judgment objectively.

Since the concept of conflict of interest is beset by a certain amount of confusion, it may be helpful to illustrate its application within the field of medical research. As noted earlier, every doctor is bound by oath "to put the life and health of my patient first". So, when physicians engaged in medical research accept drug company funding or consulting fees, or gifts or free travel, the acceptance of such benefits, and the hope for more in the future, makes them beholden to the company and thereby puts them in a conflict of interest situation. Physicians have a fiduciary duty or obligation to their patients/research subjects—a duty to put the patients' interest first—but they now have an interest, a financial and career "vested interest" in the success of the new drug being tested.

It would, of course, be naïve to deny that many conflicts of interest are not financial. Thus, a researcher's duty to exercise his judgment on behalf of his patients/subjects could be biased by considerations such as the desire for enhanced status, winning the race against scientific competitors, promotion through the academic hierarchy, and so on. It is likely not possible to eliminate completely all conflicts of interest. Nevertheless, wherever possible, society ought to strive to eliminate or, at least, to minimise, conflicts of interest. Even when there is no formal contractual obligation between medical researchers and their industrial sponsors, feelings of being beholden to the company have a tendency to influence professional judgment. By selling their good will to the companies, in return for personal benefits, researchers are guilty of betraying the trust of their subjects.

Thus, a medical researcher is in a conflict of interest situation when she has an ethical obligation to put the interests of her patients first, but she also has a private interest (pleasing a drug company sponsor, let us say, in order that grants and consulting fees continue) that has a tendency to interfere with the proper exercise of her judgment on behalf of her patient/research subject. If a researcher stands to gain monetary and/or career success by demonstrating the virtues of a new drug, and stands to lose research funding and perhaps her job if she finds that the new drug is unsafe or comparatively ineffective, then she is in a conflict of interest situation. This is true even if she does not succumb to temptation. That is, even if the researcher successfully preserves the objectivity of her judgment, it nevertheless remains true that she is in a conflict of interest situation—simply because of the presence of powerful financial and career incentives with a tendency to bias research. Carl Elliott offers a helpful analogy:

If a policeman takes money to overlook a speeding violation and then writes the ticket anyway, he has still accepted a bribe, even if he has not been influenced by it. The point is that certain people in whom public trust is placed must not have a financial interest in violating the duties carried by their institutional role. In this respect, at least, they must be financially disinterested. What is more, they must be seen to be disinterested; otherwise, the institution they represent risks falling apart.[48]

Elliott is here writing about the impropriety of ethicists accepting financial and other benefits for consulting work they do for the pharmaceutical industry, but his point applies with at least as much force when we turn to the issue of clinical researchers accepting financial benefits from industry. This point is explored in more detail below, under the heading of "What is to be done?"

Some defenders of university/industry partnerships may dismiss this application of Elliott's argument by analogy. They could point out, quite correctly, that to bribe a policeman is a criminal act, whereas a contract to accept industry funding is not illegal. When a university researcher accepts grants from industry, what have to be assessed are the terms of the contract and the understandings, explicit and implicit, between the parties. If a researcher accepts the funding and treats it as an unconditional grant—not different in kind from a government grant—then there will be no bad consequences.

To this argument, critics of university/industry partnerships are likely to respond that the risk of being blacklisted in the fierce competition for future grants could easily influence at least some researchers to tickle their research design or massage their data in order to produce pleasing (to their sponsors) results. As we have seen, there is mounting evidence in the literature indicating that this research bias seems to be occurring with considerable frequency. Of course, many companies will be deterred from egregious forms of cajolery and of bullying against biomedical researchers by the fear of critical media attention. However, a few dramatic cases, in which researchers find their careers in ruins because their findings do not enhance their sponsors' bottom line, might be sufficient, as the French say, *pour encourager les autres*. Moreover, even without explicit threats, companies have subtler ways of communicating to the biomedical research community what sort of performance is likely to enhance future opportunities for collaboration.

This is not to say that financial gain, career success, and personal prestige are in and of themselves unworthy goals. The salient point is, rather, that by putting researchers in a conflict of interest situation industry sponsorship can threaten the objectivity and reliability of research. A physician/researcher who puts herself in a conflict of interest situation leaves open the possibility that her vested interest will potentially exert an inappropriate influence on the design of the research or the collection, analysis, and disclosure of data. The studies and metastudies cited in earlier sections of this paper suggest that drug company sponsorship of research has a marked tendency to produce the kind of bias that undermines professional integrity.

If a biomedical researcher deliberately sets out to "lose" adverse data about a sponsor's drug, or consciously chooses a comparator which will artificially enhance the apparent effectiveness of the new drug, then he or she would be guilty of outright fraud. The evidence pertaining to medical fraud suggests, however, that only a small minority of scientists are corrupt in this way. The majority are honest. Honest, but often (unconsciously) biased in favour of the products of the sponsoring company. (Or generally biased in favour of new drugs, even when they are the products of a competitor company). In other words, conflicts of interest have the potential to produce dishonesty, but this may be a less common problem than their tendency to undermine the integrity of research in the subtler ways discussed above. See also the paper by Avorn J, *et al.*[49] This paper shows that doctors are probably unconsciously influenced by pharmaceutical promotion.

It is possible, as suggested earlier, to design a study that compares a new drug not to the best available alternative, but to a placebo, or to a drug already proven to be ineffective. In this way, new drugs that should not succeed commercially, because they are less good than the best already available,

may nevertheless—through heavy marketing and good salesmanship to doctors—become a commercial success. The Patented Medicine Prices Review Board reports that a mere six per cent of new drugs can be classified as "substantial improvements" over already existing treatments; the board's annual reports for 1998–2001 are cited by P Baird.[50] It seems clear, therefore, that the regulatory environment badly needs to be reinforced. Licensing bodies could insist—for example, on robust designs with adequate oversight. If one inquires, however, why university and hospital research boards and government regulatory agencies are not providing adequate oversight, the answer may turn out to be that these regulatory bodies have been "captured" by the very industries they are mandated to oversee.[51]

Researchers typically do not realise that their professional commitment to research integrity and patient safety can be compromised by their self interested pursuit of career success or financial profit or prestige. Many become indignant when this suggestion is put to them. Although I have lectured widely in North America and England on the threat to scientific objectivity posed by the financial and career benefits which the pharmaceutical industry bestows upon medical researchers, no researcher has ever admitted to me that the receipt of substantial grants, fancy trips, honoraria, consulting fees, royalty payments, or corporate share holdings has biased his or her scientific judgment. When it comes to research design or data collection and analysis, each researcher sees (or at least claims to see) his/her scientific objectivity as incorruptible. It should be mentioned that bioethicists—who are latecomers to the drug industry gravy train—seem equally confident that their judgment is not prejudicially affected by the acceptance of money and other benefits from industry (personal observation by the author).

Similarly, medical students seldom admit that the drug companies, which have graciously supplied them with free beer and pizza, or textbooks, have at the same time purchased their good will. Doctors seldom admit that their clinical judgment has been influenced by the acceptance of lavish dinners, free laptop computers, or skiing holidays to Vail, Colorado. Top university and hospital officials strenuously deny any suggestion that the receipt of donations or research funds from drug companies has skewed in any way their performance of their duties. Nor do they believe that a university's ownership of patents in new drugs being tested at the university could potentially undermine the rigour with which the university polices the integrity of the research carried out under its aegis.

"I can't be bought for ... (fill in the blank: research funding, major donations, consulting fee, royalties, Caribbean holiday, laptop computer, fancy dinner, free pizza, whatever)". Employing these or similar words, members of the biomedical research community, physicians, medical students, bioethicists, and university and hospital officials, confidently affirm that there is no harm done—certainly not to their own integrity—by the acceptance of drug company beneficences. Those who perceive such protestations as instances of hypocrisy or self deception are generally met with disbelief:

> ... few doctors accept that they themselves have been corrupted. Most doctors believe that they are quite untouched by the seductive ways of industry marketing men; that they are uninfluenced by the promotional propaganda they receive; that they can enjoy a company's "generosity" in the form of gifts and hospitality without prescribing its products. The degree to which the profession, mainly composed of honourable and decent people, can practise such self deceit is quite extraordinary.

No drug company gives away its shareholders' money in an act of disinterested generosity.[52]

These words were aimed at clinicians, but they could just as easily have been directed towards clinical researchers. The self righteousness with which biomedical researchers deny that they might themselves have been biased by acceptance of drug company money encourages the surmise that industry may understand something fundamental about human nature, something which the medical and biomedical research communities, in their naiveté, have somehow overlooked.

What the drug companies understand is that much of social life is based on reciprocity. The need to return benefit for benefit, kindness for kindness, and favour for favour is a basic motivator in virtually every human society, past or present. It behoves us, therefore, to consider that every dollar of the hundreds of millions of dollars which the companies invest in grants and gifts to researchers, hospitals and universities, doctors, and medical students is viewed by the companies as an important part of their corporate strategy. This is not meant to deny that industry has other motivations as well when it funds university research. "Genuine discovery", leading to worthwhile products, is surely one of the motives which shapes the behaviour of pharmaceutical executives. Sophisticated industry officials understand that good science can often be highly profitable and that, in the long run, bad science is likely to be exposed. Nevertheless, in the lean mean competitive world of the global marketplace, the future of a company's stock, like the career progress of its executives, will often depend on a rapidly rising "bottom line". Short term considerations, it seems all too clear, can sometimes exert considerable pressure on companies. It would be surprising if some of this pressure were not transmitted, directly or indirectly, to the scientists whose research the companies are funding.

To put this point in another way, whether intended or not, every grant and gift from a pharmaceutical company to scientists or to their university or hospital comes with strings attached. Strings that are sometimes as heavy and oppressive as lead chains.

It is also important to note that most studies in the biomedical literature are concerned with conflicts of interest at the micro level, that is, at the level of individual researchers and their published (or deliberately not published) results. A similar phenomenon arises, however, at the macro level. When institutions, such as universities and hospitals, compete for drug company research sponsorships and donations, and when such public institutions believe, perhaps correctly, that without industry money they cannot flourish, it becomes increasingly difficult for them to guard and protect traditional institutional values. In the pursuit of scientific excellence through industry funding and donations universities and their teaching hospitals can find themselves unwittingly allied with wealthy companies against their own researchers (and their own patients).

University administrators, including especially presidents and medical faculty deans, have a professional obligation to ensure that the research carried on within their institutions respects the core values of academic freedom, research integrity, and patient safety. There is a growing body of data, however, suggesting that institutional integrity is no less easily eroded than individual integrity. As Carl Elliott observes:

Corporate money is so crucial to the way that university medical centres are funded today that no threat or offers need actually be made in order for a company to exert its influence. The mere presence of corporate money is enough.[48]

Consider again the University of Toronto's behaviour in the Olivieri/Apotex and Healy/Eli Lilly cases. As we have seen, in the Olivieri/Apotex case there were legal threats made against a university researcher, Olivieri, in an effort to prevent her disclosing adverse information about the company's drug and, simultaneously, there were negotiations for a very large company gift from Apotex to the university. In the Healy/Eli Lilly case, by contrast, there is no suggestion that Healy was put on legal notice by the company whose drug he criticised, and the corporate financial donation (from Eli Lilly to CAMH) had already taken place. Nevertheless, the story played out in very similar fashion in both cases. This suggests that the presence or absence of explicit company threats—to cut off research funds, let us say—is not of great importance. When the university becomes a business, its top officials are virtually required to adopt commercial values as an adjunct to their academic values. Institutional conflict of interest *par excellence*.

WHAT IS TO BE DONE? THE REFORMIST PACKAGE

Not everyone agrees that the commercialisation of university research creates an ethical minefield for academic science. Certainly, spokespersons for industry downplay the potential for conflicts of interest. Instead, they tend to stress the many ways in which industrial sponsorship of university research has promoted the advancement of science, created beneficial new drugs, developed a market for them, and thereby made possible both corporate profits and the flourishing of scientific creativity. These claims are not without merit. Many members of the biomedical research community would endorse them with enthusiasm.

As recently as 1997, an editorial commentary in *Nature* denies outright the view that industrial sponsorship of research has resulted in serious risks of fraud, deception, or bias in presentation of data. The editor then proceeds to reject the call from other journal editors for mandatory disclosure of researchers' personal financial interests.[53] In the same vein, but a few years earlier, Kenneth Rothman, editor of the journal *Epidemiology*, writing in *JAMA*, disparaged the proposal for mandatory disclosure by researchers of their industrial ties. Rothman goes so far as to tag such proposals with the pejorative label "the new McCarthyism in science".[54]

In the 1990s, at the time these antidisclosure editorials were appearing in *Nature* and *JAMA*, only a few American scientific journals had instituted a policy of mandatory conflict of interest disclosure. By the autumn of 2001, however, growing awareness of the dangers which widespread industrial sponsorship posed to scientific objectivity led editors of many of the world's leading general medical journals to sound the alarm and jointly to strengthen their ethics requirements for authors publishing in their journals.[55] Henceforth, research published in journals such as the *New England Journal of Medicine*, the *Lancet*, the *Journal of the American Medical Association*, and the *Canadian Medical Association Journal* had to meet a newly promulgated set of ethical requirements.[56] Under these revised rules, authors are routinely compelled to disclose details of their own and their sponsor's role in the study. Moreover, the lead ("responsible") author is required to sign a statement indicating that he/she accepts full responsibility for the conduct of the trial, had full access to the data, and controlled the decision to publish. A caveat in the editorial explains, however, that not every journal editor who signed this statement will require this particular provision. The objective of these requirements is to ensure that commercial sponsors are not in a position to impose "any impediment, direct or indirect, on the publication of the study's full results, including data perceived to be detrimental to the product".[³⁵] This newly reinforced code of publication ethics, the editors tell us, is intended to safeguard "the hallmarks of scholarly independence and, ultimately, academic freedom".[³⁶]

It should also be noted that even *Nature* appears to be having second thoughts. That journal's hostility to "McCarthy-ite" scientists has been replaced, a mere four years later, by a recognition that "[t]here are circumstances in which selection of evidence, interpretation of results or emphasis of presentation might be inadvertently or even deliberately biased by a researcher's other interests".[³⁷] The current editor of *Nature*, Philip Campbell, continues to deny that "commercial interests of researchers are likely to lead to a lack of research integrity", but now concedes that "the best way to maintain readers' trust … is through a policy of transparency".[³] A 2002 article by F Van Kolfschooten, also in *Nature*, argues that disclosure is fast becoming the norm with respect to conflicts of interest in scientific research.[³⁸]

In short, the view that disclosure is the key to dealing with biomedical conflicts of interest seems to be gaining wide acceptance within the biomedical research community, even among those who were previously doubtful. Especially noteworthy is the endorsement by Stelfox *et al* in their seminal 1998 *NEJM* article on calcium channel antagonists, discussed above: "Physicians and researchers simply need to disclose their financial relationships with pharmaceutical manufacturers appropriately".[³³] Full disclosure will do the trick, they insist, because " w]e believe that the authors we surveyed expressed their own opinions and were not influenced by financial relationships with pharmaceutical manufacturers". Thus, according to Stelfox, the real problem is one of public relations: "I]t is our opinion that scientific authors are naive about public perceptions concerning such relationships [of industry sponsorship]".[³³] That is to say, the public would be upset were it to discover that scientific authors had undisclosed relationships with the sponsor whose products they were touting. To affirm the integrity of the medical profession and to maintain public confidence, according to Stelfox, it is necessary (and sufficient) that there be full disclosure of the relationships between physicians and pharmaceutical manufacturers.

Pause for a moment to consider the extraordinary claim by Stelfox and his colleagues, quoted above, that researchers (at least those they surveyed) are not influenced (even to a slight degree?) by either research funding from or their financial relationships with the pharmaceutical industry. Ironically, the Stelfox claim of non-influence comes immediately after he and his colleagues have presented evidence of a dramatic association between industry sponsorship and pro-industry results. Admittedly, since we have not yet got research to demonstrate conclusively which came first, the favourable articles or the industry funding, a certain degree of agnosticism on the question of influence is warranted. What is clearly not warranted, however, is belief in the non-influence hypothesis. Moreover, even if it turns out that in some cases the positive results came first and the industry funding then followed, such a practice, if widespread, would be a very strong inducement for researchers to design and carry out investigations likely to have industry favourable results. In short, the refusal by Stelfox *et al* even to entertain the possibility that industry funding has a tendency to bias research seems to be a matter of blind faith.

If Stelfox *et al* are mistaken in their unsupported belief, as their own data suggests they might be, then the threat to research integrity may be more than an optical illusion, and the solution they propose—full disclosure—may be inadequate to the twin tasks of ensuring research integrity and

safeguarding the public's trust in the reliability of biomedical research.

Other scholars, more seriously concerned than Stelfox and *Nature* about the corrosive effects of industry sponsorship on university research, have contributed additional reform proposals, all with a view to shoring up research integrity and public confidence. As mentioned above, the International Committee of Medical Journal Editors [ICMJE] requires, in addition to rules about disclosure of financial ties, that authors participate in the trial design, have access to data, and control publication.

Even these measures, however, seem insufficient to deal with the problem of "publication bias". Some argue that the most effective measure would be prospective registration of all trials, perhaps even all preliminary research studies. Dickersin notes that such registers already exist for several research areas[³⁹] and contends sensibly that "if treatment decisions are based on the published literature, then the literature must include all available data that is of acceptable quality".[⁴⁰] Perhaps it is time for the ICMJE to accept their own partial responsibility for a failure to deal with the problem of publication bias, and commit their journals to an editorial policy whereby the decision to publish will be based "on issues of quality and logical reasoning by the authors and not the direction and strength of study results".[⁴⁰] In other words, arguably, journal editors have a duty, in the interest of promoting research integrity, to ensure that good quality studies which happen to reach negative conclusions about a new drug are not consigned, along with their authors, to the dustbin of history. Without some such reform, researchers will continue to labour under a serious conflict of interest, but the personal interests tending to bias their results will include career advancement (via publication) rather than simply vested financial interests, which have been the main focus of the discussion so far.

Bero and Rennie suggest additional reforms which would have, they believe, the effect of improving the quality of drug studies (Bero LA, *et al*,[⁴¹] pp 209–37). They recommend, among other things, that pharmaceutical companies should support "investigator initiated research that focuses on questions that are shaped by broad scientific interests rather than narrow commercial interests" (Bero LA, *et al*,[⁴¹] pp 209–37). Indeed, just the kind of research that used to be done much more commonly a few decades ago, in the era before university/industry partnerships. They recommend that a "user fee" be imposed on drug companies to fund studies on comparative effectiveness, together with a new requirement (in order for companies to obtain government drug approval) that companies provide data comparing new drugs with available alternatives for effectiveness and cost. Their "wish list" also includes a stipulation that drug companies leave the planning and monitoring of the research design *completely* [my emphasis] to the funded investigators, and that they (the companies) not be involved in the presentation of the data—measures intended to promote balance and to minimise skewed interpretation (Bero L A, *et al*,[⁴¹] pp 209–37).

THINKING THE UNTHINKABLE: THE SEQUESTRATION THESIS

The above listed reform proposals, if rigorously implemented, would almost certainly improve the quality and scientific integrity of published biomedical research. Unfortunately, such evidence as we have suggests that the reformist package is not currently being implemented to an extent that even begins to approach what is called for in present circumstances.

A recently published (2002) national survey shows that "academic institutions routinely participate in clinical research that does not adhere to ICMJE standards of accountability, access to data, and control of publication".[39] What Schulman and his colleagues find is that, notwithstanding the importance of the new research integrity requirements, American academic institutions do not enforce them: "A[cademic institutions rarely ensure that their investigators have full participation in the design of the trials, unimpeded access to trial data, and the right to publish their findings" (Schulman K A, *et al*,[39] pp 1335). In an effort to explain this failure, Schulman *et al* suggest that "t]he current research environment may impede institutions' attempts to negotiate contract provisions that secure investigators' rights" (Schulman K A, *et al*,[39] p 1340). The phrase "current research environment" seems to refer euphemistically to the fact that North American (and many European) universities are engaged in competition with each other, and with Contract Research Organisations (CROs), for drug industry research contracts. Contract Research Organisations are private non-academic research groups, to which drug companies can turn, as an alternative to university researchers, in order to conduct the clinical trials needed for government drug licensing. Their costs are usually significantly lower than those of university researchers. Such companies typically have their own research ethics boards, the members of which will be paid by the company. This situation, needless to say, is a breeding ground for conflicts of interest. Contract research organisations with a reputation for producing favourable results for drug companies' products are likely to flourish, while those with more scrupulous standards are likely to go out of business. In other words, universities which are powerfully beholden to drug companies for research sponsorships and donations are not in a strong position to dictate ethical requirements to these same companies. Hence, the widespread failure of universities to meet their institutional obligation to protect research integrity.

As for the recommendations of Bero and Rennie, outlined above, one would have to be of an unshakably optimistic nature to believe that drug companies will voluntarily comply with any of them. This is not because drug companies never behave as good corporate citizens. Some companies are models of socially responsible behaviour. Nevertheless, every publicly traded company has a legal duty to conduct its affairs such that the best interests of its shareholders are given primacy. Alas, the best interests of shareholders do not always coincide with the best interests of patients/research subjects/the general public. When the costs of developing a new drug and bringing it to market fall in the neighbourhood of $100–$800 million (US),[40][42] it would be an unusual drug company that would willingly permit the publication of adverse data likely to scuttle its investment. To repeat an earlier quoted passage from "Dancing with the porcupine": "The duty of universities is to seek truth. The duty of pharmaceutical companies is to make money for their shareholders" (Lewis S, *et al*,[3] p 783).

One short and simple solution to the problem of protecting the research integrity of investigators and universities alike would be to prohibit outright the conflicts of interest which are responsible, in large part, for generating the problem. Carl Elliot asks us to contemplate our reaction to a judicial proceeding in which the judge was paid by one of the corporate litigants.[44] One has only to consider this prospect in order to realise that our judicial system would lose all credibility if such a practice were permitted. We require of the judiciary that it be disinterested and dispassionate. As Sheldon Krimsky points out, in an interview in the *Chronicle of Higher Education* which was quoted in the *CAUT Bulletin* (Bulletin of the Canadian Association of University Teachers): "We would not permit a judge…to have equity in a for profit prison, even if the judge disclosed it".[45]

Analogously, biomedical researchers and their universities should simply not be permitted to put themselves into situations of financial conflict of interest. If the community values public science in the public interest then it will have to be paid for by public tax dollars. Other (reformist) solutions, however plausible they may appear, are very unlikely to succeed in practice.

In the long run and overall it cannot serve the public interest to have the research agenda dictated by the corporate imperative of short run profitability. In the long run and overall it cannot be in society's interest to permit universities to forfeit public trust in the objectivity and independence of university research.

This does not mean that university originated discoveries should never be commercialised. In Western marketplace societies, many of the discoveries of fundamental research will be developed and marketed commercially. It should become the job of governments to develop new mechanisms so that a fair share of the resulting profit would be captured for the benefit of universities and hospitals—while avoiding the current funding arrangement whereby a growing number of researchers tends to become handmaidens of business, and universities become adjuncts of large corporations. University research and university researchers must be sequestered from the process of commercialisation if we want to avoid the kinds of damaging conflicts of interest described earlier.

How might such a sequestration be achieved? It would likely be difficult, or even impossible, for any national government unilaterally to change its intellectual property and patent laws. One practical possibility might be to require of any drug company which desires to bring a new drug to market that it provide to an independent institute all the funding necessary for the design and performance of a clinical trial of its drug. The institute would then allocate to qualified university and hospital researchers the task of conducting the necessary clinical trials. Clinical research would thereby become disinterested. Another promising solution to the challenge might lie in changes to the tax system. If industry profitably exploits the public's investment in scientific research, it cannot legitimately complain when a fair share of its profits from such research are recaptured through special taxation. This would constitute a partial answer to the question: if university and hospital research are no longer to be funded by industry, from which alternative source will they draw financial support? The government could provide such support through special taxes raised from corporations which make use of discoveries originating from university scientific research. Working out the details of such a proposal will be no easy task. Problems and obstacles are easy to imagine, but may not be insurmountable if society perceives a need to restore and preserve the integrity of scientific research.

The price tag for this radical proposal—that we revert to a system of public research funding—could be high, especially if it turns out not to be feasible to recapture, through taxation, most of the revenue now generated by commercialisation of university research. But there is an argument to be made that if drug research were publicly funded there would actually be a net saving, because drug costs would, in the absence of patents, be dramatically lower.[43] It is also important to note, in this connection, that failure to eliminate the conflicts of interest which currently bedevil the biomedical research community also carries a considerable price tag. The evidence on which "evidence based medicine" depends currently falls well short of the key *desideratum* of scientific reliability. If the status quo or something only mildly better than the status quo persists over time, fortunes of money will be wasted on ineffective or positively harmful treatments, and lives will be lost or blighted. Not so much because dishonest researchers will deliberately attempt to foist fraudulent results on the medical community as because ordinary decent researchers will be influenced, often unconsciously, by their understandable desire to please industry sponsors in order to achieve career success and/or financial reward.

Many within the biomedical research community will be inclined to dismiss the sequestration proposal herein advanced as the unrealistic musings of an armchair philosopher. An impartial survey of the evidence, however, can plausibly be interpreted to show that the long term costs of continued university reliance upon industry funding are likely far to outweigh the short term benefits. Certainly, the stakes are high. To continue on our present course is to risk losing the one commodity which, for physicians, universities, and hospitals, should be viewed as beyond price: the public trust.

Disclaimer: The author has not been funded by any drug company. He has appeared at three press conferences with Nancy Olivieri, at which his (unpaid) role was to analyse and evaluate the ethical issues raised by her dispute with Apotex, the Hospital for Sick Children, and the University of Toronto.

Arthur Schafer is Professor of Philosophy at the University of Manitoba and Director of the Centre for Professional and Applied Ethics.

REFERENCES

1 O'Hara J. Whistleblowing. *Maclean's Magazine* 1998 Nov:66.
2 Nathan DG, Weatherall DJ. Academic freedom in clinical research. *N Engl J Med* 2002;347:1368–70.
3 Lewis S, Baird P, Evans RG, et al. Dancing with the porcupine: rules for governing the university/industry relationship. *CMAJ* 2001;165:783–5.
4 Naimark A, Knoppers BM, Lowry FH. *Clinical trials of L1 (deferiprone) at The Hospital for Sick Children: a review of the facts and circumstances.* Toronto: Hospital for Sick Children, 1998.
5 Thompson J, Baird P, Downie J. *Report of the Committee of Inquiry on the case involving Dr Nancy Olivieri, the Hospital for Sick Children, the University of Toronto, and Apotex Inc.* Toronto: Canadian Association of University Teachers, 2001.
6 Naimark A, Knoppers BM, Lowry FH. *Commentary on selected aspects of the Report of the Canadian Association of University Teachers Committee of Inquiry on the case involving Dr Nancy Olivieri, The Hospital for Sick Children, the University of Toronto and Apotex Inc.* Toronto: The Hospital for Sick Children, 2001.
7 Thompson J, Baird P, Downie J. *Supplement to the Report of the Committee of Inquiry on the case involving Dr Nancy Olivieri, the Hospital for Sick Children, the University of Toronto, and Apotex Inc.* Toronto: Canadian Association of University Teachers, 2002.
8 The College of Physicians and Surgeons of Ontario. *Complaints committee decision and reasons. Claimant: Dr Laurence Becker; respondent: Dr Nancy Olivieri.* 2001 Dec 19:No 44410.
9 Gibson E, Baylis F, Lewis S. Dances with the pharmaceutical industry. *CMAJ* 2002;15:36–41.
10 Le Carré J. *The constant gardener.* Toronto: Penguin, 2001.
11 Ranalli P. Courage under fire [letter]. *Globe and Mail* 1998 Aug 19:A9.
12 Healy D. Good science or good business? *Hastings Cent Rep* 2000;30:19–22.
13 Elliott C. Throwing a bone to the watchdog. *Hastings Cent Rep* 2001;31:9–12.
14 Clarke C. Top scientists allege U of T academic chill. *The Globe and Mail* 2001 Sept 6:A1.
15 Bloch-Nevitt S. Addiction centre stands behind decision on hiring dispute. www.newsandevents.utoronto.ca/bin2/0106 (accessed 31 Aug 2001).
16 Creaney W, Murray I, Healy D. Antidepressant induced suicidal ideation. *Hum Psychopharmacol* 1991;6:329–32.
17 Healy D. The fluoxetine and suicide controversy. *CSN Drugs* 1994;1:223–31.
18 Healy D. Antidepressant induced suicidality. *Primary Care Psychiatry* 2000;16:23–8.
19 Somerville MA. Post-modern tale: the ethics of research relationships. *Nature* 2002;1:316–20.
20 Merton RK. *The sociology of science.* Chicago: University of Chicago Press, 1973.
21 Merges RP. Property rights theory and the commons: the case of scientific research. In: Frankel E, Miller FD Jnr, Paul J, eds. *Scientific innovation, philosophy and public policy.* Cambridge: Cambridge University Press, 1996.
22 Birch DM, Cohn G. The changing creed of Hopkins science. *Baltimore Sun* 2001 Jun 25:A1.

23 Bok D. *Universities in the marketplace.* Princeton, NJ: Princeton University Press, 2003:77.
24 Hausman DM, Kitcher P. Science, truth and democracy [book review]. *Ethics* 2003;13:423–8 at 424.
25 Zachary GP. *The endless frontier: Vannevar Bush, engineer of the American century.* Cambridge: MIT Press, 1999.
26 Diamond v Chakrabarty, US 1980;447:303.
27 Haber E. Industry and the university. *Nat Biotechnol* 1996;14:441–2.
28 Bodenheimer T. Uneasy alliance: clinical investigators and the pharmaceutical industry. *N Engl J Med* 2000;342:1539–44.
29 Krimsky S. Cited in: Kreeger KY. Studies call attention to ethics of industry support. *Scientist* 1997;11:1.
30 Pressman L. *AUTM licensing survey. FY 1999: survey summary.* Northbrook, IL: Association of University Technology Managers. Cited in: Bekelman JE, Li Y, Gross CP. Scope and impact of financial conflicts of interest in biomedical research. *JAMA* 2003;289:454–65.
31 Anon. The tightening grip of big pharma [editorial]. *Lancet* 2001;357:1141.
32 Weiss R, Nelson D. Teen dies undergoing experimental therapy. *Washington Post* 1999 Sept 29:A1.
33 Stelfox HT, Chua G, O'Rourke K, et al. Conflict of interest in the debate over calcium-channel antagonists. *N Engl J Med* 1998;338:101–6.
34 Bekelman JE, Li Y, Gross CP. Scope and impact of financial conflicts of interest in biomedical research. *JAMA* 2003;289:454–65.
35 Lexchin J, Bero KA, Djulbegovic B. Pharmaceutical industry sponsorship and research outcome and quality: systematic review. *BMJ* 2003;326:1167–74.
36 Djulbegovic B, Lacevic M, Cantor A, et al. The uncertainty principle and industry sponsored research. *Lancet* 2000;356:635–8.
37 Rochon PA, Gurwitz JH, Simms RW, et al. A study of manufacturer supported trials of non-steroidal anti-inflammatory drugs in the treatment of arthritis. *Arch Intern Med* 1994;154:157–63.
38 Shenk E. Money+science = ethics problems on campus. *The Nation* 1999 Mar 22:11–18.
39 Smith ML. Publication bias and meta-analysis. *Evaluation Education* 1980;4:22–24.
40 Dickersin K. The existence of publication bias and risk factors for its occurrence. *JAMA* 1990;263:1385–9.
41 Bero LA, Rennie D. Influences on the quality of published drug studies. *Int J Technol Assess Health Care* 1996;12:209–37, at 209.
42 Science, Innovation and Electronic Information Division, Statistics Canada. *Estimates of gross expenditures on research and development in the health field in Canada, 1970 to 1998.* Ottawa: Statistics Canada, 1999.
43 US Congress, Office of Technology Assessment, Pharmaceutical R&D. *Costs, risks and rewards,* OTA-H-522. Washington, DC: US Government Printing Office, 1993: cat no 88FO006XIB99004.
44 Okie S. Missing data on Celebrex. *Washington Post* 2001 Aug 5:A11.
45 Dieppe PA, Frankel SJ, Toth B. Is research into treatment of osteoarthritis with non-steroidal anti-inflammatory drugs misdirected? *Lancet* 1993;341:353–4.
46 Thompson D. Understanding financial conflicts of interest. *N Engl J Med* 1993;329:573–6.
47 Davis M. Conflict of Interest. *Bus Prof Ethics J* 1982;1:17–27.
48 Elliott C. Pharma buys a conscience. *Am Prospect* 2001;12:16–20.
49 Avorn J, Chen M, Hartley R. Scientific versus commercial sources of influence on the prescribing behaviour of physicians. *Am J Med* 1982;73:4–8.
50 Baird P. Getting it right: industry sponsorship and medical research. *CMAJ* 2003;168:1267–9.
51 Dukes MNG. Accountability of the pharmaceutical industry. *Lancet* 2002;360:1682–4.
52 Rawlins MD. Doctors and the drug makers. *Lancet* 1984;9:11–15.
53 Anon. Avoid financial correctness [editorial]. *Nature* 1997;385:469.
54 Rothman KJ. Conflict of interest: the new McCarthyism in science [editorial]. *JAMA* 1993;269:2782–4.
55 Davidoff F, DeAngelis CD, Drazen JM, et al. Sponsorship, authorship, and accountability. *N Engl J Med* 2001;345:825–7.
56 International Committee of Medical Journal Editors. *Uniform requirements for manuscripts submitted to biomedical journals: updated October 2001.* http://www.icmje.org/ (accessed 15 Dec 2003).
57 Campbell P. Declaration of financial interests: introducing a new policy for authors of research papers [editorial]. *Nature* 2001;412:751.
58 Van Kolfschooten F. Can you believe what you read? *Nature* 2002;416:360–3.
59 Schulman KA, Seils DM, Timbie JW, et al. A national survey of provisions in clinical trial agreements between medical schools and industry sponsors. *N Engl J Med* 2002;347:1335–41.
60 Henry D, Lexchin J. The pharmaceutical industry as a medicines provider. *Lancet* 2002;360:1590–5.
61 DiMasi JA, Hansen RW, Grabowski HG. The price of innovation: new estimates of drug development costs. *J Health Econ* 2003;22:151–83.
62 Relman A, Angell M. *The New Republic* 2002 Dec 16:27–42.
63 Anon. Conflicts of interest in biomedical research. *CAUT Bulletin* 2003 Feb:A9.
64 Baker D, Schmitt J, for Center for Economic and Policy Research. Growing pain: the expense of drugs for the elderly. http://www.cepr.net/ GrowingPain Issue Brief.htm (accessed 12 Dec 2003).

[35]

Pharma Buys a Conscience

Bioethicists increasingly find their work underwritten by pharmaceutical companies. Who passes on the ethics of ethicists?

BY CARL ELLIOTT ILLUSTRATIONS BY ALISON SEIFFER

I WAS RAISED IN A HOUSE FILLED WITH DRUG-INDUSTRY trinkets. My father has been a family doctor for more than 40 years, and drug representatives bearing gifts have visited him throughout his career. My brothers and I grew up tossing Abbott Frisbees and Upjohn Nerf balls. We took down messages on Inderal notepads, wrote with Erythromycin pens, carried Progestin umbrellas. We constructed weird Halloween costumes from models of the human hand and brain supplied by Parke-Davis and Merck. My father was no great fan of "detail men," as drug reps were called then. (These days, if you're a male physician, your detail man is likely to be an attractive young woman.) Nor did he take part in the drug industry's more outrageous marketing efforts, such as frequent-flier miles in exchange for drug prescriptions. But he saw no great harm in accepting drug samples for his patients

or toys for his children. Like virtually all doctors, he did not think that the gifts influenced him in any way.

Why pharmaceutical companies want the goodwill of doctors is no great mystery. The surprise is why they want the goodwill of someone like me. I am a philosophy professor, and I work at a bioethics center. While I do happen to have a degree in medicine, that degree is largely decorative: The only prescriptions I write these days are moral ones. Despite this difference (or maybe because of it), the pharmaceutical and biotechnological industries are funneling more and more cash into the pockets of academics who teach and study ethics. Some of it goes straight to individuals, in the form of consulting fees, contracts, honoraria, and salaries. Some of it—such as gifts to bioethics centers—is less direct. Many corporations are putting bioethicists on their scientific advisory boards or setting up special bioethics panels to provide in-house advice. While I have not yet been offered Frisbees or Nerf balls, I suspect that it is only a matter of time.

The issue of corporate money has become something of an embarrassment within the bioethics community. Bioethicists

CARL ELLIOTT *is an associate professor at the University of Minnesota Center for Bioethics and the author of* A Philosophical Disease: Bioethics, Culture, and Identity.

have written for years about conflicts of interest in scientific research or patient care yet have paid little attention to the ones that might compromise bioethics itself. Arthur Caplan, the director of the University of Pennsylvania Center for Bioethics, counsels doctors against accepting gifts from the drug industry. "The more you yield to economics," Caplan said last January, "the more you're falling to a business model that undercuts arguments for professionalism." Yet Caplan himself consults for the drug and biotech industries, recently co-authored an article with scientists for Advanced Cell Technology, and heads a bioethics center supported by Monsanto, de Code Genetics, Millennium Pharmaceuticals, Geron Corporation, Pfizer, AstraZeneca Pharmaceuticals, E.I. du Pont de Nemours and Company, Human Genome Sciences, and the Schering-Plough Corporation.

By no means does Caplan's center stand alone in its coziness with industry. The University of Toronto houses the Sun Life Chair in Bioethics; the Stanford University Center for Biomedical Ethics has a program in genetics funded by a $1-million gift from SmithKline Beecham Corporation; the Merck Company Foundation has financed a string of international ethics centers in cities from Ankara, Turkey, to Pretoria, South Africa. Last year the Midwest Bioethics Center announced a new $587,870 initiative funded by the Aventis Pharmaceuticals Foundation. That endeavor is titled, apparently without irony, the Research Integrity Project.

Bioethics appears set to borrow a funding model popular in the realm of business ethics. This model embraces partnership and collaboration with corporate sponsors as long as outright conflicts of interest can be managed. It is the model that allows the nonprofit Ethics Resource Center in Washington, D.C., to sponsor ethics and leadership programs funded by such weapons manufacturers as General Dynamics, United Technologies Corporation, and Raytheon. It also permits the former president of Princeton University, Harold Shapiro, to draw an annual director's salary from Dow Chemical Company while serving as chair of the National Bioethics Advisory Commission. Dow, of course, has been the defendant in a highly publicized lawsuit over the Dow Corning silicone breast implants as well as in numerous legal actions involving disposal of hazardous waste.

Part of the problem is aesthetic. It is unseemly for ethicists to share in the profits of arms dealers, industrial polluters, or multinationals that exploit the developing world. But credibility also is an issue. How can bioethicists continue to be taken seriously if they are on the payroll of the very corporations whose practices they are expected to assess?

LISTENING TO ELI LILLY

Last year some colleagues and I helped put together "Prozac, Alienation, and the Self," a special issue of *The Hastings Center Report*, a bioethics journal. Some of the papers that we published, including one by me, expressed worries about the extent to which antidepressants are being prescribed, especially for patients who are not clinically depressed. One paper in particular— "Good Science or Good Business?"—was especially critical of the drug industry. Its author, David Healy, is a psychopharmacologist and a historian of psychiatry at the University of Wales.

Shortly after these Prozac essays were published, Eli Lilly and Company, which manufactures Prozac, withdrew its annual gift to the Hastings Center, citing the special issue as its reason. Lilly's yearly check for $25,000 was not especially large by industry standards, but it was the Hastings Center's largest annual corporate donation. Lilly's letter to the organization was especially critical of Healy's article. Healy had previously published research indicating that some patients, particularly those who are not clinically depressed, may be more likely to commit suicide while taking antidepressants. He has also testified as an expert witness against Lilly and other drug manufacturers in lawsuits brought by family members of patients who killed themselves or others after taking antidepressants. In "Good Science or Good Business?" Healy argued that manufacturers of antidepressants have gone into the business of selling psychiatric illnesses in order to sell psychiatric drugs. Apparently, this was not the kind of bioethics scholarship that Lilly had in mind when it donated money to the Hastings Center.

THE REACTION OF BIOETHICISTS TO ALL OF THIS IS emblematic of the difficulties raised by corporate money. Some were encouraged by the response of the Hastings Center staff—particularly by the *Report*'s editors, who published the special issue without regard to Lilly's reaction. We are never hostage to corporate money, these scholars say. We can always turn it down, resign our posts, and do the right thing despite enticements to the contrary. For others, however, the fact that the *Report*'s editors faced such incentives is precisely the problem. Given enough cases where bioethicists must choose between scholarship and their corporate funders, the funders will eventually win out. In the long run, money conquers all.

But the Hastings Center episode was only the first chapter of the Healy affair. In November 2000, Healy gave a talk on the history of psychopharmacology at the University of Toronto's Center for Addiction and Mental Health (CAMH), where he was scheduled to take up a new position as director of the Mood Disorders Program. In that lecture, Healy mentioned his worries about Prozac and suicide. Shortly thereafter, the center rescinded his appointment. He was given no reason but merely informed by e-mail that CAMH did not feel that his "approach was compatible with the goals for development of the academic and clinical resource" of the clinic. CAMH officials insist that the Eli Lilly Corporation had nothing to do with the decision; yet the center is the recipient of a $1.5-million gift from Lilly. The Mood Disorders Program, which Healy was to direct, gets 52 percent of its funding from corporate sources

Whether Lilly or any other corporate funder had anything to do with Healy's dismissal is impossible to know. Even so, the trouble CAMH has had in convincing the public that industry sources were not involved points to the difficulty of discerning financial influence. Would CAMH have dismissed Healy if it had no ties to Lilly whatsoever? Does fear of being unable to attract future corporate money count as influence? Does fear of angering powerful industry-tied psychiatrists?

"Doctors fear drug companies like bookies fear the mob," says Harold Elliott, a psychiatrist at Wake Forest University. Corporate money is so crucial to the way that university medical centers are funded today that no threats or offers need actually be made in order for a company to exert its influence. The mere presence of corporate money is enough.

And researchers are probably right to be afraid. The University of Toronto itself has seen two other public scandals erupt over pharmaceutical-company funding in recent years. The most visible one involved Nancy Olivieri, a researcher at the university's Hospital for Sick Children, who was conducting clinical trials of deferiprone, a thalassemia drug, for the generic-drug manufacturer Apotex. When Olivieri became concerned about possible side effects of deferiprone, she broke her confidentiality agreement with Apotex and went public with her concerns. In response, Apotex threatened her with legal action. Rather than backing Olivieri against Apotex, the Hospital for Sick Children attempted to dismiss her. News headlines had hardly faded when Apotex promised the University of Toronto $20 million (about $13 million in U.S. dollars) in funding for molecular biology, then threatened to withdraw it if the school's then-president, Robert Prichard, did not lobby the federal government to change its drug-patent regulations. Apotex wanted rules that would be more favorable to generic-drug manufacturers. The president did as he was asked and was later forced to apologize publicly when the story broke.

Industry-sponsored bioethics programs face problems that parallel those encountered by industry-sponsored medical researchers. What do you do when your scholarly work conflicts with the goals of your industry sponsor? No one is forcing industry money on bioethics programs, but many of them are located in academic health centers, where faculty members are expected to generate money to fund their research either by seeing patients or by obtaining grants. If bioethics is seen as an activity that can attract industry sponsorship, university administrators strapped for cash will inevitably look to industry as a financial solution. All that remains is for bioethicists themselves to dispense with the ethical roadblocks.

REVIEW FOR HIRE

One of the duties routinely carried out by bioethicists is service on institutional review boards (IRBs), the local committees mandated to oversee any research undertaken in universities or hospitals in order to protect human research subjects. So central has the IRB become to the protection of research subjects that it has given its name to a leading journal, *IRB: Ethics and Human Research.* Several years ago, I served on the IRB of a psychiatric hospital, and I now see that experience as a case study in the convoluted role that corporate money has come to play in research ethics.

Soon after I joined the IRB, I found myself in sharp conflict with many other members over one recurring issue: the use of placebos in psychiatric clinical trials. When a new psychiatric drug looks sufficiently promising to be tested in human subjects, it is ordinarily tested against a control drug. If there is no effective treatment for the illness in question, that control is a placebo. Some subjects get the new drug, others get a placebo, and the researchers measure how the two compare. But if an effective treatment exists for a research subject's illness, the new drug must be tested against it, not against a placebo. The purpose of this rule is to protect subjects from harm. A patient should not get substandard treatment, such as a placebo, simply because he

or she has volunteered for a research protocol. Just as a placebo cannot ethically be given to research subjects with asthma or cancer or heart disease, one ought not be given to patients with schizophrenia or severe depression, even if they consent to the possibility. These conditions can be treated effectively with existing drugs. If an ordinary psychiatrist were to treat schizophrenia or severe depression with a placebo rather than standard therapy, he could be successfully sued for malpractice. The drugs used to treat these illnesses are not perfect, to be sure, but they have been proven more effective than placebos.

Or so I argued to the IRB. The board was reviewing industry-sponsored protocols in which patients who were severely depressed or even acutely psychotic—delusional, hallucinating, confused, tortured by their own thoughts—were being given placebos rather than effective treatments, sometimes for periods of up to eight weeks. I cited national and international ethics guidelines, even the university's own guidelines, all of which prohibited the trials. Tables were pounded. Faces turned scarlet. Blood pressures soared. Yet the IRB continued to approve many of the trials, over my objections and those of other members of the committee. The hospital administration eventually dissolved the IRB and reconstituted it with new membership.

WHY WAS THE ISSUE SO DIVISIVE? EVERYONE'S interests were involved. First of all, the pharmaceutical industry, which sponsored the trials, has a financial interest in conducting placebo-controlled trials because they usually require fewer subjects than tests with active controls and are thus less expensive. Second, the trials generated much-needed income for the hospital—and possibly for the researchers themselves. And third, many IRB members were hospital psychiatrists who conducted placebo-controlled trials for industry. Other IRB members worked under the administrative authority of senior psychiatrists who were doing this type of research. While IRB members were not privy to the financial arrangements behind these trials, clinical researchers have reportedly received $1,000 to $6,000 for each patient they've enrolled in a clinical trial, with some earning between $500,000 and $1 million a year. According to a recent article in the *Baltimore Sun,* the chair of the psychiatry department at Brown University earned more than $500,000 in fees from drug companies in 1998.

The role of corporate funding in research review does not stop with local IRBs. Researchers testing new psychiatric drugs against placebos often point out that the Food and Drug Administration requires evidence from placebo-controlled trials before it will approve a new psychiatric drug. And they are right: The FDA argues that such research is justified by its scientific merit unless it results in death or permanent disability to subjects. Yet the FDA is itself deeply compromised by industry money. The industry pays "user fees" to the FDA in order to speed up review of their products—an amount estimated to be more than $300,000 per drug. And while the FDA employs scientific experts to evaluate new drugs, a recent survey found that over half of those experts have a financial conflict of interest because of industry ties. Dr. Richard Horton, editor of Britain's prestigious medical journal *The Lancet,* has called the FDA "the servant of [the drug] industry."

Some review boards are themselves becoming corporate entities. In fact, noninstitutional review boards (NIRBs) are usually set up as profit-making ventures. They oversee industry research that is not conducted in academic medical centers. Sixty percent of industry-sponsored clinical trials are contracted out to for-profit research firms, which may in turn contract with for-profit NIRBs for ethical review. A typical NIRB will charge about $1,200 to examine a research protocol. Unlike IRBs, which are usually staffed by volunteers, most NIRBs pay their members, including their ethicists.

Defenders of for-profit review boards claim that they can operate much more quickly and thoroughly than IRBs, which depend solely on volunteers. Yet the for-profit committees are financially dependent on the companies whose research protocols they are reviewing. If a corporation does not like the results that one for-profit NIRB provides, it contracts with another. "Nothing prevents companies from searching for the most lenient NIRB," says Trudo Lemmens, an attorney and bioethicist at the University of Toronto who has published two recent studies of NIRBs. Lemmens also points out that since NIRB members are typically not guaranteed a fixed term on the board, they may be dismissed for objecting to problematic protocols.

To be fair, there is no evidence to suggest that NIRBs are performing any less competently than IRBs. In a system of research review so thoroughly compromised by industry funding, however, it is ironic that many people see the solution to inefficient review as more industry funding. For no matter how efficient NIRBs may be, they are structured so that both the body and its individual members may feel compelled to make things as easy as possible for the people who pay them.

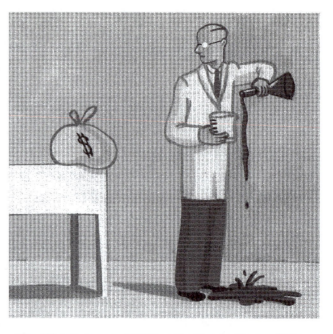

Bioethicists have paid little attention to the conflicts of interest that might compromise bioethics itself.

ASK THE EXPERTS

Earlier this year, I got an e-mail message from the CEO of a company called Foreview inviting me to become part of its "global network of experts." Foreview is a sort of corporate-academic dating service. It matches up academic "experts" with businesses seeking expertise. According to its Web site, Foreview provides its clients with "information about tomorrow's state of the economy and politics." It does this partly through its "Ask the Experts" service, which hires people like me to respond to questions posed by clients. My payment for taking part in "Ask the Experts" would be $175 per question. I was also told that this work would probably lead to more detailed consulting projects, for which I could set my own rates—but Foreview would receive a 10 percent finder's fee, capped at a maximum of $5,000.

I did not take Foreview up on its offer, which sounded a little too much like a "Dear Abby" column; but I did start to ask colleagues in bioethics about the kinds of corporate consultations they had been asked to do. The type of work available varied: testifying as an expert witness in court cases, preparing reports, giving talks at industry-sponsored meetings (often held at ski resorts or foreign vacation spots). Many biotechnology companies have set up their own bioethics advisory boards. A list of bioethicists reported to serve on such advisory boards reads like a who's who of bioethics: Nancy Dubler of Montefiore Medical, for DNA Sciences; Ronald Green of Dartmouth, for Advanced Cell Technology; Arthur Caplan of the University of Pennsylvania, for Celera Genomics and DuPont; Karen Lebacqz of the Pacific School of Religion, for Geron Corporation. Some bioethicists work pro bono while others accept fees. Evan DeRenzo, a staff member at the Center for Ethics at Washington Hospital Center, charges Janssen Pharmaceuticals by the hour to sit in on meetings, review research protocols, and help the company develop policy and educational sessions. Bruce Weinstein, formerly a faculty member in bioethics at the West Virginia University Health Sciences Center, now delivers lectures and seminars to businesses through a for-profit service called Ethics at Work. Weinstein calls himself "The Ethics Guy" and has published a self-help ethics book—*What Should I Do?*—that offers moral advice on everything from dating to personal hygiene.

Defenders of corporate consultation often bristle at the suggestion that accepting money from industry compromises their impartiality or makes them any less objective a moral critic.

"Objectivity is a myth," DeRenzo told me, marshaling arguments from feminist philosophy to bolster her cause. "I don't think there is a person alive who is engaged in an activity who has absolutely no interest in how it will turn out." Thomas Donaldson, director of the ethics program at the Wharton School, has compared ethics consultants to the external accounting firms often employed by corporations to audit their financial records. Like accountants, ethicists may be paid by the very industries they are assessing, but they are kept honest by their need to maintain a reputation for integrity.

Better to buy a bioethicist now than to be attacked by one later. The only challenge is to disguise the job so that bioethicists do not realize that they have been bought.

But the comparison of ethicists to accountants is deeply misleading. Ethical analysis does not look anything like a financial audit. If a company is cooking its books and the accountant closes his eyes to this fact in his audit, the accountant's transgression can be reliably detected and verified by outside monitors. But how do you detect the transgressions of an ethics consultant? Ethicists have widely divergent views: They come from different religious standpoints, use different theoretical frameworks, profess different political philosophies. They are also free to change their minds at any point. How do you tell the difference between an ethics consultant who has changed her mind for legitimate reasons and one who has changed her mind for money? How do you distinguish between a consultant who has been hired for his integrity and one who has been hired because he supports what the company plans to do? A savvy CEO will have no problem finding an ethicist to say virtually anything.

Yet influence is not exactly what's at issue. If a policeman takes money to overlook a speeding violation and then writes the ticket anyway, he has still accepted a bribe, even if he has not been influenced by it. The point is that certain people in whom public trust is placed must not have a financial interest in violating the duties carried by their institutional role. In this respect, at least, they must be financially disinterested. What is more, they must be seen as disinterested; otherwise, the institution they represent risks falling apart.

Judges and jurors, for instance, depend on the appearance of disinterestedness for their fragile hold on public trust. Judges get paid, of course, as do bioethicists and other academics. But the source of that payment is crucial. If we allowed judges to be paid by corporate litigators, they would soon lose their credibility—and rightly so. If bioethicists have gained any credibility in the public eye, it rests on the perception that they have no financial interest in the objects of their scrutiny.

Bioethicists who consult for industry are usually engaged in a range of other activities in which they are presumed to have a measure of distance—financially, if not ideologically—from the actions or policies in question. Students generally do not suspect that their ethics professor may be getting a paycheck from the very corporations whose actions and policies they are discussing

in class. Readers of bioethics journals do not generally suspect that the author of a paper on the ethics of stem cell research may be the part-time employee of a company conducting the research. The university that appoints an ethicist to an IRB generally does not imagine that the ethicist himself is being paid by the industries whose protocols he is expected to evaluate. Such relationships can be disclosed, of course. But even bioethicists who defend taking industry money often find disclosure a little embarrassing, and so they rarely disclose their conflicts except when it's mandatory—not in the philosophy class, not when they appear on *Nightline*, not when they are quoted in the pages of *The Washington Post* defending corporate policy. Most bioethics journals do not even require conflict-of-interest disclosures. And even when a financial relationship is disclosed, the amount of money that has changed hands is not. A reader of a scholarly article cannot tell the difference between an author who has received a hundred dollars from industry and one who has received hundreds of thousands.

T HE PROBLEM WITH ETHICS CONSULTANTS IS THAT they look like watchdogs but can be used like show dogs. What better way for a corporation to polish its image than to parade an ethics consultant before its critics? What better way to head off litigation than to run its plans by an in-house ethics board? No matter how outrageous a corporate policy, no matter how troubling a headline in the morning paper, it will be softened by the knowledge that the corporation in question has consulted with a team of ethics experts. Better to buy a bioethicist now than to be attacked by one later. The only challenge is how to disguise the job so that bioethicists do not realize that they have been bought.

Ken DeVille, an attorney and historian of medicine at East Carolina University, wonders whether bioethics will continue to be an enterprise worth pursuing once it is thoroughly infused with corporate money. "If ethicists are transformed into a bunch of corporate shills who exist only to serve the machine," he asks, "where is the honor in taking part?" Of course, DeVille's comment presumes that there is a distinction between honor and serving the machine. Once the very discipline of bioethics is itself a part of the machine, service is an honor. Laurie Zoloth, the current president of the American Society for Bioethics and Humanities, has written that the real temptations of industry associations are not financial but the honor and status of corporate consultancies. If she is right and advising a corporation is an honor, then bioethics is already making the shift from outsider to insider, from critic of the machine to loyal servant.

Still, we can all take heart: Help may be on the way. The American Medical Association's Council on Ethical and Judicial Affairs is planning a $590,000 initiative to educate doctors about the ethical problems involved in accepting gifts from the drug industry. That initiative is funded by gifts from Eli Lilly and Company, GlaxoSmithKline, Inc., Pfizer, U.S. Pharmaceutical Group, AstraZeneca Pharmaceuticals, Bayer Corporation, Procter and Gamble Company, and Wyeth-Ayerst Pharmaceutical. ◆

Part VIII
Bioethics and Public Policy

[36]

Can we learn from eugenics?

Daniel Wikler *University of Wisconsin, USA*

Abstract

Eugenics casts a long shadow over contemporary genetics. Any measure, whether in clinical genetics or biotechnology, which is suspected of eugenic intent is likely to be opposed on that ground. Yet there is little consensus on what this word signifies, and often only a remote connection to the very complex set of social movements which took that name. After a brief historical summary of eugenics, this essay attempts to locate any wrongs inherent in eugenic doctrines. Four candidates are examined and rejected. The moral challenge posed by eugenics for genetics in our own time, I argue, is to achieve social justice.

(*Journal of Medical Ethics* 1999;25:183–194)
Keywords: Eugenics; genetics; ethics; justice

I. Eugenics yesterday and today

The word "eugenics" may be unfamiliar to most people today, but for a period of about sixty-five years, roughly 1880 to 1945, both that term and the theories of human "improvement" which it denotes were in wide currency. Francis Galton, a cousin of Darwin, invented the term and launched a movement to improve the human race, or at least to halt its perceived decline, through selective breeding. His ideas spread quickly, and by the 1920s eugenics movements existed all over the world. Eugenics, a movement for social betterment clothed in the mantle of modern science, claimed the allegiance of most genetic scientists and drew supporters from the political right, left, and centre. Unfortunately for that movement, and indeed for much of mankind, eugenics was embraced by Hitler and his Nazi followers, tarnishing its name forever. After the fall of the Third Reich, eugenic ideas quickly lost their cachet, becoming virtually taboo in the United States and Europe, where the term "eugenic" is now used primarily as an epithet.

We should not forget eugenics. Eugenics casts a shadow over the use of genetics in our own era, which promises so much for health, industry, agriculture, and other fields. But that shadow is indistinct. It is often quite unclear whether a new practice in medicine or biotechnology has a eugenic cast, and whether it ought to be opposed on that ground if it does. We can learn much by studying the history of the movement and by engaging in careful moral analysis and assessment of its doctrines.

Eugenics has many lessons:

1. Eugenics is a valuable case study which demonstrates how the prestige of science can be used to disguise the moral premises and motives for a social movement, and how class, racial, and other biases can exert powerful and damaging influence over such a movement while remaining virtually invisible to its advocates. And it is another illustration of the sad thesis that good (or, at least, high-minded) intentions can lead to evil consequences.

2. Eugenics offers a perspective on the practices of our own era, the second moment in history in which the prospect for using the science of heredity to reshape society presents itself. Indeed, critics of certain practices in clinical genetics, and of some contemplated uses for the genetic technology of the future, maintain that these are eugenics in disguise. We must be able to evaluate this claim so that we can avoid the errors and wrongs of the past as we frame public policies for genetics in the future.

3. We should avoid an unthinking rejection of every eugenic thought or value. The fact that eugenicists were in favour of a particular measure or goal is not in itself sufficient reason to oppose it. We need a good analysis of which eugenic aims were wrong-headed, and why. We might judge that some of the questions to which eugenicists proposed answers ought not be ignored, and indeed that they are now given too little attention, in part because of their eugenic associations.

This paper provides both a brief history of the eugenics movement and a moral analysis of some of its tenets. I begin by recounting briefly the rise and fall of this complex international movement. I do not in any way wish to revise the very bad reputation which the eugenics movement currently suffers, and where old-style eugenics is advocated today, as in Singapore[1] and China,[2-4] conventional criticisms of these ideas still apply. When we turn to contemporary practices in clinical genetics whose status as "eugenic" is in dispute, however, the arguments must be more subtle. I argue that the label "eugenic" does in some instances apply, but that when this is the case the "eugenic" effect or intent of the practices ought not always to engender alarm or opposition.

Though we rightly reject all of the programmes practised or proposed by the eugenics movement in its heyday, I will argue that this retrospective evaluation does not point unequivocally to a rejection of any and all eugenics for the future.

II. Eugenics past

THE RISE OF EUGENICS

Though the literature of eugenics extends back to Plato, the modern movement took its cue from biology: first, Darwin's theory of natural selection, with a boost later on from Mendelian genetics. Galton understood that the theory of natural selection had important implications for understanding the development of the human species, and sought to investigate the possibility that talents and virtues of character and personality were inherited along with other traits, offering their bearers advantages in natural selection. Galton coined the term "eugenics" in 1883, defining it as the "science of improving stock—not only by judicious mating, but whatever tends to give the more suitable races or strains of blood a better chance of prevailing over the less suitable than they otherwise would have had".[5] His research, enhanced by statistical methods developed as he needed them, convinced him that society's stock of talent could be greatly enlarged if members of favoured families were to increase their rate of childbearing ("positive eugenics"). The balance should be further improved, he believed, by discouraging from reproducing those who had less to offer ("negative eugenics").

Galton's influence was nearly immediate. Darwin declared himself persuaded by his cousin's eugenic arguments, and Galton attracted a number of distinguished disciples. In Germany, the Racial Hygiene Society was formed in Berlin by 1905[6]; the English Eugenics Education Society was founded in 1907, with Galton elected honorary president the next year.[7] In the United Kingdom and the United States, the movement drew on the middle and upper-middle classes; many professionals and academics were attracted to it.[7-10] During the decades 1890-1920, eugenic ideas were advanced also in numerous non-English-speaking countries as diverse as Norway, Brazil, and the Soviet Union. Both a research programme and a popular movement, eugenics was taught at leading universities, and received attention in standard biology textbooks.

The popular eugenics movements, meanwhile, succeeded in rapidly introducing eugenic ideas into public discourse. Accounts of generations of misfits in such "white trash" family lines as the "Jukes" and the "Kallikaks" were widely publicised, warning that an unwise reproductive act could wreak havoc for generations.[8]

Following British successes at health exhibitions before the turn of the century, American eugenic organisations took a particular interest in maintaining exhibits and events at state fairs and public expositions. "Fitter Families" competitions were mounted at state fairs, with governors and senators handing out awards.[8]

The content of the eugenic programmes varied considerably. Eugenicists tended to agree that the human race was in decline, but they differed over both cause and remedy. The French and Brazilian eugenics movements were at least as concerned about neonatal care as with heredity, and their hereditarian thinking was Lamarckian—that is, they believed that parents passed on to their children characteristics acquired during their lifetimes.[11 12] Most eugenicists elsewhere accepted Galton's view, buttressed by the "germ plasm" hypothesis of August Weismann, that selection rather than environment determined heredity. Eugenicists tended to draw from this account the implication that medical care frustrated evolution by permitting the unfit to survive and reproduce (though Darwin and a number of others who held this view none the less continued to support humanitarian measures).

Eugenicists differed also in their practical proposals and legislative aims. While action on behalf of positive eugenics was limited to such mild measures as family allowances, some eugenicists (particularly in the United States and, later, Germany and Scandinavia) did not hesitate to call for coercive measures, either sexual segregation or, later, involuntary sterilisation, to prevent those imagined to have undesirable genes from propagating their kind.

In Germany, eugenics became an integral element of medical thinking, which envisioned a three-way division of health care involving medical care for the individual, public health for the community, and eugenics for the race.[13 14] Eugenics, for some, was an extension of a tradition of a social orientation in German medicine that had produced Rudolf Virchow and other pioneers of public health.

Historians have generally followed Daniel Kevles's[7] classification of eugenicists, at least in England and the United States, as either "mainline" or "reform". In the United States and

Britain, mainline eugenics was largely (but not exclusively) conservative in political orientation.

Galton was but the first of a long line of eugenicists who believed that those who excelled (at least in fields such as science and literature, where social position was insufficient for advancement) were distinguished from others in their possession of great natural, inherited talent. Indeed, the mainline eugenicists tended to believe that a person's station in life reflected his or her capabilities and could thus be used as an indication of the genes likely to be passed down to subsequent generations. To the extent that eugenics is remembered at all, what is recalled tends to be the "mainline" movement, with its conservative politics and its tendencies towards class bias, racism, and xenophobia, all of which foreshadowed the Nazis'embrace of eugenic doctrines.

In actuality, however, there once were eugenicists all over the political spectrum. The "reform" contingent, often socialists, and including many of the leading figures in the science of human genetics, accepted eugenic goals, but were unsparingly critical of the mainline eugenicists' research, biases, and proposals. Hermann Muller, an American geneticist who later won a Nobel prize for demonstrating the effect of radiation on chromosomes, insisted that natural talent could not be assessed in a society such as the United States, which did not offer equal opportunities for advancement to its citizens; only under socialism could the fit be identified as such, and then encouraged to multiply.

The labels "mainline" and "reform" do not do justice to the great variety of viewpoints and goals associated with the eugenics movements. Indeed, as Diane Paul has observed, one sign of the ubiquity of eugenic thinking was the attempt by parties on all sides of particular social disputes to further their cause by demonstrating that their recommendations would have the strongest eugenic effect.[15] Eugenics, seen as an avenue for the application of science to social problems, was attractive to some of the architects of the modern welfare state, such as the Progressives in the United States and the Scandinavian Social Democratic parties.[16]

Indeed, much of the opposition to eugenics during that era, at least in Europe, came from the right. The eugenicists' legislative successes in Germany and Scandinavia were not matched in such countries as Poland and Czechoslovakia, even though measures had been proposed there, largely because of the conservative influence in these countries of the Catholic Church.[17] The Church opposed eugenics in principle (and was virtually the only institution to do so), but this was of a piece with its opposition to abortion and con-traception: then, as now, the Church was opposed to limitations on fertility, and its opponents were often on the left.

To be sure, early eugenicists were also opponents of birth control, since they believed that its use by the upper classes exacerbated the degeneration of the gene pool. But not all eugenicists took this position. The eugenic banner was seized also by feminists, who argued that control over fertility, along with emancipation generally, permitted women to improve the race through sexual selection.

THE NAZI DEBACLE

Eugenics in Germany, while distinctive in having a medical leadership, had been marked by much the same divergences of opinion as the movements in other countries. Though numerous prominent eugenicists were racist and anti-Semitic, others were avowedly anti-racist (and some were Jews), and a number stood on the political left.[6] The Nazis imposed a uniformity of viewpoint, securing the allegiance of the many eugenicists who rallied to their cause for a thoroughly racist, nationalist eugenic programme that recognised no limits in the pursuit of "racial hygiene".

Eugenics was central to the entire Nazi enterprise, joined with romantic nativist and racist myths of the pure-bred Nordic. The emphasis on "blood" called for a purifying of the nation's gene pool so that Germans could regain the nobility and greatness of their genetically pure forbears.[18]

As Robert Proctor[14] and other historians have shown, the subsequent programmes of sterilisation, "euthanasia" of the unfit (a programme that took the lives of tens of thousands of "Aryans," mostly young children), and eventually the Holocaust itself were part of the unfolding of this central idea. The sterilisation and "euthanasia" programmes, which did not initially target Jews and other minorities, were an exercise in negative eugenics designed to improve the native German stock from its degenerated condition. Legislation barring sexual relations between Jews and "Aryans," and ultimately the Holocaust, were intended to prevent further adulteration of the "pure" German nation with inferior genes. Jews and others who contributed evil genes were the disease afflicting the German nation, which Hitler, the physician, would cure.

These measures were complemented by a range of other genetic interventions, ranging from an elaborate system of genetic courts passing judgment on the genetic fitness of those thought to harbour defective genes, to marriage advice clinics, to the Lebensborn breeding programme for SS men and other racially motivated initiatives in positive eugenics.[6] The academic fields of anthropology, biology, and medicine were reformulated in racial and eugenic terms, and the profession of medicine in Germany was compromised by its participation in government programmes of identification, sterilisation, and murder of those deemed unfit.[6] [18–20]

DECLINE AND FALL

In its first years, Nazi eugenic programmes and propaganda won the acclaim of eugenic leaders in the United States. The Nazis flattered their counterparts overseas by pointing to legislation in California and elsewhere not only as precedents but also as models, and the authors of these statutes toured Germany and filed favourable reports upon their return.[21] After the Holocaust and the defeat of the Germans, however, eugenicists in most other countries distanced themselves from German eugenics; since the Germans had presented themselves as the most consistent and purposeful of eugenicists, the movement itself fell into general disrepute. American eugenics organisations experienced amnesia over their prewar affinity with their German counterparts, spoke out against racism, and urged Americans to consider eugenics as a source of national strength. Nevertheless, the eugenics societies soon lost their followers; the American society's journal was renamed the *Journal of Social Biology*, and what had in prewar years been a virtual consensus in favour of eugenics among genetic scientists disappeared within a decade. The movement's offices were shut down, and the Rockefellers and other funding sources turned their attention to related but more reputable concerns, such as world population control, the prevention of birth defects - and to genetics and molecular biology.[22]

There is some controversy over the explanation of the sudden disappearance of eugenics from our national consciousness. The account given in the first histories of the eugenics movement was that eugenics was abandoned as the science of genetics progressed, leaving genetic scientists increasingly dubious of the central factual claims of the movement. A revisionist tradition points to the strikingly rapid repudiation of eugenics by reputable geneticists in the mid-1940s, a period marked not by any sudden increase in scientific knowledge but by the scientists' strong interest in distancing themselves from the Nazis. These accounts have different implications for the future of genetic policy. If eugenics succumbed to the advancement of science, perhaps the lid on its coffin is nailed as tightly shut as it needs to be. If, however, the retreat from eugenics was simply one of fashion, the movement has not been repudiated on the

basis of fact or even principle, and we might unthinkingly (or, worse, consciously) return to eugenics when and if fashion changes again. Finally, if clinical genetics is simply eugenics under a different name, we must achieve a clear understanding of the morality of both.

III. Is eugenic doctrine inherently evil?

The history of the eugenics movement is marked by a sorry record of pseudoscience, prejudice and bias, and, in its Nazi version, even mass murder. We can learn from eugenics that at least one movement dedicated to the betterment of humankind through genetic improvement led to terrible wrongs. But must this goal point us in the direction of evil? In the remainder of this essay, my question is whether there was, and is, a moral misjudgment, an inherent wrong, at the heart of eugenic doctrine; and, if so, in what it consists. The attempt to answer this question presents an opportunity to assess the choices open to us in the coming decades of progress in genetics. If we are to avoid the errors and sins of the eugenics movement, we will need an account of what these were. And the same holds true if we are to avoid the converse danger of refraining from justifiable remedies and interventions because we mistakenly believe them to share the taint of eugenics.

This inquiry is an uneasy hybrid of history and moral philosophy. Since our goal is to discern where the shadow of eugenics falls, the analysis has begun with a (brief) record of what eugenicists actually believed. But to comment on the applicability of their beliefs, goals, and values for the future, we must abstract from their historical context, trying instead to find themes which might apply to our own time and yet which can reasonably be attributed to the eugenicists of a century ago.

EASY TARGETS

So much that the eugenicists believed, said, and did has been repudiated that one need not look far to find their "errors". The eugenicists' scientific claims and pretensions are a case in point. Indeed, present-day warnings of a return to eugenics often amount to cautions over untenable claims in behavioural genetics, in particular the heritability of personality traits, and both genetic essentialism and determinism. Though debate continues on such claims - new discoveries of "the gene for" diverse behavioural characteristics appear frequently, and almost as frequently are later withdrawn - the bulk of the eugenicists' claims of the genetic basis of personality are now believed to be erroneous.

Similarly, there are few defenders of the violations of reproductive rights, and rights of bodily integrity, involved in eugenic involuntary sterilisation programmes - to say nothing of eugenic euthanasia, as practised on small numbers of infants in the United States and on a mass scale by the Nazis.[23] Diane Paul[24] has pointed to the development of strong guarantees of reproductive autonomy as a key difference between our own era and that of the eugenicists, one which, it would seem, would preclude the kind of artificial selection which the eugenicists had proposed.

Much the same can be said of the class biases and racism which so marked the mainstream eugenics movements in the US and UK (to the extent that one historian defined eugenics as a war on the lower classes).[10] While these biases certainly persist, anyone in the United States or Britain who openly advocated a eugenic programme that explicitly endorsed such attitudes would be quickly reprimanded.

Each of these attributes of eugenics - genetic determinism, disregard for individual rights, and racial and class bias - is so closely linked to the reputation of eugenics that warnings of a return of eugenics are often simply accusations of one of these fallacies and wrongs. If these were all that eugenics amounted to, the analogy of eugenics to Prohibition in the United States, an historical curiosity of no particular importance for our time, would be sustained, and the present paper could end at this point. Put differently, we might argue that if we try to imagine a eugenics movement from which we remove the class and racial biases, the faith that personality traits were fixed by heredity, and the conviction that the freedom of the individual to decide whether and with whom to procreate must be overridden in the name of genetic improvement, then it is not the eugenics movement we are imagining. For these attributes defined the movement.

This kind of analysis, however, comes at the cost of rejecting the definition of eugenics given by Galton, who coined the term and initiated the movement. Galton's several definitions varied over the years, but they were variations on a simple theme: using our understanding of the laws of heredity to improve the stock of humankind. In itself, this notion is not necessarily committed to genetic determinism, violations of reproductive liberty, class bias or racism. And though common in the eugenics movements of 1883 or 1933, these beliefs and attitudes also affected other social movements and programmes, and indeed the discourse of the educated classes generally. If we may carry Galton's core notion to the present, presumably more enlightened day, what sort of

programme would it entail? And will we find any hint of a eugenic original sin, a wrong present even in Galton's original conception?

IV. Five candidate wrongs

I will survey five wrongs, or putative wrongs, which might be or have been alleged to be inherent in the core eugenic doctrine of improving the stock of humankind by application of the science of human heredity. Most, I believe, are not good candidates: either they are not inherent, or they are not necessarily wrongs. But in the end, caution towards eugenics is still advised.

(I) REPLACEMENT

The first candidate wrong faults the core doctrine of eugenics on the grounds that it seeks "better" (or "fortunate") people rather than people who are made "better" (or "fortunate"). This complaint faults eugenics for posing as a doctrine of benevolence. While "human betterment" is the name of eugenics's game, according to this view, it actually betters no humans. No person's diseases are cured, and no individual's intelligence is raised, by eugenic interventions even when (and if) they are successful in their own terms. Instead, the programmes cause the world to be populated by individuals who have these advantages from their beginnings. In essence, eugenics favours healthy people over unhealthy people, and smart ones over stupid ones. That may be acceptable as a basis for choosing friends, or even employees, according to this complaint, but it is not a particularly noble social aspiration. Eugenics, in this view, does not involve any hopes for our fellow human beings, but rather a preference for the sort of fellow human beings we have.

Does this charge identify an inherent wrong in eugenics? I think not. It does locate something inherent in the doctrine - selection is what eugenics was about - but the complaint does not succeed in showing that it is really a wrong. Many social interventions of unquestioned benevolence have unintended effects on the composition of the population. As Derek Parfit[25] has taught a generation of moral philosophers, this is simply (and trivially) due to the fact that interventions with large-scale effects inevitably affect the circumstances of human reproduction, such as the moments at which people engage in sexual intercourse. This in turn determines who will be born, for when it comes to identity and fertilisation, timing is everything. Each of us is the unique product of the union of a particular sperm and a particular egg; the product of a different pair would be someone else. Macroeconomic interventions, along with most other large-scale measures, result in different sperm being united, in sexual reproduction, with different eggs, and thus change the cast of characters which will populate that part of the globe in the next generation. Yet good social policies are not a bit objectionable for that reason. It is true that these policies, unlike eugenic programmes, do not aim to determine who will be conceived and born. Nevertheless, the effect is largely the same, and it is noteworthy that they are no less laudable for that.

In any case, this complaint against eugenics proves too much. It would find fault with a woman's decision to marry one suitor rather than another because the first would be the superior parent; or another parent's decision to delay having a child until he or she was financially and emotionally ready to be a good provider and parent; and with parents who discouraged the maternal urges of an unmarried teenage daughter on similar grounds. Yet surely these choices are perfectly defensible. If the "replacement" complaint against eugenics applies to these as well, we must reject its claim to have found a serious moral flaw in that doctrine.

(II) VALUE PLURALISM

Wilhelm Johannsen, the Danish geneticist, asked in 1917, who was to set the criteria for ideal man: "But what is the ideal? Who shall be responsible for the decision? The complexity of society makes it impossible that one single human type should be the best. We need all different types of humanity."[26] It is not uncommon to find the eugenicists blamed for promoting a particular conception of human perfection, failing to appreciate the essential plurality of values and ideals of human excellence. Like others, they assumed that the ideal would be similar to themselves, or at least to those whom they most admired. Mainline eugenicists in the UK and US, largely members of the upper-middle professional classes, hoped for a society in which each person would attain their level of virtue, and despised those who failed to display the proper bourgeois values. Nazi racial hygienists, many of whom considered themselves to be of "the Nordic type", valued the Nordic type. Hermann Muller, the socialist geneticist and eugenicist, extolled a wide range of models, including Lenin, Gandhi, and Sun Yat-Sen; surely a heterogeneous group. But all of these were, like Muller himself, exceptionally brilliant men. As the question attributed to Johannsen, a scientist and reluctant eugenicist, demonstrates, the difficulty of defining human perfection was not entirely lost on the eugenicists, but the strident rhetoric of much of the mainline eugenics literature brooked

no opposition and admitted to no doubt over what constituted a "healthy" and virtuous style of life.

We might suppose, therefore, that what is wrong with eugenics is a denial of the plurality of ideals of a valuable human life. Eugenics, according to this complaint, must inevitably impose a particular vision of human perfection. Those who urge eugenics show a limitation of moral understanding and fail to realise that theirs is but one of a multiplicity of such visions, shaped differently by diverse cultural traditions and circumstances and by moral reason. This limitation in understanding is potentially harmful to people of the sort the eugenicists hope not to reproduce, since it denies to them the self respect which accompanies the aspiration to raise children in one's own image, should this be the desire of those parents.

Is this the wrong, or a wrong, inherent in eugenics? Understood as a claim about the historical eugenics movement, as opposed to the pure Galtonian ideal, I believe that the complaint is partly right but mostly wrong. If directed to the ideal itself, as it might be realised in the future, it is again mostly wrong. The complaint is right about the historical movement in that the mainline eugenicists made no secret of their ferocious, and in some cases, murderous, disdain for the very kinds of people whose fertility they wished to curb. Davenport[27] celebrated the death of a child born to a prostitute:

"I recall the impassioned appeal of a sociologist for assistance in stopping the frightful mortality among the children of prostitutes. But the daughters of prostitutes have hardly one chance in two of being able to react otherwise than their mothers. Why must we start an expensive campaign to keep alive those who, were they intelligent enough, might well curse us for having intervened on their behalf? Is not death nature's great blessing to the race?"

Oliver W Holmes, America's celebrated Supreme Court judge, wanted no more of the sort represented by the petitioner Carrie Buck, the third of "three generations of imbeciles" who had propagated "enough",[28] and in refusing her petition to remain fertile, opened the floodgates of sterilisation in American institutions.[29]

Today, we rightly abhor these sentiments, and, of course, the even more repugnant judgments about human "types" which animated the Nazis. Nevertheless, the failure to respect the plurality of values was not the central problem, even of mainline eugenics. The traits which the eugenicists believed heritable and worthy of cultivation were ones which are valued by people with widely varying ideals of personal development, plan of life, and family structure. Though some eugenicists did believe there to be particular genes for drunkenness, "shiftlessness", and the like, in the main the eugenicists focused on a very short list of traits about which there is little controversy. Intelligence dominated the list, or was the only item on it; self-control and a few other very general virtues were sometimes added. For many eugenicists, a long list of objectionable phenotypic traits, ranging from sloth to immorality, were the result of the lack of the genes thought to be necessary for these cardinal virtues. There is little real dispute over the value of these all-purpose talents, even among those who reject the class snobbery of the mainline eugenicists. Whatever one's favoured pursuit or style of living, intelligence and self-control help one make the most of it. When we consider a future eugenics programme, based on Galton's core idea, we can easily envision one that would focus exclusively on these all-purpose advantages. Value pluralism need not be an issue.

It remains true that the mainline eugenicists were anything but tolerant of personal and social ideals which differed from their own. They favoured breeding humans with an eye to intelligence and self-control because they thought that these traits were necessary if a person were to lead a "proper" kind of life, ie one like their own. Claims of this kind, for example that the poor are too stupid to understand the difference between right and wrong, or to exercise the restraint necessary for the nuclear family, resurface today in such works as Herrnstein and Murray's book, *The Bell Curve*.[30] But the transmissible characters targeted by the intervention remains one on which there is agreement regardless of differing ideals of human perfection. Value pluralism could become an issue in eugenics, even if it is not inherent in the core idea. Deaf parents who wish to abort fetuses which do not test positive for inherited deafness, and dwarf parents who want only a child with the gene for achondroplasia, hold unconventional values, and their freedom to act on them is at issue in the ethics of clinical genetics. The European parliamentary panel on genetic engineering, headed by a Green representative to the German Bundestag, held that genetic screening requires us to decide what are "normal and abnormal, acceptable and unacceptable, viable and non-viable forms of the genetic make-up of individual human beings before and after birth".[31] If we ever acquire an ability to influence personality and character through genetic choice or manipulation - to choose, for example between aggressive and gentle dispositions - this debate will be of crucial importance.

Everyone supports the goal of health, and though we do not share precisely the same concepts of health (and of disability), diversity of opinion is limited to a few disputed instances. When genetic interventions are aimed at enhancing the genome of the healthy individual, however, the scope of potential disagreement is nearly unlimited. Some of us may live long enough to see the genetic advances which will occasion such debates. Nevertheless, eugenic programmes could avoid the problem of value pluralism simply by limiting its focus to those human characters on whose desirability there is universal or widespread agreement.

(III) STATISM

In a recent address, James Watson[32] reviewed the odious history and possible future of eugenics and concluded that the most important safeguard was to eliminate any role for the state. He provided a strong case. The great wrongs visited on vulnerable people in the name of eugenics - institutionalisation, sexual segregation, sterilisation, and, in Germany, murder on a mass scale - could not have occurred without the agency of the state. In England, where the state's role was minimal, eugenics may have been offensive but it did not violate individual rights (though some of its supporters hoped for eventual acceptance of involuntary sterilisation).[33]

Since involuntary sterilisation, supported by legislation, is perhaps the most notorious wrong committed by eugenicists aside from the Nazi crimes, Watson's emphasis on the role of the state is understandable. Still, many would take issue with his contention that the state is the chief enemy. Critics of current practices in clinical genetics claim that counsellors and physicians are often, even routinely, directive towards some clients, and that this subtle coercion continues without the explicit backing of the state. Moreover, what Troy Duster[34] has called "backdoor eugenics" threatens to visit harm on the genetically disfavoured through the cumulative effect of many private decisions on the part of employers, insurers, and prospective parents. As Robert Wachbroit[35] has observed, government and society might conceivably switch roles, with the former intervening in private choice in order to preserve the liberties and wellbeing of those whose genes threaten disease or disability. In such a scenario, denying a role to the state might hasten eugenic evils rather than protecting against them. If the "backdoor" concern is justified, we ought not to conclude that the wrongs of eugenics can be avoided as long as the state forswears any eugenic intent.

Thus a strong state role is not essential for a eugenic programme. True, it may be difficult to win compliance with eugenic prescriptions without the long arm of the law. That is why Galton, imagining a fully voluntary regime, mused that eugenics might have to be instated as a civil religion in order to induce members of society to make the sacrifices required. Eugenics never attained this status, whether in the UK or elsewhere (not even in contemporary Singapore, where the head of state has been an enthusiast). The British eugenics movement was no less "eugenic" for being a citizen's movement relying on voluntary measures, and from this fact it follows that statism is not a source of wrongs inherent in the core of the eugenic programme.

(IV) "COLLECTIVISM"

An alternative analysis locates the wrong inherent in eugenics in its concern for the genetic wellbeing of the group rather than that of the individual. In this view, concern for the individual is benign. Indeed, genetic intervention might be mandatory, from the moral point of view, in certain cases. Parents who knowingly bring into being children who suffer agonising and deadly defects might be accused of "wrongful life". The fateful turn towards eugenics occurs, in this view, when we widen our interest from the individual child to the group, hoping not that our own sons and daughters will be healthy but that the population's gene pool will be improved.

This is a "collectivist" vision in the sense that the object of our concern is the group as such, while our concern with the individuals who constitute the group is primarily in the contribution which they might make towards the wellbeing of the collective.

Narrowly defined, "collectivism" doctrines are those according to which interests inhere in the collective entity or group in addition to the group's members' interests. Much of eugenic writing, whether "mainline" or "reform", was collectivist in this sense. More loosely, we might understand the label "collectivist" for eugenic doctrines or policies which locate interests only in individuals, but which condone trading of the wellbeing of some for that of others. Social Democratic eugenicists in Scandinavia, for example, were often candid in noting the burden imposed by eugenic sterilisation upon those sterilised, but justified the practice in terms of the reduced burden of dependents.[16]

According to this understanding of where the wrong in eugenics lies, a bright line can be drawn here, one that both distinguishes medical genetics from eugenics and locates the wrong inherent in

the latter. If we draw the line here, we reject the notion that parents who seek "the perfect baby" are themselves engaging in eugenics. This understanding of eugenics provides a green light to medical genetics, which can be permitted to continue its rapid development without the worry that it is revisiting the errors of the past.

But what, precisely, is the wrong which this view attributes to eugenics? Consider these three statements:

1a. I favour a genetic intervention because I want my child to have the "best" (healthiest, etc) genes.

1b. We favour genetic interventions (on behalf of each of us) because we want our children to have the "best" (healthiest, etc) genes.

1c. I favour genetic interventions (for each person in our group) because I want our children to have the "best" (healthiest, etc) genes.

If 1a is morally acceptable, surely it doesn't become wrong when voiced by several people (in the form of 1b). And how can I be faulted by endorsing that group's hope (1c)? 1b and 1c are merely the aggregate of many instances of 1a. One might expect to hear 1c uttered by, say, a health official, or a legislator who sponsors a measure which would provide genetic services to large numbers of people. Concern for the welfare of large numbers of people is part of such a person's job description.

Consider, in contrast:

2. The sum total of benefits involved in a programme of genetic interventions will be greater than the costs.

Here we seem to come closer to a "collectivist" view, for 2 does not claim that the benefits for each individual might outweigh the costs. It leaves open the possibility that some may lose while others benefit, promising only that the magnitude of the latter will be greater.

However, this appearance may, I believe, be misleading. Statements such as 2 are often made by way of justifying the use of public funds. The point of the intervention in such cases is not to save public money, for the professed (and, we may assume, the actual) goal is to ensure that as many children as possible are born with genes which make their lives go well. Given the endless competition which exists for public funds, however laudable their purpose, it always helps if one can argue that the net social cost is zero or better. This calculation has been a trump card in debates over health care allocation when played by advocates for perinatal medical care, and it might apply equally well for a programme aiming to provide better genes.

Consider, finally:

3. A programme of genetic intervention will limit the number of people who are a burden to others.

Have we, with this step, crossed the line to the "collectivist" position? And if so, does this claim partake of eugenics's original sin? The answer, I believe, is not as straightforward as it might appear.

We might begin by noting that if this claim does in fact put us on the wrong side of that imaginary moral line, we may have stepped over it a bit earlier. I just argued that a cost-benefit calculation, such as 2, need not be motivated by a wish to save society some money. But of course it could be. This might be the real goal in a particular instance even when the advocates of a programme offer it merely as a justification for the use of public funds. In either case, 2 would be in the same moral company as 3.

But is 3 "collectivist", where we understand that term as betraying concern for individuals only insofar as they add to or detract from the wellbeing of the group, and is it morally repugnant for that reason? We should note, first, that 3 is not necessarily "collectivist" in the narrow sense defined above, according to which the beneficiary is a collective entity, be it the Reich, the Revolution, or the Race, for which no sacrifice of individual wellbeing can be too great. Nazi eugenics, of course, was a collectivism of this other sort, obsessed with the glory of the reified Volk. But that is no part of the original Galtonian eugenics, at least at its core.

More to the point, the core notion of eugenics does not necessarily ask for sacrifice of any sort. Programmes which isolated or sterilised tens of thousands of people, and of course those which resorted to murder, imposed the greatest of sacrifices, but Galton's original proposal did not call for these measures. English eugenics, for all their concerns over the excess fertility of the unfit, generally proposed voluntary curbs on reproduction.[7]

In any case, the sacrifice which a eugenic programme might ask of prospective parents is likely to be much less onerous as technology develops. In Galton's day, eugenics was mainly concerned with who mated with whom and how many children resulted. For the "unfit", childlessness (even if voluntary) was the price of eugenic correctness. Today, a eugenic principle might call for prospective parents to screen pregnancies so

that the children they bring to term have the greatest feasible genetic advantages. Tomorrow, these same parents might be encouraged to avail themselves of genetic interventions to cure and to enhance. Excepting perhaps the fetuses which are aborted as a result of such a programme, no one would be asked to make sacrifices. Because parents almost always seek advantages for their children - health above all - there is a congruence between a eugenicist's concern for the public and a parent's concern for his or her child. Where there is not, a voluntary programme would leave the decision to the parent. The potential child whose conception or birth is avoided by this intervention does not count in the moral calculation which "collectivism" insists we make. Common sense must concur.

Nevertheless, this kind of eugenic programme might claim some actual, living victims. As disability-rights advocates have insisted, it is difficult to argue for public programmes on the basis of claims like 3 without suggesting, in the same act of speech, that the existence of people who are dependent on others is a fact to be regretted; and this sends the message that these lives are not, in some sense, valuable. I will not take the trouble to argue that this sentiment is reprehensible and that the opposite message ought to be the cornerstone of public policy, both in genetics and elsewhere. Every person is valuable, and not only for any contribution which he or she might make to others. The rhetoric of mainline eugenics in the UK and the US, with its denunciations of "human filth" and "human rubbish," are justification enough for the abysmal reputation of these movements, even apart from the programmes of mass sterilisation and murder which followed in their wake. Perhaps we have found, therefore, some hint of an "original sin" of eugenics. In the series 1a-1b-1c-2-3, it occurs somewhere between 2 and 3, when we begin to calculate the value of genetic improvement not in terms of the wellbeing of the individual whose genes are less likely to cause that individual to suffer, and more likely to enhance that individual's wellbeing, but for the effect which the existence of that individual might have on the wellbeing of others. But this is not quite "collectivism", and I would urge that this wrong, if it is that, be given a different rubric: unfairness.

(V) FAIRNESS

In the United States and England (though not in Germany), the fields of eugenics and public health involved different people, expert professions, journals, and aims. But the two movements shared many assumptions and attitudes. As Charlotte Muller noted in her insightful review, the gross differences in health status across racial and income lines tended to be explained in terms of heredity.[36] Burdens imposed by eugenics were justified by the analogy to public health, as Justice Holmes did, when he compared sterilisation to vaccination.[28]

Martin Pernick[37] has noted extensive overlap even in the jargon of the two fields, each of which resorted to "isolation" and "sterilisation" of the individuals who were thought to pose threats to the wellbeing of the public. Eugenics was often described in medical terms,[38] for example as an effort to prevent the spread of (genetic) disease from generation to generation. Hitler was lauded as the great doctor of the German nation, rescuing the Aryan gene pool from the genetic disease introduced by Jewish infestation.[14]

Public health had one more characteristic in common with eugenics: it created and struggled with many of the same moral problems. A persisting theme in the ethics of public health is the greater effectiveness often achievable if the interests of some are sacrificed to the interests of others. Despite the great protection Americans enjoy in the inviolability of the person, public health requirements sometimes have priority, as Holmes's reference to vaccination policy shows. How to balance these benefits and burdens is a question of distributive justice which public health programmes will always have to face.

Despite the fact that genetic technology will permit some eugenic goals to be achieved without burdening prospective parents, a public policy of providing "better" genes to future generations is bound to impose social costs. Even a fully voluntary, medically oriented programme—what is called "clinical genetics" today and which strenuously avoids any association with the eugenics of old—must answer to advocates for the disabled who claim that the wellbeing of the disabled is put at risk when genetic screening programmes try to ensure that none with their disabilities will be conceived or born. Bioethicists have warned of decreasing tolerance of differences, once we acquire the power to choose "the best", and this intolerance might impose social sanctions on those who declined to make such choices.

More concretely, it is not unreasonable to fear that if it once again becomes respectable to advocate eugenics, the wrongs of the past will return in full force. I have argued that eugenics, considered as a set of principles, need not assume genetic determinism, nor advocate or condone racism or class bias. In actual practice, however, what guarantee can there be that a eugenic programme would not be guided by these still prevalent beliefs and attitudes? Similarly, we could imagine, in

principle, a eugenic programme which avoids coercive measures, particularly sterilisation, but what assurance do we have that these measures might not eventually be viewed as justified, if public policy seeks to provide "better genes" and the benefits they might bring to society?

The ethics of eugenics and the ethics of public health, therefore, are closely related. Neither, unfortunately, has received the same attention as the ethics of personal health care. What standard of justice should be used in guiding any new eugenics? The first pages of Rawls's *A Theory of Justice* include this famous passage:

" ... Each person possesses an inviolability founded on justice that even the welfare of society as a whole cannot override. For this reason justice denies that the loss of freedom for some is made right by a greater good shared by others. It does not allow that the sacrifices imposed on a few are outweighed by the larger sum of advantages enjoyed by many. Therefore in a just society the liberties of equal citizenship are taken as settled; the rights secured by justice are not subject to political bargaining or to the calculus of social interests."[39]

This is not a bad starting position: public policy in genetics, whether or not it is termed eugenics, ought not to infringe personal liberty. But this does not necessarily call on us to avoid any risk of burdening some individuals for the sake of the genetic wellbeing of future generations. I am not personally persuaded, for example, that the threat of stigmatising the disabled requires us to abandon the effort to ensure that future generations are free of avoidable disability. But this kind of concern points us to a valid question of justice and also to an irony.

The point about justice is that genetic benefits provided in services used by a particular pair of parents may have adverse effects on others, and we are bound to reflect on the fairness of the resulting distribution of benefits and burdens. The irony is that this very admonition pulls us towards, and possibly over, the bright line which bounds that which we identified as a possible wrong inherent in the core notion of eugenics. This line is crossed when the goal of our genetic intervention is not only the wellbeing of the individual, but also the effect on others of bringing this person into the world. If we are required by distributive justice to consider the effects upon all members of the community when we contemplate genetic interventions, this moral imperative is in effect telling us to consider not only the benefit of a contemplated intervention for a particular individual, but also for others. If there is a wrong inherent in the core Galtonian eugenic project, it surely has to do with this very move, which takes us beyond the "medical" or "clinical" focus on the patient at hand (or, in the case of procreation, on the child to be) to the society as a whole. In the latter, wider view, the patient recedes from the foreground and a moral judgment is made on the basis of a calculation which takes into account the claims of many.

V. Conclusion

Where does the shadow of eugenics fall? Is there a wrong inherent in the core Galtonian eugenic programme? And what guidance might the answer to this question give us in deploying the resources of the new genetics?

One respectable position which I have not taken up directly in the above is that the core notion of eugenics may be benign, because it is trivial. No one objects in principle, according to this view, to using what we know of the science of heredity to improve the chances of future generations for achieving greater wellbeing. What rouses passionate debate are the means to be used; or the problem of value pluralism; or one of the other "easy targets" which are discussed in II, above.

Perhaps so. Much of the controversy over China's law on maternal and infant health care has indeed focused on its apparent threat of coercion, rather than its goal of a generation of healthy Chinese children.[40] But clearly some who express concern about a return of eugenics in the West are worried by the move from "medical" concern for the individual to "eugenic" ambitions for improving the gene pool in general, even if coercion is not proposed as a means to this end. Perhaps the worry is roused by the fact that this move was accompanied, early in this century, by great wrongs, harms justified by the greater good, and the fear that once the "collective" goal is established, the demand for sacrifices by individuals will not be long in coming. In some cases, however, the complaint against "eugenics" seems to be lodged against those who profess concern for the genes of humankind apart from the genes of one individual patient, whether or not the broader concern be advanced by coercion or other harms.

I do not see that much hangs on the resolution of this question. In either case, we can draw the important (if obvious) lesson that progress in genetics must pay attention to these questions of distributive justice. This very general, yet morally crucial, requirement ought to guide us now, as we decide which programmes of genetic testing and screening to undertake, and also in the future, as we contemplate the possibility of refashioning the human genome to engineer a new, perhaps improved version of homo sapiens. Done justly, the genetic wellbeing of "the group" is a proper object of concern. The question of moral importance is not whether this constitutes eugenics; it is whether it can be done fairly and justly. It wasn't, the last time it was tried.

Credits and acknowledgements

This essay overlaps my contribution to Alison Thompson and Ruth Chadwick's book, *Genetic Information: Acquisition, Access, and Control*, London: Plenum, 1998; my "Eugenic values", in *Science in Context*, 1998; 10:3–4; and parts of a forthcoming book (tentatively titled *Genes and Social Justice*), co-authored by Allen Buchanan, Dan Brock, Norman Daniels and myself, to be published by Cambridge University Press. The author is indebted to Diane Paul for help with sources and interpretations.

Daniel Wikler, PhD, is Professor in the Program in Medical Ethics, Department of History of Medicine and in the Department of Philosophy, University of Wisconsin, USA.

References

1 Chan CK, Chee HL. Singapore 1984: breeding for Big Brother. In: Chee HL, Chan CK, eds. *Designer genes: IQ, ideology, and biology*. Kuala Lumpur: Institute for Social Analysis, 1984: 4–13.
2 Beardsley T. China syndrome: China's eugenics law makes trouble for science and business. *Scientific American* 1997;Mar: 33–4.
3 Dong-Sheng S. Popularizing the knowledge of eugenics and advocating optimal births vigorously. Beijing: *Renkou Yanjiu* (Population Research)1981;4:37–41.
4 Wertz D. Eugenics: alive and well in China. *The Gene Letter* 1996;I.
5 Galton F. *Inquiries into human faculty and its development*. London: J M Dent and Sons, 1883.
6 Weindling P. *Health, race and german politics between national unification and nazism 1870–1945*. Cambridge: Cambridge University Press, 1989.
7 Kevles DJ. *In the name of eugenics*. Berkeley: University of California Press, 1985:590.
8 Rafter NH. *White trash: the eugenic family studies 1877–1919*. Boston: Northeastern University Press, 1988.
9 MacKenzie D. Eugenics in Britain. *Social Studies of Science* 1976;6: 499–532.
10 Mazumdar PMH. *Eugenics, human genetics and human failings: the eugenics society, its sources and its critics in Britain*. London: Routledge, 1992.
11 Schneider W. The eugenics movement in France, 1890–1940. In: Adams M, ed. *The well-born science*. Oxford: Oxford University Press, 1990.
12 Stepan NL. *The hour of eugenics: race, gender and nation in Latin America*. Ithaca: Cornell University Press, 1991.
13 Weiss S. The race hygiene movement in Germany. *Osiris* 1987; 3:193–236.
14 Proctor R. *Racial hygiene: medicine under the Nazis*. Cambridge: Harvard University Press, 1988.
15 Paul DB. *Controlling human heredity*. New York: Academic Press, 1995.
16 Broberg G, Roll-Hansen N. *Eugenics and the welfare state: sterilization policy in Denmark, Sweden, Norway, and Finland*. East Lansing: Michigan State University Press, 1996.
17 Roll-Hansen N. Geneticists and the Eugenics Movement in Scandinavia. *British Journal for the History of Science*. 1989;22: 335–46.
18 Burleigh M, Wippermann W. *The racial state: Germany 1933–1945*. Cambridge: Cambridge University Press, 1991.

194   *Can we learn from eugenics?*

19 Aly G, Chroust P, Pross C. *Cleansing the Fatherland: Nazi medicine and racial hygiene.* Baltimore: Johns Hopkins University Press, 1994.

20 Wikler D, Barondess J. Bioethics and anti-bioethics in Germany: what must we remember? *Kennedy Institute of Ethics Journal* 1993;3:39–55.

21 Kuhl S. *The Nazi connection: eugenics, American racism, and National Socialism.* Oxford: Oxford University Press, 1994.

22 Paul DB. The Rockefeller Foundation and the origins of Behavior Genetics. In: K Benson *et al. The expansion of American biology.* New Brunswick: Rutgers University Press, 1991.

23 Pernick M. *The black stork.* Oxford: Oxford University Press, 1996.

24 Paul DB. *Controlling human heredity.* New York: Academic Press, 1995.

25 Parfit D. *Reasons and persons.* Oxford: Oxford University Press, 1984.

26 Hansen BS. Something rotten in the state of Denmark: eugenics and the ascent of the welfare state. See reference 16: 9-76.

27 Davenport C. The eugenics programme and progress in its achievement. In: Morton A, Aldrich *et al*, eds. *Eugenics: twelve university lectures.* New York: Dodd, Mead and Co, 1922.

28 Holmes OW. Opinion in Buck v Bell, 1927, 274 US 205, 207.

29 Reilly PR. *The surgical solution: a history of involuntary sterilization in the United States.* Baltimore: Johns Hopkins University Press, 1991.

30 Herrnstein RJ, Murray C. *The bell curve.* New York: Free Press, 1994.

31 Quoted in Kevles DJ. Out of eugenics: the historical politics of the human genome. In: Kevles DJ, Hood L, eds. *The code of codes.* Cambridge: Harvard University Press, 1992.

32 Watson J. *Genes and politics: presidential address. Cold Spring Harbor Laboratory annual report, 1996.* Cold Spring Harbor, New York: Cold Spring Harbor Laboratory, 1997.

33 King D, Hansen R. Experts at work: state autonomy, social learning and eugenic sterilization in 1930s Britain. *Journal of Political Science* 1999;29:133-63 (in press)

34 Duster T. *Backdoor to eugenics.* New York: Routledge, 1990.

35 Wachbroit R. *What is wrong with eugenics? QQ Report from the Institute for Philosophy and Public Policy* 1987;7:6-8.

36 Muller C. A window on the past: the position of the client in twentieth century public health thought and practice. *American Journal of Public Health* 1985;75,5:470-5.

37 Pernick M. Eugenics and public health in American history. *American Journal of Public Health* 1997;87:1767-72.

38 Kamrat-Lang D. Healing society: medical language in American eugenics. *Science in context* 1995;8:175-96.

39 Rawls J. *A theory of justice.* Cambridge: Harvard University Press, 1971:3-4.

40 Anonymous [editorial]. China's misconception of eugenics. *Nature* 1994;367:1-2.

[37]

Abortion

Judith Jarvis Thomson

On December 30, 1994, an opponent of abortion opened fire at two Brookline clinics, killing two people and injuring five others. He then went south to spray twenty rounds of ammunition into a clinic in Norfolk, Virginia. That episode was only the most extreme in a series of recent attacks on abortion providers. In the two-year period ending in December 1994, five people were murdered and at least nine wounded in similar assaults.

With the Supreme Court's 1992 decision in *Planned Parenthood v. Casey*,1 the constitutional right to abortion seems to have become secure, at least for the time being. Concurrently, however, exercise of the right has been under increasing threat. Clinic officials report bombings, arson, and vandalism. Their insurance costs have risen, and they must pay heavily for security guards. Doctors who perform abortions are subjected to threats of violence, and they and their families are harassed; a new tactic, the malpractice suit, increases their costs.2 The number of doctors who are willing to perform abortions is therefore decreasing, and women in rural areas have to travel long distances to obtain abortions. Indeed, the pool of doctors who are able to perform abortions is likely to shrink too, because, under anti-abortion pressure, many hospitals and medical schools no longer teach abortion procedures. Clinic entries are blockaded, and even after the police are able to clear a path to the door, the women who walk it are subjected to shouted threats and insults: they are made to walk it in fear and humiliation.

Some of us had hoped that with time, opposition to abortion would become less violent, less strident, at a minimum, more open to rational debate. That has not happened. Instead, anti-abortion pressure continues to be a powerful force in politics, perhaps an increasingly powerful force. The Christian Coalition has threatened to withhold support from candidates for national office who do not oppose abortion; and it is the primary source of the many new anti-abortion initiatives now before Congress. The Republican platform has, for years, called for a constitutional amendment to ban most abortions; while Senators Robert Dole and Phil Gramm have recently said that they believe there are not enough votes in Congress to pass a constitutional amendment at this time, each has said that he would, if elected President, use the executive power to limit access to abortion.

And now we have in hand the new Papal encyclical, *Evangelium Vitae*, in which John Paul II argues, vigorously, that abortion is "murder," and condemns laws permitting abortion as "intrinsically unjust," "lacking in authentic juridical validity," and not "morally binding."3 He therefore calls on everyone to oppose both abortion and the laws that permit it.

The recent escalation of threats to exercise of the right to abortion, the continuing political power of abortion opponents, and the appearance of the new encyclical, call for a response. Those who value the abortion right should not let these things simply wash over them, as if all that matters is that the legal right was won, and occupation of the moral high ground can be left to whoever wants it. That is dangerous, both to the right itself and to the self-respect of those who value it.

Let us begin by reminding ourselves of what is at stake for women in the abortion controversy.

Some women want abortions. Why? They have a variety of reasons. The woman who is pregnant due to rape may feel devastated by the prospect of carrying and giving birth to the child of the man who violated her. The woman whose health is already at risk may not want to undergo the increased risk that carrying the fetus to term would impose on her. The woman who has already had several children, and has now been deserted by the man she lived with, may believe herself unable to supply a decent life for yet another child. A woman may discover that the child she will deliver will be horribly deformed. A woman who is preparing to embark on a career that requires hard work and single-mindedness may prefer to wait until she is in a position to give a child the attention a child needs.

Opponents of abortion seem to think that women who choose to have abortions typically do so thoughtlessly. Hence the common idea that if abortion is to be available at all, it should be available only after a 24-hour waiting period, during which time the woman can be allowed, indeed invited, to contemplate the seriousness of the step she has decided to take. Why this forced contemplation? Does any woman decide on an abortion thoughtlessly? Surely not. It should not need repeating -- over and over again -- that women who decide on abortion typically do so for weighty reasons, and that their decisions have already been preceded by serious thought.

Other women do not want abortions for themselves, but want abortions to be available to others. I have two things in mind here. First, there are the children who become pregnant. The literature on abortion typically refers to pregnant women, but 13 year-old girls are not women, they are children. Many women regard it as an outrageous idea that a child, pregnant due to rape or seduction, is morally required to carry the fetus to term. Second, and more generally, many women rightly believe that constraining access to abortion impedes the achievement of political, social, and economic equality for women. If women are denied rights over their own bodies, they are denied rights to equal participation in the work of the world; if they are not permitted to make, for themselves, such deeply important decisions as whether to bear a child, they are not permitted to occupy the status of autonomous adult, morally equal to men.

So this is an issue of great importance to women. Denial of the abortion right severely constrains their liberty, and among the consequences of that constraint are impediments to their achievement of equality. This fact is itself important, and I will return to it later.

But if abortion were murder, all that would amount to little. Suppose that a fetus is a product of rape, or that allowing it to develop would constitute a threat to the woman's health or make it impossible for her to supply a decent life to other already existing children, or that it is deformed, or that allowing it to develop would interfere with plans that are central to her life. If killing the fetus were murder, the woman would have to carry it to term, despite the burden on her of doing so. Morality, after all, does not permit us to commit murder in the name of avoiding such burdens. You certainly may not murder your five year-old child just because it is a product of rape, or because its demands on your attention get in the way of your career.

Why, then, is it to be thought that abortion is murder? A familiar argument starts from the premise that a human being's life begins at conception. (We are invited to accept that premise on the ground that the conceptus -- a fertilized human egg -- contains a biological code that will govern its entire future physical development, and therefore is already a human being.) Moreover, human beings have a right to life. A human being can forfeit that right by, for example, unjustly aggressing against another.

But, the argument continues, the fetus, at all stages of its development, is innocent of any aggression. (As the encyclical says: "No one more absolutely innocent could be imagined. In no way could this human being ever be considered an aggressor, much less an unjust aggressor.") And so the argument concludes: abortion at any stage, from conception on, is a violation of the right to life, and thus is murder.

As I said, this argument is familiar. According to Ronald Dworkin, however, opponents of abortion do not really mean it. In his interesting recent book on abortion and euthanasia,4 Dworkin argues that opponents of abortion do not really believe that the fetus has a right to life, but only something weaker, namely that "it is intrinsically a bad thing" when a fetus is deliberately destroyed (LD, p. 13). He gives two reasons for this surprising conclusion, and I will turn to them shortly. But let us first see that this idea *is* weaker.

Dworkin says that you do not have to think that a thing has a right to life in order to think it intrinsically bad to destroy it: he draws attention to the fact that there are lots of things we regard as intrinsically bad to destroy, but which we do not take to have rights to life. Great works of art, for example. So similarly, he says, you might think that destroying a fetus is intrinsically bad without thinking it has a right to life.

Now suppose it would be intrinsically bad to destroy a thing. Still, destroying it might be permissible, for it might be intrinsically worse not to destroy it. Consider a great painting, for example. Suppose that we have to choose: we must destroy the painting or a child will die. It would be intrinsically bad to destroy the painting, but intrinsically worse that a child die.

In short, where there is badness there is betterness and worseness. And if you think merely that killing a fetus in an abortion is bad, but not a violation of a right, then it is open to you to make exceptions, for it is open to you to think that something even worse will come about if it is not killed.

Dworkin's proposal, then, is this: opponents of abortion say that the fetus has a right to life, and -- given its innocence -- that abortion is therefore murder, but what they really believe is only that killing the fetus is intrinsically bad.

He gives two reasons for attributing this view to them. First, many opponents of abortion do make exceptions. For example, they are prepared to allow abortion where the pregnancy is due to rape or incest, or where the woman's life is at risk if the pregnancy continues. But if abortion was a violation of the right to life, and therefore was murder, no exceptions could be made for such cases; thus if you *think* abortion is murder, you cannot consistently also *think* that such cases are exceptions. So Dworkin's first reason for attributing to them the view that abortion does not violate a right but is only something intrinsically bad is that if we do so we can suppose that their moral beliefs are consistent.

Second, Dworkin says that it is "very hard to make sense of the idea" (LD, p. 15) that a fetus has rights from the moment of conception. Having rights seems to presuppose having interests, which in turn seems to presuppose having wants, hopes, fears, likes and dislikes. But an early fetus lacks the physical constitution required for such psychological states. How can we so much as understand the proposal that a fertilized human egg has hopes, for example? And if a man says what lacks sense, then we have at least some reason for thinking that he does not really believe what he says he believes.

For those two reasons, then, Dworkin attributes to opponents of abortion the view that abortion is not really the violation of a right but is merely intrinsically bad. He then goes on to make a case -- an impressive case -- for saying that a person who believes that abortion is merely intrinsically bad should accept the propriety of a legal regime with a constitutionally guaranteed abortion right.

Dworkin's interpretation of the views of abortion opponents is not compelling, however. Consider

John Paul II's encyclical again. It contains exactly the familiar argument I laid out above: it explicitly declares that abortion at any stage, from conception on, is "the deliberate killing of an innocent human being" and thus is a violation of "the right to life of an actual human person" and thus is "murder." Can we plausibly follow Dworkin and attribute to the Pope the view that abortion is not really a violation of the right to life, but is merely intrinsically bad? I hardly think so.5

And not simply because the Pope's words are so clear. For consider again Dworkin's first reason for attributing this view to opponents of abortion, namely the fact that they make exceptions for abortions in some circumstances (rape or incest or a risk to the woman's life), and that their moral views would therefore be inconsistent if we attributed the stronger view to them. No doubt some do make exceptions; the encyclical, however, does not. According to the encyclical: "The killing of innocent human creatures, even if carried out to help others, constitutes an absolutely unacceptable act."

What of Dworkin's second reason? How are we to make sense of the idea that an early fetus, much less a fertilized human egg, has rights?

Well, why can't we make sense of it? Here is the answer I pointed to earlier: having rights seems to presuppose having interests, which in turn seems to presuppose having wants, hopes, fears, likes and dislikes. But an early fetus, a fertilized egg, is plainly not the locus of such psychological states.

To be sure, if a fertilized egg is allowed to develop normally the resulting child *will* have wants, hopes, and fears, and thus will have interests, and it will then have rights. But this does not show that fertilized eggs have rights. Things can lack rights at one time and acquire them later. If children are allowed to develop normally they will have a right to vote; that does not show that they now have a right to vote. To show that a fertilized human egg *now* has rights one needs to produce some fact about its present, not its future.

On the other hand, it is not obvious why we should accept even the first part of the answer I pointed to. Why should we agree that having rights presupposes having interests? There is a difficulty here that we need to stop over.

What, after all, is it to have a right? Very roughly, for a person, say Alfred, to have a right that we do something is for the following to be the case: the fact that we would improve the world by not doing it does not itself justify our not doing it. Suppose, for example, that Alfred admires our antique teapot, and that we have promised to give it to him, thereby giving him a right that we will. Suppose it then turns out that Bert and Carol also admire our teapot. Perhaps the world would be better if we gave it to Bert and Carol as joint owners. (Two of the three people pleased rather than only one.) That fact does not itself justify our giving it to them rather than to him -- since by hypothesis, he has a right that we give it to him.

Again, for Alfred to have a right that we refrain from doing something is for the following to be the case: the fact that we would improve the world by doing it does not itself justify our doing it. Suppose we can save Bert's and Carol's lives by killing Alfred. Perhaps the world would be better if we killed Alfred. (Two of the three people alive rather than only one.) That fact does not itself justify our killing Alfred -- on the assumption that Alfred has a right to life, and thus a right that we not kill him.6

In short, having a right is having a certain *morally protected status*. In an earlier work, Dworkin suggested that we should think of rights as "trumps": the fact that by our act we can bring about more that is good than would otherwise come about is trumped by the fact (if it is a fact) that someone has a right that we not so act. In particular, what it is merely bad to destroy we may destroy just in the name of bringing about something better; what has a right not to be destroyed we may not destroy just in the name of bringing about something better.

So for a fetus to have a right to life is for it to have that morally protected status. The familiar argument that I set out above declares that it does. What reason is there to think it doesn't? Dworkin says that it is very hard to make sense of the idea that an early fetus, a fertilized human egg, has a right to life. It seems to me, by contrast, that the idea makes perfectly good sense. Perhaps the idea that a fetus does have that morally protected status is false. All the same, the idea that a fetus does have it cannot be bypassed as nonsense. We have to take the idea seriously.

I am in fact going to discuss only fertilized eggs, for two connected reasons. In the first place, the familiar argument I set out does not say merely that a late fetus has a right to life; it says that a fetus has a right to life from the moment of conception. If fertilized eggs have no right to life, then anyway *that* argument against abortion is blocked. But second, if that argument is blocked, then what is the opponent of abortion to replace it with? There is room for him to argue that as the fetus develops, it acquires features in virtue of which it then has a right to life, perhaps a certain level of neural development, perhaps viability, perhaps other features. That is all very well, but his making this choice commits him to thinking that some abortions are morally permissible, namely those that precede the time at which the fetus acquires the relevant features; and -- depending, of course, on his choice of features -- perhaps that most actual abortions are morally permissible. (Fully half the abortions in the United States currently take place within the first eight weeks of pregnancy, some four months before viability.7 At eight weeks, the fetus is about one-and-a-half inches long, and has only recently lost its tail.) Moreover, we can then enter discussion with him about why the features he fixes on should be thought to be the ones that make the moral difference. It is entirely possible that the outcome of such a discussion would be his taking a moral stance on abortion that is, if not the same as, then close to the stance on abortion enshrined in current law.

In sum, what needs attention is not the question "What is to be said to a person who asserts only that more or less late abortion is the killing of what has a right to life?" but rather the question "What is to be said to a person who asserts that all abortion is the killing of what has a right to life?" The vehemence of the opposition to abortion surely issues, not from the idea that a middle-to-late abortion is murder, but rather from the idea that *all* of it is. In any case, the new papal encyclical brings home to us that the stronger idea calls for a response.

So let us ask: what reason is there to deny that fertilized eggs have a right to life?

If having rights really does presuppose having interests, and that in turn presupposes having wants, hopes, fears, likes and dislikes, then -- since fertilized eggs are not the locus of such psychological states -- it follows that fertilized eggs have no rights at all, and *a fortiori* that they do not have a right to life. But why should we agree that having rights presupposes having interests?

The idea that having rights presupposes having interests seems very plausible, for reasons that emerge as follows.

Paintings, for example, have no interests. It is possible to do to a painting what is good for it: perhaps dusting it regularly is good for it. It is possible to do to a painting what is bad for it: perhaps leaving it in strong sunlight is bad for it. But dusting it regularly does not advance its interests, and leaving it in strong sunlight does not impede its interests. Doing these things may advance or impede its owner's interests, but *it* has none.

Now wronging a creature is impeding its interests unfairly. Since paintings have no interests, there is no such thing as impeding their interests unfairly, and therefore no such thing as wronging them. If we put Alfred's painting in strong sunlight, we may be impeding his interests unfairly and thereby wronging him; we are not wronging the painting.

Suppose, now, that we can improve the world by doing what is bad for a painting. We do not wrong it in so acting. Suppose also that we wrong no one else in so acting. Then our doing what is bad for the painting wrongs no one. Since, by hypothesis, our doing what is bad for the painting would improve the world, it is permissible for us to proceed.

It follows that paintings lack the morally protected status I described, and thus that they lack rights.

I think that these considerations do make the idea that having rights presupposes having interests seem very plausible. But would it be flatly unreasonable to deny that idea? I think not. Here is the difficulty. We may grant that if a thing lacks interests, then it is not possible to impede its interests unfairly, and therefore that it is not possible to wrong it. But if having rights is having the kind of protected moral status that I described, then we stand in need of an explanation of why it should be thought that a thing has that special status only if it is possible to wrong it. No doubt you can't wrong a painting. But how do we get from there to the conclusion that paintings lack the protected moral status? There is a gap here. It seems entirely reasonable to cross it, but we lack a compelling rationale for doing so.

I know of no other reason for denying that fertilized eggs have a right to life than the one that rests on the idea that having rights presupposes having interests. So I know of no conclusive reason for denying that fertilized eggs have a right to life -- thus I know of no conclusive refutation of the encyclical's assertion that they do have a right to life.

There is another side to this coin, however. While I know of no conclusive reason for denying that fertilized eggs have a right to life, I also know of no conclusive reason for asserting that they do have a right to life. Here I *do* take issue with the encyclical. For according to the encyclical, the doctrine that the fetus has a right to life from the moment of conception "is based upon the natural law" as well as "upon the written Word of God." It says that the doctrine "is written in every human heart, *knowable by reason itself*..." (my italics). But the claim that this doctrine is *known* by reason to be true simply will not do. There is nothing unreasonable or irrational in believing that the doctrine is false.

More strongly, there is nothing unreasonable in believing that the doctrine is entirely without support. There is nothing contrary to reason in refusing to lend any credence at all to the idea that fertilized eggs have a right to life.

It is important to stress this stronger claim. The encyclical says: "what is at stake is so important that, from the standpoint of moral obligation, the mere probability that a human person is involved would suffice to justify an absolutely clear prohibition of any intervention aimed at killing a human embryo." The stronger claim says that reason does not compel us to believe it more probable that an embryo is a human person than that any piece of human tissue is. If allowed to develop normally, an embryo will develop into a human person, whereas a cell in your thumb will not; it is not contrary to reason to think that that lends no weight at all to the idea that the embryo is a human person *now*.8

It pays to remember also that people who think there is no reason at all to believe that fertilized eggs have a right to life may well share a considerable amount of the morality that is accepted by people who believe that fertilized eggs do have a right to life. In his well-known speech at Notre Dame on the place of his Catholicism in his life as an elected official, Mario Cuomo said:

> those who don't [agree] -- those who endorse legalized abortions -- aren't a ruthless, callous alliance of anti-Christians determined to overthrow our moral standards. In many cases, the proponents of legal abortion are the very people who have worked with Catholics to realize the goals of social justice set out in papal encyclicals: the American Lutheran Church, the Central Conference of American Rabbis, the Presbyterian Church in the United States, B'nai B'rith Women, the Women of the Episcopal Church. These are just a few of the religious

organizations that don't share the [Catholic] church's position on abortion.9

Thus there are many people who reject Catholic doctrine on abortion, people who not only cannot be convicted of irrationality, but who act in other areas of life in a manner a Catholic respects. What this brings home to us is that a person who rejects this part of Catholic morality cannot be viewed by someone who accepts Catholic moral doctrine as thereby revealing a quite general moral disorder or deficiency. The encyclical, unfortunately, denies this. It says: "The acceptance of abortion in the popular mind, in behavior and even in law itself, is a telling sign of an extremely dangerous crisis of the moral sense, which is becoming more and more incapable of distinguishing between good and evil, even when the fundamental right to life is at stake." This does not say, but it certainly suggests, that those who reject Catholic doctrine on abortion are incapable of distinguishing between good and evil. So interpreted, it is a thoroughly groundless assault on their moral integrity.

These facts have consequences for the debate about the legality of abortion. As I reminded you at the outset, a great deal turns for women on whether abortion is or is not available. If abortion rights are denied, then a constraint is imposed on women's freedom to act in a way that is of great importance to them, both for its own sake and for the sake of their achievement of equality; and if the constraint is imposed on the ground that the fetus has a right to life from the moment of conception, then it is imposed on a ground that neither reason nor the rest of morality requires women to accept, or even to give any weight at all. A legal regime that prides itself on respect for liberty cannot in consistency constrain a deeply valued liberty on such a ground. We should be clear why. When a deeply valued liberty is constrained on a ground that the constrained are not in the least unreasonable in rejecting outright, then what is done to them cannot be justified *to* them, and imposing the constraint on them is therefore nothing but an exercise of force.

The point I make here is not just that anyone who wants to impose a severe constraint on liberty has the burden of saying why it is permissible to do so. That hardly needs saying. The point here is, more strongly, that discharging the burden requires more than merely supplying *a* reason for the constraint: the reason for the constraint has to be one that the constrained are unreasonable in rejecting. In particular, it is not acceptable to constrain access to abortion and supply by way of reason merely "The fetus has a right to life from the moment of conception." Compare the French absolutist Bossuet, who declared "I have the right to persecute you because I am right and you are wrong."10 Under a decent legal regime, people cannot persecute others on the sheer ground that (so they say) they are right and the persecuted are wrong. So similarly for severe constraints on liberty under a legal regime in which liberty is a fundamental value.

This fact breaks what some people have said is a stand-off in the abortion controversy. One side says that the fetus has a right to life from the moment of conception, the other side denies this. Neither side is able to prove its case. The people I refer to ask: why should the deniers win? Why break the symmetry by letting the deniers win instead of the supporters? The answer is that the situation is not symmetrical. What is in question here is not which of two values we should promote, the deniers' or the supporters'. What the supporters want is a license to impose force; what the deniers want is a license to be free of it. It is the former that needs the justification.

I hope it is clear that my objection to constraining access to abortion on the ground that the fetus has a right to life from the moment of conception is not that this is Catholic, and hence religious, doctrine. My objection is not that constraining the liberty on the ground of this doctrine violates the principle of separation of church and state. If the legislature constrains the liberty on the ground of this doctrine, and declares that it is entitled to do so because *God says* the doctrine is true, then the legislature does violate the principle of separation of church and state. But no sensible contemporary opponent of abortion invites the legislature to do this. The opponent of abortion instead invites the legislature to constrain the liberty on the ground of this doctrine, and to declare that it is entitled to do so because the doctrine *is* true. My objection remains.

In sum, my case here against restrictive regulation of abortion rests on three ideas. First, restrictive regulation severely constrains women's liberty. Second, severe constraints on liberty may not be imposed in the name of considerations that the constrained are not unreasonable in rejecting. And third, the many women who reject the claim that the fetus has a right to life from the moment of conception are not unreasonable in doing so. All three ideas seem to me very plausible.

There is of course room for those who accept Catholic doctrine on abortion to declare it in the public forum: the public forum is and must be open to all. But two points are worth stress.

In the first place, those who accept the doctrine ought not say that reason requires us to accept it, for that assertion is false. The public forum is as open to the false as to the true, but participants in it ought to take seriously whether what they say is true. There is already far too much falsehood in the anti-abortion movement. A recent newspaper photograph showed an anti-abortion protester holding a placard that said "Abortion kills;" that much is true. But under those words was a photograph of a baby. The baby looked to me about a year and a half old -- counting in the ordinary way, from birth, not conception. The message communicated by that placard was that abortion kills fully developed babies, and that is false, indeed, fraudulent. Exaggeration for a political purpose is one thing, fraud quite another.

But falsehood is by no means the worst that comes of pronouncements that abortion is murder. Say that often and loudly enough, and some weak-minded soul is sure to start shooting to put a stop to it -- as of course has happened, most recently in Brookline. That is the second point to stress about the public forum: what is said there has consequences. Exaggeration for a political purpose is one thing, incitement to do harm quite another.[11]

One final point, about political action. Some liberals who accept that there ought to be an abortion right are nevertheless critical of the Court's role in securing that right. They believe that if the democratic process had been left to itself -- the issue of abortion left for settlement by legislatures, whether federal or state -- the outcome for abortion rights would have been much as it is now, but without the violence. On that view, what fuels the rage of opponents of abortion is not merely that abortion is now permitted, but that it was permitted by judicial action and not left for decision by the majoritarian branch. A thoroughly convincing recent empirical study of the development of views on abortion at and since the time of *Roe v. Wade* suggests that this hypothesis about access to abortion simply is not true: it concludes that there would have been far less access to abortion than there is now had the issue been left to legislatures.[12]

And I would add that if I was correct in saying that there is nothing unreasonable in believing that at least early abortion violates no rights, and therefore that the deeply valued liberty to obtain an abortion cannot be constrained on the ground that it does violate rights, then there can be no principled objection to the settlement of the issue by the judicial rather than the legislative branch. Vindicating our fundamental liberties is, after all, exactly what courts are supposed to do.[13n]

ENDNOTES

1 112 S. Ct. 2791 (1992)

2 For a description of this new tactic, see The New York Times, April 9, 1995.

3 Pope John Paul II, The Gospel of Life [Evangelium Vitae] (New York: Random House, 1995).

Unless otherwise identified, all quotations in what follows are from that document.

4 Ronald Dworkin, Life's Dominion (New York: Vintage Books, 1994); I refer to this book henceforth as LD.

5 A number of LD's reviewers have drawn attention to the implausibility of Dworkin's idea that opponents of abortion mean only what Dworkin says they mean. (See, for example, Stephen L. Carter, "Strife's Dominion", The New Yorker, August 9, 1993.) Perhaps some do. Perhaps many do. But many do not.

6 My accounts of what it is for Alfred to have the two rights I mentioned are deliberately weak. Thus I did not say that for Alfred to have a right that we give him our teapot is for it to be the case that, come what may, we must give him our teapot, and I did not say that for Alfred to have a right that we not kill him, is for it to be the case that, come what may, we must not kill him. That is because there are circumstances in which it is permissible to infringe a right. For example, rights may conflict, in which case we must, and therefore may, infringe at least one. There are other possibilities too. My own further discussion of the possibilities appears in The Realm of Rights (Cambridge, MA: Harvard University Press, 1990). The fact that there are circumstances in which it is permissible to infringe a right is relied on by those who argue that it is sometimes permissible to kill a fetus even if it does have a right to life. Not, of course, just in the name of improving the world; rather in the name of relieving the mother of an imposition on her that she is under no duty to accede to. An extended recent discussion of these ideas may be found in Frances M. Kamm's review of LD: "Abortion and the Value of Life," Columbia Law Review 95 (1995). (Those who take this view think that while abortion may be an infringement of the right to life, it is not thereby marked as murder.) But I will not focus in what follows on the question what one may do given we assume that the fetus has a right to life. I think the time is overdue to focus on the question what weight in constitutional argument may be rested on the assertion that the fetus does have a right to life.

7 See Laurence H. Tribe, Abortion: The Clash of Absolutes (New York: Norton, 1990), p. 215. Such an opponent of abortion should welcome the release and distribution of the French drug RU-486, which is effective as an abortifacient when used within seven weeks of the last menstrual period, since its use would shrink even further the number of abortions he takes himself to have ground for thinking morally impermissible. (RU-486 is a post-implantation abortifacient. Tribe reports that high doses of some widely available birth control pills can be used - and are currently used in cases of rape - as pre-implantation abortifacients: Ovral is effective when used within three days after conception. See Tribe, p. 219. No doubt other very early abortifacients will be developed in future.)

8 I said earlier that women who decide on abortion typically do so for weighty reasons. If very early (pre-implantation) abortifacients become widely available - see footnote 7 above - many women will regard the question whether to prefer their use to the use of birth control pills as turning entirely on which choice is likely to have fewer unwanted side-effects; and there is nothing contrary to reason in thinking that that is the only relevant consideration.

9 Mario Cuomo, "Religious Belief and Public Morality: A Catholic Governor's Perspective," published in his More Than Words (New York: St. Martin's Press, 1993), p. 42.

10 This splendid remark is quoted by Susan Mendus, Toleration and the Limits of Liberalism (Atlantic Highlands, N.J.: Humanities Press, 1989), p. 7. I am grateful to Joshua Cohen for the reference.

11 Planned Parenthood responded to the Brookline killings in a newspaper ad with the headline "Words Kill," blaming pro-life rhetoric for the episode. Several days later, Mary Ann Glendon responded by blaming pro-choice rhetoric: the "language of dehumanization" that is displayed in pro-choice use of "deceptive phrases [for the fetus] like 'clump of tissue' and 'product of conception'."

After all, she asked, "how can the pro-choice movement's rhetoric fail to promote a coarsening of spirit, a deadening of conscience and a disregard for the humanity of one's opponents...?" Her explanatory leap is breathtaking. See Mary Ann Glendon's op-ed, "When Words Cheapen Life," The New York Times, January 10, 1995.

12 See Archon Fung, "Making Rights Real: Roe's Impact on Abortion Access," Politics and Society 21, no.4 (December 1993). See also Tribe, Clash, and David J. Garrow, Liberty and Sexuality (New York: Macmillan, 1994).

13 I am greatly indebted to Joshua Cohen for criticism, suggestions, and advice: I have leaned on him throughout. An early version was presented as the Keynote Address at the 1995 New England Undergraduate Philosophy Conference at Tufts University.

[38]

MORALITY AND THE LAW: SOME PROBLEMS*
Baroness Warnock

To raise the question of the relation between morality and the law may well provoke a groan, even if suppressed. It is a chestnut of a subject. My excuse for raising it is that it is worth doing so, whenever some new moral issue forces itself upon the public attention. Just such an issue is provided by the new developments in embryology. These issues have not, of course, come upon us out of a clear blue sky. But the public has begun to take cognisance of them only in the last decade. And meanwhile there is a general feeling in most countries that legislation of some kind ought to be contemplated, to regulate what has been up to now an uncontrolled field. The upshot then is inevitably a demand to relate any new legislation that may be introduced to the morality, the rights and wrongs, of the treatment of infertility, the wider use of techniques such as AID, or surrogacy or *in vitro* fertilisation, and the research that such new techniques require. This is, of course, a particular medical and social problem. But medical advances and public awareness and sensitivity are increasingly throwing up similar problems in medical ethics, as well as cases in which the principles of medicine and the law overlap. I shall concentrate on the example of treatments for infertility; but the wider applications should not be forgotten.

But, for a start, I want to narrow the issue still further.

Far and away the most important and, incidentally, the most philosophically interesting of the issues raised in the Committee of Inquiry which published its recommendations in 1984, was the issue of research using human embryos, and it is to that question that I wish to confine myself, using it as the new centre from which to survey the relation between morality and the law.

By way of introduction, it may be worth reminding you of the most notorious dispute about morality and the law, that between HLA Hart and Lord Justice Devlin, in the early 1960s. A staement of the two opposing views is contained in Hart's book, *Law, Liberty and Morality*, and Devlin's, *The Enforcement of Morals*. The issue arose from the publication of the Wolfenden Report in the early 1960s, concerned, among other things, with homosexual practices between consenting adult males. The question was whether or not the law should continue to treat such behaviour as criminal. Devlin held that there was a consensus of hostile feeling towards homosexual practices, and that the law must therefore enforce, or even reinforce such feelings and continue to treat such behaviour as criminal. Conduct that is repellent to the great majority of the public must be treated as criminal. For, in Lord Devlin's view, a shared morality is the cement that binds society together. If such shared morality is not enforced by law, society itself will disintegrate. A society is characterised by its beliefs about what is right and what wrong; without such beliefs there would be no society. To act against such a view is a kind of treason. The law could no more permit acts contrary to the shared morality than it could permit treason itself.

---

*The third Lord Morris of Borth-y-Gest Memorial Lecture given at Cardiff in November 1986.

Hart argued, on the other hand, that two moral problems must be distinguished, one primary and the other critical. At the first level, the question is whether a certain practice is right or wrong; at the second level the question is whether, if the law intervenes to criminalise the practice, the infringement of liberty involved is itself right or wrong. To make this kind of distinction is almost inevitably to introduce a kind of Utilitarian calculus into the argument. The primary question is in terms of the harm done by the practice itself; the secondary question is of the harm done, by way of infringement of liberty, invasion of privacy, or contempt for the law itself, if enforcement and conviction become too difficult.

Looking back on the controversy, which I have summarised very crudely, we may notice various important features. First and most obvious is Devlin's assumption that society has a consensus morality, and that this morality is what binds it together as one society. He did not argue that such morality can never change. He would be willing to concede that morality develops as society itself develops. But at any given time, the law must enforce what society believes to be right. The law must follow, not lead, public opinion on moral issues. Hart did not deny the existence of consensus, though I think he dissented from the view that a society could be somehow identified by its moral beliefs. His theory of morality, however, did not depend on consensus. It was the simple theory that what is right must be calculated as what is less harmful.

If the morally right is the less harmful, the wrong the more harmful) of alternative courses of conduct, people may ultimately be brought to see this. They may be *led* to a consensus, where none existed before. If people hold with passion the belief that homosexual practices between consenting males are immoral even though they do no harm, then such people can be treated by legislators as simply wrong-headed, but educable. They must learn to put aside their prejudices; or content themselves with the thought that they personally need not tangle with such practices, even though they may be permitted by the law.

The law itself has generally been judged on broadly Utilitarian grounds. Even Natural law, the other criterion sometimes invoked for distinguishing good law from bad, has usually been interpreted as if directed towards human happiness. Bentham, at any rate, in the *Principles of Morals and Legislation* set out the test: if law benefited more members of society than it harmed, produced more pleasure than pain overall, then it was a good law. If the opposite, then it was bad. For a Utilitarian, then, though law and morality are distinct, in the end each must be judged by the same standard, the balance of pleasures and pains, harms and benefits.

So, looking back, it is tempting to say that the great difference between Devlin and Hart was over what constituted morality. Was morality a matter of popular feeling, disgust and outrage, admiration and love? Or was it a matter of the aforementioned balance? If Hart was right, then in some cases the law could lead, not merely follow, public moral opinion. For there is nothing remarkable in the thought that Government, or even Parliamentary draughtsmen, might have a better insight into the overall balance of benefits and harms in any envisaged future than the public at large, unaccustomed as they would be to thinking in such broad and universal terms.

And so it is very tempting to argue that the law regulating research using human embryos should, like other laws, be drawn up from broadly Utilitarian premises. The necessity for legislation has been seen, rightly I think, to arise from the need for reassurance. The public must be given reason to feel confident that nothing too harmful will be permittted to go on in hospital laboratories. The widespread fears that exist in the public mind of nameless horrors, Frankenstein monsters, science-fiction manipulations, genetic engineering, so-called 'cloning' must as far as possible be allayed, so that sicentists can get on with medically beneficial research. Legislation must be shown to produce more good than harm, more satisfaction than pain.

Many scientists and doctors working in this field are themselves anxious that regulatory legislation should go through, so that they may know for certain what is or is not permitted. Only so can they go ahead with their research programmes in peace, certain that they are on the right side of the law. Many of them are themselves anxious about the social consequences of uncontrolled advance, and are more than willing to share the decision-making about what is ethically tolerable. Such scientists often put forward explicitly Utilitarian justification for the work they are doing. They point to the benefits to infertile couples who at present suffer extreme distress and misery through their infertility, which will come from continuing and further research. *In vitro* fertilisation programmes can increase in scope and effectiveness only by means of the use of human embryos in research. Moreover, if the freezing of human eggs is to be used as a technique in the treatment of infertility (and it has already been successfully used in Adelaide), a great deal more laboratory research needs to be done. Eggs must be unfrozen and fertilised *in vitro* in order to determine whether or not they are damaged through the process of freezing and unfreezing, as is at present suspected. Examples can be multiplied. Moreover by learning more about the very early development of the embryo ways may be found of detecting and ultimately eliminating many inherited diseases, at present severly handicapping or fatal to the child who is born with them. We may learn how to prevent spontaneous abortion; we may be able to develop new methods of contraception.

Now embryos at the very early stages after fertilisation can themselves experience no pain; indeed before the development of the central nervous system it is impossible for them to have any sensations at all, pleasurable or painful. There can thus be no question of balancing the pain of the embryo used for research against the pleasure or easement of pain experienced by the infertile or by future, unborn, children and adults. There is no contest. So research must be permitted in human embryos, for as long as it is certain it can experience no pain. When the embryo develops to the stage where it might conceivably feel pain, the research must stop.

Here then would be a framework for legislation which would be morally acceptable. There could be nothing morally wrong about a procedure which produced manifest benefits to many, with no countervailing harms to anyone. Many scientists would argue along such lines as these.

Although I am prepared to argue towards such a conclusion in the end, there is no doubt that the argument grossly oversimplifies the position. Utilitarians argue that every human counts for one, and none for more than one. (Bentham and Mill had reservations about children and savages, but we need not tangle with these.) Broadly speaking, if you have to calculate the quantity of pleasure or pain brought about by a particular policy, you must count heads, (taking into account, as well, the intensity and duration of the pleasures and pain involved). In the case of research which uses human embryos, though it is true that the embryos can feel no pain, they are, being alive, capable of being killed. And so an immediate problem arises. In the calculus of benefits and harms enjoined by Utilitarianism, the *death* of a subject is usually, and rightly, thought of as the greatest harm he can suffer. So, on this view, using embryos for research and then destroying them causes the maximum harm to the embryo, far outweighing any long-term benefits to other creatures. If, in answer to this argument, a Utilitarian says 'the calculation is between pains and pleasures of *actual people*. Embryos are not people, and so we don't have to bring them in to the calculation at all', it is immediately clear that he is not making a statement of fact, but is making a value judgment. He is saying that embryos are not *worth* considering as the equal of people, and are therefore not among those who must count for one in the utilitarian calculus. It thus becomes clear that even for an apparently straight-forward utilitarian there is no escaping the problem of decision. The decision is *how ought we to regard embryos?* Are their lives worth as much, morally speaking, as the lives of fully-formed human beings?

On this subject there is no consensus, nor anything like a consensus. If we are thinking of how the law should be drafted which would regulate the use of embryos for research, or forbid it, there is simply no possibility of saying, as Devlin said, 'the law must enforce what Society believes', because there is no one thing that society does believe with regard to the status among humans of the human embryo. Nor is this in the least surprising. Most firmly-held moral beliefs have been developed and taught over the centuries; and though some change radically (such as those relating to the necessity for women to be chaperoned), yet those that remain are generally based on beliefs that can be traced back for many centuries. No beliefs regarding human embryos fertilised and kept alive in the laboratory could possibly have this kind of pedigree. It is no wonder that people adopt radically differing attitudes towards what are, in some respects, new kinds of creature. Twenty years ago few people would even have known what a newly-fertilised embryo was like . . . how large or small, how many cells it consisted of, how it was related to the foetus and the child. Now, quite recently, such things have become relatively familiar. But we have not had time to fix on a moral view, let alone a consensus view.

There have of course been many attempts to overcome this uncertainty, by bringing discussion of the human embryo into line with the discussion of other moral subjects of a more familiar kind. For example, some people have tried to suggest that embryos should have the full protection of the law because they have *a right to life*. One move to establish this position has been to suggest that an embryo is a person or a child. The title of the first bill attempting to criminalise research, brought before Parliament in 1985, made surreptitiusly just such a move. The title of the Bill, introduced by the Rt. Hon. Enoch Powell, was *The Protection of the Unborn Child Bill*. The presumption here is that if the embryo is a human child, it will follow that is has all the rights that we accord to a child or any other person, including the right not to be used for research. But whether or not something is a person is a notoriously difficult thing to settle. Locke rightly said that the term 'person' was a forensic term, and this is to say that whether or not something is a person is not a question of fact but of decision. Someone is *deemed* to be a person, and, then, in consequence, is held to be able to own property, or sue another person, or whatever it may be. A person has rights, that is certain. But whether or not he is a person is just as much a matter of law and of judgment as is the subsequent question of what rights he has. There is a perfectly good biological sense in which a human embryo is a 'man' . . . it is, tautologically human, a member of the species *homo sapiens*. But to say that, is not *yet* to say either whether it is to count as a person nor whether it therefore has rights. Such questions are themselves matters of moral decision.

There is no help then to be found, when trying to answer the question whether an embryo has the right to live, in raising the apparently different question whether it is a person. Neither, incidentally, would it be helpful to introduce the concept of personhood if the discussion were concerned with the question whether severly deformed neo-nates, or adults in extreme pain, or irreversible coma, had the right to live or the right to die. Whether or not a living human is or is not a 'person' is the same as the question whether he has the right to live or to die, or is the bearer of rights at all. There may be good or bad reasons for making judgments, both about personhood and about rights. But it is *judgments* that are in question, not matters of fact.

The criteria most commonly suggested for deciding whether someone or something is a person (and so capable of bearing rights) are sets of characteristics which the creature must have if he is to qualify. They include, as a rule, such characteristics as 'rationality', the 'ability to value his own life', 'the ability to see into the future', and so on. But none of these criteria, insofar as they are intelligible, are satisfied by the human embryo immediately after fertilisation. So those who want to assert that such a creature is a person have to fall back on saying that it is so in virtue of its *potentiality* to acquire the necessary characteristics. If the embryo, because a potential person, is thought to be the bearer of rights, this must be because of its potential future, not its present status.

As the law stands at present of course the embryo has no rights (or only somewhat dubiously, when a doctor may be sued for damage to a child retrospectively, when it was still in the womb). So in any case when the rights of the embryo are under discussion, what is meant are not *existing legal*, but *general moral* rights. Whether or not something has a moral right is quite explicitly a question of moral judgment. It therefore seems clearest to give up talking either about personhood or about rights in the question of the status of the embryo. In the first place the two concepts are not independent but stand or fall together. But secondly, they are both, as it turns out, dependent on adopting a certain moral stance about how the embryo ought to be regarded . . . what degree of protection it ought to be afforded. To speak in such terms is overtly evaluative. To speak in terms of whether the embryo *is* a person or *possesses* rights sounds factual, and is therefore confusing.

I would therefore prefer to avoid the concepts both of personhood and of rights in the present discussion. Neither concept helps us towards that which we are seeking, namely a *moral consensus*. For this is what we would like to find if there is to be an easy solution to the question we started with . . . what is the relation between morality and the law?

For, on the one hand, a solution along the lines which Lord Devlin propounded in the 1960s depends on there being a consensus of moral feeling which it is the duty of the law to enforce and uphold. On the other hand a Utilitarian solution, like that suggested by Hart, depends on the law enforcing that which, all things considered (including the diminutions of freedom entailed in law) gives a balance of benefit over harm to those subject to the law. In the case of embryos, there is no agreed opinion of what their status ought to be, what protection they ought to be afforded. Therefore the Devlin solution fails. But so does the Utilitarian; since the balance of benefit over harm is intended by utilitarianism to apply only to human persons. The question about which there is no agreement in this case is precisely whether or not to count early human embryos among that class, whether *their* benefits and harms should or need not enter into the felicific calculus. We seem to have reached an impasse.

The British Committee of Inquiry into Human fertility and embryology was, right from the start, occupied in trying to relate possible law to the morality that we, as a committee, believed in, and that which was represented to us in the evidence we sought and sifted. And of course this morality was not self-consistent. Not only did the committee itself, though we all signed the main report, diverge (there were three dissenting opinions, only one of which is strictly relevant to my present topic); but we were by no means unanimous on the question of the basis of our moral views, even where they coincided. There were, for example, members of different religions and different races on the committee, whose philosophies, if they ever surfaced, were divergent. We were therefore faced in a most practical way with the question what ought the law to enjoin, when there is no consensus and when, on the crucial issue, Utilitarianism alone can give no sure guidance?

I say 'Utilitariansim alone' because the law *must* be justified to some extent on Utilitarian grounds. If the people in a particular community governed by law very strongly want something to be legitimised, and if those who want it criminalised will not actually suffer any harm from the practice, this is a *prima facie* reason for legitimising the practice.

But here it is necessary to raise a question which has been a problem for utilitarianism since the days of J. S. Mill. What is to count as harm? Suppose that it is mildly convenient for me to do my washing on a Sunday, and hang it out in my garden, but my neighbour believes that it is wrong to do washing on Sunday and still more wrong to hang it out in full view on the Holy Day, who is to win the argument between us? I may say that my washing does her no harm. She may reply that she is offended by it. Does Offence count as Harm? If I am offended by pornographic posters in public places, is this a valid reason for campaigning that they be taken down or that it become a criminal offence to hang them? The whole question of pornography and indeed of broadcasting and publication in general is beset by such problems. People often try to argue that pornographic literature or television programmes are harmful in the sense that they corrupt. But it is extremely difficult to establish any such causal connexion. If this claim is then withdrawn, nothing is left but offensiveness. Is being offensive or disagreeable a sufficient reason for legislation against such items? Do psychological pains count as pains? Does my distaste go into the balance against your pleasure, or is it only my physical damage that can be so weighed?

At this point someone may say that this is quite irrelevant to the question whether or not embryos should be used for research purposes. For the examples I have given are matters not of morals but of taste. The thought of a human embryo being produced in the laboratory and used for the purposes of research offends, when it does, not against *taste* but against *principle*. It is in no way comparable with the thought of Girlie magazines or with the spectacle of someone's pants on the line on a Sunday. But I do not believe that so sharp a distinction can be made. We may, most of us, understand the objection to the use of human embryos for research better than we understand the objection to washing on Sunday. But for the person who objects to the latter, sentiments of outrage may be indistinguishable. In each case the objector may feel that a sacred law has been breached.

Now it is certainly true that not all objects of strong feeling fall within the sphere of the moral. I may feel passionately that it is impossible and awful for men to wear sandals or crimplene shirts; but however strong my feelings, I would not regard the issue as one of morality, nor would I deny people's right to commit these outrages, provided I need have nothing to do with them. Not all strong feelings are moral feelings. Many are, for example, snobbish. Nevertheless I would deny that a moral objection can be seriously raised to a practice unless feelings are involved at some stage. Somewhere along the line, in the expression of a moral belief there must be a feeling, or sentiment, that the act in question would be outrageous. I do not argue that moral beliefs are matters entirely of 'intuition'; nor that they cannot be supported by reasons, of a utilitarian kind. But if the arguments are the whole of the case, if literally none but utilitarian considerations enter at any stage there is, I suggest, no difference between morality and expediency; and this becuase no *ideal* is involved. Without ideals, there can be no morality in the true sense. If this is so, then those who argue on utilitarian grounds for the use of human embryos in research have got to face the fact that they will be arguing against the strong feelings of some members of the public, and that these feelings are not trivial or irrelevant, but profound, and, in some sense, constitutive of morality itself. In dealing with morality, one cannot contrast hard-headed utilitarian *arguments*, with *'mere feelings'*.

I believe it is often hoped that moral philosophers will be able to provide reasons for beliefs that other people, not philosophers, simply hold without reason, as a matter of faith or sentiment. This is not, or not often the case. Sometimes the most a moral philosopher may be able to do is simply to notice that feelings differ.

Does this mean, as is often supposed, that a philosopher who is, in this sense, a sentimentalist, is also necessarily a relativist? I do not think so. Relativism is the theory that all moral beliefs are relative to a particular culture, a particular society or a particular time, and none is *to be preferred* to any other. In its extreme form, relativism may hold that moral beliefs are relative to the holder, What is wrong *for you* may be right *for me*. I do not think that any philosophers hold this extreme view. For, if it were true, there would be no reason for people to get so angry with one another about matters of morality. The very concept of morality itself would collapse into the concept of preference or taste in the narrowest sense. And this it refuses to do. But even leaving aside the extreme, there is no reason to identify relativism, the belief that nothing is ultimately better or worse than anything else, with the belief that morality is in some sense based as much on feelings as reason. For some feelings may be better than others. Some may, historically or culturally be more important than others, some may be so important to members of society that they *will* not give them up, indeed they *cannot* give them up.

Thus there may be within a society some absolute barriers which members of that society are not prepared to contemplate crossing; and if they are told that there are other societies in which such barriers are crossed they are prepared to say, ''then that society is wrong''. At least they may be prepared to declare that that society is one in which they could not live. For their ideals are at stake. It is here that the truth in Devlin's position lies. In the case of such a barrier, the law cannot lead people to cross it, and it should not try to do so. If one of the absolute barriers, in this society, is that female children should not be killed merely on the grounds that they are female (though we know that this is done in China, and has been done in many societies) then no law could attempt to legitimise female infanticide. Such a law, even if it were somehow or other enacted, would be disregarded and soon, by pressure of public opinion, removed. Its existence on the statute book would be a scandal. No utilitarian arguments either about the female infants themselves, nor about their families, nor about the economic needs of society as a whole would in this case carry any weight.

And so we come back to the crucial question for the Committee of Inquiry and for Parliament. Is the use of embryos in the laboratory something that must be criminalised, as entailing the crossing of one of these absolute barriers? As I have said, the Enoch Powell Bill and much of the subsequent argument has relied on the verbal designation of the embryo as a child to suggest that it is. But as I have also said, we must remember that the situation we are in is new. Research using human embryos has certainly been undertaken for a number of years, but no-one who is not a doctor or a scientist has known about it, or thought about it, until the last few years. The question legislators must ask is whether the present situation, in which research is unmonitored, unregulated and uncontrolled, is satisfactory. If it is not, then must there be a total ban on research of this kind, or can some lesser restriction be envisaged, which will recognise the special status of the human embryo, yet not treat it as if it were a child or a person?

There is a further question that may be asked. If research is to be regulated, what is the proper means of regulation? In Australia, where the issue of regulation is urgent, there is a strong feeling that legislation is inappropriate in an area which could be thought of as a matter of medical decision. Legislation has however now been introduced in the State of Victoria, prohibiting all research using human embryos. The medical profession itself is hostile to what they regard as inevitably clumsy interventions in the preserve of professional judgment and expertise. What is at issue, they argue, is the relation between doctor and patient, the doctor's entitlement to treat patients as he thinks best and his right to initiate and use the latest scientific research for the good of his patients. Any controls should come from guide-lines issued to the profession by is own members. But I would argue that, at least in this country, such guidelines would not be thought sufficient. We are perhaps a more suspicious lot, over here, and we are more prone to regard legislation as a protection rather than an unwelcome intrusion into our free-dom. There is a strong feeling, moreover, that the medical profession already takes too much power to itself; and, at the scientific end of the profession, research is too ready to go ahead out of curiousity or the desire for fame. The public would not necessarily be ready to condone, or so it feels, all the scientist might choose to do. Nothing short of legislation could satisfy the general public that outrages were not being committed behind closed doors. So, if the question is of a new piece of *legislation*, the matter must, as I have said, be regarded *partly* from a utilitarian standpoint. We come back to the old question. There is no doubt that the infertile, and children who might be born with fatal or damaging inherited diseases and many others will ultim-ately benefit from the research; the *embryos themselves* will not. How are we to weigh up the benefits and harms? It seems to me that there is here perhaps a case for the law to take a lead, and to educate people in how they may properly think of these laboratory embryos, entities which did not exist when laws of murder or infanticide were drawn up, and which have not been thought about by people in general until very recently. Some people have, as I have suggested, been ignorant of what a four-or-sixteen-cell embryo is like. They have been unaware that it is visible only under a microscope, or that it is not yet divided in the crucial ways that will determine which part of it, if any, will turn into a foetus, which part into the placenta, and whether one or two foetuses will form from the fertilised egg. Some people when they come to think of the newly fertilised egg, the early embryo, in this light may withdraw their objection to using it for beneficial medical research. For such people, legislation would be desirable as long as it limited research to embryos at this early stage of development. Such was the position of the majority of the Committee of Inquiry, including the lawyers. Most of those who argue on the other hand, that no human embryo should at any stage of its development be used for research, do so on religious grounds. And here we come, I think, to an extremely difficult problem, and a problem to be decided by different societies in different ways.

Those who propose that the human embryo should be given limited but not total protection under the law (limited, that is, in that the early embryo may be used but only for certain purposes, and only up to a fixed number of days, before it is destroyed), presuppose that, though the embryo is undoubtedly human and alive, it represents a *kind* of human life which is not so worthy of protection as other kinds, (for example, the lives of children, adults or foetuses.) Those who oppose any research whatever do so on the ground that *all* human life is equally valuable, equally worthy of the full protection of the law. This is a view generally attributed to Christianity. We are all children of the same father, and the rich, the poor, the slave, the free, the idiot or the genius are all of infinite worth. The beauty and the value of this ideal seems to be enormous. But will it really stretch to cover the four-cell embryo? Does anyone really believe that *all* human life is of the same value? I very much doubt it. Yet the short argument against the use of embryos is often of the form 'well, an embryo is human isn't it? And it's alive, isn't it? Therefore it ought not to be used for research and then killed, still less brought into existence simply for that purpose, with no chance of a proper life.'

To introduce the question of *chances* of life complicates the issue: given the present success-rate of *in-vitro* fertilisation, which is low (about 15% success after fertilisation of egg and sperm), no individual embryo, even if implanted in a uterus, has a very good chance of developing into a baby. (For that matter, given the high rate of spontaeneous abortion, *no* fertilised embryo *in utero* or *in vitro* has much of a chance.) If research were permitted, the chances of success would be higher overall, so future embryos would have a better chance. But those used for research would have none. I find it very difficult to assess the argument from chances. I will therefore return to the crucial question of equality not of *chances* of life but of *value* of life.

If a particular religion lays down that, as a matter of dogma, *all human life is of equal value*, and means to include in this dictum the newly fertilized egg, and the unconscious adult, the child in an irreversible coma, the aged patient who could be drawn back from the brink of death for a few more days, and the baby born without a brain, then so be it. Those who accept the religion presumably must also accept the dogma. We shall not expect those people to be other than totally opposed to any research using human embryos. They may say, and often do, that life begins at fertilisation, that all life is equally valuable in the eyes of God, and so all equally must be preserved. Such is, and will consistently be, the view of Judaism.

There are many people however who may even be religious and yet who do not accept any such dogma. Is it not open to those people to think for themselves whether or not the equal value of all human life is something which they must extend to the immediately post-fertilisation embryo? And then there are many people, probably a majority in Britain at present time, who are not committed to any religion at all, and who therefore necessarily have no dogma to fall back on. They must also think for themselves, and decide what value humanity as a whole should place on these early embryos. They must not, if they are consistent, assume the equal value of all forms of human life, since they are debarred from adding 'equal in the eyes of God'. In the eyes of man, equality has to be argued for. It cannot be assumed.

I must at this stage, briefly allude to, and I hope, dismiss the 'Slippery Slope' argument, the commonest of all arguments against research. There are many people who say 'I do not object to embryos being used in experiments if they are destroyed at 14 days. But I fear that once permission has been granted for experiments up to this time, the time will gradually be increased. It is better to forbid all research using human embryos than risk this erosion'. This slippery slope argument has an immense power over the ordinary public. But I do not believe that lawyers ought to be worried by it. If a law is enacted which lays down that embryos may be used for research up to and no longer than 14 days or any other firm number of days, and if going beyond this time is actually a criminal offence (not subject merely to the withdrawal of the licence to research) then there is no particular reason to fear that the law will be disregarded. Certainly the fear that it will be is no reason for refusing to introduce the law. You might as well argue that no-one should be able to obtain a licence to own firearms, for fear that once firearms were accessible to anyone, they would gradually become accessible to all. The slippery slope or foot-in-the-door argument crops up again and again in the discussion of research using human embryos often reinforced by a reference to Nazi Germany: if it is permitted to destroy human life at all, even life in the test-tube, then the next thing will be the mass destruction of any humans who are regarded as dispensable, and the holocaust will follow. The total failure of any real analogy between the extreme consequences of anti-semitism on the one hand and the limited use of pre-fourteen-day embryos on the other, need not, I hope, be laboured, especially in this company. Lawyers, as well as philosophers, are professionally accustomed to distinguishing things that differ, and they will hardly need instruction on this particular point.

Laying aside, then, the slippery slope argument, I must finally revert to the central question. How is the law to be drawn up so as to take account of what is morally acceptable or unacceptable, in the case of research using human embryos? Granted that legislation is necessary, and soon (for at present there is no regulation of research except by means of voluntary guidelines), how can Government fulfil their intention of controlling such research, but allowing some to be carried on? How can they justify such an approach, given the vociferous clamour of the abolitionists in Parliament, claiming, as they do, to speak for a majority of their constituents? Of course in the end we have to allow that Parliament must decide, in any question of legislation. And if prohibitionist laws are carried through there is no doubt that some people will claim that the law is there doing what it should, enforcing the public moral belief in the sanctity of all human life at whatever stage of development that life may be. The doubt we must feel is whether this *is* the public moral sentiment; whether members of parliament accurately distil the essence of their constituents' thought on these novel matters. Perhaps we have here a case where lawyers might lead rather than be led: where they might show themselves clear-headed though the public is muddled; and where they might try to expound the view that not all human life is equally valuable and show its practical consequences. At least they might, by debating the question, demonstrate that there are arguments to be heard on both sides. It would be paradoxical if, in what must be agreed to be a predominantly secular country, the presuppositions of fundamentalist religion should, in the end, dictate the future pattern of the law, without further debate.

Deliberating about Bioethics

by Amy Gutmann and Dennis Thompson

In some sense, bioethics was built on conflicts. Abortion, physician-assisted suicide, patients' demand for autonomy all are staple and contentious issues. And the controversies continue to proliferate. What forum best serves such debates? A look at political theories of democracy can help answer that question. The most promising for bioethics debates are theories that ask citizens and officials to justify any demands for collective action by giving reasons that can be accepted by those who are bound by the action. This conception has come to be known as *deliberative democracy*.

As controversies about bioethics proliferate, so do the forums in which they are decided. The debates take place not only in the agencies of government—legislatures, courts, and presidential commissions—but also in the institutions of society—ethics committees, institutional review boards, HMO executive committees, professional associations, and task forces of various kinds. In both society and government, these debates increasingly display, for good or ill, the characteristics of democratic politics. Political theories of democracy are therefore increasingly relevant to understanding the condition of moral debate in bioethics forums both outside as well as inside government. The most promising theories, we suggest, are those that focus on moral conflict, and call for more and better moral deliberation to deal with such conflict. These theories defend a conception that has recently come to be called *deliberative democracy*.

At the core of deliberative democracy is the idea that citizens and officials must justify any demands for collective action by giving reasons that can be accepted by those who are bound by the action. When citizens morally disagree about public policy, they therefore should deliberate with one other, seeking moral agreement when they can, and maintaining mutual respect when they cannot.

The distinctive character of this conception can be seen more clearly in contrast to the leading alternatives for dealing democratically with moral disagreement—proceduralism and constitutionalism. Proceduralists hope that if citizens agree on some basic rules of the game, they can domesticate the moral disagreement that remains by leaving it to political bargaining or by moving it off the political agenda into private life. But disagreement about procedures is often just as serious as disagreement about substance, usually because the procedural dispute covers a substantive one. Despite official statements to the contrary, the decisions of the United Network for Organ Sharing (whether based on length of the wait, or urgency of the need) presuppose moral choices. Even a seemingly neutral procedure such as a lottery for the distribution of scarce medical resources (for example, organs for transplantation) favors egalitarian values over meritocratic ones.

Amy Gutmann and Dennis Thompson, "Deliberating about Bioethics," *Hastings Center Report* 27, no. 3 (1997): 38-41.

Constitutionalists try to avoid moral disagreement by carving out a sphere of agreement on fundamental values and protecting them from the pressures of ordinary politics by assigning them to an institution like the Supreme Court. But again what should count as a fundamental value, what should be enshrined as a right, and how it should be interpreted is legitimately open to continuing challenge. Should citizens have a right to physician-assisted suicide? It is hardly obvious that this kind of question can and should be decided once and for all by courts or any authority insulated from the political process.

Deliberative democracy goes beyond proceduralism and constitutionalism by not only tolerating but encouraging continuing discussion of fundamental values in all phases of the democratic process. Deliberative democracy is the opposite of soundbite democracy, which probably provides a more accurate description of our current political life. Soundbite democracy suffers from a deliberative deficit. The din and deadlock of public life—where insults are traded, slogans proclaimed, and self-serving deals are made and unmade—certainly reveal the deep disagreements that pervade public life. But soundbite democracy does nothing to resolve those disagreements on mutually acceptable grounds and still less to help citizens live with their ongoing disagreements in a mutually respectful way.

Democracies cannot avoid disagreement, but citizens, professionals, and public officials can deliberate about their disagreements in a way that contributes to the health of a democratic society. We focus here on four important social purposes served by deliberation in democracy, and four corresponding lessons for bioethics forums. The four purposes respond to the four ineradicable sources of moral disagreement.

The first purpose is to promote the legitimacy of collective decisions. This is a response to the first source of moral disagreement—scarcity of resources. Citizens would not have to argue about how best to distribute health care or who should receive organ transplants if these goods and services were unlimited. Deliberation often cannot resolve moral disagreements because there are reasonable, indeed heart-wrenching, differences about how health care or scarce organs should be distributed. But in the face of scarcity, deliberation can help those who do not get what they want or even what they need come to accept the legitimacy of a collective decision.

The hard choices that public officials and health care professionals make should be more acceptable even to those who receive less than they deserve if everyone's claims have been considered on their merits, rather than on the basis of the party's bargaining power. Even with regard to decisions with which we disagree, most of us take a different attitude toward those decisions that are adopted merely by virtue of the relative strength of competing political interests, and those that are adopted after careful consideration of the relevant conflicting moral claims. Even deliberation that yields mutually acceptable justifications does not make up for the organ transplants that a desperately sick person fails to receive. But it can help sustain a shared sense of legitimacy that makes possible collective efforts to secure more organs in the future, and to live with one another civilly in the meantime.

To serve this legitimizing purpose in the face of disagreement, deliberative forums should expand to include the voices of as many as possible of those now excluded. Such inclusion risks intensifying moral conflict. But the benefit of taking this risk is that inclusive deliberation brings into the open legitimate moral dissatisfactions that are suppressed by power-oriented methods of dealing with disagreement. Deliberation does not seek consensus for its own sake. It seeks a consensus that can be justified reciprocally—on terms that citizens who may continue to disagree can all accept.

The second purpose of deliberation is to encourage public-spirited perspectives on public issues. This aim responds to another source of moral disagreement—limited generosity. Few people are inclined to be wholly altruistic when they are arguing about contentious issues of public policy, such as health care reform or funding for AIDS research. Deliberation in well-constituted bioethics forums responds to this limited generosity by encouraging participants to take a broader perspective on questions of common interest. John Stuart Mill presented one of the most cogent accounts of such a deliberative process. Participating in public discussions, a citizen is

> called upon . . . to weigh interests not his own; to be guided, in case of conflicting claims, by another rule than his private partialities; to apply, at every turn, principles and maxims which have for their reason of existence the common good . . .

Deliberation will not turn self-centered individualists suddenly into public-spirited citizens. Members of a bioethics commission, for example, are not automatically transformed from representatives of special interests into trustees of the public interest just as a result of talking to one another. Background conditions make a big difference and need to be considered in constituting a commission or any deliberative forum. These conditions include: the level of competence (how well informed deliberators are), the distribution of resources (how equally situated they are), and the open-mindedness of deliberators (the range of arguments they are likely to take seriously). But all we need to assume in order to urge more deliberation is that most people are more likely to take a broader view of issues, to consider the claims of more of their fellow human beings in a deliberative process that puts a premium on moral argument than in a process in which assertions of political power prevail.

Some implications for bioethics forums follow from facing up to the problem of limited generosity in this way. One is that the number or diversity of voices heard and arguments made is not the only or even most important factor in making deliberation work: the character and will of the deliberators themselves are critical. They must be willing to try to broaden their own perspective in light of what they hear in the deliberative process. They must come to the forum open to changing their own minds as well as to changing the minds of their opponents.

A related implication is that these forums are likely to work best when they are designed to resemble as little as possible the processes of power politics and interest-group bargaining. Members of bioethics committees, boards, and commissions should not think of themselves as merely delegates, even if they inevitably and quite properly bring different perspectives to the forum. They should not be chosen in a way that suggests that each represents the interests of a single constituent group, whose interests the representative is therefore bound to articulate and promote. A forum that is so organized is likely to replicate the results of interest-group bargaining.

The third purpose of deliberation, to promote mutually respectful decisionmaking, responds to an often neglected source of moral disagreement—incompatible moral values. Even utterly altruistic individuals trying to decide on the morally best standards for governing a society of abundance would not be able to reconcile some moral conflicts beyond a reasonable doubt. They would still confront, for example, the problem of abortion, which pits life against liberty. No less tractable would be other bioethics issues such as the question of whether individuals should be held responsible for health problems that are partly the product of their own choices, or the question of whether children who cannot give informed consent should ever be subjects of experimental research.

Deliberation cannot of course make incompatible values compatible, but it can help participants recognize moral merit in their opponents' claims. It can do so by helping to clarify what is at stake in a moral disagreement, encouraging deliberators to sort out self-interested claims from public-spirited ones, and to recognize those public-spirited claims that should have greater weight. Through a deliberative process, participants in a bioethics forum can isolate those conflicts, such as abortion, that embody genuinely incompatible values on both sides. Conflicts that do not involve such deep disagreement can then be easily addressed and may turn out to be more resolvable than they at first appeared to be. Some may be the result of misunderstanding or lack of information, and some may be appropriately settled by bargaining, negotiation, and compromise. In this way, deliberation helps put moral principle and moral compromise—as well as bargaining—in its place.

In the face of incompatible values, deliberative democracy calls for what we call an economy of moral disagreement. In justifying policies on moral grounds, citizens should seek the rationale that minimizes rejection of the position they oppose. By economizing on their disagreements in this way, citizens manifest mutual respect as they continue to disagree about morally important issues on which they need to reach collective decisions.

The economy of moral disagreement is not a utopian ideal. It can be seen at work in, for example, two bodies that considered the issue of fetal tissue research—the Warnock Commission in England and the Fetal Tissue Research Commission in the United States. To the extent that they recognized and respected incompatible values, commissioners helped realize the potential for mutual respect among citizens. A bioethics commission or committee may decide to focus on issues on which it can reach some reasonable consensus rather than on issues that are more likely to produce polarization. Or if it cannot avoid highly contentious issues, it should seek to help members understand the perspectives of their opponents. The quality of a commission's analysis—how well it recognizes the competing values at stake—will be at least as important as the conclusion it reaches.

But even if deliberation is possible, is it always desirable? Some might object that by raising the moral stakes, deliberative democracy turns what might otherwise have been mundane disputes into conflicts of grand moral principle, and thereby encourages no-holds-barred opposition and political intransigence. These are real risks. Moral sensitivity may sometimes make necessary political compromises more difficult. But the absence of moral reasoning also makes unjustifiable compromises more common. If a disagreement about a change in eligibility for health care turns only on the question of costs, nothing is gained by invoking principles of justice and benevolence. But when a dispute raises serious moral issues—the exclusion of certain groups such as immigrants, for example—then it is not likely to be resolved satisfactorily by avoiding arguments about justice.

The fourth purpose of deliberation is to help correct the mistakes that citizens, professionals, and officials inevitably make when they take collective actions. This is a response to the last source of disagreement, the incomplete understanding that characterizes almost all moral conflicts. A well-constituted bioethics forum provides an opportunity for advancing both individual and collective understanding. Through the give-and-take of argument, participants can learn from each other, come to recognize their individual and collective misapprehensions, and develop new views and policies that can more successfully withstand critical scrutiny. When citizens bargain and negotiate, they may learn how better to get what they want. But when they deliberate, they can expand their knowledge, including their self-understanding as well as their collective understanding of what will best serve their fellow citizens.

Some of us (and perhaps all of us sometimes) believe that we already know what constitutes the best resolution of a moral conflict without deliberating with our fellow citizens. Assuming that we know the right resolution before we hear from others who will also be affected by our decisions is not only arrogant but also unjustified in light of the complexity of issues and interests at stake. If we refuse to give deliberation a chance, we forsake not only what possibility of arriving at a genuine moral compromise but we also give up the most defensible ground for maintaining an uncompromising position: that we have tested our views against those of others.

As a little boy tugging on the coattails of Thomas Jefferson once asked (in a *New Yorker* cartoon): "If you hold those truths to be self-evident, then why do you keep on harping on them so much?" The answer from a deliberative perspective is that such claims deserve their status as self-evident truths for the purposes of collective action only if they can withstand challenge in a public forum. Jefferson himself argued for open deliberative forums, indeed even periodic constitutional conventions, in which citizens could contest conventional wisdom. An implication of taking the problem of incomplete understanding seriously is that the work of any bioethics committee, commission, or board should be regarded as provisional. Deliberative forums reach conclusions, but the conclusions should be open to challenge in a subsequent forum.

Deliberation continues through stages, as leaders present their proposals, citizens respond, leaders revise, citizens react, and the stages recur. This is what we call the reiteration of deliberation. The potential strengths (and shortcomings) of this kind of deliberation can be seen in the process that the state of Oregon adopted in the early 1990s to set priorities for its publicly funded health care under Medicaid. The Oregon Health Services Commission's priorities list, based mainly on utilitarian cost-benefit calculations, provoked much justifiable criticism (capping a tooth ranked much higher than an appendectomy). The commission then began an elaborate process of consultation, which included community meetings at which participants were "asked to think and express themselves in the first person plural . . . as members of a statewide community for whom health care has a shared value." Eventually after still more deliberation, the commission presented a revised list, which was generally regarded as an improvement over the original plan. The commission could not correct the most serious flaw in the

scheme: because only poor people were eligible, some poor people would have to sacrifice for the sake of other poor people.

Nevertheless, the process forced officials and citizens to confront a serious problem that they had previously evaded—and to confront it in a cooperative ("first person plural") spirit. As a result, even the basic unfairness in the policy was somewhat lessened in a way unexpected by the critics of the plan (and probably by its proponents as well). When the legislators finally saw what treatments on the list would have to be eliminated under the projected budget, they managed to find more resources, and increased the total budget for health care for the poor.

Although some observers saw little connection between the earlier debate and the content of the revised list, the commission did correct most of the priorities that had been widely criticized. The year-long deliberations appeared to help citizens, legislators, and health care professionals come to a better understanding of their own values—those they shared and those they did not. The experience enabled citizens and their representatives to undertake, in a more reciprocal spirit, what is likely to be a long and difficult process of setting and adjusting priorities that could eventually affect the quality of health care of all residents of the state and even some in other states.

The distribution of health care is of course not the only issue that could benefit from such reiterated deliberation. When, if ever, is medical experimentation justified in the absence of informed consent? On what basis should organs for transplantation be allocated? To what extent should government regulate research on cloning? Do physicians have a duty to treat AIDS patients? The list of contestable questions could be expanded almost indefinitely simply by collecting the topics from the table of contents of recent issues of the *Hastings Center Report*. Because moral disagreement is not likely to diminish, the need for more and better deliberation is likely to grow.

If the principles of deliberative democracy were to be more fully realized in the practices of bioethics forums, the decisions the participants reach would be more morally legitimate, public-spirited, mutually respectful, and self-correcting. Deliberation-friendly forums could help reduce our deliberative deficit. By making democracy more deliberative, we stand a better chance of resolving some of our moral disagreements, and living with those that will inevitably persist, on terms that all can accept.

Acknowledgments

Parts of this article are based on *Democracy and Disagreement* (Harvard University Press, 1996), coauthored by Gutmann and Thompson. An earlier version of this article was presented at the International Summit on Bioethics, San Francisco, 23 November 1996.

Name Index